ENCOUNTERS BETWEEN FOREIGN RELATIONS LAW AND INTERNATIONAL LAW

Foreign relations law and public international law are two closely related academic fields that tend to speak past each other. As this innovative volume shows, the two are closely interrelated and depend on each other for their mutual construction and identity. A better understanding of this relationship is of vital importance for upholding important constitutional values like democracy, the rule of law and the protection of human rights, while enabling states to engage in meaningful forms of international cooperation. The book takes a close look at the encounters between the two fields and offers perspectives for a constructive engagement between the two. Collectively, the contributions argue that the delimitation between the two fields occurs in a hybrid zone of interaction which requires both bridges and boundaries: bridges for the construction of the relationship between the two fields, and boundaries for preserving key normative expectations of both domestic and international law.

Helmut Philipp Aust is a Professor of Law at Freie Universität Berlin, Germany, and Co-Chair of the ILA Study Group 'The Role of Cities in International Law'. Publications include *Complicity and the Law of State Responsibility* (2011) and *The Interpretation of International Law by Domestic Courts* (2016, with Georg Nolte).

Thomas Kleinlein is a Professor of Law at Friedrich Schiller University Jena, Germany, where he holds the Chair of Public Law, Public International Law, EU Law and Comparative Law and is Co-Director of the Center for European Studies. Publications include *System, Order, and International Law: The Early History of International Legal Thought* (2017, with Stefan Kadelbach and David Roth-Isigkeit).

Encounters between Foreign Relations Law and International Law

BRIDGES AND BOUNDARIES

Edited by

HELMUT PHILIPP AUST
Freie Universität Berlin

THOMAS KLEINLEIN
Friedrich-Schiller-Universität Jena

CAMBRIDGE
UNIVERSITY PRESS

CAMBRIDGE
UNIVERSITY PRESS

University Printing House, Cambridge CB2 8BS, United Kingdom

One Liberty Plaza, 20th Floor, New York, NY 10006, USA

477 Williamstown Road, Port Melbourne, VIC 3207, Australia

314–321, 3rd Floor, Plot 3, Splendor Forum, Jasola District Centre, New Delhi – 110025, India

79 Anson Road, #06–04/06, Singapore 079906

Cambridge University Press is part of the University of Cambridge.

It furthers the University's mission by disseminating knowledge in the pursuit of education, learning, and research at the highest international levels of excellence.

www.cambridge.org
Information on this title: www.cambridge.org/9781108837743
DOI: 10.1017/9781108942713

First published 2021

A catalogue record for this publication is available from the British Library.

ISBN 978-1-108-83774-3 Hardback

Contents

Contributors

Niki Aloupi, Professor of Public International Law, Paris II Panthéon-Assas University

Helmut Philipp Aust, Professor of Law, Freie Universität Berlin

Stanisław Biernat, Professor of European Law, Jagiellonian University in Kraków

Curtis A. Bradley, Professor of Law, Duke University

Veronika Fikfak, Associate Professor, University of Copenhagen

Jean Galbraith, Professor of Law, University of Pennsylvania Carey Law School

Angelo Jr. Golia, Dr. iur., Senior Research Fellow (Postdoc), Max Planck Institute for Comparative Public Law and International Law in Heidelberg

JI Hua, Dr. iur., Assistant Professor of International Law, China Foreign Affairs University

Thomas Kleinlein, Professor of Law, Friedrich Schiller University Jena

Felix Lange, Dr. iur., LL.M. (NYU), M.A., Research Fellow, Berlin/Potsdam Research Group 'The International Rule of Law – Rise or Decline?'

Campbell McLachlan Q.C., Professor of Law, Victoria University of Wellington

Frédéric Mégret, full-Professor and Dawson Scholar, Faculty of Law, McGill University

Anna Petrig, Professor of International and Public Law, University of Basel, Switzerland

Michael Riegner, Dr. iur., LL.M. (NYU), researcher at Humboldt University Berlin and principal investigator in the Deutsche Forschungsgemeinschaft DFG project 'Varieties of Constitutionalism'

Prabhakar Singh, Professor, Jindal Global Law School, Sonipat

Ajla Škrbić, Dr. iur., Assistant Professor of Law, University of Business Engineering and Management Banja Luka, Bosnia and Herzegovina

Edward T. Swaine, Charles Kennedy Poe Research Professor and Professor of Law, George Washington University Law School

Dire Tladi, Professor of International Law, NRF South African Research Chair in International Law, University of Pretoria

Preface

Academic discourses on closely related issues sometimes develop in parallel, without much interaction between either track. To some extent, this is the case in the parallel universes of foreign relations law and public international law. Both fields can only exist with due acknowledgment of the other, but at times it appears as if differences and divergences between the two are overstated for the sake of solidifying one's own perspective. This present volume departs from the assumption that we need bridges as well as boundaries between foreign relations law and public international law: bridges in order to better understand the mutual dependency of the two fields, boundaries so as not to collapse one field into the other. As editors, we think that the encounters between the two fields assembled in the following pages are of a productive nature. They will hopefully contribute to a further flourishing engagement with the bridges and boundaries between foreign relations law and public international law.

Putting together this volume was made possible first and foremost by the enthusiasm with which our authors joined us on this journey, which started at the Old Castle in Dornburg close to Jena in May 2019 with an informal research workshop. Back then the first ideas for this volume developed. Our group of authors made our task as editors easy and we are grateful for various and mutual learning processes in which we engaged in the run-up to this book.

At Cambridge University Press we would like to thank Finola O'Sullivan and Marianne Nield who have steered the volume expertly to production. We are grateful to four anonymous reviewers for valuable insights which have helped to further improve the conceptual structure of the volume.

The production of this book was made possible with the financial support of various institutions. The 2019 authors' workshop was supported by the Friedrich Schiller University Jena (FSU Jena) and Freie Universität Berlin

(FU Berlin). The open access publication of this volume is enabled by support from the University Library of FU Berlin, the Faculty of Law of the FSU Jena and the Department of Law of FU Berlin.

Finally, we would like to thank our teams in Berlin and Jena for the dedicated support in preparing the manuscript for publication. Susanne Prater and Felix Schott were heavily involved in the project from the very beginning and we would like to thank them warmly for their active support. We would also like to thank Denys Forshayt, Annika Franz, Alexandra Konecny, Gundula Maxwill, Kerstin Oelstrom, Alexander Silke and Annemarie Wagner for their commitment.

Helmut Philipp Aust and Thomas Kleinlein

Table of Cases

Note on ordering: Cases are ordered alphabetically if cited with case names, otherwise the order is chronological.

INTERNATIONAL CASES

I *Permanent Court of International Justice (PCIJ)*

Case concerning certain German interests in Polish Upper Silesia, Merits, PCIJ Series A, No. 7, 1926, p. 46
Case of the S.S. 'Lotus', Judgment, Series A No. 10, pp. 10, 166
Case of the S.S. 'Wimbledon', Judgment, Series A No. 1, p. 166

II *International Court of Justice (ICJ)*

Aerial Incident of 10 August 1999 (Pakistan v. *India)*, Jurisdiction of the Court, I.C.J. Reports 2000, pp. 12, 98
Avena and Other Mexican Nationals (Mexico v. *United States of America)*, Judgment, I.C.J. Reports 2004, pp. 12, 350
Case Concerning the Arrest Warrant of 11 April 2000 (Democratic Republic of the Congo v. Belgium), Separate Opinion of Judge Bula-Bula, I.C.J. Reports 2002, pp. 100, 47
East Timor (Portugal v. *Australia)*, Judgment, I.C.J. Reports 1995, p. 90
Jurisdictional Immunities of the State (Germany v. *Italy: Greece intervening)*, Judgment, I.C.J. Reports 2012, pp. 99, 365
Land and Maritime Boundary between Cameroon and Nigeria (Cameroon v. *Nigeria: Equitorial Guinea intervening)*, Judgment, I.C.J. Reports 2002, pp. 303, 30, 52

III *Permanent Court of Arbitration (PCA)*

IV *European Court of Human Rights (ECtHR)*

V *Court of Justice of the European Union (CJEU)*

VI *African Commission on Human and Peoples' Rights (ACHPR)*

NATIONAL CASES

I *Bosnia and Herzegovina*

Constitutional Court

Decision No. U 9/00, 3 November 2000, p. 281
Decision No. U 26/01, 28 September 2001, p. 281
Decision No. U 42/01, 26 March 2004, p. 282
Decision on Admissibility, U 5/04, 27 January 2006, p. 279

II *Canada*

Supreme Court

Canada (Prime Minister) v. *Khadr* [2010] 1 SCR 44, p. 143
Operation Dismantle [1985] 1 SCR 441, p. 143
Reference re Secession of Quebec [1998] 2 SCR 217, p. 365

III *Columbia*

Constitutional Court

Case C-358/96, p. 147
Case C-379/96, p. 147
Case SU-039/97, p. 73
Case C-252/19 (LAT-445), p. 147, 344

IV *France*

1 *Conseil constitutionnel*

Decision no. 70–39 DC, 19 June 1970 – *Traité portant modification de certaines dispositions budgétaires [...] et décision du Conseil des Communautés européennes [...] relative au remplacement des contributions des États membres par des ressources propres aux Communautés*, p. 169
Decision no. 74–54 DC, 15 January 1975 – *Voluntary Interruption of Pregnancy Act*, p. 164
Decision no. 76–71 DC, 30 December 1976 – *Décision du Conseil des communautés européennes relatitve à l'élection de l'Assemblée des Communautés au suffrage universel direct*, pp. 167, 168, 169

2 *Conseil d'État*

V *Germany*

1 *Federal Constitutional Court*

2 *Higher Administrative Court for North Rhine-Westphalia*

VI *Ghana*

Supreme Court

VII *Greece*

Supreme Court

VIII *India*

1 *Supreme Court*

2 *Dehli High Court*

IX *Ireland*

Supreme Court

X *Israel*

Supreme Court

XI *Italy*

1 *Constitutional Court*

2 *Administrative Supreme Court*

3 *Supreme Court of Cassation*

4 *Tribunal of Rome*

5 *Tribunal of Florence*

6 *Tribunal of Ragusa*

XII *Netherlands*

1 *Supreme Court (Hoge Raad)*

2 *The Hague Court of Appeal*

3 *The Hague District Court*

XIII *Russia*

Constitutional Court

XIV *Singapore*

Supreme Court (sitting as Court of Appeal)

Swissbourgh Diamond Mining Company and Others v. *the Kingdom of Lesotho*, 27 November 2018, p. 223

XV *South Africa*

1 *Constitutional Court*

Kaunda and Others v. *the President of the Republic of South Africa and Others* 2005 (4) SA 235 (CC), pp. 144, 217, 218, 224

Law Society of South Africa and Others v. *President of the Republic of South Africa and Others* 2019 (3) BCLR 329 (CC), pp. 146, 147, 215, 219, 222, 223, 224, 225, 226, 227, 358

Mohamed v. *President of the Republic of South Africa* 2001 (3) SA 893 (CC), pp. 219, 221, 237

President of the Republic of South Africa and Others v. *South African Rugby Football Union and Others* 2000 (1) SA 1 (CC), p. 219

The Government of the Republic of Zimbabwe v. *Louis Karel Fick and Others*, Case CCT 101/12 [2013] (10) BCLR 1103 (CC), p. 228

The President of the Republic of South Africa and Another v. *Hugo* 1997 (4) SA 1 (CC), pp. 217, 219

Von Abo v. *the President of the Republic of South Africa* 2009 (5) SA 345 (CC), p. 219

2 *Supreme Court of Appeal*

Government of the Republic of South Africa and Others v. *Von Abo* 2011 (5) SA 262 (SCA), pp. 219, 221

Minister of Justice and Others v. *South African Litigation Centre and Others* 2016 (3) SA 317 (SCA), p. 234

Van Zyl and Others v. *the Government of the Republic of South Africa and Others* 2008 (3) SA 294 (SCA), p. 222

3 *High Court (Gauteng Division, Pretoria)*

Democratic Alliance v. *Minister of International Relations and Cooperation and Others* 2017 (3) SA 212 (GP), pp. 55, 149, 215, 235, 236

Democratic Alliance v. *Minister of International Relations and Co-operation and Others* 2018 (6) SA 109 (GP), pp. 215, 231

Von Abo v. *the Government of the Republic of South Africa and Others* 2010 (3) SA 269 (T), p. 219

4 *High Court (Trnsvaal Provincial Division)*

Von Abo v. *the Government of the Republic of South Africa and Others* [2008] ZAGPHC 226, pp. 219, 220, 237

5 *High Court (Western Cape Division, Cape Town)*

Earthlife Africa v. *Minister of Energy* 2017 (5) SA 227, p. 237

XVI *United Kingdom*

1 *Supreme Court*

Belhaj & Rahmatullah (No 1) v. *Straw & Ors* [2017] UKSC 3, pp. 144, 152
HM Treasury v. *Ahmed & others* [2010] UKSC 2, p. 153
R (Miller) v. *Prime Minister* [2019] UKSC 41, [2020] AC 373, p. 363
R (Miller) v. *Secretary of State for Exiting the European Union* [2017] UKSC 5, [2018] AC 61, pp. 55, 148, 363

2 *House of Lords*

CCSU v. *Minister for the Civil Service* [1984] UKHL 9, p. 144
Lubbe [2000] 4 All ER 268 (UKHL), p. 152
R v. *Bow Street Metropolitan Stipendiary Magistrate, ex parte Pinochet Ugarte* [1998] 2 WLR 827 (HL 1999), p. 152

3 *England and Wales Court of Appeals, Civil Division*

Blackburn v. *Attorney General* [1971] 2 All ER 1380, p. 148

4 *England and Wales High Court, Queen's Bench Division*

High Commissioner for Pakistan in the United Kingdom v. *Prince Muffakham Jah*, [2019] EWHC 2551 (Ch), p. 86
Hutchinson v. *Newbury Magistrates Court* [2000] EWHC QB 61, p. 142

5 *Court of Chancery*

XVII *United States*

1 *Supreme Court*

2 Court of Appeals, Second Circuit

3 Court of Appeals, Fourth Circuit

4 District Court for the Northern District of Alabama

Abbreviations

AC	Appeal Cases
AJCL	American Journal of Comparative Law
AJIL	American Journal of International Law
Appl. No(s).	Application Number(s)
art.	article
arts.	articles
Ass'n	Association
BCLR	Butterworths Constitutional Law Reports
BiH	Bosnia and Herzegovina
BIT	Bilateral Investment Treaty
BV	Bundesverfassung
BVerfG	Bundesverfassungsgericht/ Federal Constitutional Court
BVerfGE	Decisions of the Federal Constitutional Court
BYIL	British Yearbook of International Law
cert.	certiorari
CETA	Comprehensive Economic and Trade Agreement
cf.	confer
Ch.	Chapter
CH	Confoederatio Helvetica/Swiss Confederation
CIA	Central Intelligence Agency
Cir.	Circuit
cl./cll.	clause/clauses
cmt.	comment
col.	column
Commons	House of Commons
Cong.	Congress
Cons. Const.	Conseil constitutionnel
COP 21	Conference of the Parties 21

Corp.	Corporation
Council	Security Council
CRS	Congressional Research Service
CRT	Critical Race Theory
DCAF	Geneva Centre for the Democratic Control of Armed Forces
DEA	Directorate for European Affairs
DPA	Dayton Peace Agreement
ECHR	Convention for the Protection of Human Rights and Fundamental Freedoms (European Convention on Human Rights)
ECJ	European Court of Justice
ECtHR	European Court of Human Rights
ed.	edition
ed., eds.	editor, editors
EJIL	European Journal of International Law
EU	European Union
EWHC	The High Court of England and Wales
FAM	Foreign Affairs Manual
Fed. Reg.	Federal Register
FIU	Florida International University
FR	foreign relation
FRL	foreign relations law
FRP	foreign relations power
GATT	General Agreement on Tariffs and Trade
GHASC	Supreme Court of Ghana
G7	Group of Seven
HC	House of Commons
HPCR	Program on Humanitarian Policy and Conflict Research at Harvard University
ICJ	International Court of Justice
ICJ Rep	ICJ Reports
ICLQ	International & Comparative Law Quarterly
ICON	International Journal of Constitutional Law
ICSID Review	Foreign Investment Law Journal
ILC	International Law Commission
ILM	International Legal Materials
Inc.	Incorporated
Ins.	Insurance
Int. J. Semiot Law	International Journal for the Semiotics of Law

IO(s)	international organisation(s)
IPSR	International Political Science Review
ItCC	Italian Constitutional Court
IVG	interruption volontaire de grossesse
J CSL	Journal of Conflict and Security Law
KOF	KOF Swiss Economic Institute (Konjunkturforschungsstelle)
LQR	Law Quarterly Review
L. Rev.	Law Review
MC	Magistrate's Court
MLR	Modern Law Review
MPs	Members of Parliament
NAFTA	North American Free Trade Agreement
NATO	North Atlantic Treaty Organization
Neb. L. Rev.	Nebraska Law Review
NGO(s)	non-governmental organisation(s)
NIEO	New International Economic Order
OECD	Organisation for Economic Co-operation and Development
OHR	Office of the High Representative for Bosnia and Herzegovina
PA	Parliamentary Assembly of Bosnia and Herzegovina
PCA	Permanent Court of Arbitration
PCIJ	Permanent Court of International Justice
Res.	resolution
S.	bills originating from the Senate
SA	South Africa
SADC	Southern African Development Community
SC	Supreme Court
S Ct	Supreme Court Reporter
SCR	Canada Supreme Court Reports
SCR	Indian Supreme Court Reports
Sess.	Session
S. Exec. Rep.	Senate Executive Report
S. Con. Res.	Concurrent resolution originating in the Senate
S.J. Res.	Joint resolution originating in the Senate
S. RES.	Simple resolution originating in the Senate
TPP	Trans-Pacific-Partnership
TTIP	Transatlantic Trade and Investment Partnership
TWAIL	Third World Approaches to International Law

UCLA	University of California, Los Angeles
UK	United Kingdom
UK Const. L. Blog	United Kingdom Constitutional Law Blog
UKSC	United Kingdom Supreme Court
UKTS	United Kingdom Treaty Series
UN	United Nations
UNCLOS	United Nations Convention on the Law of the Sea
UNCTAD	United Nations Conference on Trade and Development
UN Doc.	United Nations Document (Number)
UNESCO	United Nations Educational, Scientific and Cultural Organization
UNFCCC	United Nations Framework Convention on Climate Change
UNGA	United Nations General Assembly
UNTS	United Nations Treaty Series
US	United States
US	United States Reports
USC	United States Code
USSR	Union of Soviet Socialist Republics
VCLT	Vienna Convention on the Law of Treaties
VP	vice president
VRÜ	Zeitschrift Verfassung und Recht in Übersee
WTO	World Trade Organization
ZAGPHC	Gauteng High Court

1

Introduction

Bridges under Construction and Shifting Boundaries

Helmut Philipp Aust and Thomas Kleinlein

Foreign relations law is developing very dynamically and expanding its horizons while its relationship with public international law is notoriously complex. Like an interface, foreign relations law addresses multiple and diverse questions about how the 'domestic' relates to the 'international' sphere. This volume takes a fresh look at the 'bridges' and 'boundaries' between public international law and foreign relations law. It registers the manifold encounters between the two fields in a systematic and comparative manner and addresses pressing conceptual and practical questions. Its authors analyse both traditional and more recent functions, areas and contexts considered relevant for foreign relations law and the places where foreign relations law interacts with international law. In this introduction, we develop the questions that guide their analysis of the various encounters between public international law and foreign relations law (Section I), reflect on missed encounters between the two fields (Section II), introduce the core concepts and the approach of the book (Section III), and expose its overall structure as well as contents of individual chapters (Section IV).

I THE VARIOUS ENCOUNTERS BETWEEN PUBLIC INTERNATIONAL LAW AND FOREIGN RELATIONS LAW: GUIDING QUESTIONS

New encounters between foreign relations law and international law reflect a variety of interactions between the two fields. Essentially, the places of interaction are 'hybrid' in nature and defined by both international and domestic law.[1]

[1] For an account of hybrid international/national norms, see Anthea Roberts, 'Comparative International Law? The Role of National Courts in Creating and Enforcing International Law' (2011) 60 *ICLQ* 57 at 74–81.

Foreign relations law not only 'bridges' international and domestic law or sets 'boundaries' to international law. Rather, in both capacities – as a 'bridge' and as a 'boundary' – foreign relations law is also responsive to developments in international and domestic law and, recently, subject to dynamic transformations. Due to these dynamics, the 'bridges' are constantly under (re-)construction and the boundaries keep shifting. Neither foreign relations law nor international law are fixed and stable notions.

The 'hybridity' of international and domestic law created by foreign relations law is ambivalent. If foreign relations law combines elements of both international and domestic law, this might strengthen as well as dilute the normativity of international law. On the other hand, similar concerns can be raised from the perspective of the integrity of constitutional law. Bridges significantly change landscapes, and boundaries can also considerably impact on the physical earth. In order to measure these landscapes and their transformations, the contributions to this volume address two questions: to what extent is the field of foreign relations law shaped by the normative expectations and structures of international law? Conversely, in how far is international law a product of the combined processes governed by foreign relations law and construed in the light of domestic law?

In public international law, the distinction between international and domestic law is certainly still firmly rooted in the law of treaties and the law of state responsibility. Article 27 of the Vienna Convention of the Law of Treaties (VCLT)[2] unequivocally stipulates that states cannot rely on their own domestic law in order to justify non-compliance with their obligations under international law. Yet, Article 46 VCLT is a slight opening in this regard by providing for the possibility of invalidity of an international agreement where there was a manifest violation of a provision of fundamental importance in a state party's internal law regarding the competence to conclude treaties. Article 3 of the International Law Commission's Articles on State Responsibility[3] makes a similar distinction between international and internal law, stating that the '[c]haracterization of an act of a State as internationally wrongful is governed by international law. Such characterization is not affected by the characterization of the same act as lawful by internal law'.

International law traditionally leaves it to states how to implement their international legal obligations and, in this regard, relies to a great extent on the

[2] Vienna Convention of the Law of Treaties, Vienna, 23 May 1969, in force 27 January 1980, 1155 UNTS 331.

[3] UNGA, 'Responsibility of States for internationally wrongful acts', UNGA Res. 56/83, UN Doc. A/RES/56/83, 12 December 2001.

machinery of domestic law.[4] This leeway is one of the core sites for foreign relations law, to the extent that the rules in a given constitution can grant international law a certain domestic rank and effect.[5] However, international law increasingly harbours expectations about its domestic implementation. Such expectations can impact considerably on the organization of state power. An example is the customary law requirement to hold environmental impact assessments when industrial sites are likely to produce transboundary effects.[6] Even if this might seem to be just a further obligation under international law, compliance with the 'no harm principle' under international environmental law includes a procedural element.

International institutions in charge of compliance, mostly courts, pay increasing attention to domestic procedures. In the case law of the European Court of Human Rights, scholars have even traced a 'procedural turn'.[7] One aspect of this development is that the Court takes into account domestic procedures when pronouncing on the substantive merits. This means that the quality of domestic decision-making processes influences the intensity of the Court's substantive review. A number of UN bodies like the Human Rights Committee, the Committee on the Elimination of Discrimination against Women and the Committee on the Rights of the Child promote implementation by domestic parliaments and parliamentary oversight as a complementary instrument for human rights realisation.[8]

4 Alfred Verdross and Bruno Simma, *Universelles Völkerrecht: Theorie und Praxis*, 3rd ed. (Berlin: Duncker und Humblot, 1984), para. 848.

5 Helmut Philipp Aust, 'The Democratic Challenge to Foreign Relations Law in Transatlantic Perspective' in Jacco Bomhoff, David Dyzenhaus and Thomas Poole (eds.), *The Double-Facing Constitution* (Cambridge: Cambridge University Press, 2020), p. 345 at 350–1.

6 *Pulp Mills on the River Uruguay (Argentina* v. *Uruguay)*, Judgment, I.C.J. Reports 2010, p. 14 at 82–3.

7 See, amongst others, Janneke Gerards and Eva Brems (eds.), *Procedural Review in European Fundamental Rights Cases* (Cambridge: Cambridge University Press, 2017); Thomas Kleinlein, 'The Procedural Approach of the European Court of Human Rights: Between Subsidiarity and Dynamic Evolution' (2019) 68 *ICLQ* 91 (with further references); see also for a critical analysis of this development Başak Çalı and Kristina Hatas, 'History as an Afterthought: The (Re)Discovery of Article 18 in the Case Law of the European Court of Human Rights' in Helmut Philipp Aust and Esra Demir-Gürsel (eds.), *The European Court of Human Rights: Current Challenges in Historical Perspective* (Cheltenham: Edward Elgar Publishing, 2021), p. 158.

8 On the role of parliaments in the protection and realisation of human rights, see Matthew Saul, 'How and When Can the International Human Rights Judiciary Promote the Human Rights Role of National Parliaments?' in Matthew Saul, Andreas Føllesdal and Geir Ulfstein (eds.), *The International Human Rights Judiciary and National Parliaments: Europe and Beyond, Studies on Human Rights Conventions* (Cambridge: Cambridge University Press, 2017), with references.

Beyond human rights law,[9] a 'proceduralisation' of the interface of international and domestic law can be discerned, particularly in WTO Dispute Settlement and, to a lesser extent, in international investment arbitration.[10] Arguably, this has broader implications for the interaction of foreign relations law and international law, at least in those areas of international law that are strongly 'judicialised'. Here, it is difficult to analyse the reach and authority of international law – and especially of provisions that are fairly open-ended – over domestic law independently of the authority of judicial institutions and their pronouncements.

Novel encounters like these suggest rethinking the relationship between international and domestic law and their 'site of encounter', foreign relations law. In fact, international law scholars have come to realize quite some time ago that the clear separation of international law and domestic law cannot explain phenomena of foreign administration as well as processes of integration and disintegration of states in the course of decolonization.[11] These inherently dynamic phenomena and processes presuppose the concurrent existence of international law and foreign relations law.

Public debates about the Comprehensive Economic and Trade Agreement between Canada and the EU (CETA)[12] and the aborted project of a Transatlantic Trade and Investment Partnership (TTIP) are only two examples

[9] Irrespective of the procedural approach, see, for the notion that the ECtHR's *Hirst* case raises the general issue of the authority of international law over domestic state officials, Başak Çalı, *The Authority of International Law: Obedience, Respect, and Rebuttal* (Oxford: Oxford University Press, 2015), p. 1ff.

[10] For a procedural approach to necessity and proportionality stricto sensu, see Caroline Henckels, *Proportionality and Deference in Investor-State Arbitration: Balancing Investment Protection and Regulatory Autonomy*, Cambridge Studies in International and Comparative Studies (Cambridge: Cambridge University Press, 2015), p. 149, at 149–50, 161–2; for a comparison of WTO law and international investment arbitration, see Lukasz Gruszczynski and Valentina Vadi, 'Standard of Review and Scientific Evidence in WTO Law and International Investment Arbitration: Converging Parallels?' in Lukasz Gruszczynski and Wouter Werner (eds.), *Deference in International Courts and Tribunals: Standard of Review and Margin of Appreciation* (Oxford: Oxford University Press, 2014); for a synopsis of developments in international huma rights adjudication and WTO dispute settlement, see Thomas Kleinlein, 'The Procedural Approach in International Human Rights Law and Fundamental Values: Towards a Proceduralization of the Interface of International and Domestic Law?' (2017) 14 *ESIL Conference Paper Series*, pp. 1–22.

[11] Albert Bleckmann, *Das französische Kolonialreich und die Gründung neuer Staaten: Die Rechtsentwicklung in Syrien/Libanon, Indochina und Schwarzafrika, Beiträge zum ausländischen öffentlichen Recht und Völkerrecht* (Köln: Heymann, 1969), vol. 50; Albert Bleckmann, 'Fremdherrschaft und Dekolonisierung in rechtlicher Sicht' (1971) 4 *Verfassung und Recht in Übersee* 237.

[12] Comprehensive Economic and Trade Agreement between Canada and the EU (CETA), Brussels, 30 October 2016, not in force (parts are provisionally applied), (2017) OJ L11/23.

for how deeply the 'international' is penetrating domestic legal orders. It is a truism that international law and international institutions have far-reaching implications for everybody's life. One of the prominent concerns raised by these 'mega-regionals' was about the regulatory autonomy remaining for democratic states to govern in the public interest.[13]

From the perspective of individuals, the consequences of some international legal instruments do not always differ categorically from the effects of domestic laws or executive measures, although the repercussions are usually weaker and less direct. Targeted sanctions imposed by the UN Security Council are only the most obvious example for this phenomenon.[14]

The impact of international law is not limited to the traditional sources of international treaties and customary international law (which provides for problems of democratic legitimacy of its own). It includes the secondary law produced by international organizations and many forms of what is often called 'soft law' but can also be described as informal processes of norm generation. Contrary to the actual impact of secondary law and informal instruments, which reinforces the need for democratic legitimacy, the role of domestic parliaments in their adoption and implementation is often neglected.[15]

Consequently, if ever, the claim that a clear distinction can be made between internal and external forms of state action is no longer easily tenable.[16] Rather, the strict distinction between international and internal law seems to be no more than a doctrinal remnant of the nineteenth century.

The approach of this book is to analyse not just these developments in detail, but to also take stock of the overarching narratives about foreign relations law and its relation to international law. Are there any overarching narratives which can be relied upon to look at these questions? If so, do they refer to individual jurisdictions or do they fit into more comprehensive trends?

13 Thomas Kleinlein, 'TTIP and the Challenges of Investor-State-Arbitration: An Exercise in Comparative Foreign Relations Law' in Anna-Bettina Kaiser, Niels Petersen and Johannes Saurer (eds.), *US Constitutional Law in the Obama Era: A Transatlantic Perspective* (London: Routledge, 2018); see also the contributions in Benedict Kingsbury et al. (eds.), *Megaregulation Contested – Global Economic Ordering After TPP* (Oxford: Oxford University Press, 2019).

14 Anne Peters, 'Foreign Relations Law and Global Constitutionalism' (2017) 111 *AJIL Unbound* 331 at 331.

15 For a critique, see Jan Klabbers, *The Concept of Treaty in International Law, Developments in International Law* (The Hague: Kluwer Law International, 1996), vol. 22.

16 See already Louis Henkin, *Foreign Affairs and the US Constitution*, 2nd ed. (Oxford: Oxford University Press, 1996), p. 6.

From a bird's eye view, the course of foreign relations law is rather obscured by seemingly opposite developments: In some jurisdictions, like the United States, an established foreign affairs 'exceptionalism' (with regard to justiciability or executive power) is subject to a process of 'normalisation'.[17] At least to some extent, this development is triggered by international trends (or a new perception of these trends). At the same time, and also as a consequence of international trends, other jurisdictions are just 'discovering' or developing foreign relations law as a distinct field. This raises the question whether this discovery will lead to new forms of foreign affairs exceptionalism.

II FOREIGN RELATIONS LAW AND INTERNATIONAL LAW: MISSED ENCOUNTERS?

While the encounters of foreign relations law and international law are manifold and a careful analysis serves a better understanding of both fields, scholars in the past have often focused on either foreign relations law or international law. Indeed, parts of the history of both fields can be summarised as a history of missed encounters. At times, academics from either discipline, international law and foreign relations law respectively, look at the other with a degree of scepticism. On the one hand, some international lawyers tend to view foreign relations law as a construct which primarily serves to dilute international law's normativity through domestic law categories.[18] The US pedigree of the field only further nurtures the impression of foreign relations law as a manifestation of 'American exceptionalism'. A more inward-looking approach to foreign relations law took hold in the US literature since the mid-1990s, often in the name of domestic democracy.[19] This move has been influential also outside the United States. Accordingly, on the other hand, some foreign relations law scholars, often hailing from the background of domestic constitutional law, harbour the opposite suspicion about the potentially damaging impact of international law's more lofty and looser categories which could work to the detriment of domestic constitutional principles like democracy, the rule of law and the protection of individual rights.[20]

[17] Ganesh Sitaraman and Ingrid Wuerth, 'The Normalization of Foreign Relations Law' (2015) 128 *Harvard Law Review* 1897.

[18] Cf. Anthea Roberts, *Is International Law International?* (Oxford: Oxford University Press, 2017), pp. 104–5.

[19] Curtis A. Bradley and Jack L. Goldsmith, 'Customary International Law as Federal Common Law: A Critique of the Modern Position' (1997) 110 *Harvard Law Review* 815.

[20] See, for instance, Frank Schorkopf, 'Von Bonn über Berlin nach Brüssel und Den Haag. Europa- und Völkerrechtswissenschaft in der Berliner Republik' in Thomas Duve and

On the whole, the history of the field reveals that foreign relations law is not simply the domestic – and parochial – counter-perspective to public international law. Even in the United States, the history of the field has been shaped in the beginning by staunch internationalists: Quincy Wright and Louis Henkin.[21] At any rate, recent years have seen a growing amount of interaction between the two fields of expertise. International lawyers are increasingly interested in the domestic contexts of international law. This trend has nurtured the emergence of 'comparative international law' as a research project. This new field of study is interested in the domestic contexts of international law, that is, in the 'similarities and differences in how actors in different legal systems understand, interpret, apply, and approach international law'.[22] Foreign relations law scholars demonstrate increasing awareness of how foreign relations law shapes international law.[23] Despite these developments in both fields, a gap in the literature remains with respect to an exploration of how the two fields relate to each other, how categories, concepts and principles are informed by debates and developments in the respective other field and how differences persist.

Recent years have also witnessed a growing fascination of international lawyers with the role that domestic courts can play for a more effective implementation of international law,[24] hence to some extent returning to thoughts of a 'dédoublement fonctionnel' articulated by Georges Scelle in the interwar era.[25] In other words, international law needs bridges as well as boundaries towards foreign relations law in order to become and remain workable. Similar observations are true from the perspective of foreign relations law: if the autonomy of constitutional orders is to be protected – and their central values upheld – this field of the law cannot allow for a direct and unconditional reception of categories of international law into its own

Stefan Ruppert (eds.), *Rechtswissenschaft in der Berliner Republik* (Berlin: Suhrkamp, 2018), p. 327 at 347–8.

21 Quincy Wright, *The Control of American Foreign Relations* (New York: Macmillan, 1922); Louis Henkin, *Foreign Affairs and the Constitution* (Mineola, New York: The Foundation Press, 1972).

22 Anthea Roberts et al. (eds.), *Comparative International Law* (New York: Oxford University Press, 2018).

23 Curtis A. Bradley (ed.), *The Oxford Handbook of Comparative Foreign Relations Law* (Oxford: Oxford University Press, 2019), parts II, IV and V.

24 For a recent casebook, see André Nollkaemper et al. (eds.), *International Law in Domestic Courts: A Casebook* (Oxford: Oxford University Press, 2018).

25 Georges Scelle, *Précis de droit des gens: Principes et systématique; Tome 1. Introduction: le milieu intersocial* (Paris: Sirey, 1932), p. 50; see also Antonio Cassese, 'Remarks on Scelle's Theory of "Role Splitting" (dédoublement fonctionnel) in International Law' (1990) 1 *EJIL* 210.

normative order. Some act of translation is needed, if only to assert the authority of domestic legal orders vis-à-vis 'the international'.[26] While this, from the perspective of international law, involves the establishment of boundaries, the sheer existence of foreign relations law also points to the fact that no state is an island and exists in isolation from the international community (of states) of which it forms part. If looked at from a sociological perspective focusing on the actors of the academic debate, it becomes also apparent that foreign relations law scholars need to simultaneously rely on both the bridges and the boundaries – otherwise their field of expertise would become meaningless, at least if it should not collapse into an exercise of resistance against 'foreign' elements entering the domestic legal order.

By focusing on the bridges and boundaries between the two fields, this volume also wishes to challenge too one-sided understandings of either field. It is precisely the by now established narrative of an '*Ersatz* international law'[27] that should be challenged critically. 'Comparative foreign relations law' does not have to become a counter-project to 'comparative international law' or even to public international law itself. For both fields, the treatment of bridges and boundaries raises distinct identity questions. International lawyers are notoriously sceptical of attributing too great a role to domestic law. International law scholarship might be characterised by a certain fear that its autonomy might be at risk if the role of domestic law is made too prominent.

Accordingly, this volume aims at making a conceptual as well as a practical contribution. Its conceptual contribution lies in the various attempts of the chapters in this book to sound out the complicated relationship between foreign relations law and public international law in a more context-sensitive and diverse manner than it has been undertaken so far. While this is a contribution to the world of ideas, its import is more than just theoretical. Whereas hard-nosed scholars of political science or adherents of a realist school of international relations might frown upon the relevance of public international law, various contributions to this volume – especially, but not limited to those in Part III of the volume on powers and processes – point to the pressing real world issues which are negotiated through the categories of foreign relations law and public international law. Depending on which frame is referenced, the one analytical category and legal field may weigh heavier than the other one. Yet, they always point to each other and need to be

[26] On processes of translation see Karen Knop, 'Here and There: International Law in Domestic Courts' (1999–2000) 32 *NYU Journal of International Law and Politics* 501.

[27] Originally, this phrase was coined by Dionisio Anzilotti, *Studi critici di Diritto internazionale privato* (Bologna: Cappelli, 1898), p. 104 to characterise private international law.

seen in some form of stereovision so as to portray the whole picture. Perspectives from the 'Global South' or semi-peripheral states like Bosnia and Herzegovina included in our volume show that many of their constitutional systems are heavily shaped by international law. International law is considered not just as a tool to advance the foreign policy agenda of a given state, but as a factor to be reckoned with for basic questions of the organisation of the polity.

III CORE CONCEPTS AND THE APPROACH OF THE BOOK

The approach of this volume is pluralistic. It includes various jurisdictions, perspectives and positions. However, contributors have developed their chapters against the background of a set of core concepts and notions. The plurality of approaches entails that some authors may harbour different understandings of such concepts or may even reject them in the first place. We consider this an asset rather than a liability of this collection, as it helps to reveal the essentially contested nature of notions such as 'foreign relations law'.

A *Foreign Relations Law*

'Foreign relations law' is neither a legal term of art nor is it a category of the law with wide acceptance across national legal systems. The notion refers to the part of domestic law that is generally concerned with the relationship between the outside of a state and its interior[28] and focuses on the interaction between international and domestic norms. While a proper field of foreign relations law has not materialised in all legal systems, we presuppose that any given state will have some kind of foreign relations law, at least to the extent that its constitution or other relevant legal sources provide for guidance on these issues. Most jurisdictions share rules and related case law that fulfil comparable basic functions in governing the status of international law and foreign affairs powers. Therefore, it is plausible that foreign relations law has been discovered (although relatively recently) as a field of comparative research.[29]

[28] Campbell McLachlan, 'Five Conceptions of the Function of Foreign Relations Law' in Curtis A. Bradley (ed.), *The Oxford Handbook of Comparative Foreign Relations Law* (Oxford: Oxford University Press, 2019).

[29] Curtis A. Bradley, 'Foreign Relations Law as a Field of Study' (2017) 111 *AJIL Unbound* 316; Curtis A. Bradley, 'What Is Foreign Relations Law?' in Curtis A. Bradley (ed.), *The Oxford Handbook of Comparative Foreign Relations Law* (Oxford: Oxford University Press, 2019). For earlier comparative work in this area, see the references in Thomas Kleinlein, 'Book Review:

The function of the respective body of law or cases is both to separate the internal from the external and to mediate the inward reception of international law into the domestic legal system. It is also concerned with separation of powers and the rule of law and with facilitating the external relations of the State. A further function of this body of law is to establish rules of jurisdiction and applicable law.[30] While relying on this analytical lens of 'foreign relations law', it is not our intention to contribute to a further global spread of yet another category of US law. Rather, this volume acknowledges the important tradition that foreign relations law has had in the United States and formulates invitations to rethink this category in different contexts.

B *Public International Law*

Difficult as it is to define foreign relations law, it is even more problematic to capture the meaning of public international law in a nutshell. However, some features of modern international law are of particular importance for this book. Public international law is today obviously more than a set of rules that 'governs the relations between independent states', as the Permanent Court of International Justice famously held in its *Lotus* case.[31] The horizons of international law have greatly expanded and, while international law has become a 'comprehensive blueprint for social life',[32] this expansion affected the two most foundational organizing concepts of this body of law: sources and subjects.[33] New participants have entered the international arena and the list of the recognized subjects of international law now extends beyond states to international organizations and the individual. Many other candidates for legal personality are discussed, ranging from transnational corporations to subnational actors like entities of federal states and cities.[34] This expanding list of 'actors' in the international legal system also impacts on the

Oxford Handbook of Comparative Foreign Relations Law. Edited by Curtis A. Bradley' (2020) 114 *AJIL* 539 at 539, footnote 1.

30 McLachlan, 'Five Conceptions of the Function of Foreign Relations Law', p. 21.

31 *Case of the S.S. 'Lotus'*, Judgment, Series A No. 10, p. 18.

32 Christian Tomuschat, 'International Law: Ensuring the Survival of Mankind on the Eve of a New Century' (1999) 281 *Recueil des Cours* 9 at 63–72.

33 On the importance of foundational doctrines for the operation of international law as a 'belief system', see Jean d'Aspremont, *International Law as a Belief System*, Cambridge Studies in International and Comparative Law (Cambridge: Cambridge University Press, 2018), chapters 3 and 4.

34 For an overview see Christian Walter, 'Subjects of International Law' in Rüdiger Wolfrum (ed.), *Max Planck Encyclopedia of Public International Law* (Oxford: Oxford University Press, 2012), p. 634; Jan Klabbers, *International Law*, 3rd ed. (Cambridge: Cambridge University Press, 2020), p. 74.

forms of lawmaking. The newer and less established actors tend to engage in the production of normativity on the international level, yet they still find themselves – to varying degrees – excluded from the realm of formal international lawmaking in the fields of treaty and customary international law.[35]

Also states often do not opt for the conclusion of binding international agreements but see merit in more flexible instruments of a non-binding character. The old debates about 'soft law' do not fully capture this development as many important elements of contemporary international practice are situated in an ambiguous grey zone between bindingness and mere political commitment. This is the case, for instance, with respect to the Paris Agreement on Climate Change[36] and its rather novel way of setting forth obligations which leave it to the parties to define in a first step 'nationally determined contributions' (NDCs). The 'Joint Comprehensive Plan of Action' (JCPOA) between Iran and the six powers involved in its negotiation,[37] while not binding as such, was referred to in a Security Council Resolution.[38] Hence, the 'Iran deal' was made partly binding. A third example pertains to the 'Global Compact on Safe, Orderly and Regular Migration',[39] which explicitly states that it is a non-binding political framework that at the same time synthesizes many existing obligations in the fields of human rights and migration.[40]

Taken together, international law is in a process of deformalisation.[41] For foreign relations law, this has significant impacts as the key categories of the foreign relations law of most jurisdictions seem to be premised on certain

35 This has generated interest in so-called 'informal international lawmaking', see the contributions in Joost Pauwelyn, Ramses A. Wessels and Jan Wouters (eds.), *Informal International Lawmaking* (Oxford: Oxford University Press, 2012).

36 Paris Agreement on Climate Change, New York, 22 April 2016, in force 4 November 2016, not yet in UNTS.

37 For the text of the JCPOA see UN Doc. S/RES/2231 (2015), Annex A.

38 UNSC, 'Resolution on Iran Nuclear Issue', UNSC Res. 2231, UN Doc. S/RES/2231 (2015), 20 July 2015.

39 UNGA, 'Global Compact for Safe, Orderly and Regular Migration', UNGA Res. 73/195, UN Doc. A/RES/73/195, 11 January 2019.

40 On the relationship of the Compact with the existing legal framework see Jürgen Bast, 'Der Global Compact for Migration und das internationale Migrationsregime' (2019) *Zeitschrift für Ausländerrecht* 96; Daniel Thym, 'Viel Lärm um nichts? Das Potential des UN-Migrationsrechts zur dynamischen Fortentwicklung der Menschenrechte' (2019) *Zeitschrift für Ausländerrecht* 131.

41 See already Jean d'Aspremont, 'The Politics of Deformalization in International Law' (2011) 3 *Goettingen Journal of International Law* 503; Alejandro Rodiles, *Coalitions of the Willing and International Law: The Interplay between Formality and Informality* (Cambridge: Cambridge University Press, 2018).

more or less formal understandings of the established actors and forms of international cooperation and lawmaking.

C *Hybridity As an Effect of Foreign Relations Law*

As we have seen, the growing mutual enmeshment between international law and foreign relations law creates a hybrid zone where the two meet. This hybridity takes centre stage for this book on the various encounters between foreign relations law and international law. Yet, it is important to note that we do not argue that either international law or foreign relations law respectively are hybrid in nature. While, as explained above, the strict distinction between international and internal law is of limited explanatory power today, we see great merit in upholding the rather traditional view that international law is indeed international and that foreign relations law is part of a given domestic legal system.[42] Properly understood, 'hybridity' is not a characteristic but an effect of foreign relations law. As defined above, foreign relations law encapsulates the rules of domestic law about the reception of international law and about the participation of the state and its organs in the international sphere. Asserting a hybridity of foreign relations law might indeed create the risk of diluting the normativity of one of the two or even of both fields of law. International law operates on the assumption that it is distinct from domestic law. Understanding foreign relations law as a hybrid between the international and the domestic invites the construction of an '*Ersatz* international law' for domestic purposes; a tendency that is at times identified with respect to US approaches to foreign relations law.[43]

Reliance on this distinction between public international law and foreign relations law might strike some readers as rather static in nature. Yet, upholding the traditional criteria – and, if you will, the boundaries between the two – does not preclude investigating the hybrid zone that is created by the encounters of public international law and foreign relations law. At times, the same legal question can be assessed from both perspectives. Whereas traditional dualists would defend the view that one can give starkly differing answers depending on the perspective from which the question is assessed, we argue that it is a function of both international law and foreign relations law to come

42 Helmut Philipp Aust, 'Foreign Affairs' in Rainer Grote, Frauke Lachenmann and Rüdiger Wolfrum (eds.), *Max Planck Encyclopedia of Comparative Constitutional Law* (Oxford: Oxford University Press, 2017), para. 10.

43 For a critical view in this regard see Campbell McLachlan, *Foreign Relations Law* (Cambridge: Cambridge University Press, 2014), para. 1.30.

to a solution that mediates between the two without undermining the specificities of each perspective.

This rather abstract consideration can be illustrated by reference to the ever-ongoing saga of the reach of state immunity in the Italian-German relationship. When the International Court of Justice decided in favour of Germany in the *Jurisdictional Immunities* case in 2012, it upheld a strict reading of the reach of state immunity and did not hint at the possibility of future legal developments which might accommodate the concerns of Italian courts that immunity might not be appropriate for German crimes committed in World War II.[44] While the case seemed to have been settled then, the Italian Constitutional Court struck back with its by now well-known *Sentenza* 238/2014. It found compliance with the ICJ judgment to stand in conflict with the supreme constitutional principles of the Italian constitutional order, namely the right of access to court and the right to a remedy.[45] The approach of the *Sentenza* was as categorical as the reasoning of the ICJ. The Italian Constitutional Court relied on a doctrine of 'counter-limits' (*controlimiti*) and limited its analysis to the level of Italian constitutional law, not without expressing its ambition to also influence the development of international law. One might say that this 'dialogue of courts' has created a hybrid zone where arguments from international law and foreign relations law intersect and clash with each other. While both positions seem to have opted for a 'closure' of their normative system,[46] a mutual openness for the position of the other perspective might have allowed for the construction of more bridges and the erection of fewer boundaries.

D *Dimensions of Encounters: Fields, Substance and Procedure*

Where and how do such encounters play out? For analytical purposes, we have identified three distinct yet interrelated dimensions of encounters along which the enquiry of this book is structured. This triad of fields, substance and procedure lends itself to structuring our collective endeavour in the following way.

44 *Jurisdictional Immunities of the State (Germany* v. *Italy: Greece intervening)*, Judgment, I.C.J. Reports 2012, p. 99.

45 Decision No. 238/2014 of 22 October 2014 (English version available at: www.cortecostituzionale.it/documenti/download/doc/recent_judgments/S238_2013_en.pdf, last accessed 22 January 2021).

46 Andrea Bianchi, 'Jurisdictional Immunities, Constitutional Values, and System Closures' in Curtis A. Bradley (ed.), *Oxford Handbook of Comparative Foreign Relations Law* (Oxford: Oxford University Press, 2019), p. 685.

With respect to 'fields', this book develops a number of different perspectives on how the two fields of foreign relations and public international law interact. How do the two fields perceive each other? Is the emphasis more on bridges or on boundaries? Are arguments from one field relied upon to change the law in the other? Might foreign relations law questions even be used as bargaining tools in international negotiation processes? And how do dynamics in the development of the two fields develop, for instance with respect to the overarching narrative of a foreign affairs exceptionalism versus the alleged normalisation of this field?

'Substance' allows us to catch a glimpse on the outcome of the various encounters between public international law and foreign relations law. To what ends do states and other actors pursue international cooperation? Are they conditioned by their domestic constitutions also in substantive terms? Which limits do the national constitutional framework and foreign relations law impose on the organisation of international cooperation? Does foreign relations law undergo a development of 'normalisation', meaning that the conduct of foreign relations is increasingly subjected to the constitutional and other legal standards that apply to other governmental action? If this is the case, foreign relations law will decreasingly be regarded as 'exceptional' and 'normal' constitutional standards must apply.[47]

Finally, a shift of attention to institutions and procedures also in foreign relations law is not only justified by the 'proceduralisation' of the interface of international and domestic law outlined above. The focus on 'procedure' is also warranted as large parts of foreign relations law are precisely about procedure. We argue that significant changes in the relationship between public international law and foreign relations law will materialise with respect to procedures under foreign relations law. Foreign relations law regulates the division of competences between different state organs in the field of foreign affairs and how they interact. A typical focus of this debate is the necessary amount of parliamentary participation in foreign affairs. Yet, parliamentary participation does not mean the same in a presidential system like the one of the United States and a parliamentary system as in Germany. Rather, the balance of power in foreign affairs and domestic procedures are embedded in constitutional structures and domestic legal cultures, which need to be studied carefully.

A more activist approach by some domestic courts in their control of both the executive and the legislative in foreign affairs leads to more demanding procedures. For example, the Higher Administrative Court of North Rhine-Westphalia, in March 2019, ordered the Federal Republic of Germany to take

47 Aust, 'Foreign Affairs', para. 1.

appropriate measures to ascertain whether the use by the United States of America of the Ramstein Air Base for the deployment of armed drones in Yemen takes place in accordance with international law. This decision was set aside on appeal in November 2020. While the Federal Administrative Court stressed the margin of assessment and action of the Federal Government ('*Einschätzungs-, Wertungs- und Gestaltungsbereich*') and decided in its favour, it did not deny that the state's duty to protect includes a procedural component which relates to ensuring conformity with international law. More generally, it certainly remains the case that for both courts the question of whether international law permits armed drone missions in Yemen was not a political question, but rather a legal question, to be assessed by the judiciary.[48]

IV THE STRUCTURE OF THE BOOK

The volume is structured into three main parts that analyse the three dimensions of encounters between foreign relations law and international law developed in the previous section. A first part ('Identities and Interactions') looks at varieties and variations of the field of foreign relations law and how it relates to public international law. A second part ('Sovereignty and Cooperation') analyses substantive limits to international cooperation which often stem from domestic constitutional principles. A final main part ('Powers and Processes') turns to the processing of international law obligations through domestic categories like separation of powers. These categories fulfil an important heuristic function for the structuring of our volume. They are each characterised by built-in tensions – between the identity of the respective field and its interactions with its respective 'others', between absolute sovereignty and forms of international cooperation that lead to substantial commitments and between unchecked powers and their taming in processes. The book will be concluded by some cross-cutting observations on the bridges and boundaries between public international law and foreign relations law.

A *Identities and Interaction*

The first Part, on identities and interaction, studies diverging conceptualisations of the field of foreign relations law and looks at places where one would

[48] For the decision of the OVG Münster see *Bin Ali Jaber* v. *Germany*, Judgment, 19 March 2019, 4 A 1361/15; the decision of the Federal Administrative Court is *Bin Ali Jaber v. Germany*, Judgment, 25 November 2020, 6 C 7.19; see further on the decision by the OVG Münster Helmut Philipp Aust, 'US-Drohneneinsätze und die grundrechtliche Schutzpflicht für das Recht auf Leben: "German exceptionalism"?' (2020) 75 *JuristenZeitung* 303.

not, from a traditional perspective, expect any foreign relations law. It develops a contextual account of how the various identities of the field have been shaped in encounters with different legal traditions and theoretical concerns. Furthermore, this part studies several linkages between and mutual effects of foreign relations law and international law. It analyses how foreign relations law affects the making of international law and how, vice versa, international law influences domestic rules on treaty making powers.

Felix Lange analyses the more informal and contextual influence of foreign relations law on the making of international law and, in particular, its use as a bargaining tool in treaty negotiations. With reference to the US position on the Paris Agreement on Climate Change, the chapter argues that domestic foreign relations law at times shapes the negotiation process by limiting possible outcomes. The example demonstrates potential effects of domestic constitutional design for the international legal structure.

Edward Swaine discusses how international law has homogenised foreign relations law relating to the creation and elimination of international treaty obligations – encouraging even those states that possess other constitutional agents to regard executive power as sufficient. This tendency has been fully expressed in the international law regarding ratification and is increasingly apparent in emerging practices of treaty withdrawal.

While these two contributions analyse modes of interaction between foreign relations law and international law and how this affects their respective identities, *Michael Riegner* poses the identity question on a different level. He contrasts two different perspectives on foreign relations law, one that developed in liberal democracies at the centre of geopolitical gravity and one shaped by the postcolonial contexts and historical experiences of countries at the periphery of the global political economy. The peripheral perspective is not exclusive to an essentialised 'South' but has increasing resonance and heuristic value in the 'North', highlighting contemporary transformations in liberal-democratic foreign relations law.

This insight is further corroborated by *Prabhakar Singh*'s chapter, which offers a critique of the notion of foreign relations law, formulated from an Indian perspective. The chapter traces the development of the case law of Indian courts on the resonance of international law in the domestic legal system and concludes with reflections on whether it is desirable to frame these cases as manifestations of 'foreign relations law' or whether this conceptual transplant would ignore the special situation of India as a postcolonial country. The chapter points to the difficulties in determining whether a given legal system has a field of foreign relations law and what the implications of such a finding are.

This question is also reflected on in the contribution by *Frédéric Mégret*, who asks whether there is a French variant of foreign relations law. By revisiting the idiosyncratic work of the French international law scholar and practitioner Guy de la Charrière, *Mégret* brings to the fore a starkly contrasting understanding of foreign relations law which both takes international law seriously and connects it with wider geopolitical power games. Uncovering such early and non-Anglophone voices in the effort to formulate the conceptual framework of foreign relations law can help further problematise the very notion.

The first part of the volume concludes with the contribution by *Angelo Jr. Golia*, who suggests to understand foreign relations law as a form of global administrative law. Already the categorisation as administrative law is subversive as it plays with the traditional assumption that much of foreign relations law is about high politics. Using the theoretical approach of 'Global Administrative Law' (GAL), *Golia* makes a contribution which can be understood as a particular facet of the normalisation of foreign relations law through administrative law.

B *Sovereignty and Cooperation*

Part II of the volume deals with issues of sovereignty and cooperation, two notions which are at the heart of international law and find themselves in constant tension. Sovereignty often also serves as a placeholder for constitutional values, in particular domestic democratic self-determination. Foreign relations law can mediate between these concerns and the values of international cooperation, but it can also exacerbate conflict. The theoretical debates of the beginning of the twentieth century on the tension between sovereignty and the binding force of international treaties and between monism and dualism nowadays reappear in the concepts of foreign relations law and respective case law of domestic courts. Recent years have also demonstrated that foreign relations law itself is a politically contested field, and it is exactly this field where the right balance between these conflicting values is to be struck in a dynamically developing globalised world.

Niki Aloupi sheds light on concrete examples of how this tension and the mutual imbrications can be mediated. She analyses the case law of the French Conseil Constitutionnel on 'Limitations of Sovereignty'. Since this doctrine has not the least allowed the Conseil itself to take an active role in the field of foreign relations law, *Aloupi's* contribution also demonstrates how 'substance' and 'procedure' interact.

Anna Petrig's contribution turns to another factor complicating the relationship between sovereignty and cooperation: the growing deformalisation and privatisation in international law and the impact that these developments have on the framework of democratic participation in Swiss Foreign Relations law. The chapter submits that the 'democratic participation framework' of Swiss foreign relations law is predicated on a very traditional understanding of sources and actors of international law. The chapter warns against a hollowing out of these traditional mechanisms of generating democratic legitimacy.

C *Powers and Processes*

The third and final main Part of the volume turns to powers and processes in the proverbial field where foreign relations law and international law meet. The transformations of procedures in foreign affairs and their reverberations for international law are specific examples of the interaction between foreign relations law and international law. In some legal orders, a trend towards earlier information of parliaments about imminent foreign policy decisions can be pursued. Moreover, the role of courts in foreign relations law is subject to change. In some jurisdictions, there is at least an emerging trend towards a greater role of courts in controlling the executive in foreign affairs. However, these trends do not seem to be robust but rather depend on individual subject matters and jurisdictions. While domestic procedures are themselves subject to transformation, they also impact on or transform the substance of international law foreign relations and drive innovations and change.

Dire Tladi revisits the normalisation story through the perspective of South African constitutional law. In particular, he traces how successively the role of executive discretion in this field has been diminished through case law of the courts. *Tladi* argues that the post-Apartheid constitution was a constitution made for Mandela – while subsequent case law was born out of the frustrating experience of the Zuma years. His chapter offers hence a particular perspective on the adaptability of foreign relations law to changing political circumstances – which is an important and at times overlooked factor for the implementation of international law.

The chapter by *Jean Galbraith* follows with observations on a turn from scope to process as limits to executive power in US foreign relations law. In particular, she traces how the Presidential power has undergone changes – substantive checks on the foreign affairs power were removed but at the same time substituted by procedural checks and limits. The chapter argues that international law has played a key role in this development.

In his contribution, *Stanisław Biernat* looks at the division of competences in Polish foreign relations law. He analyses how different parts of the executive – the Council of Ministers and the President – can clash with respect to their foreign affairs power and how this clash has been addressed in Polish constitutional practice.

Ajla Škrbić, in turn, focuses on the role of parliaments in creating and enforcing Foreign Relations Law from the perspective of Bosnia and Herzegovina (BiH). BiH is a unique case for the foundation of its constitutional framework in an international treaty, the Dayton Peace Agreement. Consequently, its foreign relations law, nascent as it is, is inextricably tied up in the various connections between international law and foreign relations law from the outset. In this sense, the contribution connects back to insights from the first part of the volume which highlighted the dependency of foreign relations law on international law for some states, in particular in the 'Global South'.

The contribution by *Veronika Fikfak* details how concepts of international law become appropriated in parliamentary discourses. Her case study focuses on UK parliamentary practice with respect to the use of force. She shows how the role of parliament has increased in decisions about the use of force in the UK context. At the same time, the role of international law has become ambiguous. Her chapter unearths the development that domestic approval for the use of force might be seen as a substitute for legitimation under international law. The chapter hence points to potentially troubled appropriations of international law categories in domestic contexts with uneasy repercussions for international law.

The third part of the volume is concluded by a contribution by *Ji Hua*, who looks at environmental governance and the role it plays in Chinese foreign relations law. In particular, this chapter takes the field of environmental governance as a case study to probe whether a field of foreign relations law exists in China or whether questions usually associated with foreign relations law in Western jurisdictions are processed through different categories. The chapter can hence also be read as a variation of *Prabhakar Singh*'s explorations on the existence (or not) of an Indian foreign relations law in Part I of the volume. At the same time, it tackles these questions from a more practical level with a view to the division of competences in the Chinese legal order.

D *Final Reflections*

Part IV of the volume offers two sets of final reflections from *Curtis A. Bradley* and *Campbell McLachlan*. Both contributions reflect on the overarching questions of the volume presented in this introduction through a reading of and reaction to the individual chapters.

PART I

IDENTITIES AND INTERACTION

2

Foreign Relations Law As a Bargaining Tool?

Felix Lange

I INTRODUCTION

To perceive foreign relations law as a self-standing academic subfield, perspective or theme which enlightens our understanding of the linkages between national and international law is a rather novel phenomenon.[1] In most jurisdictions an academic tradition of foreign relations law as a separate field or theme does not exist. Issues of foreign relations law such as the separation of powers in foreign affairs or the integration of international law into the domestic order are often either discussed in treatises of constitutional or international law, or in both. For instance, not only the *Oxford Handbook of the Indian Constitution* contains a chapter on the case law of the Indian Supreme Court dealing with the status of international law in the Indian legal system[2] but also the edited volume *Comparative International Law* includes a contribution addressing how the Indian Supreme Court integrates human rights law into the domestic order.[3] Moreover, if, like in the United States, a foreign relations law tradition exists, the norms of the US Constitution and the case law of the Supreme Court which relate to foreign affairs are often taught and analyzed by scholars who teach and write on international and domestic

[1] Curtis A. Bradley (ed.), *The Oxford Handbook of Comparative Foreign Relations Law* (New York: Oxford University Press, 2019).

[2] The chapter also addresses the division of competences between the executive and legislature, Lavanya Rajamani, 'International Law and the Constitutional Schema', in Sujit Choudhry, Madhav Khosla and Pratab Bhani Mehta (eds.), *The Oxford Handbook of the Indian Constitution* (New York: Oxford University Press, 2016), p. 143.

[3] Neha Jain, 'The Democratizing Force of International Law: Human Rights Adjudication by the Indian Supreme Court', in Anthea Roberts et al. (eds.), *Comparative International Law* (New York: Oxford University Press, 2018), p. 319.

(constitutional) law.[4] As the editors of this volume rightly emphasize, foreign relations law thus concerns the relationship between domestic (constitutional) law and international law. The hybrid character of foreign relations law invites us to ponder about the repercussions of domestic (constitutional) law for international law and vice versa.[5]

This contribution attempts to shed some light onto the issue of the place of foreign relations law and the bridges and boundaries it builds between constitutional and international law. It starts by studying the emergence of foreign relations law in various jurisdictions and its relationship to domestic (constitutional) law and international law. It argues that foreign relations law is best understood as a subfield or theme of domestic (constitutional) law with close linkages to international law.

But seeing the locus of foreign relations law in the domestic is only the starting point for a broader engagement with its effects on international law and vice versa. In general, the separation of foreign relations law from international law should not make us blind for studying the interlinkages and impacts of the respective fields on each other. For instance, the study of the informal and contextual influence of foreign relations law on international treaty-making seems to be worthwhile.

Therefore, this contribution analyzes one aspect of the informal use of foreign relations law in relation to international law: it discusses the possibility to rely on domestic foreign relations law as a bargaining tool in international negotiations to persuade the other negotiating parties of one's own perspective. Domestic foreign relations law might shape the negotiation process and limit possible outcomes if one actor successfully flags a certain negotiating outcome as leading to nonparticipation because of domestic veto powers. If the historic role of veto powers in treaty-making makes the threat of nonparticipation credible, the other negotiating parties might be tempted to give in and sign onto the other side's negotiating goal.

In particular, I study the evolution of the bargaining position of the United States in relation to the Paris Agreement on climate change and its connection to US foreign relations law. In the debate about the Paris Agreement, the Obama administration highlighted that the domestic constitutional rules on treaty-making call for negotiating a treaty with nonbinding provisions on climate change mitigation. Notably, the US delegation successfully stopped

[4] See for instance bio of Curtis Bradley, https://law.duke.edu/fac/bradleyc/; Jack Goldsmith, https://hls.harvard.edu/faculty/directory/10320/Goldsmith; Oona Hathaway, https://law.yale.edu/oona-hathaway, accessed September 30, 2020.

[5] Helmut Philipp Aust and Thomas Kleinlein, 'Introduction', this volume.

the adoption of a pre-negotiated final document containing language which sounded like binding commitments on climate mitigation by pointing to its foreign relations law. As I demonstrate, US foreign relations law indeed places considerable constraints on executive treaty-making without involvement of the Senate or Congress. The history of the discussions on the United Nations Framework Convention on Climate Change and the Kyoto Protocol shows that various actors regarded Senate involvement for treaties concerning climate change mitigation as obligatory.[6] However, it is also important to be aware of the ambivalence of the foreign relations law on the matter and the restraint of US courts to judicialize foreign affairs. Arguably, the Obama administration did not exhaust interpretations of its foreign relations law allowing more binding-sounding language on climate mitigation because the negotiating team itself was not eager to commit to binding language.[7] US negotiators also favored nonbinding commitments on climate mitigation for developed countries because they intended to prevent a scheme differentiating between developed and developing countries.[8] In this sense, US foreign relations law became the bargaining tool which limited the space of potential negotiating outcomes on the international plane and allowed the Obama administration to achieve the result it wanted. Even though foreign relations law can unfold this power only under very specific circumstances, the example demonstrates the potential effects of domestic constitutional design for the international legal structure.

II THE EMERGENCE OF FOREIGN RELATIONS LAW AND ITS RELATIONSHIP TO INTERNATIONAL LAW

The design of the constitutional rules addressing foreign affairs has always been an important issue during the constitution-making processes in constitutional democracies. Building on enlightenment philosophers like John Locke,[9] the founding fathers of the US Constitution debated how to allocate the competences between the branches of government in foreign affairs and the role of international treaty and customary law in the domestic legal order.[10] In the British public law tradition, William Blackstone and Albert Venn Dicey

[6] See below III.B and C.

[7] See below III.C.

[8] See below III.C.

[9] John Locke, *Second Treatise of Civil Government* (1690), s. 147.

[10] For instance, The Federalist Papers No. 75, Publius (Alexander Hamilton), 'The Treaty-Making Power of the Executive', 1788, https://avalon.law.yale.edu/18th_century/fed75.asp, accessed September 30, 2020.

contributed to an understanding of foreign affairs law as an area of executive dominance and discretion by highlighting the powers of the Crown.[11] Also, in the constitution-making processes of the nineteenth century, the emerging constitutional democracies opted for different models concerning the allocation of the foreign affairs power.[12]

The legal sciences, however, did not start to become systematically interested in issues of foreign relations law until the early twentieth century. In the United States, Quincy Wright's 1922 study on *The Control of American Foreign Relations* set the tone for the US debate on the constitutional implications for foreign affairs.[13] His discussion of the enforcement of international law in domestic courts and the powers of the President and Congress on international treaty-making and implementation, is still today regarded as an important predecessor of the contemporary debate in the United States.[14] One year later, Ernst Wolgast published his in-depth analysis of the 'Foreign Power' (*Auswärtige Gewalt*) of the German Reich addressing similar issues for the Weimar constitutional system.[15]

After the Second World War, the topic continued to stay relevant in particular in the US debate. During the 1940s, the increasing international engagement of the United States led to the emergence of congressional-executive agreements in constitutional practice causing a scholarly boom on the topic.[16] The term 'foreign relations law' developed to distinguish a separate field of study from international law and constitutional law *stricto sensu* analyzing the separation of powers in foreign affairs, the integration of international law in the US legal system and the international law applicable to the United States.[17] In 1965, the American Law Institute published the

[11] William Blackstone, *Commentaries on the Laws of England*, 4 vols. (Oxford: Clarendon Press, 1765), vol. I, p. 245; Albert V. Dicey, *Introduction to the Study of the Law of the Constitution* (London: Macmillan, 1885), p. 465.

[12] See Robert Schütze, *Foreign Affairs and the EU Constitution: Selected Essays* (Cambridge: Cambridge University Press, 2014), p. 361.

[13] Quincy Wright, *The Control of American Foreign Relations* (New York: Macmillan, 1922).

[14] Curtis A. Bradley, *International Law in the U.S. Legal System*, 2nd ed., (New York: Oxford University Press, 2015), Preface.

[15] Ernst Wolgast, 'Die auswärtige Gewalt des Deutschen Reiches unter besonderer Berücksichtigung des Auswärtigen Amtes' (1923) 44 *Archiv des öffentlichen Rechts* 1.

[16] See for instance Quincy Wright, 'The United States and International Agreements' (1944) 38 *AJIL* 341; Myres S. McDougal and Asher Lans, 'Treaties and Congressional-Executive or Presidential Agreements: Interchangeable Instruments of National Policy (pts. I and II)' (1945) 54 *Yale Law Journal* 181 and 534; Edwin Borchard, 'Treaties and Executive Agreements – A Reply' (1945) 54 *Yale Law Journal* 616.

[17] On the history of the concept see Curtis A. Bradley, 'What Is Foreign Relations Law?', in Curtis A. Bradley (ed.), *The Oxford Handbook of Comparative Foreign Relations Law* (New York: Oxford University Press, 2019), pp. 1 at 5–8.

Restatement (Second) of Foreign Relations Law of the United States with a focus on these topics and thus contributed to the successful establishment of the theme as a disparate scholarly field.[18] Around thirty years later, the scholarly consensus on issues of foreign affairs which had been enshrined in the 1987 *Restatement (Third) of Foreign Relations Law of the United States* with Louis Henkin as Chief Rapporteur was put into question.[19] Some scholars challenged assumptions about the internationalization of the US legal system and triggered a flood of positive and hostile reactions in scholarship.[20]

In other constitutional democracies, the relationship between the constitution and the international legal order has also been a popular topic of academic debates. For instance, in 1954, Western German public law professors debated the division of competences between parliament and the executive in foreign affairs as well as between the federal and state level shaping the constitutional practice of the young German Federal Republic for years to come.[21] Moreover, Klaus Vogel's 1964 programmatic essay on the internationalization of German constitutional law became a common reference point for future generations of scholars.[22] The recent establishment of *Staatsrecht III* as a distinct class of the constitutional law curriculum then triggered a substantial increase in publications on the topic.[23] In South Africa, the constitution-making in the 1990s spurred a debate about the relationship of the post-apartheid Constitution with international law.[24] The theme is frequently taken up in reaction to international law-friendly judgments of South African courts.[25] Also, the foreign relations law of supranational entities like

18 Restatement (Second) of the Foreign Relations Law of the United States (1965).

19 Restatement (Third) of the Foreign Relations Law of the United States (1987).

20 Seminal: Curtis A. Bradley and Jack L. Goldsmith, 'Customary International Law as Federal Common Law: A Critique of the Modern Position' (1997) 110 *Harvard Law Review* 815; for the new consensus see the partial revision in Restatement (Fourth) of the Foreign Relations Law of the United States (2018).

21 Wilhelm Grewe and Eberhard Menzel, 'Die auswärtige Gewalt der Bundesrepublik' (1954) 12 *Veröffentlichungen der Vereinigung der Deutschen Staatsrechtslehrer* 129.

22 Klaus Vogel, *Die Verfassungsentscheidung des Grundgesetzes für eine internationale Zusammenarbeit* (Tübingen: Mohr, 1964).

23 See for instance Frank Schorkopf, *Staatsrecht der internationalen Beziehungen* (München: Beck, 2017); Heiko Sauer, *Staatsrecht III: Auswärtige Gewalt, Bezüge des Grundgesetzes zu Völker- und Europarecht* (München: Beck, 2011); Christian Calliess, *Staatsrecht III: Bezüge zum Völker- und Europarecht*, 2nd ed. (München: Beck, 2018); Andreas Paulus, *Staatsrecht III: Mit Bezügen zum Völker- und Europarecht* (München: Beck, 2010).

24 John Dugard, 'International Law and the South African Constitution' (1997) 8 *EJIL* 77; Neville Botha, 'Treaty Making in South Africa: a Reassessment' (2000) 25 *South African Yearbook of International Law* 69.

25 Erika de Wet, 'The "Friendly but Cautious" Reception of International Law in the Jurisprudence of the South African Constitutional Court: Some Critical Remarks' (2004) 28

the European Union now receives academic attention.[26] Even though the understanding that foreign relations law is a separate field in the legal sciences is rather the exception than the rule in constitutional democracies, scholarly attention has clearly been growing.

Furthermore, a recent comparative turn sparked the interest in foreign relations law in various jurisdictions. In 2011, Campbell McLachlan's study of foreign relations law in various Commonwealth states became a key building block for the scholarly field or theme.[27] Also, the various chapters on manifold jurisdiction in the 2019 *Oxford Handbook on Comparative Foreign Relations Law* illustrate the rising scholarly interest.[28]

The maturation of foreign relations law as a disparate scholarly field or theme is accompanied by debates about its definition, place and function. In particular, various authors address the tricky relationship of foreign relations law to constitutional law and international law. The editor of the *Oxford Handbook*, Curtis Bradley, defines foreign relations law as 'the domestic law of each nation that governs how that nation interacts with the rest of the world'.[29] For him, the theme encompasses the allocation of authority on the vertical and horizontal level of a state and the role of international law before domestic courts, but not '"pure" questions' of international law.[30] Similarly, in the *Max Planck Encyclopedia of Comparative Constitutional Law*, Helmut Aust regards the separation of powers in foreign affairs, the rights of the individual when foreign relations are affected and the relationship between foreign affairs and democracy as key themes of foreign affairs law in the constitutional state.[31] Thomas Giegerich stresses in his contribution for the *Max Planck Encyclopedia of Public International Law* that '[a]lthough the foreign relations law forms that part of internal law which is most closely interlinked with international law, it remains internal law'. For him, 'there is not one worldwide foreign relations law but there are many, however, that

Fordham International Law Journal 1529; Max du Plessis and Guénaël Mettraux, 'South Africa's Failed Withdrawal from the Rome Statute: Politics, Law, and Judicial Accountability' (2017) 15 *Journal of International Criminal Justice* 361; Dire Tladi, 'A Constitution Made for Mandela, A Constitutional Jurisprudence Developed for Zuma', this volume.

26 Marise Cremona and Bruno de Witte (eds.), *EU Foreign Relations Law: Constitutional Fundamentals* (Oxford/Portland: Hart Publishing, 2008); Schütze, *Foreign Affairs*.

27 Campbell McLachlan, *Foreign Relations Law* (Cambridge: Cambridge University Press, 2014).

28 Bradley, *Comparative Foreign Relations Law*.

29 Bradley, 'What Is Foreign Relations Law?', 3–4.

30 Bradley, 'What Is Foreign Relations Law?', 3–4.

31 Helmut Philipp Aust, 'Foreign Affairs', in Max Planck Encyclopedia of Comparative Constitutional Law, August 2017, para. 5, https://oxcon.ouplaw.com/home/MPECCOL.

share certain common principles'.[32] Moreover, when foreign relations law is distinguished from related subfields like comparative international law, its domestic dimension is emphasized. As Anthea Roberts, Paul Stephan, Pierre-Hugues Verdier and Mila Versteeg stress, comparative foreign relations law examines 'the rules, institutions, and practices in different states with respect to how that state conducts relations with foreign states and other actors', whereas comparative international law assesses the different national and regional approaches to and applications of international law.[33]

Despite the grounding in domestic (constitutional) law, foreign relations law scholars are well aware of the links to international law. For some, international law is even part of foreign affairs law. In the US tradition, treatises of foreign relations law often contain chapters on the international legal rules relevant for the United States. According to Restatement the Third, foreign relations law draws its sources both from international law as applicable to the relevant state and national law, in particular constitutional law, governing that state's foreign relations.[34] Therefore, Louis Henkin situates the subject of foreign affairs law as a scholarly endeavor 'somewhere between the constitutional lawyer and the international lawyer'.[35] Similarly, Campbell McLachlan emphasizes that foreign relations law sits at the 'interface of international and municipal law' allocating jurisdiction between domestic or international courts and determining the division of competences between the three branches.[36]

The connections between international law and foreign relations law are manifold indeed, even if one assumes that foreign relations law is a subfield of domestic (constitutional) law in the respective jurisdictions and separate from international law. Doctrinal conjunctions as in article 46 VCLT[37] and as in the opening clauses of many constitutions (for instance article 51 c of the Indian Constitution; section 39 (1b) of the South African Constitution) are evidence for the close interlinkages. In some sense, foreign relations law is the bridge builder between domestic law and international law.

32 Thomas Giegerich, 'Foreign Relations Law', in Max Planck Encyclopedia of Public International Law, January 2011, https://opil.ouplaw.com/home/mpil, para. 1.

33 Anthea Roberts et al., 'Conceptualizing Comparative International Law', in Anthea Roberts et al. (eds.), *Comparative International Law* (New York: Oxford University Press, 2018), p. 9.

34 Restatement (Third) of the Foreign Relations Law of the United States § 1 (1987).

35 Louis Henkin, *Foreign Affairs and the US Constitution* (Oxford: Clarendon Press, 1996), p. viii.

36 McLachlan, *Foreign Relations Law*, pp. xxi, 18–30.

37 Vienna Convention on the Law of Treaties, Vienna, May 23, 1969, in force January 27, 1980, 1155 UNTS 331; (1969) 8 ILM 679; UKTS (1980) 58. See Aust and Kleinlein, 'Introduction', Section I; Edward T. Swaine, 'International Foreign Relations Law', this volume, Section I.

III FOREIGN RELATIONS LAW AS A BARGAINING TOOL?

Besides these doctrinal interconnections, an indirect and informal nexus between foreign relations law and international law exists. For instance, the domestic rules on treaty-making may shape how certain states negotiate international treaties and may have a substantial impact on the substantive content of a treaty. These contextual and informal linkages between foreign relations law and international law become evident when foreign relations law is used as a bargaining tool in international negotiations.

Theoretically, the possible usage of foreign relations law as a bargaining tool has been alluded to already at the end of the 1980s. The political scientist Robert Putnam is well-known for his two-level game theory in which he assesses the impact of domestic politics on international negotiations.[38] On the basis of a study of G7 summits, Putnam demonstrates how domestic interest groups affect the positions of the respective national governments in negotiations on the international level.[39] In passing, Putnam suggests a promising negotiating strategy which links domestic politics with the international negotiations. A delegation should try to convince the other negotiating parties that its suggested draft will certainly be ratified in its own national legal system while a draft more favorable to the opponent will fail in the domestic ratification procedure.[40] Putnam thus theoretically preconceives how foreign relations law could be used as a bargaining tool in international relations. A government should point to the risk of a potential veto from a domestic actor on an agreement which is in the general interest of all negotiating partners. If the government can make a credible claim that its domestic laws enable an actor to block the ratification and that the domestic actor is skeptical of the treaty arrangement, the other negotiating parties interested in collective participation in the treaty regime might accept the government's suggested draft as the only possible compromise.

Empirically, the impact of foreign relations law on international treaty negotiations is however not obvious. Because article 46 VCLT has never been successfully pleaded before an international court,[41] the domestic constitutional design does not seem to have major relevance for the legality of

[38] Robert D. Putnam, 'Diplomacy and Domestic Politics: The Logic of Two-Level Games' (1988) 42 *International Organization* 427.

[39] Putnam, 'Diplomacy and Domestic Politics', 427.

[40] Putnam, 'Diplomacy and Domestic Politics', 453.

[41] Hannah Woolaver, 'State Engagement with Treaties: Interactions between International and Domestic Law', in Curtis A. Bradley (ed.), *The Oxford Handbook of Comparative Foreign Relations Law* (New York: Oxford University Press, 2019), p. 431 at 435; see for example *Land and Maritime Boundary between Cameroon and Nigeria (Cameroon* v. *Nigeria; Equitorial*

a treaty on the international level. Moreover, even if one assumes that negotiating partners are concerned about the prospects of ratification by the respective opposite side, it is hard to assess the credibility of the argument about foreign relations law. Competing accounts about the exact contours of a domestic foreign relations law in a particular country make the assessment of limits for domestic ratification rather challenging.[42] Also, one has to touch unstable ground by making assumptions about future actions in the domestic ratification processes and envisaging a certain behavior by parliamentary veto players.

Nonetheless, this contribution argues that there exists some evidence that Putnam's envisioned strategy played a role in the context of the Paris climate change negotiations. The Obama administration successfully talked other states into adopting the US negotiating position on nonbinding commitments for climate change mitigation by pointing to its foreign relations law and potential veto players in the domestic context. Given the history of the UNFCCC and Kyoto negotiations, the Obama administration's argument about the necessity of senatorial involvement for subscribing to binding mitigation commitments was credible. However, this contribution also points to the ambivalences of US foreign relations law and highlights the reluctance of the US courts to weigh into foreign affairs. Against this background, the Obama administration arguably opted for a risk averse strategy when it comes to the nonbinding legal character of climate mitigation commitments because this was in line with another US negotiating goal to prevent a scheme which differentiates between developed and developing countries.

A *Treaty-Making under the US Constitution*

The foreign relations law of the United States establishes high hurdles for treaty participation. The US Constitution of 1789 heavily involves the Senate in the treaty-making process entailing a 'threshold [for approval of a treaty] higher than that in nearly all other advanced industrial democracies'.[43] According to US Constitution, Article II § 2, Clause 2, the President has the

Guinea Intervening), Judgment, I.C.J. Reports 2002, p. 303, 430–31, para. 265; on this see Swaine, this volume, Section I.

42 For instance, the debate on foreign relations law in the United States is characterized by strong divisions among the protagonists, for instance Peter J. Spiro, 'The New Sovereigntists: American Exceptionalism and Its False Prophets' (2000) 79 *Foreign Affairs* 9.

43 Andrew Moravcsik, 'The Paradox of U.S. Human Rights Policy', in Michael Ignatieff (ed.), *American Exceptionalism and Human Rights* (Princeton: Princeton University Press, 2005), p. 187.

power to conclude treaties with the 'Advice and Consent of the Senate' as long as 'two thirds of the Senators present concur'. The Founding Fathers bestowed the numerically smaller, expectedly more secretive Senate instead of the House of Representatives with this competence, also because Southern states regarded the senatorial blocking minority as safeguarding the US monopoly on navigation rights on the Mississippi River.[44] On the basis of the article II procedure, administration officials usually negotiate the treaty and then ask the Senate for approval of the negotiated document.[45] Some of the most important international agreements like the United Nations Charter, the NATO defence agreement, the Geneva Conventions, the Nuclear Non-Proliferation Treaty and a few human rights conventions have been concluded in this way.[46]

There exist various examples of international treaties which did not receive the consent of the Senate. Famously, the Senate did not support President Woodrow Wilson's attempt to join the Versailles Treaty after the First World War.[47] Moreover, even though the Clinton and Obama administrations endorsed human rights treaties like the Convention on the Rights of the Child, the Convention on the Elimination of Discrimination Against Women and the Convention on the Rights of Disabled People, none of these treaties received the required senatorial consent.[48] These experiences of domestic ratification failure make the threat of nonratification credible. It is quite realistic that an administration will not receive the required two-thirds majority in the Senate which has been called the 'graveyard'[49] or 'cold storage'[50] for international treaties.

However, according to US constitutional practice not every agreement negotiated at the international plane needs to follow the article II procedure in order to be ratified. Since the 1940s, so-called congressional-executive agreements emerged allowing for treaty participation of the United States

44 On this Oona A. Hathaway, 'Treaties' End: The Past, Present, and Future of International Lawmaking in the United States' (2008) 117 *Yale Law Journal* 1236 at 1278–86.

45 On the demise of the advice-criterion in the early US constitutional history, see Curtis A. Bradley and Martin S. Flaherty, 'Executive Power Essentialism and Foreign Affairs' (2004) 102 *Michigan Law Review* 545 at 626–31.

46 See Bradley, *International Law in the U.S. Legal System*, p. 84.

47 Thirty-nine senators voted in favor, fifty-five against.

48 For the US record on human rights see United Nations, Human Rights, Office of the High Commissioner, Ratification Status for United States of America, https://tbinternet.ohchr.org/_layouts/15/TreatyBodyExternal/Treaty.aspx, accessed September 30, 2020.

49 Covey T. Oliver, 'Getting the Senators to Accept the Reference of Treaties to Both Houses for Approval by Simple Majorities' (1980) 74 *AJIL* 142 at 143.

50 Louis Henkin, 'Treaties in a Constitutional Democracy' (1989) 10 *Michigan Journal of International Law* 406 at 411.

without requiring the high threshold in the Senate. For such congressional-executive agreements, the President needs advance authorization or subsequent approval of a simple majority in Congress.[51] A rising number of congressional-executive agreements have been completed in issue areas like trade, commerce and finance.[52] Moreover, sole executive agreements, which concern more technical issues, can be concluded by the President alone. Even though the US Constitution does not explicitly refer to executive agreements,[53] the Supreme Court stated in dicta that the President has 'the power to make such international agreements as do not constitute treaties in the constitutional sense'[54] and implicitly held such agreements to be valid.[55] According to the Case-Zablocki Act, the Secretary of State needs to submit every international agreement except for article II treaties within sixty days to Congress.[56]

How to distinguish between article II treaties, congressional-executive agreements and executive agreements remains a controversial question. The position enshrined in Restatement the Third '[t]he prevailing view is that the Congressional-Executive agreement may be used as an alternative to the treaty method in every instance'[57] found some support, but has also been challenged by various authors.[58] The State Department relies on the Circular 175 procedure evaluating the agreement's impact on the US as a whole and on state laws, past US and international practice in relation to similar agreements, the preference of Congress, the duration as well as the desired formal character and expediency of the agreement.[59] These criteria are not entirely clear-cut, lend themselves to interpretation and thus allow for some political discretion

51 Bradley, *International Law in the U.S. Legal System*, pp. 79–83.

52 See John Yoo, 'Rational Treaties: Article II, Congressional-Executive Agreements, and International Bargaining' (2011) 97 *Cornell Law Review* 1 at 2.

53 The Constitution refers to treaties, agreements and compacts, see for instance US Constitution Article I Section 10; Article II Section 2, Clause 2.

54 *United States v. Curtiss-Wright Export Corp.*, 299 US 304, 318 (1936).

55 See for instance *United States v. Guy W. Capps., Inc.*, 348 US 296 (1955); *Dames & Moore v. Regan*, 453 US 654 (1981); *American Ins. Ass'n v. Garamendi*, 539 US 396 (2003).

56 1 USC § 112b (1994).

57 Restatement (Third) of the Foreign Relations Law of the United States § 303, Comment e (1987).

58 For support see Hathaway, 'Treaties' End', 1236; David M. Golove, 'Against Free-Form Formalism' (1998) 73 *New York University Law Review* 1791; for critique see Laurence H. Tribe, 'Taking Text and Structure Seriously: Reflections on Free-Form Method in Constitutional Interpretation' (1995) 108 *Harvard Law Review* 1221 at 1249–78; John C. Yoo, 'Laws as Treaties?: The Constitutionality of Congressional-Executive Agreements' (2001) 99 *Michigan Law Review* 757 at 776.

59 11 FAM 720, Negotiation and Conclusion, September 25, 2006, https://fam.state.gov/fam/11fam/11fam0720.html, accessed September 30, 2020.

for each administration. More importantly, the US Supreme Court has been rather reluctant to adjudicate in foreign relations leaving it to Congress and the President to solve the dispute politically. For instance, the Court denied granting certiorari to the case challenging the conclusion of NAFTA as a congressional-executive agreement after the US Court of Appeals of the 11th circuit had dismissed the case as nonjusticiable on the basis of the political question doctrine.[60] Therefore, US courts did not develop strict limits on how to categorize certain agreements negotiated at the international level. This means that as long as there is no adjudicator to check the classification of the administration, the respective administrations possess some leeway on whether a certain agreement is an article II treaty, a congressional-executive agreement or a sole executive agreement.

B *The Obama Administration and Nonbindingness of Climate Mitigation Commitments*

The classifications of different types of agreements had a strong impact on the US position on the Paris Agreement. From the beginning of the negotiations, the administration posited that it intended an agreement with nonbinding language on climate change mitigation. More than a year before COP 21 in Paris, Todd Stern, the chief US negotiator of the Paris Agreement, stressed that 'the new agreement will be a legally binding one in at least some respects, but doesn't specify which ones'. He highlighted that the US supported a proposal by New Zealand according to which 'there would be a legally binding obligation to submit a "schedule" for reducing emissions, plus various legally binding provisions for accounting, reporting, review, periodic updating of the schedules, etc. But the content of the schedule itself would not be legally binding at an international level'.[61] One month prior to the Paris meeting, Secretary of State John Kerry told the Financial Times that the Paris climate negotiations would not lead to a treaty legally requiring reductions of carbon emissions and would be different from the Kyoto Protocol.[62] Moreover, when the US submitted its intended nationally determined contributions to

60 *Made in the USA Foundation v. United States*, 242 F 3d 1300 (11th Cir. 2001), cert. denied, 534 US 1039 (2001).

61 Todd D. Stern, 'Seizing the Opportunity for Progress on Climate', US Department of State, October 14, 2014, https://2009-2017.state.gov/s/climate/releases/2014/232962.htm, accessed September 30, 2020.

62 Demetri Sevastopulo and Pilita Clark, 'Paris Climate Deal Will Not Be a Legally Binding Treaty', Financial Times, November 11, 2015, www.ft.com/content/79daf872-8894-11e5-90de-f44762bf9896, accessed September 30, 2020.

demonstrate its commitment to climate change mitigation before COP 21 in Paris, it did not refer to these contributions as being legally binding.[63] The US delegation even explicitly rejected proposals by the European Union and small island states calling for the legal bindingness of nationally determined contributions. According to US negotiators, this would prevent high participation with and ambition within the agreement.[64]

The US delegation was even willing to risk the adoption of the negotiated document over the issue of the legal character of climate change mitigation commitments. Article 4 (4) of the final circulating draft held that '[d]eveloped country Parties *shall* continue taking the lead by undertaking economy-wide absolute emission reduction targets. Developing country Parties should continue enhancing their mitigation efforts, and are encouraged to move over time towards economy-wide emission reduction or limitation targets in the light of different national circumstances.'[65] Article 4 (4) thus clearly distinguished between the obligations of developed and developing countries.

This version of the Paris Agreement was not acceptable for the US delegation. John Kerry threatened that the US would not support the deal if the 'shall' would not be changed to 'should'.[66] According to the US delegation, the wording was smuggled into the final draft at the last minute despite the US rejection of such proposals in earlier drafts.[67] In contrast, the delegations of some developing countries claimed that the 'shall' was the agreed language and the US challenge represented an unfair last minute move to better the US position crossing a red

63 United States, Intended National Determined Contributions, March 31, 2015, www4.unfccc.int/sites/submissions/INDC/Published%20Documents/United%20States%20of%20America/1/U.S.%20Cover%20Note%20INDC%20and%20Accompanying%20Information.pdf, accessed September 30, 2020.

64 Daniel Bodansky, 'The Paris Climate Change Agreement: A New Hope?' (2016) 110 *AJIL* 288 at 297.

65 Adoption of the Paris Agreement, Proposal of the President, Draft Decision, FCCC/CP/2015/L.9, December 12, 2015, p. 21, https://unfccc.int/resource/docs/2015/cop21/eng/l09.pdf, accessed September 30, 2020. Emphasis added.

66 John Kerry, Press Availability, US Department of State, December 12, 2015, https://2009-2017.state.gov/secretary/remarks/2015/12/250590.htm, accessed September 30, 2020; see also Lisa Friedman, 'How the World Solved the "Shall" Crisis and Reached a New Climate Accord,' E&E News, December 14, 2015, www.eenews.net/stories/1060029452, accessed September 30, 2020; Melissa Eddy, 'At Climate Talks, a Few Letters That Almost Sank the Deal', The New York Times, December 14, 2015, www.nytimes.com/interactive/projects/cp/climate/2015-paris-climate-talks/at-climate-talks-three-letters-almost-sunk-the-deal, accessed September 30, 2020; John Vidal, 'How a "Typo" Nearly Derailed the Paris Climate Deal', The Guardian, December 16, 2015, www.theguardian.com/environment/blog/2015/dec/16/how-a-typo-nearly-derailed-the-paris-climate-deal, accessed September 30, 2020.

67 On this Daniel Bodansky, 'Reflections on the Paris Conference', Opinio Juris, December 15, 2015, http://opiniojuris.org/2015/12/15/reflections-on-the-paris-conference/, accessed September 30, 2020.

line on differentiation between developing and developed countries.[68] In any case, the French Presidency around Laurent Fabius yielded to the American concerns in order to save the adoption of the Paris Agreement. The Secretariat declared the 'shall' to stem from a typographical error. States thus could vote on the basis of a corrected final version incorporating the 'should' and no new negotiating around delaying the adoption had to be opened.[69]

According to the Obama administration, the key reason for why the US insisted on (re-)introducing the nonbinding 'should' into article 4 (4) of the Paris Agreement was US foreign relations law. In this view, the wording of article 4 (4) determined which actors had to be involved in the treaty-making process on the domestic level. After the adoption of the Paris Agreement, Kerry linked the drafting of article 4 (4) to the treaty-making procedure at home. In a press release, he celebrated having 'a binding agreement with respect to transparency and not having binding targets with respect to emissions or finance' as the achievement of key US negotiating goals. Otherwise 'a different kind of agreement' would have been necessary.[70] Kerry also emphasized that by correcting the perceived mistake in relation to the drafting of article 4 (4), the US 'kept faith with our own negotiating standards and what we promised to Congress and the American people'.[71] In an interview, Kerry adopted the argument of a US senator that 'this [agreement] doesn't need to be approved by the Congress because it doesn't have mandatory targets for reduction, and it doesn't have an enforcement-compliance mechanism'.[72] Other senior administration officials became even more explicit about the link with US foreign relations law. In a background briefing on the Paris Agreement, officials of the State Department stressed that 'the notion of the targets not being binding was really a fundamental part of our approach from early on' because only such an agreement does not need to be submitted to the Senate.[73] According to press reports, US diplomats were confident that the Senate did not need to be involved because the targets are nonbinding and

68 Vidal, 'How a "Typo" Nearly Derailed the Paris Climate Deal'; Meena Raman and Hilary Chiew, 'Paris Agreement Adopted after Last Minute "Technical Corrections"', Third World Network, December 15, 2015, https://twnetwork.org/climate-change/paris-agreement-adopted-after-last-minute-%e2%80%98technical-corrections%e2%80%99-0, accessed September 30, 2020.

69 Vidal, 'How a "Typo" Nearly Derailed the Paris Climate Deal.'

70 Kerry, Press Availability.

71 Kerry, Press Availability.

72 John Kerry, Interview with Chris Wallace of FOX, US Department of State, December 12, 2015, https://2009-2017.state.gov/secretary/remarks/2015/12/250595.htm, accessed September 30, 2020.

73 Background Briefing on the Paris Climate Agreement, US Department of State, December 12, 2015, https://2009-2017.state.gov/r/pa/prs/ps/2015/12/250592.htm, accessed September 30, 2020.

'[t]he elements that are binding are consistent with already approved previous agreements'.[74] In this reading, only by replacing the 'shall' with the 'should', the Senate did not have to be involved in the treaty-making process.

Moreover, the US negotiators successfully inserted the foreign relations law argument in the international debate and thus limited the potential outcome of the negotiations. Some months before COP 21, French Minister of Foreign Affairs Laurent Fabius stated in a discussion with African delegates at UN climate talks that 'we know the politics in the US. Whether we like it or not, if it comes to the Congress, they will refuse'. Fabius added that '[w]e must find a formula which is valuable for everybody and valuable for the US without going to the Congress'.[75] In the run-up to the final negotiations in Paris, EU Climate Commissioner Miguel Arias Cañete stressed that '[w]e need the United States on board, and we have to find a solution. … We understand the concerns they have because of the political situation they have in the Congress'.[76] Also in the context of the language on article 4 (4) Paris Agreement, the foreign relations law argument was crucial. According to the spokesperson for the Like-Minded Developing Countries, the EU approached the Group of Like-Minded Developing Countries and lobbied for acceptance of the last minute change citing US concerns about the involvement of the US Congress.[77] The EU apparently internalized the US foreign relations law argument and relied on it in order to keep the US in the agreement. According to some observers, the US negotiators thereby made 'the world accept the domestic constraints in the United States as a feature of international climate talks'.[78]

C *Between Real Risks and Bargaining Tool*

But how plausible was the argument of the Obama administration? Was the US negotiating position determined by domestic constraints?

74 Ed King, 'Paris Agreement "Does Not Need Senate Approval" Say Officials', Climate Home News, December 15, 2015, www.climatechangenews.com/2015/12/15/paris-agreement-does-not-need-senate-approval-say-officials/, accessed September 30, 2020.

75 Associated Press, 'Climate Deal Must Avoid US Congress Approval, French Minister Says', The Guardian, June 1, 2015, www.theguardian.com/world/2015/jun/01/un-climate-talks-deal-us-congress, accessed September 30, 2020.

76 Valerie Richardson, 'Republicans Move to Undermine Obama on Paris Climate Deal', The Washington Times, December 7, 2015, www.washingtontimes.com/news/2015/dec/7/republicans-move-to-undermine-obama-on-paris-clima/, accessed September 30, 2020.

77 Raman and Chiew, 'Paris Agreement Adopted after Last Minute "Technical Corrections"'.

78 Raymond Clémençon, 'The Two Sides of the Paris Climate Agreement: Dismal Failure or Historic Breakthrough?' (2016) 25 *The Journal of Environment & Development* 3 at 6.

It is no question that the involvement of the Senate in the treaty-making process would have placed a hurdle on the ratification of the Paris Agreement which could hardly be overcome. Since the ratification of the United Nations Framework Convention on Climate Change, the Senate had taken a skeptical position towards committing to more assertive climate mitigation obligations on the international level. While the Clinton administration negotiated the Kyoto Protocol, the Senate adopted the (nonbinding) Byrd-Hagel Resolution. With ninety-five to zero votes, the senators emphasized that 'the United States should not be a signatory to any protocol which would (A) mandate new commitments to limit or reduce greenhouse gas emissions for the Annex I Parties, unless the protocol also mandates new specific scheduled commitment for Developing Country Parties within the same compliance period, or (B) result in serious harm to the economy of the United States'.[79] By unanimously ruling out senatorial support for an agreement which differentiated in its legal bindingness for targets on greenhouse gas emission reductions between developed and developing countries, the senators put considerable pressure on the negotiating position of the administration. When after an intervention of Vice-President Al Gore the Clinton administration accepted a differentiation scheme between developed and developing countries,[80] it was obvious that the chances for passing the domestic treaty-making process were slim. It was thus no surprise that the Clinton administration did not submit the Kyoto Protocol to the Senate after signing the protocol in November 1998.[81] The Senate was regarded as the dead end of the Kyoto Protocol.

In relation to the Paris Agreement, the chances for the acceptance of a binding mitigation scheme did not look much brighter. Especially after the Republican successes at the midterm elections of 2014, Republican majorities in the Senate and the House of Representatives signalled that they would hardly support any policy initiatives of the Democratic President before the upcoming presidential elections. While the Obama administration was negotiating the Paris Agreement, the House and Senate adopted two resolutions which disputed the competences of the Environmental Protection Agency to

79 Byrd-Hagel Resolution, 105th Congress, 1st Session, S. RES. 98, https://web.archive.org/web/20100626110143/http://www.nationalcenter.org/KyotoSenate.html, accessed September 30, 2020.

80 Shardul Agrawala and Steinar Andresen, 'Indispensability and Indefensibility? The United States in the Climate Treaty Negotiations' (1999) 5 *Global Governance* 457 at 465.

81 CRS Report for Congress, 'Global Climate Change: Selected Legal Questions About the Kyoto Protocol', October 1, 2002, www.everycrsreport.com/files/20021001_98-349_75c808dae15c29b2b5a9f594598269e489f935ba.pdf, accessed September 30, 2020.

regulate climate change emissions under the Clean Air Act and blocked the legal basis for such regulations.[82] Republican Senator James M. Inhofe declared that the 'message could not be more clear that Republicans and Democrats in both the U.S. Senate and U.S. House do not support the president's climate agenda, and the international community should take note'.[83] Only a presidential veto in December 2015 against this resolution kept the door open for implementation of international commitments on climate change mitigation at the domestic level.[84]

Because of these voices and the history since the conclusion of the UNFCCC, the Obama administration knew that getting a climate treaty through the Senate was highly unrealistic. A key goal of the US delegation during the Paris climate change treaty negotiations was to ensure that the President would be able to bind the United States without seeking approval from the Senate or from Congress. Concluding the treaty as a sole executive agreement seemed to be the only promising way forward.

Moreover, a plausible argument can be made that binding commitments on climate change mitigation might have made involvement of the Senate necessary. Already during the domestic discussions on Senate approval of the UNFCCC in 1992, the domestic constitutional procedure for adopting future protocols had been discussed. In an answer to a question by the Senate Foreign Relations Committee, the Bush I administration stated that the article II procedure was needed, if a protocol adopting a targets and timetables scheme was negotiated and signed by the United States.[85] The Senate Foreign Relations Committee also expressed its view that the introduction of legally binding emission targets would require the Senate's advice and consent.[86] Accordingly, during the debate on the Kyoto Protocol with its binding scheme on targets and timetable, policy makers generally expected that senatorial advice and consent was a precondition for US ratification.

Therefore, US negotiators carefully tried to avoid resemblance with the Kyoto Protocol during the negotiations for a new agreement under the UNFCCC. In the context of the negotiations on the Copenhagen Accord,

82 S.J. Res. 23, 114th Cong. (2015); S.J. Res. 24, 114th Cong. (2015).

83 Richardson, 'Republicans Move to Undermine Obama on Paris Climate Deal.'

84 Barack Obama, 'Memorandum of Disapproval on S.J. Res. 23,' The White House, December 19, 2015, https://obamawhitehouse.archives.gov/the-press-office/2015/12/19/memorandum-disapproval-sj-res-23, accessed September 30, 2020.

85 UN Framework Convention on Climate Change, Hearing Before the Senate Committee on Foreign Relations, 102 Cong 2d Sess. 1992, 106.

86 S. Exec. Rep. No. 102-55, at 14 (1992) reported by Mr. Pell.

the US delegation suggested to use the term 'implementing agreement' for the new arrangement[87] and was successful in convincing its negotiating partners to drop the term 'protocol'.[88] Moreover, the Obama administration pushed against incorporating new financial commitments or legally binding emission targets in order to avoid involvement of the US Congress.[89]

Also, the domestic opposition was convinced that climate change mitigation obligations implied senatorial involvement, regardless of a legal or only political bindingness. In the run-up to the Paris negotiations, the Senate adopted a resolution expressing the sense of Congress that 'any agreement adopted at COP 21 containing targets and timetables, whether deemed "legally binding" or not, must be submitted to the Senate for advice and consent pursuant to Article II, section 2 of the Constitution.'[90] In reaction to the adoption of the Paris Agreement, Jim Inhofe emphasized that 'Senate leadership has already been outspoken in its positions that the United States is not legally bound to any agreement setting emissions targets or any financial commitment to it without approval by Congress'.[91]

But was foreign relations law so clear on the matter in particular when it comes to the wording of article 4 (4) Paris Agreement? Would a text stating that '[d]eveloped country Parties *shall* continue taking the lead by undertaking economy-wide absolute emission reduction targets' require the involvement of Congress?

Some observers like Dan Bodansky tend to adopt the argument of the Obama administration and put forward that 'arguably' the phrasing 'shall' would have made 'Senate or Congressional approval . . . for US participation' necessary.[92] However, as the 'arguably' signals, Bodansky is cautious not to present this legal position as the only possible view on the matter. Moreover, others have been more skeptical of the Obama administration's argument. For instance, before the conclusion of the Paris Agreement, David Wirth suggested that existing domestic federal laws and regulations allow international

87 US Submission on Copenhagen Agreed Outcome (2009), https://unfccc.int/files/kyoto_protocol/application/pdf/usa040509.pdf, accessed September 30, 2020.

88 On this David A. Wirth, 'Cracking the American Climate Negotiators' Hidden Code: United States Law and the Paris Agreement' (2016) 6 *Climate Law* 152 at 155.

89 Bodansky, 'Hope', 297.

90 S. Con. Res. 25, Congressional Record Vol. 161, No 171, November 19, 2015, www.govinfo.gov/content/pkg/CREC-2015-11-19/html/CREC-2015-11-19-pt1-PgS8166-2.htm, accessed September 30, 2020.

91 Martin Pengelly, 'Obama Praises Paris Climate Deal As "Tribute to American Leadership"', The Guardian, December 12, 2015, www.theguardian.com/us-news/2015/dec/12/obama-speech-paris-climate-change-talks-deal-american-leadership, accessed September 30, 2020.

92 Bodansky, 'Reflections on the Paris Conference.'

legally binding commitments on emissions reductions. With reference to executive authority under the Clean Air Act and the precedent of the US signature of the Minamata Convention on Mercury, he put forward that 'neither Senate advice and consent nor new congressional legislation are necessarily conditions precedent to the United States becoming party to internationally binding mitigation commitments'.[93] After the conclusion of the Paris Agreement, Wirth claimed that there is 'some – and perhaps considerable – room to argue' that enough domestic legal authority existed for subscribing to the 'shall' in article 4 (4) of the Paris Agreement.[94] In particular, Wirth points to the ambiguous phrasing of the whole article 4 (4) of the Paris Agreement when it comes to legal bindingness (inter alia the wording 'undertaking' meaning to begin something or promise something).[95]

Even if one does not subscribe to this position, the scholarly controversy demonstrates that US foreign relations law is not definite on that matter. Consequently, the question arises who decides on the limits of the foreign affairs power. In contrast to other jurisdictions, the courts in the United States are known for not weighing in on matters of foreign affairs. Despite some debate about the 'normalization of foreign affairs' in the United States,[96] the political question doctrine still is the law on the books, in particular in crucial matters of the separation of powers. As mentioned above, the Supreme Court did not hold hearing on a case concerning the distinction between article II treaties and congressional-executive agreements.[97] Moreover, the Supreme Court did also not decide on the merits of a case concerning the competences for the withdrawal from article II treaties.[98] Therefore, it is by no means certain that a US court would take up a legal challenge of the Paris Agreement containing the 'shall' on climate mitigation. It is telling that, despite some claims that the current Paris

93 David A. Wirth, 'The International and Domestic Law of Climate Change: A Binding International Agreement Without the Senate or Congress?' (2015) 39 *Harvard Environmental Law Review* 515 at 517.

94 David A. Wirth, 'Cracking the American Climate Negotiators' Hidden Code: United States Law and the Paris Agreement' (2016) 6 *Climate Law* 152 at 167.

95 Wirth, 'Cracking the American Climate Negotiators' Hidden Code', 167; for a definition of 'to undertake' see https://dictionary.cambridge.org/dictionary/english/undertake, accessed September 30, 2020.

96 Ganesh Sitaraman and Ingrid Wuerth, 'The Normalization of Foreign Relations Law' (2015) 128 *Harvard Law Review* 1897; for a critique see Curtis A. Bradley, 'Foreign Relations Law and the Purported Shift Away From "Exceptionalism"' (2015) 128 *Harvard Law Review Forum* 294.

97 *Made in the USA Foundation v. United States*, 242 F 3d 1300 (11th Cir. 2001), cert. denied, 534 US 1039 (2001).

98 *Goldwater v. Carter*, 444 US 996 (1979).

Agreement with the 'should' in article 4 (4) Paris Agreement violates US Constitution, Article II Section 2, Clause 2,[99] the matter is (as far as I can see) not litigated before courts.

Moreover, the Obama administration's rejection of the 'shall' was not only due to its foreign relations law. The US delegation also intended to prevent a scheme which differentiated between developed and developing countries. Already during the discussions about the Kyoto Protocol, many actors in the United States had dismissed asymmetrical obligations on climate mitigation between developed and developing countries pointing to potential detrimental effects for the US economy.[100] For developing countries, differentiation between binding mitigation commitments for developed countries and nonbinding rules for developing countries in the Kyoto Protocol had been a key objective expressing the principle of 'common but differentiated responsibilities' in the climate change regime.[101] However, the US delegation was no longer willing to accept this. In the Paris negotiations, the rejection of a differentiated regime similar to the Kyoto Protocol was a key negotiating position of the US delegation. In October 2014, Todd Stern stressed that an inclusive agreement with broad participation was the main goal of the United States.[102] In the context of the debate about article 4 (4) Paris Agreement, the Obama administration was concerned that the 'shall' created a distinction between binding obligations for developed countries and nonbinding obligations for developing countries.[103] Accordingly, after the adoption of the agreement, the Obama administration celebrated that the agreement did not differentiate in such a way.[104] Besides foreign relations law, the US negotiating team also had its own interest in nondifferentiation between all participants in the regime in mind.

IV CONCLUSION

This contribution demonstrates that under specific circumstances, domestic foreign relations law might have a substantial impact on international negotiations by narrowing the space for achievable outcomes.

99 Michael D. Ramsey, 'Evading the Treaty Power?: The Constitutionality of Nonbinding Agreements' (2016) 11 *FIU Law Review* 371 at 384–87.

100 See above III.B.

101 Lavanya Rajamani, 'Ambition and Differentiation in the 2015 Paris Agreement: Interpretative Possibilities and Underlying Politics' (2016) 65 *ICLQ* 493 at 506.

102 Stern, 'Seizing the Opportunity for Progress on Climate'.

103 Raman and Chiew, 'Paris Agreement Adopted after Last Minute "Technical Corrections".'

104 Background Briefing on the Paris Climate Agreement.

In the international discussions on the Paris Agreement, the US treaty-making procedure and potential veto players on the domestic level were the elephant in the room. Because the negotiating partners of the US feared that they would not get the United States on board if the Senate or Congress were involved in the domestic decision-making process, they accepted the Obama administration's insistence on nonbinding commitments for climate change mitigation. This does not mean that the Obama administration tricked its negotiating partners when referring to domestic constraints as an argument for replacing the 'shall' in article 4 (4) of the Paris Agreement with the 'should'. Given the history of nonratification of international climate treaties in the United States and the debate about binding commitments in the context of the UNFCCC, the necessity of congressional involvement for an agreement containing binding targets and timetables is plausible. Also, the risk of non-ratification by the Senate and Congress was credible because of the Republican majorities in the parliamentary bodies.

However, it is important to point to the ambiguity of US foreign relations law on the matter and the reluctance of the US Supreme Court to judicialize foreign affairs. It seems not very likely that US courts would have decided on the treaty-making process in relation to the Paris Agreement even if the final version contained the 'shall' in article 4 (4). The Obama administration arguably opted for a risk-averse strategy when insisting on incorporating the 'should' in article 4 (4) of the Paris Agreement.

A potential reason for this strategy was that the Obama administration was interested in nonbinding commitments on climate change mitigation itself. Because the administration regarded equal treatment of developed and developing countries as a key negotiating goal, the US negotiators were not willing to accept a phrasing which distinguishes between a 'shall' for developed countries and a 'should' for developing countries. In this sense, foreign relations law provided a welcome argument as a bargaining tool to convince the negotiating partners to adopt the US position.

As this example shows, the potential use of foreign relations law as a bargaining tool is limited to very specific circumstances. It seems that a state can rely on its foreign relations law as a bargaining tool if two conditions are fulfilled. First, the participation of the state in a multilateral treaty is in the interest of all other potential treaty parties because the treaty enshrines a goal which can only be achieved in a cooperative spirit. Second, the state needs to credibly claim that a veto power in its domestic setting will prevent the ratification of the treaty if the treaty does not contain provisions with the preferred outcome for the state.

The first criterion is more likely to apply to powerful states than to weaker states. Other parties probably are more interested in having China, India and the US on board as partners in a multilateral treaty regime than other small states. This is particularly true when the treaty addresses an issue to which bigger states contribute more than others. For instance, the US seems to be in a beneficial negotiating position in the climate change context because the participation of the world's second strongest emitter seems to be highly important for the success of the treaty's objectives.

The second criterion limits the use of foreign relations law as a bargaining tool to actors with a certain reputation. Given that the US Senate is widely perceived as the 'graveyard' or 'cold storage' for international treaties, the US seems to be the most likely actor to apply this negotiating strategy. In contrast, most states lack a veto player as strong as the Senate with a long history of nonratification of international treaties which makes the claim of potential nonratification credible. For instance, in India the executive alone decides which treaties it will conclude without involving parliament. In parliamentary systems like South Africa or Germany, the legislature most of the time supports the foreign policy approach of the government and approves negotiated treaties without much debate. Thus, the National Assembly and Bundestag are highly unlikely to act as a veto power.

However, also other states might point to constitutional constraints when they push for enshrining a certain rule in a treaty. It is telling that in the context of debates about how to respond to the Eurozone crisis in 2012, the head of the International Monetary Fund, Christine Lagarde, threatened to leave the room if she would hear '*Bundesverfassungsgericht*' one more time.[105] Apparently, Lagarde dismissed the argument by sceptics of the European rescue policies that a potential judgment by the German Constitutional Court might constrain the space for decision-making. Even though this example does not refer to the negotiation strategy of a state in international treaty negotiations, it demonstrates that constitutional limits might well become an argument in supra- and international debates, also outside of the US context.

Be it as it may, the Trump administration's actions in relation to the Paris Agreement are a far cry from using foreign relations law in international negotiations. The Trump administration signalled its intention to withdraw from the Paris Agreement in June 2017 and set in motion the year-long exiting

105 Kay-Alexander Scholz, 'Karlsruhe's Constitutional Monastery', Deutsche Welle, September 11, 2012, www.dw.com/en/karlsruhes-constitutional-monastery/a-16231161, accessed September 30, 2020.

process in November 2019.[106] Instead of influencing international negotiations with reference to domestic constraints, the Trump administration counts on its oil- and coal-friendly 'America First' policy.

However, it is interesting to see that the debate about the contours of foreign relations law also had repercussions for the withdrawal decision. When President Donald Trump renounced the Paris Agreement, he referred to 'serious legal and constitutional issues' since '[f]oreign leaders in Europe, Asia, and across the world should not have more to say with respect to the U.S. economy than our own citizens and their elected representatives' alluding to the noninvolvement of Congress.[107] Even though every international treaty regime might, in the view of nationalists, introduce potential elements of influence of 'foreign' actors and raise 'constitutional issues', this might be particularly worrying if Congress has not been involved in the treaty-making in the first place. Moreover, the Obama administration's decision not to involve Congress also influenced the withdrawal decision more indirectly. Trump's decision to leave without involving Congress was hardly questioned on foreign relations law grounds. Since the Paris Agreement had been concluded as an executive agreement, most scholars agree that the executive alone could withdraw from the agreement.[108] While US foreign relations law shaped the outcome of the Paris climate negotiations by limiting the space of potential outcomes, it did not constrain the executive decision-making process on the domestic level in the context of the withdrawal.

106 Emily Holden, 'Trump Begins Year-Long Process to Formally Exit Paris Climate Agreement', The Guardian, November 5, 2019, www.theguardian.com/us-news/2019/nov/04/donald-trump-climate-crisis-exit-paris-agreement, accessed September 30, 2020.

107 Statement by President Trump on the Paris Climate Accord, The White House, June 1, 2017, www.whitehouse.gov/briefings-statements/statement-president-trump-paris-climate-accord/, accessed September 30, 2020. https://www.whitehouse.gov/briefings-statements/statement-president-trump-paris-climate-accord/

108 However, see Harald H. Koh, 'Triptych's End: A Better Framework to Evaluate 21st Century International Lawmaking' (2017) 126 *Yale Law Journal Forum* 338 at 358.

3

International Foreign Relations Law

Executive Authority in Entering and Exiting Treaties

Edward T. Swaine

The nascent field of comparative foreign relations law is generating considerable, and understandable, excitement, including for the world of treaties.[1] Comparativism offers different systems the opportunity to learn from one another, and treaties offer a particularly interesting classroom. States parties are to an extent allies in a common cause, and profit mutually from a better understanding of domestic treaty-making and its constraints. Yet they are simultaneously rivals that seek to minimize the strategic opportunities afforded others – including under the agreements binding them. It is unsurprising, given these conflicting impulses, that state systems show variety in how they tackle even these common problems.

What may be more surprising is international law's apparent agnosticism. Treaties depend on foreign relations law: the latter, after all, is tasked not only with establishing domestic authority to allow states to consent to treaty obligations, but also with establishing the means by which they fulfill the resulting obligations, including through the incorporation of treaties into domestic law. Even so, international law treats structural provisions of domestic constitutions as matters of indifference. Domestic laws, the Permanent Court of International Justice once pronounced, 'are merely facts' in relation to international obligations,[2] and this view remains broadly

[1] See, e.g., Curtis A. Bradley (ed.), *The Oxford Handbook of Comparative Foreign Relations Law* (New York: Oxford University Press, 2019).

[2] See *Case concerning certain German interests in Polish Upper Silesia*, Merits, PCIJ Series A, No. 7, 1926, p. 19 ('From the standpoint of International Law and of the Court which is its organ, municipal laws are merely facts which express the will and constitute the activities of States, in the same manner as do legal decisions or administrative measures. … [T]here is nothing to prevent the Court's giving judgment on the question whether or not, in applying that law, Poland is acting in conformity with its obligations towards Germany under the Geneva Convention').

valid today.[3] For reasons suggested in this chapter, domestic *foreign relations* law is distinguishable, at least where it facilitates international law rather than posing an obstacle to it. Nonetheless, international law seems disposed against deferring to domestic legal systems, and those systems likewise seem biased against inviting external evaluation.

The supposed agnosticism of international law toward foreign relations law seems vaguely implausible – after all, treaties and customary international law foster and monitor the human rights-conferring aspects of domestic legal orders, so it is odd that they would cede everything structural, including the means by which states assume many such obligations – and does not, in any event, mean that it leaves the latter undisturbed. As others have explored, international law creates an arena in which domestic actors assume additional authority. For example, US foreign relations law has permitted the executive branch to assume a capacity for creating and terminating international obligations that has enhanced its institutional advantages over Congress.[4] Here I draw attention to a related, but materially distinct, phenomenon: how international law – specifically, treaty-law principles reflected in the Vienna Convention on the Law of Treaties (VCLT)[5] – *itself reinforces* such tendencies in domestic institutions.[6] Based on plausible, historically grounded assumptions about how states conduct foreign relations, international law has homogenized foreign relations law relating to the creation and elimination of international treaty obligations – encouraging even those states that possess other constitutional agents to regard executive power as sufficient. I examine ratification (Section I), in which this tendency is fully expressed, and then

3 James Crawford, *Brownlie's Principles of Public International Law*, 8th ed. (Oxford: Oxford University Press, 2012), p. 51; Robert Jennings and Arthur Watts (eds.), *Oppenheim's International Law*, 9th ed., 2 vols. (Essex: Longman, 1992), vol. 1, p. 83; e.g., *Case Concerning the Arrest Warrant of 11 April 2000 (Democratic Republic of the Congo v. Belgium)*, Separate Opinion of Judge Bula-Bula, I.C.J. Reports 2002, p. 100, 130–31, para. 93. See also International Law Commission, Articles on Responsibility of States for Internationally Wrongful Acts, article 3 ('The characterization of an act of a State as internationally wrongful is governed by international law. Such characterization is not affected by the characterization of the same act as lawful by internal law.').

4 Curtis A. Bradley and Jack L. Goldsmith, 'Presidential Control Over International Law' (2018) 131 *Harvard Law Review* 1201; Jean Galbraith, 'International Law and the Domestic Separation of Powers' (2013) 99 *Virginia Law Review* 987.

5 Vienna Convention on the Law of Treaties, Vienna, 23 May 1969, in force 27 January 1980, 1155 UNTS 331; (1969) 8 ILM 679; UKTS (1980) 58.

6 Much the same may be said to hold for customary international law and its formation – though the capacity of a state to eliminate customary obligations is more constrained and hence less subject to executive-branch appropriation.

withdrawal (Section II), in which it is only just emerging.[7] Such analyses seek to augment a purely comparative approach to foreign relations with a fuller recognition of the influence of international law.[8]

I RATIFICATION

Treaty law long accorded conclusive significance to treaty ratification by executives as an incident of the sovereign power of monarchs – passed along, naturally, to those with full powers to act on the sovereign's behalf.[9] This was challenged by two developments. First, beginning by the mid-nineteenth century, a practice emerged in which states adopted constitutional provisions that required legislative approval of treaties. That tendency continues largely unabated today; the subjects encompassed by such provisions have often been expanded, along with the widening scope of treaty-making generally, and there has even been an uptick in supermajority requirements.[10] Second, agreements became more varied and often more informal, resulting in many that arguably did not require approval by traditional, treaty-oriented mechanisms.[11] The first development meant that ratification was transformed from a formal and infrequent act by which sovereigns confirmed, as a matter of obligation, that their representatives had been authorized to reach agreement, into a legislative referendum on the underlying merits of the agreement. But the second development meant that ratification might sometimes be dispensed with altogether, and agreements concluded based on signature alone.[12]

7 For brevity, I use terms like 'treaty', 'ratification' and 'withdrawal' broadly (and loosely) here, so as to include distinct acts that are similar with respect to the matters under discussion – such as, respectively, 'agreement', 'accession' and 'termination'.

8 While this chapter was in draft, an important article with a comparable approach – albeit less acutely focused on the reinforcement of executive authority, and with different prescriptive impulses – was published. See Hannah Woolaver, 'From Joining to Leaving: Domestic Law's Role in the International Validity of Treaty Withdrawal' (2019) 30 *European Journal of International Law* 73.

9 See Pierre-Hugues Verdier and Mila Versteeg, 'Separation of Powers, Treaty-Making, and Treaty Withdrawal: A Global Survey', in Curtis A. Bradley (ed.), *The Oxford Handbook of Comparative Foreign Relations Law* (Oxford: Oxford University Press, 2019), p. 138 (citing Luzius Wildhaber, *Treaty-Making Power and Constitutions: An International and Comparative Study* (Basel and Stuttgart: Helbing & Lichtenhahn, 1971), p. 9).

10 See Verdier and Versteeg, 'Separation of Powers', pp. 139–41. As the authors observe, the proportion of states with such requirements dipped with the wave of new postcolonial states following World War II, but many eventually followed suit.

11 Verdier and Versteeg, 'Separation of Powers', pp. 142–47.

12 Draft Articles on the Law of Treaties with Commentaries, (1966) 2 *Yearbook of the International Law Commission* 187, 197, UN Doc. A/CN.4/SER.A/1966/Add.1 (discussing draft Article 11).

The significance for the law of treaties was hotly contested, including as to whether the violation of a state's constitutional requirement of legislative approval affected whether a nonconforming treaty nonetheless bound the state under international law. Most agreed that domestic law regulated competence to consent to treaties and (often distinctly) governed competence to notify that consent to other states. But the consequences when consent had been notified by a state official competent to that role – notwithstanding the absence of valid consent under domestic law – were unsettled, and occasioned a diverse range of views that flourished from the interwar period through the drafting of the VCLT.[13]

At one end of the spectrum, some suggested that international law treated notification by a competent notifying official as conclusive, either as a matter of dogma or based on a state's responsibility to make good the acts of its officials. At the other extreme, some regarded constitutional law as being conclusive as to both the domestic and international effectiveness of consent. In the middle were those who regarded constitutional deficiencies as potentially bearing on international efficacy, but varying as to when.[14] The Harvard Research study, after extensive canvassing of publicists, state practice and jurisprudence, decided – almost arbitrarily – to recommend codifying that '[a] State is not bound by a treaty made on its behalf by an organ or authority not competent under its law to conclude the treaty', but that a nonbound state might then be responsible for the reasonable reliance of others on its prior representations.[15] Under this approach, international law deferred to foreign relations law, but ameliorated any adverse effect on other states through a liability rule.

The matter was revisited by the International Law Commission (ILC) in drafting the VCLT. Initially, the ILC's view was similar to that of Harvard Research: for a treaty to be binding on a state, it had to be adopted 'in accordance with its constitutional law and practice through an organ competent for that purpose'.[16] Then it reversed course. The ILC's next proposal stressed state autonomy and self-help: states could always, if they chose, negotiate ratification terms that accommodated domestic processes, seek

13 For an early entry, see, e.g., Charles Fairman, 'Competence to Bind the State to an International Engagement' (1936) 30 *American Journal of International Law* 439; for a later survey, see Woolaver, 'From Joining to Leaving', 84–93.

14 For excellent surveys, see Fairman, 'Competence to Bind the State', and Harvard Research on International Law, 'Draft Convention on the Law of Treaties: Text with Comment' (1935) 29 *American Journal of International Law Supplement* 666, 992–1002.

15 Harvard Research, 'Draft Convention on the Law of Treaties', 992 (Article 21).

16 Draft Articles on the Law of Treaties, at p. 240 and n. 205 (quoting (1951) 2 Yearbook of the International Law Commission 73).

collateral arrangements, caveat their signatures, qualify full powers or improve disclosures to other states during negotiations.[17] If, despite these options, states behaved internationally in ways that were incompatible with their domestic constitutions, the proposal would be less forgiving. The draft precluded a state from invalidating its consent by invoking the violation of 'a provision of its internal law regarding competence to conclude treaties' unless that violation was 'manifest'.[18] This was later enhanced, in Article 46 of the VCLT, to define what 'manifest' meant – signifying a violation that would be 'objectively evident' to any state acting normally and in good faith – and to require that the violation also concern 'a rule of its internal law of fundamental importance'.[19]

The ILC took commentary and practice to lean, slightly, in favor of its resolution, and noted support from governments. But its conclusion also had a normative underpinning. In its view, recent treaty-making procedures had 'done all that can be reasonably demanded . . . in the way of taking account of each other's constitutional requirements'. Moreover, in most cases, states invoking the failure to abide by constitutional requirements had other motives for attempting to escape their obligations, and indulging them would threaten the security of treaty obligations.[20]

The VCLT thus wound up contributing to an important divide. Treaty law ceded to each state 'the determination of the organs and procedures by which its will to conclude treaties is formed', concerning itself 'exclusively with the external manifestations of this will on the international plane' – meaning that the international-law determination of whether a state's agent was competent to commit the state largely superseded, for international purposes, any other constitutional delicts. In principle, as the ILC explained, each government 'had the necessary means of controlling the acts of its representative and of giving effect to any constitutional requirements', and perhaps making any failings 'the clear responsibility of the Government of the State concerned' was more feasible. Any other approach, it suggested, 'would certainly be regarded as an inadmissible interference' in another state's internal affairs, particularly those that followed more dualistic approaches to the relationship between international and domestic law.[21]

[17] Draft Articles on the Law of Treaties, at p. 198 (discussing draft article 11).

[18] Draft Articles on the Law of Treaties, at p. 240.

[19] VCLT, art. 46. The rule was reinforced by Article 27, which provided that 'A party may not invoke the provisions of its internal law as justification for its failure to perform a treaty', save as indicated by Article 46.

[20] Draft Articles on the Law of Treaties, at pp. 241–42.

[21] Draft Articles on the Law of Treaties, at pp. 241–42.

This was not the only possible international rule, even by the ILC's lights. And every approach the ILC considered, not just the one it ultimately adopted, allowed states to work around the default by developing treaty practices that respected both constitutional requirements and the conclusion of treaties.[22] Unsurprisingly, though, the default it adopted was urged by governments: in practical terms, the executive representatives of governments, who were also the rule's beneficiaries. These representatives would retain primary authority over any workarounds that treaty negotiations might yield. More basically, the VCLT rule established an international-law constraint on foreign relations law. A state's representatives, rather than the state as a whole, would be entrusted (absent extraordinary circumstances) with exclusive responsibility for determining whether a state had complied with its constitutional rules, irrespective of whether those rules vested them with such responsibility or purposefully divided domestic treaty-making authority. Even in the event of manifest violations, it would ordinarily fall to those same representatives to invoke any transgression – one made through themselves or other executive-branch agents – unless the domestic legislature or some third party developed standing to do so.

There was never any illusion that this would permit the vindication of constitutional norms, even those expressed by laws regarding competence to enter into treaties. There had already been well-known instances in which Luxembourg and Argentina had acceded to the League of Nations despite violations of provisions in their constitutions requiring parliamentary approval – though there was room for disagreement as to whether these violations had been ignored as merely domestic matters or whether tacit parliamentary approvals might be surmised from their funding of League participation.[23] The ILC itself emphasized the exceptional nature of manifest violations, and even that other states had never acquiesced in attempts to invoke such violations.[24]

Subsequent assessments, and subsequent practice, only vindicate its assessment. The governments of major powers have rebuffed criticisms that they ignored the obligation to secure legislative assent, without any apparent effect

[22] This impression was reinforced by the ILC's discussion as to whether the VCLT should presume that treaties were to be ratified unless stated otherwise (the rule it initially proposed) or require ratification when a treaty so provides (the rule eventually adopted). As the ILC itself explained, its choice of default was considered substantively insignificant, and it chose the path it did to accommodate government input and avoid the problem of drafting exceptions. Draft Articles on the Law of Treaties, at pp. 197–98.

[23] For discussion, see Michael Bothe, 'Article 46', in Oliver Corten and Pierre Klein (eds.), *The Vienna Conventions on the Law of Treaties: A Commentary*, 2 vols. (Oxford: Oxford University Press, 2011), vol. II, at p. 1096.

[24] Draft Articles on the Law of Treaties, at pp. 241–42.

on their international obligations.[25] Most prominently, the International Court of Justice rejected Nigeria's contention that a bilateral declaration with Cameroon was nonbinding because the Nigerian constitution at the time required approval of its Supreme Military Council; while the provision was of 'fundamental importance' under Article 46, it was not sufficiently 'manifest', including in part because heads of state could be presumed competent.[26] A later judgment was to much the same effect, and made clear that – even though the Somali Parliament had rejected an agreement, making relatively prominent its potential authority under domestic law – that mattered little when the Prime Minister of Somalia failed to question its validity in later interactions on the international plane.[27]

It is possible that the rise in legislative authority at the national level might shape international expectations and make deviations sufficiently apparent to register as manifest, though the trend has yet to have any such effect; perhaps the nascent project on comparative foreign relations law will even assist by illuminating pertinent commonalities and differences.[28] It is unlikely, in any case, that the basic rule will be reconsidered. If anything, parallel developments suggest similar biases toward the creation of international obligations and against means by which they might be subverted. The unilateral acts doctrine, per the ILC's Guiding Principles of 2006, likewise indicates that while '[a] unilateral declaration binds the State internationally only if it is made by an authority vested with the power to do so', necessarily '[b]y virtue of their functions, heads of State, heads of Government and ministers for foreign affairs are competent to formulate such declarations'.[29]

25 Bothe, 'Article 46', at pp. 1092, 1094–96 (citing German and US examples).

26 *Land and Maritime Boundary between Cameroon and Nigeria (Cameroon* v. *Nigeria: Equatorial Guinea intervening)*, Judgment, I.C.J. Reports 2002, p. 303, 430–31, paras. 264–66; see, especially, p. 430, para. 265 (explaining that 'a limitation of a Head of State's capacity in this respect is not manifest in the sense of Article 46, paragraph 2, unless at least properly publicized', and that '[t]his is particularly so because Heads of State belong to the group of persons who, in accordance with Article 7, paragraph 2, of the [VCLT] "[i]n virtue of their functions and without having to produce full powers" are considered as representing their State').

27 *Maritime Delimitation in the Indian Ocean (Somalia* v. *Kenya)*, Preliminary Objections, Judgment, I.C.J. Reports 2017, p. 3, 24, para. 49.

28 Karen Knop, 'Foreign Relations Law: Comparison as Invention', in Curtis A. Bradley (ed.), *The Oxford Handbook of Comparative Foreign Relations Law* (Oxford: Oxford University Press, 2019), pp. 54–55 (noting 'the effect that a new baseline of knowledge about domestic law could conceivably have on the law of treaties', and that '[b]y collecting constitutional law and practice on treaties across a range of states, comparative foreign law would change, and potentially equalize, what is known about states' internal law').

29 International Law Commission, 'Guiding Principles Applicable to Unilateral Declarations of States Capable of Creating Legal Obligations, With Commentaries (2006)', (2006) 2 *Yearbook of the International Law Commission* 369, 372 (principle 4).

The emerging unilateral acts doctrine seems to be of a piece with the full powers doctrine for treaties and, more broadly, the executive capacity assumed for traditional sources of international law, insofar as it also encourages the stability of international commitments.[30] Still, this assignment of responsibility – like treaties, to a limited class of officials, without regard to what a state's foreign relations law provides – lacks the same compelling need to find an agreeable means of concluding a principal source of international law, and lacks any explicit exception for manifest violations. Interestingly, the Guiding Principles also inhibit the 'arbitrary' revocation of such commitments, with potential parallels for treaties.[31] Some governments were discontent with this exercise, but it seems to have been due primarily to the difficulty of establishing general principles – and, perhaps, the risk that they would be regarded as binding their states unintentionally – and not the risk of making international law by means that were inconsistent with domestic law.[32] The basic calculation is unsurprising. A sufficiently deliberate capacity would appeal to the political actors that may make use of it, executive officials, who might have less regard to the loss in authority suffered by others. If consulted, national legislatures might be more inclined to regard the emerging doctrine as creating a new rival to treaty-making by participative means.

II WITHDRAWAL

International law's attitude toward the domestic law regarding withdrawal from treaties is less concrete – but as a matter of inference, at least as indifferent. The VCLT allows a state to withdraw by consent or in conformity with a treaty's terms, or if the parties so intended or treaty's nature so implies.[33] Additional provisions address notice and subsequent withdrawal for cause.[34]

30 VCLT, art. 7.

31 International Law Commission, 'Guiding Principles Applicable to Unilateral Declarations of States', at 380–81 (principle 10).

32 See generally Unilateral Acts of States – Replies from Governments to the questionnaire: report of the Secretary-General, 2000, UN Doc. A/CN.4/511. Italy, at least, did indicate that legislatures might play a role, see p. 272 of the report.

33 VCLT, arts. 54, 56. In the former, any notice period is presumably dictated by the treaty; in the latter, the state gives at least twelve months' notice.

34 Where cause is invoked, a party is to notify others of its proposed withdrawal and seek their approval; if others object, disagreements are subject to a dispute resolution procedure. VCLT, arts. 65–66.

The ILC, in drafting the VCLT, noted that withdrawal serves as a safeguard when a state's consent to a treaty violates its constitutional principles.[35] Accordingly, 'a defect in [the state's] consent to be bound' – presumably, such as would satisfy Article 46 – is one of the grounds that may be invoked and notified to other states parties.[36] But nothing addresses whether there might be any 'manifest' or other constitutional violation related to the act of withdrawal *itself* – that is, addressing whether a state's invocation of some basis for withdrawal (or comparable act) might itself be impeached on the basis of a constitutional violation.[37] The VCLT incorporates notice periods, at least as defaults, presumably for the benefit of other states parties,[38] and allows the notifying state to withdraw such notice or instrument before it takes effect – including, one expects, on the basis of a constitutional violation.[39] But the practical significance is elusive. The timing in which a state can change its mind is a serious constraint.[40] In any event, the decision appears confided to

35 Draft Articles on the Law of Treaties, at p. 242 ('Confronted with a challenge under national law of the constitutional validity of a treaty, a Government will normally seek to regularize its position under the treaty by taking appropriate action in the domestic or international sphere').

36 VCLT, art. 65(1).

37 See Woolaver, 'From Joining to Leaving', 93 (conceding that 'it appears that a strictly internationalist approach is applicable in the context of treaty withdrawal'); Hannah Woolaver, 'Domestic and International Limitations on Treaty Withdrawal: Lessons from South Africa's Attempted Departure from the International Criminal Court' (2017) 111 *AJIL Unbound* 450, 454 ('Thus, a failure by the South African executive to abide by the constitutional requirement to obtain parliamentary approval could, had it been evident to other states, have resulted in the international invalidity of its consent when joining the Rome Statute, but the very same violation would not have any international legal effect on its withdrawal from the Rome Statute').

38 As noted earlier, these include a period of at least twelve months' notice when a right to withdraw is implied by a treaty, see VCLT, art. 56(2), and at least three months' notice in relation to withdrawal for one of the causes indicated by Part V. See VCLT, art. 65(2). The juxtaposition of these periods is not self-evident, but that is not of direct relevance here. Theodore Christakis, 'Article 56', in Oliver Corten and Pierre Klein (eds.), *The Vienna Conventions on the Law of Treaties: A Commentary*, 2 vols. (Oxford: Oxford University Press, 2011), vol. II, pp. 1254–55 and note 14.

39 VCLT, art. 68.

40 In principle, as to the initial notice indicated by Article 65, the period for revocation may exceed even the three months that article requires, but that is because the notice by itself accomplishes nothing – such that it may be waived by failing to execute withdrawal, as contemplated by Article 67, afterward. As regards execution, while the relevant instrument may also be withdrawn per Article 68, it also takes effect upon receipt, see VCLT, art. 78, so the window for revocation is likely to be vanishingly short. Antonios Tzanakopoulos, 'Article 68', in Oliver Corten and Pierre Klein (eds.), *The Vienna Conventions on the Law of Treaties: A Commentary*, 2 vols. (Oxford: Oxford University Press, 2011), vol. II, pp. 1566–68.

the discretion of executive-branch officials, exactly as one might expect.[41] The result, as Hannah Woolaver has observed, is that 'in contrast to international law powers to join treaties, the authority of the executive to withdraw the state from treaties in Article 67 of the VCLT is, prima facie, absolute in international law, unlimited by any checks that may exist in domestic law'.[42]

This withdrawal regime now faces challenges reminiscent of those once confronted by ratification. States are slowly retreating from the practice by which the executive is entitled to withdraw unilaterally from treaties, instead adopting new provisions that require parliamentary approval.[43] During the same period, multilateral and even bilateral treaty-making has seen a pronounced slowdown,[44] augmented (at least in the short term) by withdrawals and similar attempts at disengagement.[45] The result is that formal constitutional revision has been accompanied by high-profile instances in which executive-led attempts at withdrawal, like the United Kingdom's initial attempts to withdraw from the European Union and South Africa's (initial?) attempt to withdraw from the International Criminal Court, were slowed by judicial decisions that recognized for the first time parliamentary rights to participate in exit from certain types of treaties.[46]

41 The VCLT provides that the instruments actually executing withdrawal must be signed by the head of state, head of government, or minister of foreign affairs, or by a representative who may be asked to produce full powers. VCLT, arts. 67(2). The provision addressing the initial notice of cause, requires only that it be in writing, see VCLT, art. 65(1), but such matters are also traditionally assigned to the executive.

42 Woolaver, 'From Joining to Leaving', 95.

43 Verdier and Versteeg, 'Separation of Powers', p. 149 (describing a 'trend observers have largely missed: several countries already mandate parliamentary involvement in treaty withdrawal, and their numbers have been growing substantially in the last four decades'). Among the examples of states with explicit restrictions are Denmark, the Netherlands, Belgium and Chile, though in many more cases the restriction may be inferred from provisions governing both entry and exit into treaties or from constitutional decisions, see pp. 149–50. The authors do not, however, attempt to assess whether such a right of participation is respected in practice.

44 See, e.g., Joost Pauwelyn, Ramses A. Wessel and Jan Wouters, 'When Structures Become Shackles: Stagnation and Dynamics in International Lawmaking' (2014) 25 *European Journal of International Law* 733.

45 See, e.g., Andreas L. Paulus and Jan-Henrik Hinselman, 'International Integration and Its Counter-Limits: A German Constitutional Perspective', in Curtis A. Bradley (ed.), *The Oxford Handbook of Comparative Foreign Relations Law* (Oxford: Oxford University Press, 2019), pp. 419–24.

46 *R (Miller)* v. *Secretary of State for Exiting the European Union* [2017] UKSC 5, [2018] AC 61; *Democratic Alliance* v. *Minister of International Relations and Cooperation and Others* 2017 (3) SA 212 (GP). Brexit was ultimately effectuated, of course, with consent from the UK – and European – parliaments. European Union (Withdrawal Agreement) Act 2020, https://services.parliament.uk/bills/2019-20/europeanunionwithdrawalagreement.html, accessed July 16, 2020; European Parliament legislative resolution of January 29, 2020 on the draft Council decision on the conclusion of the Agreement on the withdrawal of the United Kingdom of Great Britain and

Despite the evolution of foreign relations law, there is no evident movement to develop international law. As with ratification, international law effectively regards executive determinations, in notifying a state's will, as exhausting treaty law's deference to domestic law, leaving any potential legislative role to be enforced solely through a state's own legal processes. This has clear appeal, both internationally and domestically, in instances where national requirements are as yet uncertain. But where national requirements are well defined, it remains troublingly clear that foreign relations law is not self-enforcing. For a number of actual or potential withdrawals – including those by the United States, a frequent flyer of sorts – justiciability principles are likely to limit the capacity of courts.[47] Even where courts are willing and ostensibly able, any domestic principle will be difficult to apply prior to a unilateral executive notice taking effect as a matter of international law.

The readiest solution would be to infer an analogous exemption for manifest violations in the withdrawal context to match that for ratification.[48] However, that is difficult as a matter of treaty interpretation. Article 46 is plainly limited to 'provisions of internal law regarding competence to conclude treaties'; that heads of government and comparable officials are elsewhere given authority to perform 'any other act with respect to a treaty' offers no textual basis for concluding that one of those acts, withdrawal, must also be constrained in the event of manifest violations.[49] Indications in the *travaux préparatoires* are mixed or negative.[50] That state practice did not support any

Northern Ireland from the European Union and the European Atomic Energy Community (XT 21105/3/2018 – C9-0148/2019 – 2018/0427(NLE)), www.europarl.europa.eu/doceo/document/TA-9–2020-0018_EN.html<int_u, accessed July 16, 2020. As for South Africa, withdrawal has been revived in the legislature, though without resolution to this point. International Crimes Bill, B 37–2017, www.justice.gov.za/legislation/bills/2017-b37-ICBill.pdf, accessed July 16, 2020. For discussion, see Laurence R. Helfer, 'Treaty Exit and Intrabranch Conflict at the Interface of International and Domestic Law', in Curtis A. Bradley (ed.), *The Oxford Handbook of Comparative Foreign Relations Law* (Oxford: Oxford University Press, 2019), pp. 360–63; Hannah Woolaver, 'State Engagement with Treaties: Interactions between International and Domestic Law', in Bradley (ed.), *The Oxford Handbook of Comparative Foreign Relations Law*, at pp. 439–43; Woolaver, 'From Joining to Leaving', 76–80.

47 See Curtis A. Bradley and Laurence R. Helfer, 'Treaty Exit in the United States: Insights from the United Kingdom or South Africa?' (2017) 111 *AJIL Unbound* 428, 432 (emphasizing other dissimilarities).

48 See Woolaver, 'Domestic and International Limitations on Treaty Withdrawal'; Woolaver, 'State Engagement with Treaties', p. 444; Woolaver, 'From Joining to Leaving', 95–103.

49 But see Woolaver, 'Domestic and International Limitations on Treaty Withdrawal', 97 (discussing Articles 2, 7 and 67 of the VCLT).

50 Professor Woolaver points to ILC commentary indicating that the evidence of authority should be the same as between consent to be bound and withdrawal, but that does not directly implicate the Article 46 obligation. Woolaver, 'Domestic and International Limitations on

such principle as a matter of customary international law – as Woolaver, a strong but judicious advocate for this interpretation, acknowledges[51] – further undermines any basis for attributing such intention to the states agreeing to the VCLT, and the lack of supportive state practice since suggests that it would be unreasonable to find any grounding in subsequent treaty practice.

To be sure, teleological or policy arguments for comparable treatment are appealing, including that the security of treaty obligations – one of the objectives of Article 46, including in limiting its exception to manifest violations only – is arguably hindered by the lack of any exception for constitutional violations regarding withdrawal, since that permits too-easy disengagement.[52] Necessarily, too, the backstops are different: while withdrawal serves as a safeguard for uncorrected constitutional violations concerning ratification, re-ratification is needed to cure withdrawal in violation of domestic law, and that tends to be more cumbersome as a matter of domestic and international procedure. Finally, it may be possible to muster additional arguments for cross-applying Article 46 and its manifest violation standard. For example, one might argue that states appearing to have withdrawn might revoke a prior notification on the ground that the relevant instrument did not 'take effect' under Article 68 if it manifestly violated a constitutional requirement of legislative participation.[53] No matter the precise basis, however, any such exemption would be doctrinally tenuous and narrow in its potential application.[54] It remains extremely unlikely that this would change so long as the manifest violation standard serves as a catchall for redressing other, potentially unknown, constitutional violations as well.

Treaty Withdrawal', 96. As she also indicates, the question of whether Article 46 standards should also be applied to withdrawal and similar matters was expressly posed, and while those raising the issue urged that the extension be reflected in text or commentary, that was expressly deferred – with the special rapporteur, Humphrey Waldock, saying it 'would require some thought' – and nothing further was done. See p. 94 (quoting ILC, 'Summary Records of the Fifteenth Session', (1963) 1 *Yearbook of the International Law Commission* 164).

51 Woolaver, 'Domestic and International Limitations on Treaty Withdrawal', 97.

52 Woolaver, 'Domestic and International Limitations on Treaty Withdrawal', 97–102; Helfer, 'Treaty Exit and Interbranch Conflict', p. 371.

53 What is required for a notification or subsequent instrument to 'tak[e] effect' under Article 68, however, is conventionally understood as meaning simply that it is received by the relevant depositary or states. VCLT, art. 78; see Tzanakopoulos, 'Article 68', p. 1567.

54 Thus Professor Helfer, who argues that the policy rationales for Article 46 warrant its application to states leaving treaties, suggests that – for that very reason – constitutional violations are essentially irrelevant under the international law of exit. Helfer, 'Treaty Exit and Interbranch Conflict', pp. 371–72.

What else might be engineered? If treaty law is to be progressively developed – or, with great difficulty, interpreted on the basis of Article 46 or otherwise – states and treaty depositories might adopt the assumption that a withdrawal must satisfy the same separation-of-powers procedures by which the state approved consent, as an international-law embodiment of the *acte contraire* doctrine. That is quite vulnerable as a general principle, given the actual discrepancy in many states between domestic laws regarding legislative approvals of ratification and withdrawal.[55] But the severity of any such rule may also be tempered. A state might overcome any such assumption by explaining its contrary (or still indeterminate) domestic principle. And the consequence – if a discrepancy was observed and remained unexplained, but withdrawal could still be approved in reasonable time – might not be to render the initial attempt invalid, thereby sustaining the full-fledged obligation, but instead to establish in the interim an obligation simply to abide by the treaty's object and purpose.[56] Still less dramatically, governments declaring withdrawal might be required by depositories or other states simply to disclose their authority and its compatibility with constitutional requirements – which might at least have the effect of making sufficiently 'manifest' any violations of a requirement to secure legislative approval.

Other solutions involve bearing possible constitutional restraints in mind while negotiating withdrawal clauses in particular treaties. The easiest lift is to restrict any immediate effect of a notice or instrument of withdrawal – for example, by restricting when withdrawal may first be effectuated, as is typical for International Labor Organization agreements, and evidenced in the Berne Convention and the Paris Agreement[57] – so as to permit legislative or judicial intervention in the case of a potentially unlawful, unilateral executive measure. More particularly, a treaty's withdrawal clause might require the disclosure of authority mentioned above, following the precedent of clauses that obligate withdrawing states to accompany their notices with explanations.[58]

55 As a commentator observed in another context, moreover, 'the notion of *acte contraire* is alien to international law'. Joost Pauwelyn, 'The Role of Public International Law in the WTO: How Far Can We Go?' (2001) 95 *American Journal of International Law* 535, 537 (discussing relationship between treaties and customary international law).

56 Cf. VCLT, art. 18.

57 See Berne Convention for the Protection of Literary and Artistic Works, Berne, September 9, 1886, as amended on September 28, 1979, in force November 19, 1984, https://wipolex.wipo.int/en/text/283698, accessed July 16, 2020, art. 35; Paris Agreement, United Nations Framework Convention on Climate Change, Report of the Conference of the Parties on the 21st Session, UN Doc. FCCC/CP/201510/Add.1, art. 28 (December 12, 2015).

58 See, e.g., Treaty Concerning Defense Trade Cooperation (US-UK), Washington and London, June 21 and 26, 2007, in force April 13, 2012, Senate Treaty Doc. No. 110-7 (2007), art. 20 (requiring 'a statement of the extraordinary events the notifying Party regards as having jeopardized its national interests' and warranting withdrawal); Treaty on the Non-Proliferation of Nuclear

III CONCLUSION

Foreign relations lawyers looking beyond their jurisdictions will naturally focus on any directly comparable national systems, but they should also consider the impact of international law on their discipline. First, international law not only provides opportunities for domestic actors that may be in tension with domestic principles, but also establishes rules that constrain foreign relations law. Second, while those rules of international law intend to respect ratification developments, they also guarantee that (in most circumstances) only constitutional rules assigning authority to the executive to communicate state decisions regarding ratification or withdrawal will be respected. As a result, these international rules have not adequately taken into account developments in legislative authority. Third, none of this is inevitable. In developing a comparative approach to foreign relations law, experts should not overlook the degree to which the effectiveness of domestic norms require attention to internationally established conditions.

Weapons, London, Washington and Moscow, July 1, 1968, in force March 5, 1970, 729 UNTS 161, art. X(1) (requiring 'a statement of the extraordinary events it regards as having jeopardized its supreme interests').

4

Comparative Foreign Relations Law between Center and Periphery

Liberal and Postcolonial Perspectives

Michael Riegner

I TAKING GLOBAL COMPARISON SERIOUSLY

Nine months before his death in a US-backed military coup, Chilean President Salvador Allende delivered an acclaimed speech to the UN General Assembly that must have been electrifying. As he concluded, the packed Assembly hall erupted into enthusiastic applause and shouts of 'Viva Allende!'.[1] Allende's 1972 speech marked an important rallying cry in the Third World's mobilization against a global economic order dominated by industrialized countries and Western multinational corporations.[2] Defending the nationalization of US-owned copper and telecommunications firms, Allende declared that '[o]ur economy could no longer tolerate the state of subordination implied in the concentration of more than 80 per cent of its exports in the hands of a small group of large, foreign companies.'[3] He mounted a spirited attack against multinational corporations' economic 'aggression' and 'imperialist intervention' into Chile's political affairs. Conscious that he was expressing a grievance shared by many developing countries, Allende concluded: 'We are witnessing a pitched battle between the great transnational corporations and sovereign States … In a word, the entire political structure of the world is being undermined.'[4] Allende's apprehension was no leftist

[1] Robert Alden, 'Mr. Allende follows outline of speech', New York Times, December 5, 1972, www.nytimes.com/1972/12/05/archives/allende-at-un-charges-assault-by-us-interests-chilean-president.html (all websites last accessed September 30, 2020).

[2] On the historical context, see Jochen von Bernstorff and Philipp Dann, *The Battle for International Law: North-South Perspectives on the Decolonization Era* (Oxford: Oxford University Press, 2019).

[3] Salvador Allende, 'Address delivered at 2096th Plenary Meeting, 4 December 1972, New York', *Official Records of the United Nations General Assembly* (1972), para. 9.

[4] Allende, *Official Records UN General Assembly*, para. 59.

paranoia: in 1973, he was ousted and died in a coup that was supported by the CIA and US-corporate interests and ushered in Augusto Pinochet's military dictatorship.[5] Beyond this extreme case, empirical research attests not only to the *economic* leverage of multinationals over many developing countries but also to the eminently *political* role transnational corporations have played in many Southern nations.[6]

Allende's speech is typically seen as a milestone towards a New International Economic Order in international law.[7] Beyond that, however, the Allende story also offers a different perspective on foreign relations law: one that is shaped by the postcolonial contexts and historical experiences of countries at the periphery of the global political economy. This perspective thus differs from conceptions of foreign relations law that developed in liberal democracies at the center of geopolitical gravity. If foreign relations law is to take global comparison seriously, it needs to take into account this peripheral perspective. Doing so not only pluralizes comparative foreign relations law and thus makes it more representative. It might also help us understand contemporary transformations of foreign relations law in Western liberal democracies, as these legal orders become less centric and more peripheral in a new multipolar geopolitical context.

Extant literature in foreign relations law is shaped by liberal perspectives from the center. As a field of study, foreign relations law is commonly thought to have originated in the peculiar context of the United States, shaped as much by its federal and presidential system as by its geopolitical centrality and dominance.[8]

5 On US involvement in the coup see Tanya Harmer, *Allende's Chile and the Inter-American Cold War* (Chapel Hill: University of North Carolina Press, 2011); Anthony Sampson, *The Sovereign State of ITT* (New York: Stein Day, 1973); United States Senate, 'First Session, Volume 7: Covert Action', *Hearings Before the Select Committee to Study Governmental Operations with Respect to Intelligence Activities*, Ninety Fourth Congress, 1975, available at www.intelligence.senate.gov/resources/intelligence-related-commissions, p. 15 f., 158 f.

6 Bastiaan van Apeldoorn and Nana de Graaf, 'The Corporation in Political Science', in Grietje Baars and Andre Spicer (eds.), *The Corporation: A Critical, Multi-Disciplinary Handbook* (Cambridge: Cambridge University Press, 2017), pp. 134–59; Lorraine Eden and Evan H. Potter, *Multinationals in the Global Political Economy* (London: Palgrave Macmillan UK, 1993); Theodore H. Moran, *Multinational Corporations and the Politics of Dependence* (Princeton: Princeton University Press, 1974); Raymond Vernon, *Sovereignty at Bay: The Multinational Spread of U.S. Enterprises* (London: Longman, 1971).

7 Cf. Sundhya Pahuja and Anna Saunders, 'Rival Worlds and the Place of the Corporation in International Law', in Jochen von Bernstorff and Philipp Dann (eds.), *The Battle for International Law: South-North Perspectives on in the Decolonization Eera* (Oxford: Oxford University Press, 2019), pp. 141–74.

8 Curtis A. Bradley, 'Foreign Relations Law as a Field of Study' (2017) 111 *AJIL Unbound* 316 at 319. But see on the nineteenth-century idea of 'Äußeres Staatesrecht' in Germany Helmut Philipp Aust, 'The Democratic Challenge to Foreign Relations Law in Transatlantic Perspective', in David Dyzenhaus, Jacco Bomhoff and Thomas Poole (eds.), *The Double-*

Most recent treatments of foreign relations law focus on one single legal order or compare a small number of 'Western' liberal democracies, typically the US, the UK, Germany or the European Union.[9] This state of affairs carries the risk, as Helmut Aust has put it, 'to fall into the trap of a self-referential, liberal, and Western mindset which takes discussions in a few jurisdictions of the "Global North" as being representative of the broader global picture'.[10]

This chapter does not address this problem by adding new legal material from the Global South to the existing comparative framework. Rather, the aim is to uncover and pluralize the theoretical assumptions and epistemic foundations of the existing comparative framework. This endeavor can draw on a longstanding critique of the epistemic limitations of traditional comparative law and on the emerging literature on a constitutionalism of the Global South.[11] Two desiderata emerge from this literature, one methodological and one epistemic: methodologically, a global comparison requires not only a more representative case selection but also increased attention to the heterogenous historical, political-economic and legal-cultural contexts that shape the meaning and function of foreign relations law in both North and South.[12] Foreign relations law is not simply a national

Facing Constitution: Legal Externalities and the Reshaping of the Constitutional Order (Cambridge: Cambridge University Press, 2020), pp. 345-75.

9 Campbell McLachlan, *Foreign Relations Law* (Cambridge: Cambridge University Press, 2014); Robert Schütze, *Foreign Affairs and the EU Constitution: Selected Essays* (Cambridge: Cambridge University Press, 2016); Curtis A. Bradley and Jack L. Goldsmith, *Foreign Relations Law: Cases and Materials* (New York: Wolters Kluwer, 2017); Helmut Philipp Aust, 'Foreign Affairs', *Max Planck Encyclopedia of Comparative Constitutional Law* (2017), http://oxcon.ouplaw.com/home/MPEC COL; Thomas Kleinlein, 'TTIP and the Challenges of Investor-State-Arbitration: An Exercise in Comparative Foreign Relations Law', in Anna-Bettina Kaiser, Niels Petersen and Johannes Saurer (eds.), *The U.S. Supreme Court and Contemporary Constitutional Law: The Obama Era and Its Legacy* (Baden-Baden: Nomos, 2018), pp. 211–28; Curtis A. Bradley (ed.), *The Oxford Handbook of Comparative Foreign Relations Law* (New York: Oxford University Press, 2019) (which does contain chapters on India, South Africa, China and Commonwealth African Countries). Conversely, standard comparative law treaties tend not to consider 'foreign relations' as a self-standing field for comparison, see e.g. Michel Rosenfeld and András Sajó (eds.), *The Oxford Handbook of Comparative Constitutional Law* (Oxford: Oxford University Press, 2013); Susanna Dorsen et al., *Comparative Constitutionalism: Cases and Materials* (St. Paul: West Academic Publishing, 2016).

10 Aust, 'Foreign Affairs', para. 6.

11 Philipp Dann, Michael Riegner and Maxim Bönnemann (eds.), *The Global South and Comparative Constitutional Law* (Oxford: Oxford University Press, 2020); Zoran Oklopcic, 'The South of Western Constitutionalism: A Map Ahead of a Journey' (2016) 37 *Third World Quarterly* 2080; Daniel Bonilla Maldonado, *Constitutionalism of the Global South* (Cambridge: Cambridge University Press, 2013); Günter Frankenberg, 'Critical Comparisons: Rethinking Comparative Law' (1985) 26 *Harvard International Law Journal* 411.

12 On contextual comparison see generally Günter Frankenberg, 'Comparing Constitutions: Ideas, Ideals, and Ideology – Toward a Layered Narrative' (2006) 4 *ICON* 439. On the combination of contextual and functionalist methods see already M. Riegner, 'Access to Information As a Human Right and Constitutional Guarantee. A Comparative Perspective'

reflection of universal international principles but remains deeply embedded in different varieties of constitutionalism, including non-liberal variants.[13] Epistemically, the challenge is thus to go beyond mere addition and to question, provincialize and pluralize the theoretical concepts and epistemic categories that prestructure the comparative inquiry.[14] Comparatists need to make explicit the underlying assumptions that define and structure foreign relations law as a field of study and to empirically test, rather than implicitly presuppose, their universal validity beyond Western liberal democracy.

This chapter pursues this approach in two steps. Section II contrasts two ideal-typical perspectives on foreign relations law, a liberal one from the center and a postcolonial one from the periphery. These perspectives differ in their approach to epistemic structure, normative functions and legal subjects of foreign relations law. These differences come into sharp relief in the legal treatment of transnational corporations, whose sociolegal reality questions categorical distinctions between international and national, political and economic, state and individual. For the purposes of this chapter, I take Salvador Allende's speech to be illustrative of this particular peripheral perspective, which was however widely shared at the time by many Third World nations and whose legacy lives on in contemporary varieties of constitutionalism in the Global South. Section III goes further and argues that the peripheral perspective is not exclusive to an essentialized 'South' but has increasing resonance and heuristic value in the 'North', as it highlights contemporary transformations in liberal-democratic foreign relations law. Again, these transformations can be studied through the changing attitudes towards transnational corporations, which represent one possible avenue for future

(2017) 50 *VRÜ / Law and Politics in Asia, Africa and Latin America* 332 at 353 ff. On case selection see Ran Hirschl, 'The Question of Case Selection in Comparative Constitutional Law' (2005) 53 *American Journal of Comparative Law* 125; Cheryl Saunders, 'Towards a Global Constitutional Gene Pool' (2009) 4 *National Taiwan University Law Review*, 1.

13 See generally Mark Tushnet, 'Editorial: Varieties of Constitutionalism' (2016) 14 *ICON* 1; Oscar V. Vieira, Uprenda Baxi and Frans Viljoen (eds.), *Transformative Constitutionalism: Comparing the Apex Courts of Brazil, India and South Africa* (Pretoria: Pretoria University Law Press, 2013); Michael W. Dowdle and Michael A.Wilkinson (eds.), *Constitutionalism beyond Liberalism* (Cambridge: Cambridge University Press, 2017); Helena A. García and Günter Frankenberg (eds.), *Authoritarian Constitutionalism: Comparative Analysis and Critique* (Cheltenham: Edward Elgar Publishing, 2019).

14 Oklopcic, 'The South of Western Constitutionalism'; Florian Hoffmann, 'Knowledge Production in Comparative Constitutional Law' in Philipp Dann, Michael Riegner and Maxim Bönnemann (eds.), *The Global South and Comparative Constitutional Law* (Oxford: Oxford University Press, 2020) pp. 41–66; Ina Kerner, 'Beyond Eurocentrism: Trajectories Towards a Renewed Political and Social Theory' (2018) 44 *Philosophy & Social Criticism* 550. On provincializing, see generally Dipesh Chakrabarty, *Provincializing Europe: Postcolonial Thought and Historical Difference* (New Delhi: Oxford University Press, 2000).

comparative research. Section IV concludes with some thoughts on the possibilities and limits of drawing lessons from historical and global comparisons.

II TWO PERSPECTIVES ON FOREIGN RELATIONS LAW: FROM CENTRE TO PERIPHERY

This following section develops and contrasts two perspectives on foreign relations law, the liberal one from the center (subsection A), and the postcolonial one from the periphery (subsection B). These should be prefaced with three caveats: firstly, they are ideal-typical perspectives that do not neatly map onto the actual law of any particular state, nor are they representative of the entire 'Global North' or 'South'. Rather, the aim is to contrast different contexts, ideological formations and epistemic structures and to offer alternative ways of thinking about foreign relations law. Secondly, ideological and epistemic difference does not hamper 'comparability' but has heuristic value precisely in uncovering implicit assumptions and teaching us as much about the self than the other. Thirdly, contrasting the two perspectives does not, at this stage, imply a normative judgment on which is the 'better' view. Normatively speaking, the peripheral view does not require abandoning questions about, and a commitment to, democracy, separation of powers and individual rights typically asked in liberal foreign relations law; but it commands a pluralized and contextualized understanding of these concepts.

A *Liberal Foreign Relations Law from the Center*

If recent handbook and encyclopedia articles are representative of the existing literature, then foreign relations law is defined, in its core, as the domestic legal norms that govern the participation of state organs in diplomatic relations and international lawmaking; beyond that, it arguably includes the domestic effects of these international activities, especially international law, and individual rights protection in internationalized situations.[15] The main research questions and normative concerns pertain to the operation of separation of powers, democracy and individual rights at the interface between the international and domestic sphere.

[15] Curtis A. Bradley, 'What Is Foreign Relations Law?', in Curtis A. Bradley (ed.), *The Oxford Handbook of Comparative Foreign Relations Law* (New York: Oxford University Press, 2019), p. 3; Aust, 'Foreign Affairs', para. 8; McLachlan, *Foreign Relations Law*, 7 ff.

These definitions and concerns are informed by a liberal perspective from the center of geopolitical gravity.[16] This perspective is shaped by specific contexts: the legal-cultural context is liberal-democratic constitutionalism. The dominant ideological influence is liberalism as it evolved in Europe and North America since the seventeenth century, embodied by intellectual forerunners like Locke, Blackstone, Mann and others.[17] Historically, it is shaped by an experience of statehood in which the nation state preexists international law and is located at the center of an imperially structured global order. Economically, these states have been capital exporting market economies, either of the liberal or coordinated variety of capitalism.[18]

The liberal, centric perspective is defined by particular ideas about the structure, function and subjects of foreign relations law: (1) its *epistemic structure* is based on a binary distinction between international and national that is rigidly applied to the political sphere, but not necessarily to the economic sphere; (2) its *normative function* is to protect internal and external, political sovereignty by allocating powers to different branches and levels of government; (3) its *agency structure* is based on two paradigmatic legal subjects: the state and the individual, who has a dual existence as a national *citoyen* and transnational *bourgeois*. In short, the liberal foreign relations law is focused primarily on relations among states and on political constitutionalism.

This perspective implies particular conceptions of sovereignty, democracy, separation of powers and rights that are embedded in the broader Western constitutional tradition. The epistemic structure of liberal foreign relations law rests on an understanding of sovereignty that establishes a binary distinction between international and national, external and internal, outside and inside. In this distinction, the national preexists, and autonomously determines its relationship to, the international. Foreign relations law is conceived as the domestic interface where this determination is made. Globalization is perceived as an external force that the state opens itself up to in choosing between 'open' or 'closed' statehood. Importantly, the distinction between international and national is applied rigidly to the political sphere but not to

16 I use 'liberal' to designate a particular constitutional tradition and political philosophy. This usage does not correspond to the meaning of 'liberal' as a position in partisan politics, where it can designate 'progressive' or 'left' in the US, or rather the opposite in Europe. Obviously, even within the meaning used here, there are different shades and traditions. On varieties of liberalism, see generally Michael Freeden, *Liberalism: A Very Short Introduction* (Oxford: Oxford University Press, 2015), 37 ff.; Duncan Bell, 'What Is Liberalism?' (2014) 42 *Political Theory* 682.

17 McLachlan, *Foreign Relations Law*, 31 ff.; Aust, 'Foreign Affairs', para. 1.

18 Peter A. Hall and David W. Soskice (eds.), *Varieties of Capitalism: The Institutional Foundations of Comparative Advantage* (Oxford: Oxford University Press, 2001).

the economic sphere. The separation of economy and politics by domestic constitutionalism is a well-known feature of nineteenth-century classical liberalism. Legally, this separation was effected by the constitutional protection of economic rights against political power – whether exercised by authoritarian executives or democratically elected legislatures. Importantly for foreign relations, as the economic sphere is separated from the state, it remains possible to imagine a 'world market' or a 'global economy', to which the liberal state opens itself by allowing for free trade and foreign investment.[19] Internally as externally, its economic role thus tends to be that of a (de)regulator.

This epistemic structure prefigures the normative functions ascribed to foreign relations law. These functions derive from a specific understanding of sovereignty in the different spheres. Sovereignty governs the political sphere, where it follows a dual logic: internationally, sovereignty translates into the requirement of state consent, typically expressed by executive actors. Internally, the logic is popular sovereignty, which requires political rights, democracy and separation of powers. Foreign relations law, then, is essentially about which of the two logics governs the interface of national and international. Importantly, this dual logic does not apply in the same way to the economic sphere, which transcends the national-international binary and remains governed at least as much by the logic of individual liberty and economic rights. Indeed, as historian Quinn Slobodian has recently shown, a key feature of normative order in the twentieth century was the extension of neo- and ordoliberal principles to the international realm: the legal separation between imperium and dominium, sovereignty and property kept economic integration possible in a world of ending empires and multiplying democratic nation states.[20]

The epistemic structure and normative functions also determine ideas about agency and legal subjectivity. The paradigmatic actors and legal subjects of liberal foreign relations law are the state and the individual. In this binary structure, the state has authority, the individual has liberty. Individual liberty is protected by rights, which differ on the national versus international, political versus economic axes: political rights are, in principle, bounded by the state: the citoyen is a national. In contrast, economic rights extend beyond the state: the bourgeois transcends the national. This idea is most developed in the European Union: supranational free movement rights have direct effect

[19] M. Fichera, 'Liberalism', *Max Planck Encyclopedia of Comparative Constitutional Law* (2017), https://oxcon.ouplaw.com/home/MPECCOL.

[20] Quinn Slobodian, *Globalists: The End of Empire and the Birth of Neoliberalism* (Cambridge: Harvard University Press, 2018).

and supremacy in domestic constitutional orders. In practice, the bourgeois is often not a human being but a legal person, typically a corporation. In liberal foreign relations law, corporations have legal subjectivity but do not constitute a separate category of actors. If they appear at all, it is under the rubric of 'informality', 'citizens or residents of other nations' or 'individuals'.[21] In the binary liberal framework, corporations simply pose a problem of attribution, and they are typically attributed to the sphere of the private individual: corporations are expressions of economic liberty and creatures of private law, a legal fiction designed to facilitate the accumulation of capital and its transnational mobility.

The result of this overall framework is neatly summed up by political theorist Christian Volk:

> What states and global governance institutions do is political, and political is equated with significant, important, primary; economic, in contrast, is equated with secondary, private, profane. Hidden behind this, of course, is also a normative program, namely that of the (democratic) self-determination of society through the state. But there is a high price to be paid for this program: The political power of private-economic actors remains invisible.[22]

B A *Postcolonial Perspective from the Periphery*

If foreign relations law emerged as an autonomous field of study in liberal democracies like the US, the UK and Germany, this does not mean that other states have no law governing foreign relations.[23] This observation implies, on the one hand, that a global comparison of foreign relations law is in principle possible. On the other hand, it carries the risk of transplanting legal concepts and epistemic categories that developed in a liberal, centric frame of reference into different contexts. As comparative law teaches us, both the meaning and the social function of legal concepts can vary with context. In the context of liberal democracies, foreign relations law may have the function of allocating jurisdiction and external powers to protect political self-determination and individual liberty.[24] But we cannot simply assume that this is true in different

[21] Aust, 'Foreign Affairs', para. 35; Bradley, 'What Is Foreign Relations Law?', p. 3; McLachlan, *Foreign Relations Law*, p. 27.

[22] Christian Volk, 'The Problem of Sovereignty in Globalized Times' (2019) *Law, Culture and the Humanities, Online First* 1 at 17.

[23] Bradley, 'What Is Foreign Relations Law?', p. 8 f.

[24] Campbell McLachlan, 'Five Conceptions of the Function of Foreign Relations Law', in Curtis A. Bradley (ed.), *The Oxford Handbook of Comparative Foreign Relations Law* (New York: Oxford University Press, 2019), pp. 21–44.

contexts shaped by different varieties of constitutionalism, geopolitical positions and epistemic frameworks.[25] Rather than assuming similarity, this chapter takes the different historical and political-economic context as starting point for an alternative perspective that looks at foreign relations law from the postcolonial periphery. 'Periphery' here designates a decentered position in the economic geography of contemporary capitalism, while 'postcolonial' refers to the condition shaped by the many legacies of colonial domination.[26]

Salvador Allende's 1972 speech can be read as manifesto of the peripheral perspective, in as much as it crystallizes formative experiences, epistemic categories and legal concepts prevalent across the Third World at the time. It captures a historical moment in which rapid decolonization gave rise to alternative political and legal imaginations in the periphery, embodied especially by the UN Declaration on Permanent Sovereignty over Natural Resources and the Declaration for the Establishment of a New International Economic Order adopted in 1974.[27] While these initiatives are often dismissed as inconsequential in *international* law, they were also an important expression of, and influence on, *constitutional* law within Third World countries. Within these legal orders, they found fertile ground in traditions of social and economic constitutionalism, inaugurated by the Mexican constitution of 1917 and the Weimar constitution of 1919, which both influenced constitutional traditions in the developing world.[28]

25 See generally Boaventura de Sousa Santos, *Epistemologies of the South: Justice against Epistemicide* (Boulder: Paradigm Publishers, 2014).

26 For a contemporary legal approach to economic geography, see Michael Dowdle, 'On the Regulatory Geography of Modern Capitalism: Putting "Rule of Law" in its Place', Oxford Centre for Socio-Legal Studies Discussion Series (2018), www.law.ox.ac.uk/sites/files/oxlaw/dowdle_putting_rule_of_law_in_its_place.pdf. Classically, Immanuel Wallerstein, *The Modern World System I* (New York: Academic Press, 1974), p. 302: 'The periphery of a world-economy is that geographical sector of it wherein production is primarily of lower ranking goods'. On the concept of 'postcolonial' in comparative law, see only Philipp Dann and Felix Hanschmann, 'Post-colonial Theories and Law' (2012) 45 *VRÜ / Law and Politics in Asia, Africa and Latin America* 12; Judith Schacherreiter, 'Postcolonial Theory and Comparative Law: On the Methodological and Epistemological Benefits to Comparative Law through Postcolonial Theory' (2016) 49 *VRÜ / Law and Politics in Asia, Africa and Latin America* 291, both with further references.

27 Mohammed Bedjaoui, *Towards a New International Economic Order* (Paris: UNESCO, 1979); Antony Anghie, 'Legal Aspects of the New International Economic Order' (2015) 6 *Humanity* 145; Ingo Venzke, 'Possibilities of the Past Histories of the NIEO and the Travails of Critique' (2018) 20 *Journal of the History of International Law* 263.

28 Roberto Gargarella, *Latin American Constitutionalism, 1810–2010: The Engine Room of the Constitution* (New York: Oxford University Press, 2013), pp. 105 ff.; David Jungbluth, *Die Entwicklung des deutschen Wirtschaftsverfassungsrechts: Von Weimar bis zum Investitionshilfeurteil* (Wiesbaden: Springer Verlag, 2018), pp. 15 ff.

In terms of ideological influences, the peripheral perspective popularized by Allende owed much to dependency theorists like Raul Prebisch and postcolonial thinkers like Franz Fanon, who sympathized with Marxist ideas all while rejecting many aspects of actually existing socialism.[29] As for liberalism, there was and is little enthusiasm for those liberal varieties that subjected the periphery to free-trade imperialism and, later on, to crippling neoliberal structural adjustment.[30] In terms of historical context, foreign relations did not begin as interstate relations but as dealings between chartered trading companies like the East India Company and local rulers.[31] The experience of statehood was also quite different: for many postcolonial states, the international preceded the national; peripheral statehood was produced and defined by international law during decolonization. The state was the only form of political organization that was legally available for collective self-determination.[32] For many new states, decolonization meant political independence but continued economic dependence: they depended on imports of capital and technology and on volatile exports of primary commodities, which were often foreign-owned or locked into unequal concessions agreements. In response, they experimented with industrial policies of import substitution and mixed or planned economies.[33]

This context gave rise to legal thinking about foreign relations that differs from the liberal-centric perspective in terms of structure, function and agency: (1) the *epistemic structure* is based on transnational and hybrid categories that transcend the binary opposition between national and international, political and economic; (2) the *normative functions* include enhancing economic self-determination, socioeconomic development and equality; (3) the *agency structure* is plural, including legal subjects ranging from state and individual to corporations, indigenous peoples and rights of nature. In short, peripheral foreign relations law is broader than the liberal one: it includes economic relations with powerful non-state actors and aspects of economic constitutionalism.

29 Matias E. Margulis, *The Global Political Economy of Raúl Prebisch* (Milton: Taylor and Francis, 2017); Frantz Fanon, *The Wretched of the Earth* (New York: Grove Press, 2004 [1961]), pp. 97 ff.

30 Andrew S. Sartori, *Liberalism in Empire: An Alternative History* (Berkeley: University of California Press, 2014).

31 Philip J. Stern, *The Company-State: Corporate Sovereignty and the Early Modern Foundations of the British Empire in India* (Oxford: Oxford University Press, 2011).

32 But see on *intellectual* alternatives Adom Getachew, *Worldmaking after Empire: The Rise and Fall of Self-Determination* (Princeton: Princeton University Press, 2019).

33 Luis Eslava, 'The Developmental State: Independence, Dependency, and History of the South', in Philipp Dann and Jochen von Bernstorff (eds.), *The Battle for International Law: South-North Perspectives on the Decolonization Era* (Oxford: Oxford University Press, 2019), pp. 71–100; Magnus Feldmann, 'Global Varieties of Capitalism' (2019) 71 *World Politics* 162; Margulis, *The Global Political Economy of Raúl Prebisch*.

This way of thinking about foreign relations law implies different conceptions of sovereignty, collective self-determination and rights. In terms of epistemic structure, the dichotomy of international and national has less historical and sociological plausibility. International law not only produced the peripheral state, but also pervaded it from the outset: international institutions midwifed, nurtured, socialized many of the new states; postcolonial law was 'modernized' in the image of Western law in 'law and development' efforts; land, natural resources and corporations were often foreign-owned; globalization was not external but internal to the state.[34] In this situation, the category of transnationalism might be a more accurate representation of peripheral relations with the rest of the world. Similarly, the separation of the political and economic spheres had less plausibility in the periphery. In the history of colonialism, sovereignty and property had been closely entangled: colonization frequently began with land acquisition, and corporate property rights often became functionally equivalent to sovereignty.[35] After the end of formal colonization, colonial hierarchies lived on in privatized property relationships. The transnational corporations symbolized this entanglement of economic and political power so vociferously denounced by Allende in this 1972 speech. This historical experience gave credit to the idea that economic relations were political, and vice versa.

These epistemic differences translated into different functions of foreign relations law. After decolonization had achieved political independence, sovereignty became closely associated with economic self-determination and development. The external and internal spheres were not differentiated by a dual logic of political sovereignty but bound together by one unitary rationality: development. Externally, peripheral sovereignty was not defined by consent to preexisting international law but conditioned on the state of development – from the mandate system to weighted voting in international financial institutions. Internally, peripheral states came into being as developmental states, whose teleology was to 'modernize' and 'catch up' with European statehood.[36] Nationalizations of 'system-relevant' enterprises, as

[34] Guy F. Sinclair, *To Reform the World: International Organizations and the Making of Modern States* (Oxford: Oxford University Press, 2017); Eslava, 'The Developmental State'.

[35] Matthias Goldmann, 'Colonial Law as a Symbolic Order: Property and Sovereignty in German Southwest Africa', *SSRN* (2019), October 28, 2018, https://papers.ssrn.com/sol3/papers.cfm?abstract_id=3274198; Brenna Bhandar, *Colonial Lives of Property: Law, Land, and Racial Regimes of Ownership* (Durham: Duke University Press, 2018); Mieke van der Linden, 'The Neglected Colonial Root of the Fundamental Right to Property: African Natives' Property Rights in the Age of New Imperialism and in Times Thereafter' (2015) 75 *Zeitschrift für ausländisches öffentliches Recht und Völkerrecht* 791.

[36] Eslava, 'The Developmental State'.

those defended by Allende in his speech, were a means to achieve economic independence, development and substantive equality. A separation of the economic and political was neither epistemically plausible nor normatively desirable. If there was a concern with separation, then it was separation of powers in the private sphere, whereas the state needed a strong executive to confront multinational corporations. Thus, the function of the law was to realize economic sovereignty, ideals of economic democracy and a measure of economic equality.

Thirdly, peripheral agency structure is not binary but plural. The state and the individual are important but not exclusive actors. There is a category of legal subjects that occupies an intermediary space between the individual and the state. Legal subjectivity and constitutional rights are granted to corporations, other collective actors like trade unions and indigenous peoples, and most recently even to nature itself.[37] Corporations are not only economic but political entities, and they have their own transnational reality independent from the private law of any particular state. As Allende put it in another speech in 1972: corporations 'have become a supranational force that is threatening to get completely out of control . . . They have their objectives, their own policies with regard to trade, shipping, international affairs and economic integration, their own view of things, their own activity, their own world.'[38]

This 'supranational' status was ensured by a variety of legal techniques: the internationalization of concession agreements and contracts between states and investors, which insulated them from the domestic law of the host state; the submission of investor-state disputes to international arbitration, which removed them from the jurisdiction of domestic courts of the host state, as became evident with the rise of such disputes in the 1990s; and finally the extraterritorial enforcement of arbitral awards in all major jurisdictions, which placed host countries at the mercy of foreign courts, often those in the investor's home state.[39] Against this quasi-supranational status, Allende asserted home state jurisdiction and the supremacy of home state law:

[37] Paola Villavicencio Calzadilla and Luis J. Kotzé, 'Living in Harmony with Nature?: A Critical Appraisal of the Rights of Mother Earth in Bolivia' (2018) 7 *Transnational Environmental Law* 397; Elena Blanco and Anna Grear, 'Personhood, Jurisdiction and Injustice: Law, Colonialities and the Global Order' (2019) 10 *Journal of Human Rights and the Environment* 86.

[38] Salvador Allende, 'Address delivered at the Inaugural Ceremony, 13 April 1972, Santiago, Chile', *Proceedings of the United Nations Conference on Trade and Development* (1973), 349, paras. 58, 60.

[39] Muthucumaraswamy Sornarajah, 'The Battle Continued: Rebuilding Empire through Internationalization of State Contracts', in Philipp Dann and Jochen von Bernstorff (eds.),

> The Chilean Constitution provides that nationalization disputes should be resolved by a tribunal which, like all tribunals in my country, has complete independence and sovereignty in the adoption of decisions ... we shall continue with undiminished determination to maintain that only the Chilean courts are competent to pass judgment in any dispute concerning the nationalization of our basic resources. For Chile, this is not merely an important problem of juridical interpretation; it is a question of sovereignty. Indeed, it is far more than this – it is a question of survival.[40]

It is this question of survival that defined the foreign relations law in much of the worlds' periphery.

Allende's reference to the Chilean constitution provides one concrete example of how the peripheral perspective translates into positive constitutional law: in July 1971, a constitutional amendment had enabled the nationalization of the copper industry by declaring that the state 'has absolute, exclusive, inalienable and imprescriptible domain over all mines' – a provision still in force at the time of writing (article 19 XXIV of the constitution of 1980).[41] While this chapter is not the place for a systematic comparison of positive legal provisions across time and space, some further examples might still serve to illustrate the theoretical points made above.

In this regard, provisions on public ownership of natural resources like the ones in Chile are not an isolated example but a recurring theme of a foreign relations law that rejects the liberal dichotomy of economy and politics, property and sovereignty. Many postcolonial constitutions introduced similar provisions that allowed for the nationalization of assets of transnational corporations and that constituted the domestic equivalent of international law claims to permanent sovereignty over natural resources.[42] Several examples thus stem from the heyday of the New International Economic Order: the

The Battle for International Law: South-North Perspectives on the Decolonization Era (Oxford: Oxford University Press, 2019), pp. 175–97.

40 Salvador Allende, 'Address delivered at 2096th Plenary Meeting, 4 December 1972, New York', para. 47, 52.

41 Ley 17450 of 16.7.1971, available at www.leychile.cl/Navegar?idNorma=29026&idParte=&idVersion=1971-07-16; on the context see Wolf Radmann, 'Staatliche Beteiligungs- und Verstaatlichungsvereinbarungen mit den ausländischen Kupferbergbaugesellschaften in Chile und Sambia' (1971) 4 *VRÜ / Law and Politics in Asia, Africa and Latin America* 301 at 317.

42 On permanent sovereignty over natural resources in international law see Nico Schrijver, *Sovereignty over Natural Resources: Balancing Rights and Duties* (Cambridge: Cambridge University Press, 2008); Sundhya Pahuja, *Decolonising International Law: Development, Economic Growth and the Politics of Universality* (Cambridge: Cambridge University Press, 2011), pp. 95 ff.

independence constitution of Angola of 1975, for instance, declared all natural resources, including oil and minerals, property of the state (article 11, today article 16 of the constitution of 2010). Iran, known to international lawyers for protracted arbitration over the nationalization of its oil industry, provides in its constitution of 1979 that 'mineral deposits' shall be at the disposal of the Islamic government (article 45), excludes foreigners from mineral extraction concessions (article 81) and prohibits agreements resulting in foreign control over natural resources (article 153). The current Constitution of Kenya (2010) not only declares all minerals and mineral oils to be 'public land' (article 61 I lit. f), but also requires parliamentary approval for the grant of natural resource concessions (article 71).[43]

Other examples come from an older constitutional tradition in Latin America, which is often associated with the Calvo doctrine in international law. Domestically, the Mexican constitution of 1917 vested ownership of natural resources like petroleum in the nation (article 27), and the Brazilian constitution of 1967 stipulated a public monopoly for petroleum exploration and exploitation (article 162, today articles 176 and 177).[44] Latin America also offers other examples beyond public ownership. Constitutional land rights of indigenous peoples, for instance, illustrate the plural agency structure of a postcolonial foreign relations law. In particular, the requirement of free, prior and informed consultation is recognized in constitutional law, either by the constitutional text like in Bolivia (article 30.II.15, 352, 403) or by constitutional case law like in Colombia.[45] In practice, this requirement can lead to quasi-diplomatic negotiations between indigenous representatives and private transnational corporations in which the state plays merely a moderating role, if at all.[46]

43 On these provisions see Petra Gümplová, 'Popular Sovereignty over Natural Resources: A Critical Reappraisal of Leif Wenar's Blood Oil from the Perspective of International Law and Justice' (2018) 7 *Global Constitutionalism* 173; Schrijver, *Sovereignty over Natural Resources*, p. 263.

44 On the significance of these provisions, see John Gledhill, '"The People's Oil": Nationalism, Globalization, and the Possibility of another Country in Brazil, Mexico, and Venezuela' (2008) 52 *Focaal* 57. On the related approach to property, see Manuel Garcia-Mora, 'The Calvo Clause in Latin American Constitutions and International Law' (1950) 33 *Marquette L. Rev.* 205.

45 From the Colombian case law, see inter alia Constitutional Court, cases SU-039/97; C-169/2001. More generally, Rachel Sieder, 'Indigenous Peoples' Rights and Law in Latin America' in César Rodríguez Garavito (ed.), *Law and Society in Latin America: A New Map* (Abingdon: Routledge, 2015), pp. 143–57.

46 Jessika Eichler, 'Indigenous Peoples' Land Rights in the Bolivian Lowlands' (2016) 5 *International Human Rights L. Rev.* 119; César Rodríguez Garavito and Carlos Baquero Díaz, 'The Right to Free, Prior, and Informed Consultation in Colombia: Advances and Setbacks' (2018), www.ohchr.org/Documents/Issues/IPeoples/EMRIP/FPIC/GaravitoAndDiaz.pdf.

While these examples all illustrate elements of the peripheral perspective in positive law, they still evince a considerable diversity in terms of actual practice and wider constitutional context, which ranges from mixed-economy constitutional democracies like Brazil to authoritarian systems like Iran. This diversity suggests that constitutionalism in the Global South is too heterogeneous to attribute one uniform peripheral perspective to its foreign relations law. If one is intent on finding a measure of convergence, an intra-regional perspective might be more promising. One example for such a regional approach to foreign relations law is regional integration in Latin America, which is still influenced by peripheral experiences. The model of regional integration espoused by Latin American states has recently been labelled as a multi-level exercise in 'transformative constitutionalism'[47] – a variety of constitutionalism that is often conceived as a 'Southern' alternative to 'Northern' liberal constitutionalism.[48]

This model of open statehood differs from its European counterpart in its differential constitutional openness for human rights and economic integration.[49] Human rights norms and case law from the Inter-American system enjoy a privileged constitutional status in contemporary foreign relations law in Latin America. This status is based on explicit opening clauses such as article 93 of the Constitution of Colombia and on incorporation doctrines like the 'block of constitutionality' and 'conventionality control'.[50] These doctrines accord international civil, political and social rights a status that is comparable to EU-type direct effect and, in some jurisdictions, supremacy. In contrast, regional economic integration and international economic law do not enjoy a similarly

[47] Armin von Bogdandy et al. (eds.), *Transformative Constitutionalism in Latin America: The Emergence of a New Ius Commune* (Oxford: Oxford University Press, 2017). For a discussion, see Michael Riegner, 'Transformativer Konstitutionalismus und offene Staatlichkeit im regionalen Verfassungsvergleich mit Lateinamerika' (2019) 67 *Jahrbuch des öffentlichen Rechts der Gegenwart* 265.

[48] The concept has multiple origins but is typically associated with Karl Klare, 'Legal Culture and Transformative Constitutionalism', (1998) 14 *South African Journal on Human Rights* 146. See also Vieira, Baxi and Viljoen, *Transformative Constitutionalism*. For a discussion of the claim of Southern particularism, see Michaela Hailbronner, 'Transformative Constitutionalism: Not Only in the Global South' (2017) 65 *American Journal of Comparative Law* 527.

[49] Armin von Bogdandy, 'Ius Constitutionale Commune en América Latina: Observations on Transformative Constitutionalism', in Armin von Bogdandy et. al. (eds.), *Transformative Constitutionalism in Latin America: The Emergence of a New Ius Commune* (Oxford: Oxford University Press, 2017), pp. 27–48.

[50] Mariela M. Antoniazzi and Pablo S. Alessandri, 'Inter-Americanization: Its Legal Bases and Political Impact', in Armin von Bogdandy et al. (eds.), *Transformative Constitutionalism in Latin America: The Emergence of a New Ius Commune* (Oxford: Oxford University Press, 2017), pp. 255–76 with further references.

privileged constitutional status.[51] And while the Inter-American human rights *acquis* protects collective rights of social groups like indigenous peoples,[52] it does not recognize rights of legal persons like corporations – unlike the European Court of Human Rights and the Court of Justice of the EU.[53] Overall, this model of regional integration thus focuses on openness towards supranational guarantees for democratic and social constitutionalism, whereas economic constitutionalism remains located at the national level – quite the reverse of the European model.

III CONTEMPORARY TRENDS: IS FOREIGN RELATIONS LAW BECOMING MORE PERIPHERAL?

The following section begins by sketching the changing context which gives the peripheral perspective increasing resonance across the North-South-divide (subsection A). Against this background, it seeks to illustrate the heuristic value of peripheral research perspectives, which shed light on three contemporary trends in foreign relations law (subsection B): the rebalancing of the relationship between property and sovereignty in investment law; the hybridization of foreign relations through state-owned enterprises; and attempts at limiting private corporate power, or quasi-sovereignty, in debates about business and human rights.

A *Changing Context: Peripheral Echoes in the Center*

In June 2018, the US White House published a report denouncing China's 'economic aggression', warning that 'Beijing's ultimate goal is for domestic companies to replace foreign companies as designers and manufacturers of key technology and products first at home, then abroad ... [C]orporate

51 Liliana Lizarazo Rodríguez and Philippe de Lombaerde, 'Regional Economic Integration and the Reality of Strong National Constitutional Powers in South America: A Comparative Analysis' (2017) 11 *International Constitutional Law Journal* 365. On the relationship of Latin American transformative constitutionalism to international economic law, see Armin von Bogdandy et al., *El constitucionalismo transformador en América Latina y el derecho económico internacional: De la tensión al diálogo* (México: UNAM/MPIL, 2018).

52 Ximena Soley, 'The Transformative Dimension of Inter-American Jurisprudence', in Armin von Bogdandy et al. (eds.), *Transformative Constitutionalism in Latin America: The Emergence of a New Ius Commune* (Oxford: Oxford University Press, 2017), pp. 337–55.

53 Cf. Anna Grear, *Redirecting Human Rights: Facing the Challenge of Corporate Legal Humanity* (Houndmills, Basingstoke: Palgrave Macmillan, 2010); Thomas Kleinlein, 'Die juristische Person des Privatrechts in der Rechtsprechung des EGMR' (2017) 65 *Jahrbuch des öffentlichen Rechts der Gegenwart* 85.

governance has become a tool to advance China's strategic goals, rather than simply, as is the custom of international rules, to advance the profit-maximizing goals of the enterprise'.[54] Soon, this political stance had legal consequences: the Chinese telecommunications company Huawei was banned by Congress from sensitive public procurement, and the US administration is pushing for Huawei's exclusion from 5G networks in the US and Western allies.[55] As other governments were pondering such a move, the UK House of Commons published a report addressing the role of social media companies in 'Disinformation and "fake news"': It found that 'malicious forces use Facebook to . . . influence elections and democratic processes – much of which Facebook, and other social media companies, are either unable or unwilling to prevent. We need to apply widely-accepted democratic principles to ensure their application in the digital age. … The big tech companies must not be allowed to expand exponentially, without constraint or proper regulatory oversight.'[56]

These statements echo some themes familiar from Allende's speech: the hybrid nature of corporations between the political and the economic; their impact on democracy; and their role in foreign relations. These echoes do not necessarily imply that Euro-America is evolving towards the South, as prominent anthropologists claim.[57] They do show, however, that peripheral ideas on foreign relations law are not exclusive to an essentialized 'South' but have increasing resonance in the changing context of foreign relations law in the 'North'. This context is marked by intensifying contestations of liberal democracy, of economic liberalism and of liberal internationalism.[58] The geopolitical context is increasingly shaped by emerging powers like China

[54] White House Office of Trade and Manufacturing Policy, *How China's Economic Aggression Threatens the Technologies and Intellectual Property of the United States and the World* (2018), available at www.whitehouse.gov/wp-content/uploads/2018/06/FINAL-China-Technology-Report-6.18.18-PDF.pdf, 1, 11.

[55] National Defense Authorization Act of 2018, Pub. L. No. 115–91, 131 Stat. 1283 (2017), s. 1656; Paul Mozur and Austin Ramzy, 'Huawei Sues US Government over what it Calls an Unfair -Ban', New York Times, March 6, 2019, www.nytimes.com/2019/03/06/business/huawei-united-states-trade-lawsuit.html.

[56] 'Disinformation and "fake news": Final Report' (2019 HC 1791), p. 5.

[57] Jean Comaroff and John. L. Comaroff, *Theory from the South: Or, how Euro-America is Evolving toward Africa* (Boulder: Paradigm, 2012).

[58] Mark A. Graber, Sanford Levinson and Mark V. Tushnet (eds.), *Constitutional Democracy in Crisis?* (New York: Oxford University Press, 2018); Manuel Castells, *Rupture: The Crisis of Liberal Democracy* (Newark: Polity Press, 2018); Thomas Piketty, *Capital in the Twenty-First Century* (Cambridge: Harvard University Press, 2014); Wolfgang Streeck, *Buying Time: The Delayed Crisis of Democratic Capitalism* (London: Verso, 2014); Dani Rodrik, 'Populism and the Economics of Globalization' (2018) 1 *Journal of International Business Policy* 12.

and by the incremental evolution of Western liberal democracies from capital exporters to capital importers, from norm shapers to norm takers.[59]

In this new multipolar context, international law is increasingly 'hitting home', and foreign relations law is evolving in response.[60] A peripheral perspective brings these transformations of foreign relations law into focus. Its main heuristic value in contemporary times is the recognition that in an economically interdependent and multipolar world, foreign relations law is not limited to political relations but requires attention to the materiality of global relations, to interferences between different varieties of economic constitutionalism, and to the interdependence of economic and political constitutionalism. Again, this general point can be illustrated by legal attitudes towards transnational corporations.[61]

B *Peripheral Perspectives on Contemporary Trends in Foreign Relations Law*

1 Rebalancing Sovereignty and Property in Foreign Investment Law

A first trend is the rebalancing of the relationship between sovereignty and property in the area of investment law. Standard narratives portray international investment law as an evolution from diplomatic protection of private property by sovereign states to a depoliticization and privatization of property disputes between investors and states.[62] Consequently, investment law has not been in the focus of liberal foreign relations law. However, host countries in the Global South have been experiencing for some time that international investment protection and arbitration can interfere with domestic constitutional principles of democracy, rule of

59 William Burke-White, 'Power Shifts in International Law: Structural Realignment and Substantive Pluralism' (2015) 56 *Harvard Journal of International Law* 1; Oliver Stuenkel, *Post-Western World: How Emerging Powers are Remaking Global Order* (Cambridge: Polity Press, 2016).

60 Aust, 'The Democratic Challenge to Foreign Relations Law in Transatlantic Perspective', at 351.

61 On renewed criticisms of corporate power, see generally Florian Wettstein, *Multinational Corporations and Global Justice: The Human Rights Obligations of a Quasi-Governmental Institution* (Stanford: Stanford Business Books, 2009); Baars and Spicer, *The Corporation: A Critical, Multi-Disciplinary Handbook*; Adam Winkler, *We the Corporations: How American Businesses Won their Civil Rights* (New York: Liveright, 2018).

62 A. Kulick, 'Narrating Narratives of International Investment Law: History and Epistemic Forces', in Stephan W. Schill, Christian. J. Tams and Rainer Hofmann (eds.), *International Investment Law and History* (Cheltenham: Edward Elgar Publishing, 2018), pp. 41–69. For the reverse trend, see now Rodrigo Polanco Lazo, *The Return of the Home State to Investor-State Disputes: Bringing Back Diplomatic Protection?* (Cambridge: Cambridge University Press, 2019).

law and human rights.[63] This peripheral experience has eventually hit home with recent controversies about TTIP, CETA and TPP in Europe and North America.[64] This is leading to re-evaluation, reform and sometimes repudiation of bilateral investment treaties and arbitration agreements across the North-South divide.[65] These reform efforts seek to recalibrate the relationship between property and sovereignty, a process which can arguably draw important lessons from peripheral legal experiences, concepts and arguments. As a recent observer put it: developed countries have learned to start worrying and love the Calvo doctrine.[66]

If one takes peripheral perspectives on the structure, function and subjects of foreign relations law seriously, then at least three issues lend themselves to further investigation. The first concerns the legal relations between foreign investors and the host states, be they contractual or hierarchical. If these legal relations are part of foreign relations, then the question of who decides about the admission of foreign investment, in what procedure and under what conditions is a critical question for foreign relations law. For jurisdictions like Germany, such criticality, or *Wesentlichkeit*, may have doctrinal consequences under prevailing doctrines of separation of powers and democracy: public relations with foreign investors may need to be increasingly subjected to parliamentary legislation instead of executive regulation.[67]

The second issue is jurisdiction. If investor-state relations are part of foreign relations, then the question of how foreign relations law allocates investment

63 Pahuja, *Decolonising International Law*, 95 ff; Muthucumaraswamy Sornarajah, *Resistance and Change in the International Law on Foreign Investment* (Cambridge: Cambridge University Press, 2015); Yannick Radi (ed.), *Research Handbook on Human Rights and Investment* (Cheltenham: Edward Elgar Publishing, 2018).

64 Kleinlein, 'TTIP and the Challenges of Investor-State-Arbitration'; Peter-Tobias Stoll, Till P. Holterhus and Henner Gött, *Investitionsschutz und Verfassung* (Tübingen: Mohr Siebeck, 2017); Rhea T. Hoffmann, *Divergenz und Transformation: Verfassungstheoretische Untersuchung des Eigentumsschutzes in der demokratischen Eigentumsverfassung und im Investitionsschutzregime* (Baden-Baden: Nomos, 2019); Ntina Tzouvala, 'The Academic Debate about Mega-Regionals and International Lawyers: Legalism as Critique?' (2018) 6 *London Review of International Law* 189.

65 Steffen Hindelang and Markus Krajewski (eds.), *Shifting Paradigms in International Investment Law: More balanced, less isolated, increasingly diversified* (Oxford: Oxford University Press, 2016); Prabhash Ranjan, *India and Bilateral Investment Treaties: Refusal, Acceptance, Backlash* (New Delhi: Oxford University Press India, 2019).

66 See generally Rodrigo Polanco Lazo, 'The No of Tokyo Revisited: Or How Developed Countries Learned to Start Worrying and Love the Calvo Doctrine' (2015) 30 *ICSID Review* 172. On potential lessons from the South, see Fabio Morosini and Michelle R. Sanchez Badin (eds.), *Reconceptualizing International Investment Law from the Global South* (New York: Cambridge University Press, 2017).

67 See generally on the constitutional implications of investment protection treaties, Stoll, Holterhus and Gött, *Investitionsschutz und Verfassung*.

disputes among host state courts, arbitral tribunals and third-country judiciaries is a key question.[68] From a peripheral perspective, the enforcement of arbitral awards against host states in third-country jurisdictions is a key interface between state and non-state legal systems. Behind seemingly technical questions regarding standards of review for annulment or non-execution of awards on the basis of public policy lurk fundamental questions of transnational legal pluralism and protection of foreign property, sovereignty, democracy and rule of law.[69]

A third issue is the domestic effect of international investment law and arbitral awards in host countries. If a domestic constitutional order contains opening clauses for international law, do these apply to international investment treaties? And what is the domestic effect of arbitral awards? This latter question was less relevant as long as tribunals awarded monetary compensation that would be paid voluntarily or be enforced against state assets abroad. But recent awards also adopt in-kind remedies. In a 2018 award in the *Chevron* v. *Ecuador* saga, the Permanent Court of Arbitration ordered Ecuador 'to remove the status of enforceability' from domestic court judgments and 'to preclude any of the [plaintiffs] from enforcing' them.[70] These judgments had required Chevron to pay damages to local residents and had been confirmed by the Ecuadorian constitutional court. Implementing such an award certainly poses delicate questions for domestic constitutional law and for the separation of powers in any constitutional order, and for foreign relations law research in general.

68 For a discussion of the relationship between domestic courts and arbitral tribunals from the perspective of transformative constitutionalism in Latin America, see René Urueña, 'Después de la fragmentación: ICCAL, derechos humanos y arbitraje de inversiones', in Armin von Bogdandy et al. *El constitucionalismo transformador en América Latina y el derecho económico internacional: De la tensión al diálogo* (México: UNAM/MPIL, 2018), pp. 59–85.

69 See generally Leon Trakman, 'Domestic Courts Declining to Recognize and Enforce Foreign Arbitral Awards: A Comparative Reflection' (2018) 6 *The Chinese Journal of Comparative Law* 174. On the annulment of arbitral awards by third countries, see Felix Boor, 'Die Aufhebung der Yukos-Schiedssprüche des Permanent Court of Arbitration vor dem Bezirksgericht in Den Haag – nur der Anfang einer langen Vollstreckungsodyssee?' (2018) 54 *Archiv des Völkerrechts* 297.

70 *Chevron Corporation and Texaco Corporation* v. *The Republic of Ecuador*, Case No. 2009–23, Second Partial Award on Track II, 30 August 2018. On this lengthy litigation, see generally Hannah Franzki and Johann Horst, 'On the Critical Potential of Law – and its Limits: Double Fragmentation of Law in Chevron vs. Ecuador', in Kerstin Blome et al. (eds.), *Contested Regime Collisions: Norm Fragmentation in World Society* (New York: Cambridge University Press, 2016), pp. 347–70.

2 Sovereignty in the Guise of Property: Hybrid Foreign Relations and State-Owned Enterprises

If international investment law is being rebalanced towards sovereignty, then sovereignty is at the same time being transformed by a symbiosis with property: state-owned enterprises, hybrid public-private entities or partly privatized corporations are increasingly internationalizing their activities.[71] In this regard, the maybe most significant transformation of foreign relations is the globalization of Chinese state-owned enterprises and the rise of foreign investment by sovereign wealth funds.[72] In a parallel development, sovereignty appears in the guises of property in large-scale land acquisition by public investors in Africa and elsewhere, which potentially disassembles territorial sovereignty of host states.[73] In all these instances, foreign relations acquire a hybrid nature – private in form but public in substance.

To analytically capture this hybridization, foreign relations law research needs a more complex account of the corporation than liberal legalism ordinarily gives. If 'corporate governance has become a tool to advance China's strategic goals',[74] as the Trump administration laments, then foreign relations lawyers need to understand non-liberal conceptions of the corporation in China and other capital exporting countries.[75] Huawei, for instance, is

[71] Michael J. Strauss, *Hostile Business and the Sovereign State: Privatized Governance, State Security and International Law* (Milton: Routledge, 2019). To peripheral countries, this is not news, if one remembers that most colonial trading companies were public-private ventures, and were treated as such by the courts, McLachlan, *Foreign Relations Law*, 49, citing the case *Nabob of Arcot* v. *East India Company* [1793] EngR 1368, (1792–1793) 2 Ves Jun 56, (1793) 30 ER 521 (Company held not to be a private person, and its agreement with a foreign ruler 'the same, as if it was a treaty between two sovereigns').

[72] Li-Wen Lin and Curtis J. Milhaupt, 'We Are the (National) Champions: Understanding the Mechanisms of State Capitalism in China' (2013) 65 *Stanford Law Review* 697; Gregory Shaffer and Henry Gao, 'A New Chinese Economic Law Order?', Univ. of California Legal Studies Research Paper Series (No. 2019–21), April 11, 2019, https://papers.ssrn.com/sol3/papers.cfm?abstract_id=3370452; Ronald Gilson and Curtis J. Milhaupt, 'Sovereign Wealth Funds and Corporate Governance: A Minimalist Response to the New Mercantilism' (2008) 60 *Stanford Law Review* 1345.

[73] Lorenzo Cotula et al., *Land Grab or Development Opportunity? Agricultural Investment and International Land Deals in Africa* (London: IIED,FAO and IFAD, 2009); Saskia Sassen, 'Land Grabs Today: Feeding the Disassembling of National Territory' (2013) 10 *Globalizations* 25; Jochen von Bernstorff, 'Who Is Entitled to Cultivate the Land? Sovereignty, Land Resources and Foreign Investments in Agriculture in International Law', in Francesca Romanin Jacu, Angelica Bonfanti and Francesco Seatzu (eds.), *Natural Resources Grabbing : An International Law Perspective* (Leiden: Brill Nijhoff, 2016), pp. 55–74.

[74] White House Office of Trade and Manufacturing Policy, How China's Economic Aggression Threatens the Technologies and Intellectual Property of the United States and the World, 1, 11.

[75] For a comparison of liberal and non-liberal conceptions of the corporation see Teemu Ruskola, 'What Is a Corporation?: Liberal, Confucian, and Socialist Theories of

formally not a public enterprise but employee-owned; but Chinese law may have other ways of establishing state control.[76] Comparing these different theoretical and legal conceptions of the corporation will be a first important avenue of research for comparative foreign relations lawyers.

A second set of questions pertains to the constitutional rights of foreign state-owned corporations. For instance, the German Federal Constitutional Court held in its 2016 decision on the phase-out of nuclear energy that Vattenfall, a Swedish state-owned enterprise, enjoyed constitutional protection of property in Germany.[77] Although the court was careful to limit its reasoning to 'exceptional cases' of enterprises owned by EU member states, there still remain many open questions for foreign relations lawyers in this regard – not least because Vattenfall has initiated parallel arbitration procedures and because the European Court of Human Rights recognizes property rights of state-owned enterprises regardless of EU membership.[78]

While granting constitutional rights to foreign state-owned enterprises limits the space for regulation in this regard, another legal institution raises even farther-reaching issues: namely, sovereign immunity and its application to state-owned enterprises in foreign courts. While the German Constitutional Court adopts a restrictive stance on *acta iure gestionis*,[79] Chinese state-owned enterprises seem to have successfully invoked sovereign immunity in US federal courts, prompting proposals for reform.[80] If granted, immunity not only poses problems from a rule of law perspective but also limits the reach of democratic economic regulation.[81]

Enterprise Organization (and State, Family, and Personhood)' (2014) 37 *Seattle Univ. Law Review*, 639.

76 Demetri Sevastopulo, 'Huawei Pulls back Curtain on Ownership Details', *Financial Times*, February 27, 2014, www.ft.com/content/469bde20-9eaf-11e3-8663-00144feab7de. See also White House Office of Trade and Manufacturing Policy, *How China's Economic Aggression Threatens the Technologies and Intellectual Property of the United States and the World*, 18 f.

77 Federal Constitutional Court, BVerfGE 143, 246.

78 *Islamic Republic of Iran Shipping Lines* v. *Turkey* (Appl. No.40998/98), Judgment of 13 December 2007. For a general discussion of the issues, see Jochen Rauber, *Zur Grundrechtsberechtigung fremdstaatlich beherrschter juristischer Personen: Art. 19 III GG unter dem Einfluss von EMRK, EU-GRCh und allgemeinem Völkerrecht* (Tübingen: Mohr Siebeck, 2019).

79 BVerfGE 16, 27 – Iranische Botschaft; BVerfGE 117, 141 – Immunität Argentiniens. For a discussion, see Rauber, *Zur Grundrechtsberechtigung*, pp. 33 f.

80 US-China Economic and Security Review Commission, 2017 Report to Congress, November 2017, www.uscc.gov/sites/default/files/annual_reports/2017_Annual_Report_to_Congress.pdf, p. 4, 29.

81 See generally McLachlan, *Foreign Relations Law*, Ch. 12.

3 Limiting or Legitimizing Private Quasi-Sovereignty: Business and Human Rights and Is Alternatives

If Northern efforts to internationalize corporate *rights* in investment law have succeeded, Southern attempts at internationalizing corporate *obligations* have failed so far: early initiatives at UN level, launched by Allende's Chile and its allies, led to the establishment of a UN Commission on Transnational Corporations in 1975 and to a soft-law code of conduct, but not to a binding legal instrument.[82] Regulation remained mostly at national level and thus vulnerable to bilateral pressures, collective action problems and regulatory arbitrage in a globalized political economy. This situation has not changed thus far with the renewed push for internationalization under the rubric of 'business and human rights', although developing countries are spearheading negotiations for a binding treaty on business and human rights, supported by China and opposed by most Western liberal democracies.[83]

The legal focus thus remains on domestic law, and thus on the foreign relations law of investor home states and host states. The current debate centers on the role of *home* states in the extraterritorial protection of human rights against corporate misconduct in host states.[84] Since the US Supreme Court has all but closed the door to the extraterritorial application of the Alien Tort Claims Act, the focus has shifted to domestic courts in Europe and to legislative projects, enacted for instance in California and in France and tabled in Germany in February 2019.[85]

82 Tagi Sagafi-nejad and John H. Dunning, *The UN and Transnational Corporations: From Code of Conduct to Global Compact* (Bloomington: Indiana University Press, 2008); Jennifer Bair, 'Corporations at the United Nations: Echoes of the New International Economic Order?' (2015) 6 *Humanity* 159; Pahuja and Saunders, 'Rival Worlds and the place of the Corporation in International Law'.

83 Surya Deva and David Bilchitz (eds.), *Building a Treaty on Business and Human Rights: Context and Contours* (Cambridge: Cambridge University Press, 2017).

84 Jennifer Zerk, 'Extraterritorial Jurisdiction: Lessons for the Business and Human Rights Sphere from Six Regulatory Areas', Harvard Corporate Social Responsibility Working Paper No. 59 (June 2010), www.hks.harvard.edu/sites/default/files/centers/mrcbg/programs/cri/files/workingpaper_59_zerk.pdf; Jochen von Bernstorff, 'Extraterritoriale menschenrechtliche Staatenpflichten und Corporate Social Responsibility' (2011) 49 *Archiv des Völkerrechts* 34; Thilo Marauhn, 'Sicherung grund- und menschenrechtlicher Standards gegenüber neuen Gefährdungen durch private und ausländische Akteure' (2015) 74 *Veröffentlichungen der Vereinigung Deutscher Staatsrechtslehrer* 373.

85 Dalia Palombo, 'The Duty of Care of the Parent Company: A Comparison between French Law, UK Precedents and the Swiss Proposals' (2019) 4 *Business and Human Rights Journal* 265; Saskia Wilks and Johannes Blankenbach, 'Will Germany Become a Leader in the Drive for Corporate Due Diligence on Human Rights?', February 20, 2019, www.business-humanrights.org/en/will-germany-become-a-leader-in-the-drive-for-corporate-due-diligence-on-human-rights.

A peripheral perspective, however, raises further questions. Firstly, from this perspective, the focus on extraterritorial home state obligations and regulations is ambivalent: it not only subjects host states to standards defined and applied elsewhere but also implies that host state legal systems are incapable, or unwilling, to dispense justice. While this may be true in some cases, it cannot be assumed for all jurisdictions, especially the many constitutional democracies with independent courts in the Global South. Indeed, a peripheral perspective might reverse the focus and ask to what extent *host* state regulation and adjudication can and should be extended extraterritorially to govern global value chains and transnational corporate conglomerates. Taking host state law seriously brings distinct regulatory approaches to the table – such as horizontal effect of fundamental rights. The idea of horizontal effect is a hallmark of transformative constitutionalism in the Global South and is used by activists and social movements against corporate abuses of powers.[86] In substance, this approach redeploys the vocabulary and legal techniques developed to restrain public authority to tame private power.

The consequences of this move for separation of powers, democracy and foreign relations remain to be fully understood. One consequence of applying fundamental rights to transnational corporations is that courts effectively become extraterritorial regulators and tend to be empowered vis-à-vis the other branches. This is potentially a problem from a liberal foreign relations law perspective; it may be less problematic for a transformative constitutionalism that prizes activist courts and an understanding of separation of powers not limited to checks and balances but also encompassing pushes and pulls. Beyond this, there are issues of separation between public and private power. Some see horizontal effect as a basis for corporate commitments to human rights, a desirable 'self-constitutionalization' of transnational enterprises and a basis for a societal constitutionalism beyond the state.[87] Others fear that a rights-based societal constitutionalism will not restrain but rather legitimize private power.[88] Likening a corporation to a state for purposes of

86 David Bilchitz, 'Constitutionalism, the Global South, and Economic Justice', in Daniel Bonilla Maldonado (ed.), *Constitutionalism of the Global South: The Activist Tribunals of India, South Africa, and Colombia* (Cambridge: Cambridge University Press, 2013), pp. 41–94; Hailbronner, 'Transformative Constitutionalism: Not Only in the Global South'.

87 Gunther Teubner, 'Self-Constitutionalizing TNCs?: On the Linkage of 'Private' and 'Public' Corporate Codes of Conduct' (2011) 18 *Indiana Journal of Global Legal Studies* 17; Gunther Teubner, *Constitutional Fragments: Societal Constitutionalism and Globalization* (Oxford: Oxford University Press, 2012).

88 Christian Scheper, '"From Naming and Shaming to Knowing and Showing": Human Rights and the Power of Corporate Practice' (2015) 19 *International Journal of Human Rights* 737. For a different notion of societal constitutionalism, see Gavin Anderson, 'Societal

human rights obligations might confirm, rather than restrain, their quasi-sovereign status. Domestic courts are faced with these controversies when pondering the legal value of corporate human rights standards in litigation.

In light of these doubts, a third and final question pertains to alternatives to the business and human rights frame from a peripheral foreign relations law perspective. Again, Allende's speech offers such an alternative perspective: his concerns and proposals were not formulated in the liberal language of rights but in the register of democracy. While ideas about economic democracy and workers co-determination have lost traction in a globalized economy dominated by (neo)liberal thinking, it may be worth reflecting on how the vocabulary of collective self-determination may be used creatively within the contemporary globalized economy. For instance, resurgent interest in inequality has led to greater space for alternative visions of corporate governance that go beyond 'shareholder democracy' and 'corporate citizenship' on the one hand, and nationalization and state ownership on the other. Such proposals are based on the premise that the corporation, conceived as a political entity, allows similar collective participation rights than the political sphere and that these rights do not depend on ownership. Rather, they allow for inclusion of workers and other stakeholders affected by corporate activities.[89] In these schemes, peripheral countries would benefit from the inclusion in corporate decision-making by virtue of their labor and affected stakeholders. This might alter the current North/South dynamics of capital exploitation by promoting economic democracy in developing countries through formally private initiatives that potentially bypass current barriers to more democratic economic reforms in highly unequal societies with unresponsive political regimes.

IV CONCLUSION

Peripheral legal ideas are not exclusive to an essentialized 'Global South' but are present in legal history, heterodox thinking and contemporary legal transformations across the North-South divide. In foreign relations law, peripheral

Constitutionalism, Social Movements, and Constitutionalism from Below' (2013) 20 *Indiana Journal of Global Legal Studies* 881. On self-regulation generally, see also A. Claire Cutler, *Private Power and Global Authority: Transnational Merchant Law in the Global Political Economy* (Cambridge: Cambridge University Press, 2003).

89 Isabelle Ferreras, *Firms as Political Entities: Saving Democracy through Economic Bicameralism* (Cambridge: Cambridge University Press, 2017); David Ciepley, 'Beyond Public and Private: Toward a Political Theory of the Corporation' (2013) 107 *American Political Science Review* 139. On a Chinese experiment in this regard, see Karita Kan, 'A Weapon of the Weak? Shareholding, Property Rights and Villager Empowerment in China' (2019) 237 *The China Quarterly* 131.

ideas are often located at the margins of, or outside, a field of study defined by a liberal perspective from the center. A peripheral perspective brings these questions into sharper focus, and it offers different answers contingent on differing geopolitical positions and epistemic foundations. This raises the question of whether there are any lessons to be learned from experiences of the periphery for our normative evaluation of present-day challenges across the North-South divide.

That question must be denied if one assumes a view of history and time that follows a liberal narrative of progress and a singular conception of modernity: The West is ahead, everyone else is catching up. If one accepts, instead, the idea of multiple modernities and nonlinear historical evolution, one may see the history of Southern countries as an inspiration – and as a warning.[90] One ironic aspect of the recent backlash against internationalism are the curious echoes of anticolonial nationalism in the language of populist nationalism – for instance, in Brexit proponents' appeals to national liberation and to individual sacrifice as necessary for achieving this goal.[91] These echoes are reason enough to recall postcolonial critiques of 'national liberation', which left unresolved the question of who would govern the nation once liberated, and who would do the sacrificing. Franz Fanon warned of the pitfalls of 'national consciousness', seeing within the liberation movements a group of bourgeois leaders who 'mobilize the people with slogans of independence, and for the rest leave it to future events' and are committed only to a 'mission [that] has nothing to do with transforming the nation; it consists, prosaically, of being the transmission line between the nation and capitalism'.[92]

90 Hoffmann, 'Knowledge Production in Comparative Constitutional Law'; Peter Wagner, *Modernity: Understanding the Present* (Cambridge: Polity, 2012).

91 Kojo Koram, 'Britain's Blindness: How did "national liberation" become a rallying cry in what was once the world's largest empire?', Dissent Magazine, February 6, 2019, www.dissentmagazine.org/online_articles/britains-brexit-blindness.

92 Fanon, *The Wretched of the Earth*, p. 100.

5

Finding Foreign Relations Law in India: A Decolonial Dissent

Prabhakar Singh

I INTRODUCTION

> [A]s a Justice of the High Court of England . . . it is my duty to apply English municipal law, including English foreign relations law . . . Questions of foreign affairs arising in English courts have . . . English law answers.[1]

Could an Indian judge, as the purveyor of the common law coming from England to India, too, identify a duty to apply Indian 'foreign relations law' (FRL), if any? Could the judge also assert that the questions of 'foreign affairs' arising before Indian courts ought to have Indian law answers? After acknowledging the presence of an established FRL in England, the British High Court in the *Muffakham Jah case* notably found for Pakistan 'a foreign relations law' but a 'constitutional law' for India.[2] We will do well to remember that while Britain does not have a written constitution, United States has one of the world's shortest written constitutions.[3] Contrarily, the Constitution of India is the postcolonial world's most detailed text. Needless to say, the Constitution is a significant lens with which to identify the possibility, or not, of an FRL within the law of the land.

In what follows, Section II investigates the origins of FRL that appears to reinforce, in the words of the Commonwealthian D.P. O'Connell, the 'essential unity of all European legal structures' that is 'founded on the moral

[1] *High Commissioner for Pakistan in the United Kingdom* v. *Prince Muffakham Jah*, [2019] EWHC 2551 (Ch) para. 85.

[2] '[V]iewed from the perspective of the law of Pakistan – including her foreign relations law' and 'I also have absolutely no doubt that, viewed from the perspective of the law of India – including in particular her constitutional law'. *High Commissioner for Pakistan in the United Kingdom* v. *Prince Muffakham Jah*, [2019] EWHC 2551 (Ch) paras. 83–84.

[3] Fali S. Nariman, *God Save the Hon'ble Supreme Court* (New Delhi: Hay House, 2018) p. 135.

concord of Western peoples'.[4] It concludes that the FRL scholars practice a convenient overlooking of the colonial history of the common law. Section III studies the significance Indian Constitution attaches to the international law of states and that of state and peoples and aliens. Since the Indian Constitution does not break free by design from common law, the Indian judges use the Constitution as well as common law to harmonise international law with Indian law. Section IV investigates how the Indian Supreme Court excludes foreign relations from judicial scrutiny. An outcome of this investigation is the fidelity of the Supreme Court to British case laws over the American precedents in its first two decades.[5] Section V discusses the Supreme Court's reading of India's postcolonial territory under the *uti possidetis* lens of international law. The study of *uti possidetis* for India is significant in that the Supreme Court has created a balance between a fractured reception of territory from the British and the postcolonial government's reception of territory within the Constitution. Indeed, the President of India has from time to time sought the Court's opinion on the executive's power of exchange of territory and cession, like with regard to Pakistan, or the Court has examined the welcoming of new territories, like Sikkim, into the Union of India. Such questions from the executive have allowed the Indian Supreme Court to affirm its Constitutional superiority with deference to the competence of the executive in territorial matters while reading international law in harmony with, what I call, a 'postcolonial common law'. Section VI concludes.

II FRL AS THE 'CONCORD OF WESTERN PEOPLES': THE COMMONWEALTH AND COLONIALISM

A *The FRL of the Commonwealth*

An FRL, in Campbell McLachlan's definition, ought to be 'a distinct field in Anglo-Commonwealth legal systems'.[6] How inclusive is this common law, however, of non settler jurisdictions such as India and Kenya, for example? 'In approaching the question of the existence or otherwise of [a] doctrine in

4 Daniel P. O'Connell, 'Unjust Enrichment' (1956) 5 *American Journal of Comparative Law* 2 at 4.

5 Exactly two decades after the Indian independence, in 1967 Justice Subba Rao, against the will of the Indian Government, read the American doctrine of 'prospective overruling' into Indian Law. Fali S. Nariman, *India's Legal System: Could it Be Saved?* (Gurgaon: Penguin Random House India, 2017 [2006]) pp. 74–5, 158–9.

6 Campbell McLachlan, 'The Allocative Function of Foreign Relations Law' (2012) 82 *British Yearbook of International Law* 349.

English law', O'Connell wrote in 1956, 'one must not only appreciate the character of the English legal system, but go further and recognize the essential unity of all European legal structures, a unity founded on the moral concord of Western peoples'.[7]

O'Connell was referring to the resistance among the English lawyers in importing a European legal idea calling into service the 'unity founded on the moral concord of Western peoples'. In the twenty-first century, McLachlan's *Foreign Relations Law* explicitly refers to only four Anglo-Commonwealth states; the United Kingdom, Australia, Canada and New Zealand,[8] effecting a further provincialisation of the 'concord of Western peoples' – the white ex-colonies of imperial Britain. Commonwealth lawyers have, as it were, gone out into the woods to pick mushrooms of various laws, if you will, for an FRL soup. The American and the British lawyers have to go mushroom-picking perhaps because they do not have the benefit of a Constitution like India's, the world's largest and enduring. Besides, India, a common law jurisdiction, is expectedly out of the consideration from both the 'concord of the Western peoples' as well as the list of jurisdictions to make an FRL from.[9] Should the FRL scholars look into the deliberations of the Indian Constitution, the conclusion would be that the advocacy for FRL is somewhat provincial.

For McLachlan, an FRL pertains to a

> whole class of legal issues and disputes, dealing with: the relationship between public international law and the municipal legal system in the control of foreign relations; the exercise of the foreign relations power by the three organs of government – its legal implications and its limits; the implications of the foreign relations power for the rights of the individual; and the treatment of the foreign state within the municipal legal system.[10]

This class is understandably large. McLachlan claims that FRL 'serves to fill a key gap by extending to the field of public powers the technique of private

[7] Daniel P. O'Connell, 'Unjust Enrichment' at 4.

[8] Campbell McLachlan, *Foreign Relations Law* (Cambridge: Cambridge University Press, 2014) refers to only four Anglo-Commonwealth states; the United Kingdom, Australia, Canada and New Zealand.

[9] Daron Acemoglu, Simon Johnson and James A. Robinson, 'The Colonial Origins of Comparative Development: An Empirical Investigation' (2001) 91 *American Economic Review* 1369 at 1370.

[10] McLachlan, 'The Allocative Function of Foreign Relations Law', 349; Campbell McLachlan, 'Five Conceptions of the Function of Foreign Relations Law', in Curtis A. Bradley (ed.), *The Oxford Handbook of Comparative Foreign Relations Law* (New York: Oxford University Press, 2019) pp. 21–43.

international law – jurisdiction and applicable law' thereby depositing FRL in the domain of the 'constitutional state'.[11]

It is well known that India inherited a common law system from British colonialism. And in 1950 India received her Constitution that was inspired by various civil and common law systems. Does India also have an FRL in the cast and mould made by the *Oxford Handbook* on FRL?[12] The *Handbook* casts a very wide net in so far as crafting an FRL is concerned. And the cast of that FRL net, for the *Handbook* editor Curtis Bradley, covers not just classic international law. For Bradley, the FRLs 'encompass the domestic law of each nation that governs how that nation interacts with the rest of the world'. We are confronted with the famous Dworkinian question then; could the 'principles' of foreign affairs be passed off as the 'law' of foreign affairs in India? I think not.

We need to first find an FRL in India. Only afterwards could we answer whether there exists or not the possibility of either bridges or boundaries between an Indian FRL and international law. If we take the FRL's scope and definition from the *Handbook* and combine it with this volume editors' expectations, we might squarely conclude that FRL for India remains primarily a constitutional reading of the international law of states and individuals.[13]

B *Overlooking Legal History*

The idiosyncratic judges, scholars, and diplomats in the geographical South should not be easily convinced by the FRL scholarship that is innocent of legal history.[14] The FRL's first impression on any Asian post-colony is that of a new blueprint of imperialism through law in the twenty-first century because, as Acemoglu, Johnson and Robinson note:

> There were different types of colonization policies which created different sets of institutions. At one extreme, European powers set up 'extractive states', [where the colonists] did not introduce much protection for private property,

[11] McLachlan, 'The Allocative Function of Foreign Relations Law', 349–50.

[12] Curtis A. Bradley, 'What Is Foreign Relations Law?' in Curtis A. Bradley (ed.), *The Oxford Handbook of Comparative Foreign Relations Law* (New York: Oxford University Press, 2019) p. 3.

[13] Venkatachala G. Hegde, 'Indian Courts and International Law' (2010) 23 *Leiden Journal of International Law* 53 at 58.

[14] A 'discursive formation of common law resulting in the transformation of the law of nations in the Indian colony rejects the idea of the periphery as only the receiver of the law. The Indian colony supplied common law to England instead.' Prabhakar Singh, 'Indian Princely States and the 19th-century Transformation of the Law of Nations' (2020) 11 *Journal of International Dispute Settlement* 365 at 387.

> nor did they provide checks and balances against government expropriation. In fact, the main purpose of the extractive state was to transfer as much of the resources of the colony to the colonizer. At the other extreme, many Europeans migrated and settled in a number of colonies, creating . . . 'Neo-Europes'. The settlers tried to replicate European institutions, with strong emphasis on private property and checks against government power.[15]

It is rather remarkable that, as a legal innovation, FRL is made up of and seeks to export to the rest of the world the common law of 'Neo-Europes' whose '[p]rimary examples' for Acemoglu, Johnson and Robinson 'include Australia, New Zealand, Canada, and the United States'.[16] How exactly does McLachlan's choice of jurisdictions map on to lands where 'Europeans migrated and settled in a number of colonies' beyond Europe? Given this obvious colonial history impacting the choice of the four jurisdictions to make and export FRL from, the postcolonial Indian should be circumspect. Whether such an FRL's legal hermeneutics, in the presence of other ways of doing law – the regular constitutional law for example – will convince the geographical South remains to be seen.[17]

Effectively, from our vantage point, the FRL scholars seem to conveniently overlook legal history.[18] There are two aspects of that overlooked legal history relevant to the postcolonial common law world. Jurist Fali Nariman reminds us of the first one: a remarkable aspect of 'legal history is that no country which had not at some time or the other been a part of the British Empire has ever *voluntarily* adopted the common law!'[19] Nariman finds it a 'stark fact' that 'whenever there was a choice between common law and the Roman law', the basis of the continental law, 'the decision has always been in favour of Roman law'.[20]

Second, the employment of private law in the service of public law is not so new. The attempts to create FRL as a new field to study law in that sense

[15] Acemoglu, Johnson and Robinson, 'The Colonial Origins of Comparative Development', 1370.

[16] Acemoglu, Johnson and Robinson, 'The Colonial Origins of Comparative Development', 1370.

[17] To the extent FRL borrows from private law made in the defence of private property and private investors, Ayyangar J. in the *Mithibarwala* case discredited that 'theory' because 'there could be no analogy between individuals and States' within 'the basic foundations of the rules of [p]ublic [i]nternational [l]aw'. *State of Gujarat* v. *Vora Fiddali Badruddin Mithibarwala*, 1964 Indlaw SC 357, para. 51.

[18] 'A recent book [on FRL] with over 46 chapters does not contain a single chapter or sustained analysis of issues of identity and/race even though the U.S. Foreign Relations paradigm is the defining framework for the book'. James T. Gathii, 'Writing Race and Identity in a Global Context: What CRT and TWAIL Can Learn From Each Other' (2020) 67 *UCLA Law Review* footnote 191.

[19] Nariman, *India's Legal System*, p. 23.

[20] Nariman, *India's Legal System*, p. 24.

mimics the McNair-Lauterpacht school of public law making by private law principles. This stoked Jessup's theoretical innovation soon after the Asian decolonisation aimed at puncturing Asian states' new-found sovereignty by invoking as the applicable law the pro-investor law of the United States.[21]

Walking through the Indian constitutional cases that have settled questions of jurisdiction and applicable law, the fulcrum of FRL's proposal, seems a good starting point for reflection.

III THE INDIAN SUPREME COURT BETWEEN PRINCIPLES, POLICY AND THE LAW

Part 5, chapter 4 of the Indian Constitution talks about 'the Union judiciary'. The Supreme Court of India currently comprises of a Chief Justice and thirty other judges appointed by the President of India.[22] Under article 143(1) the President has the powers to seek the opinion of the Court about 'a question of law or fact' which is of 'public importance'. The Court 'as it thinks fit, report[s] to the President its opinion'. Article 144 mandates that 'All authorities, civil and judicial, in the territory of India shall act in aid of the Supreme Court'. Very importantly, under article 145(5) of the Constitution:

> No judgment and no such opinion shall be delivered by the Supreme Court save with the concurrence of a majority of the Judges present at the hearing of the case, but nothing in this clause shall be deemed to prevent a Judge who does not concur from delivering a dissenting judgment or opinion.

The Indian Constitution in providing for the possibility of 'delivering a dissenting judgment or opinion' seeks to balance the majority rule principle of judicial decision-making with the constitutional mandate for judicial idiosyncrasy of separate and dissenting opinions. It bears reminding that this constitutional mandate for dissent has allowed the Indian judges to save India's democratic and secular fabric from the blades of the past and the present authoritarian governments.

A *Article 51 of the Constitution and International Law*

Article 51 of the Indian Constitution speaks most directly about international law. It reads as follows:

21 Prabhakar Singh, 'The Private Life of Transnational Law', in Peer Zumbansen (ed.), *The Many Lives of Transnational Law* (Cambridge: Cambridge University Press, 2020), p. 419.

22 The Supreme Court of India, https://main.sci.gov.in/constitution [30 September 2020].

The State shall endeavour to –

(a) promote international peace and security;
(b) maintain just and honourable relations between nations;
(c) foster respect for international law and treaty obligations in the dealings of organized peoples with one another; and
(d) encourage settlement of international disputes by arbitration.

Since article 51(c) distinguishes 'international law' and 'treaty obligations', the Indian Constitution in such ways recognises both treaty and non-treaty sources of international law. The Indian Supreme Court in the seven bench *Maneka Gandhi* ruling noted: In the context of expressions like 'security', 'public order', 'public interest' and 'friendly foreign relations', governments come and go, 'but the fundamental rights of the people cannot be subject to the wishful value sets of political regimes of the passing day'.[23] *Maneka Gandhi* thus pointed at the permanency of fundamental rights over the political nature of the executive. *Maneka Gandhi* set a fertile bed for and planted the seeds of *Vishaka* v. *State of Rajasthan* to flower later in that the former's emphasis on the 'fundamental rights' nudged the Court in the latter case to import under article 51 from an international convention on the fundamental rights for women. Justice Verma noted in *Vishaka*:

> In the absence of domestic law to formulate effective measures to check [an] evil naturally the contents of International Conventions and norms are significant for the purpose of interpretation of [fundamental rights guarantees] of the Constitutions . . . Any International Convention not inconsistent with the fundamental rights and in harmony with its spirit must be read into these provisions to enlarge the meaning and content thereof, to promote the object of the constitutional guarantee. This is implicit from Article 51(c).[24]

Article 51 remains non-justiciable for falling under 'policy' and 'principle' and not 'law' nevertheless. In other words, while one cannot directly invoke a treaty in the Supreme Court that India has not passed into a domestic law, Justice Verma, a champion of human rights, offered a useful elucidation. The Parliament has full powers to enact laws for implementing international conventions by virtue of article 253 read with Entry 14 of the Union List in the Seventh Schedule of the Constitution. And article 73(1)(a) provides that the 'executive power of the Union shall extend' to the 'matters with respect to which Parliament has power to make laws'. Next, article 73(1)(b) extends the

[23] *Maneka Gandhi* v. *Union of India*, 1978 Indlaw SC 212, para. 211.
[24] *Vishaka* v. *State of Rajasthan And Others*, 1997 Indlaw SC 2304, para. 14.

executive power 'to the exercise of such rights, authority and jurisdiction as are exercisable by the Government of India by virtue of any treaty or agreement'.

We find that the Indian Constitution distinguishes the executive's competence from the 'Parliament's power' and authority to pass a law by virtue of 'any treaty'. The executive power of the Indian Union, Justice Verma said, is therefore available 'till the parliament enacts to expressly provide measures needed to curb a gap in the law'.[25]

The executive is under the Constitution vested with residual powers up until the Parliament passes an international treaty into domestic law. The Supreme Court's firm statement of the relationship between international treaties and rights and obligations in municipal law, an assertion of dualism, can be found first in the *Maganbhai* judgment:

> The Constitution of India makes no provision making legislation a condition of the entry into an international treaty in times either of war or peace. The executive is *qua* the State competent to represent the State in all matters international and may by agreement, convention or treaties incur obligations which in international law are binding upon the State. There is a distinction between the formation and the performance of the obligations constituted by a treaty. Under the Constitution the obligations arising under the agreement or treaties are not by their own force binding upon Indian nationals or others.[26]

Essentially, *Maganbhai* distinguishes the signing of a treaty by the State from the 'performance' of obligations arising from such a treaty under the Indian law. While the executive is fully competent to sign a treaty, for the treaty to pass into domestic law the Parliament alone can do the lawmaking. Acknowledging this difference, Justice Verma astutely read article 51 as allowing international conventions and treaties becoming only a 'policy' guide for interpreting Indian law so long as such international laws do not conflict with Indian laws. In other words, international law for *Vishaka* only offers tools for interpretation and not for creating new obligations to arise without a supporting domestic law.

We can therefore hardly say that the 'directive principles' have become justiciable. They continue to remain 'principles' and 'policy' that the Court might remind the executive of, as it sometimes does, to nudge them to pass a suitable law. Article 37 of the Indian Constitution makes it very clear: 'The provisions contained in this Part [on directive principles] shall not be enforceable by any court, but the principles therein laid down are nevertheless fundamental in the governance of the country and it shall be the duty of the

25 *Vishaka* v. *State of Rajasthan And Others*, 1997 Indlaw SC 2304, para. 14.

26 *Maganbhai Ishwarbhai Patel* v. *Union of India*, 1969 SCR (3) 254, para. 79.

State to apply these principles in making laws'.[27] On balance, article 37 appears to instruct the Indian state and not the higher judiciary.[28]

We can see that for the Court instructing the executive in territorial matters is a more contested endeavour than importing justice-enhancing norms from human rights treaties. This is so because the *Vishaka* reads human rights treaties as codified customary laws but the Court generally finds no such thing as customary laws on territory. To then adjudge the Court's views on human rights treaties as a possible rejection of dualism in India is the kind of eagerness that is misleading. Little surprise that we find the anglophile Hidayatullah holding a line harder than the conservative Gajendragadkar in matters of territorial acquisition after decolonisation.[29] Nevertheless, all laws in India get oxygen from our written Constitution.

B *Common Law and the Colonial Continuity*

VP Menon – Constitutional advisor to India's last British Governor General – noted: the British 'came to trade, but stayed to rule. They left of their own will; there was no war, there was no treaty – an act with no parallel in history'.[30] India became a fully independent dominion by an Act of the British Parliament, the Indian Independence Act, 1947. The Indian Constitution article 147 therefore defined the 'interpretation' of the Constitution of India to specifically include the reading of the Indian Independence Act, 1947. Legally, as Nariman says, India did not reject common law under its Constitution.[31] Yet, as Madhav Khosla says, India did not become a case of a 'thoughtless duplication' of British laws.[32]

[27] Article 37 of the Indian Constitution of 1950.

[28] See generally, Tarunabh Khaitan, 'Directive principles and the expressive accommodation of ideological dissenters' (2018) 16 *International Journal of Constitutional Law* 389–420.

[29] Gajendragadkar for Dhavan 'was the Rooseveltian New Deal judge' and 'only in the 1970s was it discovered that this kind of judge was too closely linked with the government to credit identification with a Holmes or a Cardozo'. Rajeev Dhavan, 'Borrowed Ideas: On the Impact of American Scholarship on Indian Law' (1985) 33 *American Journal of Comparative Law* 505 at 515. Yet, as Gadbois points out, the 'Anglophile' Chief Justice of India during 1968–70, Hidayatullah and his colleague under his stewardship 'reflected views that were more conservative than during any earlier period'. George H. Gadbois Jr, *Judges of the Supreme Court of India: 1950–1989* (New Delhi: Oxford University Press, 2011), p. 136. The Nehru Government curiously enough sent the Bombay High Chief Justice MC Chagla, at the time judge *ad hoc* in the *Right of Passage* case, to the United States as India's ambassador. Chagla was later 'appointed as minister in successive governments at the centre'. Nariman, *India's Legal System*, p. 77. Should we see Nehru pollinating politics with law or vice versa?

[30] Vappala P. Menon, *The Transfer of Power in India* (Hyderabad: Orient Blackswan, 2020 [1957]) p. 436.

[31] Nariman, *India's Legal System*, p. 23.

[32] Madhav Khosla, *India's Founding Moment: The Constitution of a Most Surprising Democracy* (London: Harvard University Press, 2020) at 20.

The Indian Constitution has made the Indian Supreme Court the final authority on the reading of the Indian laws.[33] The Court has the authority to interpret the reception of international law by the municipal courts. At the core of the Indian Supreme Court's foot in the door on international law matters is India's common law tradition as well as the continuity of the colonial laws, precedents as well the various codes passed for the Indian colony after 1857, guaranteed by the Indian Constitution. Article 372(1) of the Constitution guarantees that 'all the law in force in the territory of India immediately before the commencement of this Constitution shall continue in force therein until altered or repealed or amended by a competent Legislature or other competent authority'.[34] Article 372, if you will, gives Indian judges the licence to practice comparative legal hermeneutics. With the continuity of the colonial laws guaranteed by the Indian Constitution, the Indian courts have a large say in determining and affirming the executive's international legal commitments made before 1947 that is embedded in common law.[35]

In 1964, Justice Mudholkar framed the pressing issue of common law, municipal courts, and international law in clear terms. However, 'would the position be different', Justice Mudholkar asked, 'where a particular rule of international law has been incorporated into the common law by decisions of courts?' He noted:

> Where Parliament does not modify or abrogate a rule of international law which has become part of the common law, is it open to a municipal court to abrogate it or to enforce it in a modified form on the ground that the opinion of civilized States has undergone a change and instead of the old rule a more just and fair rule has been accepted?[36]

As a matter of 'legal method', a large chunk of the arguments before the Indian Supreme Court for judicial review of the executive actions in international matters are trojan horses for importing British and American precedents. The Indian Supreme Court has under common law kept its umbilical cord with the mother British law intact even as it consistently rejected, up until the

33 Prabhakar Singh, 'Spinning Yarns from Moonbeams: A Jurisprudence of Statutory Interpretation in Common Law' (2021) 42 *Statute Law Review*, https://doi.org/10.1093/slr/hmy035, accessed 30 September 2020.

34 Article 372 (1) of the Indian Constitution of 1950.

35 '[A] rule of international law on which the several Privy Council decisions as to the effect of conquest or cession on the private rights of the inhabitants of the conquered or ceded territory is founded has become a part of the common law of this country'. *State of Gujarat* v. *Vora Fiddali Badruddin Mithibarwala*, 1964 Indlaw SC 357 (Mudholkar J.), para. 180.

36 *State of Gujarat* v. *Vora Fiddali Badruddin Mithibarwala*, 1964 Indlaw SC 357 para. 180.

1970s, the revolutionary nature of the American precedents.[37] In a protracted hermeneutical battle of the law, while the executive since 1947 has been inspired by the American independence, the Supreme Court has defended the British common law as the true law for India.[38] At the core of finding a possible FRL in India rests the local postcolonial common law, the extent of judicial review of the executive function, and the constitutional bind on the executive's competence in withdrawal from international legal obligations existing before 1947.[39]

C *The Supreme Court and Extradition of Aliens: Policy or Law?*

One of the ways to detect an FRL, McLachlan says, is to evaluate the 'question of the role of law in political matters, whether presented as a plea of non-justiciability, act of state or political question'.[40] Yet the foreign affairs exceptionalism cannot be wished away even in states where, to recall O'Connell, 'the essential unity of all European legal structures, a unity founded on the moral concord of Western peoples' is recognised. Let us see how the Indian Supreme Court has treated foreign states before it.

The *Hans Muller* case arose when the then West German Government requested the extradition of one Mr Muller for offences which he had allegedly committed in West Germany.[41] Justice Vivian Bose was admittedly forced to 'turn to a wider question' bringing the Indian Supreme Court 'to the fringe of International law'.[42] The West German Consul at Calcutta had written to the West Bengal Government on 9 October 1954 requesting that the provincial Government issue a 'provisional warrant' of arrest against Mr Muller, keeping him in custody until the West German Government could

37 'English courts have thus given effect to rules of international law by resorting to a process of incorporation'. *State of Gujarat* v. *Vora Fiddali Badruddin Mithibarwala*, 1964 Indlaw SC 357, para. 181.

38 In *Rosiline George* v. *Union of India* 1993 Indlaw SC 1535, the Indian Supreme Court declared 'rights and obligations under all international agreements' to which 'India was a party immediately before 1947, automatically devolved upon India after it achieved independence'.

39 There are no substantive limitations upon the executive from withdrawal from international commitments. Unless there is a Parliamentary process to reject an existing international obligation pre-cast in common law, the Executive cannot arbitrarily withdraw. This has been articulated in by Justice Mudholkar and Justice Lokur respectively. *State of Gujarat* v. *Vora Fiddali Badruddin Mithibarwala*, 1964 Indlaw SC 357, para. 180; *Verhoeven, Marie-Emmanuelle* v. *Union of India*, 2016 Indlaw SC 321, para. 79.

40 McLachlan, 'The Allocative Function of Foreign Relations Law', 375.

41 *Hans Muller of Nurenburg* v. *Superintendent, Presidency Jail, Calcutta*, 1955 Indlaw SC 8.

42 *Hans Muller of Nurenburg* v. *Superintendent, Presidency Jail, Calcutta*, 1955 Indlaw SC 8, para. 22.

initiate his extradition proceedings. On receipt of this letter, the West Bengal Government sent a note saying it would have 'no objection' in keeping Muller in 'detention'.

Justice Vivian Bose disagreed with the executive, here the provincial government of West Bengal. He did not find 'obvious' within Indian law the Government Secretary's proposal to keep Muller under detention and rejected the executive's position as unfounded, conceding '[t]his may not be the law in all countries'.[43] Justice Bose thought that common law courts differed from civil law states in their deference to the executive action. In India, an executive action is governed by common law in the absence of express international law, here, between India and West Germany. Effectively, Justice Bose made a distinction between the common law and the civil law approach on the role of foreign states in domestic courts. Justice Bose rejected the Indian executive's action on the detention of aliens 'without the recommendation of a court'.[44] The Supreme Court nevertheless held in India the law is that the executive Government has 'an unfettered right' to expel foreigners.

In the *Verhoeven, Marie-Emmanuelle case*, the Indian Supreme Court had an opportunity to go back to the roots of India's legal basis for foreign relations.[45] The Annexure to the *Report of the Expert Committee No. IX on Foreign Relations* contains a list of 627 treaties, conventions, agreements etc. entered into by the Government of India or by the British Government in which India or Pakistan or both were or are interested. This Annexure does not mention the Extradition Treaty between India and Chile. The precise legal issue in *Verhoeven* was whether the Expert Committee recognized the existence in 2016 of the extradition treaties between the United Kingdom and Chile, and therefore between India, the successor state to the British Indian government, and Chile.

Justice Lokur thought that all international agreements to which India (or British India) was a party would devolve upon the Dominion of India and the Dominion of Pakistan and, if necessary, the obligations and privileges should be apportioned between them. For the Supreme Court there existed 'no limitation' in the Indian Independence (International Arrangements) Order of 14 August 1947 in that it was 'only with regard to the 627 treaties' mentioned

43 *Hans Muller of Nurenburg* v. *Superintendent, Presidency Jail, Calcutta*, 1955 Indlaw SC 8, para. 35.

44 *Hans Muller of Nurenburg* v. *Superintendent, Presidency Jail, Calcutta*, 1955 Indlaw SC 8, para. 35.

45 *Verhoeven, Marie-Emmanuelle* v. *Union of India*, 2016 Indlaw SC 321, para. 79.

by the Expert Committee on Foreign Relations; rather the reference was to 'all international agreements'.[46]

IV EXCLUSION OF FOREIGN RELATIONS FROM JUDICIAL SCRUTINY

Foreign relations remain excluded from the purview of the Court thereby depositing it into the domain of 'policy' and, consequently, excommunicating it from the province of the law. The actual power of the executive and its primary competence in the field of international affairs suggest that sovereignty remains an important principle. Other common law jurisdictions would not be very different. Prime Minister Nehru, Thiruvengadam says, 'was an ardent champion of judicial review and independence' but at the same time he firmly 'believed that it was Parliament and the government of the day which would have the final say on policy decisions'.[47] And under 'our jurisprudence', Nariman reminds, 'a law can be enacted by the Parliament or state legislature but generally it comes into effect only when brought into force by a notification of the Government'.[48] Needless to add, foreign relations stand excluded from judicial scrutiny in India even as the executive could stall law-implementation on the technical ground of non-notification.

The only way 'foreign relations' as a policy could be brought within the pale of the law is by adjudging the extent of a possible judicial review of the executive actions. I discuss below, in subsection IV.A, the Court's reading of

46 *Verhoeven, Marie-Emmanuelle* v. *Union of India*, 2016 Indlaw SC 321, para. 89. Remarkably, the petitioner in *Verhoeven* relied upon the Government of India's preliminary objections to the assumption of jurisdiction by the ICJ in the *Case Concerning the Aerial Incident of 10th August 1999*. Ibid., para. 97 (citing *Aerial Incident of 10 August 1999 (Pakistan* v. *India)*, Jurisdiction of the Court, I.C.J. Reports 2000, p. 12). In a response to the executive's contention that 'the existence of a treaty is a political question and that this Court cannot go into the issue whether there is a subsisting and binding treaty', the court in *Verhoeven* found it 'difficult to fully accept the proposition in the broad manner'. Ibid., para. 111. The Delhi High Court in *Ellis case* tried to clarify the *ratio of Verhoeven*. 'The petitioner had', Delhi High Court said, 'approached the Supreme Court, *inter alia*, with the plea that there was no binding extradition treaty in terms of Section 2(d) of the [Indian Extradition] Act between India and Chile. Another plea raised before the Supreme Court was that the requisition made by the Republic of Chile, invoking the principle of reciprocity and the general principles of international law, for extraditing the petitioner from India was not maintainable. The Supreme Court did not accept either of the aforesaid submissions of the petitioner'. *Lennox James Ellis* v. *Union of India*, 2019 Indlaw DEL 14, para. 20.

47 Arun K. Thiruvengadam, *The Constitution of India: A Contextual Analysis* (New Delhi: Bloomsbury, 2017), p. 118.

48 Fali S. Nariman, *Before Memory Fades: An Autobiography* (New Delhi: Hay House, 2010), p. 82.

the UN Charter. Finally, this section studies the 'political thicket' question examined by the Indian Supreme Court in the *Sikkim* case.

A *The Indian Supreme Court and the UN Charter*

So far, we have walked through Indian case laws keeping in mind McLachlan's exposition of an FRL. One of McLachlan's stresses is upon the reception and treatment of international law in domestic courts. In this section, I will examine the Indian Supreme Court's treatment of an important regime of international law – the UN Charter.

India sent forces into Goa after the ICJ in the *Right of Passage* case ruled against Portugal having any military right of passage through Indian territory.[49] The British government at the time did not recognize India's de facto control of Goa in law (de jure). The *Monteiro* litigation before the Indian Supreme Court originated from the Goa situation where Father Monteiro having overstayed his residence permit did not apply for the Indian passport.[50] His other options were to either exit the territory of India, or take the offer of the Indian passport without which he would become an illegal 'alien' in Goa. India called her annexation lawful and valid. 'Annexation may sometimes be peaceful', Justice Hidayatullah reasoned,[51] 'as for example, Texas and Hawaiian Island were peacefully annexed by the United States or after war, as the annexation of South Africa and Orange Free State by Britain'.[52]

When a title to the new territory actually begins is not an easy question to answer. Since the 'military engagement' in Goa was only 'a few hours' duration' and 'there was no resistance at all', Justice Hidayatullah ruled: 'true annexation followed here so close upon military occupation as to leave no real hiatus'.[53] According to Justice Hidayatullah,

> [t]he occupation on December 20, 1961 was neither belligerent occupation nor anticipated occupation, but true annexation by conquest and subjugation. It must be remembered that Mr. Gardiner, counsel for Father Monteiro, concedes that the annexation was lawful. Therefore, since occupation in the

49 *Case concerning Right of Passage over Indian Territory (Merits)*, Judgment 12 April 1960, ICJ Report 6.

50 *Rev. Mons. Monteiro* v. *State of Goa*, 1969 Indlaw SC 583.

51 Monteiro is a five-judge bench ruling written by Hidayatullah, a student of McNair at Cambridge. Mohammed Hidayatullah wrote *The South-West Africa Case* (Bombay: Asia Publishing House, 1967) on the encouragement of his teacher: 'Lord McNair was responsible for my book'. M. Hidayatullah, *My Own Boswell* (New Delhi: LexisNexis, 2020 [1981]) at 87.

52 *Rev. Mons. Monteiro* v. *State of Goa*, 1969 Indlaw SC 583, para. 34.

53 *Rev. Mons. Monteiro* v. *State of Goa*, 1969 Indlaw SC 583, paras. 31, 36.

> sense used in Art. 47 [of Convention IV[54]] had ceased, the protection must cease also. We are, therefore, of opinion that in the present case there was no breach of the Geneva Conventions.[55]

The Indian justification of Goa's annexation lay in Goa being a Portuguese 'blue-water' province.[56] Due to India's brush with Portuguese colonialism in the *Right of Passage* case,[57] the decade that followed presented a change in the way Indian judges looked at international law. India had sent the Bombay High Court Chief Justice MC Chagla to sit as judge ad hoc on the *Right of Passage* bench.[58] A cosmopolitan Nehru at the time suddenly woke up to the reality of India's incomplete decolonization. The fact that Goa, Dadra, and Nagar Aveli continued to be governed by Portugal meant India stood between Lisbon and Portugal's *ultramar* province, Goa.

While India also stood between Pakistan's two overland provinces East Pakistan (now Bangladesh) and West-Pakistan (now Pakistan), New Delhi did not view these two situations, overseas and overland provinces, similarly. Portugal, in Nehru's words, presented the vestiges of colonialism, particularly after France had returned Pondicherry to India by a treaty and Britain by passing a domestic law. Judge Hidayatullah's reading of the UN Charter naturally acquires significance then. Judge Hidayatullah asserted:

> Some would make title depend upon recognition. Mr. Stimson's doctrine of non-recognition in cases where a State of things has been brought about contrary to the Pact of Paris was intended to deny root of title conquest but when Italy conquered Abyssinia, the conquest was recognized because it was thought that the state of affairs had come to stay. Thus, although the United Nations Charter includes the obligation that force would not be used against the territorial integrity of other States (Art. 2 Para 4), events after the Second World War have shown that transfer of title to territory by conquest is still recognized.[59]

[54] 4 Geneva Convention Relative to the Protection of Civilian Persons in Time of War, 12 August 1949, 75 UNTS 287.

[55] *Rev. Mons. Monteiro* v. *State of Goa*, 1969 Indlaw SC 583, para. 37.

[56] The Portuguese Permanent Representative to the UN said to the Australian diplomat Sir Owen Dixon, UN Representative for India and Pakistan, that on the Goa question 'a majority of the Council would be in sympathy with the Portuguese, whereas in the General Assembly things might go against the Portuguese'. Letter of AR Moore, May 15, 1958, in Foreign Office Files for India, Pakistan and Afghanistan, 1947–64, Doc DL 1024/2, FO371/135944 (1958) para. 1.

[57] Prabhakar Singh, 'India Before and After the *Right of Passage* case' (2015) 5 *Asian Journal of International Law* 176.

[58] Mahomedali C. Chagla, *Roses in December: An Autobiography* (Mumbai: Bhartiya Vidya Bhawan, 2018 [1973]), p. 211.

[59] *Rev. Mons. Monteiro* v. *State of Goa*, 1969 Indlaw SC 583, para. 35. The American professor Quincy Wright, the then editor of the *American Journal of International Law*, while visiting New Delhi on Ford Foundation grant found Goa to be a case of Asia's reading of the UN

We can see that the Indian Supreme Court finds the Indian Constitution, and not the UN Charter, is the applicable law in India. The reference to international law and treaty in article 51 of the Constitution only gives a 'policy' nudge to the Indian executive offering no 'law' to be applied. In December 1960, India's agent before the ICJ in the *Right of Passage* case, MC Setalvad 'expressed the opinion that there was no legal impediment in incorporating the liberated Portuguese territories into India'.[60]

B *The* Sikkim *Case: The 'Political Thicket' Question*

On 8 May 1973, the King of Sikkim, the Government of India, and leaders of the political parties representing the people of Sikkim entered a tripartite agreement.[61] Sikkim finally became a province of India in 1975. Justice LM Sharma thought the issue of Sikkim joining India was subject to the 'political questions doctrine'. In other words, 'the questions raised in the petitions pertaining' to the 'terms and conditions of accession of new territory are governed by rules of public international law' and they are as such 'non-justiciable' on the 'political questions doctrine'.[62] The territory of Sikkim was admitted into the Indian Union by an act of voluntary cession by the general consent of its inhabitants expressed on a Referendum.[63] The Court invoked the American case *Baker* v. *Carr*.[64] According to the Indian Supreme Court, the effect of *Baker* v. *Carr* 'is that in the United States of America certain controversies previously immune from adjudication were held justiciable and decided on the merits. The rejection of the "political thickets" arguments in these cases marks a narrowing of the operation of the doctrine in other areas as well'.[65] 'The submission is further that', the Court noted, 'since the terms and conditions on which Sikkim was admitted in Union of India, are political in nature, the said terms and conditions cannot be made the subject matter of challenge before this Court because the law is well settled that

Charter. Quincy Wright, 'The Goa Question' (1962) 56 *American Journal of International Law* 617–32.

60 Motilal C. Setalvad, *My Life: Law and other Things* (Mumbai: T. Setalvad & A. Setalvad, 1990 [1970]) p. 325.

61 *RC Poundyal* v. *Union of India*, 1993 Indlaw SC 1362, para. 120.

62 *RC Poundyal* v. *Union of India*, 1993 Indlaw SC 1362, para. 87.

63 *RC Poundyal* v. *Union of India*, 1993 Indlaw SC 1362, para. 88. The court here referred to A. K. Pavithran, *Substance of Public International Law Western and Eastern* (Madras: A. P. Rajendran, 1965) for which Justice Radhabinod Pal wrote the foreword.

64 *Baker* v. *Carr*, 369 US 186 (1962).

65 *RC Poundyal* v. *Union of India*, 1993 Indlaw SC 1362, para. 17.

courts do not adjudicate upon questions which are political in nature'.[66] In the *Sikkim* case, the Supreme Court moved away from *Mithibarwala* in that the Court was now open to borrow from common law jurisdictions other than England.

Sikkim joined the Union of India by an international agreement. Irrespective of this agreement, as the later Judge of the ICJ Rosalyn Higgins noted, the UN Human Rights Committee 'questioned' if the treatment of Sikkim, 'which had been overrun by force and incorporated within India, was compatible with self-determination'.[67] Although the Indian Supreme Court decided the *Sikkim* case four years after Higgins wrote about Sikkim's merger into India, Western scholars often fail to draw a distinction between India's takeover of Goa, a colonial province of Portugal, and Sikkim, an independent Asian kingdom that joined India by an international agreement and a subsequent constitutional process.

Generally speaking, if the Western opinion could so easily question a full political process expressed in the referendum in favour of joining India, and the later incorporation effected under the Constitution of India as 'overrun by force' and not 'compatible with self-determination', it is not difficult to argue that India does not see its Constitution and common law having 'a unity founded on the moral concord of Western peoples'. No wonder justice Mudholkar thought 'the law of a State can only be modified or repealed by a competent legislature of the State and not by international opinion however weighty that Opinion may be'.[68]

Generations of Indian jurists have worked overtime to cultivate and harvest British laws in postcolonial India.[69] And yet a constitutional reading of international law has remained in the Commonwealth a one-way traffic of precedents and scholarship exposing its imperial bias, the periphery never educating the centre. One does not need to remind that foreign relations are based on reciprocity. There remains an absence of references and reciprocation to Indian case laws on foreign relations in the standard FRL textbooks.

[66] The political question doctrine has been evolved in the United States to deny judicial review in certain fields. The doctrine received a setback in the case of *Baker* v. *Carr*. *Baker* v. *Carr*, 369 US 186 (1962), para. 132.

[67] Rosalyn Higgins, 'Human Rights: Some Questions of Integrity' (1989) 15 *Commonwealth Law Bulletin* 598 at 608.

[68] *State of Gujarat* v. *Vora Fiddali Badruddin Mithibarwala*, 1964 Indlaw SC 357, para. 180.

[69] Justice Vivian Bose noted Oppenheim saying the British Government had 'no power to expel even the most dangerous alien without the recommendation of a court'. *Hans Muller of Nurenburg* v. *Superintendent, Presidency Jail, Calcutta*, 1955 Indlaw SC 8, para. 35.

V THE INDIAN CONSTITUTION AND *UTI POSSIDETIS*

The Indian Constitution doubtless gives the law that the Indian Supreme Court applies. The taking and giving of territory by India too is governed by the Constitution. Territory as defined in the *Montevideo Convention* is central to the existence of a modern state.[70] Add to that the doctrine of *uti possidetis* that instructs former colonies to keep territories and honour boundaries they have received from their colonial masters. But the *uti possidetis* principle needed a reading by the postcolonial Supreme Court since the colonial masters had defeated in India – by slicing British India into two states – this principle. The new post-colonies bordering India, here Pakistan, went into a further break-up of its territories, creating new sovereign boundaries. This geopolitical situation led India to a constitutive (through the Indian Constitution) and a declaratory (by the executive) re-perfecting of its *uti possidetis* in the way discussed below.

A *Constitutional Perfecting of* Uti Possidetis

In 1959, the President of India wrote to the Indian Supreme Court for an advisory opinion about the questions of law that might arise relating to the Berubari Union as well as the Agreement relating to the exchange of Enclaves with Pakistan.[71] In the *Berubari* opinion, Justice Gajendragadkar wrote that, on a 'true construction' of article 1(3)(c) of the Indian Constitution, it was erroneous to assume that it confers specific powers to acquire foreign territories.[72] This opinion noted that cession of national territory in law amounts to the transfer of sovereignty over the said territory by the owner-State in favour of another State.[73] Justice Gajendragadkar spoke of, if you will, an implied *uti possidetis*. For him,

> It may be that this provision has found a place in the Constitution not in pursuance of any expansionist political philosophy but mainly for providing for the integration and absorption of Indian territories which, at the date of the Constitution, continued to be under the dominion of foreign States; but that is not the whole scope of Art. 1(3)(c). It refers broadly to all foreign territories which may be acquired by India and provides that as soon as they

70 Art. 1, Montevideo Convention on the Rights and Duties of States, 26 December 1933, 165 LNTS 19.

71 *Re: The Berubari Union and Exchange of Enclaves*, 1959 Indlaw SC 294.

72 *Re: The Berubari Union and Exchange of Enclaves*, 1959 Indlaw SC 294, para. 53.

73 'But though from the human point of view great hardship is inevitably involved in cession of territory by one country to the other', Gajendragradkar said, 'there can be no doubt that a sovereign state can exercise its right to cede a part of its territory to a foreign state'. *Re: The Berubari Union and Exchange of Enclaves*, 1959 Indlaw SC 294, para. 55.

> are acquired they would form part of the territory of India. Thus, on a true construction of Article 1(3)(c) it is erroneous to assume that it confers specific powers to acquire foreign territories.[74]

The Government of India in *Berubari* surprisingly did not make a distinction between boundary adjustment and cession. Nevertheless, exactly a decade later, in *Maganbhai*,[75] Justice Hidayatullah accepted and confirmed the distinction the West Bengal provincial government had made in *Berubari* between boundary adjustment and cession:

> The argument that if power to settle boundaries be conceded to the Executive, it might cede some vital part of India is to take an extreme view of things. The same may even be said of Parliament itself but it is hardly to be imagined that such gross abuse of power is ever likely. Ordinarily an adjustment of a boundary which International Law regards as valid between two Nations, should be recognised by the Courts and the implementation thereof can always be with the Executive unless a clear case of cession is involved when Parliamentary intercession can be expected and should be had. This has been the custom of Nations whose Constitutions are not sufficiently elaborate on this subject.[76]

'The power to legislate in respect of treaties lies with the Parliament', Justice Hidayatullah continued, '[b]ut making of law under that authority is necessary when the treaty or agreement operates to restrict the rights of citizens or others or modules the laws of the State'. Very importantly, '[i]f the rights of the citizens or others which are justiciable are not affected, no legislative measure is needed to give effect to the agreement or treaty'.[77] Since international law falls within the non-justiciable article 51, rights of the citizens and that of the aliens, legal or illegal, stem from India's written Constitution.[78]

[74] *Re: The Berubari Union and Exchange of Enclaves*, 1959 Indlaw SC 294, para. 53.

[75] *Maganbhai Ishwarbhai Patel* v. *Union of India*, 1969 Indlaw SC 269.

[76] *Maganbhai Ishwarbhai Patel* v. *Union of India*, 1969 Indlaw SC 269, para. 42.

[77] *Maganbhai Ishwarbhai Patel* v. *Union of India*, 1969 Indlaw SC 269, para. 79.

[78] *Sarbananda Sonawal* v. *Union of India*, 2005, Indlaw SC 404 updates on the 'law regarding deportation of aliens'. In *Louis De Raedt* v. *Union of India*, 1991, 3 SCC 664 the Supreme Court clearly held that constitutional rights available to foreigners are restricted to Article 21 of the Constitution. *Cf.* Prabhakar Singh, 'More Norms, Less Justice: The Refugees, the Republic and Everyone in Between' (2018) 39 *Liverpool Law Review* 123.

B *Declaratory Perfecting of* Uti Possidetis

While India signed an agreement to welcome Sikkim into the Union of India, almost at the same time, in 1974, the Government of India declared to accept the compulsory jurisdiction of the ICJ 'in conformity with paragraph 2 of article 36 of the Statute of the Court, until such time as notice may be given to terminate such acceptance, as compulsory *ipso facto* and without special agreement, and on the basis and condition of reciprocity, the jurisdiction of the ICJ over all disputes other than' those mentioned in the *Swaran Singh Declaration*.[79] Paragraph 10 of the declaration noted India's exclusion from the ICJ's jurisdiction:

> disputes with India concerning or relating to:
> (*a*) the status of its territory or the modification or delimitation of its frontiers or any other matter concerning boundaries;
> (*b*) the territorial sea, the continental shelf and the margins, the exclusive fishery zone, the exclusive economic zone, and other zones of national maritime jurisdiction including for the regulation and control of marine pollution and the conduct of scientific research by foreign vessels;
> (*c*) the condition and status of its islands, bays and gulfs and that of the bays and gulfs that for historical reasons belong to it;
> (*d*) the airspace superjacent to its land and maritime territory; and
> (*e*) the determination and delimitation of its maritime boundaries.

Paragraph 11 of the declaration made it retrospective. India tactically declared its exclusion of the ICJ jurisdiction, in 1974, right before the Third UNCLOS conference began. Why? Might paragraph 10(c) of India's declaration answer this? The declaration excluded from the ICJ disputes about 'the condition and status of its islands, bays and gulfs and that of the bays and gulfs that for historical reasons belong to it'.

India thus secured its *uti possidetis* in the sea before the UN Convention would fix the substantive content of the law of the sea (the UNCLOS) putting India's possessions in the sea beyond the UNCLOS.[80] India has submitted a new Declaration on 27 September 2019 replacing the 18 September 1974 Declaration. In 2019, a new *Jaishankar Declaration* excluded from the ICJ's

79 Subrahmanyam Jaishankar, 'Declarations recognizing the jurisdiction of the Court as compulsory', 17 September 2019, The ICJ, The Hague, available at: www.icj-cij.org/en/declarations/in. The 'Jaishankar Declaration' further 'expand[s] the scope of India's reservations'. Srinivas Burra, 'India's Modified Declaration on the Jurisdiction of the International Court of Justice' EJIL Talk (2 April 2020).

80 Prabhakar Singh, 'The Kashmir Question', *Deccan Herald*, 13 September 2019, p. 10.

jurisdiction 'disputes where the jurisdiction of the Court is or may be founded on the basis of a treaty concluded under the auspices of the League of Nations'.[81] By excluding from the ambit of the ICJ's compulsory jurisdiction in 2019 'disputes with the government of any State which is or has been a Member of the Commonwealth of Nations' India has attempted to put its residual *uti possidetis* beyond the ICJ's adjudication.[82]

VI CONCLUSION

The 'decisions of the Privy Council', as Fali Nariman reminds us, 'are called "opinions" because they are in the form of advice to the English Monarch' while the decisions of the House of Lords were known as 'speeches'.[83] Nehru had accepted Sir BN Rau's formulae to stay within the Commonwealth as a 'Republic' without recognising the British Monarch's moral, legal or political authority.[84] Should the British 'opinions' to the Monarch and 'speeches' in the House of Lords pre-cast in common law become 'applicable law' in India after 1950? Purshottam Tricumdass, counsel in *Mithibarwala*, had suggested that the Indian Supreme Court 'discard the theory of public international law that underlies the decisions of the Privy Council' in favour of 'the more rational, just and human doctrine' of the 'American decisions'. His 'thesis', in the words of Justice Ayyangar, 'was that the doctrines evolved by the Privy Council were conditioned by Britain being an Imperialist and expansionist power at the date when they originated and were applied' and that 'these might have been suited to the regime of a colonial power' alone.[85]

In exporting FRL, scholars from common law states seemingly exhibit a lack of sensitivity for the history of common law in British colonies. But for colonialism, common law surely could not have visited India or the other British colonies. The countries that did not suffer British colonialism chose the continental law without exception![86] In fact for Nariman 'common law' is not so much a 'law' as it is a 'unique *method* of administering justice' or, might I add, injustice. After centuries of the reception of the British common law, FRL as a new call to collapse public international law with domestic law

81 Jaishankar, 'Declarations recognizing the jurisdiction of the Court as compulsory', 17 September 2019, The ICJ, The Hague, para. 6.
82 Jaishankar, 'Declarations recognizing the jurisdiction of the Court as compulsory', 17 September 2019, The ICJ, The Hague, para. 2.
83 Nariman, *Before Memory Fades*, p. 112.
84 Sir BN Rau later become a judge of the ICJ. Setalvad, 'My Life: Law and Other Things', p. 140.
85 *State of Gujarat* v. *Vora Fiddali Badruddin Mithibarwala*, 1964 Indlaw SC 357, para. 44.
86 Nariman, *India's Legal System*, p. 24.

appears an innocuous innovation only because, as noted before, the FRL scholars overlook the colonial history of common law that jurist Nariman as well as economic historians Acemoglu, Johnson and Robinson point at.

In order to ossify the native sovereignty, the nineteenth century British colonial scholars had argued for an imperial law that was neither international law nor domestic law. Sitting in a post-colony like India, transnational law and FRL appear twins divided by time. In the twenty-first century, FRL scholars argue for a composite 'doctrine derived from public international law, private international law and municipal English law'.[87] An uncritical growth of FRL happens solely because such an 'Anglo-commonwealth' FRL does not yet recognise law, common law or civil law, of the geographical South as worthy of export. India has gone on a borrowing binge for far too long and an FRL is least desirable in a legal environment of the one-sided traffic of precedents. The common law's unwillingness for learning is not limited to her intellectual apathy for Britain's ex-colonies but extends even to continental law for which O'Connell had exhorted 'the essential unity of all European legal structures, a unity founded on the moral concord of Western peoples'.

But India has inherited a British 'legal structure' without 'a unity founded on the moral concord of Western peoples'. FRL for India remains a moral platitude of the sort O'Connell talked about in relation to Europe and England. Besides being anthropologically challenged, FRL reverses normative decolonisation while claiming to offer a bigger basket of problem-solving.

Many foreign relations issues emerge because of India's marriage to common law. The twenty-first century FRL then appears to uncritically mimic the two older common law projects; 'imperial law' of the nineteenth century Britain and 'transnational law' of the twentieth century post-war United States. We may wish to go by our written Constitution without needing, or having found, a 'foreign affairs' law. Shakespeare famously wrote 'what's in a name'. McLachlan and Bradley think otherwise; everything is in the name. The name is 'foreign relations' law. Not for India, however. Since 1950, it is constitutional law in New Delhi.

87 McLachlan, 'The Allocative Function of Foreign Relations Law', 374.

6

Foreign Legal Policy As the Background to Foreign Relations Law?

Revisiting Guy de Lacharrière's La politique juridique extérieure

Frédéric Mégret

The study of foreign relations law has been largely devoted to domestic laws as they affect foreign policy.[1] An element seems to be missing, however, somewhere between domestic and international law that is reducible to neither the constraints of domestic or international law on foreign policy. Although that element may simply be the national interest, the latter seems too crude a variable to explain alone how countries navigate not just their foreign policy generally, but its many legal dimensions specifically.

A more discreet strand of thought has looked at how national policies in relation to international law are formulated. This could be seen as including the quite specific but rich genre of writing on foreign policy legal advice and advisors (which has both a foreign policy law allocation dimension, and a foreign legal policy element)[2] although what this chapter is interested in is arguably broader and not necessarily as personalised. The key intuition here is

[1] See, for example, Curtis A. Bradley, 'What Is Foreign Relations Law?', in Curtis A. Bradley (ed.), *The Oxford Handbook of Comparative Foreign Relations Law* (New York: Oxford University Press, 2019). On this more conventional conception of foreign relations law and how it has been understood in the context of this chapter's case study, France, see the chapter by Niki Aloupi, 'The Conseil Constitutionnel's Jurisprudence on "Limitations of Sovereignty"'. Whereas the latter 'foreign relations law' stricto sensu varies quite significantly from country to country based on constitutional specificities, the attempt to theorise a 'politique juridique étrangère' arguably includes an effort to reach for something which may have local specificities but is also more functionally and universally oriented.

[2] Stephen M. Schwebel, 'Remarks on the Role of the Legal Advisor of the US State Department' (1991) 2 *EJIL* 131–5; Jesselyn Radack, 'Tortured Legal Ethics: The Role of the Government Advisor in the War on Terrorism' (2006) 77 *University of Colorado Law Review* 1–48; Lewis Johnman, 'Playing the Role of a Cassandra: Sir Gerald Fitzmaurice, Senior Legal Advisor to the Foreign Office' (1999) 13 *Contemporary British History* 46–63; Robbie Sabel, 'The Role of the Legal Advisor in Diplomacy' (1997) 8 *Diplomacy and Statecraft* 1–9; Andriy Melnyk, 'Master or Servant? International Law in the Foreign Policy Context', in

that a state's foreign policy is reducible neither to compliance with international law (as international law insists), nor to the constraints imposed by domestic law on foreign policy (as foreign relations law sometimes implicitly claims). The elaboration of the law of a state's foreign relations – rather than foreign relations law, strictly speaking – is certainly influenced by international law but is not reducible to compliance with it (even a policy of compliance with international law can be understood as a domestic policy rather than just obedience to international legal diktats). In between domestic and international law, then, lies a vibrant practice of defining what a state's policy towards international law should be that can be understood to be a central part of the definition of the law of foreign relations, albeit not strictly what is conventionally understood as 'foreign relations law'.

France may be an intriguing country to look for clues as to how to conceptualise such policies. Foreign relations law as a discipline is often seen there as a US oddity. Moreover, it is one that is seen as standing in real tension to a commitment to public international law and even as having echoes of earlier denials of its very existence – international law as really only the accumulation of the externally oriented facets of domestic law. This is particularly clear in the French perspective where the emphasis on the primacy of international law is historically combined with a very strong insistence on monism. Georges Scelle even went as far as claiming that the state had no particular pride of place, as international law was, fundamentally, not that different from domestic law.[3] Nonetheless, France, perhaps unsurprisingly for a country with a strong republican and Jacobin tradition, has also produced its own approach to the law of foreign relations, if not quite 'foreign relations law'. Rescuing that tradition that has been somewhat neglected in contemporary foreign relations law scholarship can help understand the US approach as less idiosyncratic than it is sometimes presented as being, but also help appreciate how different

Hélène R. Fabri, Emmanuelle Jouannet, Vincent Tomkiewicz (eds.), *Select Proceedings of the European Society of International Law*, 5 vols. (Oxford/Portland: Hart Publishing, 2008), vol. I, pp. 237–78; Kenneth M. Manusama, 'Between a Rock and a Hard Place: Providing Legal Advice on Military Action Against Iraq' (2011) 42 *Netherlands Yearbook of International Law* 95–121; Stephen Bouwhuis, 'The Role of an International Legal Adviser to Government' (2012) 61 *ICLQ* 939–60; Johan G. Lammers, 'The Role of the Legal Adviser of the Ministry of Foreign Affairs: The Dutch Approach and Experience' (2009) 18 *Tulane Journal of International and Comparative Law* 177–205; Fernando G. Nuñez-Mietz, 'Lawyering Compliance with International Law: Legal Advisors and the Legalization of International Politics', PhD thesis, The Ohio State University (2013).

3 Georges Scelle, *Droit international public: manuel élémentaire avec les textes essentiels* (Paris: Domat-Montchrestien, 1944); Patrick Daillier, 'L'héritage de Georges Scelle, une utopie, une théorie ou une doctrine juridique? Les trois à la fois, peut-être' (2018) 34 *Anuario Español de Derecho Internacional* 5–8.

approaches inevitably betray different conceptualisations of the relationship of the state to international law.

Published in 1983, Guy Ladreit de Lacharrière's *La politique juridique extérieure*[4] was a highly unusual book by the standards of both French international law academia and the French diplomatic service. De Lacharrière was by then a former legal advisor to the Quai d'Orsay, the seat of the foreign ministry. The book was relatively short (around 200 pages), lightly footnoted in a way that at times suggested off-the-cuff remarks rather than a standard academic treatment, but erudite and theoretically provocative. It came with the credibility and aura of de Lacharrière's experience. It seemed to pull the curtain on the making of international law in the twilight of a higher civil servant's career. It can be seen as part of a small but highly distinctive and illustrious tradition of monographs written by international lawyers with intense exposure to the state practice of international law.[5] Indeed it was praised at the time for seeming to combine in one the qualities of 'Le Sage, le Prince et le Savant'.[6] In its emphasis on state practices it has been analogised with some of the earlier work of the Russian Grigory Tunkin,[7] but it also bears mentioning that *La politique juridique extérieure* bears some affinity with Wilhelm Grewe's *Spiel der Kräfte in der Weltpolitik*[8] published at about the same time.

At the same time, the book remains somewhat obscure and a little heretical. It has never been republished since 1983 and is increasingly hard to locate outside specialised libraries. It is little known outside France, where its place is sometimes hard to gauge, and even harder to situate in a global context.[9] It has of late become the object of renewed interest, at least in francophone

4 Guy de Lacharrière, *La politique juridique extérieure* (Paris: Economica, 1983).

5 Martti Koskenniemi was director of the Division of International Law in the Finnish foreign ministry. Philip Allott was a legal adviser in the British Foreign and Commonwealth Office from 1960 to 1973. Wilhelm Grewe was involved throughout a distinguished career in the German foreign service in a variety of positions which involved international law. It is somewhat more common for US international law scholars to have worked for the State Department in some legal capacity (José Alvarez, Dan Bodansky, Anne Marie Slaughter, Lori Damrosch, etc.). See André Oraison, 'La place des jurisconsultes internationaux au sein de "la doctrine des publicistes les plus qualifiés des différentes nations"' (1998) 11 *Hague Yearbook of International Law/Annuaire de la Haye de droit international* 43–65.

6 Alain Pellet, 'Le Sage, le Prince et le Savant (A propos de "La politique juridique extérieure" de Guy de Lacharrière)' (1985) 112 *Journal du droit international* 407–14.

7 Michel Virally, 'Réflexions sur la politique juridique des Etats' in *Guy Ladreit de Lacharrière et la politique juridique extérieure de la France* (Paris: Masson, 1989), p. 394.

8 Wilhelm G. Grewe, *Spiel der Kräfte in der Weltpolitik. Theorie und Praxis der internationalen Beziehungen* (Frankfurt am Main: Ullstein Taschenbuchverlag, 1981).

9 Kolb suggests a lineage between Guy de Lacharrière and 'critical legal studies' notably in the form of the work of David Kennedy and Martti Koskenniemi but this lineage is tenuous.

academic circles.[10] Although Guy de Lacharrière was described recently as 'l'un des plus grands jurisconsultes français du XXe siècle',[11] this was, perhaps tellingly, in the *Annuaire français de relations internationales* rather than the *Annuaire français de droit international*, and by two young French public international lawyers but associated with the Centre Thucydide, which is devoted to the study of international relations. For all these reasons, de Lacharrière's book deserves a broader recognition for its contribution to our knowledge of international law 'from the inside', even as one must speculate about his relative lack of influence.

De Lacharrière had had a prestigious career by the time the book was published. He had graduated first of the concours of the Ministry of Foreign Affairs. He spoke Russian fluently and one of his first postings was in the French embassy in Moscow (1946–8). A significant part of his career was devoted to France's relationship to international organisations, including the UN and UNESCO. However, he is most keenly remembered as the legal adviser to the foreign ministry from 1969 to 1979. His most significant exposure to the trade of international law arose when he represented France at the 3rd UN Conference on the Law of the Sea that gave rise to UNCLOS, from 1979 to 1982. He had earlier on also been involved in the creation of the UNCTAD and the GATT. Subsequently, he would become a judge at the International Court of Justice and even the court's vice-president.[12]

De Lacharrière was, revealingly, never a legal academic; rather, he was a career civil servant and diplomat who sought to theorise a certain praxis of international law. Contra an international lawyers' international law ('les commentateurs'), he opposed, fundamentally, a domestic civil servant's international law ('les décideurs').[13] This chapter will re-examine this contribution in a contemporary light, weighing it against the monist and universalist assumptions of French foreign legal policy. Within the broader field of foreign relations law, the work of Guy de Lacharrière is hard to categorise. Rather than

Koskenniemi cites the book only once in *From Apology to Utopia: The Structure of International Legal Argument* (Cambridge: Cambridge University Press, 2006), p. 632.

10 Julien Cazala, 'Retour sur un classique : Guy de Lacharrière, La politique juridique extérieure' (2013) 117 *Revue générale de droit international public* 411–16; Pellet, 'Le Sage, le Prince et le Savant'; Virally, 'Réflexions sur la politique juridique des Etats'; Robert Kolb, *Réflexions sur les politiques juridiques extérieures* (Paris: Editions A. Pedone, 2015).

11 Julian Fernandez and Nicolas Haupais, 'Introduction' (2012) XIII *Annuaire français de relations internationales* 553.

12 Julien Cazala, 'Guy Ladreit de Lacharrière (1919–1987)', Société française pour le droit international, www.sfdi.org/internationalistes/lacharriere-guy-ladreit-de/, accessed 30 September 2020.

13 de Lacharrière, *La politique juridique extérieure*, p. 215.

seeing foreign relations as constrained by the domestic law framework or, for that matter, international law itself, de Lacharrière saw it as being above all determined by what he described as a state's 'foreign legal policy'.

I THE PRIMACY OF FOREIGN LEGAL POLICY

La politique juridique extérieure insisted on the centrality of the relationship between the state and its 'exterior', and argued for a voluntaristic and strategic legal foreign policy. In particular, it suggested, that if international law was international law it was because states had a 'legal foreign policy' – international law's law-ness was not immanent or metaphysical but embedded in states' defence of the national interest, opportunistic as it might be. In de Lacharrière's view, foreign legal policy towards international law was not itself entirely or even particularly determined by domestic law, as much as by concern with the national interest.[14]

His contribution to foreign relations *law* was therefore much less notable than his work on states' *politics* of international law. If anything, he tended to see foreign policy lawyers as involved in strategising about international law itself, anticipating its changes, trying to soften contradictions between positions adopted by their state over time, and understanding how evolutions in international law might affect them. In other words, the crucible of foreign relations law lied in the encounter between the national interest and the particular proclivities of the international legal order, a space that was dominated neither entirely by international law (as some academic international lawyers might imprudently presuppose) nor the national interest (as realists were too quick to conclude).

According to one of *La politique juridique extérieure's* most recognisable and paradoxical formulas: 'before international law, there are national policies towards international law',[15] this is reminiscent of the chicken-and-egg debate on the primacy of sovereignty or international law or of practice over opinio juris. But how can there be a politics of international law before international law itself? What Guy de Lacharrière rejected above all was a vision of the priority and primacy of international law, one in which law 'serait reconnu comme étant d'une nature sacrée qui le voue au respect des gouvernements et le met au-dessus des manipulations politiques. Considéré sous l'angle d'une telle dévotion, il ne pourrait faire l'objet de politiques gouvernementales'.[16]

14 de Lacharrière, *La politique juridique extérieure*, ch. I.
15 de Lacharrière, *La politique juridique extérieure*, p. 5.
16 de Lacharrière, *La politique juridique extérieure*, p. 9.

This is what might be understood as the 'immanent' conception of international law, and it is of course quite widespread.[17] It would tend to view the idea of a 'foreign legal policy' as 'sacrilegious'.[18] At the opposite extreme is a particular extreme form of the realist critique, one that would be so dismissive of international law as to find futile any notion that states have a policy towards it. As de Lacharrière puts it, 'le droit ne mériterait pas l'honneur qu'on lui ferait en ayant une politique à son égard'.[19]

Guy de Lacharrière doubted that either school reflected the practice of statecraft (as opposed, perhaps, to the scholarship of international lawyers) or was seriously entertained by those actually entrusted with safeguarding states' foreign policy legal interests. Rather than each position being represented in its pure form, however, either might taint the foreign legal policy of given states at any given moment based on its interest. This is a striking notion: the idea that views about international law are themselves influenced by a sort of *jeu de masques* that leads states to adopt the views that they need under the guise of interpreting international law. Even the insistence on respect for international law, in that context, could be understood as a foreign policy option, associated with an a priori in favour of the status quo. By the same token, too blatant an instrumentalisation of the law would be self-defeating: even realists know that if they play the international law game, they need to play it at least half-heartedly, or expose the mediocrity of their arguments.[20]

At any rate, foreign legal policy did not exist in a void and was not autonomous; it existed at the discretion and in relation to a broader national interest. The power of states was an evident element in the determination of their foreign legal policy. All other things being equal, weak states were likely to consider that an international rule of law was more advantageous; by contrast, powerful states would have a great ability to resist or withstand a finding that they had violated international law.[21] Another factor was, quite simply, the psychology and even training of those deciding in any given country and whether they were convinced of the usefulness of international law or not (although de Lacharrière noted that Nixon was a lawyer and Eisenhower a military man).[22] This is not necessarily a rejection of 'foreign relations law', but in its conspicuous ignorance of domestic law, it is an implicit

17 de Lacharrière, *La politique juridique extérieure*, p. 9.
18 de Lacharrière, *La politique juridique extérieure*, p. 9.
19 de Lacharrière, *La politique juridique extérieure*, p. 9.
20 de Lacharrière, *La politique juridique extérieure*, ch. V.
21 de Lacharrière, *La politique juridique extérieure*, pp. 138–9.
22 de Lacharrière, *La politique juridique extérieure*, p. 212.

claim that runs throughout the book about a certain exceptionality of foreign policy when it comes to domestic law.

For Guy de Lacharrière, domestic factors were quite key in explaining national variations between states.[23] The continuity of governments or something as trivial as the availability of archives were key in evaluating the risk of incoherence in foreign legal policy-making and dealing with it.[24] Perhaps more importantly, the place of law within national legal institutions stood out as relevant. For some states, the rule of law was highly important, and this was bound to have an impact: a state that despises law domestically is unlikely to embrace it internationally, for example.[25]

The constitutional framework did matter of course but only indirectly and because of its potential to shape foreign legal policy. Although foreign policy in France was a prerogative of the president, treaties stood to be adopted by the Assemblée nationale and to become law as soon as ratified. For monist states, the exact content of a treaty mattered all the more given the lack of an opportunity to subsequently adapt it into domestic law. At the same time, the absence of common law style judicial review meant that it was unlikely that France's treaty obligations would, having satisfied an a priori *contrôle de constitutionnalité*, be contested by domestic courts. This is, in turn, in contrast to common law states that are often wary of implementing their treaty obligations in domestic law lest the treaties be challenged before ordinary courts. However, de Lacharrière was well aware that in both monist and dualist countries the force of international law was not such that its violations were typically treated on a par with domestic law violations. If anything, violations of international law took importance because they were seen as also violations of domestic law.[26]

In short, the domestic element in foreign legal policy was not absent (for example, the book mentions the fact that new revolutionary governments sought to distance themselves from previous governments),[27] but it was not particularly causal from a social scientific point of view. This may be because de Lacharrière understood, rightly as it turns out in most states, that aside from procedures of ratification, much of the legal national interest stood to be defended and even defined by the executive. Treaties were negotiated by

23 The interest in such variations is, in fact, what has prompted the field of foreign relations law – understood initially as mostly a US paradigm – to increasingly effect a shift to *comparative* foreign relations law. Bradley, *Comparative Foreign Relations Law*.

24 de Lacharrière, *La politique juridique extérieure*, p. 188.

25 de Lacharrière, *La politique juridique extérieure*, pp. 208–12.

26 de Lacharrière, *La politique juridique extérieure*, pp. 208–9.

27 de Lacharrière, *La politique juridique extérieure*, p. 210.

diplomats; the decision to use force was made in the highest reaches of the state; the day-to-day conduct of relations with other states and international organisations was entirely in the hands of foreign ministries. If anything, it was the international environment that shaped the conduct of foreign legal policy, an environment that was significantly more political than legal. This was of course nowhere truer than in Fifth Republic France and de Lacharrière may have been guilty of universalising on the basis of what was in the end a fairly atypical constitutional environment. That evaluation would also stand to be relativised since the publication of *La politique juridique extérieure*, in an era marked by increasing efforts to coordinate foreign policy at the European level, parliamentary scrutiny and civil society monitoring.

Yet foreign legal policy was also not simply the translation of the national interest into an international law policy; rather, it was more broadly a governmental policy *on* international law. An example of such a policy, paradoxically, was that of states that had decided to oppose international law generally, whether newly independent or ideologically radical (the USSR, Iran, etc.).[28] In such a case, foreign legal policy could touch upon even the most fundamental aspects of international law, including state succession or the formation of customary international law. In addition, states might have a sectoral foreign legal policy concerned with particular aspects of international law only. It seems Guy de Lacharrière had in mind mostly primary rules of international law, notably the law of economic relations (including nationalisations), the law of the sea or international humanitarian law. Although states wanting to transform international law might stand out, de Lacharrière insisted that states bent on maintaining the status quo had as much of a foreign legal policy as the revolutionaries – simply that it was less visible.[29]

For Guy de Lacharrière what was striking was that no one had thought of this before and indeed that *La politique juridique extérieure* was not the object of any particular study or, for that matter, a term of art. There were isolated exceptions of course, among which John Foster Dulles[30] and Stanley Hoffmann's notion of legal strategy.[31] But the topic was not taught in universities. De Lacharrière did not designate who was responsible for this lack of interest, but at times it seems quite clear that the culprit was international law itself ('une discipline abstraite'), understood as a system of constraints rather

28 de Lacharrière, *La politique juridique extérieure*, p. 6.

29 de Lacharrière, *La politique juridique extérieure*, p. 6.

30 John F. Dulles, *War or Peace* (New York: Macmillan, 1950).

31 de Lacharrière, *La politique juridique extérieure*, p. 9; also, Stanley Hoffmann, 'International Systems and International Law' (1961) 14 *World Politics* 205–37.

than the product of uncoordinated policies that take it seriously but are not reducible to it ('la discipline concrète').[32] To de Lacharrière, this would be the equivalent of teaching international relations only without teaching foreign policy, where the study of foreign policy has, in fact, preceded the study of international relations as its own discipline. It is almost as if the study of international law had it the wrong way round: studying the system, before it has even begun to understand its agents' rationalities.

In trying to conceptualise the place of *La politique juridique extérieure* in relation to the paradigm of 'foreign relations law', then, the point might be that international law was much more significant to the conduct of foreign policy than domestic law, only not in the way that most international lawyers understood. International law was not important because it bound states, but because it provided executive branches with sophisticated opportunities to maximise the national interest, opportunities that they would be wise to understand and not ignore. Rather than an alternative to foreign relations law, *La politique juridique extérieure* is better understood as a complement to it or, even better, an inherent part of it and provides opportunities for dynamic reconceptualisation. Foreign legal policy includes both an attention to foreign relations law stricto sensu (domestic law) and to international law and, indeed, requires that one keeps an eye on how the gambits one makes on one level may ricochet on the other. Where foreign relations law as it is conventionally understood is at risk of reducing international lawmaking to a domestic *entre soi*, foreign legal policy could be understood as operating more on the interface of the domestic and the international.

II THE ROLE AND FUNCTION OF FOREIGN LEGAL POLICY

For Guy de Lacharrière the strength of having a foreign legal policy was that 'elle tend à substituer un ensemble d'actions préméditées à des comportements qui, autrement, procéderaient de la spontanéité, du réflexe, de l'instinct'.[33] Governments should not adopt positions merely on a reactive and knee-jerk basis; rather, they needed to organise themselves so as to maximise their interest over time by carefully strategising about their legal policy. However, the catch was that for de Lacharrière the national interest included a moral as well as material dimension, both on image grounds but also because, for example, even a bias in favour of the 'règne du droit dans l'ensemble de la société internationale' could turn out to be beneficial for

[32] de Lacharrière, *La politique juridique extérieure*, pp. 7–8.
[33] de Lacharrière, *La politique juridique extérieure*, p. 9.

a particular state from the point of view of its own, narrow national interest.[34] Of course, this portrayed such commitments in quite a different light than how they portrayed themselves: not some sort of Kantian a priori commitment to the law as an incarnation of reason, but a somewhat interested commitment to the law as a form of protection. Still, the grounding of support for an international rule of law in the national interest made it seem much less utopian.

In that light, states typically sought to both inscribe themselves within international law and push it in a direction that was favourable to them. Guy de Lacharrière could not fail to have been impressed as legal adviser to the French foreign ministry by the vast movement of challenge of international law that had arisen in the two previous decades as a result of the rise of the Third World. He was less inclined than some to describe what they did as 'political' and what Western states did as 'legal'. Instead, he expressed a certain understanding for their aspiration to transform international law from an oligarchic and confiscatory system into a more equal and participatory one.[35] Even the Soviet notion of international law as an instrument of class coercion found favour in principle with de Lacharrière (whose own political sensitivities one imagines to have otherwise been quite remote from material determinism), since it had the merit of expressing a clear sense of 'interest' in international law.[36]

For Guy de Lacharrière, the 'national interest' in international law arose not purely domestically, but in relation to the interests of others. The national interest was a 'preference' for the state's own well-being over the well-being of others. Yet, to be taken seriously, it also had to be enunciated in ways that resonated with the system. In the process, they would seek to pass off their national interest as entirely compatible with the common good.[37] This was perhaps a very French way of identifying the national and universal interests as coinciding. But even the most radical turn in international law (such as the one argued for by the Third World in the 1960s) was likely to be justified as consonant with the interest of the international community. The ability to speak the language of the common interest, then, was crucial to states' success in promoting their vision of international law.

At times, though, the incompatibility of one's national interest with the national interest of others would be hard to ignore, in which case one's interest

34 de Lacharrière, *La politique juridique extérieure*, pp. 13–14.
35 de Lacharrière, *La politique juridique extérieure*, p. 14.
36 de Lacharrière, *La politique juridique extérieure*, pp. 14–15.
37 de Lacharrière, *La politique juridique extérieure*, pp. 15–16.

might simply be claimed to be superior. Particularly revolutionary projects in international law had been less prone to underline the consensus, and more ready to highlight the element of struggle involved in international law.[38] Imperialism and aggression are, however, always on the other side. And in the end, de Lacharrière entertained little doubt that his fellow practitioners of international law on behalf of states implicitly acknowledged that each of them was championing a national cause, and that there would not be much use in pretending that this was otherwise. Every state tended to see the proclamations of innocence of others as merely self-serving, perhaps only because they subtly knew their own proclamations to be so.

How should one go about – if at all – reconciling opposite national interests? Guy de Lacharrière was sceptical that a formula existed that could easily be relied on. To be sure, chairs in international conferences would not tire of insisting on the importance of 'equitable and reasonable compromise'.[39] But who was to say what such a compromise entailed? How far should individual negotiators go in taking into account the interests of others? What if the opening position of one party had been plainly unreasonable? And how might each convince herself that the interest represented on the other side was as respectable as her own? And if the notion of compromise is so ambiguous, then how much of an obligation to compromise can there be? As de Lacharrière put it, 'les affirmations d'ouverture au compromis colorent donc de courtoisie l'antagonisme des préférences nationales mais en confirment surtout l'existence sans en réglementer précisément l'issue'.

Instead, the effect of foreign legal policy was to distribute the advantages and disadvantages of international law. States typically wanted to have their cake and eat it and to hold others to standards that they sought to escape for themselves. A government will be intransigent vis-à-vis the need for a manifestation of its own voluntarism, but adopt a more relaxed attitude when it comes to the consent of other states. It will protest other states' use of their veto at the Council, but will be very understanding of its own. States will formulate apparently general rules in terms that happen to narrowly suit their own characteristics. The game is a game of passing off one's interest as the general interest, but it is a 'game' nonetheless, with its rules and constraints and, indeed, its risks and dangers. For example, every rule or interpretation thereof that one puts out there is likely to be used by one's 'enemies'. Here law can be seen to have a somewhat autonomous effect: rules imply corresponding obligations; obligations are understood to be symmetrical, etc. States must

38 de Lacharrière, *La politique juridique extérieure*, pp. 19–20.
39 de Lacharrière, *La politique juridique extérieure*, p. 21.

constantly bear in mind the risk that pushing a certain abstract position in international law will come back to haunt them.

Rather than the problem of incoherence in international law itself (a non-problem as far as de Lacharrière was concerned), what intrigued was the problem of incoherence within the foreign legal policy of states. Because of the evolving national interest foundation of all foreign legal policy, states might over time be called upon to argue the opposite of what they had previously argued. Indeed, they might occasionally simultaneously adopt opposite positions in different sectors of international legal regulation where their interests differed, or even on the same issue. (De Lacharrière cites the example of the lawyer of a Third World country who simultaneously favoured the equidistance and the equitable principles approaches to maritime delimitation 'depending on which part of their coast'.[40]) Would this doom their policy and expose them to the critique of contradicting themselves?

Although politically possible, legal incoherence could sometimes be paid with a high price. Newly decolonised states who strongly defended the principle of self-determination, for example, were sometimes caught at their own game when they had to insist that it was not available to Katanga or Biafra.[41] Nonetheless, Guy de Lacharrière was sceptical that incoherence would be exposed as such, at least if it was managed well. There are, after all, many ways in which states can rationalise evolutions in their policies and distinguish the facts. They can make sure that they are evasive about why they have adopted certain options and avoid too onerous a judicial scrutiny and the threat of estoppel.[42] As to other states, although they may temporarily exploit the sin of incoherence, they are likely to be understanding of a practice that they themselves partake in.

III CONSEQUENCES FOR INTERNATIONAL LAW

But what of international law in this context? Was it anything more than the aggregate of foreign legal policies and did that not point to its fundamental instability or even futility? One of the most striking conclusions of Guy de Lacharrière was that states – as opposed to academic international lawyers – had relatively little interest in international law *in general*. They might certainly have strident opinions on certain points of international law or claim a broad commitment to it (as in the recent Franco-German 'Alliance for

[40] de Lacharrière, *La politique juridique extérieure*, p. 183.
[41] de Lacharrière, *La politique juridique extérieure*, p. 97.
[42] de Lacharrière, *La politique juridique extérieure*, p. 191.

Multilateralism'), but no state would commit itself to some general concept of what international law stood for (or only in the broadest, most rhetorical terms).[43] The challenge for someone working at the intersection of foreign legal policy and international law – as had by then become de Lacharrière's case given his ICJ functions – was to imagine what all this meant for the idea of international law, despite states' best efforts not to do so. The simplest conclusion that de Lacharrière came up with was that the existence of foreign legal policies testified to international law's existence:

> Pour que le droit international n'existe pas, alors que les politiques nationales le prennent si constamment pour objet, il faudrait supposer de la part de l'ensemble des gouvernements un singulier pouvoir d'illusion quant aux réalités de la vie internationale et une extraordinaire capacité de s'acharner sur une pure chimère.[44]

This sort of trope has long been quite familiar in discussions of international law and may not be much of a defence of the existence of international law. International law is detected indirectly through one of its effects, but this does not tell us much about whether it has any causal force or what it means to see it only through the eyes of its actors rather than, say, the perspective of the system. Moreover, international law's content and structure are very uncertain even as Guy de Lacharrière never makes the move, conceptually, to an understanding of international law as a practice. He even ponders the possibility that there are 'many international laws' each existing, perhaps, only as a figment of the imagination of a particular participant.

More interestingly, de Lacharrière saw foreign legal policy as not only a passive response to an already existing international law, but as actively involved in shaping it. De Lacharrière could not imagine states that would merely 'apply' international law in good faith, without seeking to influence it. Such a position would be non sensical precisely because the content of the law stood to be determined by its subjects' deliberations and determinations about it. In international law, 'la distinction entre l'élucidation du droit positif et l'influence sur celui-ci est particulièrement émoussée'.[45] This is particularly true of treaty-making of course – where no actor pretends that they are just implementing international law since per hypothesis there is no law to implement yet – but it is also clear in relation to customary international law where states could be mindful that what they did might participate in the production

43 de Lacharrière, *La politique juridique extérieure*, p. 195.
44 de Lacharrière, *La politique juridique extérieure*, p. 196.
45 de Lacharrière, *La politique juridique extérieure*, p. 198.

of custom. They would, as a result, become *deliberate* customary agents, encouraging or impeding its formation. After all, the very notion of opinio juris makes it clear that what states think about a norm is crucial to it becoming a norm, perhaps one of the most striking recognitions, from the point of view of international law, of a form of at least de facto foreign legal policy.

In the end, Guy de Lacharrière found that foreign legal policies were efficient, precisely because international law was their product:

> [le droit international] n'est donc pas à découvrir comme une science dont on chercherait à élucider les lois, mais à faire ou refaire. Il n'a rien de fatal et n'est donné ni par Dieu ni par la nature. Parfaitement contingent, il ne correspond à aucune nécessité transcendante mais à des convenances appréciées par des gouvernements que l'on peut désigner. C'est une politique qui a réussi, une stratégie qui a triomphé.[46]

In fact, states had a chance to influence not only this or that rule of international law, but also its very function, subject of course to the limits of political reality.

International law might be felt as an imposed law, a constraint, by some states but that was only because it was the willed law of another set of states. This is also the source of one of its weaknesses. If international law was only the manifestation of the preferences of some states generalised to the world, then violating international law should cease to appear so scandalous. Violating international law might just be an instance of 'l'opposition d'une politique à une autre'.[47] In fact, de Lacharrière noted that most states were not particularly shocked by violations of international law most of the time, and only pressed a point if it happened to conflict with their national interest: 'une certaine non-application des traités bénéficie en fait d'une indulgence très générale comme si chacun comprenait fort bien, même s'il ne juge pas opportune de le dire officiellement, qu'il est imprudent de trop blâmer chez l'autre la recherche d'une liberté que l'on entend bien revendiquer pour soi'.[48]

This notion of treaties as basically a useful technique to predetermine the future was fully compatible with frequent violations. This might seem like a fairly cavalier attitude to international law coming from a jurisconsult, but in Guy de Lacharrière's mind it did not make the mechanism of binding treaties useless; it just made it useful in a way different than that commonly understood. States embraced treaties precisely because they saw them as flexible and because they could interpret their obligations in ways that would not

46 de Lacharrière, *La politique juridique extérieure*, p. 199.
47 de Lacharrière, *La politique juridique extérieure*, p. 200.
48 de Lacharrière, *La politique juridique extérieure*, p. 201.

compromise their interest. At the same time, the treaty form remained useful as long as there was a certain 'taux de concordance' between treaty provisions and actual behaviour.[49]

In practice, did international law determine state behaviour? Guy de Lacharrière's concern was not with such systemic questions as such; rather, he was more interested in the foreign legal policy question of how international law might enter into decision-making. At times, it would be a decisive factor (for example when two equally beneficial political outcomes were available), but it could also be one element among others. Even compliance with the law was in the end a strategic element to be taken into account by states strategically. More often than not, international law intervened as a justification of decisions that would most likely have been taken on other grounds, although it might temporarily succeed in making that justification appear as causal.[50] In short, the international lawyer was often called up after the decision; more rarely before the facts.[51] But even the justification of decisions might 'retroact' on the determination of that decision, by at least affecting its modalities of execution.

The strength of de Lacharrière's analysis of international law is threefold. First, he emphasises the role of the national interest in spurring international law. The national interest is not, as in the typical realist account, a limitation on the ability of states to comply with international law; rather, it is, more productively, an orientation that dictates the kind of international law that states want and can over time seek to obtain. In short, the national interest is productive of international law because it makes international law the sort of law that states can, precisely, live with. Second, the book emphasises the relatively decentralised nature of international law-making and its bottom-up character. Contra a view of states as mere conveyor belts for the injunctions of international law, it sees them as implicated in its production, all be it with their own interest in sight. In that respect, de Lacharrière was less interested in 'respect' for or enforcement of international law than in the creation of international law. Third, the book suggests the creativity and a priori undetermined character of international law. States do not know in advance what international law's exact injunction is, at least until they have thrown their forces in the battle and sought to develop it in a direction that suits them. Contra the focus on adjudication, his emphasis on the living actors of

[49] de Lacharrière, *La politique juridique extérieure*, p. 201.
[50] de Lacharrière, *La politique juridique extérieure*, pp. 204–5.
[51] de Lacharrière, *La politique juridique extérieure*, p. 205.

international law – his role as legal adviser far more than his role as ICJ judge – is what makes for compelling reading.

In short, in being a theory of the international legal policy of states, *La politique juridique extérieure* could not avoid also being a theory of international law. Guy de Lacharrière foreshadows, in some ways, Martti Koskenniemi's work on *The Politics of International Law*.[52] Koskenniemi, in focusing on the more systemic level of international law does not start explicitly from what states' foreign legal policy should be. But as himself a former legal advisor to a foreign ministry, he is keen to construct a theory of international law that understands it as the product – inchoate, contradictory and even circular – of various discursive practices by which international lawyers in a position to do so produce its meaning. Where de Lacharrière's standpoint is one of moderate realism, Koskenniemi's is based on a more systematic critique of international law itself: international law can only be this discursive practice not specifically because states treat it that way (although that is also no doubt true), but because states *could* only treat it that way. In that respect, *La politique juridique extérieure* is aligned and converges with that later and in many ways far more sophisticated body of work in at least one fundamental respect: that of the theoretical (and not just practical) primacy of the experience of the practitioner over a more academic and contemplative approach to international law. Where de Lacharrière innovates 'in advance' of *From Apology to Utopia*[53] as it were is in his willingness to share some of the tricks of the trade by which practicing international lawyers, confronted with contradictions of their discipline, act as its sophisticated managers, for the greater good of their state and, quite possibly, of the project of international law itself. There is no place in *La politique juridique extérieure*, however, for envisaging how this exercise might be more fundamentally liberating and open up emancipatory possibilities; only the certainty of how one might go about best serving one's masters.

One common theme that runs through the book is, in that respect, the relative inadequacy of scholarly treatments of international law. Although Guy de Lacharrière was characteristically and typically diplomatic, he knew that his readership would be largely academic and that his views could be seen as a provocation to the French professorate. He noted, for example, that governments and their agents would be surprised to learn that academic international lawyers (such as Georges Scelle) thought of international law

52 Martti Koskenniemi, *The Politics of International Law* (Oxford/Portland: Hart Publishing, 2011).

53 Koskenniemi, *From Apology to Utopia*.

as attributing the state certain competencies, where their daily experience was surely that these competencies were very much the state's in the first place and in no need of recognition from outside. He also noted in relation to treaties, for example, that 'les recherches sur le caractère de dogme fondamental du principe pacta sunt servanda semblent un peu à côté de la question'.[54] However, de Lacharrière also saw the kind of distortions introduced by academic international lawyers as relatively minor as long as they were of marginal importance (and in his view no international legal theory ever created a significant obstacle to good foreign legal policy).[55]

Indeed, Guy de Lacharrière did not let these imperfections of international law stand in the way of an overall positive evaluation of its incidence. He was aware that his book might be dispiriting for scholarly observers who had 'the internal model' of law in mind and who thought that international law should promptly be reformed to be something else than it currently was – presumably something more hierarchical and institutionalised.[56] The truth of the matter, however, is that international law is exactly where states want it to be, and no less useful for it:

> le produit livré par les producteurs satisfait les consommateurs, qui sont identiques aux premiers. Les Etats, responsables du droit international, le sont aussi de ses 'faiblesses', de ses 'carences', car ils ne les sentent pas comme telles et les tiennent au contraire pour des caractéristiques précieuses; globalement, il existe une très vaste et très puissante connivence sur l'actuelle société 'anarchique' et sur la place qu'elle réserve au droit.[57]

International law, moreover, cannot improve itself by itself and, as a technique, is neutral as to its destination. If states wanted more jurisdictional control and compulsory jurisdiction, they would create it. Nothing happened by chance and no 'defect' that was intentionally there was about to be remedied. It would have been hypocritical for anyone with governmental experience to claim otherwise.

It remains that the foreign legal policy of some states is not the foreign legal policy of others, and that, for example, a rougher, more primitive international legal order may be to the benefit of a minority. Of course, nothing prevented weaker states, according to Guy de Lacharrière, from at least constituting a more integrated international legal system between themselves, and to thus announce a more cosmopolitan international law.[58] Moreover, it was

54 de Lacharrière, *La politique juridique extérieure*, p. 201.
55 de Lacharrière, *La politique juridique extérieure*, p. 203.
56 de Lacharrière, *La politique juridique extérieure*, p. 215.
57 de Lacharrière, *La politique juridique extérieure*, p. 217.
58 de Lacharrière, *La politique juridique extérieure*, p. 218.

not impossible that the concurrence of foreign legal policies would end up upgrading international law indirectly as captured in this ambiguous formula: 'les politiques juridiques extérieures manipulent le droit international, mais du même coup elles s'occupent de lui'.[59] Still, de Lacharrière may have ended up broadly satisfied with this vision of international law only because he understood it as having served his own political *commanditaires* well. But there was something almost a bit smug about the way in which he saw states as masters of their foreign legal policy, as if all states could equally afford to choose which foreign legal policy path they could adopt (consider, for example, the situation of France's former African colonies).

As Robert Kolb has pointed out, moreover, 'Il n'est sans doute pas innocent que G. de Lacharrière était le ressortissant d'un Etat se voyant traditionnellement comme Grande Puissance'.[60] His broad-brush, somewhat carefree vision of an instrumental international law worked better for France in the 1970s and 1980s than for others (although arguably he would have been the first to concede this). To this day, the vast majority of states are relatively weak powers who may find more succour in a strong international law than a sense that key powers have mastered the art of crafting the international law that works for them and that they are free to do the same. France itself has evolved somewhat in this direction as its influence declined. Still, it is not actually clear that this need always be the case: witness, for example, the discontent of a number of African states vis-à-vis the International Criminal Court, an institution that is at least relatively strong towards *them*, but on the receiving end of which they are not particularly happy to be and against whom they have waged a quite significant battle. Moreover, a commitment to a 'strong international law' (whatever that may mean), de Lacharrière would no doubt argue, is itself merely a form of foreign legal policy.

IV CONCLUSION

Guy de Lacharrière's *La politique juridique extérieure* was an odd book by French standards and has remained so ever since. It has a cult following of sorts, but is not part of the canon in the teaching of French universities. It is largely unknown beyond the borders of France and does not fit within any simple category. However, it remains a singular and refreshing contribution to the study of foreign policy, one that can be recast in light of an increasingly global interest in foreign relations law. As I have argued in this paper, de

59 de Lacharrière, *La politique juridique extérieure*, p. 218.

60 Kolb, *Réflexions sur les politiques juridiques extérieures*, p. 9.

Lacharrière was not interested in the conventional sense of that paradigm in that he largely ignored the constraints of domestic law on foreign policy. Partly, one is tempted to say, this is because he could. Under the Fifth Republic, the conduct of foreign policy is a singularly presidential prerogative, and the holders of the post (de Lacharrière served under de Gaulle, Pompidou and Giscard-d'Estaing) intended it to remain that way. A legal adviser in the foreign ministry would entertain few doubts about his position within a larger hierarchy of decision-making that foregrounded a certain *fait du prince*.

In a more than 200 page book, Guy de Lacharrière only devotes about 5 to the issue of domestic constraints.[61] To the extent that *La politique juridique extérieure* can be construed as a book on foreign relations law, then, it is one that is largely dismissive of the role of domestic law, emphasising instead domestic politics of the highest order and an almost neo-realist insistence on the place of each state within the international system with deep conservative overtones. This does not mean of course that *La politique juridique extérieure* was, instead, a matter of helping and even coaxing the state to respect its international law commitments. De Lacharrière was too wedded to a model of medium-power politics to think that his role as legal adviser was to 'represent' international law to his government. He would have scoffed at the suggestion that he was primarily an agent of international law within a national setting.

Interestingly, however, even in his role as a legal apologist for the national interest of France, he thought quite highly of international law as something that he understood to transcend that national interest. International law might well be the sum of successful foreign legal policies, but it was at least that. Moreover, one did not, at least not always, win in foreign legal policy through sheer brute force. One needed to persuade, rally, entrench certain forms of legal reasoning, in the hope that they would catch on and would, in turn, become international law. This is an exercise that conventional international lawyers would probably recognise as coming quite close to their lived experience of the making of international law.

Foreign legal relations, then, were certainly not determined by domestic law and was certainly more than the implementation of international law. It involved an intermediary element of legal statecraft, one in which states deliberately thought about their use of international law over time, calculated what they could get away with, were often brazen about adopting contradictory positions, but much less inclined to see this as contradictory or at least problematic than a pious *doctrine* speaking from outside the cenacle of power. This might not seem much of a defence of international law and indeed it is

[61] Notably, de Lacharrière, *La politique juridique extérieure*, pp. 206–10.

one that is very much at odds with how many international lawyers – most of them academics – see its promise. Yet this is no doubt on some level intended and de Lacharrière was certainly out, on some level, for a degree of provocation.

How has the book aged, and what can it tell us today? Guy de Lacharrière's treatment is very much based on his own experience as legal adviser. Although this surely gave him a first-row seat to observe the making of international law, it is also, in its own way, a limited vision for at least three reasons. First, just as de Lacharrière faults scholars of international law for focusing too much on judges, he is guilty of the symmetrical mistake, that of not focusing on judges at all. The same is true of de Lacharrière's discreet dismissal of scholars of international law; as Alain Pellet once noted, it is precisely his presentation of foreign relations as largely determined by idiosyncratic national interest calculations that militates for a strong role for *la doctrine*.[62] In fact, de Lacharrière's strong emphasis on political voluntarism could only go so far from a theoretical point of view: it helped explain the formation of international law, quite possibly its implementation, but Michel Virally specifically put the former legal adviser to task for failing to explain the very authority and legitimising function of international law, which could not themselves be derived from state will.[63]

Second, it is true that legal advisors tend to operate in a relative shadow and that his book was thus an irreplaceable testimony on a considerably important but unfairly neglected facet of international lawmaking. But international law is not exclusively a creation of states, and to the extent that it is it is hardly entirely determined by legal advisors. Indeed, in upgrading international lawmaking to a matter of policy, Guy de Lacharrière is always at risk of subtly overestimating the importance of lawyers' calculations, at the expense of general policy development. Indeed, from the point of view of the mainstream of foreign relations law, de Lacharrière's treatment is almost hubristic in its focus on the executive and the foreign ministry. It entirely neglects the role of the legislative and judicial branches in ways that are problematic now in France as in most countries. It also is oblivious to the role that civil society actors have increasingly played. *La politique juridique extérieure* would gain from being reread in light of these developments and understood as henceforth more embedded in domestic practices – precisely the gap that foreign relations law has identified. At any rate, there are greater dangers for the

62 Pellet, 'Le Sage, le Prince et le Savant', 407 at 410.
63 Virally, 'Réflexions sur la politique juridique des Etats'.

purposes of human rights or the rule of law, than states not maximising their national interest because of incoherences in their legal discourses.

Third, Guy de Lacharrière also wrote at a time of great change (decolonisation, the law of the sea) but in a context where the Cold War had frozen many options for international law. *La politique juridique extérieure* entirely ignores some areas such as international environmental law, international human rights law and international trade law, not to mention the law of European integration which has arguably such an impact on foreign relations law.[64] It is as if the conversations that animate these branches of international law did not exist for the once legal adviser to the French foreign ministry. This is in itself a striking contrast to some of his successors who have made a name for themselves as pleader before the European Court of Human Rights (Ronny Abraham) or judge at the International Criminal Court (Perrin de Brichambaud). Although a recent treatment by Robert Kolb takes de Lacharrière's book as his starting point, Kolb is more sanguine about the autonomous existence of international law and its ability, without denying the incidence of foreign legal policy, to retroact on its creators and actors. Kolb goes as far as to suggest that, next to an interest-driven foreign legal policy, is a more objective variant that is geared towards the creation of stable relations and devoted to some of the ideals of an international community.[65]

It is true that the two can at times seem hard to distinguish, as when France famously opposed the war in Iraq, in ways that could be understood to exalt international law and its prudential restraints or, more simply, to coincide with the country's geopolitical interest of the moment. Champions of international law often happen to be champions of their own interest. Certainly, legal advisers in both the UK and the US have been in the spotlight for their willingness to provide excessively supple advice in relation to torture[66] or the use of force,[67] in ways that show the limits of a purely instrumental approach to international law especially when, as is increasingly the case, civil society is watching. Indeed, one of the facets of foreign legal policy-making that has changed is the willingness of various groups and individuals to challenge it 'from below'. The days in which foreign policy was a purely regal function insulated from common politics

64 See the chapter by Aloupi, 'Limitations of Sovereignty', Section IV.
65 Kolb, *Réflexions sur les politiques juridiques extérieures*, p. 10.
66 Philippe Sands, *Torture Team: Rumsfeld's Memo and the Betrayal of American Values* (New York: Palgrave Macmillan, 2008).
67 Frédéric Mégret, '"War"? Legal Semantics and the Move to Violence' (2002) 13 *EJIL* 361–99.

and activism seem to be long gone. French foreign policy appears more constrained by its legal environment today and less administratively elitist than it may have appeared to de Lacharrière forty years ago. If not quite the constraint of foreign relations law or the command of international law, then, that is a further significant domestic constraint on foreign policy-making.

7

Judicial Review, Foreign Relations and Global Administrative Law

The Administrative Function of Courts in Foreign Relations

Angelo Jr. Golia

I INTRODUCTION: ADMINISTRATIVIZATION OF JURISDICTION AND JURIDIFICATION OF FOREIGN RELATIONS

On 19 March 2019 the High Administrative Court (OVG) of North Rhine-Westphalia (Münster) issued a decision on the legality of the use of the Ramstein military air base[1] which had been made available by Germany to the US for drone strikes in Yemen[2]. Reversing the holding of the lower court, the OVG found that the measures taken by the German government did not suffice to fulfil its positive obligations arising from the right to life. Touching on crucial diplomatic relations, this decision is remarkable for at least two reasons. First, before starting the lawsuit before German courts, the plaintiffs had already sued the US government before American federal courts, but on appeal the DC District court decided that the alleged extrajudicial killings by drone strikes were a non-justiciable political question. Second, the OVG did not only find a violation of applicable constitutional and international law, but ordered also the German government to put into place measures to ensure the

[1] *Bin Ali Jaber* v. *Germany*, Judgment, 19 March 2019, 4 A 1361/15. See Helmut Philipp Aust, 'US-Drohneneinsätze und die grundrechtliche Schutzpflicht für das Recht auf Leben: "German exceptionalism"?' (2020) 75 *Juristenzeitung* 303; Leander Beinlich, 'Germany and its Involvement in the US Drone Programme before German Administrative Courts', EJIL: Talk!, April 8, 2019, www.ejiltalk.org/germany-and-its-involvement-in-the-us-drone-programme-before-german-administrative-courts/, accessed September 30, 2020. The decision was quashed by the German Federal Administrative Court (BVerwG, *Bin Ali Jaber* v. *Germany*, Judgment, 25 November 2020, 6 C 7.19) in November 2020, as the present piece was already at the proof-editing stage. However, as pointed out by Helmut Aust and Thomas Kleinlein in the introduction to this volume, it remains the case that for both courts the question of whether international law permits armed drone missions in Yemen was not a political question, but rather a legal question, to be assessed by the judiciary.

[2] The base was used for the relay of flight control data necessary to the drone strikes.

legality of the use of the Ramstein base. Therefore, the OVG did not only review – unlike its US counterpart – the foreign policy of its own government, but also required it to manage/administer it in a different manner. This also means that, following the judgment, the German government was called to interact with the US in a way different from that originally planned, with a potential adverse impact on their otherwise (mostly) friendly relationship.

This case is exemplary of a general trend in contemporary western tradition systems towards the weakening of two fundamental dichotomies in their political-legal structures: that between domestic and foreign affairs; and that between judicial and executive/administrative power. Indeed, at least since the principle of separation of powers emerged as a distinctive feature of modern constitutionalism, western legal tradition has been built on the assumption that the public authorities performing executive/administrative functions and those performing judicial functions should be kept structurally distinct.[3] At the same time, liberal constitutions of the eighteenth and nineteenth centuries were based on a clear divide between internal and external sovereignty,[4] dealing with foreign relations (FRs) only in a limited and ostensibly value-neutral way. That is why they generally did not impose substantive obligations to the political branches of government in the management of FRs. Interestingly, in Locke's construction of the separation of powers – which did not clearly distinguish between executive and judicial power – the federative power,[5] what today is usually indicated as foreign relations power (FRP), was qualitatively different from the legislative and the executive: insofar as it could not be subject to prior legal norms, a judicial review over the exercise of federative power was conceptually inconceivable.[6] More generally, the original theories of the rule of law and liberal constitutional models did not focus

3 This stark separation did not belong to either Locke's nor Montesquieu's theories: see Jenny S. Martinez, 'Horizontal Structuring', in Michel Rosenfeld and Andras Sajó (eds.), *Oxford Handbook of Comparative Constitutional Law* (Oxford: Oxford University Press, 2012), pp. 548–49; Christoph Möllers, *The Three Branches* (Oxford: Oxford University Press, 2013), pp. 16 ff.

4 The general assumption that Hobbes was actually the originator of the dichotomy between internal and external sovereignty is contested by Theodore Christov, 'Hobbes's Janus-Faced Sovereign', in David Dyzenhaus, Jacco Bomhoff and Thomas Poole (eds.), *The Double-Facing Constitution* (Cambridge: Cambridge University Press, 2019), pp. 94–120.

5 'The power of war and peace, leagues and alliances, and all the transactions with all persons and communities without the commonwealth.'

6 See John Locke, *Two Treatises of Government* (New Haven and London: Yale University Press, 2003), § 147, p. 165. On the qualitative difference of the federative power see generally Thomas Poole, 'The Idea of the Federative', in David Dyzenhaus, Jacco Bomhoff and Thomas Poole (eds.), *The Double-Facing Constitution* (Cambridge: Cambridge University Press, 2019), pp. 54–93.

on the relationship between a single State and other States, but almost exclusively on the internal sovereignty.[7] As a consequence, they generally framed FRs as a sort of free zone where the rule of law did not apply, characterized by judicial deference and self-restraint, and therefore by a certain 'exceptionalism'.[8]

Both normative and factual developments of the twentieth century affected the divide between domestic and foreign affairs. From a normative perspective, post-war constitutions have established more institutional constraints on FRP.[9] At the same time, contemporary constitutionalism and international human rights and humanitarian law gave more relevance of the legal position of the individual, strengthening material constraints legal systems – especially in western tradition jurisdictions –[10] and turning some cosmopolitan values into binding legal principles, that is, result-oriented norms to be potentially applied as standards of review also in the field of FRs.[11] This might explain both the rise of foreign relations law (FRL) as a distinct field of legal studies and its persistently disputed

7 See Thomas Poole, 'The Constitution and Foreign Affairs' (2016) 69 *Current Legal Problems* 143 at 148 ff. (referring to a 'unilateral' constitutional model); Umberto Allegretti, 'Stato di diritto e divisione dei poteri nell'era dei conflitti asimmetrici' (2005) 11 *Dir pubb* 93 at 99–101.

8 The 'foreign affairs exceptionalism' implied in Locke's notion of federative power had a deep intellectual influence on American constitutionalism, especially through the work of William Blackstone, *Commentaries*, vol. I (Chicago: University of Chicago Press, 1979), p. 160 at 243. Classic formulations of such exceptionalism may be found in the US Supreme Court decisions *Missouri* v. *Holland*, 252 US 416 (1929); and *United States* v. *Curtiss-Wright Export Corp*, 299 US 304 (1936). See generally David Dyzenhaus, 'Hobbes on the International Rule of Law' (2014) 28 *Ethics & International Affairs* 53; Thomas M. Franck, *Political Questions/Judicial Answers. Does the Rule of Law Apply to Foreign Affairs?* (Princeton: Princeton University Press, 1992), pp. 10–30 (for the influence of British doctrine of royal prerogative on the practice of judicial abdication in the US); J. Richard Broughton, 'Judicializing Federative Power' (2006) 11 *Texas Review of Law & Politics* 283; Stephen Breyer, *The Court and the World. American Law and the New Global Realities* (New York: Vintage, 2015), pp. 15 ff.

9 See Luzius Wildhaber, *Treaty-Making Power and Constitution. An International and Comparative Study* (Basel-Stuttgart: Helbing & Lichtenhahn, 1971); Jenny S. Martinez, 'The Constitutional Allocation of Executive and Legislative Power Over Foreign Affairs: A Survey', in Curtis A. Bradley (ed.), *Oxford Handbook of Comparative Foreign Relations Law* (Oxford: Oxford University Press, 2019), pp. 97–114.

10 On the internationalization/humanization of public law see Thomas Buergenthal, 'Modern Constitutions and Human Rights Treaties' (1998) 36 *Columbia Journal of Transnational Law* 211; Chang Wen-Chen and Yeh Jiunn-Rong, 'Internationalization of Constitutional Law', in Michel Rosenfeld and Andras Sajó (eds.), *Oxford Handbook of Comparative Constitutional Law* (Oxford: Oxford University Press, 2012), pp. 1165–84; Karen Knop, 'The Spectre of Comity', in David Dyzenhaus, Jacco Bomhoff and Thomas Poole (eds.), *The Double-Facing Constitution* (Cambridge: Cambridge University Press, 2019), pp. 177–210.

11 See generally Franck, *Political Questions/Judicial Answers*, pp. 61 ff.; Deborah N. Pearlstein, 'After Deference: Formalizing the Judicial Power for Foreign Relations Law' (2011) 159 *University of Pennsylvania Law Review* 783; Ganesh Sitaraman and Ingrid Wuerth, 'The

disciplinary location.[12] Indeed, constitutional and international law together changed the normative relationship between law and FRs,[13] traditionally based on a strict interpretation of the separation of powers and on axiological neutrality.[14] From a more factual perspective, globalization processes established deep and unprecedented interdependencies among individuals, polities and systems at global level,[15] piercing national-political boundaries and therefore weakening the factual bases underpinning the domestic/foreign dichotomy.

Turning to the divide between judicial and executive/administrative power, today even Kelsen would be surprised to see how the prediction he made in the early twentieth century while discussing the theoretical foundations of constitutional adjudication – the end of the 'opposition' between judicial and executive power –[16] has come close to reality. Following the rise of principled (i.e. result-oriented)[17] norms and relative indeterminacy in contemporary

Normalization of Foreign Relations Law' (2015) 128 *Harvard Law Review* 1897; Poole, 'The Constitution and Foreign Affairs'.

12 For the debate concerning the interaction between public international law and FRL see the chapter by Curtis A. Bradley, 'Final Reflections', in this volume; Curtis A. Bradley, 'What Is Foreign Relations Law?', in Curtis A. Bradley (ed.), *Oxford Handbook of Comparative Foreign Relations Law* (Oxford: Oxford University Press, 2019), pp. 8–13; and Helmut Philipp Aust and Thomas Kleinlein, 'Introduction', this volume, arguing that the 'hybridity' between domestic (public) law and public international law is an effect rather than a characteristic of FRL.

13 See Poole, 'The Constitution and Foreign Affairs', 148 ff. (referring to a 'reflexive' or 'mutually constitutive' constitutional model). More generally see Jean-Bernard Auby, *Globalisation, Law and the State* (Oxford: Hart, 2017), pp. 80 ff.

14 This may also be read as the latest stage of a more general process, started with modernity, of formalization of politics by law. See Chris Thornhill, *A Sociology of Constitutions: Constitutions and State Legitimacy in Historical-Sociological Perspective* (Cambridge: Cambridge University Press, 2011); Torbjörn Vallinder, 'The Judicialization of Politics. A World-Wide Phenomenon: Introduction' (1994) 15 *IPSR* 91; Ran Hirschl, 'The Judicialization of Mega-Politics and the Rise of Political Courts' (2008) 11 *Annual Review of Political Science* 93.

15 See famously Anthony Giddens, *The Consequences of Modernity* (Cambridge: Polity, 1990), pp. 64 ff.

16 See Hans Kelsen, 'La garantie juridictionnelle de la constitution' (1928) 45 *Revue du droit public et de la science politique en France et à l'étranger* 197 at 212–14. At the time Kelsen wrote, public law theory was still influenced by assumptions typical of the nineteenth century administrative state, framing executives as possessing autonomous legitimation: in that context, the distinction between jurisdictional and executive/administrative functions was traditionally linked to the fact that only the exercise of the former was based on legal rules. Rejecting this criterion, Kelsen argued that the relationship of administrative/executive bodies towards law did not qualitatively differ from that of judicial bodies, especially when it comes to the norms of 'higher level'. Rather, the only real distinction lied in the different modes of organization of tribunals and executive bodies, difference that he predicted would come to an end.

17 See Robert Alexy, *A Theory of Constitutional Rights* (Oxford: Oxford University Press, 2002), pp. 47–49, and his conception of principles as result-oriented norms, i.e. norms containing 'optimisation commands'.

legal systems,[18] and the spread of judicial review mechanisms, judicial practice has progressively internalized consequentialist and teleological approaches.[19] Next to normative inputs, courts are more and more conditioned by the (expected) output of their decisions, and accommodate them to future-oriented purposes set by law in specific regulatory fields, as general or indeterminate as they may appear. Often based on balancing/proportionality techniques, domestic and international courts turn (their perception of) social expectations and policy goals, positivized in legislative, constitutional or international norms, into decisions aimed at solving and/or managing concrete issues on an ongoing basis, thus performing de facto executive/administrative functions. Therefore, rather than simple external reviewers, they increasingly act as internal participants in administrative functions. In the context of global governance, such 'administrativization' of the judicial function places courts in the broader set of global regulators,[20] thus contributing to the development and implementation of rules of coexistence, collision and cooperation among involved systems.[21]

This chapter investigates the connection between the expanding 'administrative' functions of courts and the ongoing normalization (i.e. juridification/judicialization) of FRs.[22] To that purpose, it resorts to the analytical tools of the 'global administrative law' (GAL) approach, and argues that there is a factual trend towards what may be seen as a 'global administrative law of foreign relations', that is, a transnational legal language erratically but increasingly

[18] Gunther Teubner, '"And God Laughed . . ." Indeterminacy, Self-Reference and Paradox in Law' (2011) 12 *German Law Journal* 376; Inger Johanne Sand, 'Changing Forms of Governance and the Role of Law', ARENA WP No. 00/14, www.sv.uio.no/arena/english/research/publications/arena-working-papers/1994–2000/2000/wp00_14.htm, accessed September 30, 2020.

[19] See Neil MacCormick, 'Argumentation and Interpretation in Law' (1993) 6 *Ratio Juris* 16; Gunther Teubner, 'Altera Pars Audiatur: Law in the Collision of Discourses', in Richard Rawlings (ed.), *Law, Society and Economy* (Oxford: Oxford University Press, 1997), p. 149 at 167; Klaus Mathis, 'Consequentialism in Law', in Klaus Mathis (ed.), *Efficiency, Sustainability, and Justice to Future Generations* (Berlin: Springer, 2012), pp. 3–29.

[20] See Sabino Cassese, *The Global Polity. Global Dimensions of Democracy and the Rule of Law* (Sevilla: Global Law Press, 2012); Elisa D'Alterio, 'Judicial Regulation in the Global Space', in Sabino Cassese, *Research Handbook on Global Administrative Law* (Cheltenahm: Elgar, 2016), pp. 314 ff. On the link between proportionality-based reasoning and 'administratization' of constitutional law and constitutional adjudication see Moshe Cohen-Eliya and Iddo Porat, 'Proportionality and the Culture of Justification' (2011) 59 *American Journal of Comparative Law* 463, pp. 487 ff.

[21] See Anne-Marie Slaughter, *A New World Order* (Princeton: Princeton University Press, 2004), pp. 51–61.

[22] See Sitaraman and Wuerth, 'The Normalization of Foreign Relations Law'; Carlos M. Vasquez, 'The Abiding Exceptionalism of Foreign Relations Doctrine' (2015) 128 *Harvard Law Review Forum* 305.

developed by courts in different jurisdictions, aimed at concretely managing issues falling within the scope of FRs. More specifically, the GAL approach is used, firstly, to conceptualize the function performed by courts applying FRL in the context of the increased interdependence driven by the processes of globalization and global governance. This means that, as courts increasingly participate in the 'administration' of FRs, an administrative conception can be added to and, to a certain extent, overlaps with other conceptions[23] of FRL. From this perspective, the trend towards the judicial 'administration' of FRs could be seen as the ultimate form of the – admittedly precarious and reversible – normalization of FRL. Secondly, the GAL approach is here used to categorize judicial rulings, according to the type of norms they implement or develop in the context of FRL. Here, it is possible to conceptually distinguish between norms and/or standards implemented or developed in relation to the FRs conduct of the political branches of the jurisdiction to which a given court belongs ('review norms'); and norms and/or standards implemented or developed to manage interactions with other jurisdictions or legal systems affecting FRs ('interaction norms').

Section II briefly recalls the main features of FRL (subsection II.A) and GAL (subsection II.B), mapping the analytical bases of the chapter, their conceptual assumptions, and the main challenges they face. Based on an a-systematic survey, Section III outlines a tentative taxonomy of the forms that the judicial practice takes in developing an embryonic 'global administrative law of foreign relations.' In particular, subsection III.A focuses on the 'review norms', while subsection III.B on the 'interaction norms'. Section IV concludes, summarizing the core claims and highlighting, from a more normative perspective, the potential risks of the administrativization of FRs, which may also cast doubts on the general value of GAL as a normative endeavor.

II BRINGING TOGETHER FRL AND GAL

A *The Struggles of FRL with its Scope, Sources and Functions*

FRL intersects two axes of constitutional legal theory: the relationship between domestic law and international/transnational legal systems;[24] and

[23] See Campbell McLachlan, 'Five Conceptions of the Functions of Foreign Relations Law', in Curtis A. Bradley (ed.), *Oxford Handbook of Comparative Foreign Relations Law* (Oxford: Oxford University Press, 2019), pp. 21 ff.

[24] See Anne Peters, 'Foreign Relations Law and Global Constitutionalism' (2017) 111 *AJIL Unbound* 331.

that between judicial and political branches in legal systems characterized by the constitutionalization of value choices.[25] However, although it is by now relatively well-established as a field of studies (at least in common law jurisdictions), FRL still struggles with some foundational issues,[26] concerning its scope, sources and functions.

Concerning its scope, at least two conceptions of FRL may be individuated. The first one, based on a strict dichotomy domestic/foreign, limits FRL to three macro-areas: treaty-making, -development and -termination; international and supranational integration; and use of military force.[27] A broader conception, based on a functional understanding of FRL, focuses on all the legal norms affecting the relations of a nation with the rest of the world. Under this broader conception, FRL would for example include the conflict of laws of each nation,[28] and in some cases even fields normally regarded as purely internal. A US Supreme Court decision concerning the interpretation of federal copyright law[29] may matter to manufacturers and consumers both in the US and throughout the world, with economic impacts worth billions, and potentially generating significant diplomatic frictions.[30] Likewise, a judgment of the German Federal Constitutional Court (BVerfG), holding that a specific statutory design for the surveillance powers of intelligence agencies violate the Basic Law, and forbidding the transfer of data thus obtained to other intelligence services,[31] may undermine the diplomatic position of the German government. Similarly, constitutional provisions and the related judicial rulings concerning public ownership of natural resources and property rights of corporations constitute examples of norms functionally falling withing FRL – especially from a 'peripheral perspective'.[32] In all these cases constitutional courts inevitably decide *also* on FRs issues, as in the age of globalization FRs are virtually everywhere. Therefore, the struggles of FRL

[25] See in recent scholarship Möllers, *The Three Branches*.

[26] See McLachlan, 'Five Conceptions of the Functions of Foreign Relations Law', p. 20.

[27] See e.g. Thomas Giegerich, 'Foreign Relations Law', in Rüdiger Wolfrum (ed.), *Max Planck Encyclopedia of Public International Law*, vol. IV (Oxford: Oxford University Press, 2011), p. 178 at 183.

[28] See William S. Dodge, 'International Comity in Comparative Perspective', in Curtis A. Bradley (ed.), *Oxford Handbook of Comparative Foreign Relations Law* (Oxford: Oxford University Press, 2019), pp. 701 ff.; and *Restatement of the Law Fourth, The Foreign Relations Law of the United States* (Philadelphia: ALI, 2018), pp. 148 ff and 303 ff.

[29] See *Kirtsaeng* v. *John Wiley & Sons, Inc.*, 568 US 519 (2013).

[30] See Breyer, *The Court and the World*, pp. 124–31.

[31] See BVerfG, 19 May 2020, 1 BvR 2835/17 – BND.

[32] See Michael Riegner, 'Comparative Foreign Relations Law between Center and Periphery', in this volume.

scholarship with the definition of its own analytical scope derive also from the difficulty to be coextensive with its factual scope.[33]

Regarding its sources, FRL has been traditionally conceived as a branch of domestic systems,[34] namely of their constitutional and administrative law.[35] However, following the normative developments occurred during the twentieth century, FRL has progressively come to include international law,[36] to the extent this latter applies to a specific domestic jurisdiction, or imposes on States a certain conduct in the management of their FRs, or directly regulates the conduct of individuals. Importantly, the influence of international law sources contributes to making FRL at least in part 'transnational', insofar as courts in different jurisdictions, which apply the same rules of international law or decide on similar issues concerning FRs, increasingly develop comparable and/or equivalent – albeit not identical – standards of adjudication,[37] also through reciprocal influence and cross-fertilization.[38]

This last aspect is linked to the functions attributed to FRL. Campbell McLachlan has listed five conceptions of the functions performed by FRL, namely the exclusionary, the internationalist, the constitutional, the diplomatic and the allocative.[39] While not necessarily mutually exclusive, these conceptions have different ideological roots, and potentially result in conflicting implementations by institutional actors, especially courts. Put differently: in applying FRL or in adjudicating issues related to FRs, judicial bodies may develop different understandings of their own role and the results to pursue, also depending on the underlying function attributed to FRL. However, none of these conceptions as such captures the idea that FRL has come to provide

33 See Anne Peters, 'Military Operations Abroad under the German Basic Law', in Curtis A. Bradley (ed.), *Oxford Handbook of Comparative Foreign Relations Law* (Oxford: Oxford University Press, 2019), p. 809.

34 See Giegerich, 'Foreign Relations Law', p. 178.

35 See Jean Galbraith, 'From Treaties to International Commitments: The Changing Landscape of Foreign Relations Law' (2017) 64 *University of Chicago Law Review* 167, at 1684–97.

36 On the 'double-facing' nature of FRL see McLachlan, 'Five Conceptions of the Functions of Foreign Relations Law', p. 2; and David Dyzenhaus, 'The Janus-Faced Constitution', in David Dyzenhaus, Jacco Bomhoff and Thomas Poole (eds.), *The Double-Facing Constitution* (Cambridge: Cambridge University Press, 2019), pp. 17–53.

37 See Bradley, 'Final Reflections', in this volume and, in deeper detail, Anthea Roberts et al. (eds.), *Comparative International Law* (Oxford: Oxford University Press, 2018).

38 See generally Gregory Shaffer and Carlos Coye, 'From International Law to Jessup's Transnational Law, From Transnational Law to Transnational Legal Orders', *UC Irvine School of Law Research Paper* No. 2017-02.

39 See again McLachlan, 'Five Conceptions of the Functions of Foreign Relations Law'.

concrete legal standards – potentially justiciable by courts – to 'manage' FRs on an ongoing basis.

In the light of such struggles, it seems that no single approach accounts in a comprehensive manner for some key elements of FRL, namely the mismatch between its analytical and factual scope; its 'transnationality'; its potentially 'administrative' function; and, finally, the active – be it unifying or fragmenting – role played by judicial bodies in that context.

B GAL *As an Analytical Approach to* FRL

Giving an accurate idea of GAL in few words is not easy. It has emerged together with other approaches in the galaxy of global law and postnational constitutionalism,[40] and it does not indicate a full-fledged legal system in a traditional sense.[41] Rather, it can be broken down into two main parts.

Firstly, GAL stands as an analytical/descriptive tool, referring to a *factual*[42] trend whereby a set of procedural and substantive norms – inter alia review, transparency, reason-giving, participation, *audiatur altera pars*, legal accountability and liability of administrative authority – has been increasingly developed and implemented, either formally or informally, by 'global administrative bodies' (GABs) all around the world and at different governance levels, including the domestic one. GAL focuses on the 'mechanisms, principles, practices, and supporting social understandings that promote or otherwise affect the accountability of global administrative bodies'.[43] It highlights that, when confronted with functionally differentiated issues of global concern (corruption, competition, banking supervision, terrorism, food safety, etc.), GABs of different jurisdictions and governance levels increasingly interact, often working as (either formal or informal) transnational networks. From this standpoint, GAL claims that 'much of the global governance can be understood in administrative terms, as global administration that operates in a "global administrative space" … in which the strict dichotomy between domestic and international has largely broken

40 Although it is not possible to discuss its conceptual genealogy here, see Benedict Kingsbury, Nico Krisch, and Richard B. Stewart, 'The Emergence of Global Administrative Law' (2005) 68 *Law and Contemporary Problems* 15; Sabino Cassese, 'Administrative Law Without the State? The Challenge of Global Regulation' (2005) 37 *NYU Journal of International Law and Politics* 663; Cassese, *Research Handbook*.

41 See however Benedict Kingsbury, 'The Concept of "Law" in Global Administrative Law' (2009) 20 *EJIL* 23.

42 See Lorenzo Casini, 'Global Administrative Law Scholarship', in Sabino Cassese, *Research Handbook on Global Administrative Law* (Cheltenham: Elgar, 2016), p. 554.

43 Kingsbury, Krisch, and Stewart, 'The Emergence of Global Administrative Law', 17.

down'.[44] Therefore, the label 'GAL' refers to an emerging form of transnational law, whose norms are implemented and developed by sub- and non-state administrative institutions, often with little or no involvement of political branches of governments.

Secondly, GAL embodies the normative stance of a scholarly movement towards such practices. In other words, the GAL approach does not only outline the factual implementation of a certain set of norms by administrative bodies, but also supports their spread and strengthening. It also argues that these norms and networked modes of action help to order the structures of global governance and achieve results in fields of common concern, by also strengthening their legitimacy and cooperation, and decreasing conflicts and inconsistencies among involved actors/systems. From this perspective, GABs would be also incentivized to act as transnational networks. Overall, the GAL approach claims to retains a soft normative value, aiming to bridge a relatively little gap between an 'Is' and an 'Ought' at global level, by expanding guarantees in administrative action, in fields where they have not been established yet. By these means, the GAL approach is – or claims to be – less ambitious than other 'constitutionalist' approaches to global law,[45] as it does not engage directly with the issue of unitary axiological framework(s) and global democracy.

The GAL approach deals with courts in two different yet linked ways.[46] First, they are regarded as reviewing bodies, checking the respect by GABs of the norms aimed at keeping them accountable and increasing their legitimacy. Therefore, courts implement and develop review norms on administrative action. Secondly, they are regarded as GABs themselves, especially when exercising substituting functions or working as transnational networks. In this latter case, the standards developed or implemented by courts often take the form of 'interaction norms' (margin-of-appreciation; *Solange*-like doctrines; subsidiarity; deference/comity doctrines), and are generated by courts to manage actual or virtual clashes among the systems where they operate respectively.[47] One of the merits of GAL as an analytical tool has been to

44 Nico Krisch and Benedict Kingsbury, 'Introduction: Global Governance and Global Administrative Law in the International Legal Order' (2006) 17 *EJIL* 1.

45 See Nico Krisch, 'Global Administrative Law and the Constitutional Ambition', in Petra Dobner and Martin Loughlin (eds.), *The Twilight of Constitutionalism?* (Oxford: Oxford University Press, 2010), pp. 245–66.

46 For more detailed accounts see D'Alterio, 'Judicial Regulation in the Global Space', pp. 314 ff; and Eyal Benvenisti and George W. Downs, *Between Fragmentation and Democracy. The Role of National and International Courts* (Cambridge: Cambridge University Press, 2017).

47 See Sabino Cassese, *I tribunali di Babele. I giudici alla ricerca di un nuovo ordine globale* (Rome: Donzelli, 2009).

highlight that, whether they act as reviewers of the action of GABs or as GABs themselves, courts take part of the regulation/administration of global governance.[48] Another analytical contribution of GAL is to read the interactions and reciprocal influences among courts as networks. Indeed, judicial networks, just like other information, harmonization and enforcement networks,[49] may promote convergence, compliance and cooperation among involved systems, and they are called upon to manage clashes emerging from globalization processes.[50]

In the light of these considerations, the GAL approach may provide a useful – although not exclusive – analytical/descriptive framework, at the same time accounting for the elusive scope of FRL, its 'transnationality', its 'administrative' function, and the role played by courts in managing coordination and/or fragmentation among systems. In other words, the GAL approach constitutes a viable tool to frame and understand two major tensions underlying FRL: that between its still somehow persistent 'exceptionalism' and ongoing/erratic process of normalization, where the aspiration to manage even FRs according to material legal standards meets the obstacles of the *Realpolitik*; and that between its domestic and international dimensions, where the aspiration to provide global legal standards meets the obstacles of different sources of legitimation and modes of lawmaking. The GAL approach crosscuts these tensions and may potentially offer a useful conceptual framework. Building on this core insight, the next section brings the argument further and, based on the GAL framework, outlines a tentative taxonomy of the decisions of courts 'administering' FRs.

III A (TENTATIVE) TAXONOMY OF A 'GLOBAL ADMINISTRATIVE LAW OF FRS'

Drawing a clear-cut taxonomy of the decisions taken by domestic courts in FRs matters is problematic, considering the institutional and procedural variances among different systems of judicial review. However, based on the GAL

48 See Cassese, *I tribunali di Babele*; Elisa D'Alterio, 'From Judicial Comity to Legal Comity: A Judicial Solution to Global Disorder?' (2011) 9 *ICON* 394; D'Alterio, 'Judicial Regulation in the Global Space', explicitly referring to courts as 'GAL regulators'.

49 For these categorizations see again Slaughter, *A New World Order*, pp. 51–61.

50 The persisting significant differences between administrative and judicial networks cannot be explored here, but see further Alexander Somek, 'Administration without Sovereignty', in Petra Dobner and Martin Loughlin, *The Twilight of Constitutionalism?* (Oxford: Oxford University Press, 2010), pp. 267–87; Christoph Möllers, 'Constitutional Foundations of Global Administration', in Sabino Cassese (ed.), *Research Handbook on Global Administrative Law* (Cheltenham: Elgar, 2016), pp. 114 ff.

TABLE 7.1 *Taxonomy of the Judicial Administration of Foreign Relations*

	REVIEW OF FRS ACTS/CONDUCTS ('REVIEW NORMS')	INTERACTION WITH OTHER SYSTEMS IN FRS ('INTERACTION NORMS')
JUDICIAL PROCEDURE GROUNDS	• Access/standing • Deference to executive's interpretation/findings • Justiciability doctrines • (...)	• International comity • Extraterritoriality • Self-execution doctrines • (...)
SUBSTANTIVE GROUNDS	• Legality/constitutionality • Human rights • Proportionality/reasonableness • Participation/representation • (...)	• Evaluation of other systems' respect of human rights • (...)

framework,[51] one may distinguish between (1) norms involving the application of certain standards of review on FRs acts, or of acts otherwise affecting FRs ('review norms'); (2) norms affecting the coordination/cooperation with other systems in FRs matters ('interaction norms'). Both categories may in turn be subcategorized, based on the procedural or substantive grounds. Such taxonomy is summarized above in Table 7.1.

To be sure, these categories should be seen only as a general descriptive account of the way courts generally frame the arguments underpinning their decisions in FRs matters, and may in fact overlap. For example, reasonableness/proportionality arguments are categorized *sub* the 'review norms' category, as they are mostly used as a benchmark to review domestic acts, but may often explicitly enter into considerations related to comity. Similarly, decisions based on justiciability doctrines (e.g. the British 'foreign act of State') may also give rise to interaction norms. More generally, such taxonomy does not aspire to establish strong normative divides, especially considering that the same decision may often generate *uno actu* both review and interaction norms.

A *Review Norms*

The first category, comprising the review norms implemented and/or developed on the issue as to whether to decide, includes rules on the access/standing of

[51] See above Section II.B.

private parties, the deference towards executive (either on the interpretation of relevant law or on factual findings), the justiciability of the question, etc. In this field, for the last decades domestic judicial practice has been heading – slowly, contradictorily, but constantly – towards the expansion of the courts' competence to adjudicate FRs issues, both in common law and in civil law jurisdictions. More importantly, courts seem increasingly to be reducing the use and scope of 'exceptional' doctrines of nonjusticiability (such as the US political question doctrine) and/or of deference to executives' interpretations/findings, often under the influence of international human rights law.[52] Indeed, even when they accord such deference, they increasingly give their own legal justifications as to the reasons for doing so (e.g. executive expertise).

In civil law jurisdictions, Germany is probably the most prominent example of rejection of doctrines of judicial abdication in FRs matters, even for cases involving the deployment of military force.[53] Helped by their specific cultural and institutional environment, since at least the 1954 *Status of the Saar* case,[54] through the 1983 *Pershing II* case,[55] up to the decision of the OVG Münster on the use of the Ramstein base, German courts have consistently rejected doctrines of intrinsic nonjusticiability,[56] and rather tend slightly to lower the intensity of scrutiny of the merits case.[57]

52 See e.g. ECtHR *Chevrol* v. *France* (App. No. 49636/99), Judgment (Second Section), February 13, 2003, https://hudoc.ECHR.coe.int/app/conversion/pdf/?library=ECHR&id=001-60941&filename=001-60941.pdf&TID=thkbhnilzk, accessed September 30, 2020.

53 On the contrary, French and Italian (mainly administrative) courts keep on applying doctrines of judicial abstention (*acte de gouvernement, atto politico*) in cases involving the use of military force. See *Conseil d'Etat*, No. 255905, 10 April 2003; No. 292539, 17 April 2006; No. 321470, 15 October 2008; and *Cons St*, 11 May 1966, No. 344; *Cons St*, 3 August 2000, No. 530; *Cass*, 5 June 2002, No. 8157 – *Markovic*; *Cons St*, No. 3992, 29 July 2008; Trib Rome, *Società Fincantieri*, 10 October 1991. See Moncef Kdhir, 'La théorie de l'acte de gouvernement dans la jurisprudence du Conseil d'Etat relative aux relations internationales de la France à l'épreuve du droit international' (2003) 4 *JDI* 1059; Natalino Ronzitti, 'Azioni belliche e risarcimento del danno' (2002) 85 *Rivista di dritto internazionale* 682; and Daniele Amoroso, 'A Fresh Look at the Issue of Non-Justiciability of Defence and Foreign Affairs' (2010) 23 *Leiden Journal of International Law* 933.

54 BVerfGE 4, 157 – Saarstatut.

55 BVerfGE 66, 39 – Nachrüstung, where the German Federal Constitutional Court was called to decide whether the government's authorization to the installation of nuclear missiles on German territory was compatible with international law. See also a similar decision in the UK, *Hutchinson* v. *Newbury Magistrates Court* [2000] EWHC QB 61; and, in Italy, Trib Ragusa, *Barker e altri*, 14 April 1984, (1985) 108 *Foro italiano* 21 (alluding, however, to the impossibility to adjudicate the question on the merits).

56 Whereby a judge recognizes that an applicable legal standard to decide the issue would be virtually available but abstains from adjudicating it anyway.

57 See Franck, *Political Questions/Judicial Answers*, pp. 107–25; Peters, 'Military Operations Abroad under the German Basic Law'.

Contrary to some scholarly suggestions,[58] even common law jurisdictions, where the influence of 'foreign affairs exceptionalism' is traditionally stronger, seem to participate in this trend. Importantly, in its most recent case law the US Supreme Court has increasingly rejected the use of the so-called Chevron approach in FRs matters. Such approach, intrinsically linked to the autonomous political legitimation of the executive branch in US government, compels federal courts to defer to a federal agency's interpretation of an ambiguous statute that Congress delegated to the agency to administer, and results in an almost exclusive abdication to government's agencies in interpreting the statutes.[59] Similarly, US federal courts are gradually reducing the application of the political question doctrine, even in key FRs cases such as *Zivotofsky*,[60] the Guantanamo cases[61] and, more recently, *Al Shimari*,[62] concerning alleged acts of torture committed by a private military contractor's employees towards Abu Ghraib prisoners, which vacated the lower court's dismissal based on the political question doctrine.

Other examples of this trend may be found in the case law of the Israeli Supreme Court starting from the beginning of the 1980s,[63] in the practice of the Canadian Supreme Court,[64] as well as in India,[65] UK,[66]

58 Eric A. Posner and Cass R. Sunstein, 'Chevronizing Foreign Relations Law' (2006) 116 *Yale Law Journal* 1170.

59 See Nada Mourtada-Sabbah and Bruce E. Cain (eds.), *The Political Question Doctrine and the Supreme Court of the United States* (Lanham: Lexington, 2007); Sitaraman and Wuerth, 'The Normalization of Foreign Relations Law'; Breyer, *The Court and the World*, pp. 65–87.

60 *Zivotofsky* v. *Clinton*, 566 US 189 (2012), holding that a dispute over the regulation of passports was not a political question and thus resolvable by the courts.

61 *Rasul*, 542 US 466 (2004); *Hamdi*, 542 US 507 (2004); *Hamdan*, 548 US 557 (2006); *Boumediene*, 553 US 723 (2008).

62 *Al Shimari* v. *CACI Premier Tech, Inc* (Al Shimari IV), 840 F.3d 147, 151 (4th Cir. 2016).

63 See e.g. *Segal* v. *Minister of Interior*, HCJ 217/80; *Shiran* v. *Broadcasting Authority*, HCJ 1/81; *Baransa* v. *Commander of Central Command*, HCJ, 554/81; *Ressler* v. *Minister of Defense*, HCJ 910/86, *Hilman* v. *Minister of Internal Security*, HCJ, 3123/99; *Adala* v. *Commander of Central Command*, HCJ 3799/02, affirming the justiciability of questions related to military operations, in some instances even issuing preliminary orders to stop them. See Menachem Mautner, *Law and the Culture of Israel* (Oxford: Oxford University Press, 2011), pp. 61 ff.

64 See *Operation Dismantle* [1985] 1 SCR 441, rejecting on the merits the challenge against the executive for allowing the US government to test cruise missiles over Canadian territory, but dismissing the 'political question' doctrine; and, similarly, *Canada (Prime Minister)* v. *Khadr* [2010] 1 SCR 44, concerning the modalities Canada should respond to the violation of a Canadian citizen's rights held in at the Guantanamo Bay detention facility.

65 See the evolution from *State of Rajasthan* v. *Union of India* [1977] (3) SCC 5, to *Bommai* v. *Union of India* [1994] 2 SCR 644.

66 Historically, UK courts have practiced a high degree of self-restraint towards the royal prerogative, especially in foreign affairs: see Frederick Alexander Mann, *Foreign Affairs in English Courts* (Oxford: Clarendon, 1986); Nigel D. White, *Democracy Goes to War* (Oxford:

South Africa[67] and even Russia.[68] More generally, when courts declare inadmissible a question related to FRs, they increasingly resort to the 'ordinary' tools provided by judicial procedure, such as standing requirements, although even the evolutive interpretation of these latter seems increasingly to permit a greater access of private individuals to litigate FRs issues.[69] In particular, the comparison between Germany and the US shows that, while the respective practice still differs as for the underlying legal culture and the concrete results, there is a sort of progressive alignment as for the restriction of 'exceptional' doctrines of judicial abdication.

These insights support the claim that the area of judicial reach over FRs is expanding. Such 'normalization' is a necessary precondition for claiming that the management of FRs can be conceived in terms of (co-)administration by courts. Indeed, insofar as judicial bodies increasingly address the merits of FRs cases, or declare them inadmissible based on ordinary procedural standards, they apply the same norms as for any other executive action. At the same time, the possibilities for courts to adjudicate and even 'administer' FRs issues grow.

Concerning the legal standards used on the merits, that is, the norms concerning *how* to decide on FRs issues, it is also possible to identify an expanding trend. Indeed, national courts – in the different ways permitted by their respective domestic law – increasingly use the same substantive criteria of evaluation as for ordinary domestic issues. This trend, which varies in context and intensity, does not concern only the application of constitutional/legislative norms specifically related to FRs (e.g., the content of an

Oxford University Press, 2009), pp. 283–94. However, see *CCSU* v. *Minister for the Civil Service* [1984] UKHL 9, holding that prerogative powers are as susceptible to judicial review as statutory powers; and, more recently, *Belhaj & Rahmatullah (No 1)* v. *Straw & Ors* [2017] UKSC 3, ruling that sued officials had not shown any entitlement to rely on the doctrine of the Crown act of state so as to defeat the claims brought against them. See Eirik Bjorge and Cameron Miles, 'Crown and Foreign Acts of State before English Courts: *Rahmatullah*, *Belhaj*, and the Separation of Powers', in Curtis A. Bradley (ed.), *Oxford Handbook of Comparative Foreign Relations Law* (Oxford: Oxford University Press, 2019), pp. 715–32.

67 See *Kaunda and Others* v. *the President of the Republic of South Africa and Others* 2005 (4) SA 235 (CC), already holding that courts are entitled to review decisions of the executive in the exercise of its mandate in FRs. See the chapter by Dire Tladi, 'A Constitution Made for Mandela, a Constitutional Jurisprudence Developed for Zuma', this volume.

68 See the *Chechnya* judgment of 31 July 1995, where the Constitutional court heard petitions by opposition members of the Duma, challenging the constitutionality of three presidential decrees ordering the invasion of Chechnya. The Russian case is recalled next to common law jurisdictions only because, just as these latter, it traditionally accords to the executive an extremely broad area of nonjusticiability in FRs matters.

69 See e.g. *Bond* v. *United States*, 564 US 211 (2011) (*Bond I*).

agreement or the process of treaty-making) which in some cases may lead to the invalidation of the law implementing a treaty, but also the use of constitutional general principles. These latter include both the respect of constitutional rights, often interpreted in the light of international law, and general clauses and standards such as reasonableness and proportionality. Major examples pointing to this direction may be drawn from German,[70] Italian[71] and US case law, as well as from the European Court of Justice (ECJ).[72]

Importantly, US federal courts applied proportionality/balancing techniques in issuing (or in staying) preliminary injunctions barring the enforcement of President Trump's 'travel bans'.[73] This application is particularly significant, especially when compared to the traditional 'plenary power doctrine'.[74] Similar developments may be observed in the case law on the treatment of enemy combatants in the 'war on terror'.[75]

In this context, and even though it did not resort to balancing techniques, the decision of the OVG Münster is particularly interesting. Indeed, based on a typical result-oriented norm – the obligation to protect the life and physical

70 See again Franck, *Political Questions/Judicial Answers*, pp. 107–25; Peters, 'Military Operations Abroad under the German Basic Law'.

71 See decisions nos. 54/1979, 132/1985, 128/1987, 223/1996, 238/2014 of the Constitutional court. Further, with the decision No. 135/1963, the court declared unconstitutional a decree precluding any action against decisions of the Minister of Justice in respect of seizure of goods belonging to foreign States.

72 See Case 93/78, *Lothar Mattheus* v. *Doego Fruchtimport und Tiefkühlkost eG* [1978] ECR 2203; Case 191/82, *EEC Seed Crushers' and Oil Processors' Federation (FEDIOL)* v. *Commission of the European Communities* [1983] ECR 2913; Case C-70/94, *Fritz Werner Industrie-Ausrüstungen GmbH* v. *Federal Republic of Germany* [1995] ECR I-0318958; Case C-120/94, *Commission of the European Communities* v. *Hellenic Republic* [1994] ECR I-03037; Joined Cases C-402/05 P and C-415/05 P, *Yassin Abdullah Kadi and Al Barakaat International Foundation* v. *Council of the European Union and Commission of the European Communities* [2008] I-6351; Case C-104/16 P, *Council of the European Union* v. *Front populaire pour la libération de la saguia-el-hamra et du rio de oro (Front Polisario)* [2016] ECLI:EU:C:2016:973. See Panos Koutrakos, 'Judicial Review in the EU's Common Foreign and Security Policy' (2018) 67 *International & Comparative Law Quarterly* 1.

73 See e.g. *Int'l Refugee Assistance Project*, 582 US (2017), and the *en banc* decision of the Court of Appeals for the Fourth Circuit *Vilar*, 729 F.3d 62 (30 August 2013). See Desiree C. Schmitt, 'The Doctrine of Consular Nonreviewability in the Travel Ban Cases: Kerry v. Din Revisited' (2018) 33 *Georgetown Immigration Law Journal* 55. See also *Trump* v. *Hawaii*, 585 US (2018) which, although upholding a later version of the travel ban, emphasizing deference to the executive, still applied a rational basis review.

74 Justifying the 'constitutional exceptionalism' of US immigration law with reference to the connection between the admission and removal of foreigners and 'basic aspects of national sovereignty, more particularly . . . foreign relations and the national security in immigration policies': see Matthew J. Lindsay, 'Immigration, Sovereignty, and the Constitution of Foreignness' (2012–13) 45 *Connecticut Law Review* 743.

75 See again the 'Guantanamo cases' (n. 61).

integrity deriving from article 2(2) of the German Basic Law – it held that, as the legality of the US strikes was doubtful under international humanitarian law, the right to life of the claimants might have been violated. This triggered two obligations of the German authorities: (1) to make sure, on the basis of the legal assessment of the court, whether the practice of US strikes in Yemen region is in conformity with international law as it stands – to the extent that the German territory is involved; and (2) to take measures deemed appropriate in order to work towards compliance with international law.

Another interesting instance is the *Urgenda* saga, where Dutch courts ruled that the government owes a duty of care to its citizens to provide protection against the risks posed by climate change.[76] Based on general principles of domestic civil law, reinterpreted in the light of the UN and EU climate agreements, along with international law principles and climate science, Dutch courts ordered the government to revise its policies and ensure that by the end of 2020 carbon dioxide emissions are reduced by 25 percent compared to 1990 levels, that is, more than that initially planned by the government in the context of the Paris agreement. Also in this case, based on result-oriented domestic and international norms (principle of duty of care plus reduction of greenhouse emissions), judicial bodies reviewed the legality of measures adopted by political branches, and indicated the way to manage ('administer') a given issue, namely climate change. This also implies that the court co-determined, at least indirectly, the concrete implementation of the Netherlands' international obligations. Although not immediately connected with IRs *stricto sensu*, the *Urgenda* saga is highly significant to our purposes: by judicially restricting the executive's discretion on the concrete implementation of international obligations, Dutch courts potentially set an important precedent also in fields different from climate justice, as they codetermined the possible options on the design of foreign policy.

A third exemplary case is the 2019 *SADC Tribunal* judgment of the South African Constitutional Court,[77] concerning the decision of the Southern

76 *Urgenda Foundation*, case C/09/456689/HA ZA 13-1396, 24 June 2015; *Urgenda*, Case 200.178.245/01, 9 October 2018; *Urgenda*, Case 19/00135, 20 December 2019. See Suryapratim Roy, 'Urgenda II and Its Discontents' (2019) 13 *Carbon & Climate Law Review* 130; and Otto Spijkers, 'Pursuing Climate Justice through Public Interest Litigation: the Urgenda Case', in *Völkerrechtsblog*, April 29, 2020, https://voelkerrechtsblog.org/pursuing-climate-justice-through-public-interest-litigation-the-urgenda-case/, accessed September 20, 2020.

77 *Law Society of South Africa and Others* v. *President of the Republic of South Africa and Others* (CCT67/18) [2018] ZACC 51; 2019 (3) BCLR 329 (CC), https://collections.concourt.org.za/handle/20.500.12144/34610. See Riaan Eksteen, *The Role of the Highest Courts of the United States of America and South Africa, and the European Court of Justice in Foreign Affairs* (The

African Development Community (SADC) heads of State and Government to remove the right of individual access to the SADC Tribunal. Approached by the Law Society of South Africa, the Court found that the executive's participation in the 'decision-making process and his own decision to suspend the operations' of the Tribunal to be unconstitutional, unlawful and irrational.[78] The judgment also found that the signing of the 2014 Protocol was unconstitutional, unlawful and irrational and, as a result, ordered the President to withdraw his signature, greatly restricting the executive's discretion. Importantly, the Court based its reasoning on the fact that the 2014 Protocol denied citizens of South Africa and other SADC countries the access to justice at a regional level, despite the fact that such individual access is not per se imposed by any international law obligation, not even at regional level.[79]

A final remarkable example is the judgment C-252/19 of the Colombian constitutional court.[80] Evaluating the compatibility with the domestic constitution of a bilateral investment treaty (BIT) signed with France, the court declared it 'conditionally constitutional', that is, only under specific conditions. Turning away from previous approaches,[81] the Colombian court imposed to the executive branch the negotiation and adoption of a joint interpretive note, concerning the meaning to attribute to several clauses of the BIT. Also in this case, a domestic court did not merely review the legality of executive's conduct in FRs – namely, the exercise of treaty-making power – but also imposed to take specific measures and, therefore, actively participated in the concrete management/administration of Colombia's FRs.

In other cases, judicial review of FRs conducts has come to impose participatory/procedural rights of parliaments or other actors, even when relevant domestic law does not explicitly provide for or is unclear on that point.[82] In this

Hague: Asser Press, 2019), pp. 305–11; and Tladi, 'A Constitution Made for Mandela, a Constitutional Jurisprudence Developed for Zuma', this volume.

78 *Law Society of South Africa and Others* v. *President of the Republic of South Africa and Others*, para. 97.

79 See again Tladi, 'A Constitution Made for Mandela, a Constitutional Jurisprudence Developed for Zuma', this volume.

80 C-252/19, *expediente* LAT-445, www.corteconstitucional.gov.corelatoria/2019/c-252-19.htm, accessed September 30, 2020. See Gustavo Prieto, 'The Colombian Constitutional Court Judgment C-252/19: A New Frontier for Reform in International Investment Law', EJIL: Talk!, July 29, 2019, www.ejiltalk.org/the-colombian-constitutional-court-judgment-c-252-19-a-new-frontier-for-reform-in-international-investment-law/, accessed September 30, 2020.

81 See e.g. C-358/96 and C-379/96.

82 See Pierre-Hugues Verdier and Mila Versteeg, 'Separation of Powers, Treaty-Making, and Treaty Withdrawal: A Global Survey', in Curtis A. Bradley (ed.), *Oxford Handbook of Comparative Foreign Relations Law* (Oxford: Oxford University Press, 2019), pp. 136–55, showing that there is a clear trend reflecting increased involvement of both parliamentary

regard, however, there are still significant differences between the US and other – notably European – jurisdictions. Undeniably, a field where the US political question doctrine remains almost untouchable concerns the choice on the way to internally implement or to withdraw from international agreements.[83]

On the other side of the ocean, the UK Supreme Court recently held that the government was required to obtain authorization from parliament before it could initiate withdrawal from the EU.[84] Although British scholarship has not reached a consensus as to whether the decision is in continuity with UK constitutional tradition,[85] it was mainly based on the principle of parliamentary sovereignty. However, it also relied on the principle that democratic consent mediated by (constitutional) law is necessary to take the most fundamental FRs decisions affecting the rights of British citizens, and, more generally, involving 'fundamental change in the constitutional arrangements'. The UK Supreme Court seemed thus to overcome the 1971 ruling concerning the British accession to the European Community, stating that it was beyond the jurisdiction of the courts to perform a judicial review on Parliament's rightful exercise of its powers.[86] Even more importantly, following such judgment the British parliament passed legislation empowering the Prime Minister to give to the EU Council the notice for starting negotiations for the UK's withdrawal from the EU[87] and requiring Parliamentary approval of the outcome of the government's negotiations with the EU under article 50(2) of the TEU.[88] It is therefore fair to say that, although it cannot be regarded as a direct judicialization of FRs, the high instability due to the parliamentary involvement in the Brexit negotiations is also and at least indirectly a result of that decision, that is, that of the imposition by a court of a procedural requirement on the management of a FRs issue.

and judicial branches in treaty-making in constitutional systems; and Jean Galbraith, 'From Scope to Process', this volume.

83 See *Goldwater* v. *Carter*, 444 US 996 (1979); *Made in the USA Foundation*, 56 F.Supp.2d 1226 (ND Ala 1999) which had reached the merits of the case, thus excluding that the case presented a nonjusticiable political question.

84 *R (Miller)* v. *Secretary of State for Exiting the European Union* [2017] UKSC 5, [2018] AC 61. See generally Mark Elliot, Jack Williams and Alison L. Young (eds.), *The UK Constitution after Miller* (Oxford: Hart, 2018).

85 See David Feldman, 'Pulling a Trigger or Starting a Journey? Brexit in the Supreme Court' (2017) 76 *The Cambridge Law Journal* 217; Gavin Philippson, 'Brexit, Prerogative and the Courts: Why Did political Constitutionalists Support the Government Side in Miller?' (2017) 36 *University of Queensland Law Journal* 311; Campbell McLachlan, 'The Foreign Relations Power in the Supreme Court' (2018) 134 *Law Quarterly Review* 380.

86 *Blackburn* v. *Attorney General* [1971] 2 All ER 1380.

87 European Union (Notification of Withdrawal) Act 2017.

88 European Union (Withdrawal) Act 2018.

Similar decisions were taken by the Irish Supreme Court, ruling that any new provision amending the EC/EU treaties which alters 'the essential scope or objectives' of the EC/EU requires the intervention of the people to be constitutionally valid;[89] and the BVerfG which, in its Lisbon treaty ruling, alluded to the possibility that the German people as constituent power adheres to a future European federal state through referendum, despite the fact that such institute is not foreseen by the German Basic Law.[90] In this regard, it worth recalling that some continental scholars have even taken a step further, looking for legal bases to entitle foreign subjects to challenge a State's foreign policy.[91]

Outside the European context, the major example can probably be found in South Africa. In *Democratic Alliance* v. *Minister of International Relations and Cooperation*,[92] the High Court of Gauteng was faced with a question similar to that decided by the UK Supreme Court in *Miller*, that is, the executive's withdrawal from the Rome Statute, an international treaty ratified and domesticated by the parliament, without prior parliamentary approval. Although the question is not directly addressed by the South African Constitution, in 2017 the Court, stressing the importance of public participation when withdrawing from treaties,[93] held that Section 231(2) of the Constitution, requiring parliamentary approval for treaties subject to ratification, also requires by implication parliamentary consent to withdraw from such treaties. Therefore, the notice of withdrawal was unconstitutional and invalid.

More generally, some scholars suggest that FRs issues are best addressed by judicial bodies through traditional balancing/proportionality standards of review.[94] Obviously, in deciding which values/rights to balance, and the 'weight' to give to each of them, courts inevitably exercise some discretion, which cannot

89 *Crotty* v. *An Taoiseach* [1987] IR 713, Finlay CJ, 767.

90 BVerfGE 123, 267 – Lissabon, paras. 217, 228. See however art. 146, hinting to the replacement of the Basic Law by a 'constitution freely adopted by the German people'.

91 See e.g. Umberto Allegretti, 'Costituzione e politica estera: punti preliminary' (1990) 4 *Pace, diritti dell'uomo, diritti dei popoli* 31.

92 *Democratic Alliance* v. *Minister of International Relations and Cooperation and Others* 2017 (3) SA 212 (GP) ('Withdrawal judgment'), www.saflii.org/za/cases/ZAGPPHC/2017/53.pdf. See Hannah Woolaver, 'State Engagement with Treaties: Interactions between International and Domestic Law', in Curtis A. Bradley (ed.), *Oxford Handbook of Comparative Foreign Relations Law* (Oxford: Oxford University Press, 2019), pp. 431 at 440–42 (comparing the UK Supreme Court *Miller* judgment); and Tladi, 'A Constitution Made for Mandela, a Constitutional Jurisprudence Developed for Zuma', this volume.

93 *Democratic Alliance* v. *Minister of International Relations and Cooperation and Others*, paras. 61–63.

94 See e.g. Daniele Amoroso, 'Judicial Abdication in Foreign Affairs and the Effectiveness of International Law' (2015) 14 *Chinese Journal of International Law* 99 (and the literature recalled).

but impact on a State's FRs. Also from this perspective, they might increasingly participate in the management/administration of FRs.

B *Interaction Norms*

This subsection looks at the trends concerning the interaction norms, implemented and/or developed to manage interactions with other jurisdictions or legal systems affecting FRs. Similarly to the review norms, courts may base their rulings on either procedural or substantive grounds, but such subcategorization can be even more blurred.

Such norms include the application of '(foreign) act of State' and sovereign immunity doctrines – limiting the circumstances under which courts examine the validity of foreign governments acts and the responsibility of sovereign actors – as well as other doctrines of judicial abstention (international comity, *forum non conveniens*, margin-of-appreciation, subsidiarity, *Solange*, *controlimiti*, etc.) preventing judges from evaluating the merits of a claim or grant recognition/enforcement of outer legal sources.

In particular, in common law jurisdictions – especially in the US – courts seem to explicitly take into consideration, next to strictly legal elements, *lato sensu* political elements.[95] While such attitude contributes to make their decisions more understandable, it also affects their capacity to set clear and foreseeable standards, and has been generally criticized for its unpredictability.[96] In European jurisdictions, where the choice-of-law rules are generally seen as less flexible and more predictable,[97] such elements are hidden in the folds, so to say, of legally 'pure' argumentations.

This attitude is quite apparent in the evolution of the US 'act of State' doctrine, whose scope[98] has been narrowed since 1990 by the Supreme Court,[99] limiting the case-by-case balancing in deciding whether to apply it or not.[100] More generally,

95 See Timothy A. O. Endicott, 'International Meanings: Comity in Fundamental Rights Adjudication' (2001) 92 *International Journal of Refugee Studies* 280; and, more generally, part VI of Curtis A. Bradley (ed.), *Oxford Handbook of Comparative Foreign Relations Law* (Oxford: Oxford University Press, 2019), pp. 625–732.

96 See Dodge, 'International Comity in Comparative Perspective'.

97 See Regulation (EC) No. 864/2007 of 11 July 2007 on the law applicable to non-contractual obligations (Rome II), OJ 2007 No. L199, 31 July 2007, pp. 40 ff.; Regulation (EU) 1215/2012 of 12 December 2012 on jurisdiction and the recognition and enforcement of judgments in civil and commercial matters, OJ 2012 No. L351.

98 See *Banco Nacional de Cuba* v. *Sabbatino*, 376 US 398 (1964).

99 *Kirckpatrick & Co* v. *Environmental Tectonics Corp*, 493 US 400 (1990).

100 However, subsequent federal jurisprudence was not particularly consistent: see Curtis A. Bradley, Ashley S. Deeks and Jack L. Goldsmith, *Foreign Relations Law. Cases & Materials* (New York: Wolters Kluwer, 2020), pp. 84–102.

US courts increasingly adopt reasonableness standards in deciding whether to extend the reach of domestic law or not.[101] Importantly, this 'prescriptive comity', consisting in the respect sovereign nations afford each other by limiting the reach of their laws, does not totally coincide with the 'judicial comity', whereby judges decline to exercise jurisdiction over matters more appropriately adjudged elsewhere, as it happens in the *forum non conveniens* doctrine.[102] Similarly, in the field of extraterritorial jurisdiction, it is possible to observe an – apparently paradoxical – double movement toward global coordination: while US courts seem to progressively reduce the extraterritorial reach of their jurisdiction when the legal text do not explicitly provide otherwise,[103] the European multilevel system seems to progressively expand its reach.[104]

Here, two points are worth underlining. First, in many instances courts, especially in the US, take into consideration the foreign policy dimension in order to decide a case or to interpret relevant laws, often against the positions of executive branches. This is quite apparent in the Alien Tort Statute (ATS) case law,[105] where the Court explicitly or implicitly decided the cases based on its own assessment of how to avoid diplomatic frictions. Second, reasonableness and proportionality may be applied not only to evaluate a FRs act as such, but also to extend or narrow the reach of a court's own legal system. Consequently, substantive evaluations affect procedural decisions, which only apparently do not concern the merits of a case. Indeed, in the context of decisions related to interaction norms, there is often a silent shift towards substantive standards of review, hidden in the fabric of procedural rulings.[106]

This is quite apparent when courts, in deciding whether to extend their jurisdiction extraterritorially or not, refer to the respect of human rights and/or justice in the system which would be competent. For example, before the ECJ judgment *Owusu* ruled that Regulation (EC) 44/2001 prevented its application, this was the case for the British *forum non conveniens* doctrine. In

101 For the related case law see generally Breyer, *The Court and the World*, pp. 89–164.

102 See *F. Hoffman-La Roche Ltd.* v. *Empagran S.A.*, 542 US 155 (2004).

103 See *Aramco*, 499 US 244 (1991); *Morrison*, 561 US 247 (2010); *Kiobel*, 569 US 108 (2013); *Vilar*, 729 F.3d 62 (August 30, 2013).

104 See e.g. EctHR, *Al-Skeini & Others* v. *UK* (Appl. No. 55721/07), Judgment (Grand Chamber), July 7, 2011, www.rulac.org/assets/downloads/CASE_OF_AL-SKEINI_AND_OTHERS_v._THE_UNITED_KINGDOM.pdf; *Jaloud* v. *The Netherlands* (Appl. No. 47708/08), Judgment (Grand Chamber), November 20, 2014, http://hudoc.echr.coe.int/eng?i=001-148367; and the ECJ judgment *Owusu*, Case C-281/02, *Andrew Owusu* v. *N.B. Jackson, trading as 'Villa Holidays Bal-Inn Villas' (et al.)* [2005] ECR I-01383, and their effects on the legal systems of Member States (especially the UK).

105 *Sosa*, 542 US 692 (2004); *Kiobel*, 569 US 108 (2013); *Jesner* v. *Arab Bank, PLC*, 584 US (2018).

106 See Galbraith, 'From Scope to Process', in this volume.

determining 'the more appropriate forum', British courts took into account the interests of the parties and the nature of the subject matter, and made a determination as to whether another forum was more appropriate than England. Further, they inquired as to whether 'substantive justice' would be achieved in that other forum. This second part distinguished the English test from the US test, where 'justice' is not such an explicit element.[107] Similar considerations influenced the *Pinochet* case, where the House of Lords held that (1) allegations of torture and hostage taking 'pierced the veil' of the personal jurisdictional immunity granted of Heads of State, codified in articles 28, 29 and 31 of the Vienna Convention of Diplomatic Relations (and in part II of the 1978 State Immunity Act); (2) the Crown act of state doctrine was inapplicable, as Parliament, by enacting section 134(1) of the 1988 Criminal Justice Act defining torture and section 1(1) of the 1982 Taking of Hostages Act, had shown that the conduct with which Pinochet was charged was a justiciable matter before the English courts.[108] More recently, similar arguments were the basis for the *Belhaj* decision,[109] holding that the UK government could not rely on sovereign immunity and foreign act of state to escape claims in the two cases alleging UK involvement in breaches of human rights by foreign governments in Libya.[110]

In an opposite and equal direction, domestic courts increasingly use balancing techniques, reasonableness and human rights in granting recognition or enforcement to foreign sources into domestic systems, or in granting self-executing status to international law norms. This field is notoriously explored in the European continental scholarship, as a consequence of the EU integration process. EU member States, Germany and Italy in particular, have developed similar – though not coincident – doctrines of constitutional tolerance/resistance (*Solange*, *controlimiti*), which accord or deny the 'entrance' of external legal sources under certain circumstances, and have contributed to

107 See in particular *Lubbe* [2000] 4 All ER 268 (UKHL).

108 *R* v. *Bow Street Metropolitan Stipendiary Magistrate, ex parte Pinochet Ugarte* [1998] 2 WLR 827 (HL 1999).

109 *Belhaj & Rahmatullah (No 1)* v. *Straw & Ors* [2017] UKSC 3. See again Bjorge and Miles, 'Crown and Foreign Acts of State before English Courts'.

110 Outside Europe, one may refer here again to the judgment of the South African Constitutional Court *SADC Tribunal* (n. 77), para. 11. Insofar as its reasoning is based on the denial to citizens of South Africa *and* other SADC countries of the right to access to a regional tribunal, the judgment seemed to imply that the executive, when acting in FRs, should do so in a manner that protects fundamental rights extraterritorially: see Tladi, 'A Constitution Made for Mandela, a Constitutional Jurisprudence Developed for Zuma', this volume.

the reflexive evolution of the EU system towards greater political integration and respect of fundamental rights.

These models of constitutional tolerance/resistance/jurisgeneration are increasingly invoked and applied outside the intra-EU context, as a general template to manage inter-systemic collisions.[111] The most famous example probably remains the *Kadi* saga, comprising several decisions whereby the ECJ annulled EU Regulations implementing UN Security Council resolutions imposing restrictive measures directed against persons and entities associated with Al-Qaeda, for the violation of the affected persons' procedural rights, such as the right to be heard and the requirement for an adversarial process. As a result, a source of binding international law was denied entrance and implementation into the EU legal system.[112]

A significant example of this model and its potential risks is judgment no. 238/2014 of the Italian constitutional court. Although it is not possible to provide the full procedural background, this ruling held that the norm of customary international law (CIL) concerning the jurisdictional immunity of States for *acta iure imperii*, as ascertained by the ICJ in 2012 –[113] was incompatible with the 'supreme principles' of the constitution, when applied to exclude Italian civil jurisdiction for war crimes committed by the Third Reich.[114] In particular, the Italian court recognized the ICJ's monopoly over the interpretation of CIL, proclaiming its incompetence to reassess the existence of the rule on the State immunity, and how it relates to the right to jurisdictional remedy. Secondly, claiming to adopt a balancing approach,[115] it weighted the values that – in its opinion – were at stake: the total

[111] See Nikolaos Lavranos, 'The Solange-Method as a Tool for Regulating Competing Jurisdictions among International Courts and Tribunals' (2008) 30 *Loyola of Los Angeles International and Comparative Law Review* 275 (seeing the *Solange* method as a *genus* of the *species* 'judicial comity').

[112] See in particular Joined Cases C-584/10 P, C-593/10 P and C-595/10 P, *European Commission and Others* v. *Yassin Abdullah Kadi* [2013] ECLI:EU:C:2013:518. See Matej Avbelj, Filippo Fontanelli and Giuseppe Martinico (eds.), *Kadi on Trial. A Multifaceted Analysis of the Kadi Trial* (London: Routledge, 2014). A similar case, with the same result, was decided in the UK in *HM Treasury* v. *Ahmed & others* [2010] UKSC 2.

[113] Jurisdictional Immunities of the State, 3 February 2012.

[114] For a similar case in Greece see *Areios Pagos, Prefecture of Voiotia* v. *Fed Republic of Germany*, 11/2000 (awarding damages against Germany for war crimes during World War II).

[115] See ItCC judgment No. 238/2014, paras. 3.1–3.5, para. 3.1: 'It is indeed possible to review the [constitutional] compatibility even when both norms – as in the case at issue – have constitutional status, since balancing is one of the ordinary tasks that this Court is asked to undertake in all cases within its competence.' One may question whether the subsequent reasoning constitutes an actual exercise of judicial balancing but what matters to our purposes is the fact that balancing discourse, based on principled legal norms, facilitates judicial intervention in the management of FRs.

ineffectiveness of the right to an effective jurisdictional remedy, under articles 24 of the Italian Constitution and 6 ECHR; and the State immunity recognized by international law, in this case shielding the commission of war crimes. Thirdly, it denied the 'entrance' of the CIL norm into the domestic system, thus preventing ordinary courts from implementing it.

Importantly, and first, the court at least formally accorded deference to the ICJ. As some scholars argued,[116] the court could have autonomously reassessed the scope of the CIL norm on State immunity, but rather claimed not to be allowed to do so. However, in this case 'judicial comity' did not lead to 'legal comity',[117] as it provoked a diplomatic deadlock. Secondly, the court took a position clearly in conflict with the Italian parliament and government.[118] Indeed, in its balancing it did not take into account, or did not give much weight, to other possibly involved values, for example the 'peace among nations' and the interest to friendly relationships among sovereign entities (article 11). Regardless of its legal form, this relatively discretional choice had a political impact. Thirdly, the court explicitly had a 'iurisgenerative' intent, that is, the purpose of inducing changes in international law, namely the scope of the State immunity norm,[119] and also aimed to compel the Italian government to promote further negotiations with Germany. Fourthly, in order to support its argument and the final outcome, the court explicitly relied on the ECJ's *Kadi* case law, thus trying to present its decision so as to be coherent with a broader 'transnational' judicial consensus.[120] Finally, the subsequent practice of lower courts has proved crucial in somehow managing and de-escalating the resulting diplomatic deadlock, either when they formulated settlement proposals with the German government;[121] or when they found that

[116] Giovanni Boggero, 'The Legal Implications of Sentenza No. 238/2014 by Italy's Constitutional Court for Italian Municipal Judges: Is Overcoming the "Triepelian Approach" Possible?' (2016) 76 *Heidelberg Journal of International Law* 203.

[117] See D'Alterio, 'From Judicial Comity to Legal Comity'.

[118] Aiming at avoiding diplomatic friction with Germany, in 2013 the Italian parliament added a provision to the law ratifying the 2004 New York Convention on Jurisdictional Immunities of States, excluding the Italian jurisdiction for war crimes committed by the Third Reich, even for pending proceedings. The Court also declared such provision unconstitutional and, in this sense, judgment No. 238/2014 could also be analyzed from the perspective of the 'review norms'.

[119] For a critical assessment see Raffaela Kunz, 'The Italian Constitutional Court and "Constructive Contestation": A Miscarried Attempt?' (2016) 14 *Journal of International Criminal Justice* 621.

[120] See para. 3.4.

[121] See Trib Florence, *Simoncioni*, Order March 23, 2015; and Trib Florence, *Simoncioni*, No. 2469, July 6, 2015. On this point see Daniele Amoroso, 'Italy', in Fulvio Maria Palombino (ed.), *Duelling for Supremacy. International Law vs. National Fundamental Principles* (Cambridge: Cambridge University Press, 2019), pp. 186–92.

the rule on State immunity still barred the exercise of executive jurisdiction, thus avoiding the seizure of German assets in Italy.[122]

From a more general perspective, this example is significant, as it concerns the development by a domestic court of norms regulating the relationships between an external legal system (in this case, CIL) with the domestic one. Further, it demonstrates that, while it is generally true that the '"judge judging the judge" activity heavily depends on the political influence and diplomatic relations between systems',[123] in many instances judicial rulings may run contrary to otherwise friendly relations and the reciprocal trust.

The scenario arisen from the judgment no. 238/2014 is not an isolated case but, as courts increasingly 'administer' FRs, reflects a potentially recurring scenario. Here again, and although it did not involve any interaction between judicial bodies, the decision of the OVG Münster on the Ramstein base provides a significant example. Indeed, insofar as it raised doubts on the legality of the strikes conducted through the Ramstein base by the US government, and imposed the German government to take appropriate measures in that regard, such decision generated *also* interaction norms, affecting the coordination/cooperation with other systems in FRs matters. This, however, restricted greatly the diplomatic room of maneuver of Germany, and seem to have produced a diplomatic deadlock with the US, a key strategic ally.[124]

In yet other cases, political influence and economic interests, as well as power grab considerations,[125] rather than 'humanity', might play a more direct role into the development of interaction norms. This may be the case, for example, of the use of self-executing doctrines by the US Supreme Court towards the rulings of the ICJ,[126] and by the ECJ in the field of GATT, WTO

122 Ordinary courts applied art. 39(1) of the 1957 European Convention for the Peaceful Settlement of Disputes, not involved in the decision of the ItCC. See however the judgment of the Italian Supreme Court *Cass*, No. 21995, June 25, 2019, allowing executive actions against a German state-owned company, brought by Greek plaintiffs for credits concerning Third Reich's war crimes, to proceed before Italian courts.

123 D'Alterio, 'Judicial Regulation in the Global Space', p. 317.

124 See again Aust, 'US-Drohneneinsätze', pp. 307 ff.

125 See Federico G. Thea, 'The Role of Judges in Political Struggles' (2012) 2 *Queen Mary Law Journal* 57; and, more generally, Richard A. Posner, *How Judges Think* (Cambridge-London: Harvard University Press, 2008).

126 *Medellín* v. *Texas*, 552 US 491 (2008), a case in many ways similar to judgment No. 238/2014 of the ItCC, as it held that the *Avena* judgment of the ICJ was not enforceable as domestic law, thus letting the execution of a death penalty against a Mexican national. Also in this case, the Supreme Court took a stance opposite to that of President Bush administration, and created significant diplomatic frictions with Mexico.

and international economic agreements.[127] Similarly, US courts restricted the extraterritorial reach mainly in the field of human rights protection,[128] but narrowed it only slightly as regards its instruments of (direct or indirect) government of global economy, often with the result to shield US companies from lawsuits brought by foreign nationals.[129] In these instances, domestic courts, in denying the direct effect of international binding norms, seem more concerned with preserving their domestic authority as holders of the 'final say', or with guaranteeing domestic political and/or economic interests.

IV CONCLUSION: THE ADMINISTRATIVE CONCEPTION OF FRL, ITS 'TRANSNATIONALITY' AND POTENTIAL RISKS

The necessarily a-systematic survey conducted above, based on the GAL analytical framework, seems to provide some answers to the persisting struggles of FRL scholarship. First, the GAL approach confirms the necessity to look at FRL in functional terms. At a time when the divide between foreign and domestic affairs has become almost impalpable, the (study of the) law of FRs cannot be limited to the traditional areas of treaty-making; international and supranational integration; and use of military force. To have a realistic understanding of the law/FRs relationship, the scope of FRL (and its scholarship) must include the legal fields functionally affecting FRs. Although admittedly in the age of globalization FRs are virtually everywhere, the GAL approach provides reasons to expand the scope of FRL, so as to include *at least*

[127] See ECJ, Joined Cases C-21-24/72, *International Fruit Company NV and others* v. *Produktschap voor Groenten en Fruit* [1972] ECR 01219; Case C-280/93, *Germany* v. *Council* [1994] ECR I-04973; Case C-149/96, *Portugal* v. *Council*, [1999] ECR I-08395; Case C-377/02, *Léon Van Parys NV* v. *Belgisch Interventie- en Restitutiebureau (BIRB)* [2005] ECR I-01465; Joined Cases C-300/98 and C-392/98, *Parfums Dior* and *Assco Gerüste* [2000] ECR I-11307. See also the judgment in Case C-284/16, *Slowakische Republik* v. *Achmea BV*, [2018] ECLI:EU:C:2018:158, holding that the arbitration clause contained in art. 8 of the 1991 Netherlands-Slovakia BIT had an adverse effect on the autonomy of EU law, and was therefore incompatible with it.

[128] See again the ATS case law (n. 105).

[129] See e.g. the 2010 Dodd-Frank Act: While its repressive provisions have a broad territorial reach (they can be applied each time there is a 'foreseeable substantial effect within the United States'), *Liu* v. *Siemens* AG (no 13-cv-4385, 2014 WL 3953672 (2d Cir. August 14 2014)) held that the anti-retaliation provisions protecting whistle-blowers do not apply extraterritorially, even for companies listed on the US stock exchange. See also *RJR Nabisco*, 579 US (2016) holding that the Racketeer Influenced and Corrupt Organizations Act has certain extraterritorial applications, but plaintiffs must prove injuries within the US for the act to apply; and *Jam*, 586 US (2019), where the US Supreme Court, denied absolute immunity under the International Organizations Immunity Act to the International Finance Corporation, part of the World Bank group.

all the legal fields that somehow separate the internal from the external and mediate the inward reception of international law into the domestic legal system.[130] In this regard, looking at FRL through the lenses of GAL offers another conception of (the function of) FRL in the context of legal-political globalization: the administrative one. Such conception captures the idea that the sources of FRL – be they domestic or international – provide relevant institutional actors with concrete goals and results to accomplish in the context of FRs, as well as substantive and procedural standards to 'manage' FRs, whose respect can be in turn reviewed by judicial bodies.

The functional understanding of FRL makes apparent another key element brought out by the GAL approach: the role of 'global regulators' of courts, in a domain where their influence is still underestimated.[131] The expansion of the judicial reach in FRs is not just quantitative, as more and more FRs questions are adjudicated by courts on the merits; but also qualitative, as judicial rulings affect the concrete management/'administration' of FRs. Courts – either voluntarily or involuntarily, either directly or indirectly – increasingly participate in the exercise of FRP, as they contribute to set or change the legal patters that the political branches must follow, also prospectively. This holds true even when courts adhere to the position of political branches: as courts step into the FRs arena, for analytical purposes it does not change much whether their assessments coincide to that of the executives and parliaments or not. For this reason, in highlighting the role played of courts, the GAL approach could also strengthen their self-awareness and responsiveness, just as for other GABs.

The analytical tools provided by GAL proved also useful to assess the emerging 'transnationality' in FRL, in two respects at least. Firstly, in adjudicating FRs questions judicial bodies often apply a sort of 'patchwork' of domestic and international legal sources.[132] Secondly, courts seem increasingly to develop comparable and/or equivalent argumentative models and standards of review, sometimes even explicitly recognizing reciprocal influence.[133] However, the degree of formalization of such 'common language' is probably fated to remain underdeveloped, when compared to other functionally differentiated fields which constitute the usual focus of GAL studies. Indeed, next to other factors which make judicial networks less formalized than others, in FRs matters judiciaries are 'torn between, on the

[130] See Aust and Kleinlein, 'Introduction', this volume.

[131] See however in the most recent literature Eksteen, *The Role of the Highest Courts*, assessing the role of courts applying foreign policy analysis.

[132] See e.g., the *Urgenda Foundation*, District Court of the Hague, 24 June 2015, paras. 4.35–4.86 and the Ramstein decision OVG NRW 4 A 1361/15, spec. pp. 52 ff.

[133] See, e.g., the ItCC judgment No. 238/2014, para. 3.4, recalling the ECJ's *Kadi* decisions.

one hand, [their] loyalty to the international and national rule of law and, on the other, [their] allegiance to national or organisational interests'.[134]

This point leads to a final consideration. The survey showed that the expansion of the judicial reach on FRs questions often ends up in further obstacles to the coordination of conflicting systems and to the ordering of global governance. Even the use of human rights or other substantive standards can lead to greater disorder, especially because courts' decisions highly differ as regards their hierarchization. The administrativization of FRs – a complex phenomenon driven, among other factors, by the greater relevance to the legal position of the individual, the spread of (constitutional) result-oriented norms, and a procedural turn in FRL – does not always imply greater coordination among systems, but can rather bring more disorder, conflict and unpredictability. The *Miller* judgment of the UK Supreme Court, the ItCC judgment no. 238/2014 and the ruling of the OVG Münster on the Ramstein base – the very case with which we opened this chapter – are glaring examples of the risks linked to this trend. More generally, this consideration puts somehow into question the *normative* aspirations of GAL, insofar as it advocates for the expansion of 'administrative' norms and judicial control on the exercise of power in transnational arenas, with the goal to decrease conflicts and inconsistencies among involved actors/systems, and increase their legitimacy. Although a critical assessment of such normative aspirations lies outside the scope this chapter, the administrativization of FRs, and the role played by courts in that context, constitute a hard test for the capacity of the GAL project – not only to describe, but also – to order the structures of global governance, and opens new venues for further research in the vast field of the relationship between law, FRs and global governance.

[134] Giegerich, 'Foreign Relations Law', p. 186. See also Benvenisti and Downs, *Between Fragmentation and Democracy*, pp. 145–48.

PART II

SOVEREIGNTY AND COOPERATION

8

The Conseil Constitutionnel's Jurisprudence on 'Limitations of Sovereignty'

Niki Aloupi

I 'DROIT DES RELATIONS INTERNATIONALES' AND 'FOREIGN RELATIONS LAW'

In French doctrine, the term 'droit des relations internationales' (literally translated as 'Foreign Relations Law') is not 'used to encompass the domestic law of each nation that governs how that nation interacts with the rest of the world'.[1] As a distinctive field, French 'Relations Internationales'[2] studies in a nonexclusively-legal way the interactions and communications between nations and other actors and social groups across the borders, that is, all the relations (*stricto sensu* international or *lato sensu* international including transnational ones) presenting a foreign element. Thus, political, economic and sociological considerations are taken into account in order to apprehend the international legal order. Foreign relations *law* (*droit* des relations internationals) can consequently seem ambiguous in French and therefore is often used as a synonym of public international law (droit international public). As a matter of fact, a great number of French students that are enrolled in a course 'Droit des relations internationales' in first year of law school actually study public international law. Few French law schools teach foreign relations as a distinctive discipline and even fewer have a research center specially dedicated to it.[3] As far as French foreign relations handbooks are concerned, they propose mostly three different approaches, that can also be combined between

[1] Curtis Bradley, 'What Is Foreign Relations Law?', in Curtis Bradley (ed.), *The Oxford Handbook of Comparative Foreign Relations Law* (New York: Oxford University Press, 2019), pp. 3–20.

[2] For an analysis about 'Relations Internationales' as a separate, distinctive and autonomous field in French doctrine, see Julian Fernandez, *Relations internationales*, 2nd ed. (Paris: Dalloz, 2019), pp. 1–27.

[3] Fernandez, *Relations internationales*, pp. 24–27.

them: a theoretical/doctrinal/political science approach; an historical approach; or an institutional/normative/juridical approach.[4]

Nevertheless, notwithstanding the semantics, that is, even without naming this particular field 'Foreign Relations Law' and without considering it as autonomous, the French doctrine does study 'how French law (i.e. constitutional law, statutory law, administrative regulations, and judicial decisions) interacts with the rest of the world', as well as 'the role of domestic courts in applying international law and in adjudicating cases that implicate governmental interests'.[5] In this sense, the French approach, as far as interaction between domestic law and international law is concerned, is one of a monist state that places its constitution on the summit of the hierarchy of norms and attributes to international law a supra-legislative but infra-constitutional authority (article 55 of the French Constitution 1958).

However, in a perspective where 'Foreign Relations Law' is meant to be studied as a distinctive and *a fortiori* autonomous field, this assertion is far too simplistic to truly apprehend the articulation of the French legal order with the international one. This interaction is rather complex and cannot be fully understood unless all aspects of French domestic law and more importantly French case law (in the sense of jurisprudence, since there is no *stare decisis/* binding precedent rule in French law) relative to international law have been studied. Indeed, not only the French courts jurisprudence affine, enrich or even alter the written French norms concerning domestic law/international law interaction, but also the approaches adopted by the three French Supreme Courts (Cour de Cassation, Conseil d'Etat and Conseil Constitutionnel, which is not hierarchically superior to the other two) are not always identical or even harmonized and may thus govern the relation domestic law/international law in different ways.

This chapter will focus on the Conseil Constitutionnel and its role in controlling the executive as far as the adoption of international treaties is concerned. The Conseil Constitutionnel's jurisprudence on 'limitations of sovereignty'[6] is a very interesting one and, notwithstanding its numerous

4 Fernandez, *Relations internationales*, p. 15.

5 Bradley, 'What Is Foreign Relations Law?', p. 9.

6 By 'limitations of sovereignty' doctrine this contribution refers to the doctrine of the Constitutional Council relative to the international treaties that 'jeopardize the essential conditions for the exercise of national sovereignty' and thus cannot be ratified without prior amendment of the Constitution. The term 'limitation of sovereignty' doctrine is chosen here for convenience reasons and because the whole doctrine takes as a starting point paragraph 15 of the Constitution Preamble 1946 which refers to accepted limitations to France's sovereignty. But the exact term would rather be a doctrine on 'essential conditions for the exercise of national sovereignty.'

ambiguities and grey areas, clearly reflects the strong role that the French Constitutional Council wishes to play in foreign relations law.

In its first section, this paper focuses on the role of the French Constitutional Council with regard to the review of international treaties before their ratification. Its second section offers insights on the 'limitations of sovereignty' doctrine and its criticism, whereas the third section proposes several illustrations of the Conseil Constitutionnel's jurisprudence concerning the compatibility between international treaties and the French Constitution. In its final section, this article suggests a critical assessment of this jurisprudence and argues that with the 'limitations of sovereignty' doctrine the Constitutional Council has achieved great power and discretion and has thus indirectly acquired an important role influencing the way the executive conducts its foreign relations.

II THE ROLE OF THE CONSTITUTIONAL COUNCIL IN THE CONSTITUTIONALITY REVIEW OF INTERNATIONAL TREATIES BEFORE THEIR RATIFICATION

The French Constitutional Council was created by the Fifth Republic's Constitution adopted on October 4, 1958. Initially conceived by General de Gaulle as a rather weak mechanism, feared by him because of the American precedent of what was considered as the risk of a 'judges' government', it developed an extensive and rich jurisprudence, which, combined with several constitutional modifications over the years, increased its powers and importance in the French legal order. The general growing of the Constitutional Council's role and the expansion of the possibilities of its referral also influenced its jurisprudence concerning interactions between domestic law and international treaty law.

The French Constitutional Council rules on whether proposed international treaties are in conformity with the French Constitution. This review is possible after the international treaty has been approved by the Parliament[7] and before it is ratified by the President of the French Republic. It takes place on a referral from the President of the Republic, the Prime Minister, the President of one or the other Houses (National Assembly or Senate), or from sixty Members of the National Assembly or sixty Senators. If the Council

[7] According to article 53 of the Constitution, peace treaties, trade agreements, treaties or agreements relating to international organization, those committing the finances of the State, those modifying provisions which are the preserve of statute law, those relating to the status of persons, and those involving the ceding, exchanging or acquiring of territory, may be ratified or approved only by an Act of Parliament.

asserts that the international undertaking reviewed contains a clause contrary to the Constitution, the authorization to ratify the treaty or otherwise approve the undertaking involved may be given only after amending the Constitution (article 54 of the French Constitution). According to article 61 of the Constitution, referral of certain acts and bills to the Council before their coming into force for it to rule on their conformity with the Constitution is compulsory. This is the case, amongst others, for the government bills that provide for authorization to ratify an international treaty which, although not contrary to the Constitution, would affect the functioning of the institutions.

Thus, the Constitutional Council exercises an *a priori* review on international treaties, which is compulsory in some cases and just a possibility for the President of Republic, the Prime Minister, the President of one or the other of the Houses or for sixty Members of the National Assembly or sixty Senators in all the others. This is called 'contrôle de constitutionnalité'. The Council does not however exercise a 'contrôle de conventionnalité' meaning that it does not review the conformity of French law and administrative regulations with international law (treaties, other undertakings, unilateral acts and customary law). Indeed, in its 1975 *IVG* decision,[8] the Constitutional Council asserted that such a review belongs to the administrative and judicial courts (notably Conseil d'Etat and Cour de Cassation), since international law was not a part of the French Constitution and 'bloc de constitutionnalité' (this 'constitutionality block' is composed of the Constitution 1958, its preamble, the French Declaration of Human and Civic Rights, the Preamble of the Constitution 1946 of the Fourth Republic and the Charter for the Environment 2004).

[8] Decision no. 74–54 DC – *Voluntary Interruption of Pregnancy Act*, pts. 3–7:

> 3. While these provisions confer upon treaties, in accordance with their terms, an authority superior to that of statutes, they neither require nor imply that this principle must be honored within the framework of constitutional review as provided by article 61.
>
> 4. Decisions made under article 61 of the Constitution are unconditional and final, as is clear from article 62, which prohibits the promulgation or implementation of any provision declared unconstitutional; on the other hand, the prevalence of treaties over statutes, stated as a general rule by article 55, is both relative and contingent, being restricted to the ambit of the treaty and subject to reciprocity, which itself depends on the behavior of the signatory state or states and on the time at which it is to be assessed;
>
> 5. A statute that is inconsistent with a treaty is not ipso facto unconstitutional;
>
> 6. Review of the rule stated in article 55 cannot be effected as part of a review pursuant to article 61, because the two reviews are different in kind;
>
> 7. It is therefore not for the Constitutional Council, when a referral is made to it under article 61 of the Constitution, to consider the consistency of a statute with the provisions of a treaty or an international agreement.

The Constitutional Council thus limits itself to the constitutional review of international treaties. In the 1975 Voluntary Interruption of Pregnancy Act decision, the Council asserted that '[a]rticle 61 of the Constitution does not confer on the Constitutional Council a general or particular discretion identical with that of Parliament, but simply empowers it to rule on the constitutionality of statutes referred to it'. However, when one studies the Council's case law as regards treaties and international agreements, one realizes that its 'discretion' is far more important than what the letter of the Constitution and the 1975 assertion suggest.

The 'limitations of sovereignty' doctrine has indeed allowed the Council to develop its own foreign relations law approach regarding international undertakings by France and to enjoy an important margin of appreciation while doing so. The result is that the Constitutional Council can prevent the organs in charge of France's foreign relations from undertaking some international engagements considered by it as incompatible with 'national sovereignty'. If the executive, with the agreement of the Parliament whenever necessary, insists on adopting an international treaty deemed by the Council as incompatible with national sovereignty, a modification of the Constitution will be necessary before ratification of the treaty. And indeed, as will be shown in Section IV, several examples exist where such amendments have taken place after an incompatibility decision rendered by the Constitutional Council. However, this possibility does not imply that the normativity and hierarchical position of the French Constitution is lesser than in other countries, since, in theory at least, the Constitution remains on the summit of the norms' hierarchy and its interaction with international law derives from the Constitution itself and not from international law norms. It does however highlight the power of the Constitutional Council, that can thus have an influence on the conduct of foreign relations by the executive. Also, the mere fact that amending the Constitution is envisaged in order to ratify a treaty or otherwise approve the undertaking involved, points out how important international cooperation is for the French legal order. This is also reminded in paragraph 14 of the preamble of the Constitution 1946 (which, as stated above, is actually a part of the 'bloc de constitutionnalité' used by the Council to review the constitutional conformity of law and treaties), stipulating: 'The French Republic, faithful to its traditions, shall respect the rules of public international law. It shall undertake no war aimed at conquest, nor shall it ever employ force against the freedom of any people.'

III BRIEF PRESENTATION OF THE 'LIMITATIONS OF SOVEREIGNTY' DOCTRINE AND ITS CRITICISM

The very notion of sovereignty in its external, international meaning (i.e. the fact that France as a sovereign state is not submitted to any authority superior to it and that it is only bound by undertakings that it accepted explicitly, implicitly or tacitly) is absent from the Constitution 1958, which, in article 3, only refers to internal sovereignty in these terms: 'National sovereignty shall vest in the people, who shall exercise it through their representatives and by means of referendum'.[9] However, paragraph 15 of the preamble of the Constitution 1946 refers to external sovereignty in the following terms: 'Subject to reciprocity, France shall consent to the limitations upon its sovereignty necessary to the organization and preservation of peace', thus reminding, even if it is in a somewhat inept way, the famous *Lotus* and *Wimbledon* PCIJ dicta on the right to enter into international engagements being an attribute of state sovereignty.[10] Thus, this paragraph proclaims France's sovereign right to undertake international engagements.

As part of its *a priori* review of international treaties based on article 54 of the Constitution, the Constitutional Council developed a doctrine on the respect of the 'essential conditions for exercise of national sovereignty' which indirectly refers to external sovereignty[11] although explicitly

[9] See also article 3 of the French Declaration of Human and Civic Rights (also part of the constitutionality block): 'The principle of any sovereignty lies primarily in the Nation. No corporate body, no individual may exercise any authority that does not expressly emanate from it.'

[10] *Case of the S.S. 'Wimbledon'*, Judgment, Series A No. 1, p. 25: 'The Court declines to see in the conclusion of any Treaty by which a State undertakes to perform or refrain from performing a particular act an abandonment of its sovereignty. No doubt any convention creating an obligation of this kind places a restriction upon the exercise of the sovereign rights of the State, in the sense that it requires them to be exercised in a certain way. But the right of entering into international engagements is an attribute of State sovereignty.' And *Case of the S.S. 'Lotus'*, Judgment, Series A No. 10, p. 18: 'The rules of law binding upon States therefore emanate from their own free will as expressed in conventions or by usages generally accepted as expressing principles of law and established in order to regulate the relations between these coexisting independent communities or with a view to the achievement of common aims. Restrictions upon the independence of States cannot therefore be presumed.'

[11] *N.B.* the ideas put forward in Section III of this contribution are largely inspired by an article of an important representative of the French voluntarist doctrine of international law: Jean Combacau, 'La souveraineté internationale de l'Etat dans la jurisprudence du Conseil constitutionnel français' (2001) 9 *Cahiers du conseil constitutionnel* (dossier: souveraineté de l'Etat et hiérarchie des Normes) (www.conseil-constitutionnel.fr/nouveaux-cahiers-du-conseil-constitutionnel/la-souveraineté-internationale-de-l-etat-dans-la-jurisprudence-du-conseil-constitutionnel-francais, accessed September 30, 2020); see also, in a similar vein, Andrea Hamann, 'Sur un "sentiment" de souveraineté' (2018) 21 *Jus Politicum*, 187–213 (http://juspoliticum.com/article/Sur-un-sentiment-de-souverainete-1259.html, accessed September 30, 2020); see also, Alain Pellet, 'Le Conseil constitutionnel, la souveraineté et les traités – À propos de la décision du Conseil constitutionnel du 31 décembre 1997 (Traité d'Amsterdam)' (1998) 4 *Cahiers du Conseil constitutionnel* 113 et seqq. (www.conseil-constitutionnel.fr/conseil-constitutionnel/francais/nouveaux-cahiers-du-conseil-constitutionnel/cahier-n-4/le-conseil-constitutionnel-la-souverainete-et-les-traites-a-propos-de-la-

invoking 'national' sovereignty in order to limit the executive's power to conclude international treaties when intolerable 'limitations of sovereignty' were found. The phrase – even though directly inspired by the *Lotus* dictum – is without any doubt improper. In international law, a state that transfers or limits some of its powers undertaking an international engagement does not '*limit*' its sovereignty (which is not apt to be limited) but rather *exercises* it by concluding a treaty.[12] Thus, the actual question to which the Constitutional Council answers with the 'limitations of sovereignty doctrine' is the following one: are the limitations of powers and of liberty of action (and not of sovereignty) or even the transfers of competencies undertaken by the state in its international engagement compatible with its Constitution?

The inopportune confusion caused by this 'limitation of sovereignty' expression is due to the fact that the Council refers to 'national sovereignty' in a twofold and indistinctive manner creating an erroneous amalgam between external and internal sovereignty, although the two concepts ought to be completely and carefully separated.[13] Thus, instead of clarifying the signification of paragraph 15 of the Preamble 1946, the Council, in its effort to distinguish between the 'limitations of sovereignty' that are compatible with the Constitution and those that are not, creates a rather confusing and obscure doctrine.[14] The confusion was even more important in the early beginnings of this case law. Indeed, in Decision no. 76–71 DC – *Election of the Assembly of the Communities*

decision-du-conseil-constitutionnel-du-31-decembre-1997-traite-d-amsterdam.52845.html, accessed September 30, 2020). François Luchaire, 'La souveraineté extérieure dans la Constitution française et la jurisprudence du Conseil constitutionnel', in Dominique Maillard Desgrées du Loû (ed.), *Les évolutions de la souveraineté* (Paris: Montchrestien, 2006), pp. 119–25.

12 Combacau, 'La souveraineté internationale de l'Etat dans la jurisprudence du Conseil constitutionnel français':

> *Selon cette conception, formelle et non substantielle, de la souveraineté au sens du droit international, on ne peut donc dire d'un État qu'il consent à des limitations de souveraineté à telle ou telle condition, mais qu'il considère comme compatibles avec sa souveraineté les limitations de sa liberté d'action, pour autant qu'elles respectent les conditions en cause : soit que ces traités modifient, par renonciation totale ou partielle, l'étendue du champ de la compétence internationale dont il jouissait, à titre exclusif ou concurremment avec d'autres États, ou portent atteinte à son monopole dans les domaines où elle était exclusive; soit qu'ils réduisent les pouvoirs qui lui étaient internationalement reconnus dans le cadre de cette compétence.*

13 Combacau, 'La souveraineté internationale de l'Etat dans la jurisprudence du Conseil constitutionnel français'.

14 Combacau, 'La souveraineté internationale de l'Etat dans la jurisprudence du Conseil constitutionnel français'.

by direct universal suffrage,[15] the Council distinguished between authorized 'limitations of sovereignty' and unauthorized 'transfers of sovereignty'. This unclear distinction has, fortunately, been abandoned in the case law thereafter.

IV PANORAMA OF THE CONSEIL CONSTITUTIONNEL'S JURISPRUDENCE AS TO WHICH INTERNATIONAL ENGAGEMENTS ARE NOT COMPATIBLE WITH THE FRENCH CONSTITUTION[16]

In a 1985 decision[17] about the ratification of the Sixth Protocol of the European Convention on Human Rights, the Council seemed to identify three elements as 'essential conditions for the exercise of national sovereignty', the contrariety to which would render an international treaty incompatible with the French Constitution. Firstly, to ensure the respect of the institutions; secondly, to ensure the continuity of the life of the nation; and, thirdly, to guarantee the rights and freedoms of citizens. At the time, French doctrine considered these elements to be the actual content of 'national sovereignty',[18] the limitations to which would not be tolerated. Thus, it may have seemed clear that if an international treaty limited one or more of these three 'essential conditions', it could not be undertaken without prior constitutional amendment. However, the Council showed no constancy in

[15] Decision no. 76–71 DC, December 30, 1976 – *Décision du Conseil des communautés européennes relative à l'élection de l'Assemblée des Communautés au suffrage universel direct*, pt. 1.

[16] The decisions presented in this section can be found in English in the French Constitutional Council's site: www.conseil-constitutionnel.fr/en/selection-of-dc-decisions, accessed September 30, 2020.

[17] Decision no. 85–188 DC, May 22, 1985 – *Protocole n° 6 additionnel à la Convention Européenne de sauvegarde des Droits de l'homme et des libertés fondamentales concernant l'abolition de la peine de mort, signé par la France le 28 avril* 1983, pt. 2 : 'cet engagement n'est pas incompatible avec le devoir pour l'État d'assurer le respect des institutions de la République, la continuité de la vie de la nation et la garantie des droits et libertés des citoyens'.

[18] Louis Favoreu, 'La décision du 22 mai 1985 du Conseil constitutionnel relative au Protocole no 6 additionnel à la Convention européenne des droits de l'homme' (1985) 31 *Annuaire français de droit international* 868 at 873 (www.persee.fr/doc/afdi_0066-3085_1985_num_31_1_2696, accessed September 30, 2020); see also Lucie Laithier, 'Observations sous Cons. const., 9 avril 1992, no 92–308 DC, Traité sur l'Union européenne ("Maastricht I")', in Alain Pellet and Alina Miron (eds.), *Les grandes décisions de la jurisprudence française de droit international public* (Paris: Dalloz, 2015), pp. 216 at 220–21, paras. 7 et 9; Pellet, 'Le Conseil constitutionnel, la souveraineté et les traités: À propos de la décision du Conseil constitutionnel du 31 décembre 1997 (Traité d'Amsterdam)', 113 at 117–18.

repeating these elements – and *a fortiori* clarifying their content – in the numerous decisions that followed.

Subsequently, the most important Constitutional Council's decisions resorting to the doctrine of 'limitations of sovereignty' in order to prevent the ratification of an international treaty without previous amendment of the Constitution were, and this does not come as a surprise, relative to the European Union treaties.[19] The most topical decisions in this regard will be briefly presented hereafter.

In Decision 92–308 DC – *Treaty on European Union (Maastricht I)*, the Council asserted:

> It follows from these various institutional provisions [i.e. article 3 of the French Declaration, paragraphs 14 and 15 of the 1946 Preamble and article 53 of the 1958 Constitution] that respect for national sovereignty does not preclude France, acting in accordance with the Preamble to the 1946 Constitution, from concluding international agreements relating to participation in the establishment or development of a permanent international organization enjoying legal personality and decision-making powers on the basis of transfers of powers decided on by the Member States, subject to reciprocity. However, should an international agreement entered into to this end involve a clause conflicting with the Constitution *or jeopardizing the essential conditions for the exercise of national sovereignty*, authorization to ratify would require prior amendment of the Constitution.[20]

Thus, the 'pure' unconstitutionality of a clause is presented as a distinct hypothesis from the jeopardy of the essential conditions for the exercise of national sovereignty. The Council concludes that the authorization to ratify the Treaty on European Union requires a constitutional amendment because it creates situations (concerning the establishment of Union citizenship with right to vote in municipal elections; the single monetary and exchange-rate policy and measures relating to the entry and movement of persons) in which the essential conditions for the exercise of national sovereignty were

[19] Besides the decisions analyzed thereafter see also Decision no. 70–39 DC, 19 June 1970 – *Traité portant modification de certaines dispositions budgétaires [. . .] et décision du Conseil des Communautés européennes [. . .] relative au remplacement des contributions des États membres par des ressources propres aux Communautés*; Decision no. 76–71 DC, 30 December 1976 – *Décision du Conseil des communautés européennes relative à l'élection de l'Assemblée des Communautés au suffrage universel direct*; Decision no. 91–294 DC, 25 July 1991 – *Loi autorisant l'approbation de la convention d'application de l'accord de Schengen*.

[20] Decision no. 92–308 DC – *Treaty on European Union (Maastricht I)*, pts. 12 and 13 (emphasis added).

jeopardized. As a result, the Constitution 1958 was amended and articles 88–1 and 88–2 were added.[21]

[21] As a matter of fact, every revision of the European Union treaties between 1992 and 2007 lead to a revision of the French Constitution. Title XV bearing the title 'On the European Union' and added to the French Constitution after the 1992 Decision counts nowadays the following seven articles:

> Article 88–1
> The Republic shall participate in the European Union constituted by States which have freely chosen to exercise some of their powers in common by virtue of the Treaty on European Union and of the Treaty on the Functioning of the European Union, as they result from the treaty signed in Lisbon on 13 December, 2007.
> Article 88–2
> Statutes shall determine the rules relating to the European arrest warrant pursuant to acts adopted by the institutions on the European Union.
> Article 88–3
> Subject to reciprocity and in accordance with the terms of the Treaty on European Union signed on 7 February 1992, the right to vote and stand as a candidate in municipal elections shall be granted only to citizens of the Union residing in France. Such citizens shall neither hold the office of Mayor or Deputy Mayor nor participate in the designation of Senate electors or in the election of Senators. An Institutional Act passed in identical terms by the two Houses shall determine the manner of implementation of this article.
> Article 88–4
> The government shall lay before the National Assembly and the Senate drafts of European legislative acts as well as other drafts of or proposals for acts of the European Union as soon as they have been transmitted to the council of the European Union.
> In the manner laid down by the rules of procedure of each House, European resolutions may be passed, even if Parliament is not in session, on the drafts or proposals referred to in the preceding paragraph, as well as on any document issuing from a European Union Institution.
> A committee in charge of European affairs shall be set up in each parliamentary assembly.
> Article 88–5
> Any government bill authorizing the ratification of a treaty pertaining to the accession of a state to the European Union shall be submitted to referendum by the president of the republic.
> Notwithstanding the foregoing, by passing a motion adopted in identical terms in each House by a three-fifths majority, Parliament may authorize the passing of the bill according to the procedure provided for in paragraph three of article 89.
> [Article 88–5 is not applicable to accessions that result from an Intergovernmental Conference whose meeting was decided by the European Council before July 1, 2004.]
> Article 88–6
> The National Assembly or the Senate may issue a reasoned opinion as to the conformity of a draft proposal for a European Act with the principle of subsidiarity. Said opinion shall be addressed by the President of the House involved to the Presidents of the European Parliament, the Council of the European Union and the European Commission. The Government shall be informed of said opinion.
> Each House may institute proceedings before the Court of Justice of the European Union against a European Act for non-compliance with the principle of subsidiarity.

The exact same reasoning is followed in Decision no. 97–394 DC – *Treaty of Amsterdam amending the Treaty on European Union, the Treaties establishing the European Communities and certain related instruments.*[22] This time, the 'limitations of national sovereignty' that resulted in the impossibility to ratify the treaty without prior constitutional amendment concerned the transfers of powers to the community in matters of asylum, immigration and the crossing of internal and external frontiers.

In Decision no. 2004–505 DC – *Treaty establishing a Constitution for Europe*, the henceforth classic phrase is enriched: 'When however commitments entered into for such purposes contain a clause running counter to the Constitution, *call into question constitutionally guaranteed rights and freedoms or adversely affect the fundamental conditions of the exercising of national sovereignty*, authorization to ratify such measures shall require a prior revision of the Constitution.'[23] The Council concludes that neither the assertion of 'primacy' of the European Union law, nor the title of the new Treaty or the Charter of Fundamental Rights of the European Union require a revision of the French Constitution, but that other clauses of the Constitution for Europe 'which transfer to the European Union powers affecting the essential conditions of the exercise of national sovereignty in areas or on terms other than those provided for in the Treaties referred to in article 88–2' do. This is notably so with the subsidiarity principle, with the ordinary legislative procedure, with the simplified revision procedures of the Treaty of European Union, with the new powers vested in national parliaments in the framework of the Union, and more generally with

> any provisions of the Treaty which, in a matter inherent to the exercise of national sovereignty and already coming under the competences of the Union or the Community, modify the applicable rules of decision-making, either by replacing the unanimous vote by a qualified majority vote in the

Such proceedings shall be referred to the Court of Justice of the European Union by the Government.

For the purpose of the foregoing, resolutions may be passed, even if Parliament is not in session, in the manner set down by the Rules of Procedure of each House for the tabling and discussion thereof.

Article 88–7

Parliament may, by the passing of a motion in identical terms by the National Assembly and the Senate, oppose any modification of the rules governing the passing of Acts of the European Union in cases provided for under the simplified revision procedure for treaties or under judicial cooperation on civil matters, as set forth in the Treaty on European Union and the Treaty on the Functioning of the European Union, as they result from the treaty signed in Lisbon on December 13, 2007.

22 Decision no. 97–394 DC – *Treaty of Amsterdam amending the Treaty on European Union, the Treaties establishing the European Communities and certain related instruments*, pt. 6.

23 Decision no. 2004–505 DC – *Treaty establishing a Constitution for Europe*, pt. 7 (emphasis added).

> Council, thus depriving France of any power to oppose such a decision, or by conferring decision-making powers on the European Parliament, which is not an emanation of national sovereignty, or by depriving France of any power of acting on its own initiative.[24]

In Decision no. 2007–560 DC – *Treaty of Lisbon amending the Treaty on European Union and the Treaty establishing the European Community*, the Council recalls the same compatibility clause as in 2004[25] and repeats thereafter the exact same reasoning given the similarities between the Lisbon Treaty and the aborted Constitution for Europe. However, in this 2007 decision the Council takes a step further in distinguishing European Union law and international law. Not only does it refer to article 88–1 of the Constitution as revised since the Treaty of Maastricht (indeed, since 1992, referral to article 88–1 was added to paragraphs 14 and 15 of the Preamble 1946), but also points out that 'while confirming the place of the Constitution at the summit of the domestic legal order, these constitutional provisions enable France to participate in the creation and development of a permanent European organization vested with a separate legal personality and decision-taking powers by reason of the transfer of powers agreed to by the Member States'.[26] As a matter of fact, between 1992 and 2007, the shift towards the recognition of the autonomy of the European Union legal order is subtle but clear. Whereas, for instance, in the 1997 decision, the Council still referred to an *international organization* ('in accordance with the Preamble to the 1946 Constitution, concluding international agreements for participation in the establishment or development of a permanent international organization'), in 2004, there is a referral to '[enable France to participate in the creation and development of] a *permanent European organization*', (emphasis added) and, in 2007, the balance between the place of the Constitution at the summit of the domestic legal order and the participation of France to the European Union is clearly stated. Thus, the Council takes an unambiguous position as far as the interaction between French constitutional law and European Union law is concerned. After having clarified this relation, the Council recalls once again that if 'undertakings entered into for this purpose contain a clause running counter to the Constitution' its revision is necessary.

24 Decision no. 2004–505 DC – *Treaty establishing a Constitution for Europe*, pts. 24 and 29.
25 Decision no. 2007–560 DC – *Treaty of Lisbon amending the Treaty on European Union and the Treaty establishing the European Community*, pt. 9.
26 Decision no. 2007–560 DC – *Treaty of Lisbon amending the Treaty on European Union and the Treaty establishing the European Community*, pt. 8.

The same remarks apply to Decision no. 2012–653 DC – *Treaty on Stability, Coordination and Governance in the Economic and Monetary Union*,[27] which follows an identical reasoning. However, in this decision, the Council considers that the provisions on the 'fiscal compact' and the other provisions of the Treaty are not unconstitutional. Nevertheless, this conclusion is subject to certain conditions enumerated by the Council in paragraphs 21, 28 and 30 of the decision,[28] the non-satisfaction of which would render the Treaty unconstitutional, since it is only under these conditions that the Treaty provisions 'will not infringe the essential conditions for the exercise of national sovereignty'.

Finally, Decision no. 2017–749 DC – *Comprehensive Economic and Trade Agreement between Canada*, on the one hand, and the European Union and its Member States, on the other, concerns a particular case, namely an EU *mixed agreement*: an agreement that must be signed and entered into force both by the

[27] Decision no. 2012–653 DC – *Treaty on Stability, Coordination and Governance in the Economic and Monetary Union*, pts. 8–10.

[28] § 21: Considering that the Constitution lays down the prerogatives of the Government and Parliament in the elaboration and enactment of finance laws and social security financing laws; that the principle that finance laws are to be enacted annually results from articles 34 and 47 of the Constitution and applies with respect to the calendar year; that the direct introduction of provisions of binding force and permanent character mandating compliance with rules on balanced public finances requires that these constitutional provisions be amended; that consequently, *if France chooses to give effect to the rules laid down in paragraph 1 of article 3 through provisions of binding force and permanent character, authorization to ratify the Treaty may only be granted after the Constitution has been amended* (emphasis added).

§ 28: Considering that according to the above, *if in order to comply with the commitment stated in paragraph 1 of article 3, France chooses to adopt an institutional act having the effect required under paragraph 2, in line with the second alternative stated in the first phrase of paragraph 2 of article 3, authorization to ratify the treaty may only be granted after the Constitution has been amended* (emphasis added).

§ 30: Considering that paragraph 2 of article 3 does not require that the Constitution be amended in advance, the provisions of article 8 do not have the effect of enabling the Court of Justice of the European Union to assess within this framework whether the provisions of the Constitution are compatible with the terms of this Treaty; that accordingly, *if France decides to give effect to the rules laid down in paragraph 1 of article 3 of the Treaty in accordance with the procedures stated in the second alternative in the first sentence of paragraph 2 of article 3, article 8 will not infringe the essential conditions for the exercise of national sovereignty* (emphasis added).

European Union and by each of its Member States. The Council, while following its case law on limitations of sovereignty, has thus to innovate. It asserts that

> it is its responsibility to distinguish between, on the one hand, *the stipulations of this agreement that relate to the exclusive competence of the European union pursuant to the commitments previously agreed to by France* that led to the transfer of competence agreed to by Member States, and on the other, *the stipulations of this agreement that relate to the competence shared between the European Union and the Member States or competence belonging only to Member States*. In regard to stipulations of the agreement relating to shared competence between the European Union and the Member States or a competence belonging only to Member States, it is up to the Constitutional Council, as is established in paragraph 11, to *determine if these stipulations contain a clause that is unconstitutional, calls into question the rights and freedoms guaranteed by the Constitution or runs contrary to the essential conditions for the exercise of national sovereignty*.[29]

But, as far as the previously transferred exclusive EU competence is concerned, the Council adds a condition relative this time to 'the constitutional identity of France', known from its doctrine concerning the transposition of EU Directives:

> However, if the stipulations of the agreement establish exclusive competence of the European Union, the Constitutional Council *is only asked to determine if authorization to ratify this agreement requires a constitutional review, to establish that they do not call into question a rule or a principle inherent to the constitutional identity of France*. If this is not called into question, it is up to the judge of the European Union to oversee the compatibility of the agreement with European Union law.[30]

The Council carefully examines the provisions of the Treaty, especially those relative to shared competences (the threshold to consider that a principle inherent to the constitutional identity of France is infringed being much higher), and concludes that the Comprehensive Economic and Trade Agreement between Canada, on the one hand, and the European Union and its Member States, on the other, does not contain unconstitutional clauses.

Besides the European Union treaties, and notwithstanding the gradual distinction operated by the Constitutional Council between public international law and European Union law, the doctrine of 'limitations of sovereignty' has been applied *mutatis mutandis* in other international treaties

[29] Decision no. 2017–749 DC – *Comprehensive Economic and Trade Agreement between Canada*, pts. 12 and 13 (emphasis added).

[30] Decision no. 2017–749 DC – *Comprehensive Economic and Trade Agreement between Canada*, pt. 14 (emphasis added).

signed by France.[31] Decision no. 98–408 DC – *Treaty laying down the Statute of the International Criminal Court* constitutes the most important example of an incompatibility ruling having resulted in the amendment of the French Constitution in order for an international treaty to be ratified. In this case, the incompatibility clause is formulated a little bit differently: 'Where an international agreement contains a clause *that is contrary to the Constitution or jeopardizes the rights and freedoms secured by the Constitution*, the authorization to ratify it requires revision of the Constitution.'[32] Instead of adding 'jeopardizes the rights and freedoms secured by the Constitution' to 'jeopardizing the essential conditions for the exercise of national sovereignty' like in the 2004, 2007 and 2012 decisions, the Council replaces the latter by the former. However, the reasoning and result are the same. After having found the incompatibility of several clauses of the Statute of the International Criminal Court in regards with specific articles of the French Constitution (provisions on the criminal responsibility of the holders of certain official status are contrary to the special constitutional rules governing liability of the President of the Republic, Members of the Parliament and of the Government),[33] the Council goes on to examine more generally the 'respect of the essential conditions for exercise of national sovereignty' (under a section of the decision that bears this title). The review concerns the principle of complementarity between the International Criminal Court and the national courts, the international cooperation, judicial assistance and the Prosecutor's powers, as well as the enforcement of sentences passed by the International Criminal Court. The Council finds that

> under the Statute, the International Criminal Court could be validly seized on the grounds of an amnesty statute or internal rules on limitation; in such a case, France, even if a State were neither unwilling nor unable to act, might be required to arrest and surrender to the Court a person accused of conduct covered by an amnesty or limitation period in French law; this would violate the essential conditions for the exercise of national sovereignty.[34]

31 See for instance Decision no. 85–188 DC – *Protocole n° 6 additionnel à la Convention Européenne de sauvegarde des Droits de l'homme et des libertés fondamentales concernant l'abolition de la peine de mort, signé par la France le 28 avril 1983*; Decision no. 78–93 DC 29 April 1978 – *Loi autorisant l'augmentation de la quote-part de la France au Fonds monétaire international*; Decision no. 2005–524/525 DC, 13 December 2005 – *Engagements internationaux relatifs à l'abolition de la peine de mort.*

32 Decision no. 98–408 DC – *Treaty laying down the Statute of the International Criminal Court*, pt. 12 (emphasis added).

33 Articles 26, 68 and 68–1 of the Constitution 1958.

34 Decision no. 98–408 DC, 22 January 1999 – *Treaty laying down the Statute of the International Criminal Court*, pt. 34.

It also finds that 'the power conferred on the Prosecutor to carry out these measures without the presence of the competent French legal authorities is liable to violate the essential conditions for the exercise of national sovereignty'.[35] Thus, authorization to ratify the treaty laying down the Statute of the International Criminal Court required amendment of the French Constitution.

What is interesting in this decision is the clear dichotomy between contrariety to the Constitution per se (its articles or the constitutional principles) and incompatibility with the 'respect of the essential conditions for exercise of national sovereignty'. Contrary to previous decisions on European Treaties, the Constitutional Council does not explicitly conclude here that limitation of the essential conditions for exercise of national sovereignty is *as such* unconstitutional, but rather dresses two different hypotheses that both result in the necessity of Constitution amendment.[36] Thus, the respect of the essential conditions for exercise of national sovereignty becomes an autonomous basis of review, alongside the 'bloc de constitutionnalité'. When such a 'general' infringement is asserted by the Constitutional Council, the necessary amendment of the Constitution cannot aim at this or that article (since no precise article is identified by the Council). In such a case, the only amendment leading to the possibility to ratify the international treaty is to add in the Constitution a habilitation clause (such as article 88–1 after the 1992 Decision or article 53–2 after the 1998 Decision)[37] authorizing such an undertaking as compatible with national sovereignty.[38]

Such a mechanism raises once again the question of the actual normativity of the French Constitution and of its true interaction with international (or even foreign relations) law. It is of course clear that, in theory, still nothing changes as far as the supremacy of the French Constitution in the French legal order is concerned. The mere fact that the international treaty cannot be ratified without previous amendment of the Constitution goes to show that the latter prevails normatively over the former. However, when a Constitution is over and over again amended in order for international treaties to be ratified and *a fortiori* when some of the modifications at hand consist in a simple

[35] Decision no. 98–408 DC, 22 January 1999 – *Treaty laying down the Statute of the International Criminal Court*, pt. 38.

[36] See also Combacau, 'La souveraineté internationale de l'Etat dans la jurisprudence du Conseil constitutionnel français'.

[37] 'The Republic may recognize the jurisdiction of the International Criminal Court as provided for by the Treaty signed on 18 July 1998', added to the Constitution by the Constitutional Law of June 28, 1999.

[38] For a more theoretical analysis see Combacau, 'La souveraineté internationale de l'Etat dans la jurisprudence du Conseil constitutionnel français'.

addition of a habilitation clause, it cannot be denied that such a Constitution seems less 'rigid' than the ones that leave no place to that kind of amendments. The theoretical place of the French Constitution in the hierarchy of norms may be the same as in other constitutional countries, but its actual normative density can be questioned, since the executive, the Parliament and the Constitutional Council can all influence the outcome of a constitutional amendment through their conduct of foreign relations.

V CRITICAL ASSESSMENT OF THE CONSEIL CONSTITUTIONNEL'S DIFFERENT DECISIONS THAT APPLIED THE 'LIMITATION OF SOVEREIGNTY' DOCTRINE

What is striking in this panorama of the Constitutional Council's case law – other than the relative 'hypocrisy' of the assertion concerning the absolute primacy of a Constitution that is revised as and when the ratification of a new international treaty needs it – is the rather arbitrary way in which the Council decides which limitations of sovereignty are tolerable and which are not, at least as far as the substantial content of 'national sovereignty' is concerned. Indeed, the review of those few decisions does not allow to predict for the future which international treaties will be considered by the Council as respecting the essential conditions for the exercise of national sovereignty. It does not allow either to dress an inventory of different substantial criteria (other than purely material/formal ones) taken into account by the Council in order to decide or to provide some guidelines as to how it will exercise its control power.[39] Notwithstanding the constancy of the reasoning itself, the actual arguments and results are essentially built on a case by case basis.

Concerning the actual determination of what 'national sovereignty' entails and which are the 'essential conditions' for its exercise, the only decision that tried to identify some elements was the 1985 one, as seen above. However, not only the three elements put forward in that case by the Constitutional Council did not survive in the subsequent decisions, but also and foremost the deliberation minutes of the 1985 decision indicate that there was no real intention to define 'national sovereignty' by those three elements invoked.[40] The consequence is a rather confusing case law as to why one international treaty is

[39] See also Combacau, 'La souveraineté internationale de l'Etat dans la jurisprudence du Conseil constitutionnel français'.

[40] Hamann, 'Sur un "sentiment" de souveraineté', 207, II. B.

considered to infringe the *essential* (?) conditions for the exercise of *national sovereignty* (?), whereas another international treaty is not. The consultation of several deliberation minutes (henceforth available for the earlier decisions) reinforce this impression of obscurity and arbitrariness.[41] As a matter of fact, the doctrine of 'essential conditions for the exercise of national sovereignty' is only a partial and incomplete one at best.

The only common factor that can be identified throughout the different decisions (besides the 'reciprocity' criterium invoked again and again by the Council, but also found in paragraph 15 of the Preamble 1946) is *material* concerning the *conditions* of the international engagement.[42] In short, if France maintains a certain liberty of action (for instance, to denounce the treaty even if the treaty does not actually contain a denunciation clause[43] or to invoke an exception derogatory clause in case of urgency or necessity) and if the Constitutional Council is able to review any future undertaking going further than the previous ones, then it seems that the essential conditions for the exercise of national sovereignty are respected.

However, if the Council seems to have a clear course of action as to the *material* conditions of powers' exercise that the treaty must satisfy, there is little indication (besides the mere listing of the spheres enumerated in the different decisions up to today) as to the domains in which the treaties can intervene in order for the undertaking to respect the essential conditions for the exercise of national sovereignty. Certainly, the Council asserts that 'the international agreements entered into by the authorities of the French Republic may not

[41] See analysis and long critical assessment in Hamann, 'Sur un "sentiment" de souveraineté', 207, II. B. According to the author:

> The confusion by the Council between two concepts that are alien to each other, as well as its ignorance of the singularity of State sovereignty in its international law meaning, inevitably lead to issues of State sovereignty to be measured against a famous tool of its own fabric, the 'essential conditions for exercising national sovereignty'. As an operative tool for review, this concept is consequently inadequate – and can only be inadequate, as the minutes of the Council's deliberations reveal today, given that the fate of these 'essential conditions for exercising national sovereignty' was but an accident, the product of a mistake which became 'jurisprudence constante'.

[42] Hamann, 'Sur un "sentiment" de souveraineté', 207, II.B for the distinction between material/formal elements and substantial elements.

[43] See the apparent contradiction between Decision no. 85–188 DC, 22 May 1985 – *Protocole n° 6 additionnel à la Convention Européenne de sauvegarde des Droits de l'homme et des libertés fondamentales concernant l'abolition de la peine de mort, signé par la France le 28 avril 1983*, pt. 1; Decision no. 91–294 DC, 25 July 1991 – *Loi autorisant l'approbation de la convention d'application de l'accord de Schengen*, pt. 58; Decision no. 2005–524/525 DC, 13 December 2005 – *Engagements internationaux relatifs à l'abolition de la peine de mort*, pt. 5; Decision no. 2017–749 DC – *Comprehensive Economic and Trade Agreement between Canada*, pt. 69.

adversely affect the exercise by the state of the powers that are at the core of its national sovereignty'.[44] It also refers to 'arrangements which deprive the Member States of their own powers in a matter which is vital to the exercise of national sovereignty'.[45] Still, no clear list of which those matters are is given nor the criteria to identify those matters are laid down. In other words, the 'national sovereignty' in its *substantial* meaning is not really defined by the Constitutional Council (as it is not defined by paragraph 15 of the Preamble 1946 either), although this same Council establishes itself in its case law as the 'national sovereignty's' guarantor.

Thus, the executive branch has no real guidance as to which international treaties are likely to be deemed respectful of the essential conditions for the exercise of national sovereignty by the Council and which are not. If it is free to conduct foreign relations as it wishes, and if the French legal order encourages international cooperation, the executive is never immune from a Conseil Constitutionnel's incompatibility decision resulting in a long process of a prior Constitution amendment in order for the treaty in question to be ratified. Of course, when the *a priori* constitutional review is not compulsory, referral to the Council will depend on the will of the executive (President of Republic and Prime Minister) or of the legislative (President of one or the other of the Houses or sixty Members of the National Assembly or sixty Senators). Thus, the possible interference of the Constitutional Council in the conduct of foreign relations is not without limits and its role remains closely linked to the one of the executive and the legislative branches. Still, it is clear that the Council conserves great power and discretion as to its review and its possibility to weigh upon the ratification process of the most important international treaties. In other words, its position in the management of France's foreign relations is rather significant.

44 Decision no. 92–308 DC, 9 April 1992 – *Treaty on European Union (Maastricht I)*, pt. 49.

45 Decision no. 92–308 DC, 9 April 1992 – *Treaty on European Union (Maastricht I)*, pt. 43.

9

Democratic Participation in International Lawmaking in Switzerland after the 'Age of Treaties'

Anna Petrig*

I INTRODUCTION

If someone were asked to name but one typical feature of the Swiss constitutional system, chances are high that the answer would be 'direct democracy'. Indeed, Switzerland is arguably the state granting the most far-reaching democratic participation rights in the process of lawmaking; and this holds true for both domestic and international law. Since the late 1990s, the concept of 'parallelism' – the idea that the same degree of domestic democratic legitimacy should apply to the making of international law as it does to the enactment of domestic law – has been progressively implemented. As a result, from a comparative perspective, the Swiss legal framework on democratic participation in international lawmaking is unique in terms of the actors involved, the phases during which participation is possible, and the intensity and effects it features. Despite the breadth of this legal framework, it is simultaneously very narrowly designed: in its largest parts, it is geared towards just one source of international law – treaties. The 'age of treaties', however, seems to be over and informal lawmaking increasingly supersedes formal lawmaking.

In the introduction to this book, the editors note that the 'horizons of international law have greatly expanded' and that this expansion 'affected the two most foundational organizing concepts of this body of law: sources and subjects'.[1] During the post-1945 period, states were the main players in international lawmaking, often acting under the auspices of an international organisation (IO), and treaties were the main vehicle to bring international legalisation forward. After the turn of the millennium, however, the

* I would like to sincerely thank Dr Maria Orchard, J.D./LL.M., for the editorial work on the chapter.

[1] See the introductory chapter by Helmut Philipp Aust and Thomas Kleinlein, p. 10.

international institutional landscape changed dramatically and a series of new actors appeared, which notably participate in the production of norms. While these new participants in international lawmaking are as diverse as non-governmental organisations (NGOs), transnational corporations, industry associations and regulatory agencies, they share a commonality: not one of them possesses international legal personality (yet) and, consequently, they all lack treaty-making capacity. Their normative output is thus condemned to fall short of formal international law – they cannot regulate but through informal law.

The Swiss legal framework on democratic participation in international lawmaking, being a child of its time, is largely predicated on a very traditional understanding of international law. Yet, the mentioned structural changes in international law did not go unnoticed in politics and among the broader public. In recent years, there has been a growing awareness that the Swiss mechanisms for generating democratic legitimacy need to be adjusted in light of these new (complex) realities if they are to maintain their function. Still, building new bridges in the context of informal law has proven to be far more complex than it is for treaties: what we praise as the beauties of informal lawmaking – namely that the process and actors are not being forced into a rigid corset – turn out to be the beasts when it comes to grasping the phenomenon in constitutional and statutory terms. International informal lawmaking sets boundaries on democratisation 'from below' that do not exist for treaty-making; such limits arise, for example, from the fact that the state may not even sit at the negotiating table. Overall, informal lawmaking greatly complicates the relationship between sovereignty (including domestic democratic self-determination) and international cooperation – and, to some extent, their simultaneous realisation is no easier than squaring a circle. This insight is difficult to accept for a state like Switzerland, where democratic participation in lawmaking is part of its constitutional DNA. At the same time, one tends to forget that Switzerland is one of the most globalised countries of the world and not seldom a driving force behind informal lawmaking projects.

In order to fully grasp the significance of the turn to informal lawmaking for the Swiss legal framework, which governs democratic participation in international lawmaking, it is necessary to take a step back and understand its roots, development and context. Accordingly, this chapter sets the scene by demonstrating that foreign relations law exists in Switzerland, even if this label is rarely attached to the respective set of rules. It lays out two main categories of norms belonging to it, which are those providing substantive guidance for the conduct of foreign policy and those allocating powers in this realm. This will demonstrate that foreign relations are no longer understood as an exceptional state activity subject to political discretion, and thus a prerogative of the executive, but rather as coming within the ordinary constitutional framework and being a competence jointly exercised by the government and Parliament; a result of a steady move towards normalisation[2] (Section II). It then goes on to describe that, mainly as a reaction to internationalisation, the democratic participation rights in international lawmaking were increasingly bolstered in the 1990s and the early years of the new millennium and the concept of 'parallelism', which testifies to the high degree of normalisation in the field of international lawmaking, was progressively implemented (Section III). It then discusses how the shift to informal lawmaking deprives this highly developed, but heavily treaty-oriented, democratic participation mechanism of much of its relevance, how the legislator has reacted to the rising importance of informal law, and what challenges potentially lay ahead in building new bridges (Section IV). A brief conclusion notes that not every boundary can be overcome with a bridge and that globalisation and international cooperation arguably come at a cost to democracy; yet such costs can be reduced with a domestic democratic participation framework, which is not anchored in traditional international lawmaking but reflects the complexities of contemporary international norm production (Section V).

II SWISS FOREIGN RELATIONS LAW: TOWARDS NORMALISATION

A *Is There a 'Swiss Foreign Relations Law'?*

'Foreign relations law' has been defined as encompassing 'the domestic law of each nation that governs how that nation interacts with the rest of the world', most importantly with other nations and international institutions.[3] As per Karen Knop, '[a]ll legal systems deal with foreign relations issues, but few have a field of "foreign relations law"'.[4] This statement succinctly describes the current situation in Switzerland where foreign relations law has not yet emerged as a distinct field of study or law. So far, even the term 'foreign

[2] See text belonging to n. 42 below for a definition of the term.

[3] Curtis A. Bradley, 'Foreign Relations Law as a Field of Study' (2017) 111 AJIL 316–20 at 318; in similar terms: the chapter by Aust and Kleinlein, p. 9.

[4] Karen Knop, 'Foreign Relations Law: Comparison as Invention', in Curtis A. Bradley (ed.), *The Oxford Handbook of Comparative Foreign Relations Law* (Oxford: Oxford University Press, 2019), p. 45; see also Campbell McLachlan, 'Five Conceptions of the Function of Foreign Relations Law', in Curtis A. Bradley (ed.), *The Oxford Handbook of Comparative Foreign Relations Law* (Oxford: Oxford University Press, 2019), p. 21.

relations law' has been sparsely used in writings on legal rules governing how Switzerland interacts with other subjects of international law.[5] Similarly, courses specifically entitled 'foreign relations law' are a rare occurrence in Swiss universities as compared to American universities where such courses tend to be more commonplace.[6] Nonetheless, a densely knit web of legal provisions governing Switzerland's interaction with other states and international actors is in place and continues to develop.

The Federal Constitution of 1999[7] contains a series of provisions governing foreign relations, the entirety of which is denoted as the 'external constitution' ('*Aussenverfassung*'); a term firmly rooted in the constitutional discourse since the adoption of the current constitution.[8] Indeed, the predecessor Constitution of 1874 regulated foreign relations only in fragments and left various aspects to constitutional practice.[9] The Constitution of 1999 is the first federal constitution comprising a fairly comprehensive legal framework for the conduct of foreign relations, which justifiably deserves the designation as 'external constitution'. In terms of substance, the 'external constitution' can roughly be divided into provisions allocating authority and provisions containing substantive guidance for the conduct of foreign relations.[10] These two sets of norms – to which we turn next – are specified and refined at the level of federal acts and ordinances. Further, in some fields, rules have also been developed through the case law of the Swiss

5 But see recently Odile Ammann, *Domestic Courts and the Interpretation of International Law: Methods and Reasoning Based on the Swiss Example* (Leiden: Brill Nijhoff, 2019), pp. 65–6. It must be noted, however, that the term cannot be translated into German or French in a succinct way.

6 Aspects of foreign relations law are integrated in general courses; there is no equivalent to Staatsrecht III taught in Germany (on the latter, see Helmut Philipp Aust, 'The Democratic Challenge to Foreign Relations Law in Transatlantic Perspective', in Jacco Bomhoff, David Dyzenhaus and Thomas Poole (eds.), *The Double-Facing Constitution* (Cambridge: Cambridge University Press, 2020), p. 363). Exceptional in that sense is the course 'Foreign Relations Law in Comparative Perspective' taught by Roland Portmann at the University of St. Gallen, available at https://tools.unisg.ch/handlers/Public/CourseInformationSheet.ashx/semester/FS19/eventnumber/8,492,1.00, accessed 29 June 2020.

7 Federal Constitution of the Swiss Confederation of 18 April 1999, Classified compilation 101 (hereinafter: Constitution of 1999); the entire federal law is available at www.admin.ch/gov/en/start/federal-law/classified-compilation.html, accessed 29 June 2020 (where existing, the English translation, which does not have legal force, is cited).

8 For an early reference, see Giovanni Biaggini, 'Das Verhältnis der Schweiz zur internationalen Gemeinschaft: Neuerungen im Rahmen der Verfassungsreform' (1999) *Aktuelle Juristische Praxis* 722–9, passim; see also, e.g., Roland Kley and Roland Portmann, 'Vorbemerkungen zur Aussenverfassung', in Bernhard Ehrenzeller et al. (eds.), *Die Schweizerische Bundesverfassung: St. Galler Kommentar*, 3rd ed., 2 vols. (Zürich: Dike, 2014), vol. I, p. 1097.

9 See Biaggini, 'Internationale Gemeinschaft', 723.

10 Kley and Portmann, 'Aussenverfassung', p. 1097.

Federal Supreme Court.[11] In sum, foreign relations law is not (yet) treated as a discrete field of law or study in Switzerland, but certainly exists as a matter of fact.[12]

B *Substantive Guidance for the Conduct of Foreign Policy*

The Constitution of 1999 is novel in that it spells out general foreign policy objectives.[13] Article 54(2), entitled 'foreign relations', represents the key reference point in terms of material guidance for the conduct of foreign policy.[14] Substantive orientation can further be found in various other parts of the Constitution.[15] The operationalisation and (to some extent) concretisation of these goals painted with broad brushstrokes takes place through an increasing number of federal statutes pertaining to foreign relations-related activities,[16] the adoption of treaties, and by means of foreign policy decisions by the authorities.[17]

The constitutional statements providing substantive guidance for the conduct of foreign policy feature varying degrees of abstraction and normativity.[18] Yet they share a commonality: they all testify to the legislator's heightened awareness in the 1990s of globalisation and global interdependence and the consequent growing importance of foreign relations. This phenomenon led to an incremental blending of the internal and external dimension of a state's policy[19] and the increased difficulty of clearly separating internal forms of state

[11] As per Kley and Portmann, 'Aussenverfassung', p. 1107, the significance of court decisions in the context of foreign relations has increased in recent years.

[12] This holds equally true for other jurisdictions; see, e.g., Bradley, 'Field of Study', 319, for the United States.

[13] Biaggini, 'Internationale Gemeinschaft', 723.

[14] Bernhard Ehrenzeller and Roland Portmann, 'Art. 54(2)', in Bernhard Ehrenzeller et al. (eds.), *Die Schweizerische Bundesverfassung: St. Galler Kommentar*, 3rd ed., 2 vols. (Zürich: Dike, 2014), vol. I, p. 1125.

[15] See, e.g., preamble, para. 4, and art. 2(1) and (4) setting out the goals to be pursued by the Confederation; foreign policy goals are further mentioned in provisions on specific subject matters, see, e.g., art. 101(1) on foreign economic policy.

[16] They cover a wide range of issues, such as Swiss army participation in international peacekeeping operations, development aid, the strengthening of human rights and the rule of law in third states, or the transfer of war material and related technology abroad; for a list of relevant statutes: Ehrenzeller and Portmann, 'Art. 54(2)', p. 1130.

[17] Ehrenzeller and Portmann, 'Art. 54(2)', pp. 1130–4.

[18] See Biaggini, 'Internationale Gemeinschaft', 723–4.

[19] Raffaela Kunz and Anne Peters, 'Constitutionalisation and Democratisation of Foreign Affairs: The Case of Switzerland', in Anneli Alba and Samo Bardutzky (eds.), *National Constitutions in European and Global Governance: Democracy, Rights, the Rule of Law* (Berlin: Springer, 2019), pp. 1519 and 1499.

action from external forms[20] – an insight that, as we will see, provided momentum for the normalisation of foreign affairs.

C *Allocation of Powers on Foreign Policy*

The second category of provisions of the 'external constitution' allocates power between the various levels of government (Confederation and Cantons) and branches of government (executive, legislative and judiciary). These provisions, accounting for the lion's share of the 'external constitution',[21] are more chiselled and specific as compared to those providing substantive guidance for the conduct of foreign policy. Their content is forged by the tension between the executive's claim (and need) for a certain degree of flexibility and swiftness when conducting foreign policy[22] and the quest to give due weight to federalism and democracy. The more internationalisation has progressed and the more foreign policy has shaped the domestic political environment, the more fiercely the question of vertical and horizontal allocation of powers in foreign policy has been debated.[23] Overall, the tendency is to give more weight to democracy and federalism – after all, both are foundational principles of the Constitution[24] – in order to prevent them being undermined by the externalisation of many policy areas.

As Switzerland is a federal state – the Confederation consists of 26 Cantons, which are 'sovereign except to the extent that their sovereignty is limited by the Federal Constitution'[25] – the Constitution of 1999 explicitly addresses the vertical separation of powers: foreign relations are, as per Article 54(1) of the Constitution, 'the responsibility of the Confederation', even for matters domestically falling within the competence of the Cantons.[26] This implies

20 See the chapter by Aust and Kleinlein, p. 5.

21 Matthias Oesch, 'Ein Europa-Artikel für die schweizerische Bundesverfassung', in Andreas Glaser and Lorenz Langer (eds.), *Die Verfassungsdynamik der europäischen Integration und demokratische Partizipation* (Zürich: Dike, 2015), p. 165.

22 Critically on whether a *general* need for flexibility and swiftness exists in the conduct of foreign relations: Bernhard Ehrenzeller, *Legislative Gewalt und Aussenpolitik: Eine rechtsvergleichende Studie zu den parlamentarischen Entscheidungskompetenzen des deutschen Bundestags, des amerikanischen Kongresses und der schweizerischen Bundesversammlung im auswärtigen Bereich* (Basel: Helbing Lichtenhahn, 1993), pp. 330–1.

23 Kley and Portmann, 'Aussenverfassung', p. 1103.

24 Conseil fédéral (CH), Message relative à une nouvelle constitution fédérale du 20 novembre 1996, Feuille fédérale 1997 I 1, pp. 14–15.

25 Constitution of 1999, art. 3.

26 Giovanni Biaggini, *BV Kommentar: Bundesverfassung der Schweizerischen Eidgenossenschaft* (Zürich: Orell Füssli, 2017), p. 583; Walter Haller, *The Swiss Constitution in a Comparative Context*, 2nd ed. (Zürich: Dike, 2016), p. 71; Roland Portmann, 'Foreign Affairs Federalism in

a certain erosion of cantonal competences as internationalisation progresses. It is against this background that the Constitution of 1999, by way of compensation, stipulates that the Confederation 'shall respect the powers of the Cantons and protect their interests'.[27] Moreover, the Constitution foresees a role for Cantons in foreign policy affairs, albeit a subordinate one. Concretely, Article 55 confers Cantons participatory rights in foreign policy decisions by stipulating that the Cantons 'shall be consulted' if the respective decisions 'affect their powers or their essential interests';[28] and that the 'Confederation shall inform the Cantons fully and in good time and shall consult with them'.[29] Further, Article 56, which governs relations between the Cantons and foreign states, authorises the Cantons to conduct their own foreign policy in fields in which they are competent according to domestic federalism and to conclude treaties in these areas,[30] which is fittingly dubbed 'small foreign policy' ('*kleine Aussenpolitik*').[31] This autonomous foreign policy competence and residual treaty-making capacity of the Cantons[32] is of considerable practical importance since no less than fifteen Cantons border at least one foreign state.[33]

As regards the horizontal separation of powers, the Constitution is primarily concerned with the allocation of foreign relations competences between the executive and legislative branches, viz. between the government (Federal Council) on the one hand and the Parliament (Federal Assembly) and, for certain matters, the people, or the people and the Cantons, on the other. While some constitutions are based on a rebuttable presumption in favour of executive competence, the Swiss Constitution today follows a shared power approach whereby foreign relations are a domain equally entrusted to the executive and the legislature.[34] This was not always the case. Under the

Switzerland', in Curtis A. Bradley (ed.), *The Oxford Handbook of Comparative Foreign Relations Law* (Oxford: Oxford University Press, 2019), pp. 300–1.

27 Constitution of 1999, art. 54(3).

28 Constitution of 1999, art. 55(1).

29 Constitution of 1999, art. 55(2); these participatory rights are specified in the Federal Act on the Participation of the Cantons in the Foreign Policy of the Confederation, Classified compilation 138.1 (author's translation of: Loi fédérale sur la participation des cantons à la politique extérieure de la Confédération du 22 décembre 1999) (hereinafter: Cantonal Participation Act).

30 Portmann, 'Federalism', p. 300.

31 Thomas Pfisterer, 'Art. 55' in Bernhard Ehrenzeller et al. (eds.), *Die Schweizerische Bundesverfassung: St. Galler Kommentar*, 3rd ed., 2 vols. (Zürich: Dike, 2014), vol. I, p. 1162.

32 Portmann, 'Federalism', p. 299.

33 Biaggini, 'BV Kommentar', p. 600.

34 On the two approaches: Thomas Giegerich, 'Foreign Relations Law' (last updated January 2011), in Rüdiger Wolfrum (ed.), *Max Planck Encyclopedia of Public International Law*, online edition, https://opil.ouplaw.com/view/10.1093/law:epil/9780199231690/law-9780199231690-e937, accessed 29 June 2020, para. 20; on Switzerland, see Conseil fédéral (CH), Message

Constitution of 1874, foreign policy was understood to be a prerogative of the executive whereas the role of Parliament, the people and Cantons was essentially limited to the approval of certain categories of treaties.[35] In 1994, a revision of the Constitution of 1874 was initiated. Since previous attempts had failed, the mandate for this revision was very narrowly defined, essentially consisting in an 'update' ('*mise à jour*', '*Nachführung*') rather than a redesign: its primary objective was to systematise and streamline the content of the constitutional document and to bring it in line with the then-existing constitutional practice without, however, engaging in its substantive amendment.[36] Yet, capturing 'existing constitutional practice' and drawing a line between documenting the status quo and introducing novel elements proved challenging, and foreign relations law is exemplary in this regard. The provisions (re-) defining the role of Parliament in shaping foreign policy were among the most fiercely debated aspects because they were deemed by some to overstep the 'updating mandate'.[37] Indeed, the provisions ultimately adopted reflect a paradigm shift[38] as regards the allocation of authority on foreign policy by entrenching a shared power approach. However, this change did not happen overnight but rather started crystallising in preceding years in legislation and practice.

In constitutional terms, the shared power approach is expressed as follows: Article 184(1) stipulates, from the government's perspective, that '[t]he Federal Council is responsible for foreign relations, subject to the right of participation of the Federal Assembly'; while Article 166(1) states, from the Parliament's perspective, that '[t]he Federal Assembly shall participate in shaping foreign

relative à une nouvelle constitution fédérale du 20 novembre 1996, Feuille fédérale 1997 I 1, p. 399, and Kley and Portmann, 'Aussenverfassung', p. 1105, para. 25.

35 However, some authors argued that not the constitutional text but its interpretation led to such limited role for Parliament: see, e.g., Fritz Fleiner and Zaccaria Giacometti, *Schweizerisches Bundesstaatsrecht* (Zürich: Polygraphischer Verlag, 1949), pp. 525–6; and, fifty years later, Ehrenzeller, *Legislative Gewalt*, pp. 293–300, especially p. 298.

36 Eva Maria Belser, 'Einleitung', in Bernhard Waldmann, Eva Maria Belser and Astrid Epiney (eds.), *Bundesverfassung: Basler Kommentar* (Basel: Helbing Lichtenhahn, 2015), p. 11.

37 Biaggini, 'Internationale Gemeinschaft', 722; Florent Tripet Cordier, 'Art. 152', in Martin Graf, Cornelia Theler and Moritz von Wyss (eds.), *Parlamentsrecht und Parlamentspraxis der Schweizerischen Bundesversammlung: Kommentar zum Parlamentsgesetz (ParlG) vom 13. Dezember 2013* (Basel: Helbing Lichtenhahn, 2014), pp. 1035–6; mentioning these provisions as an example where the updating of the constitutional text necessarily implies the taking on board of novel elements: Conseil fédéral (CH), Message relative à une nouvelle constitution fédérale du 20 novembre 1996, Feuille fédérale 1997 I 1, p. 47.

38 Expression used by Jörg Künzli, 'Art. 184(1)', in Bernhard Waldmann, Eva Maria Belser and Astrid Epiney (eds.), *Bundesverfassung: Basler Kommentar* (Basel: Helbing Lichtenhahn, 2015), p. 2683.

policy and supervise the maintenance of foreign relations'. In order to describe this (new) cooperative relationship, which was specified by, inter alia, the Parliament Act,[39] Swiss constitutional doctrine metaphorically refers to the executive and legislative as 'fingers of the same hand' (*'les doigts d'une même main'*,[40] *'Verhältnis zu gesamter Hand'*).[41] The inclusion of a model of shared competences and intense cooperation between the executive and the legislative in the Constitution of 1999 marks a milestone in the overall trend of erosion of the executive's monopoly over large parts of foreign relations and is strong proof of a move towards normalisation.

D *Towards Normalisation of Foreign Relations*

In the context of foreign relations law, the term 'normalisation' is used to denote the phenomenon that 'the conduct of foreign relations is increasingly subjected to the constitutional and other legal standards that apply to other governmental action'.[42] From the brief overview on the main content of the Swiss 'external constitution' follows that foreign policy is no longer regarded as 'exceptional'[43] but rather as coming within the 'normal' constitutional framework.[44]

First of all, in Switzerland, the long-held view that the principle of legality – that is, subjecting the exercise of political and administrative powers to the law – does not apply to foreign policy is now outdated.[45] In the early 1990s,

39 Federal Act on the Federal Assembly (Parliament Act) of 13 December 2002, Classified compilation 171.10, especially arts. 24 and 152; on the genesis and content of these provisions: Luzian Odermatt and Esther Tophinke, 'Art. 24', in Martin Graf, Cornelia Theler and Moritz von Wyss (eds.), *Parlamentsrecht und Parlamentspraxis der Schweizerischen Bundesversammlung: Kommentar zum Parlamentsgesetz (ParlG) vom 13. Dezember 2013* (Basel: Helbing Lichtenhahn, 2014), pp. 195–201, and Tripet Cordier, 'Art. 152', pp. 1029–44.

40 Conseil fédéral (CH), Message relative à une nouvelle constitution fédérale du 20 novembre 1996, Feuille fédérale 1997 I 1, p. 399.

41 Bundesrat (CH), Botschaft über eine neue Bundesverfassung vom 20. November 1996, Bundesblatt 1997 I 1, p. 392.

42 See the chapter by Aust and Kleinlein, p. 14; see further, e.g., Ganesh Sitaraman and Ingrid Wuerth, 'The Normalization of Foreign Relations Law' (2015) 128 *Harvard Law Review* 1897–979 at 1901.

43 The term 'foreign affairs exceptionalism' has been coined by Curtis A. Bradley, 'A New American Foreign Affairs Law' (1997) 70 *Colorado Law Review* 1089–107 at 1096, and stands for 'the view that the ... government's foreign affairs powers are subject to a different, and generally more relaxed, set of constitutional restraints than those that govern its domestic powers'.

44 See Portmann, 'Federalism', p. 302.

45 On the development of this view, see Matthias Lanz, *Bundesversammlung und Aussenpolitik: Möglichkeiten und Grenzen parlamentarischer Mitwirkung* (Zürich: Dike, 2020), pp. 37-43.

Bernhard Ehrenzeller – author of the first comprehensive treatise examining the role of the legislative in foreign policy and advocate of a shared power approach – deplored that foreign affairs were, in various respects, perceived as 'exceptional state activity' and treated accordingly.[46] Indeed, at that time, Swiss practice and prevailing doctrine viewed foreign relations as an area that cannot be regulated by law.[47] Jean Monnier put it quite bluntly by writing that 'foreign affairs are a subject matter inappropriate for codification';[48] while Luzius Wildhaber warned that legislation related to foreign policy would risk lacking substance (or even be insubstantial altogether) and could at most pertain to the allocation of powers.[49] Bernhard Ehrenzeller criticised this 'almost mythical perception of foreign policy as an area not susceptible to normalization' that prevailed at the time.[50]

Yet, at latest with the adoption of the Constitution of 1999, 'a shift away from exceptionalism' took place[51] – to use a term coined by Curtis A. Bradley in this very period of time and describing a similar phenomenon occurring in the United States.[52] As demonstrated, the Swiss Constitution provides substantive guidance for the conduct of Switzerland's foreign policy (although still in a modest way as compared to the domestic policy sphere);[53] and the move towards normalisation is further evidenced by the ever-growing body of rules and statutes concretising and operationalising these foreign policy objectives.[54] All in all, the principle of legality – a cornerstone of the rule of

46 Bernhard Ehrenzeller, *Legislative Gewalt und Aussenpolitik: Eine rechtsvergleichende Studie zu den parlamentarischen Entscheidungskompetenzen des deutschen Bundestags, des amerikanischen Kongresses und der schweizerischen Bundesversammlung im auswärtigen Bereich* (Basel: Helbing Lichtenhahn, 1993), p. 298 (in the original: 'Sonderfall der Staatstätigkeit').

47 See, e.g., Luzius Wildhaber, 'Legalitätsprinzip und Aussenpolitik', in Edouard Brunner et al. (eds), *Einblick in die schweizerische Aussenpolitik: Zum 65. Geburtstag für Staatssekretär Raymond Probst* (Zürich: Verlag Neue Zürcher Zeitung, 1984), p. 447.

48 Jean Monnier, 'Les principes et les règles constitutionnels de la politique étrangere' (1986) 127/II *Revue de droit suisse* 107–247 at 157 (in the original: 'la politique étrangère est une matière impropre à la codification').

49 Wildhaber, 'Legalitätsprinzip und Aussenpolitik', p. 455.

50 Ehrenzeller, 'Legislative Gewalt', p. 299 (in the original: 'die fast mythische Vorstellung von der Unnormierbarkeit der Aussenpolitik').

51 Portmann, 'Federalism', p. 302; on today's view that foreign relations are an area subject to and governed by law, see e.g., Astrid Epiney, 'Beziehungen zum Ausland', in Daniel Thürer, Jean-François Aubert and Jörg Paul Müller (eds.), *Verfassungsrecht der Schweiz – Droit constitutionnel suisse* (Zürich: Schulthess, 2001), p. 880; Künzli, 'Art. 184(1)', p. 2683.

52 Bradley, 'New American Foreign Affairs Law', 1104.

53 See Oesch, 'Europa-Artikel', p. 166.

54 See Lanz, 'Bundesversammlung und Aussenpolitik', p. 41; he argues that newer statutes (such as the Federal Act on the Freezing and the Restitution of Illicit Assets held by Foreign Politically Exposed Persons of 18 December 2015, Classified compilation 196.1) evidence that foreign policy issues can be governed by law.

law and laid down in Article 5(1) of the Constitution of 1999 – today extends, as a general rule, to foreign policy.[55]

The Constitution of 1999 has also heralded a shift towards normalisation as regards allocation of competences and brought foreign policy within the constitutional separation of powers framework. Foreign relations are no longer monopolised by the government but are a competence exercised jointly with Parliament. The latter has a right to steer foreign policy, notably by approving treaties[56] – a power explicitly mentioned in the Constitution[57] to which we turn now.

III ALLOCATION OF POWERS FOR TREATY-MAKING: TOWARDS DEMOCRATISATION

A *A Reaction to the Legalisation of World Politics*

One of the encounters between international law and foreign relations law that has been identified by the editors is 'procedure'.[58] Indeed, large parts of foreign relations law deal with procedure,[59] notably by distributing powers horizontally among the three branches of government;[60] and, within federal states, vertically between the various governmental levels.[61] With international law having attained enormous importance, the rules allocating powers specifically for international lawmaking today form a core aspect of foreign relations law. A vast majority of constitutions adopted by nation-states include provisions allocating powers for the conclusion of treaties.[62]

As regards the distribution of powers between the executive and legislative in treaty-making, 'a sustained trend toward greater parliamentary involvement'

55 Ehrenzeller, Legislative Gewalt, p. 371; as per Thomas Cottier, '"Tax Fraud or the Like": Überlegungen und Lehren zum Legalitätsprinzip im Staatsvertragsrecht' (2011) 130/I *Revue de droit suisse* 97–122 at 110, the principle of legality standards can be (and sometimes are) lowered in order to take the specificities of foreign policy into account.

56 See Lanz, 'Bundesversammlung und Aussenpolitik', p. 43.

57 Constitution of 1999, arts. 166(1) *juncto* 184(1).

58 See the chapter by Aust and Kleinlein, p. 13.

59 See the chapter by Aust and Kleinlein, p. 14.

60 Campbell McLachlan, *Foreign Relations Law* (Cambridge: Cambridge University Press, 2014), p. 7.

61 Giegerich, 'Foreign Relations Law', para. 39.

62 Tom Ginsburg, 'Comparative Foreign Relations Law: A National Constitutions Perspective', in Curtis A. Bradley (ed.), *The Oxford Handbook of Comparative Foreign Relations Law* (Oxford: Oxford University Press, 2019), p. 67.

has been identified and empirically backed.[63] Many constitutions require parliamentary authorisation before the executive consents to be bound by a treaty and the categories of international agreements necessitating prior approval have widened over time.[64] The shift from the executive's monopoly in treaty-making towards increasingly robust parliamentary participation can be observed in jurisdictions around the globe.[65] This transition from a complete separation of powers towards a shared power approach is commonly referred to as the 'democratisation' of the treaty-making process.[66]

The main driver behind the democratisation of the treaty-making process is the growing importance of international law in the post–Cold War period.[67] With this, an increasing number of aspects previously regulated by domestic law became matters of international law. As a consequence, they fell to the executive, which, at that time, held primary responsibility for foreign relations and were thus removed from the legislature's ambit.[68] In order to reduce the democratic deficit resulting from globalisation and enhanced international cooperation and to re-institute the constitutional balance in the realm of lawmaking, steps towards (more closely) associating Parliament with the treaty-making process were considered a necessity.[69]

B *The Concept of 'Parallelism' in Switzerland*

As regards the development of the Swiss rules allocating powers for international lawmaking, democratisation is indisputably the leitmotif as well. Already under the Constitution of 1874 and thus at a time when Swiss doctrine and practice considered foreign relations to be a prerogative of the executive, parliamentary approval was required for specific treaties.[70] As early as 1921, an

63 Pierre-Hugues Verdier and Mila Versteeg, 'Separation of Powers, Treaty-Making, and Treaty Withdrawal: A Global Survey', in Curtis A. Bradley (ed.), *The Oxford Handbook of Comparative Foreign Relations Law* (Oxford: Oxford University Press, 2019), pp. 137 and 142.

64 See, e.g., Jenny S. Martinez, 'The Constitutional Allocation of Executive and Legislative Power over Foreign Relations', in Curtis A. Bradley (ed.), *The Oxford Handbook of Comparative Foreign Relations Law* (Oxford: Oxford University Press, 2019), p. 104.

65 Verdier and Versteeg, 'A Global Survey', p. 142.

66 Term used, e.g., by Luzius Wildhaber, *Treaty-Making Power and Constitutions: An International and Comparative Study* (Basel: Helbing Lichtenhahn, 1971), p. 9.

67 In more detail, see text relating to n. 113 ff. below.

68 See Anne Peters, 'The Globalization of State Constitutions', in Janne Nijman and André Nollkaemper (eds.), *New Perspectives on the Divide Between National and International Law* (Oxford: Oxford University Press, 2007), pp. 282–3, on the democratic deficiencies resulting from globalisation.

69 See Giegerich, 'Foreign Relations Law', para. 51.

70 See Odermatt and Tophinke, 'Art. 24', p. 197.

optional referendum for treaties not containing a withdrawal clause or concluded for a duration of more than fifteen years was introduced, a move towards democratisation triggered by massive protests against a previously concluded treaty of unlimited duration concerning the Gotthard tunnel.[71] In 1977, treaties entailing accession to IOs or a 'multilateral unification of the law' became eligible for the optional referendum, while accession to organisations of supranational character or collective security were subjected to the mandatory referendum.[72] This major step in the democratisation process was deemed necessary in light of the increasing number of treaties pertaining to matters previously governed by federal acts and thus removing them from parliamentary enactment and the popular referendum.[73]

During the span of the last century, participatory rights in the treaty-making process have steadily been expanded. Yet, it was only in the late 1990s that a paradigm shift regarding democratic participation in international lawmaking occurred: the idea of reducing incongruities, which guided earlier reforms, gave way to the concept of congruence or – to use a word forged by the federal authorities in this context – 'parallelism' between domestic and international lawmaking.[74] The concept of 'parallelism' essentially entails applying the same degree of democratic legitimacy in the realm of treaty-making as is required for the enactment of domestic statutes, which means that similar democratic participation rights should be granted regardless of whether an important treaty or a federal act is being adopted.[75] Hence, it is not the form (treaty or federal act) but the normative content of a legal instrument that should be decisive for the question of whether it is subject to a referendum. This idea was (partially) implemented in 2003: in the domestic sphere, '[a]ll significant provisions that establish binding legal rules must be enacted in the form of a federal act', which is subject to the optional referendum.[76] As a consequence, all treaties containing 'important legislative provisions' or the implementation of which requires the enactment

71 Yvo Hangartner and Andreas Kley, *Die demokratischen Rechte in Bund und Kantonen der Schweizerischen Eidgenossenschaft* (Zürich: Schulthess, 2000), pp. 435–6.

72 See Hangartner and Kley, *Demokratischen Rechte*, p. 436.

73 See Conseil fédéral (CH), Message concernant de nouvelles dispositions sur le référendum en matière de traités internationaux du 23 octobre 1974, Feuille fédérale 1974 II 1133, pp. 1146–7.

74 Oliver Diggelmann, 'Verletzt die "Standardabkommen-Praxis" der Bundesversammlung die Bundesverfassung?' (2014) 115 *Schweizerisches Zentralblatt für Staats- und Verwaltungsrecht* 291–323 at 294.

75 See, e.g., Conseil fédéral (CH), Message concernant la loi fédérale sur la compétence de conclure des traités internationaux de portée mineure et sur l'application provisoire des traités internationaux du 4 juillet 2012, Feuille fédérale 2012 6959, pp. 6973–4.

76 Constitution of 1999, art. 164(1) *juncto* art. 141(1)(a).

of federal acts, were equally made eligible for the optional treaty referendum.[77]

While initially developed in the context of the optional referendum, the concept of 'parallelism' later became a general guiding principle for the allocation of powers regarding international lawmaking,[78] and even for rules governing the relationship between the Swiss legal order and international law more generally.[79] The idea of 'parallelism' is essentially the Swiss response to the hollowing out of (direct) democracy and cantonal autonomy brought about by internationalisation. It constitutes the benchmark to be attained in the effort to democratise international lawmaking 'from below'.

C *Far-Reaching Democratic Participatory Rights*

Since foreign relations law is 'undoubtedly shaped by the specific elements of each state's constitution'[80] and direct democracy being a hallmark of the Swiss constitutional system, it is hardly surprising that democratic participatory rights in international treaty-making are well-developed. From a comparative perspective, the participatory rights are arguably even unique in terms of the actors involved, the phases during which participation is possible, and regarding their intensity and effect.[81] As we will see, not only the bicameral Parliament, but also the people, Cantons, and even interested groups and political parties – albeit to a very limited degree – are granted certain participatory rights. Importantly, participation is not limited to the approval of treaties, but extends from the initiation and negotiation phase to the provisional application and termination of treaties.

77 Conseil fédéral (CH), Message relatif à l'initiative populaire 'Pour le renforcement des droits populaires dans la politique étrangère (accords internationaux: la parole au peuple!)' du 1er octobre 2010, Feuille fédérale 2010 6335, p. 6359.

78 See, e.g., the pending proposal to further implement the concept in the context of the *mandatory* referendum: Conseil fédéral (CH), Message concernant le référendum obligatoire pour les traités internationaux ayant un caractère constitutionnel du 15 janvier 2020, Feuille fédérale 2020 1195.

79 E.g., regarding the publication of legal acts, see Conseil fédéral (CH), Message relatif à la modification de la loi sur les publications du 28 août 2013, Feuille fédérale 2013 6325, p. 6343.

80 McLachlan, *Foreign Relations Law*, p. 10; see also the chapter by Aust and Kleinlein, p. 14, on the embedment of allocation of authority rules in the constitutional structures and domestic legal cultures.

81 See Kunz and Peters, 'Democratisation in Switzerland', p. 1508 (on the 'intensity of parliamentarisation'); Anne Peters and Raffaela Kunz, 'Voting Down International Law? Lessons from Switzerland for Compensatory Constitutionalism', *Völkerrechtsblog*, 3 December 2018, p. 2 (on Switzerland probably having the 'most far-reaching democratic participation rights for its citizens'); and Portmann, 'Federalism', p. 311 (on the unique interplay between federalism and direct democracy).

The initiative to participate in, or even launch, a treaty-making process with other like-minded states stems, as a general rule, from the Federal Council. Yet Parliament, through means of parliamentary procedural requests,[82] may urge the government to join a given treaty-making process.[83] The ultimate decision on the commencement of treaty negotiations remains, however, with the Federal Council.[84] Even the people can trigger treaty negotiations by requesting an amendment of the Constitution, which directs the government to commence specific negotiations.[85] The popular initiative 'Yes to Europe!', for example, entailed a constitutional amendment stipulating that '[t]he Federal Government shall enter into accession negotiations with the European Union without delay'.[86]

If the treaty is of major importance, the so-called consultation procedure is carried out at this early stage (as compared to lesser but still 'significant' treaties, for which the procedure only takes place prior to the submission of the treaty to Parliament for approval). This procedure allows any person and any organisation to express its views on the treaty to be negotiated (or to be ratified if the procedure takes place at the later stage).[87] Specific stakeholders – notably the Cantons, political parties and national umbrella organisations for the economic sector – are specifically invited to participate in the procedure,[88] the purpose of which is to associate a broad circle of actors 'in the shaping of opinion and the decision-making process' and 'to provide information on material accuracy, feasibility of implementation and public acceptance of a federal project'.[89] The latter aspect is not to be underestimated in light of the looming referendum.[90]

As mentioned, foreign relations are a federal power, which even extends to matters for which, in the internal policy sphere, the Cantons are competent. Internationalisation thus encroaches on the competences of the Cantons,

82 On the different means, see Parliament Act, art. 118 et seq.

83 Lanz, 'Bundesversammlung und Aussenpolitik', pp. 165-6.

84 CH, Directorate for European Affairs DEA, 'Yes to Europe!', last updated 27 November 2017, www.eda.admin.ch/dea/en/home/europapolitik/abstimmungen/ja-zu-europa.html, accessed 1 July 2020 (initiative was rejected in a popular vote).

85 Roger Nobs, Volksinitiative und Völkerrecht: Eine Studie zur Volksinitiative im Kontext der schweizerischen Aussenpolitik unter besonderer Berücksichtigung des Verhältnisses zum Völkerrecht (Dissertation University of St. Gallen, 2006), pp. 138–43.

86 Chancellerie fédérale (CH), 'Initiative populaire fédérale "Oui à l'Europe!"', www.bk.admin.ch/ch/d/pore/vi/vis254t.html, accessed 1 July 2020.

87 Constitution of 1999, art. 147; Federal Act on the Consultation Procedure (Consultation Procedure Act) of 18 March 2005, Classified compilation 172.061, art. 4(1).

88 Consultation Procedure Act, art. 4(2).

89 Consultation Procedure Act, art. 2(2).

90 Haller, *Swiss Constitution*, p. 244.

which are, by way of compensation, granted a series of participatory rights.[91] Apart from associating them to the consultation procedure pertaining to treaties, the Cantons must, as a rule, be consulted before treaty negotiations start.[92] The Federal Council must consider their comments; if the treaty to be negotiated affects cantonal competences, it must attach particular weight to them and provide reasons if it deviates from their positions.[93]

The determination of the negotiation mandate is an executive competence, yet the Federal Council must consult the Foreign Policy Committees[94] on 'the guidelines and directives relating to mandates for important international negotiations before it decides on or amends the same'.[95] Further, the government 'shall inform these committees of the status of its plans and of the progress made in negotiations'.[96] At times, parliamentarians also seek to influence ongoing negotiations by means of parliamentary procedural requests, by which the executive is, however, not legally bound.[97] If a treaty affects the competences (and not only the interests)[98] of the Cantons, they must be involved in the preparation of the negotiation mandate and 'shall participate in negotiations in an appropriate manner'.[99]

While the signing of treaties falls within the competence of the Federal Council,[100] the Constitution of 1999 establishes a presumption that they must be approved by Parliament.[101] Importantly, the Federal Assembly must not only approve the conclusion and amendment of treaties, but – since December 2019 and in an effort to further implement the concept of 'parallelism' – also the withdrawal from them.[102] An exception to parliamentary approval exists if the Federal Council is authorised to conclude, amend or withdraw from a treaty at its own behest by virtue of a federal act or an international treaty approved by

91 See text relating to n. 27 ff. above.

92 Cantonal Participation Act, art. 4(2).

93 Cantonal Participation Act, art. 4(3).

94 'Committees' are 'groups formed from a set number of members of Parliament' whose 'principle task is to discuss the items of business assigned to them before these are debated in the chamber'; the National Council has twelve permanent committees and the Council of States has eleven: Lexicon of Parliamentary Terms, 'Committees', www.parlament.ch/en/über-das-parlament/parlamentswörterbuch, accessed 1 July 2020.

95 Parliament Act, art. 152(3).

96 Parliament Act, art. 152(3).

97 For examples, see Lanz, 'Bundesversammlung und Aussenpolitik', p. 168.

98 Biaggini, 'BV Kommentar', p. 597.

99 Constitution of 1999, art. 55(3); Cantonal Participation Act, art. 5(1).

100 Constitution of 1999, art. 184(2).

101 Constitution of 1999, art. 166(2); Parliament Act, art. 24(2).

102 Parliament Act, art. 24(2).

Parliament.[103] Essentially, the executive is allowed to do so for treaties of 'limited scope'.[104] When approving a treaty, the Federal Assembly can also approve, amend, reject or request reservations; and the Federal Council is, generally, obliged to comply.[105] A recent addition to Parliament's participation tool-kit is the obligation of the Federal Council to consult the Foreign Policy Committees on the provisional application of a treaty later subject to parliamentary approval. If both Committees are against provisional application, the Federal Council must refrain therefrom.[106]

Finally, and this is a Swiss idiosyncrasy, various categories of treaties are subject to a popular referendum. If a treaty entails accession to an organisation for collective security or of a supranational nature, the mandatory referendum applies. Mandatory means that the referendum is carried out *ex officio*, that is, without the need for a referendum request; and its adoption requires a double majority of the people and the Cantons.[107] So far, the only mandatory referendum held was in 1986, concerning Switzerland's accession to the United Nations.[108] The optional referendum, the adoption of which only requires a majority of the people, is carried out solely at the request of 50,000 voters or eight Cantons. Subject to the optional referendum are treaties that are of unlimited duration and may not be terminated, treaties leading to the accession to an IO, and treaties containing important legislative provisions, or whose implementation requires the enactment of a federal act.[109] If no referendum is requested or the treaty passes the vote, the Federal Council is authorised to proceed to ratification.[110] Switzerland being a monist state, treaties take effect domestically as soon as they bind the state at the international plane.[111] All treaties eligible for the mandatory or optional referendum, and other treaties 'that enact law or confer

[103] Constitution of 1999, art. 166(2); Parliament Act, art. 24(2); Government and Administration Organisation Act of 21 March 1997, Classified compilation 172.010, art. 7*a*(1).

[104] Government and Administration Organisation Act, art. 7*a*(2)–(4).

[105] Claude Schenker, Départment fédéral des affaires étrangères (CH), 'Guide de la pratique en matière de traités internationaux', édition 2015, available at www.eda.admin.ch/dam/eda/fr/documents/publications/Voelkerrecht/Praxisleitfaden-Voelkerrechtliche-Vertraege_fr.pdf, accessed 1 July 2020, p. 35.

[106] Parliament Act, art. 152(3bis) and (3ter); the provision entered into force on 2 December 2019.

[107] Constitution of 1999, art. 140(1)(b).

[108] Biaggini, 'BV Kommentar', p. 1121.

[109] Constitution of 1999, art. 141(1)(d).

[110] Constitution of 1999, art. 184(2).

[111] Ammann, *Domestic Courts and the Interpretation of International Law*, p. 72.

legislative powers', must be published in the compilations of federal legislation.[112]

D *A Child of Its Time: A Strong Treaty Focus*

In Switzerland, the democratisation of international lawmaking 'from below' – along the lines of the concept of 'parallelism' – is rather advanced. Very broadly speaking, the allocation of authority in international treaty-making is no longer fundamentally different from domestic lawmaking. Normalisation and democratisation of this subset of rules of Swiss foreign relations law is accomplished to a high degree.

Yet, a limitation of the legal framework on democratic participation in international lawmaking is palpably obvious. It is geared towards just one source of international law: treaties. This treaty focus is plausible if we consider the context in which these rules originated and developed. While participatory rights have steadily expanded over the last century, they experienced a more rapid growth in the 1990s and the first years of the new millennium. This boost mirrors the 'legalisation' of world politics[113] and how international law was 'on the rise' both qualitatively[114] and quantitatively[115] speaking during this period.

This 'move to law' that arose in world politics[116] after the end of the Cold War has most notably been brought about by the conclusion of treaties. This period of time 'witnessed a striking proliferation in treaties' codifying more traditional topics of international law as well as newer ones previously understood as being unsuitable for international regulation, such as international criminal law.[117] A sharp increase in the number of treaties concluded can also be observed in Switzerland. In the first half of the 1980s, Switzerland entered

112 Federal Act on the Compilations of Federal Legislation and the Federal Gazette (Publications Act) of 18 June 2004, Official compilation 170.512, art. 3(1).

113 Judith Goldstein et al., 'Introduction: Legalization and World Politics' (2000) 54 *International Organizations* 285–399 at 386; Edith Brown Weiss, 'The Rise or the Fall of International Law?' (2000) 69 *Fordham Law Review* 345–72 at 351.

114 See, e.g., Heike Krieger and Georg Nolte, 'The International Rule of Law-Rise or Decline? Approaching Current Foundational Challenges' in Heike Krieger, Georg Nolte and Andreas Zimmermann (eds.), *The International Rule of Law: Rise or Decline?* (Oxford: Oxford University Press, 2019), pp. 12–13.

115 See, e.g., Kenneth W. Abbott, Jessica Green and Robert O. Keohane, 'Organizational Ecology and Institutional Change in Global Governance' (2016) 70 *International Organization* 247–77 at 247; and Goldstein et al., 'Legalization and World Politics', 386.

116 Goldstein et al., 'Legalization and World Politics', 385.

117 José E. Alvarez, 'The New Treaty Makers' (2002) 25 *Boston College International and Comparative Law Review* 213–34 at 216.

into around seventy treaties yearly; in the early 1990s, the number was already at 135, meaning that the figure nearly doubled in less than a decade. Between 2000 and 2003, the sheer number of roughly 210 treaties were concluded per year, which represents a growth of 55 per cent compared to the early 1990s.[118] It is against the backdrop of this changing international landscape with a 'gigantic treaty network'[119] under construction, that the Swiss concept of 'parallelism' came into being and a major expansion of democratic participation rights took place. Being a child of its time, it is nothing but understandable that the respective rules are heavily oriented towards treaties.

The years leading up to the turn of the millennium were characterised by a belief (in hindsight, some even term it a 'mantra')[120] among international law scholars that the legalisation trend would persist and that international law, and therewith the treaty 'production rate', would continue to grow exponentially.[121] Yet, 'times are changing' – as Andreas Zimmermann wrote in allusion to the Bob Dylan song – and the then 'prevailing euphoria' among international law scholars as to international law becoming increasingly and steadily more efficient, value-oriented and richer in content has since abated.[122] The contemporary views about the state and future of international law are more pessimistic: the discourse of international law being 'on the rise' turned into whether international law is 'in decline'.[123] Whether the manifestation of signs of crisis indicate the beginning of a general downward trend across all sub-branches of international law remains to be seen. What is already empirically proven, though, is the stagnation of *formal* international law.[124] The number of adopted treaties has fallen dramatically: between 1950 and 2000, the number of multilateral treaties deposited with the UN Secretary General per year was never below thirty-four; between 2005 and 2010, the count was at nine per year, and not a single multilateral treaty was deposited in

118 Oliver Diggelmann, *Der liberale Verfassungsstaat und die Internationalisierung der Politik: Veränderungen von Staat und Politik in der Schweiz* (Bern: Stämpfli, 2005), p. 2.

119 Alvarez, 'The New Treaty Makers', 218 (citing Roy Lee, 'Multilateral Treaty-Making and Negotiation Techniques: An Appraisal', in Bin Chang and Eduard Brown (eds.), *Contemporary Problems of International Law: Essays in Honour of Georg Schwarzenberger on his Eightieth Birthday* (London: Stevens, 1988), p. 158).

120 Joost Pauwelyn, Ramses A. Wessel and Jan Wouters, 'When Structures become Shackles: Stagnation and Dynamics in International Lawmaking' (2014) 25 *The European Journal of International Law* 733–63 at 733.

121 See, e.g., Alvarez, 'The New Treaty Makers', 217.

122 Andreas Zimmermann, 'Times Are Changing – and What About the International Rule of Law Then?', *EJIL: Talk!*, 5 March 2018, p. 3.

123 See, e.g., Krieger and Nolte, 'The International Rule of Law-Rise or Decline?', passim.

124 Pauwelyn, Wessel and Wouters, 'When Structures become Shackles', 734.

2011, 2012 or 2013.[125] A certain 'treaty fatigue' has spread across the international community.[126]

IV TURN TO INFORMAL INTERNATIONAL LAWMAKING: BRIDGES UNDER CONSTRUCTION

A *Informal International Law Superseding Formal International Law*

While formal lawmaking through the adoption of treaties is in decline, the demand for rules governing transnational or global phenomena is on the rise.[127] This growing need for norms is notably catered to by what is referred to as 'informal law' – that is, instruments which fall short of the traditional sources of international law[128] but are normative in the sense that they 'steer . . . behaviour or determine . . . the freedom of actors'.[129] Importantly, informal lawmaking, which progressively supersedes formal lawmaking,[130] not only differs from the latter in terms of the normative output it produces, but also regarding the process and actors involved. Informal lawmaking has been defined as:

> Cross-border cooperation between public authorities, with or without the participation of private actors and/or international organizations, in a forum other than a traditional international organization (*process informality*), and/or as between actors other than traditional diplomatic actors (such as regulators or agencies) (*actor informality*) and/or which does not result in a formal treaty or other traditional source of international law (*output informality*).[131]

Informal law is not a new means for regulating international cooperation,[132] but its occurrence and crowding out effect on formal law (most notably treaties) significantly increased after the turn of the millennium – such that informal lawmaking has been termed a 'signature development' of

125 Pauwelyn, Wessel and Wouters, 'When Structures become Shackles', 734–5.
126 Pauwelyn, Wessel and Wouters, 'When Structures become Shackles', 739.
127 See Ayelet Berman, 'Is There a Stagnation in International Law?' (2015) 109 *Proceedings of the Annual Meeting (American Society of International Law)* 71–74 at 73.
128 Berman, 'Stagnation in International Law', 71.
129 Joost Pauwelyn, 'Informal International Lawmaking: Framing the Concept and Research Questions', in Joost Pauwelyn, Ramses A. Wessels and Jan Wouters (eds.), *Informal International Lawmaking* (Oxford: Oxford University Press, 2012), p. 16.
130 Pauwelyn, Wessel and Wouters, 'When Structures become Shackles', 734.
131 Pauwelyn, 'Informal International Lawmaking', p. 22.
132 Berman, 'Stagnation in International Law', 73.

contemporary global governance.[133] While various reasons account for the rise of informal international law,[134] the 'dramatic' changes in institutions of global governance[135] in recent years are a key factor. Traditionally, the main players in international lawmaking were states and IOs; the latter, occasionally referred to as 'treaty machines', played a central part in treaty-making.[136] José Alvarez noticed that the proliferation of treaties has been 'aided and abetted by the concomitant rise in intergovernmental organizations' and that the age of treaties is therefore 'not incidentally also the age of IOs'.[137] In the early 2000s, however, the formation of new IOs slowed markedly.[138] Simultaneously, the number of non-state actors active at the international level – notably in the 'production of normativity'[139] – multiplied. They are a diverse group, ranging from NGOs and transnational corporations to industry associations and regulatory agencies.[140] As they have yet to acquire international legal personality, they lack treaty-making capacity; as a consequence, any normative instrument they adopt is informal in nature.[141]

B *The Development of 'Soft Participatory Rights' for 'Soft Law'*

In recent years, awareness of the potential of informal law (similar to that of formal law) to limit the domestic policy space has grown considerably among Parliament and the broader public. For a while, the Migration Pact was the epitome of the 'encroachment potential' of informal law. Meanwhile, the discussion moved beyond this specific instrument and turned into a more principled one: how to involve Parliament more closely in 'soft law projects'.[142]

133 Jean Galbraith and David T. Zaring, 'Soft Law as Foreign Relations Law' (2014) 99 *Cornell Law Review* 735–94 at 745.
134 See, e.g., Brown Weiss, 'The Rise or the Fall of International Law?', 352.
135 See Abbott, Green and Keohane, 'Organizational Ecology and Institutional Change', 247 and 271.
136 José E. Alvarez, *International Organizations as Law-makers* (Oxford: Oxford University Press, 2005), pp. 275–6.
137 Alvarez, 'The New Treaty Makers', 217.
138 Abbott, Green and Keohane, 'Organizational Ecology and Institutional Change', 247.
139 See the chapter by Aust and Kleinlein, p. 11.
140 Anne Peters, 'Compensatory Constitutionalism: The Function and Potential of Fundamental International Norms and Structures' (2006) 19 *Leiden Journal of International Law* 579–610 at 592–3.
141 Berman, 'Stagnation in International Law', 73.
142 See The Federal Council (CH), 'Parliament to be more closely involved in soft law projects', 27 June 2019, www.admin.ch/gov/en/start/documentation/media-releases.msg-id-75590.html, accessed 1 July 2020.

While the debate on democratic participation in informal lawmaking gained momentum with the Migration Pact, it is far from novel in Switzerland. Rather, the role of Parliament in the making of 'non-binding instruments' has been discussed time and again – often in connection with 'soft law' in the fields of banking, finance and tax. As early as 1985, a member of Parliament requested the Federal Council to consider rejecting an OECD recommendation on banking secrecy.[143] The request was rebuffed with the competent Federal Chancellor replying that the government did not intend to enter into a binding obligation and, consequently, had no reason to consult Parliament 'in advance – and certainly not in advance! – on what it must do'; rather, it would be for the executive to decide on Switzerland's position as long as it did not legally oblige the country.[144] The answer is reflective of the allocation of powers as it stood under the Constitution of 1874, where foreign relations matters were a prerogative of the executive.

It was only under the Constitution of 1999, which conceives foreign relations as a shared competence requiring close cooperation between the executive and legislative branches, that things changed. In 2002, the Parliament Act was adopted, Article 152 of which obliges the executive to inform the Foreign Policy Committees 'regularly, comprehensively and in good time of important foreign policy developments'; and to consult and update them on 'important plans' ('*orientations principales*', '*wesentliche Vorhaben*').[145] As per the common understanding, the notion of 'important plans' includes 'soft law' projects of a certain significance.[146] Yet, the implementation of Article 152 of the Parliament Act has been far from frictionless; Parliament – or at least some of its members – has felt bypassed by the government on more than one occasion.[147]

As a consequence, the notion of 'important plans' of Article 152(3) of the Parliament Act was clarified by including Article 5*b* in the Government and Administration Organisation Ordinance in 2016, which defines two instances in which the Foreign Policy Committees must be consulted. First, if the implementation of recommendations of IOs or multinational fora requires

143 Bulletin officiel de l'Assemblée fédérale (CH), Conseil national, 1985, vol. III, Interpellation urgente Eisenring: Recommendation de l'OECD concernant le secret bancaire (85.435), p. 1070.

144 Interpellation urgente Eisenring: Recommendation de l'OECD concernant le secret bancaire, p. 1075 (author's own translation).

145 Parliament Act, art. 152(3); the Foreign Policy Committees and other parliamentary committees can also *request* to be informed and consulted: Parliament Act, art. 152(5).

146 Tripet Cordier, 'Art. 152', p. 1040.

147 For a detailed account, see Francesco Naef, 'Soft Law und Gewaltenteilung: Über die Kunst der Legiferierung durch die Katzenklappe' (2015) 8 *Aktuelle Juristische Praxis* 1109–21 at 1115–19.

the enactment or substantial revision of a federal act. Second, if a failure to implement exposes Switzerland to risk of serious economic disadvantage, sanctions, isolation or damage to its political reputation, or if other serious disadvantages for Switzerland are to be expected.[148] This long-winded wording not only testifies to the fact that informal law may exert a certain compliance pull on states, but also to the difficulty of defining instances that trigger consultation rights in abstract terms.

The newly introduced provision soon came under fire, in part for enshrining parliamentary rights in an ordinance, which can be modified or revoked by the government alone, rather than a formal law.[149] Moreover, despite the more detailed description of the instances in which Parliament must be consulted, it again felt bypassed – notably in the context of the Migration Pact. It is against this background that the Foreign Policy Committee of the Council of States tasked the government to report on the 'growing role of soft law in international relations' and 'the resulting creeping weakening of Parliament's democratic rights' and to consider possible amendments of Article 152 of the Parliament Act.[150] All things considered, the propositions put forward in the report to better associate Parliament in the making of 'soft law'[151] are neither novel nor revolutionary, yet the report's significance may lay elsewhere. While the Federal Council has long been rather reserved about further increasing parliamentary participation in the field of 'soft law', it now 'considers it a priority to create the necessary conditions for Parliament to better assess soft law instruments and, on this basis, to exercise its right to participate in a more targeted manner.'[152]

C *Demands for 'Hard Participatory Rights' for 'Soft Law'*

The democratisation of informal lawmaking 'from below' is arguably more developed in Switzerland than in many other jurisdictions, but it is still

148 Ordonnance sur l'organisation du gouvernement et de l'administration du 25 novembre 1998, Receuil systématique 172.010.1.

149 See, e.g., Conseil national (CH), Groupe PDC, interpellation 18.4112, 'Participation du Parlement aux décisions portant sur du droit souple: Absence de ligne claire du Conseil fédéral', 28.11.2018.

150. Conseil des Etats (CH), Commission de politique extérieure, postulat 18.4104, 'Consultation et participation du Parlement dans le domaine du droit souple ("soft law")', 12 November 2018 (author's own translations).

151 For the various options, see Conseil federal (CH), 'Consultation et participation du Parlement dans le domaine du droit souple ("soft law")', Rapport du Conseil federal en réponse au postulat 18.4104, Commission de politique extérieure CE, 12 novembre 2018 (hereinafter: Federal Council, 'Soft Law Report'), pp. 18–19.

152 Federal Council, 'Parliament to be more closely involved in soft law projects'.

relatively embryonic when compared with democratic participation in treaty-making. In terms of actors, only parliamentary committees (and, among them, mainly the Foreign Policy Committees) are granted information and consultation rights – not Parliament as a whole, let alone the people, Cantons or broader public.[153] As regards the phases and intensity, solely a right to be informed and consulted during the making of informal law is granted, but not the veto power that Parliament, the people and Cantons possess vis-à-vis certain categories of treaties through parliamentary approval or referenda. Broadly speaking, nothing more than 'soft participatory rights' are available for 'soft law', while 'hard participatory rights' are reserved for 'hard law' – that is, treaties. For a long time, the discussion surrounding the expansion of democratic participation rights centred on the scope of information and consultation rights. With the Migration Pact, however, the reform discussion took on a new dimension: a rather widely supported claim for 'hard participatory rights' in informal lawmaking was formulated. No less than three different parliamentary committees – the composition of which reflects the strength of the political parties of the respective parliamentary chamber[154] – instructed the Federal Council not to sign the Migration Pact during the UN Conference in Morocco in December 2011 and to submit it to Parliament for approval.[155] Individual requests even tabled the question whether the people and Cantons, by means of popular referendum, should have the final say on Switzerland's participation.[156]

To shrug off the call for 'hard participation', which took shape in the context of the Migration Pact, as a purely populist manoeuvre would not do the matter justice.[157] Admittedly, had the Pact pertained not to migration, but say civil aviation, it would have sparked very little debate;[158] moreover, various parliamentary requests on the matter had populist undertones. For example, the Swiss People's Party unleashed a barrage of criticism about Switzerland's

153 As it is the case for treaties, see above Section III.C.

154 Parliament Act, art. 43(3).

155 Conseil national (CH), Commission des institutions politiques, motion 18.4093, 'Pacte de l'ONU sur les migrations: Soumettre à l'Assemblée fédérale la décision d'approbation', 19 October 2018; Conseil des Etats (CH), Commission des institutions politiques, motion 18.4103, 'Pacte de l'ONU sur les migrations: Soumettre à l'Assemblée fédérale la décision d'approbation', 8 November 2018; Conseil des Etats (CH), Commission de politique extérieure, motion 18.4106, 'Pacte mondial des Nations Unies sur les migrations: Soumettre à l'Assemblée fédérale la décision d'approbation', 12 November 2018.

156 See, e.g., Conseil national (CH), A. Glarner, interpellation 18.3842, 'Pacte de l'ONU sur les migrations: Participation démocratique et validité intraétatique', 26 September 2018.

157 Peters and Kunz, 'Voting down international law?', p. 4.

158 Federal Council, 'Soft Law Report', p. 16.

leading role in the making of the Pact – even asking whether the Swiss ambassador should incur liability for having facilitated the process.[159] Hence, to some extent, the debate on democratic participation in informal lawmaking has been hijacked by the right-wing populist party in order to make political capital. At the same time, various requests – especially those emanating from parliamentary committees[160] – seem to have been truly spurred by the concern that informal lawmaking suffers from democratic deficits. It is arguably this broader, cross-party call for 'hard' participation that ultimately led to the Federal Council's decision not to sign the Pact in December 2018 and to submit the decision to Parliament. Yet the government tried its best not to set a precedent, stressing that according to the current rules on allocation of powers, namely Article 184(1) of the Constitution, it is authorised to sign the Pact in its own competence, and that the decision to submit it to Parliament was taken solely for political (not legal) reasons. Consequently, the Federal Council formally rejected the parliamentary requests asking for the Pact's submission to Parliament but acted in conformity with the requests as a matter of fact.[161]

At this juncture, it is difficult to tell whether the decision to submit the Migration Pact to Parliament for approval (which, as of January 2021, has yet to happen) broke through the glass ceiling in terms of limiting participation in informal law to 'soft participatory rights'. At the time of writing, discussions on whether to grant 'hard participatory rights' are ongoing. A parliamentary initiative submitted in the National Council, which requests adaptation of the rules on allocation of authority in a way that foresees parliamentary approval for 'soft law', is currently pending. Concretely, it suggests to submit to Parliament those informal instruments that involve compliance-monitoring, from which reporting obligations arise, if non-compliance may constitute a breach of the principle of good faith, or if its implementation is likely to require the enactment or amendment of a federal act.[162] In the Council of States, the Foreign Policy Committee suggested to establish a subcommission specifically tasked with evaluating the need for legislative action in order to ensure parliamentary participation in informal lawmaking.[163] As a

[159] Conseil national (CH), T. Matter, question 18.5601, 'Pacte de l'ONU sur les migrations: Conséquences pour les responsables', 26 November 2018.

[160] See n. 155 above.

[161] See the answer of the Federal Council provided in response to the three motions mentioned in n. 155 above.

[162] Conseil national (CH), Groupe de l'Union démocratique du centre, initiative parlementaire 18.466, 'Approbation du droit non contraignant par l'Assemblée fédérale', 29 November 2018.

[163] Conseil des Etats (CH), 'Nouvelle législature: Perspectives en matière de politique extérieure', Communiqué de presse, 14 January 2020, www.parlament.ch/press-releases/Pages/mm-apk-s-2020-01-14.aspx, accessed 6 July 2020.

result, both parliamentary chambers are currently considering how meaningful 'soft participation' in informal lawmaking could be granted and whether 'soft law' is even amenable to 'hard participatory rights'.

D *Challenges in Building New Bridges*

To sketch out detailed construction plans for building new bridges between informal international lawmaking and domestic democratic participation proves challenging. Applying the provisions available in the context of treaties by analogy[164] will not work in many cases, while designing specific rules for informal lawmaking is no easy feat. This is not surprising given that the phenomenon is negatively defined as lawmaking that dispenses with certain formalities traditionally linked to international law,[165] coupled with the complicating factor that informality can relate to different elements – actors, process and output.[166] This makes informal lawmaking a multifaceted and complex phenomenon that is 'hard to grasp in domestic constitutional terms'.[167] Still, discussion has started on how to extend 'soft participation rights' and whether to grant 'hard participation rights' in informal lawmaking.

The Swiss debate turns on 'soft *law*';[168] hence, there seems to be common ground that only 'legislative'[169] informal instruments, and not those dealing with a concrete situation, should qualify for 'hard participatory rights' – even though this is not the case for treaties.[170] Otherwise, Parliament would stray too far into the territory of the executive, which – despite the far-reaching soft participatory rights of Parliament[171] – retains the ultimate decision-making power for the 'operational conduct' of foreign policy.[172] Consensus also seems

164 As has been done for other *formal* sources of (international) law: Anna Petrig, 'Sind die parlamentarische Genehmigung und das Referendum im Außenbereich auf völkerrechtliche Verträge beschränkt? Eine Untersuchung anhand von Kompetenztransfers an Völkerrechtsakteure' (2018) 78 *Heidelberg Journal of International Law* 93–146.

165 See definition in text relating to n. 131 above.

166 Joost Pauwelyn, Ramses A. Wessels and Jan Wouters, 'An Introduction to Informal International Lawmaking', in Joost Pauwelyn and Jan Wouters (eds.), *Informal International Lawmaking* (Oxford: Oxford University Press, 2012), p. 2.

167 Peters and Kunz, 'Voting Down International Law?', p. 4.

168 See, e.g., Federal Council, 'Soft Law Report', passim.

169 The term is defined in Parliament Act, art. 22(4).

170 E.g., a treaty determining a border that is of unlimited duration and that may not be terminated is eligible for the referendum as per Constitution of 1999, art. 141(1)(d)(1); see also Publications Act, art. 3(2) stating 'The Federal Council may decide that treaties . . . that are not legislative in their nature be published in the AS.'

171 Constitution of 1999, art. 166(1).

172 Lanz, 'Bundesversammlung und Aussenpolitik', p. 223.

to emerge that the 'importance' of an informal instrument should be the criterion used to decide whether and to what degree democratic legitimacy is necessary (*'critère de l'importance'*, *'Kriterium der Wesentlichkeit'*), which aligns well with the standard already applying to (domestic and international) formal law.[173] Such a material criterion may dispel the argument that expanding democratic participation to informal law would flood Parliament with submissions – by comparison, only 5 per cent of all treaties concluded by Switzerland are approved by Parliament, while the other 95 per cent are of 'limited scope' and thus fall in the sole competence of the executive.[174] True, to specify the criterion of 'importance' is far from clear and the assessment may change over time;[175] yet the challenge is not idiosyncratic to informal law but exists equally with regard to formal law. Under domestic law, Article 164(1) of the Constitution sets out which matters must be regulated in federal acts, which are enacted by Parliament and subject to the optional referendum. The provision is applied by analogy in order to assess whether a treaty contains 'important legislative provisions' and is thus eligible for the optional referendum.[176] While various commentators have expressed doubt as to whether Article 164 of the Constitution provides (much) guidance at all,[177] having a (partly deficient) abstract definition of the instances where 'hard participation rights' apply is still preferable over putting the decision entirely at the discretion of the authorities. Apart from considerations of treating equal cases equally,[178] a high value is attached to the idea that the referendum should not feature a 'plebiscitary' character – which, in Swiss parlance, means that its exercise must not depend on the will of the authorities,[179] but

173 See Federal Council, 'Soft Law Report', pp. 14–16; the referendum on accession to an IO is an exception to the rule: see Anna Petrig, 'Das Referendum zum Beitritt zu internationalen Organisationen: Nach 40 Jahren Bestand ein (überflüssiges) Relikt?' (2017) 136/I *Revue de droit Suisse* 339–66 at 359–63.

174 Kathrin Alder und Lukas Leuzinger, 'Schweizer Selbstbestimmung: Die wichtigsten Fakten zu den internationalen Verträgen' *Neue Zürcher Zeitung online* (Zürich, 15 November 2018) www.nzz.ch/schweiz/die-bedeutung-des-internationalen-rechts-in-zahlen-ld.1433328?reduced=true, accessed 6 July 2020.

175 See concerns expressed in Federal Council, 'Soft Law Report', pp. 15–16.

176 Bundesamt für Justiz (CH), Gutachten vom 6. Januar 2004 zuhanden der aussenpolitischen und staatspolitischen Kommissionen von National- und Ständerat, überarbeitet im Mai 2004, VPB 2004 Nr. 4, p. 1077, at 1087.

177 See, e.g., Pierre Tschannen, 'Art. 164', in Bernhard Ehrenzeller et al. (eds.), *Die Schweizerische Bundesverfassung: St. Galler Kommentar*, 3rd ed., 2 vols. (Zürich: Dike, 2014), vol. II, p. 2684.

178 Constitution of 1999, art. 8(1).

179 This essentially happened with the Migration Pact.

be granted if predefined criteria are met. For some authors, this even amounts to a feature of direct democracy.[180]

Turning back to the requirements for subjecting informal law to 'hard participatory rights', it seems that only those with a high degree of normativity should qualify: if normativity is low, the impact on the domestic sphere is negligible and thus no enhanced democratic legitimacy is warranted. In its 'Soft Law Report', the Federal Council proposes a matrix for assessing the normativity of an informal instrument. The y-axis measures the 'will to shape' ('*volonté d'agir*', '*Gestaltungswille*'), while the x-axis indicates the degree of 'will to enforce' ('*volonté d'imposer*', '*Durchsetzungswille*') a specific instrument; the higher an instrument figures on the two axes, the higher its normativity.[181] With this, the long-held argument against democratic participation in the making of 'soft law' – that it is not legally binding – seems to have finally lost its persuasive power and the normativity of informal law is being recognised.

The Swiss debate has circled around the concept of 'soft law' and is thus mainly concentrated on the output.[182] However, in order to conceptualise democratic participation properly, the focus should not just be on 'law' – but on 'lawmaking'. Actors and processes – that is, the chain of activities and decisions leading to a specific output and the forum in which this takes place – are of equal importance. This is why the concept of 'informal lawmaking', which captures all these dimensions, is more beneficial to framing the discussion on democratisation 'from below' as compared to 'soft law' (apart from the fact that there is often nothing particularly 'soft' about informal law).[183] Since the current debate has been intensified by the legal quagmire surrounding the Migration Pact, the perception of actors and processes in informal lawmaking – which impact potential bridges and boundaries for domestic democratic participation in informal lawmaking – may be slightly distorted. It is indeed a rather simple game to subject the Pact to 'hard participation rights', that is, to parliamentary approval and even a referendum. The treaty analogy works well since there is neither actor informality (states adopted the instrument within the UN system) nor process informality (the negotiations took place in proceedings that could equally apply to a treaty and the Pact was ultimately adopted and signed by states at an intergovernmental conference). The sole distinction from formal

180 See, e.g., Andreas Auer, Giorgio Malinverni and Michel Hottelier, *Droit constitutionnel suisse*, 3rd ed., 2 vols. (Berne: Stämpfli, 2013), vol. I, pp. 204–5.

181 Federal Council, 'Soft Law Report', p. 12.

182 See, e.g., Federal Council, 'Soft Law Report', passim.

183 See, e.g., Pauwelyn, Wessel and Wouters, 'When Structures become Shackles', 743.

law is that the Pact falls short of a treaty.[184] In many instances, however, both process and/or actor informality will be much more pronounced, which makes democratic participation more challenging – if not entirely meaningless or impossible.

In treaty-making, states are the main actors: they negotiate, adopt, sign and ratify treaties. In informal lawmaking, this may be very different; states may be just one of the actors involved or even be absent altogether from the negotiating table. The latter holds true if informal law stems from what Michael Bothe aptly refers to as 'private norm entrepreneurs'.[185] In the field of the law of armed conflict, for instance, a series of informal meetings have taken place over the past decades, during which (often old-fashioned) international rules were clarified, restated or updated in light of new technological or societal phenomena.[186] Interestingly, Switzerland was an active player in this field of law in the 'age of treaties' and continues to be one in times of informal lawmaking. The experts attend these processes in a purely personal capacity,[187] and states are not official participants, but may – for the sake of legitimacy, authority and thus efficiency of the instrument in question – still be involved, be it consultations on drafts or as observers (especially states sponsoring the process[188]).[189] Since states do not sit at the negotiating table, at least not officially, these processes may not even fall under the definition of informal lawmaking provided above, which requires '[c]ross-border cooperation between *public* authorities'.[190] Yet, to pretend that the output produced has no normative value also seems to miss the point.[191] Be that as it may, this

184 Discussing whether it is a treaty or an informal instrument: Anne Peters, 'The Global Compact for Migration: to Sign or Not Sign?' EJIL: Talk!, 21 November 2018, pp. 2–3.

185 Michael Bothe, 'Private Normunternehmer im Völkerrecht: Gedanken zur Fortentwicklung des Völkerrechts durch nicht-staatliche Institutionen', in Holger P. Hestermeyer et al. (eds.), *Coexistence, Cooperation and Solidarity: Liber Amicorum Rüdiger Wolfrum* (Leiden: Martinus Nijhoff, 2012), pp. 1399–412, passim; the term 'norm entrepreneur' seems to go back to Cass R. Sunstein, 'Social Norms and Social Roles' (1996) 4 *Columbia Law Review* 903–68.

186 Bothe, 'Private Normunternehmer', pp. 1402–4.

187 See, e.g., The Programme on Humanitarian Policy and Conflict Research (HPCR), *Manual on International Law Applicable to Air and Missile Warfare* (Cambridge: Cambridge University Press, 2013), p. xi.

188 See, e.g., the invitation of donor countries (among them Switzerland) to participate in the deliberations of the following manual: HPCR, Manual on International Law Applicable to Air and Missile Warfare, p. xi.

189 Bothe, 'Private Normunternehmer', pp. 1407–8; e.g., also in the case of the Manual on International Law Applicable to Air and Missile Warfare, see p. 1404.

190 See definition in text relating to n. 131 above (emphasis added).

191 See, e.g., the *San Remo Manual on International Law Applicable to Armed Conflicts at Sea*; Natalino Ronzitti, 'Naval Warfare' (last updated June 2009), in Rüdiger Wolfrum (ed.), *Max*

type of informal lawmaking suggests that certain features of informal lawmaking may set boundaries for domestic democratic participation.

In terms of process, a key difference between informal lawmaking and treaty-making is that a formalised procedure exists for the latter.[192] For treaties it is thus much easier to determine where to build bridges along the route from initiating negotiations to the entry into force of an instrument. Informal lawmaking is not subjected to a standardised procedure, and this is praised as its competitive advantage vis-à-vis treaties. Moreover, at the outset, how a specific process should evolve is often (deliberately) left open and is only specified as it goes along. Such a 'wait-and-see approach' lowers the entry hurdle for negotiations and allows for adjustments – towards more or less formality – along the route. The Montreux Document is exemplary as a process of informal lawmaking in which formality increased over time. When it was launched by Switzerland and the International Committee of the Red Cross in 2006, a group of only seventeen states – those most affected by the phenomenon – were involved in the negotiations, which were of a rather informal character.[193] Today, the instrument can be 'supported' by any state or IO by submitting a letter or diplomatic note, based on a template, to the Swiss Federal Department of Foreign Affairs.[194] While very informal at the beginning, the process in the end is nearly the equivalent of signing and ratifying a treaty. At the outset, domestic democratic control would have only made sense for the seventeen participating states, while today any state can 'support' the document and could, before doing so, request parliamentary approval. Whether democratic participation 'from below' is possible and meaningful must thus be assessed for a specific process and the answer may change over time – a striking contrast from the route taken for treaties.

A further (and certainly not last) difference between treaties and informal instruments pertains to the possibility that states can dodge the latter's effects and implement a domestic 'disapproval' of the instrument at the international

Planck Encyclopedia of Public International Law, online edition, https://opil.ouplaw.com/view/10.1093/law:epil/9780199231690/law-9780199231690-e342, accessed 6 July 2020, para. 2, writes that this 'private codification' has 'over time, acquired considerable weight and several navy manuals refer to it as an authoritative statement of existing law'.

192 See Vienna Convention on the Law of Treaties, Vienna, 23 May 1969, in force 27 January 1980, 1155 UNTS 331.

193 *The Montreux Document on pertinent international legal obligations and good practices for States related to operations of private military and security companies during armed conflict*, www.eda.admin.ch/dam/eda/en/documents/aussenpolitik/voelkerrecht/20192511-montreux-document_EN.pdf, accessed 6 July 2020, pp. 9 and 41.

194 Montreux Document Forum, 'How to Join', www.mdforum.ch/en/how-to-join, accessed 6 July 2020.

level. If Parliament or the people do not approve a specific treaty, the Swiss Federal Council will simply abstain from ratifying it and no legal obligation accrues from it for Switzerland. For informal law, it is much more difficult to explain how, why, when and who comes into the maelstrom of its normativity. At times, it may be possible to formally endorse, sign or support the instrument – whether refraining from doing so is sufficient to dispel its effects is debatable. The Federal Council correctly notes in its report that informal law may even impact states not having participated in the making of a specific instrument.[195] This triggers the question of what the executive is obliged to do at the international level if Parliament or the people rejects a specific informal instrument.

V CONCLUSION

This discussion suffices to demonstrate that designing meaningful mechanisms for generating democratic legitimacy is much more difficult in the context of informal international lawmaking than it is for formal international lawmaking. Yet, if these mechanisms shall continue performing their function, it is necessary to adapt them to structural changes of international law as expeditiously as possible. Otherwise the pendulum will swing back and the executive will regain powers in international lawmaking, which have been pushed back over the years in favour of greater involvement of Parliament, the people and Cantons.

The expanding horizons of international law in terms of actors and sources have repercussions on foreign relations law across the globe. The impact of informal lawmaking on the democratisation of international law 'from below', however, appears to have not yet received the necessary academic and practical attention. This is surprising in light of the great value attached to the democratisation of international lawmaking in the context of treaties and the fact that most jurisdictions' mechanisms do not apply to informal law.[196] Academic literature is a mirror to this finding: it is extremely rich in terms of parliamentary involvement in treaty-making, but very scant when it comes to informal lawmaking. By way of example, Alejandro Rodiles recently wrote that the trend towards informal lawmaking 'has gone completely unnoticed by the

[195] Federal Council, 'Soft Law Report', p. 8.

[196] As per Leonard F. M. Besselink, 'Informal International Lawmaking: Elaboration and Implementation in the Netherlands', in Ayelet Berman et al. (eds.), *Informal International Lawmaking: Case Studies* (The Hague: Torkel Opsahl Academic EPublisher, 2012), p. 106, informal law does not require parliamentary approval in any Western state.

Mexican literature'.[197] Jean Galbraith and David T. Zaring likewise note that in the United States, there is 'exhaustive academic literature' on treaties and that 'similar literature exists with regard to the foreign relations law dimensions of customary international law', but informal international instruments 'by contrast, get barely a nod in the foreign relations law literature'.[198] Arguably, the discussions on the lack of democratic control of the Migration Pact was a catalyst for more intense debate in the future.[199]

Comparative foreign relations law certainly has the potential to unearth the various facets of the problem and to enlarge the pool of potential solutions on how to democratise informal international lawmaking 'from below'. Yet, even if the most perfect bridges were built – in such a combined and common effort – the very characteristics of international informal lawmaking sets some insurmountable boundaries. This leads back to the two central questions raised by the editors in the introduction to this book: 'To what extent is the field of foreign relations law shaped by the normative expectations and structures of international law? Conversely, in how far is international law a product of the combined processes governed by foreign relations law and construed in light of domestic law?'

Domestic mechanisms on democratic participation can only fulfil their purpose if they mirror the structures of international law – notably its sources – as accurately as possible. The Swiss rules on democratic control of treaty-making are a good example: having been drafted during the 'age of treaties', they had to be adapted and are still in process of being reviewed so as to be fit for purpose in the age of informal lawmaking. As regards the impact on international law 'from below', a crucial difference seems to exist between formal and informal lawmaking. As regards formal sources, notably treaties and customary international law, states are the masters of their creation.[200] Hence, states – through their domestic (foreign relations) law – have a better grip and control of the process. They may similarly monopolise the creation of informal law if actors and/or process feature a very low degree of informality (as in the case of the Migration Pact), but may not be even officially on board if

197 Alejandro Rodiles, 'Executive Power in Foreign Affairs: The Case for Inventing a Mexican Foreign Relations Law', in Curtis A. Bradley (ed.), *The Oxford Handbook of Comparative Foreign Relations Law* (Oxford: Oxford University Press, 2019), p. 128.

198 Galbraith and Zaring, 'Soft Law as Foreign Relations Law', 753.

199 See, e.g., Frank Schorkopf, 'Der Deutsche Bundestag und der Migrationspakt: Anlass zur Stärkung der parlamentarischen Beteiligung an völkerrechtlichen Soft Law-Prozessen?' (2019) 3 *Zeitschrift für Ausländerrecht und Ausländerpolitik* 90–96, passim.

200 See Bothe, 'Private Normunternehmer im Völkerrecht', p. 1404, on states' monopoly in the creation of formal international law.

the actors and/or processes are characterised by a high degree of informality (like the example of 'private norm entrepreneurs' suggests). Informal lawmaking may thus, in some instances, have much more of a 'life of its own' than formal law and be immune to democratisation 'from below'. Hence, in the context of informal lawmaking, bridges can be built, but not every boundary can be overcome.

Internationalisation came at a cost to democracy in the 'age of treaties', and such costs will increase further in times of informal international lawmaking. The increased use of informal lawmaking will exacerbate the tension between sovereignty – understood as a 'placeholder for constitutional values, in particular domestic democratic self-determination'[201] – and cooperation. However, when discussing (the limits of) democratisation 'from below', one tends to forget that Switzerland not only ranks number one in certain globalisation indexes,[202] but it is not seldom a driving force behind (laudable) informal lawmaking processes. This situation is exemplary for Dani Rodrik's more generalised finding that 'we cannot simultaneously pursue democracy, national determination, and economic globalization'[203] – or, to put it more bluntly, you can't have your cake and eat it too.

201 See the chapter by Aust and Kleinlein, p. 17.

202 In the KOF Globalisation Index 2019, which measures the economic, social and political dimensions of globalisation, Switzerland ranks number one in the overall index combining de facto and de jure globalisation: ETH Zurich, 'KOF Globalisation Index', https://kof.ethz.ch/en/forecasts-and-indicators/indicators/kof-globalisation-index.html, accessed 7 July 2020.

203 Dani Rodrik, *The Globalization Paradox: Why Global Markets, States, and Democracy Can't Coexist* (Oxford: Oxford University Press, 2011), p. xviii.

PART III

POWERS AND PROCESSES

10

A Constitution Made for Mandela, A Constitutional Jurisprudence Developed for Zuma

The Erosion of Discretion of the Executive in Foreign Relations

Dire Tladi

I AN INTRODUCTION

The field of law that is the subject of this book, foreign relations law, is referred to in South Africa simply as constitutional law or, the intersection of constitutional law and international law. It does not concern the rules of international law as such but may well concern processes that may lead to the making of international law, whether practice for the purposes of customary international law and, more often, treaty-making conduct. Contestations over who participates in international activities on behalf of the state, and under what circumstances international engagements on behalf of the state may be pursued (or abandoned) fall within this area.

Three recent cases in South Africa illustrate some of the contestations that may play themselves out over the limits of the right to engage in foreign relations. The judgments in question are the *Democratic Alliance* v. *Minister of International Relations and Cooperation* concerning the decision of the government to withdraw from the Rome Statute (hereinafter the *Withdrawal* judgment),[1] *Law Society of South Africa* v. *President of South Africa* (hereinafter the *SADC Tribunal* judgment),[2] and *Democratic Alliance* v. *Minister of International Relations and Cooperation* concerning the decision of the government to confer or recognise spousal immunities of Grace Mugabe, the spouse of former late President of Zimbabwe (hereinafter the *Grace Mugabe* decision).[3] While all three judgments addressed international law questions,

1 *Democratic Alliance* v. *Minister of International Relations and Cooperation and Others* 2017 (3) SA 212 (GP).

2 *Law Society of South Africa and Others* v. *President of the Republic of South Africa and Others* 2019 (3) BCLR 329 (CC).

3 *Democratic Alliance* v. *Minister of International Relations and Co-operation and Others* 2018 (6) SA 109 (GP).

these international law questions were not the central legal questions to the disputes. Rather, the central questions in all three cases concerned the distribution of competence between branches of government in relation to the conduct of foreign relations – constitutional lawyers may refer to the doctrine of the 'separation of powers'. These judgments have a number of things in common. First, all three concern the powers of the executive in foreign relations, and the limits thereof. Second, all three judgments concern judicial review of decisions made by the executive during Zuma administration. Third, in the judgments, the courts came to the conclusion that the decisions by the executive had been unlawful. In the interest of full disclosure, I should declare that I had been involved in *some* way in all three matters before the courts – I will describe my personal involvement when discussing each case. Given space constraints, I will discuss the Constitutional Court judgment in the *SADC Tribunal* in detail and only briefly touch upon the other two, which were not delivered by the apex court.

The decisions, to varying degrees, reflect an interesting trend in which the courts have slowly but surely eroded the discretion of the executive in foreign relations to the point where it can hardly be termed discretion. Much of this erosion has developed, it seems, because of a mistrust of the Zuma administration, leading one commentator in a social media platform to quip that South Africa has a 'constitution written for a President like Mandela and a constitutional jurisprudence made for a President like Jacob Zuma'.[4] This chapter will assess the decisions emanating from these cases principally from the perspective of the distribution of competence in the conduct of foreign relations. It proceeds from two premises which, decisions in question notwithstanding, have not been challenged as doctrine and remain, at least in rhetoric, the law in South Africa. First, the executive, even in the conduct of foreign relations, is constrained by the Constitution and the courts are not only permitted, but are duty-bound, to determine whether the executive has consistently with the Constitution. Second, while the courts are tasked with holding the executive accountable for its exercise of public power, the executive has a wide margin of discretion which ought not be interfered with lightly. In the next section of this chapter, the basis of these two premises is traced.

4 The phrase 'A Constitution made for a President like Mandela and a constitutional jurisprudence made for a President like Zuma' is borrowed from a facebook post by the recently appointed director of the Centre for Applied Legal Studies, Tshepo Mandlingozi.

II MANDELA'S CONSTITUTION: EXECUTIVE DISCRETION IN FOREIGN RELATIONS

South African courts, in the Apartheid years – before the international law-friendly years[5] – applied British concepts such as 'the act of state doctrine' and the related 'prerogatives' in matters pertaining to the conduct of foreign relations by the executive, with the result that the executive's conduct was beyond review. Under these traditional concepts, the executive had an almost unfettered discretion in the conduct of foreign relations,[6] and, in order 'to avoid judicial intrusion into the domain of the political branches', courts were required 'to refrain from sitting in judgment on the acts' covered by such doctrines.[7] These concepts however, do not fit neatly into South Africa's constitutional model which, in addition to being an international law-friendly framework, has also been termed a deliberative constitution.[8] Under this constitutional framework all exercise of public power, including the executive's conduct of foreign relations, must be subject to judicial scrutiny to ensure compliance with the Constitution.[9] This important constitutional principle raises the question of the appropriate standard for the review of the executive's conduct in matters of foreign relations.

In my view, the question was appropriately answered in a well-reasoned and rigorous judgment by the Constitutional Court in *Kaunda* v. *the President of the Republic of South Africa.*[10] In *Kaunda* the court determined that though courts are entitled to review decisions of the executive in the exercise of its

[5] For the description of the South African constitutional framework as international law-friendly see Neville Botha, 'Justice Sachs and the Interpretation of International Law by the Constitutional Court: Equity or Expediency?' (2010) 25 *Southern Africans Public Law* 235–50. See Dire Tladi, 'Interpretation of Treaties in an International Law-Friendly Framework: The Case of South Africa', in Helmut Aust and Georg Nolte (eds.), *The Interpretation of International Law by Domestic Courts: Uniformity, Diversity, Convergence* (Oxford: Oxford University Press, 2016).

[6] See e.g. Michael Bayzler, 'Abolishing the Act of State Doctine' (1986) 134 *University of Pennsylvania Law Review* 325–98; David Gordon, 'The Origin and Development of the Act of State Doctrine' (1976–1977) 8 *Rutgers Camden Law Journal* 595–616, at 595 ('As early as 1674, English courts declined to rule on the validity of foreign acts of state. This policy was adopted by the United States Supreme Court only twenty years after the Court's inception').

[7] Mark Haugen and Jeff Good, 'Evolution of the Act of State Doctrine: W.S. Kirkpatrick Co. v. Environmental Tectonics Corp. and Beyond' (1991) 13 *University of Hawaii Law Review* 687–714 at 688.

[8] See Dikgang Moseneke, 'Transformative Constitutionalism: its Implications for the Law of Contract' (2009) 20 *Stellenbosch Law Review* 3–13.

[9] *The President of the Republic of South Africa and Another* v. *Hugo* 1997 (4) SA 1 (CC), at para. 13.

[10] *Kaunda and Others* v. *the President of the Republic of South Africa and Others* 2005 (4) SA 235 (CC). For discussion of *Kaunda* see Dire Tladi and Polina Dlagnekova, 'The Act of State

mandate in foreign relations, in doing so they should 'give particular weight to the government's special responsibility for and particular expertise in foreign affairs' and therefore afford 'wide discretion ... in determining how to deal' with such foreign relations matters.[11] According to the Constitutional Court, the courts could, for example, intervene if a decision was irrational.[12] Importantly, the court stressed that the fact that the courts could review a decision of the executive in the conduct of foreign relations did 'not mean that courts *would substitute their opinion for that of government*' or order a particular course of action in the conduct of foreign relations.[13]

There is a second principle laid out in *Kaunda* which may be of some relevance for some of the analysis in this chapter. In rendering its decision, the court considered whether the Bill of Rights in the Constitution applies extraterritorially – this is referred to in the court's decision as extraterritoriality in a constitutional context.[14] The court stated that the Constitution 'provides a framework for the governance of South Africa', is 'territorially bound and has no application beyond our borders'.[15] Foreigners are entitled to the protection offered by the constitution while in South Africa but lose any such protection 'when they move beyond the borders'.[16] The court emphasised that the 'bearers of the rights [in the constitution] are people in South Africa' and that '[n]othing suggests that it is to have general application, beyond our borders'.[17]

Doctrine in South Africa: Has Kaunda Settled a Vexing Question?' (2007) 22 *South African Public Law* 444–56.

11 *Kaunda and Others* v. *the President of the Republic of South Africa and Others* 2005 (4) SA 235 (CC), at para. 144. Elsewhere the Court stated quoted with approval, a judgment in the German Federal Constitutional Court in the *Hess* decision BVerfGE 55, 349–70, at 395–6: '... the Federal Basic Law grants the organs of foreign affairs wide room for manoeuvre in the assessment of foreign policy issues ...'.

12 *Kaunda and Others* v. *the President of the Republic of South Africa and Others* 2005 (4) SA 235 (CC), at para. 79.

13 *Kaunda and Others* v. *the President of the Republic of South Africa and Others* 2005 (4) SA 235 (CC), at para. 79.

14 *Kaunda and Others* v. *the President of the Republic of South Africa and Others* 2005 (4) SA 235 (CC), at para. 36.

15 *Kaunda and Others* v. *the President of the Republic of South Africa and Others* 2005 (4) SA 235 (CC), at para. 36.

16 *Kaunda and Others* v. *the President of the Republic of South Africa and Others* 2005 (4) SA 235 (CC), at para. 36.

17 *Kaunda and Others* v. *the President of the Republic of South Africa and Others* 2005 (4) SA 235 (CC), at para. 37. At para. 54, in a slightly different, but still relevant, context, the Court noted that the Bill of Rights 'binds the South African government, but does not bind other governments'.

Although *Kaunda* was decided during the presidency of Thabo Mbeki, it was built on jurisprudence developed under the Mandela administration.[18] This jurisprudence not only advanced as a matter of principle (rhetoric) the idea of discretion and the notion that the courts ought to not substitute their own opinion for that of government, but actually applied said principle. The only time, during the Mandela–Mbeki administrations, when the rhetoric appeared not to be followed was in the *Von Abo* cases – which incidentally has interesting backstory connection with *Law Society of South Africa* v. *President*.[19] The *Von Abo* cases are interesting series of cases in which one man, *Von Abo*, sued the government for failing to protect his farming and business interests in Zimbabwe. The North Gauteng High Court, though paying lip-service to the jurisprudence of *Kaunda*, found that the government was indeed duty-bound to intervene diplomatically to protect the commercial interests of Mr Von Abo in Zimbabwe.[20] In a subsequent judgment on the damages, the Pretoria High Court proceeded to hold the government accountable on the basis of, inter alia, the failure to enter into a bilateral investment agreement with Zimbabwe (*Von Abo II*).[21]

Although the Pretoria High Court judgments in the *Von Abo* cases were eventually overturned by the Supreme Court of Appeal for not being consistent with the standard for the judicial review of acts of the executive in the conduct of foreign relations set by the Constitutional Court in, inter alia, *Kaunda*,[22] it is worth describing the salient themes of the *Von Abo* High Court judgments which, it seems, have been adopted in the new constitutional jurisprudence on the test for executive decisions in the conduct of foreign relations. The applicant in *Von Abo* had sought an order, inter alia, requiring

18 It was built in particular on the jurisprudence on the appropriate test for executive decisions such as *The President of the Republic of South Africa and Another* v. *Hugo* 1997 (4) SA 1 (CC) and *President of the Republic of South Africa and Others* v. *South African Rugby Football Union and Others* 2000 (1) SA 1 (CC) and *Mohamed and Another* v. *President of the Republic of South Africa and Others* 2001 (3) SA 893 (CC), although the latter concerned events that took place a few months after the end of the Mandela presidency.

19 See *Law Society of South Africa and Others* v. *President of the Republic of South Africa and Others* 2019 (3) BCLR 329 (CC).

20 *Von Abo* v. *the Government of the Republic of South Africa and Others* [2008] ZAGPHC 226. This judgment was the subject of a critique in Dire Tladi, 'The Right to Diplomatic Protection, the Von Abo Decision and One Big Can of Worms: Eroding the Clarity of Kaunda' (2009) 1 Stellenbosch Law Review 14–30. When approached to confirm the order of the High Court, the Constitutional Court declined on account of procedural grounds not related to the substance. See *Von Abo* v. *the President of the Republic of South Africa* 2009 (5) SA 345 (CC).

21 *Von Abo* v. *the Government of the Republic of South Africa and Others* 2010 (3) SA 269 (T).

22 *Government of the Republic of South Africa and Others* v. *Von Abo* 2011 (5) SA 262 (SCA).

the government to, within thirty days, 'take all necessary steps to have the Applicant's violation of his rights by the Government of Zimbabwe remedied',[23] remedies that the court granted in whole. There had also been a prayer, which was eventually abandoned by the Applicant but which the Court still felt the need to address, namely to 'force the respondent to join ICSID' – a treaty regime for the settlement of investment dispute.[24] Both of these prayers seem to be far-reaching, policy matters concerning the conduct of foreign relations.

Although the Applicant had abandoned its prayer concerning ICSID, the Court nonetheless proceeds identify reasons why the government should join ICSID.[25] These are policy consideration that courts are ill-equipped to consider. For example, while noting that joining ICSID would be greatly beneficial to South Africans investing in foreign states,[26] it does not consider that joining ICSID opens South Africa to suit from investors from other states that might challenge basic foundational policies of the government such as Black Economic Empowerment. The court felt so strongly about this policy question of joining ICSID that, notwithstanding the abandonment of the prayer by the Applicant, it decided to keep it on the table:

> The fact that the prayer for this specific relief was abandoned … does not mean, in my view, that the consistent failure on the part of the respondents to join ICSID and make a serious attempt to enter into a Bilateral Investment Treaty ('BIT') with Zimbabwe with the view to protecting its nationals investing in that country should not come under the spotlight … .[27]

With respect to the broader question of intervening in executive decisions in the conduct of foreign relations, without assessing the appropriate standards in the particular case, the Court simply states that, on the basis of the 'guidelines' provided by the Constitutional Court in *Kaunda*, 'it appears that there need not be an actual refusal on the part of the Government to grant diplomatic protection before a court will intervene … '.[28] In assessing the judgment of the

23 *Von Abo* v. *the Government of the Republic of South Africa and Others* [2008] ZAGPHC 226, at para. 19 et seq.

24 *Von Abo* v. *the Government of the Republic of South Africa and Others* [2008] ZAGPHC 226, para. 26.

25 *Von Abo* v. *the Government of the Republic of South Africa and Others* [2008] ZAGPHC 226, at paras. 29–37.

26 *Von Abo* v. *the Government of the Republic of South Africa and Others* [2008] ZAGPHC 226, at paras. 29 and 31.

27 *Von Abo* v. *the Government of the Republic of South Africa and Others* [2008] ZAGPHC 226, at para. 37.

28 *Von Abo* v. *the Government of the Republic of South Africa and Others* [2008] ZAGPHC 226, at para. 143.

Pretoria High Court in *Von Abo*, I have previously made the following general critique:

> The judgment quotes large extracts from the *Kaunda* majority [judgment], dissenting and concurring [opinions], mixes them together in a *potpourri* approach and then declares an outcome. The congruence between this outcome and *Kaunda* is assumed and therefore never properly examined. The differences between the majority, minority and concurring [opinions] are never explored.[29]

The essence of *Von Abo*, contrary to the majority in *Kaunda*, is that the Government has a duty to provide diplomatic protection. Not only that, the court in *Von Abo* orders very specific ways to achieve this objective, including seeking a bilateral investment treaty or joining ICSID, in a way that makes nonsense of the *Kaunda* judgment's call for wide discretion because of the nature of the playing arena, namely foreign relations. As noted, this judgment was eventually overturned by the Supreme Court of Appeal for its failure to respect the wide margin of discretion required by *Kaunda*.[30] This respect for the discretion of the executive in foreign relations has not meant that the courts have simply found in favour of the executive. In instances where the executive has clearly violated the constitution, the courts have not been shy to appropriately censure the executive.[31]

III ZUMA'S CONSTITUTIONAL JURISPRUDENCE: DISCRETION? WHAT DISCRETION?

A *The* SADC Tribunal *Decision*

I begin with the *SADC Tribunal* judgment, first because it was delivered by the Constitutional Court and second because of the three decisions, it is the most problematic and the one whose reasoning most offends the *Kaunda* doctrine of a very wide margin of discretion in foreign relations. The SADC *Tribunal* judgment concerned the decision of the Southern African Development Community (SADC) heads of state and government to remove

29 Tladi, 'The Right to Diplomatic Protection', 24.

30 *Government of the Republic of South Africa and Others* v. *Von Abo* 2011 (5) SA 262 (SCA).

31 For an example of a decision in which the Court held that the conduct of the executive in foreign relations was unconstitutional is *Mohamed and Another* v. *President of the Republic of South Africa* 2001 (3) SA 893 (CC) where the court held that the decision to render a Tanzanian national to the United States where he was subject to the possibility of the death sentence was contrary to the Constitution.

the right of access to the *SADC Tribunal* for individuals and other non-state entities. The Constitutional Court was approached by the Law Society of South Africa and others seeking an order to find that the president of South Africa, by signing the protocol establishing a new tribunal without such access had violated the constitution. In a hard-to-follow judgment penned by the chief justice, Mogoeng Mogoeng, the court found that the president's participation in the 'decision-making process and his own decision to suspend the operations' of the tribunal to be unconstitutional, unlawful and irrational.[32] The judgment also found that president's signing of the 2014 Protocol[33] was unconstitutional, unlawful and irrational and the court, as a result, directed the president to withdraw his signature.[34] My criticism of the judgment relates not only to the outcome, but to the reasoning, and to this point it may be added that a judgment built around the concurring opinion of justices Cameron and Froneman would be *less* objectionable, but ultimately also problematic.[35]

There is much that is open to critique – and little saving grace – in the *SADC Tribunal* judgment, both in terms of the order and the reasoning. But before delving into the analysis of the judgment, a related case concerning a South African diamond mining company, Swissbourgh, whose mineral rights in Lesotho had allegedly been expropriated to make way for the Lesotho Highlands Water Project, is worth referring to. The owner of the company, Mr Josias van Zyl, a South African national, first approached the South African courts (in the pre-Zuma years) seeking diplomatic protection, but was unsuccessful.[36] The cases are related to the *SADC Tribunal* judgment because, subsequent to the impugned decision of the SADC Summit concerning the tribunal, Swissbourgh filed an investment claim with the Permanent Court of Arbitration against the government of Lesotho claiming that its participation in the decision-making process that led to the taking away of the right of individual access to the *SADC Tribunal* – referred to in all the

32 *Law Society of South Africa and Others* v. *President of the Republic of South Africa and Others* 2019 (3) BCLR 329 (CC), para. 97.

33 Protocol on the Tribunal in the Southern African Development Community adopted on 21 February 2014, available at https://ijrcenter.org/wp-content/uploads/2016/11/New-SADC-Tribunal-Protocol-Signed.pdf, accessed 30 September 2020. There has not yet been ratification by Parliament of this Protocol pursuant to the President's signature.

34 *Law Society of South Africa and Others* v. *President of the Republic of South Africa and Others* 2019 (3) BCLR 329 (CC), para. 97.

35 *Law Society of South Africa and Others* v. *President of the Republic of South Africa and Others* 2019 (3) BCLR 329 (CC), para. 97; concurring opinion judges Cameron and Froneman, paras. 98–104.

36 *Van Zyl and Others* v. *the Government of the Republic of South Africa and Others* 2008 (3) SA 294 (SCA).

relevant papers of those papers as the 'shuttering of the Tribunal' – was a violation of its rights under the SADC Treaty regime, including the investment protocol. It will be noted that the claims of Swissbourgh are similar to those raised by South African Law Society before the South African courts. In the Swissbourgh matter, I served as expert witness for the government of Lesotho, focusing on the rules of state responsibility under international law and the decision-making processes in SADC, providing both a written report and being cross-examined by counsel for Swissbourgh.[37] In a majority judgment of two to one, the arbitral tribunal determined that Lesotho's participation in the decision-making process to shutter the tribunal did constitute a violation of international law and that Lesotho could be held liable for the damages[38] – incidentally, the one dissenting opinion came from a former South African judge of appeal, judge Petrus Millar Nienaber.[39] Because the arbitration was held under the PCA rules, the courts of Singapore had jurisdiction to review the arbitration award to determine whether the arbitral tribunal had jurisdiction. Lesotho had argued, inter alia, that the arbitral tribunal had not had jurisdiction precisely because its participation in the decision-making process did not establish international responsibility. After an earlier high court judgment affirmed Lesotho's claim, the highest court of Singapore, the Court of Appeal, finally overturned the arbitral award on the basis, inter alia, that the participation of Lesotho in the SADC decisions did not breach the relevant of international law as had been argued by Swissbourgh.[40]

Consistent with the *Kaunda* jurisprudence, the *SADC Tribunal* judgment begins by acknowledging that while public power must always be exercised within constitutional bounds, the president ought not to be 'unnecessarily constrained in the exercise of constitutional power'.[41] Yet, in what follows, the court departs from the *Kaunda* line of reasoning in at least two material ways.

37 The expert report is on file.

38 *Swissbourgh Diamond Mines and Others* v. *the Kingdom of Lesotho*, Permanent Court of Arbitration Case-2013–29, Partial Final Award on Merits and Jurisdiction, 18 April 2016. The judgment remains confidential but is on file with the author. I am able to share the outcome because, due to the appeals process in the courts of Singapore described further below, the outcome is for all intents and purposes, public.

39 *Swissbourgh Diamond Mines and Others* v. *the Kingdom of Lesotho*, Permanent Court of Arbitration Case-2013–29, Partial Final Award on Merits and Jurisdiction, 18 April 2016, dissenting opinion Justice Petrus Millar Nienaber.

40 See *Swissbourgh Diamond Mining Company and Others* v. *the Kingdom of Lesotho*, Court of Appeal of Singapore, 27 November 2018. For an accessible summary, see 'Top court dismisses appeal on arbitration award', www.straitstimes.com/singapore/courts-crime/top-court-dismisses-appeal-on-arbitration-award <30 September 2020>.

41 *Law Society of South Africa and Others* v. *President of the Republic of South Africa and Others* 2019 (3) BCLR 329 (CC), at para. 2.

First, the court's reasoning seems to imply that the executive, when acting in foreign relations, should do so in a manner that protects fundamental rights extraterritorially. Second, the court's judgment, both in terms of its reasoning and in terms of *dispositif* leaves very little discretion for the executive.

The extraterritorial rationale of the court's judgment is evident early on when it states that the 'only avenue open to those [in Zimbabwe] aggrieved by having been deprived of their land in that constitutionally sanctioned manner was the Tribunal'.[42] The court then states that the 'President, together with leaders of other SADC [states], *decided to* eviscerate the possibility of the states ever being held to account for perceived human rights violations, non-adherence to the rule of law or undemocratic practices'.[43] For this reason the court states, that South Africa, through the actions of its president, 'were party to denying citizens of South Africa and other SADC countries access to justice at a regional level'.[44] Yet, leaving aside that this statement is made *before any analysis* of the issues takes place, this seems to go against *Kaunda's* admonition that the 'bearers of the rights [in the Constitution] are people in South Africa' and that '[n]othing suggests that it is to have general application, beyond our borders'.[45] The impugned decisions are decisions taken at an international forum, in a foreign country, with no apparent impact in South Africa at all. The extraterritorial nature of the conduct is buttressed by the assertion that the unconstitutionality flows from an alleged breach of a rule under international law.

The judgment, furthermore, leaves very little discretion, if any, for the executive in the conduct of foreign relations. The judgment's conclusions that the impugned decisions are unlawful, irrational and unconstitutional are based on a single pillar, namely that they are in breach of South Africa's international law obligations. Given the far reaching nature of the decision – constraining the executive's role in international forums and even declaring the signature of a treaty to be unlawful – one would have expected a detailed and rigorous assessment of the claim that the impugned decisions were in breach of international law.[46] Yet there is no assessment of this claim at all.

42 *Law Society of South Africa and Others* v. *President of the Republic of South Africa and Others* 2019 (3) BCLR 329 (CC), para. 11.

43 *Law Society of South Africa and Others* v. *President of the Republic of South Africa and Others* 2019 (3) BCLR 329 (CC), at para. 14 (emphasis added).

44 *Law Society of South Africa and Others* v. *President of the Republic of South Africa and Others* 2019 (3) BCLR 329 (CC), at para. 15.

45 *Kaunda and Others* v. *the President of the Republic of South Africa and Others* 2005 (4) SA 235 (CC), at para. 37.

46 A more detailed analysis of the international law questions in the judgment can be found in a forthcoming article Dire Tladi, 'The Constitutional Court's Judgment in the SADC Case: International Law Continues to Befuddle' (2020) 10 *Constitutional Court Review* 129–43.

There appears to be two possible bases, none of which are really tested, for the court's assertion that the treaty has been breached. The first is what the court refers to as 'the entrenchment of a human rights culture, a democratic order and adherence to the rule of law' and the obligation on the SADC summit not to disturb these values.[47] The content of this 'obligation' is never described nor is it ever explained how the decision to adopt the 2014 Protocol breaches this obligation. In other words, does this 'entrenchment-obligation' require the existence of a tribunal in which individuals will have direct access? This certainly does not go without saying since the UN Charter itself has a human rights-entrenchment clause,[48] yet the UN does not have a tribunal with the right of access of all individuals of UN member states. The closest the court comes to any sort of description, let alone analysis, of this 'obligation' is a footnote reference to article 4 of the treaty and the preamble. Yet, article 4 of the treaty simply provides that the SADC and its member states shall act in accordance with a number of enumerated principles, including 'human rights, democracy and the rule of law'.[49] None of these principles imply, let alone require, the existence of a tribunal, even less so one with the right of individual access.

To the extent that article 4(c) might be said to refer to a right of access to an effective judicial remedy under international law, this is a right that applies in national systems. There is no right, whether under the SADC Treaty[50] or general international law, to access to an international tribunal (I include regional courts under the rubric of international courts).[51] It is disconcerting

47 *Law Society of South Africa and Others* v. *President of the Republic of South Africa and Others* 2019 (3) BCLR 329 (CC), at para. 51.

48 See e.g. arts. 55 and 56 of the Charter of the United Nations, San Francisco, 26 June 1945, 1 UNTS XVI.

49 See especially art. 4(c) of the Treaty of the Southern African Development Community.

50 Treaty of the Southern African Development Community, Windhoek, 17 August 1992, available at www.sadc.int/files/5314/4559/5701/Consolidated_Text_of_the_SADC_Treaty_-_scanned_21_October_2015.pdf, accessed 30 September 2020.

51 See e.g. United Nations Human Rights Committee, General Comment No. 32 – Article 14: Right to equality before courts and tribunals and to a fair trial, CCPR/C/GC/32, 23 August 2007, commenting on article 14 of the International Covenant on Civil and Political Rights: 'This guarantee not only applies to courts and tribunals addressed in the second sentence of this paragraph of article 14, but must also be respected whenever domestic law entrusts a judicial body with a judicial task' (para. 7); see also para. 18, which states: 'The notion of a "tribunal" in article 14, paragraph 1 designates a body, regardless of its denomination, that is established by law, *is independent of the executive and legislative branches of government* or enjoys in specific cases judicial independence in deciding legal matters in proceedings that are judicial in nature. . . .' (emphasis added) and the '. . . failure of a State party to establish a competent tribunal to determine such rights and obligations or to allow access to such a tribunal in specific cases would amount to a violation of article 14 if such

that the court seems oblivious to, or perhaps simply chose to ignore, the fact that the African Commission of Human and Peoples Rights had recently addressed the question of whether the shuttering of the tribunal's access to individuals amounted to a breach of the right of access to courts and effective judicial remedies in an application filed by Luke Munyandu Tembani who, incidentally was also second applicant in the Constitutional Court application.[52] In its well-reasoned decision, the African Commission concludes that the right of access to courts applied to national courts and not to international courts and, therefore, that the impugned decision of the SADC Summit was not contrary to the right of access to courts.[53]

The second possible basis for the conclusion that the impugned decision was a breach of South Africa's international law obligation is that the SADC summit did not follow the appropriate procedures under the relevant SADC treaties. According to the court, the adoption of the new 2014 Protocol was unlawful because 'the Treaty has never been amended so as to repeal its provisions relating to individual access to the Tribunal, human rights, the rule of law and access to justice'.[54] In the view of the court, the jurisdiction of the Court could only be 'lawfully tampered with in terms of the provisions of the [SADC] Treaty that regulate (*sic*) its amendment'.[55] The SADC Treaty, and indeed other SADC instruments including the 2001 Protocol[56]

limitations *are not based on domestic legislation*, are not necessary to pursue legitimate aims such as the proper administration of justice, or are based on exceptions from jurisdiction deriving from international law such, for example, as immunities, or if the access left to an individual would be limited to an extent that would undermine the very essence of the right' (emphasis added). See also art. 8 of the 1948 Universal Declaration of Human Rights is instructive in this respect. It provides that everyone 'has the right to an effective remedy by the competent national tribunals for acts violating the fundamental rights', UN General Assembly, Universal Declaration of Human Rights, 10 December 1948, 217 A (III); art. 13 of the European Convention on Human Rights provides for the right to an 'effective remedy before a national authority', Convention for the Protection of Human Rights and Fundamental Freedoms, Rome, 4 November 1950, 213 UNTS 221.

52 *Luke Munyandu Tembani and Benjamin John Freeth (represented by Norman Tjombe)* v. *Angola and Thirteen Others*, Communication 409/12, www.achpr.org/public/Document/file/English/achpr54_409_12_eng.pdf <30 September 2020>.

53 *Luke Munyandu Tembani and Benjamin John Freeth (represented by Norman Tjombe)* v. *Angola and Thirteen Others*, Communication 409/12, www.achpr.org/public/Document/file/English/achpr54_409_12_eng.pdf <30 September 2020>, at paras. 139, 144 and 146.

54 *Law Society of South Africa and Others* v. *President of the Republic of South Africa and Others* 2019 (3) BCLR 329 (CC), para. 53.

55 *Law Society of South Africa and Others* v. *President of the Republic of South Africa and Others* 2019 (3) BCLR 329 (CC), para. 49.

56 Protocol on Tribunal in the Southern African Development Community, Windhoek, 7 August 2000, www.sadc.int/files/1413/5292/8369/Protocol_on_the_Tribunal_and_Rules_thereof2000.pdf, accessed 23 September 2020.

establishing the tribunal, require a two-third majority for amendment and dissolution of any SADC institutions.[57] Yet the court, beyond stating that the SADC instruments required a two-thirds majority, does not test whether the procedures under the SADC instruments were complied with or not. The closest to any kind of assessment of whether the impugned decisions were made in accordance with a procedure that was consistent with the relevant instruments is the assertion by the Court that instead of the 'three quarters majority', the Summit 'sought to amend the Treaty through a protocol, thus evading compliance with the Treaty's more rigorous threshold of three-quarters of all of its Member States'.[58] It states, without explanation, that the decision of SADC 'evidences a failure to adhere to the provisions or proper meaning of the Treaty',[59] without applying the methodology for treaty interpretation under international law.

An assessment of the adherence to the procedure of the SADC summit would require, first, an interpretation of the relevant instruments and second, the description of the procedure followed. The court does neither of these. It is the case that the while instruments require a two-thirds majority, the impugned decision by SADC was adopted by consensus. Whether the consensus procedure falls foul of the two-thirds majority requirement is a matter to be determined through interpretation. This is particularly the case since SADC only ever adopts decisions by consensus, even where a two-thirds majority is required.[60] This consensus-decision-making-process arguably

57 See art. 36(1) of the SADC-Treaty provides that an amendment of the treaty 'shall be adopted by a decision of three-quarters of all Members of the Summit'. Art. 37(3) Protocol of the Tribunal in the Southern African Development Community, Windhoek, 7 August 2000, www.sadc.int/files/1413/5292/8369/Protocol_on_the_Tribunal_and_Rules_thereof2000.pdf, <30 September 2020>, states that '[a]n amendment to this Protocol shall be adopted by a three (3) quarters of all the members of the Summit . . .'. Moreover, the SADC-Treaty provides that Art. 22(11) provides that '[a]n amendment to any Protocol that has entered into force shall be adopted by a decision of three-quarters of the Member States that are Party to the Protocol'. Article 37(3) of the 2000 Protocol.

58 *Law Society of South Africa and Others* v. *President of the Republic of South Africa and Others* 2019 (3) BCLR 329 (CC), at para. 49. See also at para. 52 ('More importantly, the Tribunal is an institution of SADC and the Treaty requires a "resolution supported by three-quarters of all members to dissolve . . . any institution"').

59 *Law Society of South Africa and Others* v. *President of the Republic of South Africa and Others* 2019 (3) BCLR 329 (CC), at para. 51.

60 See e.g. para. 8.2.4.1 of the Records of the Summit Decision of August 2007 amending the Tribunal Protocol to 'facilitate trade disputes in the SADC Region'; Decision 6 of the Records of the Summit Decision of August 2008 amending the Treaty to provide for two Deputy Executive Secretaries and the abolition of the Integrated Committee of Ministers; Decision 10 on the Amendment of Article 6 of the Tribunal Protocol; Summit Decision 15 on the amendment of SADC Treaty so as not to provide for a specific number of Deputy

constitutes subsequent practice within the meaning of article 31(3)(b) of the Vienna Convention, which should be taken into account in determining whether the SADC decisions are consistent with the relevant instruments.[61] As the International Law Commission has noted, subsequent practice under article 31(3)(b) of the Vienna Convention 'may serve to clarify the meaning of a treaty by narrowing, widening or otherwise determining the range of possible interpretations, including any scope for the exercise of discretion which the treaty accords to the parties'.[62] It is worth mentioning that the Constitutional Court itself, in *Zimbabwe* v. *Fick*, accepted without question the amendment to article 16 of the SADC Treaty (concerning the tribunal), even though that amendment was adopted by consensus and not by a recorded vote.[63] There is thus a settled practice, over an extended period of time, in which SADC member states have made decisions by consensus, even where the requisite treaty provides for a threshold of two-third majority. This would indicate that the impugned decisions were adopted consistently with the 'authentic'[64] interpretation of parties to the SADC instruments which ought to have been taken into account in the assessment of whether those decisions were procedurally valid.

In addition to not considering the role of subsequent practice, the court also failed to consider that adopting a new treaty, even one inconsistent with a previous treaty is not unlawful under international law. As a general matter,

Executive Secretaries. See Compilation of Summit and Council Records of Decisions, available at www.sadc.int/documents-publications/show/7813, accessed 30 September 2020.

61 Article 31(3)(b) of the Vienna Convention on the Law of Treaties, Vienna, 23 May 1969, 1155 UNTS 331.

62 ILC 2018, Draft Conclusions on Subsequent Agreements and Subsequent Practice in Relation to the Interpretation of Treaties, *Report of the International Law Commission, Seventieth Session*, General Assembly Official Records (A/73/10), Draft Conclusion 7.

63 *The Government of the Republic of Zimbabwe* v. *Louis Karel Fick and Others*, Case CCT 101/12 [2013] (10) *BCLR* 1103 (CC), at para. 10 ('The amendment alluded to above was effected by the Summit in terms of the Agreement Amending the Treaty of the Southern African Development Community (Amending Agreement). Article 16(2) of the Treaty was amended to provide for the Tribunal Protocol to be an integral part of the Treaty, obviously subject to the adoption of the Amending Agreement'.). See art. 18 of the 2001 Agreement Amending the Treaty of the Southern African Development Community. The Agreement was adopted on 14 August 2001. See Communiqué of the SADC Summit of 2001 August, Malawi Blantyre, para. 23.

64 See draft conclusion 3 of the ILC 2018 Draft Conclusions on Subsequent Agreements and Subsequent Practice in Relation to the Interpretation of Treaties, *Report of the International Law Commission, Seventieth Session*, General Assembly Official Records (A/73/10), ('Subsequent agreements and subsequent practice under article 31, para. 3 (a) and (b) [of the Vienna Convention], being objective means evidence of the understanding of the parties as to the meaning of the treaty, are authentic means of interpretation, in the application of the general rule of treaty interpretation in article 31'.).

rules of international law, including treaty rules, are *jus dispositivum* and can be derogated from or modified by subsequent rules of international law.[65] This includes treaty rules concerning access to courts and certainly includes rules of amendments. The only exception to this basic rule of international law is the operation of peremptory norms of general international law (*jus cogens*).[66] It is clear that the court does not believe that the right of individual access to the *SADC Tribunal* is a peremptory norm since it accepts that the provisions could have been amended through the 'correct procedure'. Nor does the court assert that the amendment provisions themselves are of a peremptory character. This being the case, the normal rules of successive treaties laid out in the Vienna Convention would, even if in the absence of the application of article 31(3)(b), be relevant. Article 59 of the Vienna Convention provides for the termination of one treaty by entry into force of another if 'it appears from the later treaty or is otherwise established' that the parties to the previous treaty intend for it to be replaced.[67] This rule is not subject to the provisions of the previous treaty.[68] The 2014 Protocol is explicit that the 2000 Protocol 'is replaced with effect from the date of entry into force of' the 2014 Protocol.[69] Even though the 2014 Protocol is inconsistent with the 2000 Protocol, it is hard to imagine how the adoption of a subsequent treaty repealing an old treaty – a situation contemplated by the Vienna Convention – could be unlawful. At any rate, the problem with the Court is not *only* its conclusion but also its failure to engage with the methodology of international law by addressing this and other rules of interpretation.

It is hard to imagine what policy space, or discretion, is left for the executive, after the *SADC Tribunal* judgment. To borrow from the words of *Kaunda* the Constitutional Court does not 'give particular weight to the government's special responsibility for and particular expertise in foreign affairs' and certainly does not afford it 'wide discretion ... in determining how to deal'.

65 *North Sea Continental Shelf cases (Federal Republic of Germany/Denmark; Federal Republic of Germany/Netherlands)*, I.C.J. Reports 1969, p. 3, para. 72. See for discussion *First Report of Special Rapporteur (Dire Tladi) on* Jus Cogens (A/CN.4/793), paras. 66–7.

66 *North Sea Continental Shelf cases (Federal Republic of Germany/Denmark; Federal Republic of Germany/Netherlands)*, I.C.J. Reports 1969, p. 3, para. 72. See for discussion *First Report of Special Rapporteur (Dire Tladi) on* Jus Cogens (A/CN.4/793), paras. 66–7. See also generally, Draft Conclusions on Peremptory Norms of General International Law (*Jus Cogens*), *Report of the International Law*, General Assembly Official Records (A/74/10), 147.

67 Article 59 of the Vienna Convention ('A treaty shall be considered terminated if all the parties to it conclude a later treaty relating to the same subject and ... [it] appears from the later treaty or is otherwise established that the parties intended that the subject matter be governed by that treaty ...').

68 See *ibid.*

69 Article 48 of the 2014 Protocol.

Moreover, this judgment, again contrary to the admonition of *Kaunda*, substitutes its own policy preferences for those of the government: the government, as a policy matter, accepted the position of other SADC members to have a tribunal without individual access, but the court preferred a tribunal with such access. The judgment provides a good illustration for why courts should avoid replacing their own policy-preferences for the government's, particularly in the area of foreign relations. The judgment treats the executive's participation in the decision of 2012 to dissolve the *SADC Tribunal* as a simple choice between supporting the shuttering or not. It shows a complete ignorance for the fact that states have other choices, including not blocking consensus of decisions they are not fully supportive of, or of being agnostic. The court does not even grapple with the decision-making processes to determine whether there was a vote, or if the decisions were adopted by consensus, if there was a vote whether South Africa supported the motion or abstained. Under the *SADC Tribunal* judgment, the decision of the South Africa to support, abstain from or not support, a resolution in any organ of an international organisation, including the UN General Assembly, the United Nations Security and the African Union, can be overturned by the courts if the decision does not accord with the policy preferences of the court.

B *The Democratic Alliance cases*

The *SADC Tribunal* judgment is notable not only because it is handed down by the apex court, but also because of how far-reaching it is. The judgment concerned the type of decision that one would expect a court to give the greatest of discretion to the executive – one that took place outside the borders of the country, concerned organs of an international organisation and had little impact on South African law or South African circumstances. Yet the erosion of the discretion of the executive by the courts is not isolated. Two cases brought by the Democratic Alliance and decided by the High Courts of Gauteng – the *Grace Mugabe* and *Withdrawal* decision – provide further examples of decisions by courts concerning the exercise of discretion by the executive in foreign affairs.

The *Grace Mugabe* judgment concerned the decision of the South African foreign minister to confer immunities on Grace Mugabe, at the time the spouse of Robert Mugabe (then head of state of Zimbabwe).[70] The decision emanated from the now infamous alleged assault by Grace Mugabe on

[70] In the interest of transparency, I should declare that at the time of the relevant events, I served as Special Adviser to the foreign minister and was intimately involved in the decision-making.

a South African woman, Gabriella Engels, in Johannesburg. The assault took place during the SADC summit of 2017 but before the arrival of Robert Mugabe – although there is some dispute as to whether Grace Mugabe was in South Africa for the summit or for personal reasons, this question is in fact immaterial to the legal issues and the question of the discretion. The decision was made pursuant to section 7(2) of the Diplomatic Immunities and Privileges Act[71] which provides as follows:

> The Minister may in any particular case if it is not expedient to enter into an agreement as contemplated in subsection (1) and if the conferment of immunities and privileges is in the interest of the Republic, confer such immunities and privileges on a person or organisation as may be specified by notice in the *Gazette*.

In the midst of a media storm surrounding the events, and in response to a note verbal from the Embassy of Zimbabwe, the minister conferred immunity on the First Lady in accordance with section 7(2) of the act. In a letter to the National Commission of Police, the Director-General of the Department of International Relations and Cooperation stated that the discretion accorded to the minister under the section was not absolute and required 'the Minister to consider all the facts and circumstances' and further noted that any decision she takes 'must be reasoned'.[72] The letter provides a detailed account of the facts and circumstances taken into account by the Minister, but these can be summarised as follows:

(i) the rule of law and the need to ensure that the law protected South African citizens;
(ii) that Grace Mugabe was the First Lady of neighbouring and that prosecuting her would negatively affect relations between South Africa and Zimbabwe and may even affect relations between South Africa and other African states;
(iii) that South Africa was chair of SADC and the ongoing SADC Summit would be thrust the SADC Summit into chaos if the First Lady were arrest and prosecuted; and
(iv) that under customary international law spouses of heads of state were entitled to derivative immunity.

[71] Diplomatic and Immunities Act, No. 37 of 2001, www.gov.za/sites/default/files/gcis_document/201409/a37-010.pdf <30 September 2020>.

[72] The full letter is quoted in *Democratic Alliance* v. *Minister of International Relations and Co-operation and Others* 2018 (6) SA 109 (GP), at para. 6.

The court, however, declared that the decision of the minister was unconstitutional and set it aside it. First, it cast doubt on the assertion that spouses of heads of state are entitled to derivative immunity *ratione personae*. Although derivative immunity of the immediate family of a head of state, especially the spouse, is generally accepted,[73] the court dismisses the contention on the basis that 'at least two other national courts' have rejected this view.[74] Yet, both cases relied on by the court are not authority for the view that spouses of heads of state are not immune from the foreign criminal jurisdiction. First, the Belgian judgment in *Mobutu* v. *SA Cotoni*,[75] cited by the court did not concern immunity from criminal jurisdiction but rather immunity from civil jurisdiction. These two types of immunities are different and cannot just be conflated.[76] An illustration of the fact that, as a matter of international law, the rules pertaining immunity in civil proceedings ought not to be simply transposed to immunity in criminal proceedings, is the *Jurisdictional Immunities of States* case, where the International Court of Justice, while concluding that there are no *jus cogens* exceptions to immunity from civil jurisdiction, noted that the same was not necessarily true for immunity from foreign criminal jurisdiction.[77] This is not to say that rules relating to civil

73 See for discussion Joanne Foakes, *The Position of Heads of State and Senior Officials in International Law* (Oxford: Oxford University Press, 2014), p. 104. While there are discrepancies on the scope, what is not questioned is that spouses benefit from this type of immunity when in the company of the heads of State. See in this respect, Robert Jennings and Arthur Watts (eds.), *Oppenheim's International Law*, 9th ed., 2 vols. (Harlow: Longman, 1992), Vol. 1: Peace, Parts 2 to 4, 1039 et seq. ('[With respect to Family members], [e]xcept in so far as they may regarded as part of the Head of State's retinue, their exemption from [jurisdiction is] more questionable, *except in the case of the Head of State's spouse*') (emphasis added). See also Arthur Watts, 'The Legal Position in International Law of Heads of States, Heads of Governments and Foreign Ministers' (1994) 247 *Recuile de Cours de l'Académie de Droit International de La Haye* 9–30.

74 *Democratic Alliance* v. *Minister of International Relations and Co-operation and Others* 2018 (6) SA 109 (GP), at para. 24.

75 Cited in *Preliminary Report on Immunity of State Officials from Foreign Criminal Jurisdiction by Roman Kolodkin, Special Rapporteur* (A/CN.4/604), 29 May 2008, at para. 126. I note that the High Court did not consult the judgment itself but rather relied on an account of the judgment offered in the Kolodkin report and erroneously suggested that the judgment was in German ('The judgment is in German. The summary herein is drawn from the report' of Roman Kolodkin).

76 See for discussion *Third Report of the Special Rapporteur (Dire Tladi) on Peremptory Norms of General International Law* (Jus Cogens) (A/CN.4/714), at para. 124.

77 *Jurisdictional Immunities of the State (Germany* v. *Italy: Greece intervening)*, Judgment, I.C.J. Reports 2012, p. 99, para. 91 ('The Court concludes that, under customary international law as it presently stands, a State is not deprived of immunity by reason of the fact that is it is accused of serious violations of international human rights law or the international law of armed conflict. In reaching that conclusion, the *Court must emphasise* that it is addressing *only* the

proceedings are not at relevant at all, since they have been used as a basis to define the head of state as including their spouses.[78] Second, the Belgian court in the *Mobutu* case did not exclude derivative immunity of the immediate family. Rather, that Court excluded the children of the president of Zaire from the scope of such derivative because they had reached and passed the age of majority and, as such, were not his immediate family. The same is true of the other authority relied on, namely W v. *Prince of Liechtenstein*, in which the Austrian Supreme Court denied derivative immunity.[79] As in the *Mobutu* case, W v. *Prince of Liechtenstein* concerned civil immunity and, more importantly, derivative immunity was excluded not because the Court did not recognise its existence but rather because sisters and brothers of the head of state were not regarded as part of the immediate family. If anything, these authorities would support derivative immunity but restrict its scope of application to the immediate family, which the spouse of a head of state would most certainly be. The relevant part of paragraph 24, in which these two cases are discussed, is in fact taken, verbatim from the preliminary report of the International law Commission Special Rapporteur on the topic of immunity (and sometimes without acknowledgement).[80] However, the judgment is misleading and quotes the report out of context. In the report, in the preceding paragraph, the special rapporteur confirms the view of the minister that this 'jurisdictional immunity . . . also extends, in such circumstances, to the closest accompanying family members . . .'.[81] Having referred to the two cases utilised as the only two cases in which derivative immunity was denied,[82] the special rapporteur then places them in context by stating that 'in the two cases . . . in which the courts declined to recognise the immunity of the' the relevant

immunity of the State itself from the jurisdiction of the courts of other States; the question of whether, and if so to what extent, immunity might apply in criminal proceedings against an official of the *State is not in issue in the present case*') and at para. 87, noting that the *Pinochet* case 'concerned the immunity of a former Head of State from the criminal jurisdiction of another State, not the immunity of the State itself in proceedings designed to establish its liability to damages' (emphasis added). This similar sentiment has been expressed in other cases, e.g. *Yousuf* v. *Samantar*, 699 F.3d 763, 776-77 (4th Cir. 2012), at para. 124. See also ILC Summary Records, Tladi (A/CN.4/SR.3425), at 14.

78 Foakes, *The Position of Heads of State*, p. 104.

79 Cited in the *Preliminary Report on Immunity of State Officials from Foreign Criminal Jurisdiction by Roman Kolodkin, Special Rapporteur* (A/CN.4/604), 29 May 2008, at para. 126.

80 *Preliminary Report on Immunity of State Officials from Foreign Criminal Jurisdiction by Roman Kolodkin, Special Rapporteur* (A/CN.4/604), 29 May 2008, at para. 126.

81 *Preliminary Report on Immunity of State Officials from Foreign Criminal Jurisdiction by Roman Kolodkin, Special Rapporteur* (A/CN.4/604), 29 May 2008, at para. 125.

82 *Preliminary Report on Immunity of State Officials from Foreign Criminal Jurisdiction by Roman Kolodkin, Special Rapporteur* (A/CN.4/604), 29 May 2008, at para. 126.

family members 'the rulings were based on the fact that the persons concerned were not among the immediate family of the Head of State and were not dependent on him'.[83] The court's use of these authorities is thus, at best a misunderstanding, and at worst a misrepresentation of the authorities in question. The false impression is also created in the judgment that the Kolodkin report rejected spousal immunity while the report clearly believed spousal immunity to be part of customary international law.[84]

The court's judgment is based on another significant error. The court relies on section 6(a) of the Foreign States Immunities Act which, according to the court, excludes the immunity of Mr Mugabe in cases of 'death or injury of any person'.[85] If, so the understanding of the court goes, Robert Mugabe did not enjoy immunity because section 6(a) excludes of the Foreign States Immunities Act excludes immunity in the case of 'death or injury', then Grace Mugabe could not, herself, have enjoyed immunity as it was derivative. This reflects a complete lack of understanding not only of international law but of the immunity legislation in South Africa. Immunity *ratione personae* from foreign criminal jurisdiction is not addressed *at all* in the Foreign States Immunities Act which addresses the immunity of the *state itself from civil proceedings*.[86] Immunity *ratione personae* from foreign criminal jurisdiction in South Africa is governed by the Diplomatic Immunities and Privileges Act[87] and, as recognised by the Supreme Court, it knows no exception both under international law.[88] According to the court, in the *Al Bashir* judgment, the only exception is the relation to International Criminal Court arrest and surrender proceedings.[89]

83 *Preliminary Report on Immunity of State Officials from Foreign Criminal Jurisdiction by Roman Kolodkin, Special Rapporteur* (A/CN.4/604), 29 May 2008, at para. 127.

84 *Preliminary Report on Immunity of State Officials from Foreign Criminal Jurisdiction by Roman Kolodkin, Special Rapporteur* (A/CN.4/604), 29 May 2008, at para. 127.

85 *Democratic Alliance* v. *Minister of International Relations and Co-operation and Others* 2018 (6) SA 109 (GP), at paras. 39–40.

86 See John Dugard. 'Immunity', in John Dugard et al., (eds.), *Dugard's International Law: A South African Perspective*, 5th ed. (Cape Town: Juta, 2018), p. 347 et seq.

87 Section 4(1)(a) of the Diplomatic Immunities and Privileges Act of 2001 provides that a head of State enjoys such immunity 'from the criminal and civil jurisdiction of the courts … in accordance with rules of customary international law'. I note, though this is not critical, that even if the Foreign States Immunities Act were relevant, as the later law, the Diplomatic Immunities and Privilege would trump it.

88 *Minister of Justice and Others* v. *South African Litigation Centre and Others* 2016 (3) SA 317 (SCA).

89 *Minister of Justice and Others* v. *South African Litigation Centre and Others* 2016 (3) SA 317 (SCA).

On the basis of these two flawed bases, the court decides to overturn a decision of the executive based on a discretion expressly granted by legislation. It does not even assess whether the discretion was exercised correctly. The discretion accorded to the executive in the conduct of foreign relations in *Kaunda* and confirmed by the Diplomatic Immunities and Privileges Act is ignored in favour of the policy preference of the judiciary. Let me pause to say, it is correct that at the time judgment Grace Mugabe did not, under customary international law, enjoy the derivative immunity referred to in the decision of the minister, because that immunity applies only to the spouse of *a sitting head of state* and when in the *presence of the head of the state*. The question is not whether Grace Mugabe had immunity or not, the question is whether the minister had the right, acting under the Diplomatic Immunities and Privileges Act and in the exercise of the executive competence in foreign relations, to confer such immunities.

The second Democratic Alliance case, the *Withdrawal* judgment, concerned the decision of the South African government to withdraw from the Rome Statute of the International Criminal Court without parliamentary approval. The reasoning in the *Withdrawal* judgment is not as objectionable as the SADC *Tribunal* and *Grace Mugabe* judgment. Indeed, though I don't fully agree with the decision, I believe it is a reasonable judgment and, at least on the surface, perhaps even more rational than what I believe is the objectively correct interpretation of the law.[90] As the court stated, the *Withdrawal* judgment concerned 'the separation of powers between the national executive and parliament in international relations and treaty-making'.[91] In this case, the High Court determined that South Africa could withdraw from a treaty entered into after the approval of parliament, only after parliament itself had approved the withdrawal. According to the court, 'there is no question that the power to conduct international relations and to conclude treaties has been

90 The relevant events also took place while I was adviser to the Foreign Minister. Here, I should say, my legal views were at variance with my political views. Contrary to my legal views, expressed in this chapter, my political views were as follows: First, given the judgment of the Supreme Court of Appeal in the *Al Bashir* judgment, it was unnecessary to withdraw. A careful reading of the *Al Bashir* judgment suggested that the problem was not the Rome Statute at all, but rather South Africa's domestic implementation legislation. Rather than withdraw, all South Africa needed to do was to amend it's the Rome Statute Implementation Act and its problems would disappear. If, however, it was deemed necessary to withdraw, parliamentary approval should be obtained because, while my legal position was that it was unnecessary, it was difficult to imagine a South African court accepting such an argument, even in the absence of the 'Zuma-jurisprudence'.

91 *Democratic Alliance* v. *Minister of International Relations and Cooperation and Others* 2017 (3) SA 212 (GP), at para. 1.

constitutionally conferred upon the executive'.[92] This power, however, is not unfettered and requires 'the national power to engage parliament'.[93] In this context, it accepts that 'the formulation of a policy to withdraw from the Rome Statute therefore no doubt falls within the national executive's province'.[94] However, in the view of the court, the 'approval of an international agreement' by parliament 'creates a social contract between the people of South Africa' and the national executive, requiring parliamentary approval before the executive seeks to withdraw from an agreement so approved.[95]

Although I do not share in this interpretation, I am not inclined to be too critical of this decision, nor would I ascribe it necessarily *solely* to the emergence of the 'Zuma jurisprudence'. This is because the reasoning seems logical and is not based on any obviously flawed logic. There is, however, an alternative construction of section 231(2) of the Constitution[96] which would grant greater autonomy to the executive in the conduct of foreign relations – for the record, this alternative interpretation was never presented by counsel for the government whose argument were rather convoluted.[97] My own reading of section 231(2) is that it requires parliament to approve international agreements before the executive can ratify such agreements. Yet, the approval by parliament is nothing more than that – an approval or, to put it more colloquially, permission to ratify. The approval itself does not bind the republic to the obligation contained in the treaty nor does it bind the executive into ratifying the relevant treaty. The approval is intended to confirm that the treaty is consistent with South Africa's legal framework and that the executive *may, if*

92 *Democratic Alliance* v. *Minister of International Relations and Cooperation and Others* 2017 (3) SA 212 (GP), para. 35.

93 *Democratic Alliance* v. *Minister of International Relations and Cooperation and Others* 2017 (3) SA 212 (GP), at para. 35.

94 *Democratic Alliance* v. *Minister of International Relations and Cooperation and Others* 2017 (3) SA 212 (GP), at para. 45.

95 *Democratic Alliance* v. *Minister of International Relations and Cooperation and Others* 2017 (3) SA 212 (GP), at paras. 52 and 53.

96 Section 231 of the South African Constitution provides as follows: 'An international agreement binds the Republic only after it has been approved by a resolution in both the National Assembly and the National Council of Provinces …', www.gov.za/sites/www.gov.za/files/images/a108-96.pdf, accessed 30 September 2020.

97 The government, in essence, argued that 'parliament approval is only required in order for a treaty to become binding'. See, *Democratic Alliance* v. *Minister of International Relations and Cooperation and Others* 2017 (3) SA 212 (GP), at paras. 38–9. There was also a similarly confusing argument that a notice of withdrawal under international law does not require parliamentary approval (at para. 40). This latter point is accurate but irrelevant. The question was not whether the notice of withdrawal was valid under international law, surely it was. Rather the question was whether it was valid under domestic law.

it wished, proceed with the ratification process.[98] If approval is nothing more than permission to become party, then whether South Africa becomes a party to the said treaty or not, or becomes party and then decides to withdraw, does not undermine the parliamentary approval. To put it simply, parliamentary approval establishes a right to join the treaty not an obligation to become (or remain) a party. This, however, is only one possible approach to section 231(2) – one which would give the executive greater discretion to make policy choices in foreign relations – and the Court chose another, equally reasonable approach.

IV CONCLUSION

Under the South African constitutional framework, all exercise of public power is subject to judicial review to ensure consistency with the constitution. This includes the executive's conduct of foreign relations. Yet the Constitutional Court has, in several judgments, recognised that the nature of foreign relations requires significantly more discretion for the executive than the exercise of public power in other contexts. The test established by the Court to determine whether that conduct in foreign relations is consistent with the Constitution is rationality. Under this general test, the executive should be given a wide margin of discretion and the courts should interfere with policy choices made by the executive only in exceptional cases. Moreover, the courts should avoid substituting their own policy preferences for those of the executive. With the exception of one case of the High Court, which was eventually overturned by the Supreme Court of Appeal,[99] in the pre-Zuma era, the courts did not unnecessarily intervene unless there was a clear and unjustified breach of the constitution.[100]

In the Zuma era, while the courts have continued to pay lip-service the constitutional doctrine of deference, they have shrunk the discretion accorded to the executive to the extent that it is nothing but an empty shell. Under this new judicial oversight framework, it is the courts, based on the policy preferences of the judges, who determine what treaties South Africa may or may not enter into, whether to call for a vote or accept consensus in international forums, how and whether to vote where a vote is called for in such forums and whether to accord or not to accord immunities. While, given the Zuma

98 See in this regard *Earthlife Africa* v. *Minister of Energy* 2017 (5) SA 227, at para. 114 noting agreements requiring approval of parliament are those that 'generally engage or warrant the focussed attention or interest of Parliament'.

99 *Von Abo* v. *the Government of the Republic of South Africa and Others* [2008] ZAGPHC 226.

100 An example of a case where the Court did intervene is *Mohamed and Another* v. *President of the Republic of South Africa* 2001 (3) SA 893 (CC).

administration's corruption-riddled tenure, very often the courts' policy preferences are understandable, it is a dangerous path when courts begin to assume the role of policy-maker, no matter how laudable the policy may be – after all, the road to hell is paved with good intentions.

It is still too early to tell whether the Zuma-era approach will continue in the Ramaphosa era, particularly since not a single foreign relations-related decision of the Ramaphosa administration is yet to be challenged. However, because the courts have, while constraining the discretion of the executive, maintained, at least as rhetoric, the *Kaunda* balance, underdoing the Zuma-era jurisprudence should not be too difficult.

11

From Scope to Process

The Evolution of Checks on Presidential Power in US Foreign Relations Law

Jean Galbraith

A core challenge for foreign relations law – as with all public law – is how to constrain decision-makers and yet enable them to be effective. Power and flexibility are necessary to successful governance, but they are also the keys to despotism. The challenge of this conundrum underlies much of political theory and constitutional law.

In the United States, the original solution was an innovative distribution of powers between various branches of government. The Framers of the US Constitution gave certain powers to Congress, as set forth in the Constitution's Article I, and certain powers to the President, as set forth in its Article II.[1] A third branch – the courts – could resolve constitutional disputes between these branches in appropriate cases. By disaggregating government into separate strands, the Framers believed that these 'constituent parts may, by their mutual relations, be the means of keeping each other in their proper places'.[2]

Over time, however, this distribution of powers has changed with respect to foreign affairs. The core story, often told, is of the rise of presidential power.[3] The original constitutional design sought to require congressional approval for non-defensive uses of force, Senate approval for important international agreements, congressional control over international commerce, and arguably a general principle of congressional control with respect to foreign affairs. Yet in today's world, the President has considerable authority to initiate non-defensive uses of force,

[1] See US Constitution, arts. I and II.

[2] James Madison, 'Federalist No. 51', in Clinton Rossiter (ed.), *The Federalist Papers* (New York: New American Library, 1961).

[3] For two of many such accounts, see Arthur M. Schlesinger, Jr., *The Imperial Presidency* (Boston: Houghton Mifflin, 1973); Eric A. Posner and Adrian Vermeule, *The Executive Unbound: After the Madisonian Republic* (Oxford: Oxford University Press, 2010).

make international agreements without Senate approval, act in relation to foreign commerce without the assent of the current Congress, and more generally assert the 'lion's share' of control over foreign affairs.[4]

As the scope of the President's power has grown, however, it has also become subject to more process-based requirements. Transparency and regularity are now often expected and not infrequently mandated with respect to uses of executive power related to foreign affairs. These requirements do not stem from the US Constitution but rather from a web of diffuse sources, including US congressional law, US executive branch practice, and various aspects of international law. This new set of constraints serves to some degree as a substitute for the original constitutional constraints.

This book chapter describes these twin developments in relation to presidential foreign affairs power – the erosion of scope-based checks and the rise of process-based checks. It argues that international law has played a role in both developments. In closing, it considers the extent to the changes described here may have relevance for the practice of other nations.

Throughout the chapter, the terms 'scope-based' and 'process-based' are used in a distinct and perhaps idiosyncratic way. They are used not in relation to the entire power of the federal government, but rather more narrowly in relation to the power of the President and the executive branch that works under him or her. The term 'scope-based' (and related terms) refer to *what the President has the legal authority to do as a matter of domestic law amid congressional silence*. The term 'process-based' (and related terms) refer to *how this legal authority is to be exercised*. By way of example, the question of whether the President has the domestic legal authority to bomb Syrian government facilities in response to Syria's use of chemical weapons against its own citizens is treated here as an issue of scope. By contrast, the question of whether, with respect to such a use of force, the President has satisfied any legal requirements relating to notice, consultation, reporting, and reasoned decision-making is treated as an issue of process. Distinctions between scope and process are always complicated at the margins, but the two concepts nonetheless serve as useful frames for thinking about the scope of executive power.[5]

4 Edward S. Corwin, *The President: Office and Powers, 1787–1948*, 3rd ed. (New York: New York University Press, 1948), p. 208.

5 The use of these concepts inevitably depends on one's vantage point. Because I focus here on the power of the executive branch rather than on the power of the federal government as a whole, I consider the President's power to use force to be a 'scope-based' issue – a question of *what* the President can do unilaterally. If I were focusing on the power of the federal government as a whole, I might consider the overall extent of the US government's power to use force under the US Constitution and international law to be a 'scope-based' issue but the question of how power is divided within the various branches of the federal government to be a 'process-based' issue. And if

I THE EROSION OF SCOPE-BASED CONSTITUTIONAL CHECKS ON THE PRESIDENT'S FOREIGN RELATIONS POWERS

Perhaps inevitably, consideration of US foreign relations law starts with the US Constitution. Its Framers sought to provide the US government with a full panoply of foreign affairs powers, but they spread control over these powers between Congress and the President. In the years since, however, the scope of presidential power has increased. The President now considers himself or herself able as matter of scope to undertake a vast swath of decision-making related to US foreign affairs without the affirmative approval of Congress.

By way of illustration, consider the following four foreign affairs powers:

- *Uses of Force*. The text of the Constitution allocates to Congress numerous powers related to war, including the power to declare war, while making the President commander-in-chief.[6] Over time, however, the President has come to assert more and more concurrent power with respect to the initiation of uses of force.[7] The US executive branch still recognizes that a full-scale war likely requires congressional authorization, but many substantial uses of force in the twentieth and twenty-first centuries have been initiated without congressional authorization.[8]
- *International Agreements*. The text of the Constitution provides that the President shall have power to make treaties with the advice and consent of two-thirds of the Senate.[9] While some agreements do still go through this process, in practice Presidents have also come to make international agreements, including very important ones, through several other alternative processes. Some of these agreements are made with clear congressional authorization, but others are made by the executive branch acting either alone or in reliance on a vague statutory

I were focused on the power of the United States rather than of its government, I might consider it a 'process-based' issue whether the US government had a particular power or instead would need a constitutional amendment to have that power. My focus throughout this chapter, however, is on the power of the presidency.

6 US Constitution, arts. I § 8, cll. 11–14 and II § 2, cl.1.

7 For a discussion of this development and of its relationships to international law on the use of force, see generally Curtis A. Bradley and Jean Galbraith, 'Presidential War Powers as an Interactive Dynamic: International Law, Domestic Law, and Practice-Based Legal Change' (2016) 91 *New York University Law Review* 689.

8 For a recent articulation of the legal views of the executive branch on this issue, see Steven A. Engel, Assistant Attorney General, Office of Legal Counsel, 'April 2018 Airstrikes Against Syrian Chemical-Weapons Facilities: Memorandum Opinion for the Counsel to the President', US Department of Justice, May 31, 2018, www.justice.gov/olc/opinion/file/1067551/download, accessed April 3, 2020.

9 US Constitution, art. II § 2, cl. 2.

provision.[10] These agreements may not have the power to alter US domestic law, but they can serve as binding international commitments on the part of the United States.

- *Commerce.* The text of the Constitution provides Congress with the authority to regulate foreign commerce.[11] Unlike with respect to uses of force and international agreements, the President typically does not assert independent constitutional authority over foreign commerce. Nonetheless, the President has very substantial control in practice over the regulation of foreign commerce, as existing congressional statutes delegate considerable authority in this domain to the President. The imposition of the various tariffs by the Trump administration are recent examples.[12]
- *Overall Control over Foreign Affairs.* The text of the Constitution does not set forth a general foreign affairs power. It is at best debatable whether the text of the Constitution should be read as granting such a power to the President, and indeed there is considerable evidence from the timing of the Framing suggesting that if such a power exists, it should lie with Congress.[13] Nonetheless, such a power is often asserted by the executive branch to lie with the President.[14]

10 See generally Jean Galbraith, 'From Treaties to International Commitments: The Changing Landscape of Foreign Relations Law' (2017) 84 *University of Chicago Law Review* 1675 (discussing the development of these agreements and the extent to which they are subject to separation-of-powers constraints).

11 US Constitution, art. I § 8, cl. 3.

12 See Timothy Meyer and Ganesh Sitaraman, 'The Power To Declare Trade War', Lawfare Blog, March 23, 2018, www.lawfareblog.com/power-declare-trade-war, accessed April 3, 2020 (describing how vaguely worded preexisting statutes have served as authorizations for these tariffs).

13 This evidence includes Congress's constitutional power to make laws 'necessary and proper' for executing the constitutional powers of the US government, US Constitution, art. I § 8, cl. 18; the President's obligation to 'take care that the laws be faithfully executed', US Constitution, art. II § 3; and the broader backdrop underlying the concept of executive power at the time, see generally Julian Davis Mortenson, 'Article II Vests Executive Power, Not the Royal Prerogative' (2019) 119 *Columbia Law Review* 1169.

14 See Charles J. Cooper, Assistant Attorney General, Office of Legal Counsel, '*Memorandum Opinion for the Attorney General Regarding the President's Compliance with the "Timely Notification" Requirement of Section 501(b) of the National Security Act*', US Department of Justice, December 17, 1986, www.justice.gov/file/23891/download, accessed April 3, 2020 (concluding that the President has 'plenary authority to represent the United States and to pursue its interests outside the borders of the country, subject only to limits specifically set forth in the Constitution itself and to such statutory limitations as the Constitution permits Congress to impose by exercising one of its enumerated powers'); see also, e.g., Stephen E. Boyd, Assistant Attorney General, Office of Legislative Affairs, *Letter to Eliot L. Engel,*

The rise of the President's foreign affairs powers undoubtedly has multiple causes. In a famous concurring opinion written during the 1950s, Supreme Court Justice Robert Jackson pointed to the political prestige of the President, the rise of the party system, and the perceived need to address urgent situations over time as likely causes for 'the gap that exists between the President's paper powers and his real powers'.[15]

The structure of the international legal system may itself have contributed to the rise in the President's foreign affairs powers vis-à-vis Congress.[16] At various points in time Presidents or their lwyers have pointed to international law in justifying claims of presidential power. With respect to war powers, for example, executive branch actors drew on nineteenth-century international legal conceptions of sovereignty in defending a unilateral presidential authority to use force in the protection of citizens abroad.[17] Also in the nineteenth and later in the twentieth century, Presidents and their lawyers pointed to international law in arguing for a narrow construction of what amounts to a 'war' requiring congressional approval.[18] With respect to international agreements, executive branch decision-makers also sometimes drew on international legal principles in defending the domestic constitutional right of the President to enter into these agreements without the advice and consent of the Senate.[19]

That the President's scope-based foreign affairs powers have grown vis-à-vis Congress does not mean that these powers are without scope-based limits.

Chairman, House Committee on Foreign Affairs, US Department of Justice, May 7, 2019, www.justice.gov/ola/page/file/1160886/download, accessed April 3, 2020 (citing this 1986 memorandum in claiming that draft legislation would be unconstitutional to the extent that it 'require[d] the President to adopt a [particular] foreign policy').

15 *Youngstown Sheet & Tube Co.* v. *Sawyer*, 343 US 579, 651–54 (1952) (Jackson, J., concurring).

16 For an elaboration of this argument, see generally Jean Galbraith, 'International Law and the Domestic Separation of Powers' (2013) 99 *Virginia Law Review* 987.

17 Bradley and Galbraith, 'Presidential War Powers', 712–18 (giving examples).

18 Galbraith, 'International Law and the Domestic Separation of Powers', 1021–23, 1024–25 (giving examples).

19 Galbraith, 'International Law and the Domestic Separation of Powers', 1028–33. Similarly, executive branch lawyers pointed at times to international legal practice in justifying the unilateral domestic constitutional power of the President to terminate treaties made with the advice and consent of the Senate. See, e.g., Memorandum from Green Haywood Hackworth, Legal Advisor of the Department of State, Abrogation of Treaties (27 January 1936), quoted in (1943) 5 *Digest of International Law* 328 ('A contention that the action of the President in denouncing a treaty must be submitted to . . . the Senate . . . would seem to be questionable for the reason that when the President has given notice of the desire of this Government to terminate a treaty, the failure of . . . the Senate to approve does not alter the situation . . . [as] the foreign government may decline to accept a withdrawal of such notice').

There remain some situations in which the President needs congressional approval in the domain of foreign affairs, although the contours of these situations are often ill-defined. And while preexisting congressional law often serves to authorize presidential action with respect to foreign affairs – as in the example of tariffs – there are also some statutes that place limits on the President's foreign affairs powers.[20] Additionally – and importantly – there are limits on presidential power separate and apart from those grounded in the separation of powers. The President is also subject to limits stemming from international law and from constitutional protections for individual rights.[21] For all these limits, however, the scope of presidential power remains vast with respect to foreign affairs.

II THE RISE OF PROCESS-BASED CHECKS ON PRESIDENTIAL POWER

There is a corollary to the rise of the President's scope-based powers. This is the development of more process-based rules with respect to *how* the President should exercise foreign affairs powers. These rules are not grounded in US constitutional law, but rather come from congressional statutes, executive branch regulations, and broader principles of public law manifested through the practice of the US administrative state. Significantly, some of these process-based limits also stem from international law or more generally from the way in which the US executive branch interfaces with the international legal system. Although the limits imposed by these process-based checks are different in nature from scope-based checks, they nonetheless have a constraining effect on presidential power.

20 One notable example is the provision in the War Powers Resolution requiring that the President withdraw US armed forces from hostilities after sixty days unless the President has received affirmative approval from Congress to continue the hostilities. 50 USC § 1544(b). Some administrations have questioned the constitutionality of this provision and even more administrations have interpreted it narrowly. Nonetheless, it is thought to have had some constraining effect on practice. David P. Auerswald and Peter F. Cowhey, 'Ballotbox Diplomacy: The War Powers Resolution and the Use of Force' (1997) 41 *International Studies Quarterly* 505.

21 The enforcement of these limits can be a challenge. The United States has pulled away from the jurisdiction of international courts, and US domestic courts have imposed various barriers to review over claims tied to foreign affairs, particularly ones rooted in international law. See, e.g., *Medellín* v. *Texas*, 552 US 491 (2008) (holding that certain types of international treaty obligations require congressional implementing legislation in order to give rise to domestic legal claims enforceable by the federal courts).

A *Process-Based Checks Grounded in US Domestic Law and Practice*

The Framers of the US Constitution were not solely interested in deciding *who* had the power to do *what*. They also had an interest in *how* power was exercised. They were conscious of the values of transparency and orderly process, though recognizing that aspects of some foreign affairs might benefit from secrecy. This consciousness, however, did not manifest itself in the form of procedural rules set out for the executive branch about how to conduct its business, including its foreign policy. What few procedural rules there were instead were aimed at Congress, including a clause encouraging Congress to establish Rules of Proceedings and another clause requiring it to publish Journals of Proceedings.[22] The issue of process rules for the executive branch was not one which they addressed in the text of the Constitution, other than some thin provisions about consultation with ministers and with Congress that left considerable room for presidential discretion.[23]

The absence of process-based requirements on the executive branch in the text of the US Constitution does not mean that such requirements are absent from US foreign relations law. Rather, these process-based requirements exist, but they are deemed to be nonconstitutional in nature.

Congress is one important source of process-based limits on the President's foreign affairs powers. The War Powers Resolution passed by Congress in the 1970s requires the President to meet certain consultation and reporting requirements with respect to the initiation of hostilities.[24] The Case-Zablocki Act similarly sets out various process-based requirements for the executive branch to follow with respect to international agreements that are not made through the process set out in the Constitution's Treaty Clause, including a reporting requirement.[25] Both of these statutes were passed against

[22] US Constitution, art. I § 5, cll. 2 and 3 ('Each House may determine the Rules of its Proceedings … Each House shall keep a Journal of its Proceedings, and from time to time publish the same, excepting such Parts as may in their Judgment require Secrecy').

[23] US Constitution, art. II § 2, cl. 1 ('[The President] may require the Opinion, in writing, of the principal Officer in each of the executive Departments, upon any Subject relating to the Duties of their respective Offices') and § 3 ('He shall from time to time give to the Congress information of the State of the Union').

[24] 50 USC § 1542 ('The President in every possible instance shall consult with Congress before introducing United States Armed Forces into hostilities … and after every such introduction shall consult regularly with Congress until United States Armed Forces are no longer engaged in hostilities'); 50 USC § 1543 (requiring the President to give notice to Congress within forty-eight hours of various actions, including the introduction of US troops into hostilities, and to subsequently provide periodic updates to Congress).

[25] 1 USC § 112b (requiring that the text of such agreements be transmitted to Congress or the relevant congressional committee within sixty days of their entry into force and imposing other procedural requirement, including that 'an international agreement may not be signed or

a backdrop of congressional recognition that the President's foreign affairs powers had grown in scope since the time of the Framing. They therefore reflect, at least in part, a deliberate choice to make process-based limits available as a partial substitute for now eroded limits on scope. Similarly, in the trade context, trade statutes delegating power tend to fold in some process requirements.[26] In these statutes, Congress is both providing the executive branch with increased scope to exercise power and setting out requirements with respect to how it is to be exercised. Finally, separate and apart from statutes, the 'soft' oversight powers that congressional committees have in terms of opening investigations and holding hearings can serve as process-related incentives for thoughtful executive branch decision-making.[27]

A second important source of process-based requirements is the executive branch itself. The President is the head of an enormous bureaucracy (or perhaps more aptly of many enormous bureaucracies). In the foreign affairs decision-making space, as with domestic affairs, the executive branch has developed numerous internal rules and procedures for how its affairs are to be conducted. Some such processes are set forth in executive orders issued by the President, which typically last across administrations in the absence of repeal.[28] Others lie within specific agencies. With respect to international agreements, for example, the State Department has long-standing regulations addressing the process by which these are to be made.[29]

The importance of regular process can potentially be amplified by the expectations of US domestic courts. As mentioned earlier, US courts have

otherwise concluded on behalf of the United States without prior consultation of the Secretary of State').

26 By way of example, the steel and aluminum tariffs imposed by the Trump administration on many nations were done pursuant to a statute that requires the US Secretary of Commerce to follow certain procedural steps in investigating whether to recommend the imposition of tariffs. See 19 USC § 1862 (providing, among other things, that the Secretary of Commerce is to undertake interagency consultations as appropriate and 'if it is appropriate and after reasonable notice, hold public hearings or otherwise afford interested parties an opportunity to present information and advice relevant to such investigation').

27 See generally Josh Chafetz, 'Congress's Constitution' (2012) 160 *University of Pennsylvania Law Review* 715 (discussing these oversight powers).

28 By way of example, Executive Order 12,333 from 1981 continues to provide a regulatory framework for the conduct of US intelligence activities related to foreign affairs. See Executive Order 12333, 46 Fed. Reg. 59941 (1981). For a broader discussion of US intelligence practice, see Samuel J. Rascoff, 'Presidential Intelligence' (2016) 129 *Harvard Law Review* 633; see also at 637 (describing 'presidential intelligence' as 'the White House's sustained, routinized, and process-driven governance of American spying').

29 Known as the C-175 Procedure, these regulations can be found at 11 FAM §§ 720–27. The original C-175 procedure was promulgated in the 1950s. See US Department of State Circular No. 175 of 13 December 1955, in (1956) 50 AJIL 784.

developed a variety of doctrines related to jurisdiction and justiciability that can prevent them from reaching the merits of cases, and these doctrines can have particular power in cases related to foreign affairs. Where courts do have jurisdiction, however, they may be open to claims of procedural irregularity or pretextual decision-making. The fast-and-loose approach to procedure that characterized so much of the Trump administration was plainly a source of concern to many judges, even though one of its most dubious decisions was upheld by a closely divided Supreme Court.[30]

B *Process-Based Checks Grounded in the Interface with International Law*

The international legal system itself provides some process-based checks as well. So much of foreign relations law is about engagement through international organizations. With engagement through these systems comes acceptance of their process-based requirements. This is another way through which certain procedural norms, including transparency, can be brought to bear on the US executive branch.

One set of such process-based checks is tied to participation in the ordinary business of an international organization. While plenty of diplomacy is carried out in back rooms, various international legal regimes incorporate forms of transparency into their operating procedures. To give a simple example, the US executive branch cannot unilaterally keep all observers out of a major UN conference.[31] More generally, to the extent that international legal regimes are premised around open dialogue, the executive branch must engage in such dialogue in order to act effectively through the regimes.[32] Just as US executive

30 In *Trump v. Hawaii*, 585 US __, 138 S Ct 2392 (2018) the Supreme Court upheld the travel ban imposed by the Trump administration on immigrants and visitors seeking to enter the United States from several Muslim-majority countries by a 5–4 vote. In dissent, Justice Sotomayor aptly argued that evidence of President Trump's animus towards Muslims, combined with the shaky administrative process by which the travel ban was imposed, would lead 'a reasonable observer [to] conclude that the Proclamation was driven primarily by anti-Muslim animus, rather than by the Government's asserted national-security justifications'. *Trump* v. *Hawaii*, at 2438–44 (Sotomayor, J., dissenting).

31 For discussion of the process by which observer status is granted, see 'Formal Procedures for Granting Observer Status' (2008) UN Juridical Yearbook 439 ('In practice, the General Assembly has adopted resolutions granting observer status to various organizations and entities').

32 Constraints through dialogue can exist in bilateral relations as well, although this dialogue is presumably less likely to be conducted in the public sphere. See Ashley Deeks, 'Checks and Balances from Abroad' (2016) 83 *University of Chicago Law Review* 65, 68 (observing that if 'one recognizes that US national security increasingly relies on relationships with foreign partners, then the idea that the executive responds to foreign critiques and concerns to enable ongoing partnerships has bite').

branch actors are aware of the prospect of congressional oversight, so too are they aware of the prospect of international criticism. If the President chooses to invade Grenada, for example, his representatives must be prepared to defend this choice to the Security Council – and to cast a public veto of a resolution condemning this action.[33] Although the executive branch representatives are nominally defending the decisions of the United States, in practice the decisions they are defending are often ones made specifically by the President as opposed to ones that are also explicitly authorized by Congress.

A further set of process-based checks could potentially stem from the way in which international legal regimes use reporting and review mechanisms as enforcement devices. Partly because of the difficulty in getting states to agree to other remedies, treaty regimes rely heavily on reporting requirements. This is true with regard to many substantive areas of international law and especially in the human rights context.[34] The reporting process can both shine a light on state behavior and serve as a focal point for international and domestic pressure aimed at particular state polices.[35] Because of the relative insularity of the United States and the various other ways in which information related to the United States is transparent, it is unclear how much additional transparency these reporting requirements bring to US practice. But at least in

[33] See Richard Bernstein, 'U.S. Vetoes U.N. Resolution "Deploring" Grenada Invasion', New York Times, October 29, 1983, www.nytimes.com/1983/10/29/world/us-vetoes-un-resolution-deploring-grenada-invasion.html, accessed April 3, 2020 (noting the 11–1 vote, with 3 abstentions and noting that '[a]mong the 63 countries that requested to speak in the Security Council debate, only a small number of Caribbean nations defended the invasion . . . [and n]early all the rest condemned it with varying degrees of harshness').

[34] For a general discussion, see Abram Chayes and Antonia Handler Chayes, *The New Sovereignty: Compliance with International Regulatory Agreements* (Cambridge, MA: Harvard University Press, 1998), p. 154 (describing the role of reporting requirements and noting that their 'incidence . . . is so high that they seem to be included almost pro forma in many [international] agreements, with little concern about cost or implementing capacity'). For some of the considerable literature on human rights reporting requirements, see, e.g., Philip Alston and James Crawford (eds.), *The Future of UN Human Rights Treaty Monitoring* (Cambridge: Cambridge University Press, 2000); Gudmundur Alfredsson, Jonas Grimheden, and Bertrand G. Ramcharan (eds.), *International Human Rights Monitoring Mechanisms: Essays in Honour of Jakob Th. Möller* (Leiden: Martinus Nijhoff Publishers, 2009); Jasper Krommendijk, *The Domestic Impact and Effectiveness of the Process of State Reporting under UN Human Rights Treaties in the Netherlands, New Zealand and Finland: Paper-pushing or policy prompting?* (Cambridge: Intersentia, 2014).

[35] See Cosette D. Creamer and Beth A. Simmons, 'The Dynamic Impact of Periodic Review on Women's Rights' (2018) 81 *Law and Contemporary Problems* 31 (finding that 'self-reporting [by states] has a significant positive effect on women's rights' and considering the mechanisms that might underly such an effect).

theory, they are another way in which the executive branch must publicly account for its choices – and more generally for US behavior.

C *Presidential Power in an Age of Process-Based Checks*

As Congress's scope-based checks on presidential power have dwindled, process-based checks have grown. It is difficult to measure the practical effect of this trade-off. Process-based checks are not as formally robust as scope-based checks. They do not serve as an absolute bar to action, but rather go to how the decision to undertake this action should be reached and to what extent the action and the related decision-making process should be done in a way that is transparent and therefore subject to evaluation and criticism. Are these lighter process-based checks more or less normatively desirable than robust scope-based checks? The answer may depend upon the particular context. It is possible, for example, to be supportive of the current system with respect to the making of international agreements yet more skeptical about it with respect to uses of force.

The presidency of Donald Trump tested the power of process-based checks. Executive branch lawyers in the Trump administration took robust positions on the scope of presidential powers. This was true both with respect to the President's constitutional powers and with respect to how broadly to read preexisting delegations in congressional statutes. At the same time, the Trump administration showed little respect for orderly internal process within the executive branch.[36] Yet the Trump administration remained subject to process constraints in other ways, including from Congress. With respect to the use of force, for example, Congress lacked the votes necessary to override a presidential veto and impose scope-based checks on presidential power.[37] But in 2018 and 2019 Congress legislated to incorporate stronger reporting requirements with respect to the legal and policy justifications offered by the

36 See, e.g., W. Neil Eggleston and Amanda Elbogen, 'The Trump Administration and the Breakdown of Intra-Executive Legal Process' (2018) 127 *Yale Law Journal Forum* 825, 847 (discussing these challenges, including the ones that arise when 'a President wakes up one morning and decides to change a policy by tweet without involving [the] extensive apparatus' of 'a full array of experts at the National Security Council, the State Department, the Central Intelligence Agency, the Department of Homeland Security, the Department of Justice and other agencies').

37 See Jean Galbraith, 'Contemporary Practice of the United States: U.S. Drone Strike in Iraq Kills Iranian Military Leader Qasem Soleimani' (2020) 114 *AJIL* 313, 320 (describing how both the House and the Senate passed resolutions stating that the executive branch lacked the authority to use force aggressively against Iran, but that there were not enough votes for these resolutions to overcome a presidential veto).

executive branch for uses of force.[38] It remains to be seen what long-term effects, if any, such process-based requirements have on the outcomes of presidential decisions with respect to foreign relations.

III SCOPE, PROCESS, AND COMPARATIVE PRACTICE

US foreign relations law offers a unique set of bridges and boundaries. With its presidential system of government, eighteenth-century constitutional text, and distinctive role on the international stage, the United States has developed a set of foreign relations law practices that are all its own and that are often impenetrable. For the lay person, the well-educated lawyer, the foreign practitioner – maybe everyone but the expert in the specific field, US foreign relations law is excruciatingly hard to understand. Indeed, one of the ironies of the shift from scope-based limits to process-based limits described above is that it is untransparent to most observers.

Other countries undoubtedly strike different balances between scope-based checks and process-based checks on the power of the executive. In the United Kingdom, for example, there has been a recent rise in scope-based checks on executive power, including the developing constitutional convention requiring parliamentary authorization for certain uses of force and the UK Supreme Court's decision that parliamentary approval would be required for the treaty withdrawal underlying Brexit.[39] In Germany, the Basic Law was amended in the 1990s such that the new Article 23 set forth both scope-based and process-based limits on executive branch decision-making with respect to German participation with the European Union.[40] These developments place

38 See Scott R. Anderson and Erica Newland, 'Why the Trump Administration May End up in Court Over War Powers Reporting', Lawfare Blog, February 28, 2020, www.lawfareblog.com/why-trump-administration-may-end-court-over-war-powers-reporting, accessed April 3, 2020 (describing these new requirements).

39 See, e.g., Katja S. Ziegler, 'The Use of Military Force by the United Kingdom: The Evolution of Accountability', University of Leicester School of Law Research Paper No. 18–09, December 12, 2018, https://papers.ssrn.com/sol3/papers.cfm?abstract_id=3300107, accessed April 3, 2020 (discussing the rising constitutional convention with respect to parliamentary approval for at least certain kinds of uses of force); *R (Miller)* v. *Secretary of State for Exiting the European Union* 2017 [UKSC] 5, www.bailii.org/uk/cases/UKSC/2017/5.html, accessed April 3, 2020 (concluding that parliamentary approval was necessary prior to the government's giving the requisite treaty notice of withdrawal from the Treaty on European Union); see also Curtis A. Bradley and Laurence R. Helfer, 'Treaty Exit in the United States: Insights from the United Kingdom or South Africa' (2018) 111 *AJIL Unbound* 428 (discussing not only the UK Supreme Court decision but also a similar decision reached by the High Court of South Africa).

40 German Basic Law, art. 23 (providing as translated, for example, that '[b]efore participating in legislative acts of the European Union, the Federal Government shall provide the Bundestag with an opportunity to state its position' and setting out various ground rules regarding the

constitutional limits on executive power in foreign affairs, unlike the US pattern of long-standing erosion of such limits.

Although the US trajectory of limits on executive power in foreign relations law may be distinctive to the United States, the impact of this trajectory has broader implications. The transition between the Obama administration and the Trump administration demonstrated the instability that can come from the combination of strong presidential foreign affairs powers and a polarized US electoral process. In the future, it is possible that the US Supreme Court will restore more scope-based checks on the President's foreign affairs powers or that Congress will reclaim some powers with respect to trade and other economic sanctions that it has delegated to the President. But unless and until that happens, continuity in US foreign relations practice will depend heavily on process-based constraints.

roles to be played by the Bundestag, Bundesrat, and Länder in the course of decision-making); see also BVerfG, Judgment of the Second Senate of 19 June 2012 – 2 BvE 4/11 -, www.bverfg.de/e/es20120619_2bve000411en.html, accessed April 3, 2020 (reading art. 23 broadly to apply to certain other international agreements closely connected with the European Union).

12

Division of Competences in the Field of Foreign Relations in the Polish Constitutional System

Stanisław Biernat

I INTRODUCTION

The legal issues of foreign relations fall within the area between international law and the national law of particular states.[1] These problems may therefore be analyzed from both or either of these points of view. The following considerations will be conducted from the perspective of Polish law. In this legal system, foreign relations law is not treated as a separate branch but as part of constitutional law. Along the axis: exceptionalism – normalization,[2] Polish law is situated on the side of the latter.

The political and socioeconomic transformations of the state began in the late 1980s and early 1990s. The foundations of liberal democracy and market economy were laid then. As early as in 1989, the first changes to the then binding Communist constitution were introduced and developed in the following years. The current Constitution dates from 1997.[3] It should be added that Poland joined the European Union in 2004.[4]

[1] See the chapter by Helmut Philipp Aust and Thomas Kleinlein, 'Introduction', this volume.

[2] Aust and Kleinlein, 'Introduction', at pp. 6, 14.

[3] 'Konstytucja Rzeczypospolitej Polskiej z dnia 2 kwietnia 1997' ['The Constitution of the Republic of Poland'] (1997) 78 *Dziennik Ustaw [Journal of Laws]* item 483 as amended.

[4] Treaty between the Kingdom of Belgium, the Kingdom of Denmark, the Federal Republic of Germany, the Hellenic Republic, the Kingdom of Spain, the French Republic, Ireland, the Italian Republic, the Grand Duchy of Luxembourg, the Kingdom of the Netherlands, the Republic of Austria, the Portuguese Republic, the Republic of Finland, the Kingdom of Sweden, the United Kingdom of Great Britain and Northern Ireland (Member States of the European Union) and the Czech Republic, the Republic of Estonia, the Republic of Cyprus, the Republic of Latvia, the Republic of Lithuania, the Republic of Hungary, the Republic of Malta, the Republic of Poland, the Republic of Slovenia, the Slovak Republic, concerning the accession of the Czech Republic, the Republic of Estonia, the Republic of Cyprus, the Republic of Latvia, the Republic of Lithuania, the Republic of Hungary, the Republic of Malta, the Republic of Poland, the Republic of Slovenia and the Slovak Republic to the European Union, OJ2003, No. L 236, September 23, 2003, p. 17.

An examination of the rules concerning foreign relations in a state that regained its sovereignty relatively recently, after the liberation from Soviet domination, deserves attention. Poland was previously unable to pursue an independent foreign policy. The following considerations will focus on how foreign relations are regulated in the provisions of the Polish Constitution and constitutional practice and analyze both executive powers and activities of the Parliament in the field of foreign relations. This matter will be presented in the broader context of the features of the state's political system which have been shaped and have been evolving since 1989.

II THE POLISH CONSTITUTION, INTERNATIONAL LAW AND SEPARATION OF POWERS

There is an important provision in the Constitution which determines the place of international law in the national legal order.[5] Pursuant to article 9, '[t]he Republic of Poland shall respect international law binding upon it'. In addition, the Constitution regulates the functions, tasks and competences of state authorities in the field of foreign relations. It is worth noting that the aforementioned issues were not regulated in the Constitution during the communist times.

Foreign relations form a separate area of state activity. Their specificity lies in their being directed outside of the country and towards foreign partners. Despite these specificities, foreign relations should be treated as a part of the general policy of the state together with its internal policy or, rather, with many policies in particular areas of the state's activity.[6] Consistency of all policies and rules and compliance with constitutional values is therefore required.[7]

The starting point for further analysis is one of the main principles of the Polish constitutional and legal system: the separation of powers. It is expressed in article 10 of the Constitution of 1997:

5 Andrzej Wasilkowski, 'Przestrzeganie prawa międzynarodowego (art. 9 Konstytucji RP)' ['Observance of international law (article 9 of the Polish Constitution)'] in Krzysztof Wójtowicz (ed.), *Otwarcie Konstytucji RP na prawo międzynarodowe i procesy integracyjne [Opening of the Constitution of the Republic of Poland to international law and integration processes]* (Warsaw: Wydawnictwo Sejmowe, 2006), pp. 9–30.

6 Leszek Garlicki, 'Konstytucja a "sprawy zewnętrzne"' ['The Constitution and "external affairs"'] (2007) 4 *Przegląd Sejmowy*, pp. 195–96.

7 Ryszard Piotrowski, 'Konstytucyjne uwarunkowania polityki zagranicznej' ['Constitutional determinants of foreign policy'], in Ryszard M. Czarny and Kamil Spryszak (eds.), *Państwo wobec współczesnych wyzwań. Zagadnienia prawa konstytucyjnego [The state in the face of contemporary challenges. Issues of constitutional law]* (Torun: Wydawnictwo Adam Marszałek, 2012), pp. 272–87.

(1) The system of government of the Republic of Poland shall be based on the separation of and balance between the legislative, executive and judicial powers.
(2) Legislative power shall be vested in the Sejm and the Senate, executive power shall be vested in the President of the Republic of Poland and the Council of Ministers, and the judicial power shall be vested in courts and tribunals.

The principle of separation of powers was restored in Poland in the early 1990s. Previously, the principle of 'unity of state power' had applied for several decades. The highest authority of state power was formally the Sejm (Parliament), although in reality the state was governed by the communist party.

An analysis of the current legal arrangements in the field of foreign relations shows that the tasks and competences in this area are granted to authorities belonging to different branches although their participation is unequal. The roles that have been provided for the various state authorities in this area are, on the one hand, a manifestation and, on the other, a result of the constitutional system which has been adopted.

III EXECUTIVE POWERS IN THE FIELD OF FOREIGN RELATIONS

The executive power is of the utmost importance in this area and will receive a great deal of further attention. This is not surprising; on the contrary, it is a typical situation in many states with a long tradition.[8]

A characteristic of the executive branch in Poland is its duality expressed in article 10(2) of the Constitution. Functions, tasks and competences are vested separately in the President and the Council of Ministers (the Government). The duality was introduced by the first constitutional amendments after the collapse of the communist system in 1989. The constituent authorities of the executive are separated from each other and each have their own legitimacy.

Article 127(1) and (2) provide

(1) The President of the Republic shall be elected by the Nation, in universal, equal and direct elections, conducted by secret ballot.
(2) The President of the Republic shall be elected for a 5-year term of office and may be re-elected only for one more term.

[8] This trend is observed to be weakening. See Garlicki, 'Konstytucja a "sprawy zewnętrzne"', p. 196.

The President therefore derives his democratic legitimacy directly from the will of the sovereign nation.

In turn, the Council of Ministers (the Government) benefits from the support of the parliamentary majority in the Sejm – the first chamber of the Polish Parliament. The Government's legitimacy therefore derives from the principles of representative democracy (articles 4(2), 154 and 155).

The issues of foreign relations law in Poland concern largely the distribution of tasks and competences between these two segments of the executive power. The tasks and competences of both segments in the area in question have undergone a characteristic evolution after the change of the political system in 1989.

A *The Temporary 'Small Constitution' of 1992 and Separation of Powers between the President and the Council of Ministers*

In 1992, a law of constitutional rank, commonly referred to as the 'Small Constitution', was passed, which was intended to be temporary.[9] The need to issue it came about when it turned out that it would take more time to pass a new, 'full' Constitution, because of the controversy surrounding its future content.[10]

It is important to note that the tasks and competences in the field of foreign relations were not clearly separated in the Small Constitution between the two executive segments, that is, the President and the Council of Ministers. They were assigned to both of these authorities.[11]

The Small Constitution stated in article 28 that:

(1) The President of the Republic of Poland shall be the supreme representative of the Polish State in internal and international relations.

9 'The Constitutional Act of 17 October 1992 on the mutual relations between the legislative and executive institutions of the Republic of Poland and on local self-government' (1992) 84 *Dziennik Ustaw [Journal of Laws]* item 426. The adoption of 'Small Constitutions' for transition periods during the political changes became a Polish tradition in the twentieth century. Such statutes were passed in 1919, 1947 and 1992.

10 Ryszard Chruściak, 'Mała konstytucja z 1992 r.' ['The Small Constitution of 1992'] (2007) 5 *Przegląd Sejmowy*, pp. 89–110.

11 On the position of the President before the entry into effect of the Constitution, Piotr Tuleja and Krzysztof Kozłowski, 'Komentarz do art. 126 Konstytucji' ['Commentary to Article 126 of the Constitution'], in Marek Safjan and Leszek Bosek (eds.), *Konstytucja RP Komentarz [Constitution of the Republic of Poland, A Commentary]* (Warsaw: C. H. Beck, 2016), vol. II, p. 566; Marian Grzybowski and Anna Dobosz, 'Pozycja ustrojowa Prezydenta RP a jego kompetencje w stosunkach zewnętrznych państwa' ['The President's political position and his competences in the State's external relations'] (2018) 9 *Horyzonty Polityki* pp. 132–37.

(2) The President shall ensure observance of the Constitution, safeguard the sovereignty and security of the State, the inviolability and integrity of its territory as well as upholding international treaties.

In addition, article 32(1) provided that 'The President shall exercise general control in the field of foreign relations.'

In turn, as regards the second segment of the executive, the Small Constitution provided in article 51(1) that '[t]he Council of Ministers shall conduct the internal and the foreign policy of the Republic of Poland'. Furthermore, article 52(2) point 7 stated that '[t]he Council of Ministers shall maintain the relations and shall conclude treaties with governments of other states and with international organisations'.

It followed from the cited provisions that the separation of tasks and competences between the President and the Government was difficult.[12] It was impossible to easily separate the 'exercising of the general control in the field of foreign relations' which was the competence of the President, from 'conducting the internal affairs and the foreign policy of the Republic of Poland' which, in turn, was the responsibility of the Council of Ministers. The reasons for the imperfections of these provisions were largely due to the complex political situation. Many small parties were represented in the Parliament in the early 1990s, which made it difficult to achieve a stable majority for a clear concept of executive power. As a result, compromise solutions were adopted, which were not very consistent though.[13] The state of the then constitutional provisions posed a risk of establishing two separate foreign policies, specifically when the President and the Government came from different political parties.[14] The legal concepts contained in the Small Constitution could create conflicts and tensions, especially as the President sought to expand his competences at the expense of those of the Government.[15] It also had to do with the strong personality of President Lech Wałęsa. For example, the President caused the development of the practice of his consenting to the appointment of the Foreign Minister and the National Defence Minister by the Sejm. It happened, although according to its article 61, the Small Constitution provided for the President expressing only a legally nonbinding opinion. It should be concluded, however, that

12 Ryszard Mojak, 'Stanowisko konstytucyjne Prezydenta Rzeczypospolitej Polskiej w Małej Konstytucji' ['Constitutional position of the President of the Republic of Poland in the Small Constitution'], (1993) 2 *Przegląd Sejmowy*, pp. 68–110.

13 Chruściak, 'Mała konstytucja z 1992 r.', pp. 96–97.

14 Grzybowski and Dobosz, 'Pozycja ustrojowa Prezydenta RP', pp. 136–37.

15 Chruściak, 'Mała konstytucja z 1992 r.', p. 103.

despite the aforementioned problems and controversies, the unity of Polish foreign policy was not threatened.[16]

B *The Constitution of 1997 and 'Rationally Modified Parliamentarianism'*

1 Predominance of the Council of Ministers in Foreign Affairs

The legal structures of the presently binding Constitution of 1997 are partly a reaction to the above mentioned provisions of the Small Constitution and doubts as to their application.[17]

The intention of the founders of the Constitution was to eliminate the overlap of tasks and competences between the Government and the President and avoid the danger of potential conflicts. Therefore, the Constitution made a stricter separation of the role of the two segments of executive power. This pertained not only to the area of foreign relations even though it became most conspicuous there.[18]

During several years of work on subsequent draft constitutions, various political models and relations between the authorities were considered, referring to both the experiences of previous years of political transformation and models taken from other states. The proposals included both the presidential system with a dominant role of the President, and the parliamentary and cabinet system with a strong government and a ceremonial role of the President. Various intermediate solutions were also proposed.[19]

As a result, a concept was adopted which is not the realization of any of the above models in their pure form. The constructions expressed in the Constitution are referred to as the adoption of the model of 'rationally modified parliamentarianism',[20] even though it is not a commonly used

16 Garlicki, 'Konstytucja a "sprawy zewnętrzne"', p. 198.

17 Tuleja and Kozłowski, 'Komentarz do art. 126 Konstytucji', p. 570; Dariusz Dudek, 'Komentarz do art. 146 Konstytucji' ['Commentary to article 146 of the Constitution'], in Marek Safjan and Leszek Bosek (eds.), *Konstytucja RP Komentarz [Constitution of the Republic of Poland, A Commentary]* (Warsaw: C. H. Beck, 2016), vol. II, pp. 729–32.

18 Maria Kruk, 'Konstytucyjny system rządów. Założenia i praktyka' ['Constitutional system of government. Assumptions and practice'], in Ewa Gdulewicz, Wojciech Orłowski and Sławomir Patyra (eds.), 25 *lat transformacji ustrojowej w Polsce i Europie Środkowo-wschodniej [25 years of political transformation in Poland and Central and Eastern Europe]* (Lublin: Wydawnictwo Uniwersytetu Marii Curie-Skłodowskiej, 2015), pp. 13–62 at 34–35.

19 Tuleja and Kozłowski, 'Komentarz do art. 126 Konstytucji', pp. 568–70.

20 Anna Chorążewska, 'Dualizm egzekutywy i jego konsekwencje: Casus sporu o reprezentację Polski w Radzie Europejskiej' ['Dualism of the executive power and its consequences: Casus of the dispute over the representation of Poland in the European Council'], in Tadeusz Mołdawa and Jarosław Szymanek (eds.), *Instytucja prezydenta. Zagadnienia teorii*

expression. It is characterized by a strong position of the Council of Ministers and of the Prime Minister, supported by the parliamentary majority. The President does not play a decisive role in this model. However, his functions and tasks are not purely representative and decorative. They are more important, although limited.[21] It can only be added, as a side note, that the aforementioned expression departs from the term *parlementarisme rationalisé* known in the French constitutional law literature.[22] A comparison of the two segments of the executive power leads to the conclusion that the Constitution gave priority to the Council of Ministers (the Government). In particular, the Council of Ministers, headed by the Prime Minister, was entrusted with conducting foreign policy.[23]

The limitation of the President's competences in the field of foreign relations resulted from the already mentioned intention to eliminate the phenomenon of overlapping tasks and competing powers by both segments of the executive. It should be noted that the inconsistencies that occurred before the

i praktyki na tle doświadczeń polskich oraz wybranych państw obcych [The institution of the president. Issues of theory and practice against the background of Polish and selected foreign countries' experiences] (Warsaw: Elipsa Dom Wydawniczy 2010), pp. 29–52 at 35; Jerzy Ciapała, 'Spór kompetencyjny' ['The dispute of competence'], in Leszek Garlicki, Marta Derlatka and Marcin Wiącek (eds.), *Na straży państwa prawa. Trzydzieści lat orzecznictwa Trybunału Konstytucyjnego [Guarding the rule of law. Thirty years of the Constitutional Tribunal's jurisprudence]* (Warsaw: Wolters Kluwer, 2016), pp. 760–81 at 767; Dudek, 'Komentarz do art. 146 Konstytucji', p. 724.

21 Ciapała, 'Spór kompetencyjny', p. 769; Tuleja and Kozłowski, 'Komentarz do art. 126 Konstytucji', pp. 563–64, 570.

22 In France, this term means a parliamentarian system of government modified by the mechanisms introduced in the constitutional solutions after World War II to limit the political game between the Parliament and the Government to provide protection against system degenerations and government instability. See Louis Favoreu et. al., *Droit constitutionnel* 10th ed. (Paris: Dalloz, 2007), p. 360.

23 Małgorzata Masternak-Kubiak and Artur Preisner, 'Realizacja konstytucyjnego podziału kompetencji organów państwa w stosunkach zewnętrznych' ['Implementation of the constitutional division of competences of state authorities in external relations'], in Krzysztof Wójtowicz (ed.), *Otwarcie Konstytucji RP na prawo międzynarodowe i procesy integracyjne [Opening of the Constitution of the Republic of Poland to international law and integration processes]* (Warsaw: Wydawnictwo Sejmowe, 2006), pp. 109–36 at 114; Garlicki, 'Konstytucja a "sprawy zewnętrzne"', p. 196; Piotrowski, 'Konstytucyjne uwarunkowania polityki zagranicznej', p. 273; Lech Mażewski, 'Prowadzenie polityki zagranicznej w Rzeczypospolitej Polskiej' ['Conducting foreign policy in the Republic of Poland'] (2009) 3 *Ruch Prawniczy Ekonomiczny i Socjologiczny*, pp. 9–18 at 9; Bartłomiej Opaliński, 'Funkcjonowanie władzy wykonawczej z perspektywy 15 lat obowiązywania Konstytucji Rzeczypospolitej Polskiej z 1997 r.' ['Functioning of the executive power from the perspective of 15 years of the 1997 Constitution of the Republic of Poland'], in Stanisław Biernat (ed.), *Konstytucja Rzeczypospolitej Polskiej w pierwszych dekadach XXI wieku wobec wyzwań politycznych, gospodarczych, technologicznych i społecznych [The Constitution of the Republic of Poland in the first decades of the 21st century in the face of political, economic, technological and social challenges]* (Warsaw: Biuro Trybunału Konstytucyjnego, 2013), pp. 217–30 at 219–20.

entry into force of the Constitution could theoretically be removed by granting a dominant position to either the Council of Ministers (government) or the President. The decision of the authors of the Constitution to adopt the first of these solutions can be partly explained by the intention to weaken the influence of President Lech Wałęsa, who, for all that, had lost the presidential election even before the Constitution was passed.

The provisions of the Constitution illustrate the assessment presented above.[24] In accordance with its article 146(1), '[t]he Council of Ministers shall conduct the internal affairs and foreign policy of the Republic of Poland'. Furthermore, the Council of Ministers 'exercise[s] general control in the field of relations with other States and international organizations' (article 146 paragraph 4 item 9) and 'conclude international agreements requiring ratification as well as accept and renounce other international agreements' (article 146 paragraph 4 item 10). The provisions set out above were supplemented by a general clause in article 146(2), according to which '[t]he Council of Ministers shall conduct the affairs of the State not reserved to other State authorities or local government'. This implies a presumption of competence for the benefit of the Council of Ministers, amongst others, in matters of foreign relations, unless another provision explicitly confers competence on another state authority. The position of the Prime Minister who is the head of the Council of Ministers is also strong.[25]

It follows from the abovementioned provisions that the Constitution granted to the Council of Ministers certain tasks and competences which had previously been vested in the President under the Small Constitution. This reduced the risk of conflicts which, however, could not be entirely avoided, as it would yet transpire.[26]

2 The Constitutional Role of the President of the Republic in Foreign Affairs

The President's role in the field of foreign relations based on the Constitution of 1997 is not unequivocal.[27] Generally speaking, his role has weakened in

24 Mażewski, 'Prowadzenie polityki zagranicznej w Rzeczypospolitej Polskiej', pp. 9–11; Bartosz Szczurowski, 'Komentarz do art. 133 Konstytucji' ['Commentary to article 133 of the Constitution'], in Marek Safjan and Leszek Bosek (eds.), *Konstytucja RP Komentarz [Constitution of the Republic of Poland, A Commentary]* (Warsaw: C. H. Beck 2016), vol. II, pp. 632–35; Dudek, 'Komentarz do art. 146 Konstytucji', pp. 760–63; Grzybowski and Dobosz, 'Pozycja ustrojowa Prezydenta RP', pp. 138–42.

25 Chorążewska, 'Dualizm egzekutywy i jego konsekwencje', pp. 35–36.

26 Garlicki, 'Konstytucja a "sprawy zewnętrzne"', p. 197; Ciapała, 'Spór kompetencyjny', p. 768.

27 Marian Grzybowski and Piotr Mikuli, 'Realizacja konstytucyjnych kompetencji Prezydenta RP w sferze stosunków międzynarodowych' ['Implementation of the constitutional competences of the President of Poland in the sphere of international relations'], in

comparison with the previous legal status. The earlier formula that the President exercises general control in the field of international relations was not maintained because this task was assigned in the Constitution to the Government.

In order to present the role of the President in the light of the Constitution, it is necessary to distinguish his functions and tasks from his powers (competences). This distinction extends to the whole activity of the President, including the field of foreign relations.

The President's most important functions defining his position in the constitutional setup of the state are set out in article 126(1) of the Constitution:

> The President of the Republic of Poland shall be the supreme representative of the Republic of Poland and the guarantor of the continuity of State authority.

In turn, the President's main tasks are defined in article 126(2):

> The President of the Republic shall ensure observance of the Constitution, safeguard the sovereignty and security of the State as well as the inviolability and integrity of its territory.

Commentators stress that article 126 of the Constitution indicates the symbolic role of the President as the authority embodying the state and the majesty of the Republic of Poland also in external relations.[28] The President performs this role, on a continuous basis, in various forms at home and abroad, often in a solemn manner. The above-mentioned provisions indicate the general position of the President as a defender of the most fundamental values of the state.

However, the provisions cited above alone are not a sufficient source of the powers for the President to adopt legal acts or undertake other activities having legal effects.

Marian Grzybowski (ed.), *System rządów Rzeczypospolitej Polskiej. Założenia konstytucyjne a praktyka ustrojowa [System of government of the Republic of Poland. Constitutional assumptions and political practice]* (Warsaw: Wydawnictwo Sejmowe 2006), pp. 51–64; Masternak-Kubiak and Preisner, 'Realizacja konstytucyjnego podziału kompetencji organów państwa w stosunkach zewnętrznych', p. 111; Garlicki, 'Konstytucja a "sprawy zewnętrzne"', pp. 196–97; Piotrowski, 'Konstytucyjne uwarunkowania polityki zagranicznej', pp. 274–75; Mażewski, 'Prowadzenie polityki zagranicznej w Rzeczypospolitej Polskiej', pp. 11–13; Opaliński, 'Funkcjonowanie władzy wykonawczej z perspektywy', p. 222; Dudek, 'Komentarz do art. 146 Konstytucji', pp. 743–44; Grzybowski and Dobosz, 'Pozycja ustrojowa Prezydenta RP', pp. 137–42.

28 Chorążewska, 'Dualizm egzekutywy i jego konsekwencje', pp. 37–38; Ciapała, 'Spór kompetencyjny', p. 773; Grzybowski and Dobosz, 'Pozycja ustrojowa Prezydenta RP', pp. 137, 142–47.

With regard to the President's powers, the Constitution has adopted the concept expressed in article 126(3):

> The President shall exercise his tasks within the scope of and in accordance with the principles specified in the Constitution and statutes.

This means that for the President's actions to have legal effects there must be legal basis contained in specific provisions of the Constitution apart from article 126 or in the legislative acts of Parliament.[29] There is therefore no presumption that the President has the competence for the performance of its tasks, since such presumption is provided for the Council of Ministers (article 146(2)). The actions of the President which have legal effects are referred to in the Constitution as 'official acts' (article 141(1)).

An analysis of the Constitution shows that the provisions that define the President's competence to undertake actions that have legal effects in the field of foreign relations are not numerous. Such is the nature of article 133(1):[30]

> The President of the Republic, as representative of the State in foreign affairs, shall:
> 1) ratify and renounce international agreements, and shall notify the Sejm and the Senate thereof;
> 2) appoint and recall the plenipotentiary representatives of the Republic of Poland to other states and to international organizations;
> 3) receive the Letters of Credence and recall diplomatic representatives of other states and international organizations.

These are competences traditionally held by the Head of State. It is noteworthy that ratification of some international agreements is of paramount importance, although the actual conclusion of agreements is a competence of the Council of Ministers (article 146(4) point 10). In turn, the President's power to appoint ambassadors gives him the possibility to influence the staff policy in the foreign service.

The requirement for the President to have a specific legal basis for the exercise of his powers includes acts which produce legal effects (official acts). However, there are no restrictions for the President to undertake various types of activities that do not produce legal effects, but generate political consequences, domestically and abroad. From the legal point of view, they are

29 Masternak-Kubiak and Preisner, 'Realizacja konstytucyjnego podziału kompetencji organów państwa w stosunkach zewnętrznych', p. 112; Chorążewska, 'Dualizm egzekutywy i jego konsekwencje', p. 37; Tuleja and Kozłowski, 'Komentarz do art. 126 Konstytucji', p. 575.

30 Grzybowski and Mikuli, 'Realizacja konstytucyjnych kompetencji Prezydenta RP', pp. 52–54.

treated as nonbinding actions.[31] They consist in making visits abroad, receiving representatives of other states, making speeches, declarations, etc. Sometimes the mere presence of the President in a particular place and time demonstrates the great importance Poland attaches to a given event. Such activity of the President serves the purpose of carrying out the functions and tasks contained in article 126(1) and (2) of the Constitution.

With regard to actions which have legal effects, that is to say, official acts, an important distinction should be made between the ways in which the President exercises his powers.[32]

Some competences are carried out independently and do not require the approval of other state authorities. They are referred to in the legal literature as the President's prerogatives. A closed catalogue of prerogatives is contained in article 144(3) of the Constitution. In the field of broadly defined foreign relations it is only the ordering of the promulgation of an international agreement in the Journal of Laws (*Dziennik Ustaw*) of the Republic of Poland that is in the nature of a prerogative (article 144(3), (7)).

In principle, however, official acts of the President require for their validity the signature of the Prime Minister (article 144(2)).

All of the aforementioned powers of the President set out in article 133(2) of the Constitution are exercised following this procedure. Making the issuance of the acts listed therein dependent on the countersignature of the Prime Minister additionally limits the role of the President in the field of foreign relations. It is the Prime Minister who bears political responsibility before the Sejm.[33]

It should be noted that the dominant role of the Council of Ministers in the exercise of the executive power compared to that of the President, not only in the area of foreign relations, leads to the identification of a significant inconsistency.[34] As already mentioned, the President is elected by citizens in direct and universal vote. This model of election determines his strong democratic legitimacy, which, as a natural consequence, should give him broad powers. In the light of the Polish Constitution, however, despite the recognition of the President as the supreme representative of the Republic of

[31] Chorążewska, 'Dualizm egzekutywy i jego konsekwencje', pp. 38–39; Szczurowski, 'Komentarz do art. 133 Konstytucji', pp. 631–32; Grzybowski and Dobosz, 'Pozycja ustrojowa Prezydenta RP', pp. 139, 142–44.

[32] Szczurowski, 'Komentarz do art. 133 Konstytucji', p. 631; Grzybowski and Dobosz, 'Pozycja ustrojowa Prezydenta RP', p. 143.

[33] Grzybowski and Mikuli, 'Realizacja konstytucyjnych kompetencji Prezydenta RP', p. 59; Kruk, 'Konstytucyjny system rządów', p. 42.

[34] Kruk, 'Konstytucyjny system rządów', pp. 35–42; Dudek, 'Komentarz do art. 146 Konstytucji', p. 743.

Poland, his powers to carry out actions that produce legal effects are limited.[35] In such a state of affairs, Presidents have attempted to strengthen their position and reduce the discrepancies between the broad democratic mandate of the President and his political role on the one hand and the real influence in the field of internal policy and foreign relations on the other.[36] This happened especially in cohabitation situations when the President and the Prime Minister came from other political formations and that caused tensions.[37] The most conspicuous example of a conflict caused by the President's belief that his powers are excessively limited was the dispute over the representation of Poland in the European Council.

3 Overlapping Competences and Duty to Cooperate

Despite the delineations made in the Constitution, some tasks in the field of foreign relations belong to both segments of the executive power.[38] The tensions this may cause between them could potentially be mitigated by the introduction of an obligation for the President to cooperate with the Government.[39] It is already the preamble that characterizes the Constitution

35 Kruk, 'Konstytucyjny system rządów', p. 35.

36 Garlicki, 'Konstytucja a "sprawy zewnętrzne"', p. 198.

37 Dudek, 'Komentarz do art. 146 Konstytucji', p. 743–44; Grzybowski and Dobosz, 'Pozycja ustrojowa Prezydenta RP', p. 141.

38 Grzybowski and Mikuli, 'Realizacja konstytucyjnych kompetencji Prezydenta RP', pp. 61–64; Garlicki, 'Konstytucja a "sprawy zewnętrzne"', p. 197; Opaliński, 'Funkcjonowanie władzy wykonawczej z perspektywy', pp. 223, 225–26; Tuleja and Kozłowski, 'Komentarz do art. 126 Konstytucji', p. 575.

39 Masternak-Kubiak and Preisner, 'Realizacja konstytucyjnego podziału kompetencji organów państwa w stosunkach zewnętrznych', pp. 110–12.; Zbigniew Witkowski, 'Dyrektywa "współdziałania władz" jako element organizujący życie wspólnoty państwowej w świetle Konstytucji RP z 2 kwietnia 1997 r.' ['Directive of the "cooperation of authorities" as an element organizing the life of the state community in the light of the Polish Constitution of 2 April 1997'], in Jan Wawrzyniak and Marzena Laskowska (eds.), *Instytucje prawa konstytucyjnego w dobie integracji europejskiej [Institutions of constitutional law in the era of European integration]* (Warsaw: Wydawnictwo Sejmowe 2009, pp. 139–45; Chorążewska, 'Dualizm egzekutywy i jego konsekwencje', p. 40–41; Opaliński, 'Funkcjonowanie władzy wykonawczej perspektywy', pp. 224–25; Maciej Pach, 'Dyrektywa współdziałania władz w Konstytucji RP z 1997 roku jako przykład ustrojowego *wishful thinking*' ['Directive on the cooperation of the authorities in the Constitution of the Republic of Poland of 1997 as an example of political wishful thinking'], in Stanisław Biernat, *Konstytucja Rzeczypospolitej Polskiej w pierwszych dekadach XXI wieku wobec wyzwań politycznych, gospodarczych, technologicznych i społecznych [The Constitution of the Republic of Poland in the first decades of the 21st century in the face of political, economic, technological and social challenges]* (Warsaw: Biuro Trybunału Konstytucyjnego, 2013), pp. 205–16; Ciapała, 'Spór kompetencyjny', pp. 775–77; Szczurowski, 'Komentarz do art. 133 Konstytucji', pp. 634–35; Grzybowski and Dobosz, 'Pozycja ustrojowa Prezydenta RP', p. 141.

of the Republic of Poland as 'the fundamental law for the State, based on . . . cooperation between the public powers'.

The obligation in question has been made concrete in the context under consideration here in article 133(3) of the Constitution: 'The President of the Republic shall cooperate with the Prime Minister and the appropriate minister in respect of foreign policy.'

This provision is to be understood as an obligation of the President to cooperate with the Prime Minister and the Minister of Foreign Affairs in various forms. The obligation to cooperate is assumingly not unilateral, but lies with the Prime Minister and the Minister of Foreign Affairs, too. The provisions of the Constitution do not clarify what the cooperation is about: whether it is about mutual information, coordination of activities or whether it is required to bring about a consensus of positions. Cooperation may include agreeing on foreign policy directions as well as coordinating actions on the international arena. It should be conducted in good faith with a view to avoiding conflicts.[40]

C *Constitutional Conflict over the Representation of Poland in the European Union*

The Constitution was passed seven years before Poland acceded to the European Union. Therefore the Constitution does not contain any provisions relating to the EU and Poland's membership therein. However, there are provisions in the Constitution that enabled Poland to become a member of the Union.[41] Article 90 of the Constitution contains 'European clause' which served as the political and legal basis for the accession to the Union. In turn, article 91 defined the position in the legal system in force in Poland of international agreements, including EU Treaties and the law established by international organizations, that is, also EU secondary law.

In 2009, the Constitutional Tribunal ruled on the conflict concerning who is to represent Poland in the European Council.[42] The President was of the opinion that it was his responsibility. The Prime Minister, on the other hand,

[40] Such position was taken by, e.g., the Constitutional Tribunal in its decision of 20 May 2009 (Ref. No. Kpt 2/08).

[41] Stanisław Biernat, 'Offene Staatlichkeit: Polen' ['Open Statehood: Poland'], in Armin von Bogdandy, Pedro Cruz Villalón and Peter M. Huber (eds.), *Handbuch Ius Publicum Europaeum* (Heidelberg: C. F. Müller, 2008), pp. 243–75.

[42] Maria Kruk, 'Glosa do postanowienia TK z 20 maja 2009 (sygn. akt Kpt 2/08)' ['Annotation on the Constitutional Court decision of 20 May 2009 (Ref. No. sygn. akt Kpt 2/08)'] (2010) 1 *Przegląd Sejmowy* 174–88; Jerzy Jaskiernia, 'Współdziałanie Prezydenta i Rady Ministrów w sferze polityki zagranicznej' ['Cooperation between the President and the Council of

who came from another political party, considered this to be a competence vested in the Government and did not agree to change the practice under which the Prime Minister sat on the European Council. The President was even denied access to a government plane to travel to Brussels. However, the President took part in the European Council meeting together with the Prime Minister. Thereafter, the Prime Minister applied to the Constitutional Tribunal to resolve the dispute over the competence to represent Poland in the Council. The Tribunal issued its first ever decision of this kind, based on article 189 of the Constitution.[43]

In this ruling, the Tribunal settled the competence dispute by considering it in the wider context of the role of the state authorities in dealing with the EU institutions. It was important to establish whether the division of tasks and competences between state authorities in EU matters was the same as in the field of foreign relations. As the Constitution does not contain provisions on the separation of tasks and competences of both segments of the executive in relations with the EU, the Constitutional Tribunal decided to settle the competence dispute submitted to it on the basis of general constitutional provisions. The starting point was the conviction that relations with the European Union do not fall within the scope of either internal policy or external relations, but show, at the same time, the characteristics of both areas.

An analysis of the Constitution led the Constitutional Tribunal to the conclusion that it is the Council of Ministers (the Government) that is generally competent in European affairs due to its position as an authority with general power in the field of both home affairs and foreign relations. The Prime Minister, who heads the Government, is authorized to represent Poland in the European Council and to express Poland's position in this forum.

However, there can be no question of the Government's exclusivity in European matters. The constitutional position of the President as the supreme representative of the Republic of Poland and his tasks specified in article 126(2) of the Constitution, is not without relevance either. The Constitutional Tribunal stated that in (rather exceptional) cases, when issues falling within the scope of the President's tasks would be discussed by the European Council, he may decide to represent Poland in this EU institution. In such

Ministers in the sphere of foreign policy'] (2010) 6 *Państwo i Prawo*, pp. 3–18; Mażewski, 'Prowadzenie polityki zagranicznej w Rzeczypospolitej Polskiej', pp. 14–15; Ciapała, 'Spór kompetencyjny', pp. 760–81; Tuleja and Kozłowski, 'Komentarz do art. 126 Konstytucji', p. 571; Dudek, 'Komentarz do art. 146 Konstytucji', p. 744.

43 Judgment of May 20, 2009 Ref. No. Kpt 2/08, http://trybunal.gov.pl/fileadmin/content/omowienia/Kpt_02_08_EN.pdf, accessed June 26, 2020.

situations, however, the President would be obliged to present the position determined by the Council of Ministers.

The Tribunal stressed that the state cannot pursue two foreign or European policies and the division of competences while ensuring the consistency of operation by all state authorities is essential.[44] An important place in the judgment under discussion is occupied by considerations concerning the obligation of the President to cooperate with the Prime Minister and the Minister of Foreign Affairs resulting from the already mentioned provisions of the preamble and article 133(3) of the Constitution.

The final conclusions of the Constitutional Tribunal's ruling may be summarized as follows: in the first place the Tribunal put forward the principle of cooperation between the public powers, expressed in the Preamble and article133(3) of the Constitution of the Republic of Poland. The obligation to cooperate rests with the President of the Republic of Poland, the Council of Ministers and the Prime Minister (who presides over the Council of Ministers), while exercising their constitutional duties and powers. As a rule it is the Council of Ministers which determines the stance of the Republic of Poland to be presented at a given session of the European Council. The Prime Minister presents the agreed stance there (article 146(1), article 146(2) and article146(4), (9) of the Constitution). The President, as the supreme representative of the Republic, may, however, decide to participate in a particular session of the European Council, if he finds it useful for the exercise of his duties, specified in article 126(2) of the Constitution. The participation of the President in a given session of the European Council requires his cooperation with the Prime Minister and the competent minister in order to ensure uniformity of actions taken on behalf of the Republic of Poland in the relations with the European Union. Such a cooperation enables the President to refer to the stance of the Republic of Poland determined by the Council of Ministers. It also makes possible to specify the extent and manner of the intended participation of the President in a session of the European Council.

D *The Role of the President of the Republic in Practice*

1 The President As the Supreme Representative of the Republic of Poland

The constitutional arrangements outlined above according to which the President has a strictly defined and limited power to take actions with legal effect do not mean that successive Presidents are passive in the field of foreign

44 This attests to the adoption of the concept of 'normalization' in foreign relations law. See Aust and Kleinlein, 'Introduction', p. 14.

relations. Indeed, Presidents are very active in this area.[45] This can be illustrated by the endeavors of Polish President Andrzej Duda in several months of 2019. During this time, the President made many foreign visits and met with his counterparts from other states. Sometimes the anniversaries of various important events were an opportunity to make such visits.[46] A separate category were multilateral conferences with Heads of State on a variety of political or social issues.[47] The President's participation was aimed at emphasizing the significance and rank of these meetings and conferences for Polish interests.

The results of these visits were various documents signed by the Polish President and his partners from other countries. However, these were not international agreements and were not legally binding. They expressed the political will of the Republic of Poland and other participating countries.

2 The President As Commander-in-Chief of the Armed Forces of the Republic of Poland

Separate mention should be made of events in external relations with the participation of the Polish President where he acted not only as the supreme representative of the Republic of Poland (article 126(1)) guarding the sovereignty and security of the state (article 126(2)), but also as the Commander-in-Chief of the Armed Forces of the Republic of Poland (article 134(1)). An example of such activity is the participation of the Polish President in the meeting of the North Atlantic Council in London (3–4 December 2019) on the 70th anniversary of NATO and the signing of the London Declaration issued by the Heads of State and Government.[48] The Declaration reaffirmed, inter alia, the commitment to article 5 of the Washington Treaty. It should be noted in this context that the practice developed in the past of Poland being represented at NATO summit meetings by the President. The President is always accompanied by the Minister of National Defence, which reflects the requirements for cooperation provided for in the Constitution (article 133(3)).

45 In early 2021, it was even announced the plan to create an Office of International Policy in the Chancellery of the President.

46 www.president.pl/en/news/art,1079,joint-statement-by-the-presidents-of-the-republic-of-lithuania-and-the-republic-of-poland-on-the-occasion-of-the-450th-anniversary-of-the-union-of-lublin.html, accessed June 26, 2020; www.president.pl/en/news/art,1144,president-commemorates-battle-of-the-bulge.html, accessed June 26, 2020.

47 www.president.pl/en/news/art,1115,v4-meeting-starts-in-lany-czech-republic.html; www.president.pl/en/news/art,1119,president-warns-against-cohesion-cap-funding-cuts.html, accessed June 26, 2020.

48 www.president.pl/en/news/art,1139,london-declaration-.html?fbclid=IwAR2qSZMqeJHWiSbbYqDWvhUNK83llD4wD-ekvCXVBH6rsCw9LVhzSn49ZFc, accessed June 26, 2020.

Poland's foreign policy is largely aimed at strengthening state security considering the sense of threat from Russia. The United States is considered to be the main guarantor of state security within NATO as well as beyond the framework of this Alliance. In the area of political and military cooperation with the United States, successive Polish Presidents have been very active. The result of many years' efforts is the presence of 4,500 American soldiers on the Polish territory. The President's activity was also maintained in 2019. It was manifested by two joint declarations of the Presidents of both countries. These were the Joint Declaration on Defense Cooperation Regarding US Force Posture in Poland (June 2019) and the Joint Declaration on Advancing Defense Cooperation (September 2019).

In the first of these declarations of June 12, 2019,[49] the United States announced an increase in its military presence in Poland in the near future by about 1,000 additional soldiers. This will was sustained in the second declaration. Poland, on the other hand, promised to provide and maintain the jointly agreed infrastructure for an initial package of additional projects at no cost to the United States. Poland is also planning to provide additional support to the US Armed Forces, going beyond the NATO standard of support by the host country. The declaration then listed the intended specific undertakings for increasing defense cooperation in Poland. The second declaration of September 23, 2019 is an extension and detail of the first one.[50] It lists the locations of particular US military units in Poland.

These declarations are important political documents for Poland, but do not have direct legal effects. This is evidenced by the emphasis in both declarations on the common will to strive for the conclusion of international agreements and arrangements necessary for the implementation of increased cooperation in the field of infrastructure and defense, including improvement of the functioning of the US armed forces in Poland. It follows therefrom that the declarations under discussion have a preparatory value in relation to future international agreements.

The above review shows that the President's role in the field of foreign relations is not limited to his formal competence to undertake actions with legal effects. The political implications are no less important. It should be added that the current President of Poland is considered by many observers as

49 www.president.pl/en/news/art,1069,joint-declaration-on-defense-cooperation-regarding-us-force-posture-in-the-republic-of-poland.html, accessed June 26, 2020.

50 www.president.pl/en/news/art,1107,joint-declaration-on-advancing-defense-cooperation.html, accessed June 26, 2020.

a politician who is not independent, but subject to the influence of the ruling Law and Justice (PiS) party and its powerful Chairman Jarosław Kaczyński.

IV ACTIVITIES OF THE PARLIAMENT IN THE FIELD OF FOREIGN RELATIONS

The dominance of the executive in the field of foreign relations is undeniable. However, this does not mean exclusivity in this area. Relevant is also the activity of the Parliament[51] which in Poland consists of two chambers: the Sejm and the Senate. The role of the Parliament in the field of foreign relations deserves attention because of its democratic legitimacy stemming from direct elections.

1 *Declaration of a State of War and Conclusion of Peace and Ratification of Treaties*

The Sejm – the Parliament's first chamber – has, in the light of the Constitution, a two-fold competence to take decisions in the field of foreign relations. First, under article 116(1), 'the Sejm shall declare, in the name of the Republic of Poland, a state of war and the conclusion of peace'.[52] The Constitution details it in article 116(2):

> The Sejm may adopt a resolution on a state of war only in the event of armed aggression against the territory of the Republic of Poland or when an obligation of common defence against aggression arises by virtue of international agreements. If the Sejm cannot assemble for a sitting, the President of the Republic may declare a state of war.

Second, the Parliament gives its consent in the form of a statute to the ratification of major international agreements.[53] In accordance with article 89(1)

> ratification of an international agreement by the Republic of Poland as well as renunciation thereof, shall require prior consent granted by statute – if such agreement concerns:

51 Masternak-Kubiak and Preisner, 'Realizacja konstytucyjnego podziału kompetencji organów państwa w stosunkach zewnętrznych', pp. 118–21; Garlicki, 'Konstytucja a "sprawy zewnętrzne"', pp. 198–201; Mażewski, 'Prowadzenie polityki zagranicznej w Rzeczypospolitej Polskiej', p. 13.

52 Masternak-Kubiak and Preisner, 'Realizacja konstytucyjnego podziału kompetencji organów państwa w stosunkach zewnętrznych', pp. 118–20.

53 Grzybowski and Mikuli, 'Realizacja konstytucyjnych kompetencji Prezydenta RP', pp. 54–61.

1) peace, alliances, political or military treaties;
2) freedoms, rights or obligations of citizens, as specified in the Constitution;
3) the Republic of Poland's membership in an international organization;
4) considerable financial responsibilities imposed on the State;
5) matters regulated by statute or those in respect of which the Constitution requires the form of a statute.

In addition, specific, more demanding rules for ratification with the participation of both chambers of the Parliament refer to the international agreement based on article 90(1) of the Constitution. Pursuant to this provision, '[t]he Republic of Poland may, by virtue of international agreements, delegate to an international organization or international institution the competence of State authorities in relation to certain matters'. This provision concerned the Accession Treaty of Poland joining the EU.

A statute, granting consent to the ratification of such an agreement shall be passed by the Sejm by a two-thirds majority vote in the presence of at least half of the statutory number of its Members, and by the Senate by a two-thirds majority vote in the presence of at least half of the statutory number of Senators. The consent to the ratification may also be granted in a nationwide referendum (article 90(2) and (3)).

2 *Control over the Activities of the Council of Ministers in the Field of Foreign Relations and the Parliamentary Foreign Affairs Committee*

From the parliamentary perspective, noteworthy is the competence to exercise control over the Government. In accordance with article 95(2) of the Constitution, the Sejm shall exercise control over the activities of the Council of Ministers within the scope specified by the provisions of the Constitution and statutes. Clearly, the scope of parliamentary control is broader than the field of foreign relations. The activities of the Parliamentary Foreign Affairs Committee are of great practical importance. The Committee discusses current issues of the Government's foreign policy. In addition, the Committee initiates legislative work, expresses its opinion on the correctness of procedures for the ratification of international agreements and provides its opinions on candidates for positions related to the state's foreign policy.[54]

[54] Jerzy Jaskiernia, 'Charakter prawny i funkcje Komisji Spraw Zagranicznych Sejmu RP' ['Legal nature and functions of the Foreign Affairs Committee of the Polish Sejm'] (2004) 6 *Polski Przegląd Dyplomatyczny* 25–130; Masternak-Kubiak and Preisner, 'Realizacja konstytucyjnego podziału kompetencji organów państwa w stosunkach zewnętrznych', p. 121; Garlicki, 'Konstytucja a "sprawy zewnętrzne"', p. 200.

Periodically, the Sejm holds debates on the foreign policy which is presented by the Minister of Foreign Affairs. This provides an opportunity for the parliamentary opposition to take a stand. It should be stressed, however, that the President's activity in the field of foreign relations remains beyond the Parliament's control.[55]

It can be concluded that, apart from the Parliament's competence in the process of ratification of international agreements, the Parliament's role in the field of foreign relations lies in providing opinions and inspiring the activities of the Council of Ministers. Control over the Government is general in its nature. The Parliament's real influence on the executive in this area depends largely on the qualifications and determination of Members of the Sejm dealing with international affairs in a given term of office.

3 *Parliamentary Activity in EU Affairs*

Poland's membership in the European Union has opened new fields of parliamentary activity. As already mentioned, EU affairs do not fall within the division of state activities into internal and external affairs and contain elements of both. The role of the Parliament in the European affairs is defined by EU and Polish law. The Lisbon Treaty has significantly strengthened the position of national parliaments. The various forms of participation of national parliaments in the Union's political life and the related competences are formulated in the extensive article 12 TEU which should be mentioned in the first place.[56] In this context, reference should also be made to two protocols which have the legal power of treaties. They regulate the procedures for EU institutions to observe the principle of subsidiarity and assessment, in this respect, of draft EU legislation by the parliaments of the Member States.[57] The Polish Parliament is also involved in these procedures.

As far as Polish law is concerned, reference should be made to the Act of 2010 on the Cooperation of the Council of Ministers with the Sejm and Senate on Matters Related to the Membership of the Republic of Poland in the European Union.[58] Pursuant to the provisions of this Act, the Council of

55 Grzybowski and Dobosz, 'Pozycja ustrojowa Prezydenta RP', p. 145.

56 Tobias Lock, 'Articles 10–12', in Manuel Kellerbauer, Marcus Klamert and Jonathan Tomkin (eds.). *The EU Treaties and the Charter of Fundamental Rights. A Commentary* (Oxford: Oxford University Press, 2019), pp. 108–23 at 118 ff.

57 Protocol (No 1) on the Role of National Parliaments in the European Union (OJ 2016 No. C202, 7 June 2016, pp. 203–05 and Protocol (No 2) on the Application of the Principles of Subsidiarity and Proportionality (OJ 2016 No. C202, 7 June 2016, pp. 206–09).

58 'Ustawa z dnia 8 października 2010 r. o współpracy Rady Ministrów z Sejmem i Senatem w sprawach związanych z członkostwem Rzeczypospolitej Polskiej w Unii Europejskiej'

Ministers is obliged to cooperate with both chambers of the Parliament in a number of areas: making European Union law, bringing actions before the Court of Justice of the European Union by the Sejm and the Senate, creating Polish legislation implementing European Union law, giving opinions on candidates for certain posts in the European Union as well as in connection with representatives of the Council of Ministers holding the presidency of the Council. The cooperation according to the statute in question consists mainly in the provision by the Government of information, to a broad extent, to parliamentary committees competent for European affairs, consultations and opinions on the Government's intended activities. The statute in question introduces procedures to ensure efficient cooperation.

V CONCLUSION

The above considerations have illustrated the existence of various factors determining the performance of tasks and competences in the field of foreign relations in a country which just over thirty years ago gained the possibility to act independently on the international and European arena. The arrangement of political forces reflected in the parliamentary composition during the drafting and adoption of the Constitution determined the choice of the structure of the state system, including the dualism of the executive power and, within it, the relationship between the Council of Ministers (the Government) and the President. In addition to the constitutional solutions, of great relevance are the changing external conditions as well as the personality traits of politicians performing the functions of president, prime minister, ministers or members of parliament. Thanks to these characteristics, even in the unchanged constitutional state, there may be differences in the real significance of particular authorities in such an important and sensitive area as foreign relations.

Worth noting at this point are the processes of transformation of the Polish state system towards authoritarianism noticeable after 2015.[59] These processes are taking place without any amendment to the Constitution, although with an interpretation of its provisions departing from what was commonly approved previously. Essentially, undemocratic changes are being made through new statutes and changes in the application of the old ones. Most

(2010) 213 *Dziennik Ustaw [Journal of Laws]* item 1395. Dudek, 'Komentarz do art. 146 Konstytucji', pp. 747–48.

59 Wojciech Sadurski, *Poland's Constitutional Breakdown* (Oxford: Oxford University Press, 2019).

observers assert that certain of these statutes are unconstitutional. This unconstitutionality, however, cannot be effectively examined considering the loss by the Constitutional Tribunal of its prestige and public trust. The independence of courts, including the Supreme Court, has been significantly weakened.

The aforementioned political transformations have an effect on Poland's foreign relations. They result in impairing the state's reputation in the international arena due to the undermining of the principles of democracy and the rule of law. The European Union responded to these developments.[60] Proceedings under article 7 TEU have been pending before the Council of the European Union since 2018.[61] These were initiated by the European Commission which believes that there is a clear risk of a serious breach by this Member State of the values referred to in article 2 TEU, and in particular the rule of law. The ECJ has issued several judgments ruling on the violation by Poland of the rule of law with regard to the judiciary.[62] Poland's position in the European Union has weakened. Even if there is no formal Polexit, its increasing marginalization is to be expected.

The developments in Poland are also condemned by numerous international organizations. Poland is getting more and more isolated on the international arena.

The changes in the practice of Poland's foreign relations in recent years are invisible in an analysis limited to constitutional considerations only. In the exercise of their constitutional tasks and competences, including in the field of foreign policy, both the President and the Government headed by the Prime Minister as well as the parliamentary majority, are subject to the will of the Chair of the ruling party (PiS).

60 Armin von Bogdandy, Piotr Bogdanowicz, Iris Canor, Christoph Grabenwarter, Maciej Taborowski, Matthias Schmidt, *Defending Checks and Balances in EU Member States,Taking Stock of Europe's Actions*, (Berlin, Heidelberg: Springer, 2021), https://link.springer.com/book/10.1007%2F978-3-662-62317-6.

61 Armin Hatje and Lubos Tichý (eds.), *Liability of Member States for the Violation of Fundamental Values of the European Union*, Europarecht Beiheft 1 (Baden-Baden: Nomos, 2018).

62 Judgments of the Court of Justice: Case C-619/18, *European Commission* v. *Republic of Poland* [2019], ECLI:EU:C:2019:531; Case C-192/18, *European Commission* v. *Republic of Poland* [2019], ECLI:EU:C:2019:924; Joined Cases C-585/18, C-624/18 and C-625/18, *A. K. and Others* v. *Sąd Najwyższy* [2019], ECLI:EU:C:2019:982.

13

The Role of Parliaments in Creating and Enforcing Foreign Relations Law

A Case Study of Bosnia and Herzegovina

Ajla Škrbić

I INTRODUCTION

The growing importance of foreign relations law raises the question of whether the traditional exclusion of parliaments from a country's foreign affairs is wrong and utterly flawed. While there are practical benefits in seeing foreign relations as belonging only to the executive branch, this approach undermines the potential for national parliaments to engage in developing this area of law.[1] Hence, in this chapter I examine the role of parliaments in foreign relations law taking Bosnia and Herzegovina (BiH) as an example.

BiH is particularly interesting in this regard for several reasons. Firstly, BiH has a unique constitutional framework and special relationship with international law due to the Dayton Peace Agreement (DPA).[2] Even though this uniqueness is in a certain tension with the approach to discuss the general question of the role of parliaments in foreign relations law, the example of BiH is interesting because it can show that the impact of parliaments on foreign relations law depends on parliaments' role in a state and effective use of their competencies. Secondly, BiH has an extremely complex and multilevel system of state organisation as a result of the same treaty. Finally, the complex internal structure combined with weak institutions and the absence of

[1] This doctrine has its origin in Locke's 'Two Treatises of Government' (1689) and is later confirmed in Montesquieu's 'The Spirit of Laws' (1748), Blackstone's 'Commentaries on the Laws of England' (1765), as well as Dicey's 'Lectures Introductory to the Study of the Law of the Constitution' (1885). Cf. Campbell McLachlan, *Foreign Relations Law* (Cambridge: Cambridge University Press, 2014), pp. 149–218.

[2] General Framework Agreement for Peace in Bosnia and Herzegovina (Dayton Peace Agreement), Paris, 14 December 1995, (1996) 35 ILM 89, 172.

a dedicated law on foreign relations[3] leads to a large number of actors (international and domestic) that can and has a major role in creating and implementing foreign policy.

In this chapter, I will first provide some general information on the constitutional design in BiH, on the institutions established by the Constitution, and the general separation of powers as arranged by the Constitution. I will further examine the foreign relations law of BiH and the respective competencies of the Parliamentary Assembly of BiH (PA) in the implementation of the foreign policy. I argue that foreign affairs should be analysed as a matter of the distribution of powers between the executive and legislative branch, and not the exclusion of the foreign affairs power from the legislature.[4] Finally, the chapter will turn to foreign relations law as a field of scholarship and research in this country. The chapter ends with conclusions and recommendations. This part of the chapter addresses some of the practical issues related to the smaller and larger role of the legislature in shaping foreign policy. It also addresses the future perspective of the role of parliaments in the issue under examination.

II A GENERAL CONSTITUTIONAL AND LEGAL FRAMEWORK IN BIH

BiH is rather unique when it comes to (subsection A) its internal organisation and (subsection B) its relation to international law. This special position of BiH is owed to a violent international armed conflict that lasted on Bosnian territory from 1992 to 1995 and ended with the signing of the DPA with the Annex 4 serving as the Constitution for BiH.

A *Internal Organisation of Bosnia and Herzegovina*

One of the main questions raised during the negotiations of the DPA was a question of how to organise the internal structure of BiH. In an effort to end the war, the DPA was negotiated and signed by all three parties to the conflict,

3 Even though this is also the case with many other states, I believe it is a problem when it comes to weak and divided states such as BiH. Namely, the existence of a distinct law with clear rules and guidance could introduce a cohesion in foreign policy and reduce the possibilities for excuses for self-interested conduct of political parties in foreign policy. Or, referring to what Dire Tladi has addressed in his chapter, I believe that current BiH statutes that deal with foreign relations are written for strong, independent and rule-of-law committed actors, whereas in BiH, quite the opposite is true.

4 This goes in line with the finding of Campbell McLachlan (Cf. McLachlan, *Foreign Relations Law*, p. 150).

that is BiH, Croatia, and Serbia (along with the representatives from the European Union (EU), France, Germany, Italy, Russia, the United Kingdom and the United States). With so many parties to the agreement, the provisions therein represented a compromise of the parties' respective interests. Consequently, the DPA achieved its main purpose of ending the war, but it left in place the ethnic division established by war. More specifically, the solutions provided by the DPA succeeded in preserving BiH as a sovereign state; however, it divided BiH into two parts: the Federation of BiH (decentralised and predominantly with Bosniac and Croat population) and Republika Srpska (relatively centralised and predominantly with Serb population). Furthermore, the Federation of BiH was divided into ten cantons with great powers and competencies. However, the complexity of the state organisation does not end there. In addition to these two Entities (and cantons in Federation of BiH), the town of Brčko became an independent district in 1999, being the only part of BiH not governed by the DPA.

As regards the institutions established by the Constitution and the issues of separation of powers as arranged by the Constitution, they are weak and reflect the ethnic divisions in BiH.[5] This is an expression of a balance of power and a drafting compromise between the warring DPA parties.[6] Against this background, all governmental functions and powers not expressly assigned to the institutions of BiH are within the jurisdiction of the Entities.[7] As a consequence, many important areas such as education or the police apparatus have been constitutionally placed under the jurisdiction of the Entities, which is not the case for the field of foreign policy, however.[8]

The weak position of national institutions is further complicated by their ethnically defined structure.[9] In addition, each of the constituent

[5] The institutions on the state level include the PA, the government (Council of Ministers), the Presidency, the Constitutional Court, and the Central Bank (BiH Constitution, Articles IV–VII).

[6] Marko Joseph, 'Five Years of Constitutional Jurisprudence in Bosnia and Herzegovina: A First Balance' (2004) *European Diversity and Autonomy Papers 7/2004*, p. 6.

[7] BiH Constitution, Article IV(3)(a).

[8] BiH Constitution, Article III(1)(a).

[9] For example, the PA is bicameral and encompasses a House of Representatives and a House of Peoples (BiH Constitution, Article IV). The members of the House of Representatives are directly elected in the Federation of BiH (two-thirds of members) and in the Republika Srpska (one-third of members), while the members of the House of Peoples are indirectly elected by the parliaments of the Entities [BiH Constitution, Article IV(1) and (2)]. Here, two-thirds of members are elected from the Federation of BiH (and include five Bosniacs and five Croats), while the remaining one-third of members are elected from Republika Srpska (five Serbs).

Even the Constitutional Court for which the Constitution does not contain express rules on an ethnic quota has ethnically defined structure. Namely, the Court has nine members. Six of peoples[10] has a veto power over all essential decision-making, that is, is entitled to invoke the 'vital interest' that enables them to block every proposal they deem harmful to their respective peoples.[11] This may, and very often does, paralyse the national institutions. It is worrying also for foreign policy which is a responsibility of the tripartite Presidency.[12] Even though the Constitution of BiH declares that the Presidency shall endeavour to adopt all Presidency decisions by consensus, and the conducting of foreign policy is particularly emphasised in this regard,[13] this procedure may lead to stalemate of the Presidency and foreign policy. Namely, if no consensus is reached, two members of the Presidency may adopt a decision. However, the dissenting member may then declare a proposed decision to be destructive of a 'vital interest' of the Entity from the territory from which he/she was elected.[14] In that case, a separate proceeding for the resolution of a dispute will be initiated.[15] Accordingly, each of the constituent peoples may have a final say in the Presidency and foreign policy, which goes in line with my claim regarding a large number of actors that can have a major role in foreign policy in BiH.

them are selected by the Entities, while the remaining three members are appointed by the President of the European Court of Human Rights (ECtHR), again pointing to the unique openness to international law. And although there is no constitutional or other rule on an ethnic quota for local judges, for the two positions allocated to the Republika Srpska, the judgeships are always filled by Serbs; and for the four positions allocated to the Federation of BiH, two judgeships are filled by Bosniacs while two are filled by Croats.

10 Pursuant to the Preamble of the Constitution, Bosniacs, Croats and Serbs are described as 'constituent peoples'.

11 The fact that the term 'vital national interest' is not defined in the BiH Constitution presents a further challenge.

12 BiH Constitution, Article V(3)(a).

The Presidency has to comprise one Bosniac, one Croat and one Serb. Hence, anyone identifying other than a member of constituent peoples is ineligible for Presidency. However, it is noteworthy that the candidates for every function in BiH are 'self-defined' and can even change their ethnic affiliation throughout the time. This issue was raised after it came to light that several individuals (in connection to some prominent functions at the state and Entity levels) have changed their ethnicity in order to be eligible for certain functions and to be 'a representative' of a certain constituent peoples.

13 Cf. Article V(2)(c) of the Constitution.

14 Again, this is supposed to ensure equality of the ethnic groups.

15 Pursuant to the Article V(2)(d) of the Constitution, such a decision will be referred immediately to the National Assembly of Republika Srpska (if the declaration was made by the member from that territory), to the Bosniac Delegates of the House of Peoples of the Federation (if the declaration was made by the Bosniac member), or to the Croat Delegates of that body (if the declaration was made by the Croat member). Finally, if the declaration is confirmed by a two-thirds vote of those persons within ten days of the referral, the challenged Presidency decision will not take effect.

Finally, in addition to these state-level institutions, both Entities, the Federation of BiH and Republika Srpska, have their own separation of powers-structures.[16] Furthermore, the Brčko District has its own division of powers.[17] Also, both Entities have their own Constitutions, while the Brčko District has the Statute of the Brčko District of BiH.[18]

B *BiH and International Law*

The Constitution of BiH and the DPA have led to a special situation of BiH vis-à-vis international law. The fact that the Constitution is a part of an international treaty enables it to be interpreted as a treaty defined by the 1969 Vienna Convention on the Law of Treaties.[19] Furthermore, its content makes BiH uniquely open to international law. This is the result of the DPA makers trying to develop and to guarantee pluralism and non-discrimination of both the majority and minority in BiH with respect to the application and protection of the whole range of different legal instruments and human rights and freedoms. This is best demonstrated by:

- The direct applicability of the fundamental freedoms of the European Convention of Human Rights (ECHR) and its Protocols;[20]

16 They have their own parliaments, governments, presidents and an extensive network of courts.

17 Its legislative power is exercised by the District Assembly, the executive power is exercised by the District Government, while the judicial power is exercised by the District courts.

18 Hence, even though having a very complex administrative division, BiH does not have a supreme court, or any other court of last resort or court of appeal, ensuring a uniform application of laws in BiH. Along with the Constitutional Court, the only court on the state level is the so-called State Court. Quite interesting and in line with my claim regarding Bosnian internationalised structure, the judges and prosecutors of the State Court were until 2012 appointed from international staff. This certainly fostered easier introduction of international legal solutions into national legal framework and institutions.

On the other hand, Federation of BiH and Republika Srpska *do* have their own Supreme Courts, as well as lower courts.

19 Vienna Convention on the Law of Treaties, Vienna, 23 May 1969, in force 27 January 1980, 1155 UNTS 331; (1969) 8 ILM 679; UKTS (1980) 58.

20 BiH Constitution, Article II(2), sentence 1. Although there are differing views on what the obligation to directly apply the ECHR means, the prevalent conclusion is that the rights and freedoms under the ECHR form directly applicable law which require no special transformation procedure. For different conclusion see Decision on Admissibility and Merits, U 106/03, 27 October 2004, where the Constitutional Court comprehended 'direct applicability' in a way that ordinary courts are under the obligation to directly apply the rights and freedoms set forth in the ECHR without taking into account the laws which are contrary to them and without forwarding the issue of the constitutionality of those laws to the Constitutional Court (Constitutional Court of Bosnia and Herzegovina, Decision on Admissibility and Merits, U 106/03, 27 October 2004, www.ustavnisud.ba/dokumenti/_bs/u-106–03-26086.pdf, accessed

- The provision on the absolute supremacy of ECHR and its Protocols over all other law;[21]
- The provision on an additional fifteen international conventions on human rights and protection of national minorities to be applied in BiH;[22]
- The provision stating that the general principles of international law shall be an integral part of the law of BiH and the Entities;[23]
- The provision that highlights that no amendment to the Constitution may eliminate or diminish any of the rights and freedoms referred to in Article II, or alter this provision.[24]

Furthermore, the DPA has established the Office of the High Representative (OHR)[25] as an ad hoc international institution responsible for overseeing implementation of civilian aspects of the DPA.[26] The OHR has the status of

17 July 2020, in English: www.ustavnisud.ba/dokumenti/_en/u-106–03-26086.pdf, accessed 17 July 2020). However, the Court later changed its position (see Constitutional Court of Bosnia and Herzegovina, Decision on Admissibility and Merits, AP 1603/05, 21 December 2006, www.ustavnisud.ba/dokumenti/_hr/AP-1603–05-102456.pdf, accessed 17 July 2020, para. 37). Cf. Christian Steiner et al., *Constitution of Bosnia and Herzegovina: Commentary* (Sarajevo: Konrad Adenauer Stiftung, 2010), pp. 105–7.

21 BiH Constitution, Article II(2), sentence 2. This provision was contested among some scholars due to its ambiguity. The first issue was whether the ECHR has priority over the laws of BiH or both in relation to the laws and the Constitution. Since the BiH Constitution was written in English and has not been officially translated in the official languages of BiH, the problem could have not been solved by reading the respective constitutional provision. However, it seems that the Constitutional Court of BiH is of view that the ECHR is not above the Constitution (see Decision on Admissibility, U 5/04, 27 January 2006, where the Constitutional Court held that the ECHR cannot have superior status over the Constitution, since the superior status and constitutional power of the ECHR in BiH stem from the BiH Constitution itself, www.ustavnisud.ba/dokumenti/_bs/u-5–04-71799.pdf, accessed 21 April 2020, in English: www.ustavnisud.ba/dokumenti/_en/u-5–04-71799.pdf, accessed 26 April 2020).

The second issue was whether this provision invokes all ECHR Protocols or just the ones that were in force on the day of entry into force of the BiH Constitution. It seems logical that the Constitution drafters had *all* protocols in mind since they used the notion of 'protocols' without enumeration, as was the case with the International Covenant on Civil and Political Rights, for example. (cf. Christian Steiner et al., *Constitution of Bosnia and Herzegovina: Commentary* (Sarajevo: Konrad Adenauer Stiftung, 2010), p. 159).

22 Annex I to the BiH Constitution. Since they are integral part of the Constitution, they too have priorities over all other laws in BiH.

23 BiH Constitution, Article III(3)(b).

24 BiH Constitution, Article X(2).

25 The Austrian diplomat Valentin Inzko has filled this post since March 2009.

26 The civilian aspect of the DPA is a non-military aspect of the peace settlement set forth in Annex X of the DPA. It entails a wide range of activities, including the continuation of humanitarian aid efforts for as long as necessary, the rehabilitation of infrastructure and reconstruction of the economy, the establishment of political and constitutional institutions

a diplomatic mission to BiH and its main task is to ensure that BiH evolves into a peaceful and viable democracy, as well as to serve as the final authority for interpretation of the DPA on the civilian implementation of the peace settlement.[27] The High Representative has the power to impose decisions in cases where BiH authorities are unable to agree or where important issues are being considered or require resolution. Consequently, in the past, the High Representative has removed elected officials from office, imposed numerous laws and bylaws, and banned individuals from running for office, among other measures.[28]

Its work has been challenged in front of different courts. The main takeaway from these efforts has been that the foundation for the OHR's legislative acts lies in international law[29] and, therefore, it cannot be challenged by courts (whether it is the Supreme Court of the Federation of BiH or Republika Srpska, the State Court of BiH, the Constitutional Court of BiH or even the ECtHR).[30] However, it is worth noting that after its adoption, relevant

in BiH, the promotion of respect for human rights and the return of displaced persons and refugees, and the holding of free and fair elections.

27 Dayton Peace Agreement, Annex X, Article V.

28 The laws he imposed or amended are many and even include amendments to the Entity constitution and the declaring unconstitutional a law adopted by the PA. For instance, he imposed the laws on the transfer of competencies from the Entities to the state level, laws on privatisation, new currency, citizenship, the freedom of movement, the customs tariffs schedule, the law on foreign investment, the law on the flag, on the coat of arms of BiH, the laws on privatisation of banks and enterprises, on telecommunications, on the common driving licence, the Law on the Court of BiH, etc. Among the most challenged OHR decisions were the ones on removing from office civil servants or elected public officials (that even included a member of the Presidency of BiH and the President of an Entity) – mostly for non-cooperation with the International Criminal Tribunal for the Former Yugoslavia (ICTY) but also for corruption, mismanagement of public assets, interference with the judiciary, or not carrying out duties as a judge. The number of his interventions is indeed extensive. For example, only in one day in 2004, the OHR removed fifty-nine members of the political leadership of Republika Srpska because of their non-cooperation with the ICTY (list available at: www.ohr.int/list-of-removed-and-conditionally-removed-officials-by-the-high-representative/). The number of interventions reached 153 per year at the high point of the OHR's activities (see Constance Grewe and Michael Riegner, 'Internationalized Constitutionalism in Ethnically Divided Societies: Bosnia-Herzegovina and Kosovo Compared' (2011) 15 *Max Planck Yearbook of United Nations Law* 1, 56, and Karin Oellers-Frahm, 'Restructuring Bosnia-Herzegovina: A Model with Pit-Falls', in A. von Bogdandy and R. Wolfrum (eds.), *Max Planck Yearbook of United Nations Law*, Volume 9 (The Netherlands: Koninklijke Brill, 2005), pp. 179–224 at 208).

29 Its mandate derives from Annex X of the DPA, the relevant resolutions of the United Nations (UN) Security Council, and the Bonn Declaration.

30 See, e.g., ECtHR, *Kalinić and Bilbija* v. *Bosnia and Herzegovina* (Appl. Nos. 45541/04 and 16587/07), Admissibility Decision (Fourth Section), 13 May 2008, http://hudoc.echr.coe.int/eng?i=001–86652, accessed 21 April 2020; Office of the High Representative in Bosnia and

legislation becomes part of domestic law and is consequently reviewable by the Constitutional Court.[31] More specifically, although the OHR is acting on the basis of international law, legislation that it adopts replaces acts of the PA and becomes part of domestic law (and, in accordance with the Constitution, all acts, regardless of who adopts them, are reviewable by the Constitutional Court). Therefore, the Constitutional Court *can* review the constitutionality of the content of legislation enacted by the OHR, but *not* whether there was enough justification for the OHR to enact the legislation in the first place.

It is thus not surprising that the work of the OHR has been, and still is, highly criticised.[32] The main criticism is that the OHR has de facto, unlimited legal powers that are contrary to the essential democratic principles it promotes. On the other hand, there are also legitimate arguments that, due to the ethnic composition of BiH institutions and institutions on the substate level, the intervention of the OHR is welcome and often necessary.

In my view, even though the objections to the OHR are justified, its work (as well as the work of other international actors in BiH) is indeed still necessary. However, three points of concern stand out: first, its role should be more transparent and better explained to the citizens. Second, it should use its powers more effectively in critical situations for which it is made (which has been not the case since the former and most active High Representative Paddy Ashdown has left office). Finally, it should work towards enabling domestic actors to work fully independently.

Not only BiH, but also the Brčko District has a 'special supervisor'. However, in 2012 the High Representative announced that the Brčko Supervisor would suspend his functions while retaining all his authority, as he believed that the District's institutions now have the capacity to address their challenges on their own. Thus, while the Special Representative position

Herzegovina, Order on the Implementation of the Decision of the Constitutional Court of Bosnia and Herzegovina in the Appeal of Milorad Bilbija et al, No. AP-953/05, 23 March 2007, www.ohr.int/?p=64783, accessed 21 April 2020; Constitutional Court of Bosnia and Herzegovina, Decision No. U 26/01, 28 September 2001, www.ustavnisud.ba/dokumenti/_hr/u-26-01-51291.pdf, accessed 21 April 2020, in English: www.ustavnisud.ba/dokumenti/_en/u-26-01-51291.pdf, accessed 26 April 2020.

31 See, e.g., Constitutional Court of Bosnia and Herzegovina, Decision U 9/00, 3 November 2000, www.ustavnisud.ba/dokumenti/_bs/u-9-00-12134.pdf, accessed 26 April 2020, in English: www.ustavnisud.ba/dokumenti/_en/u-9-00-12134.pdf, accessed 26 April 2020, 83–93.

32 In August 2019, leaders of BiH's leading political parties have signed an Agreement on the Principles of Establishing Authorities in BiH, which includes the creation of preconditions for the OHR's departure from BiH. Nevertheless, this departure is explicitly conditioned by a positive assessment of the political situation in BiH based on full respect for the DPA, which the OHR itself, along with the UN Security Council and the Peace Implementation Council should assess.

continued to exist, the full responsibility for the District's affairs were devolved to local administration.

Finally, the Constitution has articles that deal with the Entities' relations with international law. Namely, the relations between them and foreign states are regulated in Article III(2)(a) and (d) of the Constitution. Pursuant to these provisions, Entities may establish 'special parallel relationships' with neighbouring states if these relationships are consistent with the sovereignty and territorial integrity of BiH. Each Entity may also enter into agreements with states and international organisations with the consent of the PA. However, the PA may provide by law that certain types of agreements do not require such consent.[33]

C *Shortcomings of the Current System*

Although very open to international law and explicitly securing the enjoyment of the rights and freedoms to all persons in BiH without discrimination on any grounds, the BiH Constitution should and has been subject to a large amount of criticism. The main reason is its discriminatory nature, since it discriminates the very persons it should protect. The citizens not belonging to the mentioned 'constituent peoples' are being discriminated against, since they are ineligible to stand for election for certain prominent positions in BiH. However, it is not just them: Bosniacs, Croats, and Serbs are also discriminated against based on the territory in which they live (e.g. a Serb member of the Presidency may only be directly elected from the territory of Republika Srpska, thus discriminating all Serbs in the Federation by disabling them to choose 'their' representative in the Presidency).

This has led to several lawsuits against BiH before the ECtHR.[34] The most famous and widely discussed case among them is the Case of Sejdić and Finci.[35]

33 Several agreements on these special parallel relationships were signed. However, some of them (between Republika Srpska and Serbia in particular) were criticised due to their alleged unconstitutionality (see, e.g., Constitutional Court of Bosnia and Herzegovina, Decision U 42/01, 26 March 2004, www.ustavnisud.ba/dokumenti/_bs/u-42-01-12264.pdf, accessed 26 April 2020, in English: www.ustavnisud.ba/dokumenti/_en/u-42-01-12264.pdf, accessed 26 April 2020).

34 See ECtHR, *Sejdić and Finci* v. *Bosnia and Herzegovina* (Appl. Nos. 27996/06 and 34836/06), Judgment (Grand Chamber), 22 December 2009, ECHR 2009-VI, 273; *Zornić v. Bosnia and Herzegovina* (Appl. No. 3681/06), Judgment (Fourth Section), 15 July 2014, http://hudoc.echr.coe.int/eng?i=001-145566, accessed 21 April 2020; and *Šlaku* v. *Bosnia and Herzegovina* (Appl. No. 56666/12), Judgment (Fifth Section), 26 May 2016, http://hudoc.echr.coe.int/eng?i=001-163056, accessed 21 April 2020.

35 It was the first time the ECtHR declared a constitutional provision of a state party to be in violation of the ECHR. Namely, Mr Sejdić (Bosnian national of Roma ethnicity) and Mr Finci (Bosnian national of Jewish ethnicity) complained that the BiH Constitution prevented

However, even after more than ten years since the delivery of this judgment, the necessary reforms in BiH have not been adopted.[36] This has led to the characterisation of the situation in BiH by the Committee of Ministers of the Council of Europe as a manifest breach of the country's obligations under the ECHR, as well as of its undertakings as a member state of the Council of Europe.[37] Thus, even though the BiH Constitution is continuously described as uniquely open to international law, the truth is that not all of its provisions are in line with international law. The scars of the war in the 1990s remain deeply enshrined in how BiH functions in general and the DPA continues to be the basis for the present political divisions of BiH.

The 'world's most complicated system of government'[38] has consequences for the foreign policy as well. The prominent role of the constituent peoples in

them from being candidates for the Presidency of BiH and the House of Peoples of the PA solely on the ground of their ethnic origins. The ECtHR held that BiH had violated Article 14 of the ECHR and Article 3 of Protocol No. 1 as regards to the applicants' ineligibility to stand for election to the House of Peoples of the PA, as well as Article 1 of Protocol No. 12 as regards to the applicants' ineligibility to stand for election to the Presidency. And while the ECtHR judgment recognised that BiH has a particularised system designed to ensure peace in the 1990s, it noted that a mechanism of power sharing with careful balancing of the rights of all, not just some, communities is possible and needs to be introduced (ECtHR, *Sejdić and Finci* v. *Bosnia and Herzegovina* (Appl. Nos. 27996/06 and 34836/06), Judgment (Grand Chamber), 22 December 2009, ECHR 2009-VI, 273, para. 48.).

36 Status of Execution of the Judgment in *Sejdić and Finci*, http://hudoc.exec.coe.int/eng?i=004-3141, accessed 21 April 2020.

The amendments to the BiH Constitution were introduced only once in 2009 with an Amendment that established the constitutional status of the Brčko District (Amendment I to the Constitution of BiH, Official Gazette of BiH, 25/09). All other attempts to amend the Constitution were unsuccessful since, pursuant to Article X(1), the Constitution may be amended only by a decision of the PA, including a two-thirds majority of those present and voting in the House of Representatives. Hence, BiH political leaders (through BiH institutions and with the agreement of all three 'constituent peoples') need to reach an agreement on the content of reforms. It is evident, though, that the nationalist political leaders want the status quo to be preserved as it enables them to stay in power. Thus, it does not seem likely that the Case of *Sejdić and Finci* will be implemented in the near future.

37 Council of Europe, Department for the Execution of Judgments of the European Court of Human Rights, 'Sejdić and Finci – After 10 years of absence of progress, new hopes for a solution for the 2022 elections', 22 December 2019, www.coe.int/en/web/execution/-/sejdic-and-finci-after10-years-of-absence-of-progress-new-hopes-for-a-solution-for-the-2022-elections, accessed 21 April 2020.

Also, in the following cases on similar issues, the ECtHR stated that the failure of BiH to introduce constitutional and legislative reforms is not only an aggravating factor as regards to the BiH's responsibility under the ECHR for an existing or past state of affairs, but also a threat to the future effectiveness of the ECHR machinery (see, e.g., ECtHR, *Zornić* v. *Bosnia and Herzegovina* (Appl. No. 3681/06), Judgment (Fourth Section), 15 July 2014, http://hudoc.echr.coe.int/eng?i=001-145566, accessed 21 April 2020, para. 40.).

38 Alberto Nardelli, Denis Džidić and Elvira Jukić, 'Bosnia and Herzegovina: the World's Most Complicated System of Government?', *The Guardian*, 8 October 2014, www.theguardian.com

the national institutional system combined with the substantial involvement of the international community leads to foreign policy being governed by a number of different and sometimes opposing actors. The domestic ethnically divided institutions (controlled by the same political parties for thirty years) disable genuine political change, making it impossible to reach decisions against the will of the ruling elites. On the other hand, the power of the international community represented through the OHR not only makes BiH foreign relations law dependent on international law but it also allows the previously mentioned domestic political actors to evade the political responsibility for their (in)actions. This reality does not lead to strengthened capacities of BiH institutions in exercising foreign affairs, nor does it lead to creation and implementation of common external goals. It only undermines institutional actions in the domain of foreign affairs and leads to political stalemate and institutional ineffectiveness.

Interestingly, the dependency of BiH foreign relations law on international law seems to be somewhat similar to the states in the 'Global South', as explained by Michael Riegner in his chapter. Notwithstanding the fact that BiH does not belong to the Global South, its foreign relations law, just like foreign relations law of the states in the 'Global South', does not shape the outside world as much as the outside world shapes their internal sphere. And although BiH's constitutional structure adds a new layer of complexity to the study of foreign relations law, there is a similarity in terms of the openness to and acceptance of international law, which is expressed in their respective constitutions. By allowing a special status of international law within their domestic legal systems, these states try to derive the formal validity of their constitutions from international law, to modernise their image and to build up their reputation within the international community. Hence, the transnational and hybrid categories of their foreign relations law transcend the binary opposition between national and international, political and economic, while the normative functions of their foreign relations law include enhancing economic self-determination, socio-economic development and equality.[39] All these states also share a similar goal: to take a more prominent role in the international community, which makes their foreign policy issues more relevant over time.

/news/datablog/2014/oct/08/bosnia-herzegovina-elections-the-worlds-most-complicated-system-of-government, accessed 21 April 2020.

39 See the chapter by Michael Riegner, p. 69.

III BOSNIA AND HERZEGOVINA'S FOREIGN RELATIONS LAW

The foreign policy of BiH is implemented through the Presidency of BiH,[40] the Ministry of Foreign Affairs of BiH,[41] and the resident and non-resident diplomatic and consular missions of BiH.[42] There is no dedicated law on foreign relations in BiH yet.[43] Moreover, until March 2018, the only document specifically regulating foreign relations law in BiH were the three-pages-long General Guidelines on and Priorities of Conducting the Foreign Policy of BiH.[44] However, there are many other laws (including the Constitution) that deal implicitly with foreign relations.[45]

'The General Guidelines on and Priorities of Conducting the Foreign Policy of Bosnia and Herzegovina' established the following as the priorities of BiH's foreign policy:

- Preservation and protection of the independence, sovereignty, and territorial integrity of BiH within its internationally recognised borders;
- Full and consistent implementation of the DPA;

40 See the responsibilities of the Presidency in Article V(3) of the BiH Constitution.

41 See the responsibilities of the Ministry of Foreign Affairs in Article 8 of *Zakon o ministarstvima i drugim tijelima uprave Bosne i Hercegovine* [Law on Ministries and Other Bodies of Administration of BiH], Official Gazette of BiH, 83/17, available in English at: www.ohr.int/laws-of-bih/public-institutions/.

42 There are also other local bodies that indirectly deal with foreign relations of BiH, such as the Ministry of Foreign Trade and Economic Relations of BiH, the Ministry of Defense of BiH, the Ministry of Security of BiH, the Ministry of Human Rights and Refugees and the Ministry of Communications and Transport.

43 However, its adoption is foreseen in the new Foreign Policy Strategy of BiH 2018–2023, www.predsjednistvobih.ba/vanj/?id=80826, accessed 21 April 2020, p. 2.

Also, a significant part of foreign relations law is covered by *Zakon o postupku zaključivanja i izvršavanja međunarodnih ugovora* [Law on the Procedure of Concluding and the Execution of International Treaties], Official Gazette of BiH, 32/13 (see part IV of this chapter).

44 Ministry of Foreign Affairs of Bosnia and Herzegovina, 'The General Guidelines on and Priorities of Conducting the Foreign Policy of Bosnia and Herzegovina', 26 March 2003, www.mvp.gov.ba/vanjska_politika_bih/osnovni_pravci_vanjske_politike_bih/?id=2, accessed 21 April 2020.

45 Some of them are the previously mentioned Law on the Procedure of Concluding and the Execution of International Treaties, Law on Ministries and Other Bodies of Administration of BiH, *Zakon o Vijeću ministara BiH* [Law on the Council of Ministers of BiH], *Zakon o državnoj službi u institucijama BiH* [Law on Civil Service in the institutions of BiH], etc. Further, throughout the years, there were several legal acts that dealt with foreign relations law in BiH (e.g. *Platforma za djelovanje Predsjedništva Republike Bosne i Hercegovine u ratnim okolnostima* [Platform for the Action of the Presidency of the Republic of BiH under War Conditions] and *Uredba sa zakonskom snagom o vršenju inostranih poslova* [Decree with the Force of Law on Conducting Foreign Policy and the Rules on Inner Organization of the Ministry of Foreign Affairs]). More on that in: Jasmin Hasić and Dženeta Karabegović (eds.), *Bosnia and Herzegovina's Foreign Policy Since Independence* (Cham: Palgrave Macmillan, 2019), pp. 27–30.

- BiH inclusion into European integration processes;
- Participation of BiH in multilateral activities; and
- Promotion of BiH as a partner in international economic relations.[46]

However, in March 2018, the Presidency of BiH decided to revise these guidelines and it adopted 'The Foreign Policy Strategy of Bosnia and Herzegovina 2018–2023' (hereinafter Strategy) establishing a wider framework on the activities of the relevant institutions of BiH in the realm of foreign relations law.[47] The Strategy was adopted in accordance with the constitutional competencies of the Presidency,[48] and the institutions of BiH are obliged to implement it.

Given that the global situation has changed since 2003 (the growing problem of terrorism and radicalism, the refugee crisis, challenges that the EU faces, etc.), the Strategy proposes several novel approaches to address these global challenges. However, it does not bring anything that has not been previously confirmed as foreign policy goal by the competent legislative and executive bodies of BiH.

Hence, this document states as its goal the establishment of a wider framework and guidelines on the activities of the relevant institutions of BiH in the realm of foreign policy.[49] It also emphasises the necessity for the Ministry of Foreign Affairs of BiH to prepare every two years a draft action plan with detailed objectives and priorities on the implementations of the Strategy.[50] In addition, it reiterates the obligation of the same Ministry in monitoring the implementation of the Strategy, as well as the Ministry's duty to annually inform the Presidency of BiH on the

46 Ministry of Foreign Affairs of Bosnia and Herzegovina, 'The General Guidelines on and Priorities of Conducting the Foreign Policy of Bosnia and Herzegovina', 26 March 2003, www.mvp.gov.ba/vanjska_politika_bih/osnovni_pravci_vanjske_politike_bih/?id=2, accessed 21 April 2020.

47 It is unknown when and where the consultations for the adoption of such an important document took place or who was involved in the process since the media, academia, experts and relevant non-governmental organisations were surprised when this was announced (cf. Davor Vuletić, 'Towards New Foreign Policy Strategy of Bosnia and Herzegovina 2018–2023', Friedrich-Ebert-Stiftung Sarajevo, November 2018, http://vpi.ba/wp-content/uploads/2019/01/Towards-New-Foreign-Policy-Strategy-of-BiH-2018-2023.pdf, accessed 21 April 2020, p. 6).

Concurrently, the 2003 General Guidelines on and Priorities of Conducting the Foreign Policy of BiH were adopted with the consultations with the academia, nongovernmental organisations and business community (see Vuletić, 'Towards new Foreign Policy Strategy').

48 BiH Constitution, Article V(3)(a).

49 The Presidency of Bosnia and Herzegovina, 'Foreign Policy Strategy of Bosnia and Herzegovina 2018–2023', 13 March 2018, www.predsjednistvobih.ba/vanj/?id=80826, accessed 21 April 2020, p. 2.

50 The Presidency of BiH, 'Foreign Policy Strategy 2018–2023', p. 2.

efficiency of its implementation and suggests measures on redefining of the Strategy.[51]

As regards the principles of the foreign policy of BiH, the Strategy emphasises openness, equality, reciprocity, peaceful cooperation, and non-interference in internal affairs of other countries, as well as the protection and promotion of the BiH's own basic constitutional principles, such as constitutionality, sovereignty, territorial integrity and the rule of law.[52] Also, the respect for and protection of human rights and fundamental freedoms and the fight against all forms of violent extremism are stated as priority principles.[53] In addition and due to the uniquely complex political structure of BiH, the Strategy underlines the importance of the principle of consensus in every public appearance of foreign policy actors in the country.[54] Finally, efficiency, transparency, responsibility for the results achieved, together with the universally endorsed principles of international law and the general principles of diplomatic practice are among the principles of the implementation of BiH's foreign policy.[55]

The central part of the Strategy refers to the pillars of BiH's foreign policy. Those pillars are the strategic directions and dynamic guidelines of the foreign policy of BiH within which the objectives of the Strategy shall be pursued. These pillars are, first 'security and stability', second 'economic prosperity', third the 'protection of the interest of BiH's nationals abroad and international legal cooperation' and fourth and finally the 'promotion of BiH in the world'.[56]

These pillars are intertwined and depend on one another. Thus, economic prosperity cannot be achieved without the security and stability of BiH, while the promotion of BiH in the world is not possible without the protection of BiH's interests and cooperation of BiH in international institutions.[57]

In addition, the importance of BiH's integration in EU and NATO, as well as dedication to values of the UN are highlighted.[58] Indeed, it can be said that

51 The Presidency of BiH, 'Foreign Policy Strategy 2018–2023', p. 2.
52 The Presidency of BiH, 'Foreign Policy Strategy 2018–2023', pp. 3–4.
53 The Presidency of BiH, 'Foreign Policy Strategy 2018–2023', p. 4.
54 The Presidency of BiH, 'Foreign Policy Strategy 2018–2023', p. 3.
55 The Presidency of BiH, 'Foreign Policy Strategy 2018–2023', p. 4.
56 The Presidency of BiH, 'Foreign Policy Strategy 2018–2023', pp. 5–13.
57 The Presidency of BiH, 'Foreign Policy Strategy 2018–2023', p. 5.
58 This was followed by the accusations by the then President of Republika Srpska Milorad Dodik (and current Serb member of the Presidency of BiH) towards the then Serb member of the Presidency Mladen Ivanić that, by accepting NATO integration provisions, he attempted to rebut the 2017 Resolution on the Protection of the Constitutional Order and the Proclamation of the Military Neutrality of Republika Srpska. The Resolution is available at: www.narodnaskupstinars.net/?q=la/akti/ostali-akti/rezolucija-o-zaštiti-ustavnog-poretka-i-proglašenju-vojne-neutralnosti-republike-srpske, accessed 21 April 2020.

from 1997 onwards,[59] all foreign relations policies of this country have been focused on BiH's membership in the EU, and anything done by the relevant actors in BiH is expected to be done with the EU integration as a primary goal in mind.[60]

There are both legal and political considerations associated with the compliance of Bosnian institutions and political actors with EU foreign policy declarations. Each country aspiring to become an EU member has committed itself to gradually align its policies and practices with the EU's foreign policy activities, which is demonstrated through the adoption of foreign policy declarations and the eventual implementation of the measures that may result from them. Therefore, the majority of agreements signed jointly between BiH and EU, as well as BiH acts passed after its decision on the accession to the EU, highlight the duty of an increasing convergence of positions of BiH with the EU.[61] In addition, this is important as it shows that BiH is trustworthy and can act in accordance with the obligations arising from concluded and accepted agreements as well as from any other obligation stemming from the European integration process.

However, the practice of the BiH institutions shows something different. Political actors in BiH work on the above-mentioned priorities and principles in only a declaratory fashion (and sometimes not even that). This has been emphasised by the European Commission, too.[62] For example, the Strategy highlights the membership in NATO as one of the BiH's priorities. However,

[59] In 1997, the EU Council of Ministers established political and economic requirements for the development of bilateral relations with BiH.

[60] The Strategy also emphasises that the foreign policy of BiH should work more intensely to achieve:
- More comprehensive and efficient participation in important international events;
- Promotion of tourism and business trips to Bosnia and Herzegovina;
- Promotion and capacity building of the 'country of origin' concept aimed at exporters of goods and services;
- Better and more comprehensive presentation in the international media;
- Usage of contemporary communication technologies for promotion of Bosnia and Herzegovina's values;
- Further enhancement of cultural relations with other states and regions.

(Cf. The Presidency of BiH, 'Foreign Policy Strategy 2018–2023', p. 13).

[61] See, e.g., the Foreign Policy Strategy itself, or Article 10(2) of the Stabilisation and Association Agreement Between the European Communities and their Member States, of the one part, and Bosnia and Herzegovina, of the other part, Luxembourg, 16 June 2008, in force 1 June 2015, http://dei.gov.ba/dei/bih_eu/sporazum/glavni_text/default.aspx?id=1172&langTag=en-US, accessed 21 April 2020.

[62] European Commission, Commission Staff Working Document, Bosnia and Herzegovina 2018 Report, Accompanying the document: Communication from the Commission to the European Parliament, the Council, the European Economic and Social Committee and the Committee of the Regions, 2018 Communication on EU Enlargement Policy, 17 April 2018, https://ec.europa.eu/neighbourhood-enlargement/sites/near/files/20180417-bosnia-and-herze

the current chairman of the Presidency of BiH Milorad Dodik almost daily declares that BiH membership in NATO is unacceptable.[63]

The second problem is that the three-member Presidency of BiH (as well as other BiH's institutions) do not share the same views on a number of domestic and international issues. This is a major obstacle for every decision that must be made in BiH. For example, BiH has not yet recognised Kosovo as an independent state due to the lack of unanimity within the Presidency of BiH. Namely, Serb members of the Presidency throughout the years have always opposed this recognition as their policies are usually in line with Serbia.[64] The Ministry of Foreign Affairs is united with them on this issue as well.[65] Their stance is determined by the stance of Republika Srpska, which is strongly opposed to the recognition of Kosovo.[66] BiH is therefore currently the

govina-report.pdf, accessed 21 April 2020, p. 3: 'Bosnia and Herzegovina's alignment with EU Common Foreign and Security Policy has yet to be improved'.

63 A significant amount of research confirms that BiH is not acting in accordance with what it has committed to. For example, in the period 2014–17, BiH did not support any of the more than 20 EU declarations related to Moscow's actions in Ukraine and cyber-attacks directed at the EU member states for which the EU accuses Russia (Denis Hadžović, 'Where is the Foreign Policy of Bosnia and Herzegovina Shaped?', Centre for Security Studies – BH, 7 February 2018, http://css.ba/press-release-where-is-the-foreign-policy-of-bosnia-and-herzegovina-shaped/, accessed 21 April 2020, p. 2.). Furthermore, between January 2018 and January 2019, in fourteen cases political actors in BiH did not join foreign policy positions or EU declarations directed against Russia's actions that endangered the sovereignty and territorial integrity of Ukraine and Georgia (S. Degirmendžić, 'The Conduct of Foreign Policy Shows the Pro-Russian Commitment of our Officials', *Avaz*, 7 April 2019, https://avaz.ba/vijesti/bih/473386/hadzovic-vodenje-vanjske-politike-pokazuje-prorusku-opredijeljenost-nasih-zvanicnika, accessed 21 April 2020). Given that many important political actors from Republika Srpska and the media they control are openly endorsing Russia against the EU, and taking into account slow progress made by BiH on its road towards EU accession, many civil society organisations in BiH claim that even after the adoption of the Strategy, the foreign policy of BiH is more in line with the pro-Russian than pro-European views.

64 For example, current Serb member of the Presidency Milorad Dodik has made threats even while he was a Prime Minister of Republika Srpska, stating that he will act on secession of Republika Srpska from BiH if Kosovo becomes independent (comparing the secession of Kosovo from Serbia with the potential secession of Republika Srpska from BiH).

65 Minister of Foreign Affairs (Bosnian Serb) highlighted that the issue of recognising Kosovo will not even be considered while he occupies the office and during the mandate of the current Council of Ministers. See Oslobođenje, 'Crnadak: No recognition of Kosovo or decision on MAP', 30 April 2019, www.oslobodjenje.ba/vijesti/bih/crnadak-nema-priznanja-kosova-niti-odluke-o-map-u-453466, accessed 21 April 2020.

66 In 2008, National Assembly of Republika Srpska even adopted a resolution denouncing the unilateral declaration of independence of Kosovo and declaring that, if a majority of EU and UN states recognise Kosovo's independence, it would consider it as a precedent and signal it could declare its own secession from BiH. This resolution also called upon all officials from Republika Srpska to prevent BiH from recognising Kosovo's independence. See Narodna skupština Republike Srpske, 'Rezolucija o nepriznavanju jednostrano proglašene nezavisnosti Kosova i Metohije i opredjeljenjima Republike Srpske', 22 February 2008, www.narodnaskupstinars.net

only country in the region other than Serbia that has not recognised Kosovo. This complicates not only the movement of people ('it is easier to get to London than to Priština') but also economic cooperation (e.g., in response, Kosovo at one point introduced 100 per cent Tariff on the import of goods from BiH).

The situation in BiH foreign affairs is nevertheless not all bad. From its independence onwards, BiH has presided over the UN Security Council and the Council of Europe, has been preparing applications for admission to memberships in NATO and EU, has contributed to international crisis management, peacekeeping and peace building missions worldwide, and has been solving its disputes with other states before international courts.[67] BiH has demonstrated that, even though it has been grappling with its own uniquely complex system of government, it has somehow succeeded in implementing some of its foreign policy goals. However, it is without question that BiH lacks an effective institutional apparatus and a clear strategy on foreign relations.[68]

IV THE ROLE OF THE PARLIAMENTARY ASSEMBLY OF BOSNIA AND HERZEGOVINA IN BOSNIAN FOREIGN RELATIONS LAW

The role of the PA in the foreign policy of BiH is not much emphasised in the Constitution or any of the BiH laws. Pursuant to the Constitution, foreign policy is a responsibility of the institutions of BiH,[69] more specifically of the Presidency. Thus, the Presidency is responsible for conducting the foreign policy of BiH, for appointing ambassadors and other international representatives of BiH, for representing this country in international and European organisations and institutions and for seeking membership in such organisations and institutions of which BiH is not a member.[70] Furthermore, the

/?q=la/akti/ostali-akti/rezolucija-o-nepriznavanju-jednostrano-proglašene-nezavisnosti-kosova-i-metohije-i-opredjeljenjima-republike-srpske, accessed 21 April 2020.

67 Hasić and Karabegović, *Bosnia and Herzegovina's Foreign Policy*, p. 3.

68 Hasić and Karabegović, *Bosnia and Herzegovina's Foreign Policy*, p. 4.

69 In contrast to matters that fall into the responsibilities of the Entities.

70 BiH Constitution, Article V(3)(a)–(c).

The Constitutional Court however emphasised that the PA has responsibility for enacting legislation as necessary to implement decisions of the Presidency in the area of foreign policy (see Constitutional Court of Bosnia and Herzegovina, Decision on Admissibility and Merits, U 9/07, 4 October 2008, paras. 16, 18 and 21, www.ustavnisud.ba/dokumenti/_bs/U-9-07-214754.pdf, accessed 13 July 2020, in English: www.ustavnisud.ba/dokumenti/_en/U-9-07-214754.pdf, accessed 13 July 2020).

Presidency is also responsible for negotiating, denouncing and ratifying treaties of BiH.[71] Finally, its competencies include coordination of the country with international and nongovernmental organisations in BiH.[72]

The Law on Ministries and Other Bodies of Administration of BiH details these issues further. It regulates that the Ministry of Foreign Affairs is responsible for the implementation of the foreign policy of BiH and development of BiH's international relations.[73] However, it sets out that this should be done in accordance with the positions and directions of the Presidency of BiH. What is more, the same Ministry is responsible for proposing the adoption of positions concerning the issues of interest for foreign policy activities and the international position of BiH, as well as for representing BiH in foreign relations, and carrying out the professional tasks in relation thereto.[74] Pursuant to the regulations set out in the same Law, the Ministry of Foreign Affairs is responsible for proposing to the Presidency of BiH the establishment and termination of diplomatic or consular relations with other states, the cooperation with international organisations, as well as the preparation and organisation of international meetings and agreements.[75] Moreover, its competencies also include preparing documents, analyses, information, and other materials serving the needs of the bodies competent for the foreign policy implementation.[76]

Nevertheless, for the reasons listed below, the role of the PA in the foreign policy of BiH is not insignificant.

Firstly, it has been highlighted that the Presidency is responsible for negotiating, denouncing, and ratifying treaties of BiH. However, it cannot do so without the consent of the PA.[77] This is confirmed by the Law on the Procedure of Concluding and the Execution of International Treaties.[78] Hence, even though the Law stipulates that international treaties on behalf of BiH are concluded by the Presidency of BiH,[79] the Presidency must, for the

[71] BiH Constitution, Article V(3)(d).

[72] BiH Constitution, Article V(3)(h).

[73] Law on Ministries and Other Bodies of Administration of BiH, Article 8 (available in English at: www.ohr.int/laws-of-bih/public-institutions/).

[74] Law on Ministries and Other Bodies of Administration of BiH, Article 8.

[75] Law on Ministries and Other Bodies of Administration of BiH, Article 8.

[76] Law on Ministries and Other Bodies of Administration of BiH, Article 8.

[77] BiH Constitution, Article V(3)(d).

The consent of the PA is published in the Official Gazette of BiH (see Council of Europe, Committee of Legal Advisers on Public International Law (CAHDI), Expression of Consent by States to be Bound by a Treaty, Analytical Report and Country Reports, 23 January 2001, https://rm.coe.int/168004ad95, accessed 11 July 2020, p. 226).

[78] Law on the Procedure of Concluding and the Execution of International Treaties, Articles 15–17.

[79] Law on the Procedure of Concluding and the Execution of International Treaties, Article 3(1).

purpose of obtaining the prior approval for ratification, submit the concluded international treaty to the PA. The Presidency should also submit a detailed explanation of the need and conditions for concluding a considered treaty.[80] Thus, the PA decides to give (or not) prior consent for the ratification of an international treaty, while the Presidency, upon obtaining that consent, decides on the ratification of an international treaty. Additionally, the Council of Ministers is responsible for implementing international treaties, and shall notify the Presidency and the PA about said implementation at least once a year.[81]

Secondly, even though the Presidency shall decide on the cancellation or withdrawal from an international treaty (either on its own initiative or at the proposal of the Council of Ministers), it cannot do so without the prior approval of the PA.[82]

Thirdly, it has been emphasised that the Ministry of Foreign Affairs is responsible for proposing the adoption of positions concerning the issues of interest for foreign policy activities and the international position of BiH, as well as for representing BiH in its foreign relations, and carrying out the professional tasks in relation thereto. However, it should report on these activities to, among others, the PA.[83]

The controlling role of the House of Representatives of the PA is also reflected in its authority to confirm the appointment of the Council of

80 Law on the Procedure of Concluding and the Execution of International Treaties, Article 15.

81 Law on the Procedure of Concluding and the Execution of International Treaties, Article 30.

The Law on the Procedure of Concluding and the Execution of International Treaties stipulates that the Council of Ministers of BiH is responsible for the execution of international treaties through the competent institutions of BiH and the Entities. International treaties which establish direct obligations for BiH are executed by the competent institutions of the state administration whose competence covers areas regulated by those treaties, while the treaties which are concluded by BiH, and which establish obligations for domestic legal persons, are directly executed by those legal persons.

There is however no explicit provision defining the rank of international treaties in domestic law or provision regulating the introduction of international treaties in domestic law as condition for their applicability. The Constitution also does not provide any clarification on the matter (see generally Constitutional Court of Bosnia and Herzegovina, Decision on Admissibility and Merits, U 5/09, 25 September 2009, www.ustavnisud.ba/dokumenti/_bs/U-5-09-290456.pdf, accessed 10 July 2020, in English: www.ustavnisud.ba/dokumenti/_en/U-5-0 9-290456.pdf, accessed 10 July 2020). The ratified and published international treaties are directly applicable and incorporated into domestic law by promulgation and publication in the Official Gazette of BiH (see Council of Europe, Expression of Consent by States to be Bound by a Treaty, pp. 225–7).

82 Law on the Procedure of Concluding and the Execution of International Treaties, Article 33(2).

83 Law on Ministries and Other Bodies of Administration of BiH, Article 8.

Ministers of BiH, to oversee and control its work, and to vote no confidence when deemed necessary.[84]

Furthermore, the House of Representatives has several Permanent Committees, including, among others, the Committee on Foreign Affairs.[85] Its jurisdiction is to monitor the conduct of foreign policy and to consider all issues in the field of international relations and foreign affairs.[86] This includes a role in adopting legislation in the field of foreign affairs.[87] This also includes engaging with the cooperation of BiH with international organisations and the international community, as well as inter-parliamentary cooperation with the respective parliamentary committees of other countries. In addition, the Committee considers granting and revoking consent to the ratification of international treaties, agreements and conventions.[88] The role of the Committee can also be important when it comes to the cancellation or withdrawal from an international treaty.[89] Therefore, perhaps the biggest influence of the PA on BiH's foreign policy may be made through the work of this Committee. Nevertheless, this influence will depend on its very members. In fact, some of its Chairs have done everything in their power to minimise the role of the Committee.[90] As a result, the internal division and complexity of BiH have its impact on the work of this Committee as well.[91] It seems as this Committee in BiH exists only formally. For example, the 2017 annual report of the Committee states that the Committee has held twelve sessions and adopted four conclusions. The average attendance of its members

84 See the responsibilities of the PA in Article IV(4) of the Constitution.

85 They are not defined in the Constitution but in *Poslovnik Predstavničkog doma Parlamentarne skupštine BiH* [Rules of Procedure of the House of Representatives], Official Gazette of BiH, 97/15.

86 Article 43 of Rules of Procedure of the House of Representatives.

87 The Rules of Procedure of the House of Representatives requires this Committee to be consulted 'for the purpose of obtaining its opinion on the principles on which the proposed law is based' (Articles 106 and 109). If the House does not accept opinion of the Committee, it must request that the Committee provides a new opinion (taking into account the debate conducted at the session of the House). This process can be repeated two times at most, after which the legislative procedure shall be suspended in case that the opinion is not adopted (see Articles 113 and 121).

88 For the full list of Committee's competencies see Article 45 of the Rules of Procedure of the House of Representatives of the PA.

89 In accordance with Article 139 of the Rules of Procedure of the House of Representatives, prior approval of the PA which is required in this regard means, among others, that the House of Representatives will have to seek the opinion of the competent committee on the matter.

90 The Secretary of the Committee on Foreign Affairs, personal communication, April 2019.

91 For example, it is not uncommon for Committee members to form a single-ethnic delegation when meeting with members of other countries' foreign affairs committees (Hasić and Karabegović, *Bosnia and Herzegovina's Foreign Policy*, p. 235).

to its sessions was 70 per cent, and the sessions lasted on average 39.5 minutes. Therefore, the members of the Committee spent only eight hours in a whole year working on their tasks. Moreover, in the same year, this Committee had a meeting only with the Committee on Foreign Affairs of the Parliament of Italy. If compared to the previous reports, it seems also that the work of the Committee is decreasing and becoming less influential.[92] Even though the Committee's dependence on the work of other state organs is one of the reasons of its lack of efficiency, one of the main reasons is certainly the reluctance of its members to use the competencies given to them in the realm of foreign relations. Therefore, the Committee on Foreign Affairs has never effectively scrutinised the actions of the executive and its work is without practical effect in shaping the BiH's foreign affairs.[93]

In conclusion, it is obvious that the PA has instruments to influence the foreign policy of BiH. Certainly, a function that is primarily linked to the PA *is* the legislative function.[94] However, in executing such a role the PA has ways to influence the foreign relations, too. Thus, the role of PA in this area is indirect but can be significant. I believe that this is primarily due to two explanations: first, the legislature may slow down the executive in the conduct of foreign policy (and thus should not have any bigger role in this area). Second, it is important to have a certain level of control of the executive in carrying out the functions entrusted to it (ensuring therefore that the PA has a system of checks and balances). Namely, the PA's size and probable non-expertise in foreign relations law are not practicable for foreign policies to be made by parliament directly. Members of the PA are not used to making and dealing with foreign policies. However, they are representatives of the people. On the contrary, the government and the ministries are used to working on foreign aspects and to doing so quickly. Since 'good

[92] For example, in 2016, the Committee held fifteen sessions and adopted two conclusions. The average attendance of Committee members to its sessions was 81.66 per cent, and the sessions lasted forty-one minutes on average. Further, the Committee considered and granted positive opinions for the ratification of sixty-three international treaties and had meetings with three foreign committees on foreign affairs. As regards the legislative activity, the Committee did not do activities proposed in the Work Plan because the draft laws did not enter the parliamentary procedure.

In 2015, the Committee held eighteen sessions and adopted eleven conclusions. The average attendance of Committee members to its sessions was 74 per cent, and the sessions lasted fifty minutes on average. Further, the Committee considered and granted positive opinions for the ratification of seventy-seven international treaties. Finally, in 2015, the Committee did not do activities proposed in the Work Plan either because the draft laws did not enter the parliamentary procedure.

[93] Similar in Hasić and Karabegović, *Bosnia and Herzegovina's Foreign Policy*, p. 235.

[94] BiH Constitution, Article IV(4).

scrutiny makes for good government',[95] the PA should and does have the means at its disposal to monitor the executive, to scrutinise its practice, and to keep it in appropriate bounds, ensuring both openness and efficiency. Its members should not be indifferent to issues of foreign relations. This does not mean they challenge executives but that they strengthen them.[96]

However, the PA is currently mostly interested in domestic politics and the ethnic divisions, which brings foreign relations barely in its focus. Its members were largely elected because of their nationalist sentiment and membership in a particular political party, allowing the ruling elites to capture the PA. Also, the peculiar relationship between the international community and the PA (as well as other national institutions) has consequences for BiH foreign relations law too. The power of the OHR to act in substitution for the domestic institutions makes it a very relevant actor in BiH foreign affairs. Moreover, while acting as domestic institution, the OHR places himself above the domestic legal system, making BiH a unique example in this regard. Even though the OHR acts only if the PA had failed to act, and although his actions are less frequent than before, the mere fact that he possesses these powers contributes to the erosion of the boundaries between the domestic and international domain. Consequently, BiH foreign relations law is developing in the various and quite special connection between international and domestic law.

V FOREIGN RELATIONS LAW AS A FIELD OF SCHOLARSHIP IN BOSNIA AND HERZEGOVINA

When it comes to the foreign relations law as a field of scholarship and research in BiH, it has been seen mostly as a part of the political and not legal scholarship. There have been virtually no scholars with exclusive and foremost expertise in this area. Most of the scholars have seen it as a part of some other, 'bigger' discipline, such as international relations or political science.

As far as law professors are concerned, international law professors and national law professors are partly isolated from each other, and they mostly teach one discipline or the other, although it is not uncommon that the same

95 Robin Cook, Leader of the House of Commons, 'Modernisation of the House of Commons: A Reform Programme for Consultation', December 2001, www.publications.parliament.uk/pa/cm200102/cmselect/cmmodern/440/44003.htm, accessed 21 April 2020.

96 Andrés Malamud and Stelios Stavridis, 'Parliaments and Parliamentarians as International Actors', in Bob Reinalda (ed.), *The Ashgate Research Companion to Non-State Actors* (Farnham: Ashgate, 2011), pp. 101–15 at 103.

professor teaches courses in both public international law and public law fields. In addition, curricula for the courses are generally separated from one another and provide little connection between the disciplines.[97] Therefore, most courses either do not touch upon foreign relations law at all, or only sporadically mention it (for example, Public International Law curricula and/ or Constitutional Law curricula). Thus, foreign relations law is taught scarcely and mostly within Public international law or/and Constitutional Law courses.

The state of affairs in BiH is comparable to other jurisdictions like China. As Congyan Cai explains with respect to Chinese foreign relations law,[98] few international lawyers at Chinese universities know constitutional law well and, vice versa, few constitutional law professors have much knowledge of international law.[99] Another similarity concerns the manner in which China and BiH conduct foreign relations; namely, the fact that political expediency is routinely invoked to justify the obscurity and low transparency in activities in foreign relations.[100] Finally, as in China, in BiH, there are two recent developments in foreign relation law that merit attention. The first concerns a recent important legislative initiative concerning foreign relations (explained earlier in this chapter). The second is related to the fact that recently this area began to grow in academic importance. Specifically, there has been an increase in the number of books and papers on the subject.[101] Also, there are growing numbers of faculties and special study programs with a particular focus on foreign relations.[102] Accordingly, it can be said that with the rise of BiH foreign relations, the interest for this topic is expanding

97 Unlike for example law schools in the United States, which have a more flexible structure that allows faculty to more easily cross historic subject matter divides. See the chapter by Curtis A. Bradley, p. 343.

98 Congyan Cai, 'Chinese Foreign Relations Law' (2017) 111 *AJIL Unbound* 336. See also Section II in JI Hua, 'China and Global Environmental Governance: Coordination, Distribution and Compliance', in this volume.

99 Cai, 'Chinese Foreign Relations Law', 336.

100 Cai, 'Chinese Foreign Relations Law', 336–7.

101 See, e.g., Hasić and Karabegović, *Bosnia and Herzegovina's Foreign Policy*; and Bernhard Stahl and Soeren Keil (eds.), *The Foreign Policies of Post-Yugoslav States: From Yugoslavia to Europe* (Basingstoke: Palgrave Macmillan, 2014).

102 See, e.g., the Faculty of Political Science and International Relations at the Sarajevo School of Science and Technology, the Faculty of International Relations and Diplomacy at the University of Herzegovina, or special study programs such as International and Public Relations at the International University of Sarajevo, International Relations and Diplomacy at the Faculty of Philosophy at the University of Tuzla, and Master's degree program in International Relations and Diplomacy at the American University in BiH.

as well. Yet, this still remains a largely unexplored research area in the legal discipline.

VI CONCLUSION

My main conclusion is that the impact of parliaments on foreign relations law depends on their role in a state and effective use of their competencies. Their means to impact the conduct of foreign relations become more diverse with the strengthening of their role in a state. Looking at the example of BiH, it seems that this impact can be seen mostly in the ratification of international treaties, in the use of committees on foreign affairs, and in the annual checks and reports. Nevertheless, the development of foreign relations law demands constant adaptation of methods of its implementation. I believe this competency should be used to a full extent as the increase in this practice can improve the quality and transparency of foreign affairs. However, both internal and external factors affect this effectiveness. Individual members of parliament (and its committee on foreign affairs) can also make a major contribution to this effectiveness. As a result, their personal views are vitally important.

This is especially true for BiH because its complicated internal system adds another layer of complexity to BiH foreign relations. Here, not only the political parties but also state institutions (as well as institutions on the substate level) are mainly organised along ethnic lines. With the general lack of trust between different ethnic groups, it is almost impossible to reach consensus on many questions. This makes BiH ineffective on a daily basis, including on foreign relations law. In this regard, a solution must be found to enact a constitution that institutes a legitimate form of government and guarantees the protection of all ethnic groups, while at the same time creating the shared political identity that transcends the dominant ethnic allegiances.[103]

However, Bosnia's extremely complex and multilevel system of state organisation is not the only feature that makes BiH special when it comes to foreign relations. Its constitutional structure also creates unique relationship between international and domestic sphere and has consequences for foreign relations law too. In particular, the OHR's powers make BiH dependent on foreign actors' decision-making process. The OHR can substitute himself for the national authorities, including the PA, and can even overrule the PA's decisions. This makes the boundaries between 'international' and 'domestic' more fluid and can greatly affect the foreign relations law as well.

103 Grewe and Riegner, 'Internationalized Constitutionalism in Ethnically Divided Societies', 4.

When it comes to foreign relations law in BiH, it is necessary to strengthen co-operation between the PA and the executive branch in the creation and implementation of foreign policy, as well as to strengthen the co-operation of the Committee on Foreign Affairs with parliamentary counterparts from other states. In addition, the importance of foreign relations law and major changes in the world order require an assessment of the effectiveness of the current system in achieving the goals set out in the 2018 Strategy. Currently, each and every conduct constituting relations of BiH with other countries is actually the result of improvisation arising from this general document. It is necessary to regulate this field by a more comprehensive act, which is also something that professional diplomats have been lobbying for since 2001.[104] It is also important to involve all relevant actors in drafting this act (from the academic community to business actors). This could reduce the possibilities for self-interested conduct of political parties in foreign policy, while leading to the development of foreign policy that is in the interest of BiH and its citizens.[105] It is therefore necessary to concretise the 2018 Strategy with clear directives for foreign affairs on the basis of the priority interests of BiH. The executive should remain the main figure in foreign relations law, but the scrutiny, guidance, and support of the PA must be enhanced. Otherwise, the potential of the PA will be wasted unnecessarily.

In conclusion, it is true that the traditional doctrine generally excludes parliaments from any role in the conduct of foreign affairs and that there are indeed practical benefits in seeing foreign relations as belonging only to the executive branch. However, the traditional approach seems much less persuasive today as it undermines the potential for national parliaments to engage in developing this field of law. The legislative branch can certainly add another layer of scrutiny and expertise to the foreign relations law. Therefore, the emphasis needs to be on the construction of more 'bridges' and the erection and shifting of fewer 'boundaries', respectively.

104 Davor Vuletić, 'Towards New Foreign Policy Strategy', p. 7.

105 Of course, discretion based on coordination and consensus is required in the conduct of foreign relations. However, when it comes to divided states such as BiH, more transparency is needed.

14

War, International Law and the Rise of Parliament

The Influence of International Law on UK Parliamentary Practice with Respect to the Use of Force

Veronika Fikfak

In foreign relations law, the power to wage war is inherently an executive power.[1] It is the government that declares war or sends the military forces into battle. Yet, increasingly, the prerogative to engage in military action has been open to scrutiny by domestic parliaments. This trend was first noted in 1990, when Lori Damrosch argued that there was a trend 'towards parliamentary control over the decision to introduce troops into situations of actual or potential hostilities'.[2] In relation to the Gulf War she noted a 'striking pattern of parliamentary approvals for decisions to commit military support, including votes in the US Congress, the French Assemblée nationale, and the Parliaments of Italy, Canada, Australia, the Netherlands, Greece, Turkey and Spain'.[3] Similarly, the NATO bombing against the then Federal Republic of Yugoslavia in 1999 triggered 'intensive parliamentary

[1] The latest in the series of reports, which affirm this position is: 'The Role of Parliament in the UK Constitution: Authorising the Use of Military Force', Report of the Public Administration and Constitutional Affairs Committee, 06 August 2019, www.parliament.uk/business/committees/committees-a-z/commons-select/public-administration-and-constitutional-affairs-committee/news-parliament-2017/parliament-military-force-report-published-17–19/, accessed on 30 September 2020. Prior reports are mentioned throughout this paper and include: Ministry of Justice, 'The Governance of Britain', Policy paper, CM 7170; Ministry of Justice, 'The Governance of Britain: War Power and treaties: Limiting Executive powers', CM 7239; Ministry of Justice, 'The Governance of Britain: Constitutional Renewal', White Paper, Cm 7342-I; Ministry of Justice, 'The Governance of Britain: Review of the Executive Royal Prerogative Powers: Final Report', October 2009; House of Lords, Constitution Committee, 'Constitutional arrangements for the use of armed force', 2nd Report 2013 – 14, HL Paper 46; and Joint Committee on Human Rights, 'The Government's policy on the use of drones for targeted killing', 2nd Report 2015 – 16, HC 574.

[2] Lori F. Damrosch, 'Is There a General Trend in Constitutional Democracies Toward Parliamentary Control over War-and-Peace Decisions?' (1996) 90 *ASIL Proceedings* 36, 36.

[3] Tom Ruys, Luca Ferro, Tim Haesebrouck, 'Parliamentary War Powers and the Role of International Law in Foreign Troop Deployment: Decisions the US-Led Coalition against

deliberations' in all participating states[4] as did the 2003 Iraq invasion.[5] In relation to both conflicts, the legality of intervention was highly disputed. Since then, the involvement of parliaments around the world has become a fait accompli. The Netherlands Constitution, for example, was revised to require the Government to inform Parliament prior to deployment of forces abroad,[6] the French Constitution also similarly strengthened the position of Parliament,[7] whilst other countries changed legislation to define the precise role of the legislature in the context of deployment of armed forces abroad.[8] In all of these cases, the role of Parliament has been strengthened so that it could provide *support* or *approval* for military action and for troops on the ground.[9] The votes in national parliaments provide legitimacy to the decisions made and give the impression that the Government was held to account by the people's representatives.[10] In some cases, for example when national parliaments had effectively vetoed the Government's plans for military actions,

"Islamic State" in Iraq and Syria' (2019) 17 *ICON* 118–50 citing Lori F. Damrosch, 'Democratization of Foreign Policy and International Law, 1914–2014' (2014) 21 *ILSA Journal of International and Comparative Law* 281, 287–8; see also Lori F. Damrosch, 'The Interface of National Constitutional Systems with International Law and Institutions on Using Military Forces: Changing Trends in Executive and Legislative Powers' in Charlotte Ku and Harold K. Jacobson (eds.), *Democratic Accountability and the Use of Force in International Law* (Cambridge: Cambridge University Press, 2003) 50; Michael Bothe and Andreas Fischer-Lescano, 'The Dimensions of Domestic Constitutional and Statutory Limits on the Use of Military Force' in Michael Bothe, Mary E. O'Connell and Natalino Ronzitti (eds.), *Redefining Sovereignty: The Use of Force after the Cold War* (Ardsley: Transnational Publishers, 2005) p. 203.

4 Bothe, Fischer, 'The Dimensions of Domestic Constitutional and Statutory Limits', p. 203.

5 Wolfgang Wagner, Dirk Peters and Cosima Glahn, 'Parliamentary War Powers Around the World, 1989–2004 A New Dataset' (2010) DCAF Occasional Papers No. 22, p. 25.

6 See Article 100, which was included anew into the Dutch Constitution, see: The Netherlands, Raad van State, *Rijkswet van 22 juni tot verandering in de Grondwet van de bepalingen inzake de verdediging*, 22 June 2000, Staatsblad van het Koninkrijk der Nederlanden, Jaargang 2000, p. 294.

7 France, Congrès, *Loi constitutionelle n° 2008–724 de modernisation des institutions de la Ve République*, 24 July 2008, Journal Officiel de la République Française, NOR: JUSX0807076L (amending Article 35 of the French Constitution of 28 September 1958, which before only provided for involvement of Parliament in cases of declaration of war).

8 German Parliamentary Participation Act: Germany, Bundestag, *Gesetz über die parlamentarische Beteiligung bei der Entscheidung bewaffneter Streitkräfte im Ausland*, 18 March 2005, Bundesgesetzblatt I, p. 775.

9 Philippe Lagassé, 'Parliament and the War Prerogative in the United Kingdom and Canada: Explaining Variations in Institutional Change and Legislative Control' (2017) 70 Parliamentary Affairs 280, 280.

10 Ruys, 'Parliamentary War Powers and the Role of International Law in Foreign Troop', 118; Damrosch, 'Democratization of Foreign Policy and International Law', 288 and 292; Louis Henkin, *How Nations Behave: Law and Foreign Policy*, 2nd ed. (New York: Columbia University Press, 1979) p. 64.

there is even talk of a quasi-sharing of powers between the Executive and the Legislature.[11]

In the context of the United Kingdom, these developments are captured in my recent monograph, *Parliament's Secret War* (co-authored with Hayley Hooper).[12] In the monograph, we contextualise the recent emergence of a constitutional convention, which requires that the House of Commons should have an opportunity to debate an intervention before troops are committed. The Convention, which was adopted in response to the Iraq invasion and recognised by subsequent Governments, has been hailed as historic and is said to represent a real shift in power from the Government to Parliament. In this context, the book makes a strong argument about how international institutions and international law more generally have facilitated this move: on one side, by failing to provide legal bases for interventions on the international level (e.g. Security Council) thus creating a lacuna for national legislatures to step in, and on the other side, by giving parliamentarians the necessary international law terminology on the basis of which they could assess the legality (and legitimacy) of the use of force. The book makes clear that 'international law' has influenced domestic parliamentary discourse in several ways.

This chapter presents the empirical evidence to support the arguments made in and serves as a precursor to *Parliament's Secret War*. Through discourse analysis, I seek to empirically trace how international law influences domestic parliamentary language. In this regard, I am interested in how members of Parliament understand and explain their role in the context of decisions to use force. I show how by merely looking at the debates in Parliament, one can conclude that after Iraq there has been a change in power-relations between the Government and Parliament. Tracing the terminology used by MPs, I reveal the decline of the term 'Government' and the rise of the reference to the 'House'. This terminology suggests a shift of focus (and perhaps power) from the Government to the House. The chapter maps out how this shift is mirrored in the increased relevance of international law and specifically the question surrounding the legality of the military intervention. It is this question – and particularly the experience of Iraq – that has reshaped the debates in the UK Parliament vis-à-vis the Government. When

[11] Veronika Fikfak and Hayley Hooper, *Parliament's Secret War* (Bloomsbury: Hart Publishing, 2018).

[12] Fikfak and Hooper, *Parliament's Secret War*; Some of the international law points are also previously made by Nigel White *Democracy goes to War* (Oxford: Oxford University Press, 2009). For the historical argument on the topic, see Rosara Joseph, *The War Prerogative: History, Reform, and Constitutional Design* (Oxford: Oxford University Press, 2013).

the legal basis is ambiguous, Parliament reaches for the 'international law' toolbox to assert its responsibility. The presence of 'international' concerns in parliamentary discourse then fluctuates depending on the clarity of the basis for the intervention. The investigation also reveals that as MPs become more and more involved and informed on issues of war, the deference shown to international institutions and their evaluation of the situation decreases. MPs appear to become more confident in referring to traditional international terms and more competent to make decisions about interventions themselves.

I WHO HAS POWER?

Prior to the Iraq war, the involvement of the House of Commons in debating a potential military intervention was limited. The House was traditionally engaged after the Government made its decision on intervention and more specifically, after the start of hostilities. According to Tony Blair, this tradition required that the Prime Minister make a statement in the House of Commons, followed by a question and answer session or a potential debate. Yet, these debates never ended in a vote, which would explicitly support or reject the military engagement. Instead, a procedural motion of adjournment was called, allowing the Government to preserve face even when seriously criticised.

In 2003, the questions surrounding the legality of the intervention in Iraq without an explicit Security Council Resolution triggered an important debate in the UK as to the role of the Westminster Parliament. In response to previous disputes, such as Suez and Kosovo, in which MPs were denied an opportunity to debate or have a meaningful vote, concerns were raised that 'The question of whether British troops are committed to action ought to require the dignity of a more meaningful procedure'.[13] In face of a strong revolt from Labour backbenchers and the resignation of Robin Cook, MPs were – for the first time – given an opportunity to vote *prior to the start of hostilities* about whether they supported the war or not.

The Iraq example could be an anomaly in an otherwise consistent practice of governments from both sides of the isle which had sidelined Parliament. Yet, the eventual discovery that no nuclear weapons existed, and the clear illegality of the invasion triggered a period of introspection in the UK.[14] A number of committees and inquiries debated the issue of the appropriate

[13] Robin Cook, *The Point of Departure* (London: Simon & Schuster Ltd, 2003) pp. 187–8.

[14] Andrew Blick, 'Emergency Powers and the Withering of the Royal Prerogative' (2014) 18 *The International Journal of Human Rights* 195–210.

role for Parliament on questions of military action. The reports (aptly called as *Taming the Prerogative* and *Governance of Britain*) underlined the need for the Government to be 'accountable to Parliament for the use of prerogative powers just as for things done under statutory or common law authority'.[15] The main complaints made against the traditional arrangements were that the Government was usually only 'accountable after the event'.[16] This allowed it to take decisions in a vacuum and escape accountability by providing a reason for intervention only when troops were already on the ground. By that point, most of the strategic decisions had already been taken and a step back from military action would be potentially embarrassing and dangerous for the troops. The involvement of Parliament only at this late stage – effectively as a confirmatory organ – greatly demeaned the House of Commons.[17] In this regard, the 2003 Iraq vote could not be treated only 'as an act of generosity by the Government for which we had to be grateful at the time'[18] but had set a precedent for the future.

As a consequence, by 2011 consensus had arisen around the position that 'any major military action should have explicit parliamentary approval'.[19] The Government acknowledged this in the Cabinet Manual by recognising a new 'convention ... that before troops were committed the House of Commons should have an opportunity to debate the matter and said that it proposed to observe that convention except when there was an emergency and such action would not be appropriate'.[20] This recognition of the role of Parliament in sending troops into battle redefines the relationship between the Government and the House of Commons. The convention puts the traditional arrangements under which the Government is the sole source of the deployment power under question and as a consequence, the old arrangements are no longer sufficient. If 'Parliament should be the source of Government's power', this requires a different role for the Commons.[21] In this context, the timing of

15 House of Commons Public Administration Select Committee, 'Taming the Prerogative: Strengthening Ministerial accountability to Parliament', 4th Report, 2003–04, HC 422, p. 8.

16 House of Commons Public Administration Select Committee, 'Taming the Prerogative', p. 8.

17 Hansard, HC, vol. 398, col. 373, 22 January 2003, Tam Dalyell.

18 House of Commons, 'Taming the Prerogative', [22], William Hague MP, later Foreign Secretary, who argued in favour of a statutory basis for parliamentary approval.

19 House of Commons, 'Taming the Prerogative', p. 8.

20 HM Government, *The Cabinet Manual: A guide to laws, conventions and rules on the operation of Government*, 1st ed. (London: The Stationary Office, 2011) [5.38]. House of Commons Political and Constitutional Reform Committee, 'Constitutional Implications of the Cabinet Manual', 6th Report of 2010–2011, HC 734, [61]; Andrew Blick, *The Codes of the Constitution* (Oxford: Hart Publishing, 2016).

21 House of Lords, Select Committee on Constitution, 'Waging War Parliament's role and responsibility', 15th Report, 2005–06, [43] and S Payne, vol. II: Evidence, 17.

its involvement is key – the Commons has to be involved *prior* to deployment. In this case, the debate and vote can serve to question the Government about its decision and strategy and Parliament can ultimately provide approval for the exercise of the deployment power. The whole issue can 'be better scrutinised, better thought through, better prepared and the decision would be better made'.[22]

Since the Manual's publication in 2011, the House of Commons has been given the opportunity to debate military deployments in relation to Syria, against Islamic State (IS) in Iraq and most recently against IS in Syria. Instead of voting on procedural motions, these are now put as substantive questions of support and approval of governmental actions. Today, MPs could argue that the practice of putting the question to the House on a substantive motion has developed into a binding convention, which requires the House's involvement every time the Government contemplates military action.[23] Although the timing of this debate and vote is still inconsistent (sometimes *prior*, other *after* the fact), the substantive involvement suggests a fundamental shift in the role of Parliament.

This story of the birth of the constitutional convention and the role and responsibility of the House of Commons in the context of decisions to use force can also be traced in the choice of terminology used by MPs in debates of the House. Nine debates are mapped out on the graph below – from Korea 1950, to Suez 1956, Gulf 1991, Kosovo 1999, Iraq 2003, Libya 2011, Syria 2013, ISIL in Iraq 2015 and Syria 2018.[24] The picture reveals a clear story of the *decrease* in the (linguistic) relevance of 'Government', eclipsed by an *increase* in the

[22] House of Lords, Select Committee on Constitution, 'Waging War' Evidence, 17, citing Clare Short.

[23] On constitutional conventions: John A. G. Griffith, 'The Political Constitution' (1979) 42 *Modern Law Review* 1; David Feldman, 'Constitutional Conventions' in Matt Qvortrup (ed.), *The British Constitution: Continuity and Change and the Influence on Europe – A Festschrift for Vernon Bogdanor* (Oxford: Hart Publishing, 2013) 94, 94; A Tomkins, 'In Defence of the Political Constitution' (2002) 22 *Oxford Journal of Legal Studies* 157–75 and Graham Gee and Grégoire C. N. Weber, 'What Is a Political Constitution?' (2010) 30 *Oxford Journal of Legal Studies* 273–99; Joint Committee on Conventions, 'Conventions of the UK Parliament', HL 265-I (2006).

[24] I employ a basic frequency analysis, which counts the number of times a certain word appears in the text analysed, followed by a word-in-context analysis. I also look at the relative importance of the words studied, taking into account how long the debate was (e.g. how many terms appear in it and how frequently). In total, I analyse nine debates on the use of military force: Hansard, HC, vol. 477, col. 485–596, 05 July 1950, (Korea); Hansard, HC, vol. 558, col. 2–149, 12 September 1956 (Suez); Hansard, HC, vol. 183, col. 734–826, 15 January 1991 (Gulf); Hansard, HC, vol. 329, col. 573–668, 19 April 1999 (Kosovo); Hansard, HC., vol. 401, col. 760–858, 18 March 2003 (Iraq); Hansard, HC, vol. 525, col. 700–807, 21 Mar 2011 (Libya); Hansard, HC, vol. 566, col. 1425 ff. 29 Aug 2013 (Syria 2013); Hansard, HC, vol. 603, col.

relevance of 'the House'. After the experience of Iraq in 2003, the importance of the House of Commons can be visible as a slight bump on the graph. A further and considerable increase in the relevance of the 'House' can be seen in the context of the 2013 vote in which MPs vetoed the proposed intervention of the Government in Syria against Assad, a day labelled as a 'historic night' and 'a victory for Parliament'.[25] After this defeat of the Government's motion to deploy troops to Syria, commentators even argued that the decision of Prime Minister Cameron to comply with the vote in the House suggests the so-called 'consultation' convention has solidified into a binding constitutional convention regulating relationship between two institutions of the constitution and that as a consequence Westminster Parliament had acquired a type of veto-power over decisions on military action.[26] This, however, appears to have been the peak of Parliament's power. Since then, subsequent governments (under Theresa May) appear to have taken a step back and the extent of power that Parliament has over these issues remains unclear.[27] This fluidity is visible on Figure 14.1 as references to 'the House' decrease after 2013.

The terms 'House' and 'Government' cannot be seen in isolation from what they require: The growing reference to the 'House of Commons', for example, is mirrored by the relevance of the terms such as 'responsibility' and 'duty' to refer to MPs' role, as well as the appearance of the terms 'constitutional convention',[28] all of which become more widely used after 2003. For example, although MPs

323–501, 02 December 2015; Hansard, HC, vol. 639, col. 39 ff., 16 April 2018: https://hansard.parliament.uk/commons/2018–04-16/debates/92610F86-2B91-4105-AE8B-78D018453D1B/Syria, accessed on 30 September 2020. More generally on frequency textual analysis, see Martin Weisser, 'Basic Frequency Analysis – or What Can (Single) Words Tell Us About Texts?' in Martin Weisser (ed.), *Practical Corpus Linguistics: An Introduction to Corpus-Based Language Analysis* (Bridgewater: Wiley, 2015) p. 146. Textual analysis is increasingly used in law: Jack G. Conrad and L. Karl Branting, 'Introduction to the Special Issue on Legal Text Analytics' (2018) 26 *Artificial Intelligence Law* 99–102.

25 Tim Stanley, 'Syria Vote: This Historic Night Was a Humiliation for David Cameron But a Victory for Parliament', *The Telegraph* (29 August 2013); Robert Hutton and Thomas Penny, 'Historic Vote Sees Cameron Defeated by Lawmakers on Syria', *Bloomberg Online* (20 August 2013); James Hallwood, 'The Syria Vote Was a Triumph of Parliamentary Sovereignty' *New Statesman* (30 August 2013).

26 Gavin Phillipson, '"Historic" Commons Syria Vote: the Constitutional Significance (Part I)', *UK Constitutional Law Association blog* (19 September 2013), https://ukconstitutionallaw.org/2013/09/19/gavin-phillipson-historic-commons-syria-vote-the-constitutional-significance-part-i/, accessed on 30 September 2020.

27 Veronika Fikfak and Hayley J. Hooper, 'Whither the War Powers Convention? What Next for Parliamentary Control of Armed Conflict after Syria?', *UK. Const. L. Blog* (20 April 2018), https://ukconstitutionallaw.org/, accessed 30 September 2020.

28 This is not shown on the graph but the line overlaps with 'responsibility'.

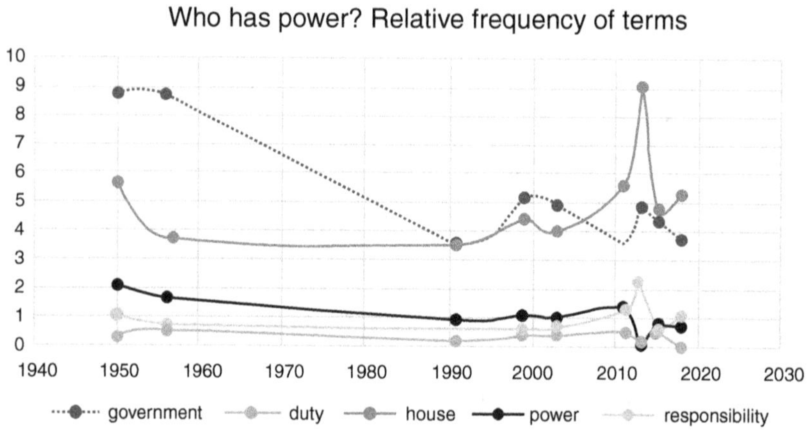

FIGURE 14.1 Who has power? Relative frequency of terms

initially had no 'legal or constitutional right to decide the matters [of military deployment]', they had a 'duty to represent the people'.[29] In contrast, after 2011 MPs insist that 'the new convention places a *responsibility* on Members of Parliament to weigh up the arguments and vote according to their conscience'.[30] 'Being a Member of Parliament is a great honour, but it carries *responsibility*: the responsibility for deciding whether one agrees with the Government of the day'.[31] If before the focus was on helping and supporting Government, now this new responsibility requires parliamentarians to hold the Government to account. If military intervention will be waged with the approval of Parliament, then 'with deeper engagement comes greater responsibility',[32] a responsibility, which MPs cannot abdicate.

The convention therefore not only appears to shift the discourse about the power from the Government to Parliament, it also very clearly changes how MPs perceive their own function.

II THE ROLE OF INTERNATIONAL LAW IN DOMESTIC PARLIAMENTARY DISCOURSE

When the constitutional convention was emerging, the most frequently asserted reason for its birth and recognition was the idea of increasing the

[29] Hansard, HC, vol. 177, col. 774–5, 6 September 1990 (Tony Benn).
[30] Hansard, HC, vol. 603, col. 367, 2 December 2015, Alan Johnson, emphasis added.
[31] Hansard, HC, vol. 329, col. 609, 19 April 1999, Tony Benn, emphasis added.
[32] Hansard, HC, vol. 639, col. 8, 16 April 2018, Jo Swinson, emphasis added.

accountability of the Government to the House.[33] The aim was therefore to democratize the prerogative power. Yet, in *Parliament's Secret War*, we put forward a different argument – one that questions whether the idea of accountability was the main driving force in the recognition of the convention. Instead, we argue that the consistent failure of the Security Council to act and support military action in certain conflicts, created a 'lacuna', which 'could be filled by domestic legislatures'.[34] The failure of the international community to provide authorisation for action in the context of Kosovo, Iraq, Syria and Yemen, etc., had prompted subsequent governments to turn inwards and look to their own parliaments to provide legitimacy for their action. The developments on the international sphere have therefore triggered a 'domestication' of decision-making.[35] In the UK, this has placed Westminster Parliament centre stage and has made MPs primary decision-makers on decisions to use force.[36]

The shift of decision-making from the international sphere to the domestic, however, 'has not resulted in a more domestically focused discourse. Instead, the discussions in the House have focused precisely on those questions which the international community should have resolved – questions of the legality of the use of force'.[37] In many ways, Westminster Parliament appears to be carrying out similar functions as the Security Council – for example, testing whether there is enough basis to support military action proposed by their Government.

33 Charlotte Ku, Harold K. Jacobson, *Democratic Accountability and the Use of Force in International Law*; Hans Born, H Hanggi, 'The Use of Force under International Auspices: Strengthening Parliamentary Accountability', DCAF, Policy Paper No 7, 2005.

34 Fikfak, Hooper, *Parliament's Secret War*, p. 52. See also James Strong, 'The Accidental Prerogative: Why Parliament Now Decides on War' (2015) 17 *British Journal of Politics and International Relations* 604 ff.; Julian Borger and Bastien Inzaurralde, 'Russian Vetoes Hurt UN Security Council's Legitimacy, says US', *The Guardian* (23 September 2015), www.theguardian.com/world/2015/sep/23/russian-vetoes-putting-un-security-council-legitimacy-at-risk-says-us, accessed 30 September 2020.

35 Jean Galbraith and Curtis Bradley, 'Presidential War Powers as an Interactive Dynamic: International Law, Domestic Law, and Practice-Based Legal Change' (2016) 92 *NYU. L. Rev.* 689 at 689; the 'domestication' of course allows for unilateral interventions: Colin R. G. Murray and Aoife O'Donoghue, 'Towards Unilateralism? House of Commons Oversight of the Use of Force' (2016) 65 *International and Comparative Law Quarterly* 305–41; Nico Krisch, 'Unilateral Enforcement of the Collective Will: Kosovo, Iraq, and the Security Council' (1999) 3 *Max Planck Yearbook of United Nations Law* 59–103.

36 Note, for example, how President Obama drops the planned intervention in Syria in 2013, after Westminster Parliament fails to support Cameron's motion for military action; See film by Greg Barker, *The Final Year* (HBO, 2017); Kenneth R. Mayer, 'Executive Power in the Obama Administration and the Decision to Seek Congressional Authorization for a Military Attack against Syria: Implications for Theories of Unilateral Action' (2014) *Utah Law Review* 821 ff.

37 Fikfak, Hooper, *Parliament's Secret War*, p. 48.

This can be clearly seen in the graph below.[38] Looking at the different disputes of the last seventy years, it is clear that those which have a clear international authorisation (Gulf War and Korea),[39] raise little if any concerns about international law. For example, in relation to Korea, MPs talk about the 'authority of international law' and the need for Britain to 'act up to [its] supreme international obligations'.[40] In these cases, the additional support and legitimacy that a national parliament could provide to an already authorised international action is minimal and MPs therefore appear not to be too concerned or worried about international norms. References to 'international' law are minimal.[41]

In contrast, the peaks of debate about international law can be seen clearly (on Figure 14.2) in cases where the international basis for the intervention is unclear or ambiguous: after Iraq 2003, most references to international law are made in the context of the 2013 Syria debate and in 2018. However, the most visible peak of concern about 'international' legality of military action can be seen in relation to the 1956 Suez crisis, in which Britain helped Israel and France in the nationalization of the Suez Canal. The action was condemned by the international community, but the Security Council failed to condemn the nationalisation due to France and Britain's veto.[42] In the Suez debate, which followed in the House, there were 302 references to 'international' law. Later, in 2003, Iraq generated 98 references.

Developments on the international level have therefore created *space* for domestic parliaments, but they have also – at least indirectly – imposed a responsibility on MPs to not allow themselves to be used strategically in a manner that enables the Government to fill the void at international law level. As the Constitutional Committee in its *Waging War Report* found:

> Given the absence of legal restraint on the deployment power under domestic law, the rules of international law on the use of force take on an enhanced significance as the only apparent limitation on the prerogative. Domestic legality does not pre-empt international law. In other words,

38 Note also the change in how the intervention is referred to. The term war appears to be limited to situations in which ground troops are sent into battle. This is different when airstrikes are debated – there the terminology turns to 'action'.

39 SC Resolution 82 (1950) and SC Resolution 660 (1990), followed by SC Resolution 661 (1990) imposing economic sanctions, and SC Resolution 665 (1990) authorizing naval blockade to enforce embargo against Iraq.

40 Hansard, HC, vol. 477, col. 493, 5 July 1950 (Attlee).

41 These generate the fewest absolute references to 'international law' and 'international': e.g. twenty-eight and seventy-one.

42 Vetoes used on 30 October 1956 at Security Council meetings nos. 749 and 750.

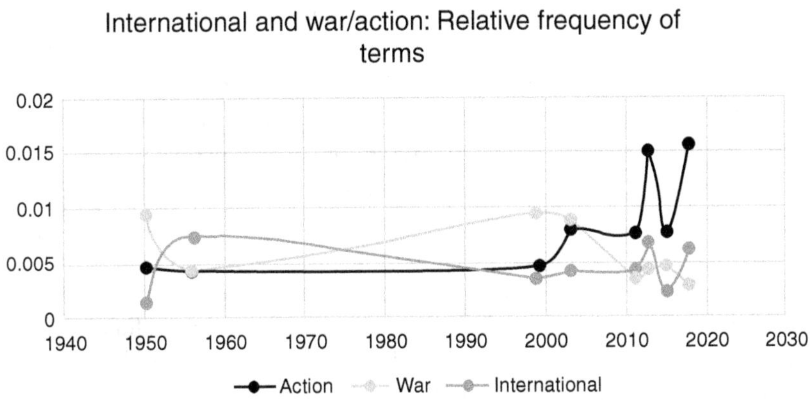

FIGURE 14.2 International and war/action: relative frequency of terms

> action, which may not be unlawful under domestic law, could be in violation of international law.[43]

In fact, looking closely at debates, international law appears to provide MPs with the framework and language with which they can carry out their functions. In Suez, for example, MPs underlined that the UK as a member of the United Nations had 'steadfastly avoided any international action which would be in breach of international law or, indeed, contrary to the public opinion of the world. We must not, therefore, allow ourselves to get into a position where we might be denounced in the Security Council as aggressors, or where the majority of the Assembly were against us.'[44] Others equally recognized what was at stake: 'are we to live under a regime of international anarchy or international law? … We all recognise that [the Charter] has its limitations. … But nevertheless it has sufficient authority for one to say that no action that we take … should be in derogation of the Charter, much less in contradiction of it'.[45]

In Iraq, when debating potential military action, MPs objected that 'The action against Iraq is, I believe, pre-emptive, and therefore demands even greater international support and consensus than other sorts of intervention. We do not have it. Such isolation entails a genuine cost and danger. It undermines the legitimacy that we must maintain to tackle the many threats to global security'.[46]

43 House of Lords, Select Committee on Constitution, 'Waging War' Evidence, 17, p. 15.
44 Hansard, HC, vol. 558, col. 19, 12 September 1956, Hugh Gaitskell.
45 Hansard, HC, vol. 558, col. 114, 12 September 1956, J. E. S. Simon.
46 Hansard, HC, vol. 401, col. 798, 18 March 2003, John Denham.

These concerns run through the debates that seek to fill the void left by unauthorised, unilateral military interventions. In fact, MPs appear to have internalised international concerns about the legality of the proposed action and worry about how they will be perceived by the international community.[47] For this reason, when the Government makes its case to MPs, it does so in a similar manner as it would before the United Nations – by referring to the Charter and presenting the intervention as 'necessary' and 'proportionate'. In turn, MPs – in effect invited to step into the shoes of the Security Council and support the use of force – pick up on this *international* language of 'necessity' and 'proportionality' and use the same terminology to assess and evaluate the legitimacy of the proposed military intervention. The graphs below show clearly how in the debates of the Commons the use of the terms 'necessary' and 'proportionate' – to refer to the appropriate extent and scope of the use of force – have skyrocketed since the Iraq War.[48] Before 2004, MPs barely made use of this terminology to discuss the use of military action (bar the blatant exception of Suez). Even in relation to the Falklands Islands, where the intervention was defined as one of self-defence, the necessity and proportionality were not high on the agenda. After 2004, both terms 'necessary' and 'proportionate' feature prominently as seen in Figure 14.3 (e.g. in the context of debates concerning Libya 2011 – 'necessary', Syria 2013 – 'proportionate', Syria 2015 – both).

The graphs in this section portray the lessons from Iraq clearly: since 2004, MPs regularly require that the Government seek a legal opinion about potential military action and make a clear case as to the legality of the intervention.[49] But their expectations do not stop there – an assessment of proportionality of the action is also expected and MPs themselves will query this element of the

[47] The idea of internalisation of international norms into domestic sphere is best made by H. Koh, 'Transnational Legal Process' (1996) 75 *Neb. L. Rev.* 181; Compare for example the efforts to internalise international norms through domestic courts: Veronika Fikfak, 'English Courts and the "Internalisation" of the European Convention on Human Rights – Between Theory and Practice' (2013–14) 5 *Cambridge Journal of International and Comparative Law – The UK Supreme Court Yearbook* (2015) 183–214; ' International Law Before English and Asian Courts: Finding the Judicial Role in the Separation of Powers' (2013) 3(2) *Asian Journal of International Law* 271–304.

[48] Though note the variations in the use of the term 'necessary': aside from Suez, the peaks appear to be consistent with internationally authorised actions (Libya and ISIS in Iraq). On who gets to define meaning to terms, see Benedict Burnett and Veronika Fikfak, 'Domestic Courts' Reading of International Norms: A Semiotic Analysis' (2009) *Int J Semiot Law* 22, Art. no. 437 and Veronika Fikfak, 'Judicial Strategies and their Impact on the Development of the International Rule of Law' in Machiko Kanetake and André Nollkaemper, *The Rule of Law at the National and International Levels* (Bloomsbury: Hart Publishing, 2016) p. 45.

[49] Hansard, HC, vol. 566, col. 1426, 29 August 2013, Caroline Lucas asking about why only two paragraphs of Attorney General's opinion in relation to Syria 2013 were published.

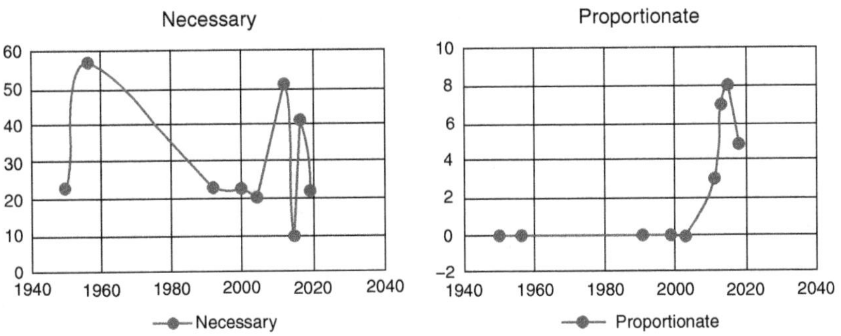

FIGURE 14.3 Use of terms ‘necessary’ and ‘proportionate’

intervention throughout the debate. The ‘proportionality’ graph shows beautifully how before 2003, no assessment of proportionality took place in the Commons. Since then, however, MPs are not only informed about what international law requires but also concerned that the country complies with its requirements.

It is clear from what has been said that whilst international concerns have always been at the heart of debates in Parliament (partly due to the international nature of war), with the birth of the War Powers Convention after 2003, interest in international law has steadily increased, driven by the need for accountability. This need was more pronounced in situations where military intervention had no clear authorisation from the Security Council, that is, in the case of Syria 2013 and airstrikes in Syria in 2018. The graph below shows clearly how the enhanced involvement of the ‘House’ (and the power associated with it) and the need to hold the Executive to account for the proposed ‘action’ directly correlates with the House’s attention to ‘international’ concerns. Since 2003, when the Pandora’s box for enhanced parliamentary involvement was opened, the three lines (and seen on Figure 14.4) appear to move almost in parallel. The strong link between the ‘international’ and the power and relevance of the ‘House’ is therefore clear.

III THE IMPLICATIONS FOR INTERNATIONAL LAW

Governments have turned to domestic parliaments strategically, inviting them to fill the lacuna left by the international community (e.g. Security Council). MPs appear to have accepted this challenge and have become increasingly more confident and more competent to discuss the use of military action in terms usually preserved for the Security Council. The question however arises

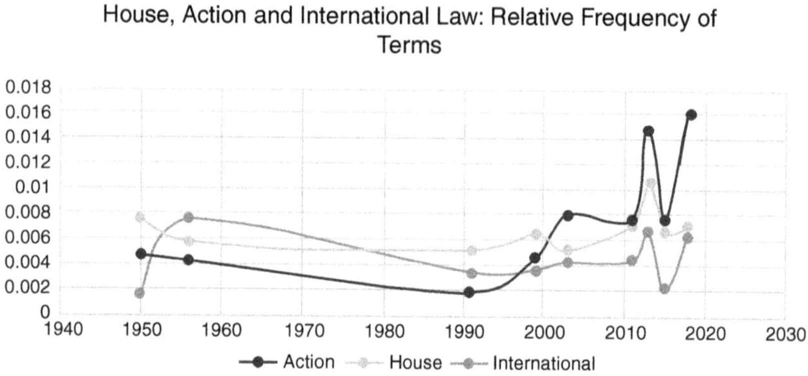

FIGURE 14.4 House, action and international law: relative frequency of terms

as to whether the new role of the Commons has – at least internally – increased or decreased the relevance of the United Nations and the Security Council. And what does Westminster Parliament's decision to act instead of the Security Council mean for the international community and for international law?

From the view of debates in Parliament, it is clear that references to the 'United Nations' have importantly decreased. If in Korea, Suez and during the Gulf war, the United Nations was in the forefront of MPs minds, this is no longer the case. Since 2011, when the War Powers Convention was officially recognised and the position of the Commons solidified in relation to decisions to use force, these references have fallen even further. A similar trend can be seen in relation to the 'Security Council'. Whilst references to the Council have remained steady throughout the sixty years, since 2011 there has been a steep drop in their appearance in debates in the House (as seen in Figure 14.5). It is this drop which is perhaps the most remarkable: once the issue of the use of military action is 'domesticated' through the War Powers Convention, references to the UN, the Security Council and even the 'international community' become so rare that regardless of whether the use of force is authorised or not, these external bodies/audiences appear to become less relevant in the domestic debate.[50] As the position of the Commons to have a say on the matter is solidified and MPs

50 Tony Blair, 'Doctrine of the International Community' Speech in Economic Club (Chicago, 24 April 1999), http://webarchive.nationalarchives.gov.uk/+/www.number10.gov.uk/Page1297, accessed 30 September 2020; more generally on the disappearance of the international community: Georges Abi Saab, 'Whither the International Community' (1998) 9 *EJIL* 248–65; Sean D. Murphy, 'The Doctrine of Pre-emptive Self-Defence' (2005) 50 *Villanova Law Review* 699–748; W. Michael Reisman, 'Unilateral Actions and the Transformations of

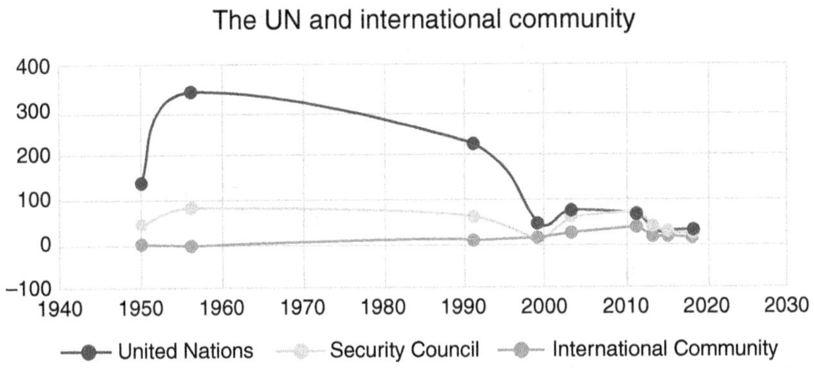

FIGURE 14.5 The UN and international community

become more involved and informed on issues of war, the deference shown to international institutions and their evaluation of the situation decreases.

This is confirmed by the most recent 2019 report of the Public Administration and Constitutional Affairs Committee, which investigates the role of Westminster Parliament in debates to authorise the use of military force. The aim of the report is to explore the scope of the War Powers Convention and the role of Parliament vis-à-vis the Government after the Iraq, Libya and Syria 2013, 2015 and 2018 experiences. Although the report mentions the UN Charter (once and in footnotes!), it does not refer to the United Nations, the Security Council or the international community.[51] Even more, the term 'international law' does not appear in the report.[52] The document is therefore clearly concerned to situate Parliament in the domestic sphere, rather than define its role vis-à-vis international institutions or the international community. In the domestic sphere, Parliament can claim to have a say in authorising military action, or as some commentators asserted even a 'de facto veto power',[53] but its role – which emerged due to a lacuna created by the international community – does not remain inextricably linked to the international sphere. Although international terminology may be used

the World Constitutive Process: The Special Problem of Humanitarian Intervention' (2000) 11 *EJIL* 3–18.

51 'Role of Parliament' Report, which refers to the National Security Council, para. [72].

52 There are some references to international coalitions, audiences and once even to obligations. 'Role of Parliament' Report, paras. [19], [85] and footnote 48.

53 'Role of Parliament' Report, S Payne in para. [44].

by Parliament to assess the legal basis for an intervention, international actors do not appear to feature in Hansard debates.

The shift of decision-making from the international sphere to the domestic has important implications for international law. The sidelining of international institutions not only as fora of decision-making but as fora with expertise in international law signposts a move towards unilateralism and isolationism.[54] As Murray and O'Donoghue put it:

> We challenge the underlying assumption that Parliament's interventions mark an indisputably positive development in constraining the use of force. When coupled with the focus upon the doctrine of humanitarian intervention which has accompanied many controversial exercises of UK military force since the end of the Cold War, the involvement of Parliament in the decision-making process risks hollowing out UN Charter safeguards. … Relying upon domestic assemblies to provide the sole necessary authorization point for certain uses of force might appear to offer a means to unblock international institutional processes – but this course turns away from international constraints upon the use of force and opens the door to new forms of unilateralism.[55]

Murray and O'Donoghue for example show that in the domestic legislatures claims to self-defence have been stretched far beyond what international law envisages, to include collective self-defence in relation to Afghanistan, situations of pre-emptive self-defence, and targeted killings.[56] Similarly, *Parliament's Secret War* maps out how multiple legal bases are being used by the Government before UK Parliament to make claims about the legality of military action, even though international law excludes accumulation of such arguments (e.g. self-defence versus authorised action).[57] Both of these practices 'complicate the question of whether a use of force complies with

54 Reisman, 'Unilateral Actions and the Transformations of the World Constitutive Process', p. 12; Kenneth R. Mayer, 'Executive Power in the Obama Administration and the Decision to Seek Congressional Authorization for a Military Attack against Syria: Implications for Theories of Unilateral Action' [2014] *Utah Law Review* 821 at 821; Harold Hongju Koh, 'Syria and the Law of Humanitarian Intervention Part II: International Law and the Way Forward' *Just Security* (2 October 2013), http://justsecurity.org/2013/10/02/koh-syria-part2, accessed 30 September 2020; Carsten Stahn, 'Between Law-Breaking and Law-Making: Syria, Humanitarian Intervention and "What the Law Ought to Be"' (2014) 19 *J. CSL* 25 at 46.

55 Murray and O'Donoghue, 'Towards Unilateralism?', pp. 305 and 341.

56 Hansard, HC, vol. 599, col. 26, 7 September 2015 (Cameron).

57 Fikfak and Hooper, *Parliament's Secret War*, p. 61, which links the issue to one of expertise: see pp. 58 ff. More generally, on the interaction between international and domestic levels and 'who knows best', see Veronika Fikfak, 'Kadi and the Role of the Court of Justice of the European Union in the International Legal Order' (2013) 15 *Cambridge Yearbook of European Legal Studies* 587–617.

international law'.[58] On international level, such claims would not be (or indeed are not successful) since the UK cannot control action of other States, yet domestically they succeed because the legislature is 'more susceptible to executive influence'.[59] This is especially true in the UK, where due to the fusion of power between Government and Parliament and the control the former enjoys in the Commons, its decisions are regularly upheld by the House.[60]

Ultimately, the victim of the process of 'domesticating decisions on military action has been international law, and in particular the UN Charter. By acting instead of the UN and by using international law language, governments have sought to sideline the international community and invited parliamentarians to aid them in redefining what is legally permissible'.[61] These examples have contributed to the development of customary international law on the use of force, which lives in parallel to and competes with the UN Charter. In this regard, as Hans Blix has commented, national governments – supported by their own legislatures – have become 'global policemen', acting without or even contrary to UN mandate, writing their own rules for the use of force.[62] Such unilateralism undermines the original basic tenets of the Charter, undermines the international institutions that are responsible for its enforcement, and ultimately leads to fragmentation of international law.

IV CONCLUSION

This chapter traces the influence of international law on the birth of the consultation convention, which has allowed the UK Parliament to be increasingly involved on questions of war. Through discourse analysis, it shows how the way in which members of Parliament understand and explain their role in the context of decisions to use force changed, especially after Iraq. Tracing the terminology used by MPs, I reveal the decline of the term 'Government' and the rise of the reference to the 'House'. MPs speak of their own 'duty' and 'responsibility' to weigh up arguments on the use of force and hold the

58 Murray and O'Donoghue, 'Towards Unilateralism?', p. 307.

59 Murray and O'Donoghue, 'Towards Unilateralism?', p. 305.

60 Walter Bagehot, *The English Constitution* (Oxford: Oxford University Press, 2009) p. 11; O. Hood Phillips 'A Constitutional Myth: Separation of Powers' (1977) 93 *LQR* 11–13; Stanley Alexander De Smith, 'The Separation of Powers in New Dress' (1966–67) 12 *McGill Law Journal* 491–6. The debates on Brexit are really the rare anomaly in the history of the Commons, but are reflective of a deep division in the Commons and around the country.

61 Fikfak and Hooper, *Parliament's Secret War*, p. 64, slightly reworded.

62 Hansard, HC, vol. 566, col. 1464, 29 August 2013 (Llwyd).

Government to account. This shift in terminology is mirrored in the increased relevance of international law and specifically the question surrounding the legality of the military intervention. The presence of 'international' concerns in parliamentary discourse fluctuates depending on the clarity of the basis for the intervention. When the legal basis is ambiguous, Parliament reaches for the 'international law' terms like 'necessity' and 'proportionality' to assert its responsibility and hold the Government to account. The importance of international law, however, is not limited to the 'borrowing' of the international law toolbox. Indeed, the failure of international institutions to provide legal bases for interventions in cases like Kosovo, Iraq, Syria and Yemen, has created room for national parliaments to be involved on these questions in the first place. But as questions on the use of force are 'brought home' and 'domesticated', this has not led to a reinforced relevance of the international community or its institutions. The investigation for example reveals that as MPs become more informed and confident to discuss issues of war, the deference shown to international institutions and their evaluation of the situation decreases. References to the 'United Nations' and the 'Security Council' disappear from Hansard debates. Even more, the Government is able to persuade MPs about the legality of the use of force in ways that would not be acceptable at international level. These examples show how increasingly international law is being developed at domestic level independently of international institutions and often unilaterally, by Governments acting only through and with the support of their own parliaments. Gradually, from conflict to conflict, such unilateral action is contributing to the development of customary international law on the use of force, which competes and potentially contradicts with arrangements under the UN Charter. Although hailed as a historic step in the direction of heightened accountability, the recent empowerment of domestic parliaments on issues of the use of force counterintuitively suggests that the future of the international law on the use of force appears to be 'domestic'.

15

China and Global Environmental Governance

Coordination, Distribution and Compliance

Ji Hua[*]

I INTRODUCTION

Foreign relations law defines the foreign relations power of subjects of international law.[1] It encompasses the domestic law of each nation that governs how that nation interacts with the rest of the world.[2] In China, there is no field of foreign relations law recognised as such. Rather, the questions animating foreign relations law are deeply entrenched in fragmented provisions among hundreds of different legal texts. Given this fragmentation, this chapter focuses on the negotiation, conclusion, approval and implementation of international environmental treaties and agreements. In 1972, the opening of the Stockholm Environmental Conference marked the beginning of international environmental law and global environmental cooperation. As a part of international law, the functioning of international environmental law largely depends on the willingness and national capacities of states. Since many environmental problems have consequences that reach beyond national jurisdictions, domestic environmental laws and policies will impact other states and global environmental governance. The focus of this chapter is on law and practice concerning Chinese foreign relations law on global environmental governance. It will look into how China has been constructing its foreign relations law relating to environmental governance both nationally

* The views expressed are my own and do not necessarily reflect the positions of my university or any of its components. Unless otherwise indicated, translations of Chinese law provisions are not official.

1 Thomas Giegerich, 'Foreign Relations Law', *Max Planck Encyclopedia of International Law* (January 2011).

2 Curtis A. Bradley, 'What Is Foreign Relations Law?', in Curtis A. Bradley (ed.), *The Oxford Handbook of Comparative Foreign Relations Law* (New York: Oxford University Press, 2019), p. 1.

and globally and will propose that Chinese foreign relations environmental law and policy be conceived as a basic structure of foreign relations law.

The next part of this chapter will demonstrate the current status of Chinese foreign relations law and how Chinese international law scholarship perceives it (Section II). It will be highlighted that a comprehensive field of Chinese foreign relations law is so far only a product of scholars' efforts. The third part of the chapter will address why Chinese law does not include a general foreign relations statute (Section III). I maintain that traditional doubts, caution and silence from the law constitute three main factors. Yet, since 1972, the relationship between environmental governance in China and its global counterpart has turned out to be rather dynamic. This dynamic relationship has been developed and reinforced by 'Chinese environmental diplomacy', which helps to explain its role in Chinese 'foreign relations environmental law and policy' (Section IV). As Campbell McLachlan wrote, the 'distribution of foreign relations power between the organs of government' is one of the functions of foreign relations law.[3] Therefore, in the fifth part of the chapter, I will explore how powers of Chinese public authorities have been allocated with regard to the negotiation, conclusion, approval and implementation of international environmental treaties and global environmental institutions (Section V). I propose that Chinese administrative organs have developed a coordinated approach to 'external environmental relations'. In part six, I will discuss the legal status of environmental treaties in China, their place in Chinese law and mechanisms of implementation (Section VI). The conclusion will briefly summarise the main findings on the encounters between global environmental law and governance and Chinese 'external environmental relations' (Section VII).

II DEBATES ON CHINESE FOREIGN RELATIONS LAW

The history of foreign relations law as a field of study in China is relatively short. A Chinese international law scholar, Professor Liu Renshan of Zhongnan University of Economics and Law, pinpointed that Chinese foreign relations law is an important part of the Chinese legal system. He proposed that 'foreign relations law' entails an interconnected and composite legal system comprised of laws, regulations and other normative legal documents dealing with external relations.[4] According to his account, this field of

[3] Campbell McLachlan, 'Five Conceptions of the Function of Foreign Relations Law', in Curtis A. Bradley (ed.), *The Oxford Handbook of Comparative Foreign Relations Law* (New York: Oxford University Press, 2019), p. 25.

[4] Liu Renshan (刘仁山), ZHONG GUO DUI WAI GUAN XI FA SHI ZHONG GUO FA LV TI XI DE ZHONG YAO ZU CHENG BU FEN (中国对外关系法是中国法律体系的重要

the law fulfils two specific functions: first, it defines the allocation of powers in foreign affairs, such as which public organs have the right to declare war, deploy peacekeeping forces, send envoys or negotiate and approve international treaties. Second, it governs how international law becomes a part of Chinese law. With regard to these two functions, he listed three categories of sources in Chinese law, the constitution, special laws[5] and provisions[6] concerning foreign relations. Furthermore, he emphasised that Chinese international lawyers should explore relationships between international law and Chinese domestic law. In May 2016, a conference on 'Chinese Foreign Relations law: A New Agenda' stressed the importance of international legal research and practice, especially on matters affecting China and the Chinese people. From then on, a few Chinese scholars have devoted themselves to the topic. Based on his previous research, Liu Renshan extended his proposals on current drawbacks of China's foreign relations law – namely lack of systematicity, illogical legislative gaps and lack of applicability – and made suggestions how to organise it in a more systematic manner.[7] On the basis of his analysis of Chinese courts' contributions to international law,[8] Cai Congyan, Professor of International Law at Xiamen University School of Law, emphasised the

组成部分) [Chinese Foreign Relations Law is one of important part of Chinese Legal System] (2009) *Law and Social Development* 151–53 at 151.

[5] In general, there are ten basic laws in the Chinese legal system, which are 'Constitution', 'Administrative Law', 'Social Law', 'Economic Law', 'Civil Law', 'Criminal Law', 'Commercial Law', 'Environmental law', 'Litigation and non-litigation procedure Law' and 'Military Law'. In China, a 'special law' is a single law regulating a specialised legal issue. For example, in order to specify the legislative power and procedure of 'the National People's Congress and the Standing Committee of the National People's Congress' stipulated in the 'Constitution of the People's Republic of China', the National People's Congress promulgated 'Law on Legislation of the People's Republic of China'. The law on legislation is one of the 'special laws'. For readers who may be interested, see Lin Li, *The Chinese Road of the Rule of Law* (Beijing: China Social Sciences Press & Springer Nature Singapore, 2018), pp. 80–4.

[6] 'Provisions' in this chapter refers to specified articles resolving foreign relations or foreign-related legal issues. An example for a special provision is Article 9 of the ZHONG HUA REN MIN GONG HE GUO XING FA 2017 XIU ZHENG (中华人民共和国刑法2017修正) [Criminal Law of the People's Republic of China (2017 Amendment)] (promulgated by the National People's Congress, 4 Dec. 2017, effective on 4 Dec. 2017). It provides that Chinese Criminal Law is applicable to universal crimes under international treaties.

[7] He proposed three arguments in his article: (a) taking 'Foreign Relations Law' as one essential part in Chinese legal system by legislation; (b) clarifying territorial application of international treaties and customs; (c) upholding roles of international law in cultivating new lawyers. See Liu Renshan(刘仁山), ZUO WEI YI FA ZHI GUO ZHI FA DE ZHONG GUO DUI WAI GUAN XI FA (作为依法治国之法的中国对外关系法) [Chinese Foreign Relations Law as a law ruling the country] (2016) 3 *Studies in Law and Business* 131–42.

[8] Cai Congyan, 'International Law in Chinese Courts during the Rise of China' (2016) 110 *American Journal of International Law* 269 at 269–88.

importance of Chinese foreign relations law, mapped its current structure[9] and sketched the functions of Chinese domestic courts in the interpretation and implementation of international law.[10] Overall, current voices in Chinese scholarship focus primarily on the 'significance, status and proposed structure' of Chinese foreign relations law. The current work of these scholars is mostly constructive and extrapolated from theoretical considerations. There is no statute on foreign relations law in the current Chinese legal system. However, that does not mean that foreign relations law does not exist or does not have practical relevance. To the contrary, the questions animating foreign relations law are deeply entrenched in fragmented provisions among hundreds of different legal texts.

Recently, China has proposed a programme on rule of law in foreign relations, which may lead to the official establishment of foreign relations law as a field of law in the near future. On 31 October 2019, the Central Committee of the Communist Party of China adopted fifteen major decisions on 'Adhering to and Improving the Socialist System with Chinese Characteristics and Promoting the Modernization of the State Governance System and Capabilities'.[11] Among these, the thirteenth decision focused on 'independent foreign policy of peace and promotion of the building of one community of human destiny', advocating five objectives on foreign relations and law, which are 'establishment of foreign-related institutional mechanisms', 'coordination of foreign exchanges on part of the People's Congress, the central government, the Central Committee of the Communist Party, the military, local governments, and people's organizations', 'strengthening the Party's overall planning and coordination of all Party external work', 'strengthening the rule of law in foreign relations' and 'establishment of a legal system for work related to foreign states'. The thirteenth decision symbolises that the Chinese government is pursuing a systematic construction

9 Cai Congyan, 'Symposium on Comparative Foreign Relations Law: Chinese Foreign Relations Law' (2017) 111 *American Journal of International Law Unbound* 336–40.

10 Cai Congyan (蔡从燕), ZHONG GUO QUE QI DUI WAI GUAN XI FA YU FA YUAN DE GONG NENG ZAI ZAO (中国崛起、对外关系法与法院的功能再造) [Rise of China, Foreign Relations Law and the Re-construction of Functions of Courts] (2018) 71 *Wuhan University Journal* 130–43.

11 The Central Committee of the Communist Party, 'Decisions on Adhering to and Improving the Socialist System with Chinese Characteristics and Promoting the Modernization of the State Governance System and Capabilities' (Chinese Version), available at www.xinhuanet.com//mrdx/2019-11/06/c_138532143.htm, accessed 30 September 2020. The Central Committee of the Communist Party is the core authority branch in China. According to the 'Constitution of the Chinese Communist Party', the Party exercises overall leadship over all areas of endeavor in every part of the country including developing the rule of law.

of 'foreign relations law'. For the Chinese government, the next step is how to shape its structure and define its scope of application. We will need to assess in the future the impact of this ambition of the government.

III THE 'UNDERDEVELOPED' FOREIGN RELATIONS LAW IN CHINA

Two factors contribute to explaining why foreign relations law is so far underdeveloped in China: China's traditional perspectives on international law (subsection A) and the silence of Chinese law (subsection B).

A *Traditional Perspectives on International Law: Doubt and Caution*

China's traditional perspectives on international law depend on the historical experience of certain diplomatic practices.[12] Some authors have characterised the Chinese modern period (from 1840 to 1949) to be 'semi-colonial and semi-feudal'.[13] During this period, the first acquaintance with international law is the treaty of Nanking (1842),[14] the first unequal treaty in Chinese diplomatic history influencing Chinese attitudes towards international law.

After 110 years of fighting against aggressors, the government of the People's Republic of China, established in 1949, perceived international law as a Western instrument against socialism. Until 1966, China adopted a strategy of 'Start All Over Again', which means that the new Chinese government would stay away from the Western legal system. During the Cultural Revolution (1966 to 1976), China's diplomacy was still in progress, for example, to retrieve legal rights in the UN and participate in the Stockholm environmental conference, even if international legal research had been ceased. From 1949 to 1978, before the 'Reform and Opening-up Policy' was adopted, two characteristics were constitutive for China's approach towards international law: first, a suspicion towards traditional international law that primarily protected developed states to the detriment of most undeveloped nations and, second, respect for the principles of 'sovereignty', 'territorial integrity', 'independence', 'equality' and 'mutual respect'. After the

12 For the history of Chinese international law, see Xue Hanqin, *Chinese Contemporary Perspectives on International Law: History, Culture and International Law* (Leiden, Boston: Martinus Nijhoff Publishers, 2012), pp. 13–67; Cai Congyan, *The Rise of China and International Law: Taking Chinese Exceptionalism seriously* (New York: Oxford University Press, 2019), pp. 41–99.

13 Duan Jielong (ed.), *International Law in China: Cases and Practices* (Beijing: Law Press China, 2011), p. 164. For a history of the 'Semi-Feudal and Semi-Colonial' in China, see e.g. Immanuel C. Y. Hsü, *The Rise of Modern China* (New York: Oxford University Press, 2000), pp. 168–613.

14 Cai, *The Rise of China and International Law*, p. 52.

adoption and implementation of the 'Reform and Opening-up Policy' in 1978, China revived international law research and teaching and promoted interactions between international law and diplomacy. From 1979 on, China became a participant of and contributor to the international legal order, for example, it joined over 300 multilateral treaties and 130 international organisations.[15] With the expansion of its opening-up policy, China became aware of the role of international law in protecting national interests. In its foreign relations, China successfully requested the Alabama Court of the United States of America to dismiss the case of the *Huguang Railway Bonds*[16] on the grounds of absolute jurisdictional immunity and non-payment of odious debts by appointing its legal counsel to make an appearance on behalf of China in 1984.[17] Another example, the *Guanghua Dormitory* (or *Khoka-ryo* student dormitory) case (1987–2007)[18] portrays China's recognition and succession practices in international law.

In 2014, the Chinese government adopted a strategy of a 'socialist rule of law'.[19] The strategy emphasised that 'China will vigorously participate in the formulation of international norms, promote the handling of foreign-related economic and social affairs according to the law, strengthen its discourse power and influence in international legal affairs, . . . safeguard the proper interests of its citizens and legal persons abroad, and foreign citizens and legal persons in China'.[20] It can be taken from this that China is serious about shaping a new international law order based on their understanding of the principles of 'sovereignty' and 'cooperation'.[21] While the idea of a 'socialist rule of law' as

15 Wang Zonglai and Hu Bin, 'China's Reform and Opening-up and International Law' (2010) 9 *Chinese Journal of International Law* 193–203 at 194.

16 *Russel Jackson, et al.* v. *The People's Republic of China*, 550 F. Supp. 869 (U.S. District Court, N. D. Ala. 1982).

17 For general description on the process of the case, see Xue, *Chinese Contemporary Perspectives on International Law*, p. 87 (footnote 180 included).

18 The entire case has not been officially reported yet. As for factual and legal analysis, see Shen Jianming, 'Revisiting the Disability of the Non-Recognized in the Courts of the Non-Recognizing States and Beyond: The Departure of the in re Guanghua Liao Courts from the Rules' (1990) 5 *Florida International Law Journal* 401–70. For a general account of the procedural history of the case, see Xue, *Chinese Contemporary Perspectives on International Law*, p. 51 (footnote 84 included).

19 Rogier Creemers and Jeremy Daum, 'CCP Central Committee Decision concerning Some Major Questions in Comprehensively Moving Governing the Country According to the law Forward', available at https://chinacopyrightandmedia.wordpress.com/2014/10/28/ccp-central-committee-decision-concerning-some-major-questions-in-comprehensively-moving-governing-the-country-according-to-the-law-forward/, accessed 30 September 2020.

20 See above, note 19.

21 Anne Peters, 'After Trump: China and Russia move from norm-takers to shapers of the international legal order', available at www.ejiltalk.org/after-trump-china-and-russia-move-from-norm-takers-to-shapers-of-the-international-legal-order/, accessed 30 September 2020.

such cannot tell us how China will attain these objectives through specific actions, it forms the background also for the growing scholarly interest in a Chinese foreign relations law.

B *The Silence of Chinese Law on Foreign Relations*

As far as international law is concerned, China's Constitution only specifies which organs have the authority to conclude and approve a treaty.[22] The 'Law on the Procedure of the Conclusion of Treaties', adopted by the Standing Committee of the National People's Congress in 1990, enumerates three categories of treaties that shall be concluded by three corresponding public authorities[23] but does not stipulate the status of treaties in the Chinese legal system. There is also no systematic law concerning how an approved treaty will be implemented in the Chinese legal order. The Civil Procedure Law provides that international treaties shall prevail unless China has formulated reservations.[24] But the logic of 'primacy' cannot be applied to other areas of the law. In WTO law and the law of sea, China adopts the mode of 'transformation', which means that specific domestic laws ensure compliance with approved treaties. Consequently, fragmentation and unpredictability characterise the current status of international treaty application in China. As Professor Cai has pointed out, fragmentation and unpredictability also imply

22 ZHONG HUA REN MIN GONG HE GUO XIAN FA 2018 XIU ZHENG (中华人民共和国宪法2018年修正) [Constitution of the People's Republic of China (2018 Amendment)] (promulgated by the National People's Congress, 11 Mar. 2018, effective on 11 Mar. 2018). Article 89 (8) provides that the State Council governs foreign affairs and concludes treaties and protocols with foreign countries. Article 67 (15) entails that the Standing Committee of the National People's Congress decides on the ratification or abrogation of treaties and important agreements concluded with foreign states.

23 ZHONG HUA REN MIN GONG HE GUO DI JIE TIAO YUE CHENG XU FA (中华人民共和国缔结条约程序法) [Law of the People's Republic of China on the Procedure of the Conclusion of Treaties 1990] (promulgated by the Standing Committee of the National People's Congress, Dec. 28, 1990, effective on Dec. 28, 1990). Article 6–8 identify three categories of treaties signed in the name of: (i) the People's Republic of China; (ii) the Central People's Government; (iii) a Governmental Sub-division or Department. The 1990 Law is *'lex specialis'* to the 'Constitution of the People's Republic of China (2018 Amendment)' on the conclusion of treaties.

24 ZHONG HUA REN MIN GONG HE GUO MIN SHI SU SONG FA 2017 XIU ZHENG (中华人民共和国民事诉讼法2017年修正) [The Civil Procedure Law of the People's Republic of China (2017 Amendment)] (promulgated by the Standing Committee of the National People's Congress, 27 Jun. 2017, effective on 1 Jul. 2017). Article 260 provides that '[w]here there is any discrepancy between an international treaty concluded or acceded by the People's Republic of China and this law, the provisions of the international treaty shall prevail, except clauses to which the People's Republic of China has formulated reservations'.

flexibility,[25] and the purpose of this flexible attitude and approach is to progressively find adequate solutions.

IV CHINESE FOREIGN RELATIONS ENVIRONMENTAL LAW AND POLICY

While Foreign Relations Law in general is still underdeveloped in China, it can be said that Chinese foreign relations environmental law and policy conforms to a basic structure of foreign relations law. Before discussing the allocation of China's public powers in global environmental governance and the legal status of environmental treaties in China as key topics of foreign relations law in Sections V and VI of this chapter, I will sketch the encounters of international and domestic environmental law and governance that have resulted from Chinese environmental diplomacy since the 1970s (subsection A) and have led to congruent basic legal principles of Chinese and international environmental law (subsection B).

A *Chinese Environmental Diplomacy*

Chinese environmental diplomacy has contributed to international and national environmental law. Chinese environmental diplomacy began in 1972,[26] which also marks the beginnings of international environmental law. In 1972, the Chinese government sent delegations to participate in the Stockholm Conference. It was also the first time that China participated in a multilateral conference for the protection of the environment. Unfortunately, the issues in this conference were not deeply discussed in China because of the 'Cultural Revolution'. This 'revolution' plunged the legal system and social order into chaos. However, it did not stop the progress of Chinese diplomacy, for example, the Government of the People's Republic of China was recognized as 'the only legitimate representatives of China to the United Nations' in 1971.[27] The reason why China still participated in the Stockholm Conference was that China expected the conference to open valuable opportunities for interacting with the Western world without

25 Cai, 'International Law in Chinese Courts during the Rise of China', 273.

26 Zhang Haibin (张海滨), LUN ZHONG GUO HUAN JING WAI JIAO DE SHI JIAN JI QI ZUO YONG (论中国环境外交的实践及其作用) [The Practice and Function of China's environmental diplomacy] (1998) 3 *International Politics* 38–44 at 38.

27 'Restoration of the lawful rights of the People's Republic of China in the United Nations', UN Doc. A/RES/2758(XXVI).

damaging core national interests.[28] The first Prime Minister of the People's Republic of China, Zhou Enlai (周恩来), asked delegations to positively express ideas, policies and understanding and promote independence, economy and solidarity with 'third-world' countries.[29]

Stockholm turned out to offer an opportunity for pushing forward domestic environmental protection in China. Learning from global environmental problems at the conference, the delegations reported to Prime Minister Zhou that China also experienced serious environmental degradations. In 1973, the State Council opened the first conference on national environmental protection in Beijing, which put environmental protection on the national agenda. In its aftermath, China adopted a series of laws and regulations. China's Constitution (1978) firstly provided that China protects the environment and natural resources, prevents and eliminates pollution and other public hazards.[30] The most remarkable evidence is that the Standing Committee of the National People's Congress adopted the first comprehensive environmental protection law in 1979.[31]

Chinese environmental diplomacy was not limited to be a learner. From the 1990s onwards, China became active in promoting its understanding of international cooperation. At the 1992 Rio Conference, China and other developing countries insisted that the notion of 'Common but differentiated Responsibilities' be one of the guiding legal principles in global environmental governance.[32] China proposed that industrialised countries should take leading responsibilities for tackling global environmental problems not only for their historical contributions but also for their comparative higher capabilities. At last, the Rio legal instruments reflect this proposal.[33] The principle of

28 Lv Jie (吕杰), ZHONG GUO HUAN JING WAI JIAO YU GUO NEI HUAN JING BAO HU (中国环境外交与国内环境保护) [China's Environmental Diplomacy and Domestic Environmental Protection] (2003) 13 *China Population, Resources and Environment* 11–15.

29 Wang Zhijia (王之佳), *ZHONG GUO HUAN JING WAI JIAO* (中国环境外交) [*China's environmental diplomacy*] (Beijing: China Environment Press, 1999), p. 107.

30 Article 11, ZHONG HUA REN MIN GONG HE GUO XIAN FA 1978 (中华人民共和国宪法 (1978)) [Constitution of the People's Republic of China (1978)] (promulgated by the National People's Congress, 5 Mar. 1978, effective on 20 Sep. 1978, invalidated on 4 Dec. 1982).

31 ZHONG HUA REN MING GONG HE GUO HUAN JING BAO HU FA SHI XING (中华人民共和国环境保护法试行) [Environmental Protection Law of the People's Republic of China (For Trial Implementation)] (promulgated by the Standing Committee of the National People's Congress, 26 Dec. 1989, effective on 26 Dec. 1989).

32 'Statement by H.E. Mr. Li Peng, Prime Minister of the People's Republic of China', in 'Report of the United Nations Conference on Environment and Development: Statements Made by Heads of State or Government at the Summit Segment of the Conference', UN Doc. A/CONF.151/26/Rev.1 (vol. III), p. 36.

33 Principle 7 of the 'Rio de Janeiro Charter/Declaration on Environment and Development', UN Doc. A/CONF.151/26.

'Common but differentiated Responsibilities' has been one of guiding principles in Chinese environmental diplomacy.[34]

B Congruent Basic Legal Principles of Chinese and International Environmental Law

To better understand Chinese foreign relations environmental law and policy, it is necessary to take into account those Chinese environmental legal principles which overlap with international environmental law. This exercise helps to identify connections and understand official attitudes towards Chinese foreign relations law on environmental governance. Articles 4 and 5 of the Chinese 'Environmental Protection Law (2014 Revision)' manifestly stipulate four basic legal principles.

The first principle is the 'coordination of economic and social development with environmental protection'.[35] Before the 2014 revision, Chinese environmental protection was coordinated with economic and social development.[36] In other words, the purpose of environmental protection is to fully realise economic development. After the revision, environmental protection shall be equal to economic development. The principle of coordination, in essence, is consistent with the principle of sustainable development in international law.[37]

The second principle is 'prevention first'. Generally, the principle holds that any pollution and risk of pollution should be prevented or controlled before they

34 Wang, *China Environmental Diplomacy*, p. 205. For the latest state practice, please see 'Statement by China on Behalf of BASIC at the Opening Plenary of COP25', available at www4.unfccc.int/sites/SubmissionsStaging/Documents/201912111926–STATEMENT%20BY%20CHINA%20ON%20BEHALF%20OF%20BASIC%20AT%20THE%20OPENING%20PLENARY%20OF%20COP25.pdf, accessed 30 September 2020.

35 ZHONG HUA REN MIN GONG HE GUO HUAN JING BAO HU FA 2014 XIU DING (中华人民共和国环境保护法2014修订) [Environmental Protection Law of the People's Republic of China (2014 Revision)] (promulgated by the Standing Committee of the National People's Congress, 24 Apr. 2014, effective on 1 Jan. 2015). Article 4 provides that 'protecting the environment is a fundamental national policy of the state. The state shall adopt economic and technological policies and measures conducive to economically and cyclically utilizing resources, protecting and improving the environment and enhancing the harmony between mankind and nature to coordinate economic and social development with environmental protection'.

36 Article 4 of the 'Environmental Protection Law of the People's Republic of China (1989)': 'The plans for environmental protection formulated by the state must be incorporated into the national economic and social development plans; the state shall adopt economic and technological policies and measures favourable to environmental protection so as to coordinate the work of environmental protection with economic construction and social development'.

37 *Pulp Mills on the River Uruguay (Argentina v. Uruguay)*, Judgment, I.C.J. Reports 2010, p. 14, para. 177. See Jin Ruilin (金瑞林) and Shu Min (舒旻), HUAN JING FA DE JI BEN YUAN ZE (环境法的基本原则) [Basic Principles in Environmental Law] in Jin Ruilin (ed.), *Environmental Law* (Beijing: Peking University Press, 2016), p. 35.

are created. In international environmental law, prevention as a principle only underscores the obligation of states to prevent environmental damage within and beyond their own jurisdiction. Article 5 of the Chinese Environmental Protection Law provides that environmental protection should be focused on prevention. Both public and private entities and individuals should take responsibilities for preventing risks and damages. The three techniques usually applied under the principle in China – environmental impact assessment, environmental standards and environmental monitoring – are consistent with international environmental practices.

The third principle, 'public participation', as enshrined in Principle 10 of the Rio Declaration, has been transformed into Chinese environmental law. It is applied in public information, environmental management and impact assessment, class action etc. In 2015, the Ministry of Environmental Protection issued an order on 'Measures for Public Participation in Environmental Protection', which portrays special communication channels (letters, faxes, email, '12369' tip-off hotline, public hearings, notification and financial support) to facilitate the participation of non-state actors in environmental decisions.

'Polluter pays', the fourth principle, evolved from the Organisation for Economic Co-operation and Development (OECD) and highlights the 'internalization' of environmental costs and the assumption of the 'burden' by environmental polluters and beneficiaries.[38] Based on the OECD Recommendations[39] and the Rio Declaration,[40] Chinese environmental law broadens its contents by incorporating an environmental tax law,[41] rules on the insurance for environmental liability[42] and a compensation mechanism for ecological protection.[43]

38 Principle 16 of Rio de Janeiro Charter/Declaration on Environment and Development.

39 OECD 'Recommendation on Guiding Principles concerning International Economic Aspects on Environmental Policies' (26 May 1972) OECD Doc C (1972) 128, (1972) 12 Acts of the Organisation 225; OECD 'Recommendation on the Implementation of the Polluter-Pays Principle' (14 Nov. 1974) OECD Doc C (74) 14 Acts of the Organisation 535; OECD 'Recommendation on the Application of the Polluter-Pays Principle to Accidental Pollution' (25 Jul. 1989) OECD Doc C (89) 88, 28 ILM 1320.

40 Jin and Shu, 'Basic Principles in Environmental law', p. 45.

41 ZHONG HUA REN MIN GONG HE GUO HUAN JING BAO HU SHUI FA 2018 XIU ZHENG (中华人民共和国环境保护税法2018修正) [Environmental Protection Tax Law of the People's Republic of China (2018 Revision)] (promulgated by the Standing Committee of the National People's Congress, 26 Oct. 2018, effective on 26 Oct. 2018).

42 Article 6 of ZHONG HUA REN MIN GONG HE GUO HAI YANG HUAN JING BAO HU FA 2017 XIU ZHENG (中华人民共和国海洋环境保护法2017修正) [Marine Environmental Protection Law of the People's Republic of China (Amendment 2017)] (promulgated by the Standing Committee of the National People's Congress, 4 Nov. 2017, effective on 5 Nov. 2017).

43 GUO WU YUAN BAN GONG TING GUAN YU JIAN QUAN SHENG TAI BAO HU BU CHANG JI ZHI DE YI JIAN (国务院办公厅关于健全生态保护补偿机制的意见)

The above four principles are stipulated in both international and Chinese environmental law. The normative congruence on the level of principles has been recognised in the Chinese official position on national and international environmental governance in general.[44]

V THE ALLOCATION OF CHINA'S PUBLIC POWERS IN GLOBAL ENVIRONMENTAL GOVERNANCE

The allocation of powers to negotiate, conclude and approve treaties and agreements is one of the core issues in foreign relations law. Due to fragmentations and complexities in international environmental law, and silences in Chinese constitutional law, Chinese departmental regulations provide for different functions for the respective public authorities in individual treaty regimes.[45] This section will analyse the allocation of China's public powers in global environmental governance. In 2018, China has completed the 'State Council Institutional Reform Plan'.[46] After the reform, the power to negotiate all multilateral environmental treaties was transferred to the Ministry of Ecology and Environment. However, the competence of the Ministry is not exclusive. I will first set out the administrative actors involved in China's 'external environmental relations' (subsection A) before I turn to the allocation of powers in the conclusion and approval of environmental treaties and agreements (subsection B) and in international cooperation with global environmental institutions (subsection C).

A *Administrative Organs Involved in 'External Environmental Relations'*

More than one Chinese administrative organ is taking action in global environmental governance, such as negotiations, conclusion and approval of international environmental treaties and international cooperation. These collective and coordinated actions of administrative organs are based on their allocated powers.

[Opinions of the General Office of the State Council on Improving the Compensation Mechanism for Ecological Protection] (promulgated 28 Apr. 2016, effective on 28 Apr. 2016).

44 See n. 32 above; Liu Nengye, 'China's Position on International Environmental Issues', in Qin Tianbao (ed.), *Research Handbook on Chinese Environmental Law* (Cheltenham: Edward Elgar Publishing, 2015), pp. 368–94; Wang, *China Environmental Diplomacy*, pp. 201–5.

45 Before 2018, the National Development and Reform Commission took the leadership in climate change negotiations.

46 NPC Observer, 'A Guide to 2018 State Council Institutional Reforms (Further Updated)', available at https://npcobserver.com/2018/03/14/a-guide-to-2018-state-council-institutional-reforms/, accessed 30 September 2020.

In general, it is the State Council that conducts Chinese foreign affairs including the negotiation and conclusion of international treaties.[47] In practice, the Ministry of Foreign Affairs has been empowered to negotiate international environmental treaties on behalf of the People's Republic of China and the Chinese government. To achieve division of powers and goal congruence, China has devised a scheme of 'external coordination' in multilateral environmental agreements negotiations. In other words, there is not one single public organ that is empowered to negotiate global environmental treaties or agreements.

At present, there are over ten administrative departments involved in the process of external coordination, which consists of three steps. First, the Ministry of Foreign Affairs plays a role as the 'Window Unit'. The Ministry of Foreign Affairs traces and notifies the everyday development of all issues. Secondly, the Ministry of Foreign Affairs will contact public authorities and assign specific issues to them on the basis of relevance and expertise. For example, matters involving green technologies or forestry will be assigned to the Ministry of Science and Technology and the Ministry of Agriculture and Rural Affairs respectively. The authorities entrusted with the exercise of these assigned powers will set up specialised study groups to propose ideas and draft documents on their own. After respective investigations, all these groups will gather together to exchange ideas, draft, revise and finalise position papers for international negotiations. However, this coordination does not work well all the time. Due to the multifaced nature and complexity of environmental issues, different public organs might propose conflicting environmental policies and goals affecting the process of 'external coordination' in environmental diplomacy.[48]

B *Allocation of Powers on Conclusion and Approval of International Treaties and Agreements*

Article 89 of China's Constitution provides for the functions and powers exercised by the State Council. Item 8 of this article clearly empowers the Council to conduct foreign affairs and conclude treaties and agreements with foreign states, which is also provided in Article 3 of the 'Law of the People's Republic of China on the Procedure of the Conclusion of Treaties'.

47 Article 89(9) of China's Constitution (2018 Amendment).

48 Li Jinhui (李金惠), Jia Shaohua (贾少华) and Tan Quanyin (谭全银) (eds.), *HUAN JING WAI JIAO JI CHU YU SHI JIAN (环境外交：基础与实践)* [*Environmental Diplomacy: Basis and Practice*] (Beijing: China Environmental Press, 2018), p. 119.

Questions of approval are more complex. According to the Constitution, two public authorities shall be involved, the Standing Committee of the National People's Congress[49] and the President of the People's Republic of China.[50] Article 3 of the Law on the Procedure of the Conclusion of Treaties stipulates that the Standing Committee of the National People's Congress is competent to approve treaties and important agreements, while the President shall approve treaties and important agreements in pursuance of the decisions of the Standing Committee of the National People's Congress. The authority of approval of the President of the People's Republic of China is derived from the Standing Committee of the National People's Congress. In practice, none of China's international treaties and agreements has been approved by the President. It is noteworthy that the Standing Committee of the National People's Congress only approves 'treaties and important agreements'.[51]

1 Approval of Certain Treaties by the Standing Committee of the National People's Congress

The 'Law of the People's Republic of China on the Procedure of the Conclusion of Treaties', literally understood, fully empowers the Standing Committee of the National People's Congress to approve all international treaties. Article 7 enlists the 'treaties and important agreements' that shall be approved by the Standing Committee of the People's Congress:

(1) treaties of friendship and cooperation, treaties of peace and other treaties of a political nature;
(2) treaties and agreements concerning territory and delimitation of boundary lines;
(3) treaties and agreements relating to judicial assistance and extradition;
(4) treaties and agreements which contain stipulations inconsistent with the laws of the People's Republic of China;

49 See n. 23 above.

50 See n. 23 above.

51 In Chinese law, treaty (TIAO YUE, 条约) and agreement (XIE DING, 协定) have different meanings. Strictly speaking, a treaty is a written agreement between states and relates to matters of general concern. An agreement, written or unwritten, usually prescribes in detail the line of conduct which will be followed between states or between states and foreign legal persons with regard to specific issues. Also see George Grafton Wilson, *Handbook of International Law* (St. Paul: West Publishing Co., 1910), pp. 191–4. In international law, the two terms can be used interchangeably, however, agreement is more general. See Robert Kolb, *The Law of Treaties: An Introduction* (Cheltenham: Edward Elgar Publishing, 2016), p. 24.

(5) treaties and agreements which are subject to ratification as agreed by the contracting parties;
(6) other treaties and agreements subject to ratification.

The following remarks will focus on environmental treaty practice with respect to Article 7 paragraphs 4 to 6.

Firstly, according to Article 7 paragraph 4 of the 'Law of the People's Republic of China on the Procedure of the Conclusion of Treaties', if provision(s) in an international environmental treaty or agreement depart from existing national law, the Standing Committee has exercised the power of approval over the instrument, for example, the 1989 Basel Convention on the Control of Transboundary Movements of Hazardous Wastes (approved in 1991),[52] the 1992 United Nations Framework Convention on Climate Change (approved in 1992)[53] and the 1992 Convention on Biological Diversity (approved in 1992).[54]

Secondly, Article 7 paragraph 5 provides that the Standing Committee shall approve an international treaty or agreement that shall clearly be subject to ratification as agreed by the contracting parties. For example, the Committee approved the Convention for the Protection of the World Cultural and Natural Heritage[55] in 1988.[56] The most recent case is the Convention on the Prohibition of Military or Any Other Hostile Use of Environmental Modification Techniques,[57] which was approved in 2005.

In practice, the Standing Committee has exercised its power according to Article 7 paragraph 6, the so-called 'miscellaneous clause'. The Committee is competent if a new agreement or protocol substitutes an old one that was subject to approval or actually approved by the Committee. For example, in 2006, the 1996 Protocol to the 1972 Convention on the Prevention of Marine Pollution by Dumping of Wastes and Other Matter[58] was approved based on the notion of 'succession of treaty'[59] because the 1972 Convention was also

52 Basel Convention on the Control of Transboundary Movements of Hazardous Wastes and their Disposal, Basel, 22 March 1989, in force 5 May 1992, 1673 UNTS 57.

53 United Nations Framework Convention on Climate Change, New York, 9 May 1992, in force 21 March 1994, 1771 UNTS 107.

54 Convention on Biological Diversity, Rio de Janeiro, 5 June 1992, in force 29 December 1993, 1760 UNTS 79.

55 UNESCO Convention for the Protection of the World Cultural and Natural Heritage, Paris, 16 November 1972, in force 17 December 1975, (1972) 11 ILM 1358.

56 Article 31 (1) of the UNESCO Convention.

57 Convention on the Prohibition of Military or Any Other Hostile Use of Environmental Modification Techniques, New York, 10 December 1976, in force 5 October 1978, 1108 UNTS 151.

58 Protocol to the Convention on the Prevention of Marine Pollution by Dumping of Wastes and Other Matter, London, 7 November 1996, in force 24 March 2006, (1997) 36 ILM 1.

59 Article 23 of the 1996 Protocol to the 1972 Convention on the Prevention of Marine Pollution by Dumping of Wastes and Other Matter stipulated that 'the protocol will supersede the

subject to approval by the Standing Committee. Two further recent examples are the 2013 Minamata Convention on Mercury[60] and the 2015 Paris Agreement,[61] which were approved by the Committee in 2016. Although both treaties were neither subject to the national constitutional procedure nor successors of earlier treaties, the Committee still approved them because of their significant implications to environment and human health.[62]

2 Approval of Other Agreements by the State Council

Article 7 of the 'Law of the People's Republic of China on the Procedure of the Conclusion of Treaties' defines the realm of agreements that shall be approved by the Standing Committee. Those agreements that do not fall under one of the six items of Article 7 may be subject to approval by the State Council. For example, the State Council approved the 2000 Cartagena Protocol on Biosafety to the Convention on Biological Diversity[63] in 2005. The question is when does the State Council exercise its power. No statute specifies those circumstances that empower the State Council.

It is unclear how allocated powers function in international environmental agreements that do not fall under Article 7 of the Law of the People's Republic of China on the Procedure of the Conclusion of Treaties. The Standing Committee virtually approved several environmental agreements affecting human health or environment that do not fall under Article 7 without further legislation. As for the State Council, no statute supports its power of approval even if the power has been practically exercised. I would prefer to identify these practices as 'unpredictable' consequences caused by 'legal *lacuna*'. To achieve predictability, Chinese law should further clarify how to allocate the two public authorities to exercise powers on approval on the grounds of existing practices.

Convention as between Contracting Parties to this Protocol which are also Parties to the Convention'.

60 Minamata Convention on Mercury, Kumamoto, 10 October 2013, in force 16 August 2017, available at www.mercuryconvention.org/ (last accessed: 30 September 2020).

61 Paris Agreement to the United Nations Framework Convention on Climate Change, Paris, 12 December 2015, in force 4 November 2016, Doc. FCCC/CP/2015/10/Add.1.

62 Yi Li (易立), LUN QUAN GUO REN DA CHANG WEI HUI JUE DING PI ZHUN HE JIA RU HUAN JING BAO HU LEI TIAO YUE DE QUAN LI (论全国人大常委会决定批准和加入环境保护类条约的权力) [The Powers of Conclusion and Acceptance of International Environmental Agreements of the Standing Committee of the National People's Congress] (2017) 39 *Journal of China Three Gorges University (Humanities & Social Sciences)* 67–73 at 70.

63 Cartagena Protocol on Biosafety to the Convention on Biological Diversity, Montreal, 29 January 2000, in force 11 September 2003, 2226 UNTS 208.

C Allocation of Powers in International Cooperation with Global Environmental Institutions

Apart from concluding international environmental treaties or agreements, China has been also active in cooperating with global environmental institutions. Among these, two institutions, the 'Global Environmental Facility' and the 'South-South Cooperation Fund' reflect how Chinese public powers interact in international environmental cooperation, as shown in Table 15.1 below.

1 Cooperation with the 'Global Environmental Facility'

Allocation of powers is also an issue with regard to the operation of the Global Environmental Facility (GEF), which is advocated by China.[64] As a founding member, contributing and recipient country, China has carried out a productive cooperation with the GEF since May 1994.[65] Until the end of 2019, China has been granted 1,855.84 million US dollars funding from the GEF for 213 projects concerning, inter alia, climate change, land degradation and biodiversity.[66] Without financial assistance from global contributions, it would be difficult to upgrade Chinese environmental governance. The Chinese government announced that it will prepare to implement all plans supported by the GEF. The GEF can be the major financial resource to realise national environmental protection with bilateral cooperation.[67]

In practice, the Ministry of Finance plays the role of a 'Focal Point' in the GEF. Due to its financial nature, all plans and activities should be in accordance with considerations of the national macro-economy, which is instructed by the National Development and Reform Commission (国家发展与改革委员会). To achieve efficient collaboration, the Ministry of Finance and the Ministry of Ecology and Environment jointly established the 'Secretary Office of China-GEF' in 2002.[68] The Office identifies, reviews, monitors and assesses all programmes proposed by the Ministry of Finance. If a proposed

[64] The 'Global Environmental Facility' is the largest and a permanent financial mechanism to assist developing countries to implement programmes regarding international environmental protection. *See* Rudolf Dolzer, 'Global Environmental Facility (GEF)', *Max Planck Encyclopedia of International Law* (2010).

[65] China is one of thirty-six donor countries to the GEF Trust Fund. However, no data shows the specific donation amounts until submission.

[66] See the website of the 'GEF', available at www.thegef.org/country/china, accessed 30 September 2020.

[67] Lin Gan, 'Global Environmental Policy in Social Contexts: The Case of China' (1992) 5 *Knowledge and Policy* 30–50 at 34.

[68] See the website of 'GEF and China', available at www.gefchina.org.cn/gefyzg/xmgk/201603/t20160316_24277.html, accessed 30 September 2020.

programme is accepted by the Secretary Office, the Ministry of Finance will notify GEF. GEF finally decides whether the programme would be approved.

2 Launching and Building the 'South-South' Cooperation Fund

China is not only receiving assistance, but also contributing to environmental financing. In 2015, Chinese President Xi Jinping launched the proposition to set up a 'South-South' Cooperation Fund at the United Nations Development Summit. In his speech, he proposed that China would contribute two billion dollars to support developing countries to implement the '2030 Sustainable Development Goals'. To effectively implement the fund, the Ministry of Commerce promulgated the 'Consultative Draft on Application and Administration of the South-South Cooperation Fund' in 2016.[69] According to this draft, the Ministry of Commerce will administer the approval, management and supervision of funding programmes. If a foreign entity intends to receive assistance, it shall submit application files to its corresponding commercial organ or representative office in China. The Commercial Representative Offices affiliated to Chinese embassies and consulates abroad will assist the Ministry to manage and supervise the programme when the international application is approved.

VI THE LEGAL STATUS OF INTERNATIONAL ENVIRONMENTAL TREATIES IN CHINA

By the end of 2019, China is a state party to ninety-nine multilateral, seventy regional and bilateral environmental treaties, agreements and protocols, which almost cover all environmental areas. With the increasing number of international environmental agreements particularly two questions arise, which are another core issue of foreign relations law: the place of international environmental agreements in the Chinese legal system (subsection A) and how international treaty provisions become part of Chinese law (subsection B). This section of the chapter will address these two issues in the light of the applicable Chinese law, with a focus on international environmental law.

69 In China, before a new legislative instrument is introduced, the administrating organ will promulgate it online and ask for public participation. The 'Consultative Draft on Application and Administration of the South-South Cooperation Fund' was promulgated on 9 September 2016, and open to public participation from 9 October 2016. The draft has not been transformed into law until submission. An English translation is not available. The Chinese text can be found at the website of the 'Department of Treaty and Law of the Ministry of Commerce of the People's Republic of China', http://tfs.mofcom.gov.cn/article/as/201609/20160901387579.shtml, accessed 30 September 2020.

TABLE 15.1 *Allocated Functions of China's Public Authorities in International Environmental Issues*[70]

Name of Public Authority	General Allocated Functions
Ministry of Foreign Affairs	Convening of negotiations on international conventions
Ministry of Ecology and Environment	Negotiation of Multilateral Environmental Agreements
Ministry of Science and Technology	Administration and Implementation of ecological scientific technologies
Ministry of Agriculture and Rural Affairs	Sustainable development in rural and agricultural matters
Ministry of Finance	Collecting and allocating international finance
Ministry of Transport	Building and promoting digital and low-carbon transportations
Ministry of Water Resources	Hydropower stations constructions
Ministry of Housing and Urban-Rural Development	Energy efficient housing
Ministry of Commerce	Attracting environmental-related international trade and investment funds
China Meteorological Administration	International climate sciences cooperation

A *The Place of Environmental Agreements in Chinese Law*

An approved international treaty occupies an uncertain place under Chinese law. Under constitutional law, the hierarchy in the system of Chinese environmental law follows the hierarchy of public authorities:[71] comprehensive environmental law and standards adopted by the Standing Committee of the National People's Congress; environmental regulations and standards adopted by the State Council; departmental regulations adopted by Central Ministries and Commissions.[72] Very few Chinese scholars contend that the legal nature of approved treaties or agreements depends on the hierarchy of public authorities. According to this view, for instance, an international environmental treaty can be equal to environmental law when it was approved by the

70 The content of the table is compiled by the author. For more detailed information, see n. 48 above.

71 For 'the legislative structure and hierarchy of public authorities of the People's Republic of China', see Chen Jianfu, *Chinese Law: Context and Transformation* (Leiden: Brill Nijhoff, 2016), pp. 229–78; Perry Keller, 'Sources of Order in Chinese Law' (1994) 42 *The American Journal of Comparative Law* 711–59 at 728.

72 See Jin Ruilin and Shu Min, 'Basic Principles in Environmental law', pp. 49–56.

Standing Committee.[73] I am very sceptical about this proposition. The standard of 'hierarchy' shall be strictly limited in the context of Chinese lawmaking. It is implausible that the status of treaties or agreements could be arbitrarily determined by the hierarchy of the approving authority without any basis in a statute.

B *Methods of Implementation*

China has been always upholding that it will conform to international law irrespective of whether this contradicted its national law and policy. Yet, current Chinese law does not provide a specific approach to implement international legal obligations. In accordance with existing practice, some legal scholars contend that there are three ways for international treaty provisions to become part of China's domestic law: transformation through legislation (subsection 1), execution by administrative measures (subsection 2) and direct application of international treaties (subsection 3).[74] These observations are confirmed by the practice of Chinese environmental law.

1 Transformation through Legislation

The process of transformation generally takes place in two alternative ways. A first option is the enactment of special legislation. Generally, it is the State Council that promulgates departmental regulations. For example, in order to implement the Basel Convention on the Control of Transboundary Movements of Hazardous Wastes and their Disposal,[75] the Regulations on the Safety Management of Hazardous Chemicals[76] were adopted in 2013. The second approach is the incorporation of treaty obligations into existing laws by amendment or revision.

73 See e.g. Jiang Hong (江虹), GUO JI FA YU GUO NEI FA GUAN XI DE SI KAO (国际法与国内法关系的思考) [Reflections on Relationships between International Law and Domestic Law] (2014) 3 *Journal of Liaoning Administration College* 43–5; Wu Hui (吴慧), GUO JI TIAO YUE ZAI WO GUO GUO NEI FA SHANG DE DI WEI JI YU GUO NEI FA CHONG TU DE YU FANG HE JIE JUE (国际条约在我国国内法上的地位及与国内法冲突的预防和解决) [Status of International Treaties in the Chinese Law System and How to Prevent and Manage Conflicts] (2000) 2 *Journal of the University of International Relations* 23–8.

74 Xue Hanqin and Jin Qian, 'International Treaties in the Chinese Domestic Legal System' (2009) 8 *Chinese Journal of International Law* 299322; Charles R. McElwee, *Environmental Law in China: Managing Risk and Ensuring Compliance* (New York: Oxford University Press, 2010), pp. 689.

75 Basel Convention on the Control of Transboundary Movements of Hazardous Wastes and their Disposal, Basel, 22 March 1989, in force 5 May 1992, 1673 UNTS 57.

76 WEI XIAN HUA XUE PING AN QUAN GUAN LI TIAO LI 2013 XIU DING (危险化学品安全管理条约2013修订) [Regulations on the Safety Management of Hazardous Chemicals (2013 Revision)] (promulgated and amended by the State Council of the People's Republic of China, 7 Dec. 2013, effective on 7 Dec. 2013).

The typical example is that the State Council adopted the 2018 Amendment of the Regulation on the Administration of Ozone Depleting Substances[77] to fulfil legal obligations under the Vienna Convention for the Protection of the Ozone Layer[78] and the Montreal Protocol on Substances that Deplete the Ozone Layer.[79]

2 Execution by Administrative Measures

Sometimes, administrative measures may be adopted to address harsh environmental problems, since it is time-consuming to transform international legal obligations into statute. Hence, administrative organs or offices may be authorised to promulgate regulatory documents.[80] The most recent case is the Chinese government's 'no' to foreign garbage, which is a matter governed by the Basel Convention. In 2017, under the approval of the State Council, the General Office of the State Council issued a 'Notice on the Issuance of the Implementation Plan for Prohibiting the Entry of Foreign Garbage and on the Advancement of the Reform of the Solid Waste Import Administrative System'.

3 Direct Application

Chinese environmental laws provide for general objectives, obligations and accountabilities. Normally, supplementary provisions address how an international environmental treaty will be dealt with when it is not in conformity

77 XIAO HAO CHOU YANG CENG WU ZHI GUAN LI TIAO LI 2018 XIU ZHENG (消耗臭氧层物质管理条例2018修正) [Regulations on the Administration of Ozone Depleting Substances] (promulgated and amended by the State Council of the People's Republic of China, 19 Mar. 2018, effective on 19 Mar. 2018).

78 Vienna Convention for the Protection of the Ozone Layer, Vienna, 22 March 1985, in force 22 September 1988, 1513 UNTS 293.

79 Montreal Protocol on Substances that Deplete the Ozone Layer, Montreal, 16 September 1987, in force 1 January 1989, 1522 UNTS 3.

80 To implement the 'Clean Development Mechanism' in the Kyoto Protocol, two administrative measures were issued. QING JIE FA ZHAN JI ZHI XIANG MU YUN XING GUAN LI BAN FA 2011 XIU DING (清洁发展机制项目运行管理办法2011修订) [Measures for the Operation and Management of Clean Development (2011 Revision)] (promulgated by the National Development and Reform Commission, Ministry of Science and Technology, Ministry of Foreign Affairs and Ministry of Finance, 3 Aug. 2011, effective on 3 Aug. 2011); ZHONG GUO QING JIE FA ZHAN JI ZHI JI JIN GUAN LI BAN FA 2017 XIU ZHENG (中国清洁发展机制基金管理办法2017修正) [Measures for the Administration of the Clean Development Mechanism Fund (2017 Amendment)] (promulgated by the Ministry of Finance, National Development and Reform Commission, Ministry of Foreign Affairs, Ministry of Science and Technology, Ministry of Environment and Ecology (formerly referred to as 'Ministry of Environmental Protection'), Ministry of Agriculture and Rural Affairs (formerly referred to as 'Ministry of Agriculture') and China Meteorological Administration, 29 Dec. 2017, effective on 1 Jan. 2018).

with national laws. Out of twenty-seven national laws only two explicitly define the status of international environmental treaties in case of conflicts.[81]

Article 96 of the Marine Environmental Protection Law (2017 Amendment) states that:

> Where an international treaty regarding marine environment protection concluded or acceded to by the People's Republic of China contains provisions differing from those contained in this Law, the provisions of the international treaty shall apply; however, the provisions about which the People's Republic of China has reservations shall be excepted.[82]

This provision reflects that international environmental treaty law prevails over national law in the field of marine protection. It also proves that direct applicability of environmental treaties has been presupposed in Chinese environmental law, although very few environmental laws directly pinpoint the approach. Since most provisions in environmental treaties are vague, national law normally is not in conflict with treaty provisions but concretises them for special circumstances.

VII CONCLUSION

China does not have a systematic law and practice concerning foreign relations. Its two characteristics of fragmentation and unpredictability can be explained by historical doubts and cautions towards international law, a western-dominated discourse and system of international law, and silence on the part of China's Constitution. Chinese environmental diplomacy helps to further comprehend Chinese foreign relations environmental law and policy. While there is no field of foreign relations law recognised as such in China, Chinese foreign relations environmental law and policy conforms to a basic structure of foreign relations law. China devised and operated distributed authorities through external coordination in international environmental treaty negotiations. According to the law and administrative regulations, the Standing Committee and the State Council are empowered to ratify or conclude international environmental treaties or agreements under special

81 Another example: Article 90 of ZHONG HUA REN MIN GONG HE GUO GU TI FEI WU WU RAN HUAN JING FANG ZHI FA 2016 XIU ZHENG (中国人民共和国固体废物污染环境防治法2017修正) [Law of the People's Republic of China on the Prevention and Control of Environmental Pollution Caused by Solid Wasters (2016 Revision)] (promulgated by the Standing Committee of the National People's Congress, 7 Nov. 2016, effective on 7 Nov. 2016).

82 See n. 42 above.

conditions. A ratified treaty becomes part of the Chinese legal system. To achieve compliance, Chinese legislative authorities may adopt transformation, executional measures or direct application.

The overall picture painted in this chapter hence points to a nuanced answer to the question of the existence of a Chinese foreign relations law: it does not exist as a separate field, but there are many components of Chinese domestic law which fulfil typical functions of a foreign relations law. In particular, they help to construct bridges and establish boundaries between public international law and the Chinese legal framework. Further research on the prevalence of similar conditions of the Chinese legal framework for other fields of international cooperation would be a welcome addition to the global scholarship on foreign relations law as well as public international law.

FINAL REFLECTIONS

16

The Dynamic and Sometimes Uneasy Relationship Between Foreign Relations Law and International Law

Curtis A. Bradley

The Oxford Handbook of Comparative Foreign Relations Law, published in 2019, ambitiously sought 'to lay the groundwork for a new field of study and teaching'.[1] The present volume usefully complements that effort by focusing, from a comparative perspective, on how foreign relations law interacts with international law. In this concluding chapter, I reflect on the relationship between these two bodies of law, drawing on examples from this volume and also from the *Handbook*. As will become evident, foreign relations law and international law have important and often underappreciated effects on each other, sometimes in ways that are constructive and mutually reinforcing, but at other times in ways that produce potential conflict.

I DEFINING FOREIGN RELATIONS LAW

As defined in the *Oxford Handbook*, foreign relations law is 'the domestic law of each nation that governs how that nation interacts with the rest of the world'.[2] Such domestic law can take a variety of forms, including constitutional law, statutory law, administrative regulations, and judicial decisions. It can also include constitutional customs, or 'conventions', that may or may not have legal status.[3] Much of this law, at least in constitutional

[1] Curtis A. Bradley, 'Preface', in Curtis A. Bradley (ed.), *The Oxford Handbook of Comparative Foreign Relations Law* (Oxford: Oxford University Press, 2019).

[2] Curtis A. Bradley, 'What Is Foreign Relations Law?' in Curtis A. Bradley (ed.), *The Oxford Handbook of Comparative Foreign Relations Law* (Oxford: Oxford University Press, 2019), p. 3. One can also describe certain international institutions, most notably the European Union, as having a body of foreign relations law. See Bradley, 'Preface'.

[3] For example, in Japan, the distinction between treaties that need to be submitted to the legislature for approval and agreements that can be concluded unilaterally by the executive branch is regulated by the 'Ohira Principles', a nonbinding set of standards promulgated by

democracies,[4] concerns allocations of authority between political actors, such as the authority to represent the nation in diplomacy, to conclude and terminate international agreements, to recognize foreign governments and their territories, and to initiate or end the use of military force.[5] In federal systems, these allocation issues are not only horizontal but also vertical, extending to the relations between national and subnational institutions. Foreign relations law also encompasses issues relating to the role of the courts in transnational cases, such as whether certain issues are 'non-justiciable' and thus subject entirely to political branch determination, whether and to what extent courts should give deference to the views of the executive branch, and the types of relief that courts are allowed to issue when they find that the executive branch has acted unlawfully.

Because foreign relations law under this definition is a type of domestic law, it is analytically distinct from a nation's international legal obligations.[6] This distinction between foreign relations law and international law is not meant to suggest anything about the status of international law within a domestic legal system. Nations differ in the extent to which they are positioned towards either the 'monistic' or 'dualistic' ends of the spectrum with respect to the domestic status of international law, and these differences are themselves part of their foreign relations law.

One virtue of defining foreign relations law as a form of domestic law is that it facilitates comparative analysis. Unlike international law, foreign relations

a Japanese foreign minister. See Tadaatsu Mori, 'The Current Practice of Making and Applying International Agreements in Japan', in Curtis A. Bradley (ed.), *The Oxford Handbook of Comparative Foreign Relations Law* (Oxford: Oxford University Press, 2019), ch. 11.

4 Comparative study may reveal differing national conceptions of what is or should be encompassed by foreign relations law. See, for example, Michael Riegner, 'Comparative Foreign Relations Law between Centre and Periphery: Liberal and Postcolonial Perspectives', this volume, p. 60, which suggests that postcolonial states may have a different perspective than liberal democracies about the functions of foreign relations law.

5 There are allocation issues even in non-democracies. For discussion of foreign relations law issues relating to China, see, for example, Ji Hua, 'China and Global Environmental Governance: Coordination, Distribution and Compliance', this volume, p. 317; Congyan Cai, 'International Law in Chinese Courts', in Curtis A. Bradley (ed.), *The Oxford Handbook of Comparative Foreign Relations Law* (Oxford: Oxford University Press, 2019), ch. 31.

6 See also Thomas Giegerich, 'Foreign Relations Law' (January 2011), in *Max Planck Encyclopedia of Public International Law*, available at https://opil.ouplaw.com/view/10.1093/law:epil/9780199231690/law-9780199231690-e937 ('The concrete form and content of a State's foreign relations law is within its domestic jurisdiction and thus beyond the range of international law.').

law makes no claim of universality and instead accepts that nations can and will have different approaches.[7] And there are many reasons why the content of foreign relations law might vary from nation to nation. It is not surprising, for example, to find differences between constitutional arrangements developed after World War II and those developed earlier. Parliamentary and presidential systems are also likely to reflect somewhat different approaches to questions of the separation of powers. In addition, understandings of the judicial role likely differ among countries, including as between civil law and common law countries. The particular domestic politics of a country can also have an important influence on the content of its domestic law, including its foreign relations law. Furthermore, foreign relations law may be affected by a nation's geopolitical status and sense of its national interest, and these will obviously vary, both among individual countries and over time.[8]

Another virtue of treating foreign relations law and international law as analytically distinct is that it allows for a consideration of the relationship between these bodies of law, including a consideration of the 'bridges' and 'boundaries' that are the focus of the present volume. As discussed below, there is an interactive dynamic between foreign relations law and international law, with each body of law having effects on the other.

Despite the benefits of using this definition for purposes of analysis, it should be emphasized that any sharp distinction between foreign relations law and international law will be artificial in practice. International law can and often is applied as domestic law, either directly or through some act of domestic incorporation. Moreover, even when international law is not applied directly, courts often construe domestic law in light of international legal obligations, and executive actors often exercise their discretion with such obligations in mind. Foreign relations law, as defined in the *Oxford Handbook*, includes the domestic rules governing such application and interpretation but not the international legal obligations themselves. The term could be defined more broadly, however, to include at least some aspects of international law.[9]

7 To be sure, even when nations ostensibly have the same international obligations, they may interpret them differently, and it may be fruitful to explore such differences. See, for example, Anthea Roberts et al., *Comparative International Law* (Oxford: Oxford University Press, 2018).

8 See also Frédéric Mégret, 'Foreign Legal Policy as the Background to Foreign Relations Law? Revisiting Guy de Lacharrière's *La politique juridique extérieure*', this volume, p. 108, which suggests that in studying differing national approaches to foreign relations, it is important to consider not only a nation's domestic law but also its particular policy orientation towards international law.

9 Any attempt to include international law within the definition of foreign relations law will encounter difficult line-drawing questions. Does one include all of a nation's international

Foreign relations law, however it is properly defined, has long been a more developed field of study and teaching in the United States than in most other countries. It is not entirely clear why this is so. The United States has the oldest written Constitution in the world, and accommodating that Constitution to a radically changed international environment, as well as a substantially different US role in that environment, may present unique challenges. In addition, the United States has a unique brand of federalism that tends to generate complex legal issues, especially as globalization has blurred the line between foreign and domestic affairs. Law schools in the United States also may have a more flexible structure than in many other countries, allowing faculty to more easily cross historic subject matter divides.

Whatever the reasons, there now appears to be growing interest outside the United States in foreign relations law. In 2014, Campbell McLachlan published an important and wide-ranging treatise on Commonwealth foreign relations law, a treatise cited by the UK Supreme Court in its landmark *Miller* decision concerning Brexit.[10] A number of important works have also been published in recent years focusing on EU foreign relations law, addressing issues such as the process for concluding international agreements and the role of federalism that are similar to the foreign relations law issues faced by individual nations.[11] The *Oxford Handbook*, which has forty-six chapters by authors from around the world, will hopefully stimulate further international interest in the subject. Likewise, the present volume highlights the potential interest in foreign relations law by scholars from a wide variety of countries. As a result, this is an especially good time to be thinking both about the nature of this body of law and about similarities and differences in how nations address it.

legal obligations? Only those that have the status of domestic law? Only those that are enforceable by the courts?

10 Campbell McLachlan, *Foreign Relations Law* (Cambridge: Cambridge University Press, 2014), cited in R *(on the Application of Miller and another)* v. *Secretary of State for Exiting the European Union*, [2017] UKSC 5, para. 57, www.supremecourt.uk/cases/docs/uksc-2016–0196-judgment.pdf, accessed September 30, 2020.

11 See, for example, Marise Cremona and Bruno de Witte (eds.), *EU Foreign Relations Law: Constitutional Fundamentals* (Oxford: Hart Publishing, 2008); Piet Eeckhout, *EU External Relations Law*, 2nd ed., (Oxford: Oxford University Press, 2011); Ramses A. Wessel and Joris Larik, *EU External Relations Law: Text, Cases and Materials* (Oxford: Hart Publishing, 2020). See also Joris Larik, 'EU Foreign Relations Law as a Field of Scholarship' (2017) 111 *AJIL Unbound* 321.

II FOREIGN RELATIONS LAW'S EFFECTS ON INTERNATIONAL LAW

There a variety of ways in which foreign relations law can affect international law. Most directly, a nation's foreign relations law can affect the manner in which a nation engages with international law – for example, the domestic process that it must follow in order to join or implement a treaty. Sometimes such foreign relations law will, at least as a practical matter, act as a constraint on a nation's ability to engage or comply with international law – for example, by requiring that multiple domestic institutions agree on such engagement or compliance. If so, this will have an impact on international law's development.[12] In some cases, domestic courts may even require that governmental actors take certain actions to ensure the compatibility of international law with domestic constitutional law. A noteworthy example is the Colombian Constitutional Court's 2019 decision conditioning the constitutionality of a bilateral investment treaty between Colombia and France on the issuance of a particular interpretive declaration by the two countries.[13]

Sometimes foreign relations law will affect not only international law's primary rules, but also its secondary rules that govern how international law is made. Indeed, this has long been the case. For example, when some nations began separating the treaty power between executives and legislatures after the American and French revolutions of the late eighteenth century, international law began to relax expectations that signature of a treaty carried with it an obligation to ratify the treaty.[14] Similarly, in part spurred by American practice arising from its divided treaty power, international law came to allow for treaty reservations at the time of ratification (and international law on that subject has since evolved to take account of changes in the nature of treaty-making, including most notably the rise of multilateral conventions).[15] Today, the

[12] In other instances, a nation might be able to use its foreign relations law to its advantage in international negotiations, as Felix Lange notes in his chapter for this volume, 'Foreign Relations Law As a Bargaining Tool?' See also Robert D. Putnam, 'Diplomacy and Domestic Politics: The Logic of Two-Level Games' (1988) 42 *International Organization* 427.

[13] See Gustavo Prieto, 'The Colombian Constitutional Court Judgment C-252/19: A new frontier for reform in international investment law', EJIL: Talk!, July 29, 2019, www.ejiltalk.org/the-colombian-constitutional-court-judgment-c-252-19-a-new-frontier-for-reform-in-international-investment-law/, accessed September 30, 2020. See also Angelo Jr. Golia, 'Judicial Review, Foreign Relations and Global Administrative Law. The Administrative Function of Courts in Foreign Relations', this volume, p. 130.

[14] See J. Mervyn Jones, *Full Powers and Ratification* (Cambridge: Cambridge University Press, 1946), pp. 76–80.

[15] See Curtis A. Bradley, *International Law in the U.S. Legal System*, 3rd ed., (Oxford: Oxford University Press, 2020), p. 38.

foreign relations laws of many countries divide the treaty power between the executive branch and the legislature, at least for certain types of agreements,[16] making these international law rules even more significant.

Importantly, the normative goals of foreign relations law will not always align with the normative goals of international law. For example, there is an effort in some countries to give their legislatures a stronger role in foreign relations decision-making, such as with respect to treaty-making and the use of military force. Doing so might lead to greater deliberation and democratic input, but it will not inevitably promote greater international cooperation. It is not uncommon, for example, for legislatures to fail to approve treaties or other international law efforts favored by the executive branch. There may also be a recent trend towards making foreign relations law more 'administrative' in nature, and thus potentially subject to greater judicial oversight. But, as Angelo Jr. Golia notes in his chapter for this volume, such a shift 'does not always imply greater coordination among systems, but can rather bring more disorder, conflict and unpredictability'.[17]

Sometimes a greater role for legislative or judicial involvement in foreign relations law will even lead to breaches of international law that might not have occurred under executive control. This is one way of understanding the much-discussed *Medellin* v. *Texas* litigation in the United States. In holding that legislative action was needed in order to convert the US obligation to comply with a decision of the International Court of Justice into domestic law,[18] the Supreme Court made it much more difficult for the United States to comply. Indeed, even now, many years after the decision, Congress has still not enacted the requisite legislation.[19] The US experience with amendments to its sovereign immunity statute in recent years similarly highlights how legislatures may not always prioritize international law compliance. The US Congress has created various exceptions to sovereign immunity for terrorism-related conduct, despite concerns raised by the executive branch that such

[16] See Pierre-Hugues Verdier and Mila Versteeg, 'Separation of Powers, Treaty-Making, and Treaty Withdrawal', in Curtis A. Bradley (ed.), *The Oxford Handbook of Comparative Foreign Relations Law* (Oxford: Oxford University Press, 2019), ch. 8.

[17] See Golia, 'Judicial Review, Foreign Relations and Global Administrative Law', p. 158.

[18] See *Medellín* v. *Texas*, 552 US 491, 525–26 (2008) ('The responsibility for transforming an international obligation arising from a non-self-executing treaty into domestic law falls to Congress.').

[19] Proposed legislation designed to facilitate US compliance with the obligations of consular notice that were at issue in *Medellin* was introduced in Congress in 2011, but the legislation was not adopted. See Consular Notification Compliance Act, S. 1194, introduced in Senate on June 14, 2011.

exceptions may not be consistent with international law and might expose the United States to reductions in its own sovereign immunity abroad.[20]

Another widely discussed example is the 2014 Italian constitutional court decision issued in response to the ICJ's decision in *Germany* v. *Italy* concerning the international law of sovereign immunity. In holding that the international law of immunity recognized by the ICJ was incompatible with Italian constitutional law and thus inapplicable in the domestic legal order, the court contributed to placing Italy in potential breach of its international obligations. In doing so, it acted contrary to the position of both the executive and legislative branches in Italy, which were prepared to accept the ICJ's decision.[21] In these and other examples of potential conflict between foreign relations law and international law, there can be reasonable debates about which body of law should bear more of the blame. One interesting issue for future scholarly analysis would be whether and to what extent each of the two bodies of law has some responsibility to coordinate with the other.[22]

III INTERNATIONAL LAW'S EFFECTS ON FOREIGN RELATIONS LAW

Not only does foreign relations law affect international law, but international law also in turn affects foreign relations law. As an initial matter, the foreign relations powers that must be allocated under foreign relations law are

20 For example, in 2016, Congress enacted the Justice Against Sponsors of Terrorism Act over President Barack Obama's veto. In his veto message, Obama expressed concern that, by creating a new exception to immunity, the Act 'would upset longstanding international principles regarding sovereign immunity, putting in place rules that, if applied globally, could have serious implications for U.S. national interests'. See Barack Obama, 'Veto Message from the President, S. 2040', the White House, September 23, 2016, https://obama whitehouse.archives.gov/the-press-office/2016/09/23/veto-message-president-s2040, accessed September 30, 2020. Of course, sometimes legislatures do play close attention to international law or are otherwise influenced by it. See, for example, Veronika Fikfak, 'War, International Law and the Rise of Parliament – The Influence of International Law on UK Parliamentary Practice with Respect to the Use of Force', this volume, p. 299.

21 See Golia, 'Judicial Review, Foreign Relations and Global Administrative Law', p. 153 et seq. See also Andrea Bianchi, 'Jurisdictional Immunities, Constitutional Values, and System Closures', in Curtis A. Bradley (ed.), *The Oxford Handbook of Comparative Foreign Relations Law* (Oxford: Oxford University Press, 2019), ch. 38.

22 Another interesting example of domestic foreign relations law imposing a limit on the implementation of an ICJ ruling is a 2014 decision from Colombia's constitutional court requiring that a treaty be concluded in order to implement an ICJ decision limiting Colombia's maritime rights. See Monica Garcia, 'Colombia Court Backs Santos in Sea Boundary Dispute with Nicaragua', Reuters, May 3, 2014, www.reuters.com/article/colom bia-nicaragua-dispute/colombia-court-backs-santos-in-sea-boundary-dispute-with-nicaragua-i dUSL2N0NP03L20140503, accessed September 30, 2020.

themselves often defined by international law, which regulates the rights and obligations of sovereign nations.[23] For example, if a national constitution assigns the power to 'declare war' to a particular national actor, one would need to consult international law in order to have a full understanding of the potential scope and significance of this authority. More generally, as a matter of explication, it will often be necessary to know the international law backdrop in order to understand elements of foreign relations law, such as foreign relations law relating to treaty-making and interpretation, extraterritorial regulation, and sovereign immunity.[24]

Moreover, while international law generally purports to be agnostic about domestic constitutional arrangements, in fact it sometimes assumes or favors certain arrangements. In particular, international law tends to assume, at least as a default, executive control over aspects of foreign relations. As a result, international law can make it more difficult for nations to rein in executive authority in the foreign relations area. This is evident, as Edward Swaine notes in his chapter for this volume, in the international law governing treaty termination.[25] The Vienna Convention on the Law of Treaties presumes that notices of treaty withdrawal received from heads of state are valid and, unlike for treaty formation, does not provide for any domestic process justification for voiding such notice. To be sure, international law does not require that states give unilateral withdrawal authority to their executives, and it is possible that domestic institutions could resist the exercise of such authority. In recent years, national courts in both the United Kingdom and South Africa famously insisted on legislative involvement in treaty withdrawals. But the effectiveness of such domestic checks will depend on a state's

23 See, for example, *United States* v. *Curtiss-Wright Export Corp*, 299 US 304, 318 (1936) ('As a member of the family of nations, the right and power of the United States in that field are equal to the right and power of the other members of the international family. Otherwise, the United States is not completely sovereign.').

24 The American Law Institute's (2018) *Restatement (Fourth) of the Foreign Relations Law of the United States* 2, observes that, because it 'deals with two distinct legal systems, namely domestic law bearing on foreign relations and relevant portions of international law, it must address both'.

25 See Edward Swaine, 'International Foreign Relations Law: Executive Authority in Entering and Exiting Treaties', this volume, p. 46. See also Hannah Woolaver, 'State Engagement with Treaties: Interactions Between International and Domestic Law', in Curtis A. Bradley (ed.), *The Oxford Handbook of Comparative Foreign Relations Law* (Oxford: Oxford University Press, 2019) ch. 24; Hannah Woolaver, 'From Joining to Leaving: Domestic Law's Role in the International Legal Validity of Treaty Withdrawal' (2019) 30 *European Journal of International Law* 73.

particular laws and institutions.[26] International law, as currently structured, does not itself facilitate legislative involvement in treaty withdrawals.

Executive authority is favored under international law in other ways as well. The Vienna Convention sets forth only very narrow grounds for invalidating treaties concluded in violation of domestic law: according to article 46 of the Convention, the violation must not only concern 'a rule of [the nation's] internal law of fundamental importance', but the rule must also be 'manifest'. In part because of this provision, the US Senate did not approve the Convention when President Nixon submitted it in the 1970s: the Senate Foreign Relations Committee was concerned that this provision might bind the United States to international agreements made by the president without the two-thirds Senate consent required by article II of the Constitution, because that requirement might not be considered 'manifest' given the extensive US practice of concluding agreements outside of this process.[27] Again, of course, national institutions could resist executive aggrandizement in this area. In 2017, for example, the Ghanaian Supreme Court held that Ghana's president had acted unconstitutionally in concluding an agreement with the United States without obtaining parliamentary approval, and it specifically declined to follow the US practice of allowing executive agreements.[28] But, as for treaty withdrawal, any such domestic resistance will obtain little support from international law.

Yet another way that the Vienna Convention may empower executives is its treatment of signing obligations. Under article 18 of the Convention, a nation that signs an international agreement is 'obliged to refrain from acts which would defeat the object and purpose' of the treaty 'until it shall have made its intention clear not to become a party to the treaty'. This is true even for nations that require legislative approval prior to the ratification of treaties. As a result, executives in such nations can potentially create treaty-related obligations through unilateral action. In the United States, this may have happened when the Clinton administration signed the Rome Statute for the International Criminal Court in 1999, knowing that the incoming Bush

[26] For an explanation of why the United Kingdom and South African decisions are unlikely to have much relevance to US law, see Curtis A. Bradley and Laurence R. Helfer, 'Treaty Exit in the United States: Insights from the United Kingdom or South Africa?' (2017) 111 *AJIL Unbound* 428.

[27] See Anna M. Frankowska, 'The Vienna Convention on the Law of Treaties before United States Courts' (1988) 28 *Virginia Journal of International Law* 281 at 296–98.

[28] See *Banful* v. *Attorney General and Another,* (J1/7/2016) [2017] GHASC 21 (June 22, 2017), available at https://ghalii.org/gh/judgment/supreme-court/2017/21, accessed September 30, 2020.

administration was not supportive of the Statute. The Bush administration then 'unsigned' the Convention by announcing that it had no intention of ratifying it.[29]

These examples also suggest that, especially in nations in which the scope of executive authority over foreign relations is unclear, executives may be able to leverage international law as a way around domestic constraints. Another potential example of this phenomenon concerns the use of military force. Even in nations that require legislative approval for some uses of force, executives may seek to rely on international law, such as UN Security Council authorization, as an alternative or supplementary source of authority. This happened in the United States, for example, in connection with the Korean War.[30]

Another example of international law's potential effect on foreign relations law concerns the increasingly administrative nature of international law. A significant amount of international law is made today not through high-level negotiations between foreign ministries but rather through international institutions, lower-level negotiations between domestic administrative agencies, and various forms of 'soft law'.[31] This development tends to further enhance executive authority over foreign relations, for a number of reasons: executive agents tend to represent nations in international institutions, administrative law tends to be centered in the executive branch, and less formal agreement-making may not be subject to the usual domestic requirements for treaty-making.[32] In response to this development, as Jean Galbraith notes in her chapter for this volume, legislatures may need to enhance process-based constraints on the exercise of executive authority.[33]

[29] See Curtis A. Bradley, 'Unratified Treaties, Domestic Politics, and the U.S. Constitution' (2007) 48 *Harvard International Law Journal* 307 at 311–12.

[30] See Curtis A. Bradley and Jean Galbraith, 'Presidential War Powers as an Interactive Dynamic: International Law, Domestic Law, and Practice-Based Legal Change' (2016) 91 *New York University Law Review* 689 at 735–36.

[31] See Anna Petrig, 'Democratic Participation in International Law-Making in Switzerland after the "Age of Treaties"', this volume, p. 180 (discussing how 'informal law-making greatly complicates the relationship between sovereignty (including domestic democratic self-determination) and international cooperation').

[32] For an account of increased executive branch control over international law in the United States, see Curtis A. Bradley and Jack L. Goldsmith, 'Presidential Control Over International Law' (2018) 131 *Harvard Law Review* 1201.

[33] See Jean Galbraith, 'From Scope to Process: The Evolution of Checks on Presidential Power in U.S. Foreign Relations Law', this volume, p. 239. For discussion of a legislative effort in Spain along these lines, see Carlos Espósito, 'Spanish Foreign Relations Law and the Process for Making Treaties and Other International Agreements', in Curtis A. Bradley (ed.), *The Oxford Handbook of Comparative Foreign Relations Law* (Oxford: Oxford University Press, 2019), ch. 12.

Sometimes international law itself requires or favors certain processes of decision-making, and when it does so this can also affect foreign relations law. In their introductory chapter for this volume, Helmut Aust and Thomas Kleinlein give the example of a requirement of environmental impact assessments,[34] a requirement that may as a practical matter empower certain administrative agencies at the domestic level. Investment law is another example where international law may in effect mandate certain domestic processes, as well as the substance of some aspects of the domestic law applied in these processes.[35] The ICJ's 2004 decision in *Avena*, which was at issue in the *Medellín* litigation referenced above, is also an example of international law being construed to impose a domestic process requirement, namely judicial review of the convictions and sentences of certain individuals who had been imprisoned without proper consular notice,[36] although the United States still has not implemented the requirement.

In addition to these horizontal separation of powers effects, international law may also affect vertical issues relating to federalism. In a variety of ways, international law tends to favor national over subnational control over foreign relations. For example, unless a treaty provides otherwise, it is deemed, as noted in article 29 of the Vienna Convention, to apply throughout the entire territory of a party. Similarly, under the international law of state responsibility, nations are viewed as responsible for the conduct of their territorial units, and they are not allowed to rely on their internal law, including internal law relating to federalism, as a justification for a failure to comply with their obligations.[37] Although these presumptions in favor of national rather than subnational control of foreign relations law are understandable in a system of Westphalian nation-states, they can make it more difficult for constitutional values relating to federalism to be maintained, especially as international law increasingly overlaps with matters of traditional domestic regulation.

34 See Helmut Philipp Aust and Thomas Kleinlein, 'Introduction', this volume, p. 3.

35 See, for example, Julian Arato, 'The Private Law Critique of International Investment Law' (2019) 113 *American Journal of International Law* 1 at 50 (arguing that '[international investment law] and [investor-state dispute settlement] have together generated rudimentary, but surprisingly broad, swathes of international private law – disciplining domestic policy space in underappreciated ways, and distorting the logic and functions of whole fields of domestic private law in relation to foreign investors').

36 See *Avena and Other Mexican Nationals (Mexico* v. *United States of America)*, Judgment, I.C.J. Reports 2004, para. 140. ('[T]he legal consequences of this breach have to be examined and taken into account in the course of review and reconsideration. The Court considers that it is the judicial process that is suited to this task.').

37 See International Law Commission, 'Responsibility of States for Internationally Wrongful Acts', 2001, arts. 4(1), 32, United Nations Office of Legal Affairs, 2005, https://legal.un.org/ilc/texts/instruments/english/draft_articles/9_6_2001.pdf, accessed September 30, 2020.

IV CONCLUSION

One of the virtues of studying foreign relations law, as noted at the outset of this chapter, is that it allows for an exploration of the rich and evolutionary relationship between foreign relations law and international law, a topic that has been under-explored in the literature. The present volume makes an important contribution in addressing that relationship from a range of perspectives, and it will undoubtedly spur additional scholarship on the topic. In addition to its scholarly value, the volume should be of interest to lawyers and policy-makers in both the domestic and international domains because it highlights how legal rules developed in one of these domains can have important, and not always beneficial, effects in the other.

17

The Present Salience of Foreign Relations Law

Campbell McLachlan

I POPULISM, CONSTITUTIONAL LAW'S EXTERNAL FACE AND INTERNATIONAL LAW

The choices that states make about how their internal constitutional systems relate to the world outside – the *inter*national – are not accidental. They reflect fundamental decisions about how open or closed the state is to international law[1] and about the level at which governance decisions that affect societies are made. Despite this, the legal relationship between the domestic and the international is under-theorised. It has been characterised by a 'dichotomy [which] remains perhaps the least investigated of all the fundamental divisions in our political lives'.[2]

The fissure between the municipal and the international has been exposed to view – and exploited – by the contemporary rise of so-called 'populism' in many states. A key tenet of populism has been a form of exclusionary identity politics that, mobilising popular sovereignty, creates a division between 'the people' and the other, seen in Hobbesian terms as the enemy outside.[3] Populism makes a claim to sociological legitimacy – that society should not be controlled by external forces – that leads to a turn against 'elites, supranational agreements, international judicial institutions or economic powers'.[4] The result is a context in which 'international law is invoked, but in what

1 Helmut Philipp Aust, 'The Democratic Challenge to Foreign Relations Law in Transatlantic Perspective', in Jacco Bomhoff, David Dyzenhaus and Thomas Poole (eds.), *The Double-Facing Constitution: Legal Externalities and the Reshaping of the Constitutional Order* (Cambridge: Cambridge University Press, 2020), p. 345.

2 David Armitage, *Foundations of Modern International Thought* (Cambridge: Cambridge University Press, 2013), p. 10.

3 Jan-Werner Müller, *What Is Populism?* (London: Penguin Books, 2017), p. 3.

4 Paul Blokker, 'Populist Governments and International Law: A Reply to Heike Krieger' (2019) 30 *EJIL* 1009 at 1012.

seems an increasingly antagonistic way, amounting often to a dialogue of the deaf'.[5]

Despite the central importance of the external face of populism, surprisingly little attention has been paid to its legal significance, in comparison to its internal constitutional implications.[6] The populist challenge to international law is particularly concerned with the boundary between the international and the domestic, in which national sovereignty – linked with the popular sovereignty of 'the people' – is invoked as the key concept. In legal terms, this means that the challenge presented by the external face of populism is not only about the way in which states interact on the plane of international law, in the discourse between states and in their engagement with and within international institutions. It is also, perhaps even principally, about the relation between the internal law and institutions of the state on the one hand and international law on the other. This is the domain of foreign relations law.

The result is that the renewed attention given to foreign relations law as a field of *comparative* study (and not merely an American *Sonderweg*)[7] comes at a time when the legal doctrines are being tested and debated to an unprecedented extent in many states in ways that expose to view the underlying policies and principles served by the law in this area. Yet this is not only a linear story about the enlargement of executive power fuelled by popular mandate. In constitutional democracies, it also is an account of the ways in which the other organs of government, the legislature and the courts, articulate their own role.

The publication of the present collection of chapters – the fruit of a well-conceived symposium – therefore presents an opportunity to reflect on the manner in which foreign relations law mediates the relation between the domestic and the international legal realms at a time when this is a hotly contested boundary. This is not simply an exercise in comparing legal techniques. Rather, it invites consideration of a larger question: what is foreign relations law *for*?

It is possible to examine that question (as I have done elsewhere) as one of the perspective or conception of the function of foreign relations law with

5 James Crawford, 'The Current Political Discourse Concerning International Law' (2018) 81 *Modern Law Review* 1.

6 But see for important interventions: Philip Alston, 'The Populist Challenge to Human Rights' (2017) 9 *Journal of Human Rights Practice* 1; Heike Krieger, 'Populist Governments and International Law' (2019) 30 *EJIL* 971. For a more general survey: (2018) 49 *Netherlands Yearbook of International Law* 1–220.

7 Detlev F. Vagts, 'American International Law: A *Sonderweg*?', in Klaus Dicke et al. (eds.), *Weltinnenrecht. Liber Amicorum Jost Delbrück* (Berlin: Dunker & Humblot, 2005), p. 835.

which the field is approached.[8] Seen in this way, both the scope of the field and the development of specific legal doctrines will be affected by whether foreign relations law is conceived as designed to maintain the exclusion of the international from the domestic realm; or alternatively to facilitate the reception of international law into the domestic sphere. It may bring the conduct of foreign relations within the domestic constitutional sphere or concern itself with the external conduct of diplomatic relations between states. Finally, it might be reconceived as a conflict of laws for public law, performing an allocative function on questions of jurisdiction and applicable law as they arise in the external exercise of public power. In this latter perspective, the field draws upon elements of public and private international law as well as constitutional law, even if (like private international law itself) it must always remain a part of the domestic law of each state.

This book shines a specific spotlight on the relationship between comparative foreign relations law and public international law. Amidst what Edward Swaine describes as 'the considerable, and understandable, excitement regarding the nascent field of comparative foreign relations law',[9] it is worth pausing to ask what implications this might have for the development of international law itself. Is the turn to foreign relations law, as Anthea Roberts has suggested, 'an inherently conservative move'?[10] After all, foreign relations law had been until recently hardly recognised as a field outside the United States. There it has taken a pronounced inward turn in the most recent generation of scholarship. Is it not more than coincidental that it should be exported as a comparative field at a time when the rise of populism, in the United States and elsewhere, increasingly resists the role of the international in the domestic polity?

What effect might the development of comparative foreign relations law as a field have on public international law itself? Helmut Aust and Thomas Kleinlein argue in their Introduction that 'it is precisely this by now established narrative of an "*Ersatz* international law" that should be challenged critically'.[11] But in order to do so, it is first necessary to consider that narrative. Section II will enquire whether, and if so how, an increased focus on foreign

8 Campbell McLachlan, 'Five Conceptions of the Function of Foreign Relations Law', in Curtis A. Bradley (ed.), *The Oxford Handbook of Comparative Foreign Relations Law* (Oxford: Oxford University Press, 2019), p. 21.
9 See the chapter by Edward T. Swaine, p. 46.
10 Anthea Roberts, *Is International Law International?* (New York: Oxford University Press, 2017), p. xx.
11 See the chapter by Helmut Philipp Aust and Thomas Kleinlein, p. 1 at 8.

relations law might itself undermine international law or create an '*Ersatz* international law'.

The balance of this chapter considers two lines of response. Its central argument is that a renewed focus on the *relation between* international law and foreign relations law, which the present collection adopts, might in fact address such a critique.

Section III argues that, once the more extreme rhetoric of the populist critique of international law is stripped away, the debate exposes to view the importance of reconnecting the external and internal aspects of sovereignty. Populist leaders have adopted (and often appropriated for their own purposes) a much more deep-seated and genuine concern about the exercise of popular sovereignty vis-à-vis governance at the global level, which should not be dismissed. Brexit is emblematic of the reignition of a much larger and critically important debate about how 'the people' of a nation are to determine the manner in which they are to engage with the world. This is not a new issue, though it has been sharply re-exposed to view in the present era. In this debate, there is no necessary dissonance between international law – which retains as a peremptory norm the principle of self-determination[12] – and the viability of a national constitution founded on representative democracy. On the contrary, it is the populist claim of an exclusive executive right to speak for the people in foreign relations that we should question.

Section IV then suggests a second important line of response. This is precisely that recognising the concerns of foreign relations law to be legal concerns (as opposed to the exercise of executive discretion in a zone of non-law) enables consideration of the interaction between the domestic constitution and international law as one concerned with the interaction of legal systems. In other words, it necessitates treating international law as law and the domain of foreign relations as not being purely political but as bounded by law. This is not about treating all exercises of foreign policy as constrained by law, still less as necessarily subject to domestic adjudication. Rather it requires us to take seriously the extent to which the executive foreign affairs function is bound by the international law obligations that it assumes on behalf of the state.

The diverse chapters collected in the present volume cast important light on a set of legal questions that arise out of a governance dilemma that many states now face with increasing urgency. It may well be impossible, as Dani Rodrik

12 International Law Commission, 'Draft Articles on Responsibility of States for Internationally Wrongful Acts, with commentaries' (2001) II(2) *Yearbook of the International Law Commission* 31 at 85.

has suggested, to have 'hyperglobalization, democracy and self-determination all at once'.[13] But, even if we put aside 'hyperglobalisation', we must still find a way to reconcile popular engagement in the process of government at the national level with the necessity of international cooperation.

II AN *ERSATZ* INTERNATIONAL LAW?

In order to challenge critically the idea that foreign relations law is a kind of *Ersatz* international law, as the editors of this volume invite us to do, it is first necessary to examine the nature of the charge. How might it be said that the emergence of foreign relations law, as a discipline on a global comparative scale, could adversely affect international law itself? Here experience in the United States, as the country in which foreign relations law as a distinct subject has the greatest prominence, may be instructive.

In an important contribution to the debate about the emergence of the field of comparative foreign relations law, Karen Knop identifies three anxieties about the effect of the creation of such a field on public international law itself in light of the American experience.[14] In the first place, she notes that the study of foreign relations law has displaced international law in many American law schools, with the consequence that students are 'less likely to approach public international law as a legal system than instrumentally as one possible tool in the legal toolkit for solving transnational problems'.[15] In the second place, she suggests that foreign relations law may end up taking dualism to its ultimate end. This 'deep dualism'[16] discounts the legal quality of international law, such that 'the field of foreign relations law is structured as a divide between an internal realm in which law is the default and an external realm in which foreign relations is the default'.[17] In the third place, she identifies the risk that foreign relations law distorts the operation of international law: by inserting domestic concerns into the operation of international law; by encouraging non-compliance with international law at the national level, inserting boundaries derived from domestic constitutional law; or by opening the potential that domestic courts will simply misconstrue its obligations.

[13] Dani Rodrik, *The Globalization Paradox: Democracy and the Future of the World Economy* (New York: W.W. Norton, 2012), p. 200.

[14] Karen Knop, 'Foreign Relations Law: Comparison as Invention', in Curtis A. Bradley (ed.), *The Oxford Handbook of Comparative Foreign Relations Law* (Oxford: Oxford University Press, 2019), p. 3.

[15] Knop, 'Comparison as Invention', p. 51.

[16] Citing Alejandro Lorite Escorihuela, 'Cultural Relativism the American Way: The Nationalist School of International Law in the United States' (2005) 5 *Global Jurist Frontiers* 1.

[17] Lorite Escorihuela, 'Cultural Relativism the American Way', 54.

These concerns cannot be ignored, at least insofar as they are observable in the contemporary American context. Jens Ohlin argues in his book *The Assault on International Law* that the development of doctrines in US constitutional law that enhance executive discretion in foreign relations went hand-in-hand with scholarship that sought to undermine the determinate and binding character of international law.[18]

Recent experience also exposes the risk of blurring important lines of distinction between the operation of international and national law. Naz Modirzadeh describes how, after 9/11, international humanitarian law became 'at best a set of tools that could be operationalized alongside constitutional law, human rights law, and criminal law and procedure' in a form of 'folk international law'.[19]

Nor are these trends limited to the United States. John Finnis, arguing that the executive in the United Kingdom has no obligation to abide by the state's international law obligations, writes: 'International law remains, like it or not, a defective example of law. The criteria for its formation and identification remain opaque, controverted, and manipulable without redress'.[20]

Chapters in this volume bear out some of the concerns that Knop identifies. Felix Lange shows how the insertion of the domestic constitutional law limitations of the United States into the negotiations shaped the outcome of the Paris Agreement on climate change at the international level, while providing no subsequent constraint on the executive decision to withdraw at the domestic level.[21]

Foreign relations law may also encourage the priority of constitutional law concerns over international law obligations. Angelo Golia recounts the refusal of the Italian Constitutional Court to give effect to the judgment of the International Court of Justice in the dispute between Germany and Italy on sovereign immunity for acts committed in World War II, in which it cited supreme principles of the constitution.[22] As Curt Bradley observes, 'the

18 Jens David Ohlin, *The Assault on International Law* (New York: Oxford University Press, 2015). For an early important essay calling attention to this trend see: Peter J. Spiro, 'The New Sovereigntists, American Exceptionalism and Its False Prophets' (2000) 79 *Foreign Affairs* 9.

19 Naz K. Modirzadeh, 'Folk International Law: 9/11 Lawyering and the Transformation of the Law of Armed Conflict to Human Rights Policy and Human Rights Law to War Governance' (2014) 5 *Harvard National Security Journal* 225 at 257.

20 John Finnis, 'Ministers, International Law, and the Rule of Law', Judicial Power Project, 2 November 2015, https://judicialpowerproject.org.uk/ministers-international-law-and-the-rule-of-law/, accessed 5 May 2020.

21 See the chapter by Felix Lange.

22 See the chapter by Angelo Jr Golia, discussing Decision No. 238/2014 of 22 October 2014 (Italian Constitutional Court); *Jurisdictional Immunities of the State (Germany v. Italy: Greece intervening)*, Judgment, I.C.J. Reports 2012, p. 99.

normative goals of foreign relations law will not always align with the normative goals of international law'.[23]

A closer embrace of international law at the national law level may also lead to its misapplication. Dire Tladi argues in his critique of the South African Constitutional Court judgment in the *SADC Tribunal* case that 'the problem with the Court is not *only* its conclusion but also its failure to engage with the methodology of international law'.[24]

To these concerns, the rise of populism adds the prospect of an increasing outright withdrawal of states from the international legal system, facilitated by the exercise of an unbound executive discretion to withdraw within many domestic constitutions.[25] This is a trend of which President Trump's announced withdrawals from the Paris Agreement and the Iran Nuclear Accord – both so recently and painstakingly negotiated – are emblematic. Yet the evidence of withdrawal, in particular from submission to international dispute settlement, is in fact much more widespread.[26] Examples include the United Kingdom's withdrawal from the jurisdiction of the European Court of Justice under Brexit; the increasing challenge to the jurisdiction of the European Court of Human Rights; the threatened collective withdrawal of African states from the International Criminal Court; and the withdrawal of a number of key states from investment treaty arbitration.[27] In each case, there is a striking similarity in one of the key strands in the arguments for withdrawal. Those objecting to the conferral of a power of adjudication over states upon international tribunals allege that this creates a democratic deficit. International judges, described as unaccountable international elites, are said to take decisions that constrain the power of peoples to exercise their popular sovereignty by determining the direction of their societies for themselves. They assert that this undermines the essence of the sovereignty of states.

International law has seemed curiously impotent in the face of these newly emboldened assertions of sovereignty, though I have argued elsewhere that international law does place checks on withdrawal, recognising that it is an act that is not a matter of purely unilateral discretion, since of its nature it affects the interests of other states parties.[28] The question that this phenomenon raises

23 See the chapter by Curtis A. Bradley, p. 345.
24 See the chapter by Dire Tladi, p. 229, discussing *Law Society of South Africa and Others v. President of the Republic of South Africa and Others* 2019 (3) BCLR 329 (CC).
25 See the chapter by Edward T. Swaine.
26 Campbell McLachlan, 'The Assault on International Adjudication and the Limits of Withdrawal' (2019) 68 *ICLQ* 499, and the detailed references therein.
27 McLachlan, 'The Assault on International Adjudication', 507–10.
28 McLachlan, 'The Assault on International Adjudication', pt. IV.

in the present context is whether a closer engagement between international law and foreign relations law is capable of nourishing new insights into the concept of sovereignty in its double-facing aspect: external and internal.[29] Such a constructive engagement might furnish one possible set of responses to the critique outlined above. It is to this question that we must now turn.

III IS SOVEREIGNTY INDIVISIBLE?

Modern international lawyers have a tendency to regard the sovereignty of states as something of an embarrassment – an inconvenient truth. In the last edition of *Oppenheim* that he edited in 1955, Hersch Lauterpacht concludes a passage on 'The problem of sovereignty in the twentieth century' with the optimistic suggestion that 'progress in International Law, the maintenance of international peace and, with it, of independent national States, are in the long run conditioned by a partial surrender of their sovereignty'.[30] Forty years later, Louis Henkin concluded in 1995 that 'for legal purposes at least, we might do well to relegate the term sovereignty to the shelf of history as a relic from an earlier era'.[31] James Crawford insists in 2005 that the term sovereignty as a legal term can only mean 'the totality of powers that States may have under international law. By contrast, as a political term its connotations are those of untrammelled authority and power and it is in such discourse that the term can be problematic'.[32]

The view of international lawyers that sovereignty is unhelpful in legal terms stands in stark contrast to its persistence. This is not only in international political discourse, in which, for instance, Brexit was cast as 'a fight for the very sovereignty of our nation';[33] and President Trump repeatedly invoked at the rostrum of the UN General Assembly the notion that: 'The future does not belong to globalists. The future belongs to patriots. The future belongs to sovereign and independent nations . . .'.[34] It also finds its way into international legal discourse. The Beijing Declaration adopted by the first South-South Human Rights Forum in 2017 resolves that: 'The international community's

[29] The author is indebted to David Dyzenhaus for the term 'the double-facing constitution'. See Bomhoff, Dyzenhaus and Poole (eds.), *The Double-Facing Constitution*.

[30] Lassa Oppenheim and Hersch Lauterpacht (eds.), *International Law: A Treatise*, 8th ed. (London: Longmans, Green & Co, 1955), pp. 122–4 at para. 70.

[31] Louis Henkin, *International Law: Politics and Values* (Dordrecht: Martinus Nijhoff Publishers, 1995), p. 10.

[32] James Crawford, *The Creation of States in International Law*, 2nd ed. (Oxford: Oxford University Press, 2006), p. 33.

[33] The Spectator, 15 December 2018.

[34] Statement of President Trump to the UNGA, 24 September 2019, UN Doc. A/74/PV.3, p. 11.

concern for human rights matters should always follow international law and the universally recognized basic norms governing international relations, of which the key is to respect national sovereignty'.[35] So too the proposal for collective withdrawal from the International Criminal Court considered by an Open-ended Ministerial Committee of the African Union in January 2017, invoked the need to '[p]reserve the dignity, sovereignty and integrity of Member States'.[36]

The comparative failure of international lawyers to engage with the concept of sovereignty, in both its internal and external aspects, may, as John Jackson presciently warned in 2003, actually promote the persistence of sovereignty fictions such as 'the notion that absolute power is concentrated at the head of a nation-state'. Jackson argued that an attempt to bury the concepts of sovereignty 'without adequate replacements could lead to a situation in which pure power prevails: that, in turn, could foster chaos, misunderstanding, and conflict, like Hobbes' state of nature, where life is "nasty, brutish, and short"'.[37]

Jackson was writing at a time of great expansion in the ambition of international institutions and was driven by a perception of the entirely new set of pressures that this was creating for 'nation-state governments trying to deliver the fruits of their important achievements to their constituents'.[38] In other words, he was concerned about the effect of exercises of sovereignty on the plane of international law on the maintenance of popular sovereignty in national constitutions. Seen in this light, the rise of populism has simply exposed to view what Blokker calls a 'deeper, intrinsic tension in the post-war international legal order between democratic self-government on the one hand, and a universalistically understood international regime, on the other'.[39]

This is a serious concern that lies at the heart of several of the chapters in this volume. It is not to be dismissed as mere populist rhetoric. Aust and Kleinlein suggest in their Introduction that 'Sovereignty often serves as a placeholder for constitutional values, in particular domestic democratic self-determination'.[40] As Anna Petrig puts it, discussing the Swiss constitutional debate about the Migration Pact: 'To shrug off the call for "hard

35 Beijing Declaration, 8 December 2017, p. 8.

36 African Union, 'Withdrawal Strategy Document – Draft 2', 12 January 2017.

37 John H. Jackson, 'Sovereignty-Modern: A New Approach to an Outdated Concept' (2003) 97 *AJIL* 782 at 794.

38 Jackson, 'Sovereignty-Modern', 797.

39 Blokker, 'A Reply to Heike Krieger', 1014.

40 See the introductory chapter by Helmut Philipp Aust and Thomas Kleinlein, p. 17.

participation", which took shape in the context of the Migration Pact, as a purely populist manoeuvre would not do the matter justice'.[41]

International law resists conflating the question of the sovereignty of a state on the international plane with the 'constitutional lawyer's question of supreme competence within a particular State'.[42] At the same time, there is a strong strain in foreign relations law, which finds its philosophical origins in John Locke's idea of the 'federative power' that would leave the conduct of foreign relations in the hands of the executive.[43] On the face of it, these two claims seem to contradict rather directly the notion, now so widely exploited by the populist leaders, of the importance of a direct link between 'the people' and the exercise of independent sovereignty on the international plane, for which the Brexit referendum is emblematic.

Yet a closer focus on the relation between the international and the domestic dimensions of sovereignty and on the contribution of, respectively, international law and constitutional law might assist our understanding of this relationship. In his highly original monograph *Sovereignty* published in 1933, Hermann Heller argued for the indivisibility of sovereignty. He wrote:

> If a state is sovereign, it is the universal decision-making unit in its territory; the existentiality of the decision-making unit prohibits splitting sovereignty into the sovereignty of a state law and a separate international law sovereignty. … The highest independent decision-making power is always the mark of one and not two facts.[44]

In his view, it was essential to liberate the idea of the sovereign person from the 'bloodlessness' of a 'conceptual phantom labelled the state'.[45] He located sovereignty in the people as the body politic, but, distancing himself from Carl Schmitt's conception of a 'voluntaristic dictatorship' he insisted that the people may only govern through the appointment of representatives 'juristically dependant magistrates' that represent the common will.[46]

Several of the chapters in this volume examine the development of mechanisms that seek to enhance and protect democratic involvement in the decisions of states on the international plane, which comparative research

[41] See the chapter by Anna Petrig, p. 203.

[42] Crawford, *The Creation of States*, 33.

[43] John Locke, *Two Treatises of Government, Second Treatise* (London 1690), II, para. 147.

[44] Hermann Heller, *Sovereignty: A Contribution to the Theory of Public and International Law*, English translation of the 1927 original edition, edited and introduced by David Dyzenhaus (Oxford: Oxford University Press, 2019), p. 140.

[45] Heller, *Sovereignty*, pp. 104, 106.

[46] Heller, *Sovereignty*, p. 108.

shows is a global trend.[47] Both Ajla Škrbić and Stanislaw Biernat consider the case for an enlarged parliamentary role in controlling the executive's use of the foreign affairs power.[48] Niki Aloupi shows how the *Conseil Constitutionnel* in France mediates the effect of international commitments upon national sovereignty, through its decisions on whether a constitutional amendment is required as a condition for the ratification of a treaty.[49]

Veronika Fikfak, who considers the development of British parliamentary practice on the use of force against the background of a much broader comparative trend, argues that this development is not only about the accountability of the executive to Parliament. Examining the parliamentary debates, she suggests that, in the process, a direct link has been forged between the questions of the lawful use of force at international law and Parliament's responsibility at the national level to decide to authorise the use of force.[50] In the process, the international law issues become domesticated.

These trends, important though they are, still fall short of Heller's conception of indivisible sovereignty through the exercise of the ultimate power of decision on foreign affairs by the elected representatives of the people. Nevertheless, recent experience in the United Kingdom concerning the decision to withdraw from the European Union gives support to this idea. Brexit concerned an exercise of the foreign affairs power: the decision to withdraw from a Treaty (and the whole complex of international arrangements that flow from it). The process in the United Kingdom began with that most un-British of constitutional devices: a resort to direct popular democracy through the medium of a referendum. Immediately thereafter the executive (vociferously backed by elements in the Press) attempted to treat this as a mandate that could be executed by a straightforward exercise of its foreign affairs prerogative.[51]

In two landmark cases, the Supreme Court demurred, decisively finding in favour of Parliamentary sovereignty, that is: the principle that the sovereignty of the people may only be exercised through their representatives (however chaotic the results may be) and that this principle applies as much to foreign

47 Pierre-Hugues Verdier and Mila Versteeg, 'International Law in National Legal Systems: An Empirical Investigation' (2015) 109 *AJIL* 514; Pierre-Hugues Verdier and Mila Versteeg, 'Separation of Powers, Treaty-Making, and Treaty Withdrawal: A Global Survey', in Curtis A. Bradley (ed.), *The Oxford Handbook of Comparative Foreign Relations Law* (Oxford: Oxford University Press, 2019), p. 135.

48 See the chapters by Ajla Škrbić and Stanislaw Biernat respectively.

49 See the chapter by Niki Aloupi.

50 See the chapter by Veronika Fikfak.

51 For a detailed account of the background see: Campbell McLachlan, 'The Foreign Relations Power in the Supreme Court' (2018) 134 *Law Quarterly Review* 380.

relations as it does in other spheres. The first case directly concerned the decision to notify withdrawal. The second concerned a decision to prorogue Parliament while withdrawal negotiations were ongoing.

In *Miller (No. 1)*,[52] the Court rested its decision on the ground that the decision of the executive to withdraw would necessarily change the law applicable within the United Kingdom, something that only Parliament was competent to do. In this way, the Court could present the outcome as upholding the 'dualist system' that separated the international from the national and in turn the executive foreign affairs function from the legislative function of Parliament. It was only because the nature of withdrawal from EU law necessarily transgressed that line that the court had to intervene, since 'the dualist system is a necessary corollary of Parliamentary sovereignty . . . it exists to protect Parliament not ministers'.[53]

In *Miller (No. 2)*,[54] however, the issue could not be analysed as an application of dualism in law-making. The Court recognised that what was really at stake in the prorogation of Parliament was not merely an internal question of the distribution of powers between the executive and Parliament, but also one that went to the heart of Parliament's ability to scrutinise the executive conduct of foreign affairs. The constitutional significance of that power of supervision was one that Dicey early identified. He accepted that 'it is not Parliament but the Ministry, who direct the diplomacy of the nation'.[55] At the same time, Ministers were constantly accountable to the House of Commons for the exercise of that power. In this way, he thought 'The prerogatives of the Crown have become the privileges of the people'.[56] For the Supreme Court, the principle of 'Parliamentary accountability' is 'no less fundamental to our constitution than Parliamentary sovereignty' since: 'By these means, the policies of the executive are subjected to consideration by the representatives of the electorate, the executive is required to report, explain and defend its actions, and citizens are protected from the arbitrary exercise of executive power'.[57]

Does this mean that the sovereignty of Parliament now includes the sovereign power of decision on all matters of foreign affairs? The answer is still

[52] *R (Miller)* v. *Secretary of State for Exiting the European Union* [2017] UKSC 5, [2018] AC 61.

[53] *R (Miller)* v. *Secretary of State for Exiting the European Union* [2017] UKSC 5, [2018] AC 61 at [57].

[54] *R (Miller)* v. *Prime Minister* [2019] UKSC 41, [2020] AC 373.

[55] Albert Venn Dicey, *Introduction to the Study of the Law of the Constitution*, 2nd ed. (London: Macmillan & Co., 1886), p. 394.

[56] Dicey, *The Law of the Constitution*, p. 396.

[57] *R (Miller)* v. *Prime Minister* [2019] UKSC 41, [2020] AC 373, 406 at [46].

probably not: the gradual increase in Parliamentary supervision of treaty-making and the growth of a convention with regard to prior consultation on the war power do not amount to a full assumption of power. Nor would this be consistent with the important value of the separation of powers in constitutional government that requires a balance to be maintained between the three organs of government. Nevertheless, the 'crisis' test that Heller invites us to apply has demonstrated, at least in this one contemporary example, the need in the last resort to find a single holder of sovereign power within the state. Within a democratic state, that holder can only be the constitutionally appointed representatives of the people.

How, then, can this domestic constitutional law point be connected with international law in a way that supports the idea of an *indivisible* sovereignty? The answer lies in one of the most central organising principles of the post-War system of international law: the principle of self-determination.

The principle is enshrined in the United Nations Charter as one of the principal purposes of the Organisation, being 'respect for the principle of equal rights and the self-determination of peoples'.[58] It has been subsequently developed through law-making resolutions of the General Assembly on Colonial Peoples[59] and on Friendly Relations[60] and as the first human right in the International Covenants.[61] In the latter, in common article 1, it finds its expression in the following way:

> (1) All peoples have the right to self-determination; by virtue of that right they freely determine their political status and freely pursue their economic, social and cultural development.
> (2) All peoples may, for their own ends, freely dispose of their natural wealth and resources without prejudice to any obligations arising out of international economic co-operation, based on the principle of mutual benefit, and international law. In no case may a people be deprived of its own means of subsistence.

58 Charter of the United Nations, San Francisco, 26 June 1945, entered into force 24 October 1945, 1 UNTS 16, Art. 1(2).

59 UNGA, 'Declaration on the Granting of Independence to Colonial Countries and Peoples', UNGA Res. 1514 (XV), UN Doc. A/RES/1514 (XV), 14 December 1960.

60 UNGA, 'Declaration on Principles of International Law concerning Friendly Relations and Co-operation among States in accordance with the Charter of the United Nations', UNGA Res. 2625 (XXV), UN Doc. A/RES/2625 (XXV), 24 October 1970 ('Friendly Relations Declaration').

61 International Covenant on Economic, Social and Cultural Rights, New York City, 16 December 1966, entered into force 3 January 1976, 993 UNTS 3, Art. 1; International Covenant on Civil and Political Rights, New York City, 16 December 1966, entered into force 23 March 1976, 999 UNTS 171, Art. 1.

(3) The States Parties to the present Convention, including those having responsibility for the administration of Non-Self-Governing and Trust Territories, shall promote the realization of the right to self-determination and shall respect that right, in conformity with the provisions of the Charter of the United Nations.

In turn it has been developed and implemented through the practice of the United Nations. No single principle has more profoundly transformed the international legal system.[62] Respect for it as 'one of the essential principles of contemporary international law'[63] is an obligation *erga omnes*, which all states have a legal interest in protecting.[64]

The point here is that the self-determination creates an explicit link between international law and the 'people' who are and remain the holders of the right.[65] Self-determination as a legal principle has both driven the emergence of new States and limited the validity of attempts to create new states that do not meet its criteria. But for present purposes, its significance lies in its enduring application *internally* within the framework of an existing state.[66] In this way, international law supports the essential connection between the internal and the international role of self-determination: between the people and their right to determine their political organisation. So, renewed attention to the connection between international law and foreign relations law may shed new light on the meaning of popular sovereignty and its relation to the right to self-determination.

This point is important because the international law principle of self-determination is no populist charter, licensing the will of the majority to the exclusion of the human rights of individuals. Its expression as a matter of customary international law in the Friendly Relations Declaration includes the provision that: 'Every State has the duty to promote through joint and separate action universal respect for and observance of human rights and fundamental freedoms in accordance with the Charter'.[67] The same principle adds, in its savings clause, that the consequence of due observance of the principle of equal

62 Crawford, *The Creation of States*, Ch. 3; Marcelo Kohen, 'Self-Determination', in Jorge Viñuales (ed.), *The UN Friendly Relations Declaration at 50* (Cambridge: Cambridge University Press, 2020), Ch. 7.

63 *East Timor (Portugal* v. *Australia)*, Judgment, I.C.J. Reports 1995, p. 90, para. 29.

64 *Legal Consequences of the Separation of the Chagos Archipelago from Mauritius in 1965*, Advisory Opinion, 25 February 2019, para. 180.

65 For a recent exploration of this idea in the context of election interference see: Jens David Ohlin, *Election Interference* (Cambridge: Cambridge University Press, 2020), Ch. 4 'The Promise of Self-Determination'.

66 *Reference re Secession of Quebec* [1998] 2 SCR 217, 282 at [126].

67 Friendly Relations Declaration, principle 5, paragraph 3.

rights and self-determination of peoples is that the State is 'thus possessed of a government representing the whole people belonging to the territory without distinction as to race, creed or colour'.[68] The insertion of the right in the international human rights covenants has the same consequence that it is to be read together with all of the other rights protected thereunder.

There is a second respect in which a focus on the relationship between international law and foreign relations law may also prove productive. That lies in treating seriously its starting premise: that international law constitutes a distinct legal system, and that part of the function that foreign relations law may perform within a domestic legal system is to provide rules of reception, or, put more broadly, rules that manage the interaction between legal systems by determining which legal system has jurisdiction over which issues and what law applies. It is to this aspect that we must now turn.

IV INTERNATIONAL LAW AS LAW

In their Introduction, Aust and Kleinlein reject the idea that international law or foreign relations law are 'hybrid in nature'. They seek to uphold 'the rather traditional view that international law is indeed international and that foreign relations law is part of a given domestic legal system'. Nevertheless, they argue that 'foreign relations law encapsulates the rules of domestic law about the reception of international law' and that 'upholding the traditional criteria … does not preclude investigating the hybrid zone that is created by the encounters of public international law and foreign relations law'.[69]

This approach may provide a potential way of pursuing Knop's suggestion that '[o]ne way forward may lie in noticing and questioning the strong law/politics distinction at play in both foreign relations law and the international law that it threatens to displace, discount, or distort'.[70] In other words, it may answer the distinction – implicit or explicit in some contemporary foreign relations law scholarship – between a relatively positivist approach to binding law at the domestic constitutional level and the assumption that, beyond the state, the international arena can be characterised only by foreign relations and not by binding law.

The partially revised American Law Institute *Restatement (Fourth) Foreign Relations Law* 2018 makes the point that, because a restatement of foreign relations law 'deals with two distinct legal systems, namely domestic law

68 Friendly Relations Declaration, principle 5, paragraph 7.
69 See the chapter by Helmut Philipp Aust and Thomas Kleinlein, p. 12.
70 Knop, 'Comparison as Invention', p. 58.

bearing on foreign relations and relevant portions of international law, it must address both'.[71]

How might a renewed focus on treating the interface between international law and domestic constitutional law as one of the interaction between legal systems actually make a difference? In the first place, it might challenge the utility of conventional ways of analysing the reception of international law in domestic legal systems as one determined by the distinction between dualist and monist systems. Recent comparative research has shown that this traditional distinction does not correctly explain the actual rules of recognition applicable in states that are traditionally regarded as being 'monist' or 'dualist'.[72] The true position is much less black and white.

'Monist' states must still maintain procedures for treaty review and ratification to ensure legislative control over the making of laws that are to be applicable internally within the state. 'Dualist' states, even if they maintain strict rules of separation between treaty obligations and domestic law may still accept that customary international law is 'part of the law of the land'.[73] When they do so, this is not because international law is referred to in the interpretation of a norm of municipal law. Rather it is because international law is applicable to the determination of the issue within the municipal legal system. It is applicable because a rule of recognition of municipal law so provides, and therefore subject to the terms on which municipal law admits the international law rule. But it is nevertheless applicable as law.[74]

A consideration of the internal effect of the international legal obligations assumed by states might also lead us to question deep dualism in another respect. It would challenge another mistaken dualist proposition that international law obligations sound only on the international plane and produce no domestic effects. It would do so by demonstrating that the essential corollary of the allocation to the executive of the power to conduct foreign affairs and to enter into treaties is that the executive assumes a concomitant obligation to comply with the international law obligations that it has assumed. Such a requirement (which is supported in the case of the United Kingdom by several centuries of practice) ensures that the state abides by the international

[71] American Law Institute, Restatement (Fourth) of the Foreign Relations Law of the United States (2018), Introduction.

[72] Verdier and Versteeg, 'International Law in National Legal Systems', 514.

[73] William Blackstone, *Commentaries on the Laws of England*, 9th ed. reprint (Oxford: Strahan, Cadell and Prince, 1783) Bk IV, p. 67. See the Indian Supreme Court authorities cited in the chapter by Prabhakar Singh.

[74] The point is developed fully in Campbell McLachlan, *Foreign Relations Law* (Cambridge: Cambridge University Press, 2014), Ch. 3.

law obligations that it has assumed through the persons that contract on its behalf and represent it in foreign relations.[75]

The result of treating foreign relations law as concerned with the interaction of the different legal systems that are in play in questions of foreign relations 'admits of a larger variety of relevant bodies of law. It also has the potential to develop a more complex account of dualism'.[76] In rejecting a 'fixed law/politics opposition' it would subject foreign relations questions to the principle of legality, not conceived narrowly as the municipal law of any particular state, but rather as determining the issue according to the applicable law, whether that be municipal law or international law.

A further benefit of such a focus is that it may provide a better means of doing comparative foreign relations law on a global basis. Michael Riegner, in his chapter for this volume, highlights the contingency of the set of choices for foreign relations law created by the Western constitutional tradition.[77] He points out that this tradition assumes the pre-existence of the state and then poses the foreign relations law question as a set of choices about the relation of the state to international law at the interface. He argues that 'the distinction between international and national is applied rigidly to the political sphere but not to the economic sphere'.[78]

By contrast, in the colonised Third World, 'foreign relations did not begin as inter-state relations but as dealings between chartered trading companies like the East India Company and local rulers. The experience of statehood was also quite different: for many postcolonial states, the international preceded the national: peripheral statehood was produced and defined by international law during decolonization'.[79] A search for models of foreign relations law in the Global South would, as the Latin American example that he discusses illustrates, open up the possibility of transformational constitutionalism, a model of regional integration that emphasises social not economic rights, which remain much more closely subject to national control.[80] We might note in this regard how closely the formulation of the right to self-determination in Article 1 of the International Covenants links the right of peoples to determine

75 Campbell McLachlan, 'The Double-Facing Foreign Relations Function of the Executive and Its Self-Enforcing Obligation to Comply with International Law' in Bomhoff, Dyzenhaus and Poole (eds.), *The Double-Facing Constitution*, Ch. 13.

76 Knop, 'Comparison as Invention', p. 60.

77 See the chapter by Michael Riegner, pp. 60 et seqq.

78 See the chapter by Riegner, pp. 65–66.

79 See the chapter by Riegner, p. 69.

80 See the chapter by Riegner, p. 74.

political status (paragraph 1) to their right to control economic resources (paragraph 2).

V CONCLUSION

If comparative foreign relations law proves itself really capable of embracing different perspectives as to the relation between a national constitution and international law that treats both as law, it might rise above a mere comparison of differences. It might then dispel the concern that, as a discipline, it may cannibalise the study of international law, creating in the process an *Ersatz* or 'folk' international law. In doing so it may shed new positive light on a compelling issue of our age on which foreign relations law sits, whether as bridge or boundary, namely: how to redefine the relation between the nation state and the international realm in ways that give real meaning to both the right of peoples to self-determination and the community interest shared by all humanity to secure our common future.

Index

www.ingramcontent.com/pod-product-compliance
Lightning Source LLC
LaVergne TN
LVHW011700200926
848484LV00004B/1012
* 9 7 8 1 1 0 8 8 3 7 7 4 3 *